Reaching
Adolescents
The Young Adult Book
and the School

Reaching Adolescents

The Young Adult Book and the School

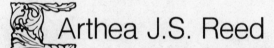 Arthea J.S. Reed

University of North Carolina
at Asheville

Holt, Rinehart and Winston

New York Chicago   San Francisco
Philadelphia   Montreal   Toronto   London
Sydney   Tokyo   Mexico City
Rio de Janiero   Madrid

Photo acknowledgments: *Cover by Ken Karp; pp. ii, 5, 19, 36, 44, 79, 118, 144, 161, 233, 237, 278, 304, 322, 337, 372 and 406 by Mary Jo Brezny; p. 87 by Jaime Armstrong; p. 174 by Charlotte–Mecklenberg Schools; p. 352 by Furman Owens; p. 431 by University of North Carolina at Asheville Graphics Department.*

Library of Congress Cataloging in Publication Data

Reed, Arthea J. S.
  Reaching adolescents.

  Includes bibliographies and indexes.
    1. Youth—Books and reading.   2. Literature—Study and teaching
(Secondary) 3. Education, Secondary. I. Title.
Z1037.A1R43   1985   028.5′5   84-12905

ISBN 0-03-069342-X

CBS College Publishing
Holt, Rinehart and Winston
The Dryden Press
Saunders College Publishing

to Don

Preface

More than five years ago I first put pen to paper to write a textbook that had been developing inside my head for a decade, more or less. The book, which has come to be called *Reaching Adolescents: The Young Adult Book and the School* (the title of the text has gone through many mutations; my favorite still remains "Are You There, God? It's Me, Margaret's Teacher"), was first conceived in 1968. At that time I was an ill-prepared first-year English teacher of high school sophomores. The young adults I was assigned to teach did not fit my middle-class image of fifteen-year-olds. They appeared to me to be undisciplined, unmotivated, uninterested (and uninteresting), and altogether illiterate. I suffered through six months of attempting to force into their heads the material in the literature anthology. At every turn my altogether illiterate sophomores outwitted me. They lost their books or left them in their lockers. They became deathly ill during class and had to flee to the restroom. They argued with their classmates and with me. They slept through my oral readings. They threw spit wads at classmates who attempted to answer questions. The coup de grace was one of my all-time favorite literary works, Shakespeare's *Romeo and Juliet*. They mocked me, my love of literature, and the Bard; they stole my class notes.

I went home to my husband in tears. I needed a new "plan of attack," as I perceived it. I spent the evening inventing "appropriate" punishments: ten points off the final grade for uttering an unsolicited remark, detention for an incomplete paper, a phone call to parents each time a grade lower than 75 was recorded on a quiz, and other similar acts of retribution. Donald, my partner of six months of wedded less-than-bliss (these unthankful teenagers were destroying my marriage), wiped my tears and listened to my ranting and ravings as I prepared my onslaught.

By 10:00 P.M. I had prepared my purple encyclical, to be duplicated and given unceremoniously to my students the next day. I read it aloud with great expression. When I had finished, I asked my husband, "Well, what do you think of that? That should work, shouldn't it?" (I really didn't want him to answer.)

Donald walked over to me, put his arm around my shoulder, and said, "Yes, no doubt it will have some effect. It will do two things for sure: make them hate you and hate to read. You're too kind and care too much about kids and about books to carry that off, Charlie."

I started to cry. But through my tears and a night without sleep came a new birth. I threw away my purple prose and decided to go into the classroom with my defenses down and, for the first time, really listen to my students. The next day, as the students entered the room—expecting to find a raving maniac, no doubt—they found instead the real me, perched on top of my desk (not behind the podium, for the first time that year). Without a lesson plan, I began, "Well, you've convinced me; you hate English. I'm a slow learner, but now I'm convinced. I don't understand why, and I'd like to find out."

And find out I did. At first the students were hesitant to talk, as they had every right to be. They had learned to dislike and distrust me through my dislike and distrust of them. But when they opened up, they talked nonstop for a week. During that week I learned how books, school, and teachers had become their enemies. Together we began to plan a new approach to teaching and learning. Through my students I learned about books written for young adults. One of the students who worked in a book distribution center brought me a copy of a new book by S. E. Hinton, *The outsiders*. (I think he stole it, but I didn't dare ask.) I read the book with great enthusiasm. The next day he queried, "Did you like it?"

"Did you know that S. E. Hinton person's only sixteen? Could we read it in class?"

I didn't have any other copies of the book, but there was no reason I could not read it aloud. And so began my love of young adult literature. Those kids in my class did have sparkling eyes! I glimpsed them as I read. The depth of their understanding was remarkable. Sometimes their questions and comments could not wait until I came to a good stopping point. They would blurt them out, and we would be off on a thirty-minute discussion. Often they were discussing without me. I was having a wonderful time; this was the way teaching was supposed to be. My students were enthusiastic. So enthusiastic, in fact, that they were asking for more books. Soon they were discovering new books and authors and sharing them with me and with one another.

But alas, my euphoria did not last. Not because the kids were not excited, but because I realized that I was not teaching what I was expected to teach. I decided not to scrap my slowly growing English program, but instead to seek ways, with the help of the students, to add the skills and concepts of the English classroom to the motivational reading program. I posed the problem to them, explaining that their parents, the school, and the community expected them to be learning certain things in the sophomore English class. They protested that they had not learned anything before. "What are we supposed to learn, anyway?" I decided to show them by giving each one a copy of the state's guidelines for sophomore English. With the help of these students I began to develop a curriculum that included all aspects of English required in secondary school classrooms, and much more. The curriculum included books, books, and more books.

That summer I made a commitment to read two young adult books per week, a commitment I have kept through the years. Since 1968 I have taught in two public school systems, one urban and one rural. I have taught English, journalism, history, and a year-long course in the humanities. I have acted as a director of instruction for a county school system and a supervisor of student teachers. In these positions I have observed thousands of teachers of young adults. This book is a compilation of what I have observed and disovered through experience and observation. My first class of students taught me to teach. They taught me the value of beginning instruction with the student. Since that time I have gained significant data to support what a group of incredibly intelligent fifteen-year-olds already knew.

ORGANIZATION. *Reaching Adolescents* is divided into four parts. The first, a rationale, is based on the research of psychologists, learning theorists, educators (teacher researchers as well as university researchers), and parents.

Part Two is a comprehensive examination of young adult literature by theme and genre. This section makes no attempt at literary criticism; rather, it catalogues and annotates the world of literature for the young adult reader. It can be read as is or can be used as a reference as teachers plan to incorporate young adult books into the curriculum.

Part Three, which deals with methodology, discusses techniques for incorporating young adult books into most of the classrooms of the middle and the secondary school. Throughout the five chapters of this section a wide variety of unit plans that incorporate young adult books are featured. Chapter 7 presents the methodological framework, the thematic unit, and presents a model thematic unit. Chapters 8 and 9 are devoted to incorporating young adult books into the English and social studies classrooms. Chapter 10 discusses methodology for using young adult literature in reading, science, mathematics, physical education, music, and art classrooms. Chapter 11 deals with techniques for making books come to life no matter what the subject area.

The final part of the book gives the teacher, librarian, parent, and university instructor a succinct and complete report of the review and bibliographic information available in the field of literature for young adults. It discusses ways to build a classroom library. Because of the recent concern about censorship of classroom and library materials, a final chapter is included that suggests a positive approach to that problem.

AUDIENCE. *Reaching Adolescents* is designed to be used in college and university classes in young adult (or adolescent) literature, children's literature, reading, and language arts, and as a supplemental text in various middle and secondary school methods classes. The book is appropriate for teacher education and library science students, and is one that students will want to retain for their personal professional library. It is filled with bibliographic information and teaching ideas that can be immediately incorporated into the classroom. For this reason, it is also an excellent resource for all in-service classroom teachers at the middle- and secondary-school level.

Writing Style

Reaching Adolescents was written with the reader in mind. The tone of the book is conversational. At the same time the style is appropriate for instructional purposes in a college or university course. The parts of the book allow the instructor to divide the course into four distinct units. The excerpts from young adult books that appear throughout the text give the instructor the opportunity to introduce students to some of the best and most popular young adult books. The student, teacher, librarian, or parent who reads this book will be motivated to begin a campaign to read young adult books on a regular basis.

FEATURES. The major task of the text is to provide scholarly information about young adult literature, presented in a readable fashion, and to offer an arsenal of ideas for incorporating young adult literature into the classroom.

Anthological Asides. The phrase "Anthological Aside" was coined to explain the intent of the excerpts from young adult books that appear throughout the text. These excerpts were selected to give the reader a sampling of the best and most popular young adult books. In addition, their placement as "asides" in the text was designed to illustrate points the author makes about the young adult, the books, and their use in the classroom.

Author Quotes. The quotations from authors of young adult books that are featured in the text were selected to support points made about the field of young adult literature, writing young adult books, and introducing the books to young readers. Instructors of university courses can use them as discussion starters or as beginning places for additional research.

Unit Plans and Annotated Bibliographies. Throughout the book, particularly in the section entitled "Methodology," unit plans and bibliographies are presented. The unit plans were chosen for their successful incorporation of young adult books into the subject area curriculum, as well as their presentation of skills and concepts essential to the study of the discipline. All of the unit plans were developed by the classroom teachers whose names appear on the plans.

Case Studies. Case studies are cited to exemplify theory or methodology throughout the book. The studies are based on my own observations or teaching experiences. Since these observations occurred over a period of fifteen years, it was impossible to recall accurately the names of all the teachers mentioned. Therefore, the names on the studies are not the names of actual classroom teachers.

The History of Young Adult Literature at a Glance. Appendix B, a brief timeline of young adult literature, is designed to give the reader an overview of the most popular reading material of young adult readers prior to the rise of the young adult market. The second section of the timeline is a compilation of some of the "cutting edge" books of the young adult literary field. In addition, the timeline includes events that have influenced the reading tastes of young adults, the books used in classrooms, and the books available in libraries and stores.

The timeline can be an excellent teaching and learning tool in the university classroom. Students can participate in research about reading tastes of young readers throughout history, as well as in discussions about the effect of major historical events on young adult literature. They can add their own titles and authors to the timeline by examining major events of the day that may affect the reading interests of young adults. After considering these events, students can predict changes in reading tastes and classroom and library reading fare.

Chapter Bibliographies. At the end of each chapter is a complete bibliography of the young adult titles that appear in that chapter. Most of the bibliographies are divided by theme or genre. The bibliographies are designed to help the reader locate the books in both hard and soft cover.

Each bibliography also includes a list of suggested readings for studying the information presented in the chapter in more depth. The suggested reading list at the end of Chapter 12 gives addresses for obtaining information about review and bibliographic sources.

Some chapter bibliographies incude films and other audiovisual material to use in conjunction with young adult books.

ACKNOWLEDGMENTS. A project such as *Reaching Adolescents* involves the time and support of many people. First and foremost, thanks go to my students, past and present, who taught me, through example, most of what my heart and my gut know about teaching. The students who first passed on to me their enthusiasm for young adult books deserve special thanks. The students in my adolescent literature classes at the University of North Carolina at Asheville who contributed experiences of their own adolescence, their adolescent children, and their students were also essential to the completion of this project.

The experiences of hundreds of outstanding teachers fill the pages of this book. Without them the story could not be told. They have provided me with new insights and a renewed respect for the power of books and of teaching.

Thanks go to my colleagues. Verna Bergemann, University of North Carolina at Asheville, was a constant source of support and strength needed to see this project through. Critical, supportive feedback essential to the successful completion of the manuscript was provided by Hugh Agee, University of Georgia; Alethea Hilbig, Eastern Michigan University; and M. Jerry Weiss, Jersey City State College.

Special thanks go to the marvelous schools and teachers who allowed me to photograph their students as they interacted with books: Joanne Bartsch, science teacher at Asheville Country Day School; Helen Fairbanks, English teacher at Asheville High School; Gail Latrop, language arts, social studies, and mathematics teacher at Brevard Middle School; Kate McConnaughey, English and art teacher at Christ School; Reed Finley, English teacher at Christ School; Carole Browning, reading teacher at Erwin Middle School; Patsy Scales, librarian at Greenville Middle School; and Rebecca Devet, "the poetry lady" in the Charlotte/Mecklenburg Schools. Thanks also go to Mary Ann Osby and Mary Lou West, parents who believe in reading with their children.

Two grants from the University of North Carolina at Asheville and the Southern Regional Education Board kept the project from dying.

The support and love of friends and family can never be underestimated in the completion of a long, time-consuming project. Thanks go first to Jan Scroggs, my friend and secretary, who typed this manuscript twice, and then some. My good friend Phyllis Lang, editor of the *Arts Journal,* edited the final manuscript and indexed the text. My mother, Martha Staeger, read the initial manuscript for errors and helped Phyllis with the indexing. My loving husband, Donald, became a better cook and housekeeper during the five years of this project. Without his intellectual and emotional support the project would have been impossible. And thanks to all the rest of you who seemed to know when not to ask, "How's the book going?"

Finally, thanks go to my editors at Holt: David Boynton, who initiated the project; Barbara Leffel, who renewed my enthusiasm for it; and Earl McPeek, and Herman Makler, who carried it through production.

A.J.S.R.

About the Author

Arthea J. S. Reed, known to her colleagues, students, family, and friends as "Charlie," is an associate professor of education at the University of North Carolina at Asheville. She has recently been named editor of *The ALAN Review,* published by the Assembly on Literature for Adolescents of the National Council of Teachers of English. *The ALAN Review* is the only international journal devoted solely to the study and review of literature and media produced for young adults. In addition, Dr. Reed is the author of a forthcoming book for parents, *A parent's guide to books for young adults.*

Because of her interests in reading and writing, the teaching of reading and writing, and encouraging children to read and write, she has

focused much of her energy on two projects. She is codirector of the Mountain Area Writing Project (a site of the North Carolina and National Writing Projects), which encourages teachers to become writers and researchers as they teach their students to write. She was the first director of the Young Authors' Project, which has involved over 150,000 students, parents, librarians, administrators, and teachers from western North Carolina. Through the project, thousands of children have published their own writing in "classroom publishing companies," and their books have been widely displayed. The current focus of the Young Authors' Project relates to Dr. Reed's interest in parents, young adults, and books. The project is giving its attention to developing school- and community-based programs in which adolescents and parents communicate through young adult books they read together.

Prior to teaching at the university, Dr. Reed received a Ph.D. at Florida State University and taught junior and senior high school English and social studies. In addition she has been director of instruction for a county school system and a college and university administrator. Dr. Reed's continuing concern for young adults keeps her in the classrooms for many hours per week. Her work in the schools leads to many speaking engagements and frequent consultation with teachers, administrators, librarians, and parents.

Contents

Contents

Contents

Contents

Anthological Asides

Reaching
Adolescents
The Young Adult Book
and the School

Part One
A Rationale for Using Young Adult Literature in the Secondary School Classroom

 **1** Why Should Young Adult
Literature[1] Be Used in
the Classroom?

The Stages of Reading Development

In recent decades the public has become increasingly concerned with the lack
of reading skills among students in secondary school classrooms. Many people
claim that the teenagers of today cannot read, at least not so well as the critics
read when they attended school twenty or thirty years ago. Others believe that
teenagers do not read, at least not as much or the same quality of material as
was read by students of previous generations. Those of us who work daily with
adolescents know that both these views are simplifications of the reading problems that we see in our classrooms.

Dan Jackson (1980), a junior and senior high school teacher in Spotswood,
New Jersey, tells of his career as a nonreader in the Bronx schools:

> *The crowd I grew up with in the Bronx during the 1960s had plenty of
> style and color, no geniuses as far as I know, and not much class. But*

[1] *Young adult literature, adolescent literature,* and *juvenile literature* are all terms that describe
(1) literature written or marketed primarily for teenagers; (2) books to whose main characters the
teenager can personally relate (usually young people between the ages of twelve and twenty-five);
(3) stories with an uncomplicated, often single plot line; (4) books with plots that address the concerns of young adults. For the purposes of this text, literature that is not written or marketed for
young adults, but which attracts a young adult readership, will be included.

quite a few of us had the cheek or the need to do things our own way. That's how we played. That's how we partied. And that's how we read books. John, for example, went wild with Catullus one year for no apparent reason. He would recite romantic or sexy lyrics halfway through our beer-blasts. Ten years down the line, he became probably the only IBM specialist whose first trip to Europe was highlighted by a visit to see the Catullus manuscripts in Venice. Fred liked Maugham. He read The Moon & Sixpence, Of Human Bondage, Cakes and Ale, *and at least eight other works, while falling into and failing out of three high schools. And his vision of the world was shaped by those unrequired readings.*

The girls were no different. Lorraine hated the three high schools she attended, but read enough detective fiction to compile a bibliography for a dissertation. Marian was bookish and bright. She even stayed in the same school for four years. None of us were ever surprised when she showed up at Orchard Beach with Siddhartha, Père Goriot, *or* The Brothers Karamazov.

Sweeper and Razz liked only sports stories, which they weren't allowed to read in school. Bill's teacher thought this passion for Jules Verne was "just a stage." Ronny had a problem with his penchant for Sartre; what teacher would believe that a kid from the Bronx was really reading Nausea *for the third time?*

So, along with the streets, the crowds and the noise, along with the ghosts, flowers and animals that filled our walks in Poe Park, the Botanical Gardens and the Bronx Zoo, we all had this other thing in common: our schools didn't recognize or exploit our enthusiasm for reading.[2]

Can Dan read? Can John read? What about Fred, Lorraine, Marian, and the others—can they read? The answer for all these is the same—of course they can read!

But do they read? Is reading detective stories really reading? Are books by Catullus or Maugham considered "real" books? Does Sartre count? Are Sweeper and Razz, who like only sports stories, reading? Of course, they are all reading, not the books chosen by their teachers, perhaps, but they are all enthusiastically reading.

Dan Jackson wasn't a very good student in school; he was too busy reading, learning, and living. He failed English and Latin and was told that he was not college material. Dan Jackson is not alone. I was in the lowest reading group in my fifth-grade class, the Ostriches (we always had our heads in the sand), but the summer between fifth and sixth grades I devoured every Agatha Christie novel I could find.

I received a note the other day from an eighth-grade teacher. "I'm concerned about my kids' reading motivation," she wrote, "not because they are not motivated, but because school is destroying it. I saw bright kids who made

[2]As published in *Media & Methods, American's Magazine of the Teaching Technologies,* March 1980, pp. 14–17.

4

D's and E's in reading this year and suffered a real setback in their reading because they were bored and turned off by the reading program. I'm afraid some of these kids will think they have reading problems when really the problem is with the program.''

Like Dan Jackson and his friends, many students love to read, but they don't love to read what the schools have chosen for them. They want to read Sartre or Verne or Christie or Blume or Jakes or Lipsyte or Cormier.

Why? What's wrong with Dickens and Shakespeare and Plato and the history text? Nothing. Nor is there anything wrong with the Dan Jacksons in the classroom who refuse to read them. The problem is not that Dan, and teenagers like him, can't read. For surely a teenager who has the ability to read Catullus can read Dickens. Without a doubt, a student who has plowed through *Nausea* ad nauseam has the stomach to read a history text. Nor is the problem that they won't read. (I am reminded of the fourth-grade teacher who complained to a mother that her son was reading ''books'' during history class.)

Then what is the problem?

The problem is that we're forcing our students to move directly from Dick and Jane, or whatever they are reading in the latest basal series, to Dickens, Shakespeare, Plato, and the history text. We expect them to jump directly from childhood into adulthood. We forget what we learned in our adolescent psychology courses, we forget about developmental stages, we forget about the needs hierarchy. In short, we do not help our students bridge the gap between their complete dependency on us and their emerging independence.

Adolescents who love to read can find a quiet spot even in a schoolyard.

■ ■ ■ **An Anthological Aside**

At Least, We Don't Have to Read Them Aloud . . .

LOIS DUNCAN

The hand of the clock moved forward one final click. The bell rang. And Mr. Griffin stepped through the doorway into the classroom, pulling the door shut behind him.

The day had officially begun.

Never once could Susan recall a morning when Mr. Griffin had not been standing in front of them at the precise moment the bell stopped ringing. Other teachers might saunter in late, delayed in the teachers' lounge for a last drag on a cigarette or a final swallow of morning coffee. Other teachers might pause in the hall to secure a button or tie a shoestring. Other teachers might sometimes not appear at all while unorganized substitutes stumbled over their lesson plans and finally gave up and let everybody out early.

But Mr. Griffin was there always, as reliable as the bell itself, stiff and straight in a navy blue suit, white shirt, and tie, his dark hair slicked flat against his head, his mouth firm and uncompromising beneath the small, neatly trimmed mustache.

His eyes moved steadily up and down the rows, taking silent roll as the buzz of conversation dwindled and faded to silence.

"Good morning, class," he said.

Susan answered automatically, her voice joining the uneasy chorus.

"Good morning, Mr. Griffin."

"Please take out your homework assignments and pass them to the front. Miss Cline, will you collect them, please?"

Susan opened her notebook and withdrew the sheets of lined paper on which she had carefully printed the verses she had composed the night before.

In the seat behind her, Jeff raised his hand.

"Mr. Garrett?"

"I don't have mine finished yet, Mr. Griffin. There was a basketball game last night, and I was one of the starters."

"That must have created a great problem for you, Mr. Garrett."

"I couldn't very well skip the game, could I?" Jeff said. "The team was counting on me. We were playing Eldorado."

"Basketball is indeed an important reason for attending high school,"

Abridged from Lois Duncan, *Killing Mr. Griffin* (Boston: Little, Brown, 1978), pp. 10–16. Copyright © 1978 by Lois Duncan.

Mr. Griffin said in an expressionless voice. "The ability to drop balls through baskets will serve you well in life. It may keep your wrists limber into old age."

"Mr. Ruggles, your hand is raised. Do you have a similar disclosure to make?"

"I did the assignment, sir," David said. "It blew out of my notebook. I'll redo it tonight."

"I have never accepted late papers on windy days. Miss Cline?"

"I didn't understand the assignment," Betsy said. Her eyes were wide and worried. "How can anybody write a final song for Ophelia when she's already said everything there is to say? All that about rosemary being for remembrance and everything? Nothing happens to her after that except she drowns."

"There are those who might consider suicide an event of some importance in a young woman's life," Mr. Griffin said dryly. "Are there any other comments?" The room was silent. "Then will those of you who were able to find some final words for poor Ophelia, please pass them forward?"

At least, we don't have to read them aloud, Susan thought in relief. That was a possibility she had not thought about last night when she sat at the desk in her room, letting the words pour from her pen onto the paper. There, caught by the magic of the painful story, she had let herself *become* Ophelia— lonely, alienated from the world, sickened with the hopelessness of her love, gazing into the depths of the water that would soon become her grave.

Only this morning as she was leaving the house had the horrible thought occurred to her—what if he makes us read the songs in class? There was no way that she could have done that. Too much of Susan lay exposed in the neatly printed verses, intermixed with the person of Ophelia.

Now she scanned her words again—

> Where the daisies laugh and blow,
> Where the willow leaves hang down,
> Nonny, nonny, I will go
> There to weave my lord a crown.
>
> Willow, willow, by the brook
> Trailing fingers green and long,
> I will read my lord a book,
> I will sing my love a song.
>
> Though he turn his face away,
> Nonny, nonny, still I sing,
> Ditties of a heart gone gray
> And a hand that bears no ring.
>
> Water, water, cold and deep—

"Miss McConnell, have you completed your meditation?" Mr. Griffin's voice broke in upon her.

"I'm sorry." Susan felt her face growing hot with embarrassment. "I was just—just—checking the spelling." Hurriedly she thrust the papers into the hand of the girl in front of her.

"An excellent idea, but it might have been done before now. As for those who have no paper to turn in, you may consider your grade F for this assignment. Now, open your books, please, to the first scene in Act Three."

"But, Mr. Griffin, that's not fair!" Jeff burst out. "If we missed doing the assignment we should be allowed to make up!"

"Why is that, Mr. Garrett?"

"Other teachers take late papers!" Jeff said. "In fact, most teachers don't give assignments at all on game nights. Dolly Luna—"

"What Miss Luna does is no concern of mine. She teaches her class according to her policies," Mr. Griffin told him. "My own policy happens to be to teach English literature. If students wish to take part in extracurricular activities, that's fine, but they should be just that—extra. Any student who allows them to interfere with his academic responsibilities must be prepared to accept the consequences."

"And the consequences are F's, is that it?" Jeff's voice was shaking with outrage. "Well, there happen to be a lot of us who think there's more to life than trying to outdo Shakespeare! When we *do* turn stuff in, it comes back so marked up that nobody can read it. Spelling, grammar, punctuation— everything's got to be so blasted perfect—"

"Cool it, boy," Mark Kinney said quietly. He sat slouched in his seat in his usual don't-care position, his odd, heavy-lidded eyes giving him a deceptively sleepy appearance. "Jeff's sort of overexcited, Mr. G., but what he's getting at is that we're most of us seniors in this class. We need this credit to graduate."

"Darned right, we do!" Jeff sputtered. "By dumping F's out wholesale, you may be knocking a bunch of us smack out of graduation. It's not fair to us or to our parents or even to the school! What are they going to do next fall with twenty or so of us all back trying to get one lousy English credit!"

"It's interesting to contemplate, isn't it?" Mr. Griffin said mildly. "But I'd advise you not to be lulled into a false sense of security by the thought that it can't be done. I am quite capable of holding back anyone I feel has not qualified for a passing grade, a fact which your friend Mr. Kinney can support."

His hand slid into his jacket pocket and brought out a small, plastic vial. Without seeming to so much as glance at it, he snapped it open, took out a pill, and popped it into his mouth. Then he recapped the vial and placed it back in the pocket.

"Please, open your books to *Hamlet*, Act Three, Scene One. We'll now review for a quiz I have scheduled for Monday. You do have your book with you, don't you, Mr. Garrett?"

"Yes, I do—sir," Jeff said hoarsely.

The wind continued to blow. Gazing through the window toward the parking lot, Susan could barely make out the rows of cars, veiled as they were by swirling dust. Out of this wild, pink world a bird came flying, half blinded, carried by the wind, and crashed headlong into the windowpane. Its beak crumpled against the glass, and it seemed to hang there an instant, stunned by the impact, before it dropped like a feather-covered stone to the ground below.

Poor thing, Susan thought. Poor little thing.

Poor bird. Poor Ophelia. Poor Susan. She had a sudden, irrational urge to put her head down on the desk and weep for all of them, for the whole world, for the awful day that was starting so badly and would certainly get no better.

From his seat behind her she heard Jeff Garrett mumble under his breath, "That Griffin's the sort of guy you'd like to kill."

■ ■ ■

Not all students are able to take on the adult world at the same rate. Some sixteen-year-olds read Shakespeare with such maturity that the rhythm and power of his words can be captured in their own writings. Others are unable to understand simple assignments given by teachers and are totally lost in a morass of Elizabethan English. Furthermore, the sixteen-year-olds who read with the maturity of an adult may be unable to face the world of their adolescence, while the teenagers who lack simple interpretive skills are well adjusted and comfortable. All of these young people, however, can enjoy reading and find answers in the books they read, if they are directed to books that are appropriate for them. As Dan Jackson writes:

> As the world of our childhood crumbled, we turned more and more to books for answers. We searched frantically for characters who had done what we hoped to do: survive ... feel joy ... find love. It was important to look in books for people who could do what was rarely done by the train conductors and cops who worked with our fathers. It was important to consider the countless stories that have bittersweet endings in order to learn whatever sorrow teaches, and to better appreciate the joy that seemed so elusive to us at that age. It was as important to do all this as it had been to make believe we were Yogi Berra or Whitey Ford or Mickey Mantle when, in earlier years, we played stickball outside Yankee Stadium.[3]

The three stages of reading growth were outlined by Margaret Early in 1960. According to Early, the primary stage of development is characterized by unconscious enjoyment. The reader, or listener in the case of prereading chil-

[3]Ibid., pp. 14–17.

dren, displays delight for no apparent reason. Anyone who has read the same story to a three-year-old at least a hundred times has been witness to this first stage of reading development, which begins at infancy and continues through the beginning and middle years of elementary school.

The second stage of development is added to the first usually by the late elementary or early junior high school years, when the reader is willing to exert effort to increase pleasure in reading. The reader enjoys the book vicariously, becoming a part of the story. This is the stage that Jackson and his friends entered when their "childhood crumbled."

> ☐ *From the raw material of life—the people we know and admire, the characters we meet in books, film, and television—we form and nourish the personal myths that guide our lives.*
> FRANK MCLAUGHLIN
> *"Place of fiction in the development of values"* [4]

Early's second stage of reading development usually corresponds with the egocentric years of adolescence. We adults may recall those years in our own lives with amazement and wonder how we survived. The years of drag racing on the interstate, cruising Main Street, buying beer with a borrowed ID, smoking dope, shoplifting at Woolworth's, walking by the lifeguard stand five hundred times a day, playing the radio until our eardrums were numb . . . the years of proms and books and friends and tears and demonstrations and petitions and political passion and love. . . . This second stage most often coincides with teenagers' search for self amid the need to be accepted by others, particularly their peers.

The reason Dan Jackson and his friends did not read in school, but read enthusiastically outside school, is that their teachers forgot about, or did not know about, the second stage in reading development. They assumed that students were ready to appreciate literature for its aesthetic value. The aesthetic, or third, stage of reading development allows readers to bring all their creative ability to the work of literature. Readers use their past experiences, their previous reading, their ideas and values to help in appreciating the work. At this stage readers possess a "deeper feeling for mankind." This feeling replaces the early "narrow concern for oneself" evidenced in the second stage of reading development (Early 1960). Dan Jackson's teachers did not allow Dan and his friends to go through the second stage of reading development in the classroom; according to Early, this stage cannot be bypassed if the reader is going to progress to the next stage. Therefore, Dan and his friends were forced to progress through the "narrow concern for oneself" stage on their own, while their teachers were requiring them to read Dickens and Shakespeare and Plato for their aesthetic value.

[4]Ibid, pp. 18–21.

□   *Through words we contemplate the world, establish a destiny, ask questions. (Who are we? Where are we? Where are we going?) We use language to answer the questions. How do we get to be who we are? Through language.*
ROBERT COLES
keynote address / IRA Convention / Atlanta, Ga. / April 1979

Conflicting Needs of the Adolescent

The second, or "narrow concern for oneself," stage of reading development usually occurs during the early teenage years, when adolescents are seeking affirmation of the self through their peer group and possibly through personal, peer-group-acceptable accomplishments.

The psychologist Abraham Maslow contends that the egocentric nature of the adolescent is a normal progression through basic human needs. Normal human beings must meet the basic needs of belongingness, love, and esteem before they can become productive, self-actualized adults.

> *My strong impression is ... that some proportion of youth rebellion groups—I don't know how many or how much—is motivated by profound hunger for groupiness, for contact, for real togetherness in the face of a common enemy, any enemy that can serve to form an amity group simply by posing an external threat. The same kind of thing was observed in groups of soldiers who were pushed into an unwanted brotherliness and intimacy by their common external danger, and who may stick together throughout a lifetime as a consequence. Any good society must satisfy this need, one way or another, if it is to survive and be healthy.*[5]

If Dan Jackson's teachers had remembered Maslow's hierarchy of needs, they might have helped Dan and his friends bridge the gap between stages one and three of reading development. According to Maslow, the basic human needs are these: (1) physiological needs (homeostasis, or the body's automatic efforts to maintain a constant, normal state of the bloodstream and appetites, or preferential choices of foods, indicating chemical shortages); (2) safety needs (security; stability; dependency; protection; freedom from fear, anxiety, and chaos; need for structure, order, law, limits; strength in the protector; and so on); (3) social affection (belongingness or love); (4) self-esteem (strength, achievement, adequacy, mastery and competence, confidence, independence and freedom, and reputation or prestige); (5) understanding (the desire to know); (6) aesthetic needs (the desire for beauty); and (7) self-actualization (self-fulfillment, or reaching one's full potential).

---

[5]Abraham H. Maslow, *Motivation and personality,* 2d ed. (New York: Harper & Row, 1954), p. 44. Reprinted by permission of Harper & Row, Publishers, Inc.

■ ■ ■ **An Anthological Aside**

It's the Climbing That Makes the Man

ROBERT LIPSYTE

"Let me tell you what it's like." Donatelli walked toward Alfred until they were standing face to face. His square head settled down into the crisp collar of his open-throated, short-sleeved white shirt. He had almost no neck.

"You get up at five-thirty in the morning, before the gas fumes foul the air, and you run in the park. That's to build up your legs and wind. You run smooth and easy, a little faster and a little longer each day. You run every day, rain or snow, unless you're too sick. Then you go home and eat breakfast. Juice, two boiled eggs, toast, and tea. You go to school?"

"I work."

"You don't eat too much lunch, it just makes you slow and tired. No fried foods, no beans, no cabbage, no pies and cakes, no soda. After work you come to the gym. Jump rope, stretching exercises, sit-ups, push-ups, deep-knee bends. You do them until you can't do any more, then start all over again. You go home, have a good dinner. Meat, green vegetable, fresh salad, milk, fruit. You're asleep by nine o'clock. . . . You'll do it for a week, maybe two. You'll feel a little better physically, but all your friends, your family, will say you're a fool. You'll see other people smoking and drinking and staying out late, eating anything they want, and you'll start to think you're a fool, too. You'll say to yourself, 'All this sacrifice, and I'll probably never even get to be a good fighter.' And you'll be right, nine times out of ten. . . . People will try to drag you down. Some will laugh at you for wanting to be a fighter. And others will tell you you're so good you don't need to train, to go to bed early. How far did you go in school?"

"Eleventh grade."

"What happened?"

"I quit."

"Why?"

"Didn't seem like any reason to stay."

"What makes you think you won't quit here too?" . . .

"I want to be somebody."

"Everybody is somebody."

"Somebody special. A champion."

Donatelli's thin lips tightened. "Everybody wants to be a champion. That's not enough. You have to start by wanting to be a contender, the man coming up, the man who knows there's a good chance he'll never get to the top, the man who's willing to sweat and bleed to get up as high as his legs and his brains and his heart will take him. That must sound corny to you."

"No."

"It's the climbing that makes the man. Getting to the top is an extra reward."

Aunt Pearl leaned over his shoulder and filled his glass. "When I was seventeen, Alfred . . . don't look at me like that, I was seventeen, too . . . a man came by the house. He was from the Apollo Theater. Said he heard me singing in the church choir. Wanted to sign me up for a stage show. No star part, you understand, I'd be in a chorus. Wear a fancy dress. They'd teach me some dance steps."

She walked around the table, holding the milk container with two hands. "Was we ever excited, me and Dorothy and Ernestine, your momma. Couldn't sign a contract because I was underage, and my momma, your grandma, wouldn't sign for me. She said that stage shows were sinful. Be shameful, one of her daughters struttin' around, showin' off. I'd end up no good."

She sat down, her fingers tightening on the container. "How I talked with her, and I cried, and Dorothy and Ernestine, they begged her, too. The more we begged the harder she set her face. Sinful. Shameful. No good."

"You never told me 'bout that."

"No secret. You just always been so closed into yourself, Alfred."

"What happened?"

"Nothing. The man went away. I met your Uncle John, and we went together a long time before my momma would give her blessing. She said he didn't have enough money in the bank. How that man worked. Night and day he worked. We got married, and he got sick soon after Charlene came along. He never did get to see the twins. Passed on a month before they came."

Her hands tightened and twisted on the container, and milk spurted out onto her lap. Alfred came around the table and put his hands on Aunt Pearl's shoulders.

"He woulda been real pleased with them. Nice girls," he said softly.

She was sobbing. "I don't say I woulda been a star or anything. I don't know what I'm saying."

"But you would of liked to try," said Alfred.

"Yes."

He held her shoulders until they stopped heaving.

"Thanks, Alfred. You're a comfort." She wiped her eyes and looked up into his. "I didn't even ask if you won your fight."

"I won it."

She reached up and stroked his face. "And it didn't even taste sweet, the winning, did it, honey?"

"No."

"You gonna quit this thing now?"

"No."

The bell rang.

"You want him to continue?" asked the referee.

Donatelli's pale blue eyes were narrow.

Henry's voice, shrill and loud. "Gotta let him, Mr. Donatelli, gotta."

"Let him fight," said Donatelli.

The bell rang.

The crowd was roaring deep in its gut, ocean waves that lapped at the ring, that drowned all pain and all feeling, drowned all sound but the drumming of leather against flesh. Everything was wet and sticky. Everything was sweat and blood. There were three Hubbards now, all of them hazy, jab at the middle one, hook the middle one. They stood toe to toe in the center of the ring, whacking, slugging, thumping back and forth, flinging sweat, elbows, fists, knees, jab the middle one, hook the middle one. *Thunk.* Alfred felt his mouthpiece fly out, hook the middle one, pop-pop, iron pipes, sledgehammers, meat hooks, go ahead, throw everything you got, you gonna have to, gonna stand here all day and all night and take what you got and give it right back, gonna hang in forever, gonna climb, man, gonna keep climbing, you can't knock me out, nobody ever gonna knock me out, you wanna stop me you better kill me.

The bell rang, but neither of them heard it, grunting, straining, slugging, and then everyone was in the ring pulling them apart, grabbing their gloves.

" . . . by unaminous decision . . . Elston Hubbard."

The referee held up Hubbard's right arm, and his manager held up the left, but Hubbard broke loose and ran across the ring, throwing his arms around Alfred. They hugged each other, crying because it was over, and Hubbard gasped, "You tough, baby."

All the way up the aisle, people were reaching out to touch Alfred's robe. "Great fight, kid . . . beautiful . . . real heart, Brooks . . ."

■ ■ ■

Maslow tells us that needs are usually met in order, although there is a good bit of overlap and one need may be much stronger for some people. Further, he claims, a person can become stuck on one need and therefore be unable to move to higher-level needs. This produces a great deal of frustration.

Why Should Young Adult Literature Be Used in the Classroom?

For the last ten years I have conducted an informal survey of parents and teachers of teenagers. I have asked them to check the level of the hierarchy at which they find most teenagers. Usually, the check marks appear at number 3, social affection. Often, the checks appear on number 4, self-esteem. At times, the checks appear between social affection and self-esteem. I have never found a check placed beside any other level of the hierarchy. Therefore, adults who live or work closely with teenagers believe that most teens are attempting to meet the needs of social affection and self-esteem. Many of us observe a struggle between these two needs.

Janet was an adolescent facing this struggle. When I first met Janet she was a student in my ninth-grade composition class. I remember the first paper she handed in—it was beautiful. I wondered how I could possibly teach her anything. Her paper was so impressive I read it to the class. Of course I didn't use her name, but everyone knew whose paper it was. For Janet, this was the worst kind of torture. She was one of those children who are not only intelligent but also talented, beautiful, athletic, and very popular. She was not about to give up that popularity. Overt intelligence in Janet's peer group was clearly unacceptable. Therefore, she stopped handing in papers in my composition class. However, Janet's intelligence caused a conflict for her. In order to be socially acceptable, Janet believed she should not exhibit her intelligence. On the other hand, her intelligence was part of her, and her self-esteem required acknowledging it. Janet resolved her internal struggle in an antisocial way.

In the wee hours of a Sunday morning I received a phone call from a hysterical Janet. When she calmed down, she told me she was in a church and had taken the hymnals and thrown them through the windows. In her adolescent mind the community was at fault for her internal conflict between the needs for social approval and for self-esteem. So she had lashed out against the church, a visible symbol of her community.

This struggle to meet social affection and self-esteem needs is also evidenced in the developmental reading stage of adolescents, the "narrow concern for oneself" stage of reading choice and appreciation.

A study completed in 1977 by Lance Gentile and Merna McMillan, who attempted to determine why many teenagers won't read, helps show how a teenager's struggle to meet needs may affect in-school reading. The study found ten factors that contribute to what the authors call the "reluctant reader syndrome."

1. Many students "equate reading with ridicule, failure, or exclusively school-related tasks."
2. "Some people are not excited by ideas. Many are driven to experience life directly rather than through reading."
3. "A great number of adolescents do not want to sit, and in some cases are incapable of sitting, for prolonged periods."
4. "Adolescence is a time of intense egocentrism."

5. "Many young people demand to be entertained. They have developed little understanding or appreciation of intrinsic rewards. . . ."
6. Many "students are pressured at home as well as in school to read! read! read! Persistent stress proves counterproductive."
7. "Many young people grow up in an atmosphere void of reading material."
8. "Reading may be considered 'antisocial activity' by many adolescents."
9. "Many classroom texts and supplemental reading materials are dull to look at."
10. "Some adolescents view reading as part of the adult world and automatically reject it."[6]

The Teacher's Role

As teachers of young adults, not only do we have the responsibility to encourage reading, but also, in the words of Robert Lipsyte, we have a chance to change minds. We can make a difference for the young adults in our classrooms by developing curricula that encourage them to read books that help teenagers move from the "narrow concern for oneself" stage of reading appreciation to the aesthetic, creative stage of reading development. We can make a difference for our students by assisting them in locating good literature that helps meet their needs and may even change their minds.

☐ *When you write for adolescents, you have a chance to change minds.*
ROBERT LIPSYTE
author of The contender / *IRA Convention* / *Atlanta, Ga.* / *April 1979*

Adolescent literature provides books that help young adults meet their needs. The student who is struggling with the conflict between peer acceptance and feelings of self-worth can be directed to Robert Cormier's *The chocolate war,* the story of a young boy who must decide whether being accepted by his peers is more important than what he believes is right. The ending of the book does not show the reader that the decision is easy, nor does it prove that a person who chooses the ethical course is always the victor, but it does show the struggling young adult that he or she is not fighting alone.

Young people who feel rejected by their parents can find a friend in the heroine of M. E. Kerr's *Dinky Hocker shoots smack!* Dinky, a fat girl who feels rejected by her mother's apparent lack of concern for her as she pursues a career of social concern for others, finds both solace and pain in overeating. In

[6]Reprinted by permission of Lance Gentile, Merna McMillan, and the International Reading Association.

an attempt to gain her mother's attention, she scrawls the phrase of the book's title all over town.

Young adults who feel alone and rejected by their peers may enjoy a book such as Jean Little's *One to grow on.* Janie is a quiet, plain girl who is convinced that no one could care about her for herself. Therefore, she often invents stories that make her life seem more exciting. In her loneliness, she falls prey to girls who use her in a variety of ways. Slowly, Janie learns to believe in herself, and this new confidence helps her find true friendship.

Those of us who teach young adults can assist them in selecting literature that will help them to meet their needs. But first we must become familiar with the books written for and/or enjoyed by young adults. Then we must find ways to incorporate this literature into the regular classroom curricula. We must help our students build a bridge from their childhood reading to the mature reading of an adult; we must help our students close the gap between their lower-level needs of social acceptance and self-esteem to their higher, full-potential needs. We must allow the Dan Jacksons of our classrooms to find answers to the problems created by their crumbling childhood worlds in books we keep in our classroom libraries, books by Sartre, Verne, Christie, Blume, Lipsyte, Cormier, Paterson, Holland, Duncan, L'Engle, and others. Through young adult literature we can help our students become mature readers, while they are answering the questions that must be answered by healthy adolescents.

Discovering and Using the Interests of Teenagers

At times the assignments we ask our students to complete do not meet their needs, do not matter to them, and are uninteresting. Consequently, the students often are unsuccessful in reaching the educational objectives we have set for the assignment, sometimes because they have not even attempted to begin it. One of the ways to increase student success in the completion of assignments is to make them interesting and motivational. The key to creating interesting assignments is knowledge of the students' interests.

> *How could I set up a school program when I know so little about the students it was meant to serve?*
>
> *I began again. This time I went to the students. What's wrong with your English class, I asked, that causes you to turn it off the way you do? You're out to lunch during your English class, I said, and I want to know why. They told me why: They told me that it didn't make any difference about them. That the teacher didn't like them so they didn't like the teacher. She didn't talk like she wanted you to understand. And never nothing to read that was any good, even if you wanted to read. What difference does it make anyway? (Fader and McNeil 1966, p. 9)*

Of course, this bleak picture of the secondary school English classroom is not true of most classrooms. Many classrooms are colorful symbols of the exciting learning that happens within them; they are covered with student work; they have wall-to-wall books, magazines, and newspapers; there are comfortable little nooks for escaping to read a good book; the teacher cares and smiles often.

How can we turn our classrooms into exciting centers of learning? As Dan Fader told us in 1966, we must begin with the students. If the classrooms are to become places that interest and excite adolescents, the classrooms must be theirs. If the curriculum is to meet their needs, help them develop new interests, and make a difference, then it must be based on who "they *are.*" The students "must be met where they are before they can be led to where they *should be* (i.e., where *we* are)" (Fader and McNeil, pp. 9–10).

This does not mean "watering down" the content of the subject area; nor does it mean excluding the "classics"; nor does it mean eliminating the basics; nor does it mean teaching only what interests the students today. It means bridging the gap between childhood and adulthood so that the content can be taught in a more sophisticated way. It means reading books like *Death be not proud: A memoir* (Gunther) and *Ronnie and Rosey* (Angell) so that works such as *On death and dying* (Kübler-Ross) and *For whom the bell tolls* (Hemingway) can be more easily understood and appreciated. It means learning vocabulary within the book the student is reading, rather than in isolation. It means broadening interests by beginning with something the student understands, such as *Anne Frank: The diary of a young girl,* and moving to a complete study of the Holocaust.

But before we can begin our classes, we must get to know our students. We must know what "turns them on." This is not as difficult as it sounds. It does not mean that we can do no planning before we meet the students. It does mean that we must first be aware of the general interests of teenagers, and second learn the individual interests of the students in our classes. We can begin our planning with a knowledge of what we know about adolescents.

GENERAL INTERESTS OF TEENAGERS. George Gallup, in conjunction with the Associated Press, periodically publishes a Youth Survey. The survey (see Table 1-1) can give us a general understanding of the interests of teenagers. Using this survey is only a starting point for getting to know the teenagers in our classrooms. Other studies of youth interests can provide valuable information.

In a study (Table 1-2) of the interests of high school students, N. T. Gill (1980) found that these students "appear to express interests that reflect national values" and that "girls at this age level are still the more romantic of the species" (p. 166). He concludes that "the solution for preventing and correcting both disharmony in the classroom and general apathy toward education . . . may very well be nothing more complicated than simply to discover ways of making our schools into centers of interest rather than compounds of boredom" (p. 166).

The classroom, which is a colorful symbol of learning, is filled with books, books, books—some of them written by the students themselves.

Table 1-1 Gallup Youth Survey, 1979

HOBBIES
(Percentages based on those who have hobbies.)

	Both sexes	Boys	Girls
Outdoor activities	25%	27%	23%
Handicrafts, domestic arts	20	20	19
Playing musical instruments	18	12	24
Reading	17	8	26
Creative arts	16	10	22
Collecting	10	12	7
Mechanics	7	15	*
Listening to music	7	6	8
Driving cars, motorcycles	4	5	2
Watching TV, movies	3	2	4
All others	14	14	13
TOTALS	141%	131%	148%

ACADEMIC STANDING

	Above average	Average or below	White-collar household	Blue-collar household
Outdoor activities	23%	27%	23%	27%
Handicrafts, domestic arts	21	18	19	21
Playing musical instruments	20	15	20	17
Reading	20	14	16	18
Creative arts	17	15	20	12
Collecting	9	11	9	10
Mechanics	6	9	5	9
Listening to music	6	8	8	6
Driving cars, motorcycles	2	5	2	6
Watching TV, movies	3	3	4	2
All others	15	12	14	12
TOTALS	142%	137%	140%	140%

*Less than one percent.
Source: Copyright © 1979 by George Gallup. Used by permission of the Associated Press.

READING INTERESTS OF TEENAGERS. Other studies of teenage interests indicate that boys have a narrower range of reading interests than girls. After a ten-year study of young adult interests, Jo M. Stanchfield (1973) concluded that this narrower range of interests in male readers may account, in part, for their greater difficulty in learning to read.

Stanchfield (1962) found that junior high school boys are primarily interested in outdoor life, exploration and expeditions, sports and games, sea adventure,

Table 1-2 Comparison of High School Student Interests

Rank order of female interests	Rank order of male interests
Boys	Girls
Love	Sex
Life	Life
People	Cars
Peace	Love
Animals	Sports
Travel	Peace
Sex	Movies
Movies	People
Pop Music	Travel
Cars	Animals
Sports	Motorcycles
God	Pop Music
Cooking	God
Generation Gap	Countries
Countries	School
School	Generation Gap
Teachers	Voting Age
Motorcycles	Wild West
Voting Age	Cooking
Death	Teachers
Drugs	Death
Vietnam	War
War	Vietnam
Wild West	Hippies
Hippies	Drugs
Communism	Communism
Girls	Boys

Source: N. T. Gill, Comparison of high school student interests across three grade and ability levels, *High School Journal* (1980). Reprinted by permission of the University of North Carolina Press.

science fiction, mystery and detective stories, outer space, and humor. In short, male junior high school readers prefer excitement, suspense, and the unusual, rather than the romance that female teenagers enjoy. Other researchers have confirmed these results in more recent studies (Shores 1964, Culliton 1974, Ritt 1976). Similar reading interests were found in male senior high students. Studies conducted by Smith and Eno (1961) and Culliton (1974) showed that senior high boys preferred mystery, adventure, sports, science fiction, sea stories, comedy, animal stories, and career interest.

DETERMINING THE INTERESTS OF SPECIFIC TEENAGERS. Knowing the general interests of teenagers is not enough, however. We must learn the interests of the teens in our community and in our classroom. As I travel around the six public high schools in the county in which I live and work, I see many differences from school to school. The difference begins with dress. In one local school all the boys wear baseball hats. In another high school, not more than ten miles away, wearing a brimmed cap is grounds for instant ridicule.

Other differences are far less obvious. At one school there is nothing more important than football, the team, the cheerleaders, pep rallies, and all the other hoopla that surrounds high school athletics. At another school, football takes a back seat to cars, cycles, cruising, dragging, and the Friday-night races. In another school it is much more acceptable for a girl to play on the basketball team than to be a cheerleader. In a school six miles away, girl basketball players are socially unacceptable. In order to be an effective teacher in any school we must know the school, the community, and the students.

It is essential if we are to successfully instruct our students in our subject area that we know them—what makes them cry, what makes them laugh, what makes them sing. If we know these things about our students, we can use their interests to turn them on to our subject.

There are many interest inventory techniques that can be used to determine our students' interests. Some are quite simple. A sentence-completion test can be designed to assess student reading, recreational, and content area interests.

The incomplete sentence test could incorporate sentences that pertain more specifically to the unit of study. For example, in a history class studying World War II, the items might include:

In studying wars I am most interested in _____. *I saw the movie*

_____ *that dealt with WW II. My* _____ *fought in*
(name of movie)   (family member)

_____.
(particular war)

Figure 1.1 An Incomplete Sentence Test

1. The best book I have ever read is _____.

2. The best movie I have ever seen is _____.

3. I often read the magazine _____.

4. In history I like studying _____ best.

5. On a free Saturday afternoon I am likely to be found _____.

6. My favorite television show is _____.

7. The "neatest" place I have ever visited is _____.

8. I would like to visit _____ more than anywhere in the world.

9. I'd rather be _____.

10. If I could meet anyone in the world (living or dead), it would be _____.

Some interest inventories are much more complex. For example, each student can be asked to draw a coat of arms that best represents him or her. One section of the shield might contain a symbol that represents recreational interests, another family life, a third educational interests, and a fourth reading or viewing interests. The top of the coat of arms might be the single symbol that the student believes best depicts the most important aspect of his or her life.[7]

Teenagers today are interested in and excited by many things. If we can use their interests to design curricula, we can turn our classrooms into exciting centers of learning, and we can capture the enthusiasm with which the students read *Mad* or tabulate baseball stats or write letters to friends. If we incorporate young adult literature into our classroom bibliographies, we can assist our students in learning new concepts by beginning where the students are, with the knowledge they already possess. We can create classrooms that are "centers of interest rather than compounds of boredom" (Gill 1980, p. 166). We can make the learning that students do in school as meaningful as the learning they do outside of school.

YOUNG ADULT BOOKS, TEENAGE INTERESTS, AND CLASSROOMS. There are young adult books appropriate to every subject area. For example, Harry Mazer's *The last mission* is a gripping tale about an enlisted teenager who becomes an aircraft gunner. This World War II story shows the horror of a mission that turns out to be the last for every member of the crew except the young gunner. This is only one example of the thousands of young adult books appropriate in history classes.

Fiction and nonfiction books are useful in science classrooms as well. The nature books of Jean Craighead George teach more than facts about our environment; they teach the necessity for maintaining an environmental balance for all living creatures. George's fiction books, such as *Julie of the wolves,* are marvelous tools for developing student interest in studies of animal life and nature. Nonfiction works written for adolescent readers can awaken scientific fervor in many young adults. Titles such as Randall Eaton's *The cheetah, nature's fastest racer* are interesting nonfiction companions to the fiction books on the science classroom shelf. The student who develops an interest in animal life through fiction can be directed toward this beautiful, informative book and many others like it.

Our job is to find the books that are useful in our classroom. We must determine which books are likely to be of interest to our students based on information that has been gathered from interest inventories, and direct the student toward these books. The reward is in watching the content area we love come to life for a previously unmotivated student.

[7]An excellent source for interest-inventory techniques is Blackburn and Powell 1976.

Building Bridges

The task of the teacher of young adults is to help students build bridges from childhood to emerging adulthood. In order to assist in the construction, teachers must understand that every student is different. No two people progress through the teen years at the same physiological pace, with the same needs, with identical interests, with equal intellectual maturity.

> ☐ *Everybody has a bridge.... For everyone there is a bridge that brings back all the pain of growing up....*
> MAYA ANGELOU
> *author of* I know why the caged bird sings / *during a question-and-answer session with Asheville, N.C., high school students* / *March 1983* / *referring to a bridge in Stamps, Ark., that racially divided the town*

Literature written for young adults allows readers to see themselves in a book, to read the book with ease and interest, and to gain new information that relates the new to the familiar world of young adulthood. Through young adult books readers are assisted in meeting their needs by reading about characters who

Table 1-3 Novels to Be Used as Bridges to Adult Reading

Books read by young adult readers	"Classics"
Crompton, Anne E. *A woman's place*	*The return of the native*
Peyton, K. M. *Flambards*	
Flambards in summer	*Silas Marner*
Trease, Geoffrey. *Message to Hadrian: An adventure story of ancient Rome*	*Caesar's commentaries*
Townsend, John Rowe. *The summer people*	*Pride and prejudice*
Hemingway, Ernest. *The old man and the sea*	
Graham, Robin, and L. T. Derek *Dove*	*Moby Dick*
Eyerly, Jeannette. *Bonnie Jo, go home*	
Blume, Judy. *Forever*	*The scarlet letter*
Tolkien, J. R. R. *The Hobbit*	
Adams, Richard. *Watership down*	*The pilgrim's progress*
Adams, Richard, *Shardick*	
Peyton, K. M. *The Beethoven medal*	*Wuthering Heights*
Rivera, Geraldo. *A special kind of courage: Profiles of young Americans*	*Profiles in courage*
Peck, Richard. *Representing super doll*	*Vanity Fair*
Kerr, M. E. *Gentlehands*	*Great expectations*
George, Jean C. *Julie of the wolves*	*Walden*
Ney, John. *Ox goes north: More trouble for a kid at the top*	
Ney, John. Ox: *The story of a kid at the top*	
Ney, John. *Ox under pressure*	*The great Gatsby*
Kerr, M. E. *The son of someone famous*	

Source: Compiled by Charlotte Kutscher, Librarian, Asheville High School Library, Asheville, N.C., 1979.

face and resolve similar problems and conflicts. However, as teachers we want our students to move beyond the world of the young into the world of the adult, emotionally and intellectually. The literature of the young adult is not an end, but a means. It allows the young reader to progress beyond the books read for childhood pleasures to the aesthetic, intellectual reading of the mature adult. Many young adult books are appropriate bridges to this world of mature adult reading (see Table 1-3).

The secondary school classroom should be a place where each student, like Jesse in Katherine Paterson's *Bridge to Terabithia,* "came to be knighted. After [he] stayed for a while and grew strong [he] had to move on. . . ." The teacher must discover materials and develop methods that allow each student to "push back the walls of his mind and make him see beyond to the shining world—huge and terrible and beautiful and very fragile." The secondary school classroom teacher must help each student build a bridge to adulthood by beginning all instruction with the student's needs, interests, and abilities. And through the instruction, the teacher must help the student find new worlds.

■ ■ ■ **An Anthological Aside**

Building the Bridge

KATHERINE PATERSON

He woke up Saturday morning with a dull headache. It was still early, but he got up. He wanted to do the milking. His father had done it ever since Thursday night, but he wanted to go back to it, to somehow make things normal again. He shut P.T. in the shed, and the dog's whimpering reminded him of May Belle and made his headache worse. But he couldn't have P.T. yapping at Miss Bessie while he tried to milk.

No one was awake when he brought the milk in to put it away, so he poured a warm glass for himself and got a couple of pieces of light bread. He wanted his paints back, and he decided to go down and see if he could find them. He let P.T. out of the shed and gave the dog a half piece of bread.

It was a beautiful spring morning. Early wild flowers were dotting the deep green of the fields, and the sky was clean and blue. The creek had fallen well below the bank and seemed less terrifying than before. A large branch was washed up into the bank, and he hauled it up to the narrowest place and laid it bank to bank. He stepped on it, and it seemed firm, so he crossed on it, foot over foot, to the other side, grabbing the smaller branches which grew out from the main one toward the opposite bank to keep his balance. There was no sign of his paints.

He landed slightly upstream from Terabithia. If it was still Terabithia. If it could be entered across a branch instead of swung into. P.T. was left crying piteously on the other side. Then the dog took courage and paddled across the stream. The current carried him past Jess, but he made it safely to the bank and ran back, shaking great drops of cold water on Jess.

They went into the castle stronghold. It was dark and damp, but there was no evidence there to suggest that the queen had died. He felt the need to do something fitting. But Leslie was not here to tell him what it was. The anger which has possessed him yesterday flared up again. *Leslie, I'm just a dumb dodo, and you know it! What am I supposed to do?* The coldness inside of him had moved upward into his throat, constricting it. He swallowed several times. It occurred to him that he probably had cancer of the throat. Wasn't that one of the seven deadly signs? *Difficulty in swallowing.* He began to sweat. He didn't want to die. Lord, he was just ten years old. He had hardly begun to live.

Abridged from Chapter 13, "Building the Bridge," pp. 118–28, in *Bridge to Terabithia.* New York: Thomas Y. Crowell, 1977. Copyright © 1977 by Katherine Paterson. Reprinted by permission of Harper & Row, Publishers, Inc.

Leslie, were you scared? Did you know you were dying? Were you scared like me? A picture of Leslie being sucked into the cold water flashed across his brain.

"C'mon, Prince Terrien," he said quite loudly. "We must make a funeral wreath for the queen."

He sat in the clear space between the bank and the first line of trees and bent a pine bough into a circle, tying it with a piece of wet string from the castle. And because it looked cold and green, he picked spring beauties from the forest floor and wove them among the needles.

He put it down in front of him. A cardinal flew down to the bank, cocked its brilliant head, and seemed to stare at the wreath. P.T. let out a growl which sounded more like a purr. Jess put his hand on the dog to quiet him.

The bird hopped about a moment more, then flew leisurely away.

"It's a sign from the Spirits," Jess said quietly. "We made a worthy offering."

He walked slowly, as part of a great procession, though only the puppy could be seen, slowly carrying forward the queen's wreath to the sacred grove. He forced himself deep into the dark center of the grove and, kneeling, laid the wreath upon the thick carpet of golden needles.

"Father, into Thy hands I commend her spirit." He knew Leslie would have liked those words. They had the ring of the sacred grove in them.

The solemn procession wound its way through the sacred grove homeward to the castle. Like a single bird across a storm-cloud sky, a tiny peace winged its way through the chaos inside his body.

"Help! Jesse! Help me!" A scream shattered the quietness. Jess raced to the sound of May Belle's cry. She had gotten halfway across on the tree bridge and now stood there grabbing the upper branches, terrified to move either forward or backward.

"OK, May Belle." The words came out more steadily than he felt. "Just hold still. I'll get you." He was not sure the branch would hold the weight of them both. He looked down at the water. It was low enough for him to walk across, but still swift. Suppose it swept him off his feet. He decided for the branch. He inched out on it until he was close enough to touch her. He'd have to get her back to the home side of the creek. "OK," he said. "Now, back up."

"I can't!"

"I'm right here, May Belle, You think I'm gonna let you fall? Here." He put out his right hand. "Hold on to me and slide sideways on the thing."

She let go with her left hand for a moment and then grabbed the branch again.

"I'm scared, Jesse. I'm too scared."

"'Course you're scared. Anybody'd be scared. You just gotta trust me, OK? I'm not gonna let you fall, May Belle. I promise you."

She nodded, her eyes still wide with fear, but she let go the branch and took his hand, straightening a little and swaying. He gripped her tightly.

"OK, now. It ain't far—just slide your right foot a little way, then bring your left foot up close."

"I forgot which is right."

"The front one," he said patiently. "The one closest to home."

She nodded again and obediently moved her right foot a few inches.

"Now just let go of the branch with your other hand and hold on to me tight."

She let go the branch and squeezed his hand.

"Good, you're doing great. Now slide a little ways more." She swayed but did not scream, just dug her little fingernails into the palm of his hand. "Great. Fine. You're all right." The same quiet, assuring voice of the paramedics on *Emergency,* but his heart was bongoing against his chest. "OK. OK. A little bit more, now."

When her right foot came at last to the part of the branch which rested on the bank, she fell forward, pulling him down.

"Watch it, May Belle!" He was off balance, but he fell, not into the stream, but with his chest across May Belle's legs, his own legs waving in the empty air above the water. "Whew!" He was laughing with relief. "Whatcha trying to do, girl, kill me?"

She shook her head a solemn no. "I know I swore on the Bible not to follow you, but I woke up this morning and you was gone."

"I had to do some things."

She was scraping at the mud on her bare legs. "I just wanted to find you, so you wouldn't be so lonesome." She hung her head. "But I got too scared."

He pulled himself around until he was sitting beside her. They watched P.T. swimming across, the current carrying him too swiftly, but he not seeming to mind. He climbed out well below the crab apple and came running back to where they sat.

"Everybody gets scared sometimes, May Belle. You don't have to be ashamed." He saw a flash of Leslie's eyes as she was going to the girls' room to see Janice Avery. "Everybody gets scared."

"P.T. ain't scared, and he even saw Leslie . . ."

"It ain't the same for dogs. It's like the smarter you are, the more things can scare you."

She looked at him in disbelief. "But you weren't scared."

"Lord, May Belle, I was shaking like Jello."

"You're just saying that."

He laughed. He couldn't help being glad she didn't believe him. He jumped up and pulled her to her feet. "Let's go eat." He let her beat him to the house.

When he walked into the basement classroom he saw Mrs. Myers had already had Leslie's desk taken out of the front of the room. Of course, by

Monday Jess knew, but still, but still, at the bus stop he looked up, half expecting to see her running up across the field, her lovely, even, rhythmic run. Maybe she was already at school—Bill had dropped her off, as he did some days when she was late for the bus—but then when Jess came into the room, her desk was no longer there. Why were they all in such a rush to be rid of her? He put his head down on his own desk, his whole body heavy and cold.

He could hear the sounds of the whispers but not the words. Not that he wanted to hear the words. He was suddenly ashamed that he'd thought he might be regarded with respect by the other kids. Trying to profit for himself from Leslie's death. *I wanted to be the best—the fastest runner in the school—and now I am.* Lord, he made himself sick. He didn't care what the others said or what they thought, just as long as they left him alone—just so long as he didn't have to talk to them or meet their stares. They had all hated Leslie. Except maybe Janice. Even after they'd given up trying to make Leslie miserable, they'd kept on despising her—as though there was one of them worth the nail on Leslie's little toe. And even he himself had entertained the traitorous thought that now he would be the fastest.

Mrs. Myers barked the command to stand for the allegiance. He didn't move. Whether he couldn't or wouldn't, he didn't really care. What could she do to him, after all?

"Jesse Aarons. Will you step out into the hall. Please."

He raised his leaden body and stumbled out of the room. He thought he heard Gary Fulcher giggle, but he couldn't be sure. He leaned against the wall and waited for Monster Mouth Myers to finish singing "O Say Can You See?" and join him. He could hear her giving the class some sort of assignment in arithmetic before she came out and quietly closed the door behind her.

OK. Shoot. I don't care.

She came over so close to him that he could smell her dimestore powder.

"Jesse." Her voice was softer than he had ever heard it, but he didn't answer. Let her yell. He was used to that.

"Jesse," she repeated. "I just want to give you my sincere sympathy." The words were like a Hallmark card, but the tone was new to him.

He looked up into her face, despite himself. Behind her turned-up glasses, Mrs. Myers' narrow eyes were full of tears. For a minute he thought he might cry himself. He and Mrs. Myers standing in the basement hallway, crying over Leslie Burke. It was so weird he almost laughed instead.

"When my husband died"—Jess could hardly imagine Mrs. Myers ever having had a husband—"people kept telling me not to cry, kept trying to make me forget." Mrs. Myers loving, mourning. How could you picture it? "But I didn't want to forget." She took her handkerchief from her sleeve and blew her nose. "Excuse me," she said. "This morning when I came in, someone had already taken out her desk." She stopped and blew her nose again. "It—it—we—I never had such a student. In all my years of teaching. I shall always be grateful—"

He wanted to comfort her. He wanted to unsay all the things he had said about her—even unsay the things Leslie had said. Lord, don't let her ever find out.

"So—I realize. If it's hard for me, how much harder it must be for you. Let's try to help each other, shall we?"

"Yes'm." He couldn't think of anything else to say. Maybe some day when he was grown, he would write her a letter and tell her that Leslie Burke had thought she was a great teacher or something. Leslie wouldn't mind. Sometimes like the Barbie doll you need to give people something that's for them, not just something that makes you feel good giving it. Because Mrs. Myers had helped him already by understanding that he would never forget Leslie.

He thought about it all day, how before Leslie came, he had been a nothing—a stupid, weird little kid who drew funny pictures and chased around a cow field trying to act big—trying to hide a whole mob of foolish little fears running riot inside his gut.

It was Leslie who had taken him from the cow pasture into Terabithia and turned him into a king. He had thought that was it. Wasn't king the best you could be? Now it occurred to him that perhaps Terabithia was like a castle where you came to be knighted. After you stayed for a while and grew strong you had to move on. For hadn't Leslie, even in Terabithia, tried to push back the walls of his mind and make him see beyond to the shining world—huge and terrible and beautiful and very fragile? (Handle with care—everything—even the predators.)

Now it was time for him to move out. She wasn't there, so he must go for both of them. It was up to him to pay back to the world in beauty and caring what Leslie had loaned him in vision and strength.

As for the terrors ahead—for he did not fool himself that they were all behind him—well, you just have to stand up to your fear and not let it squeeze you white. Right, Leslie?

Right.

Bill and Judy came back from Pennsylvania on Wednesday with a U-Haul truck. No one ever stayed long in the old Perkins place. "We came to the country for her sake. Now that she's gone . . ." They gave Jesse all of Leslie's books and her paint set with three pads of real watercolor paper. "She would want you to have them," Bill said.

Jess and his dad helped them load the U-Haul, and noontime his mother brought down ham sandwiches and coffee, a little scared the Burkes wouldn't want to eat her food, but needing, Jess knew, to do something. At last the truck was filled, and the Aaronses and the Burkes stood around awkwardly, no one knowing how to say good-bye.

"Well," Bill said. "If there's anything we've left that you want, please help yourself."

"Could I have some of the lumber on the back porch?" Jess asked.

"Yes, of course. Anything you see." Bill hesitated, then continued. "I meant to give you P.T.," he said. "But"—he looked at Jess and his eyes were those of a pleading little boy—"but I can't seem to give him up."

"It's OK. Leslie would want you to keep him."

The next day after school, Jess went down and got the lumber he needed, carrying it a couple of boards at a time to the creek bank. He put the two longest pieces across at the narrow place upstream from the crab apple tree, and when he was sure they were as firm and even as he could make them, he began to nail on the crosspieces.

"Whatcha doing, Jess?" May Belle had followed him down again as he had guessed she might.

"It's a secret, May Belle."

"Tell me."

"When I finish, OK?"

"I swear on the Bible I won't tell nobody. Not Billy Jean, not Joyce Ann, not Momma—" She was jerking her head back and forth in solemn emphasis.

"Oh, I don't know about Joyce Ann. You might want to tell Joyce Ann sometime."

"Tell Joyce Ann something that's a secret between you and me?" The idea seemed to horrify her.

"Yeah, I was just thinking about it."

Her face sagged. "Joyce Ann ain't nothing but a baby."

"Well, she wouldn't likely be a queen first off. You'd have to train her and stuff."

"Queen? Who gets to be queen?"

"I'll explain it when I finish, OK?"

And when he finished, he put flowers in her hair and led her across the bridge—the great bridge into Terabithia—which might look to someone with no magic in him like a few planks across a nearly dry gully.

"Shhh," he said. "Look."

"Where?"

"Can't you see 'um?" he whispered. "All the Terabithians standing on tiptoe to see you."

"Me?"

"Shhh, yes. There's a rumor going around that the beautiful girl arriving today might be the queen they've been waiting for."

■ ■ ■

Anthological Asides in Chapter 1

Duncan, L. *Killing Mr. Griffin.* Little, Brown, 1978. Dell, 1979.
Lipsyte, R. *The contender.* Harper & Row, 1967. Bantam, 1979.
Paterson, K. *Bridge to Terabithia.* Crowell, 1977. Avon, 1979.

Titles Mentioned in Chapter 1

Adams, R. *Shardick.* Simon & Schuster, 1957, 1974.
————. *Watership Down.* Macmillan, 1972. Avon, 1975.
Angell, J. *Ronnie and Rosey.* Bradbury, 1977 Dell, 1979.
Blume, J. *Forever.* Bradbury, 1975. Pocket Books, 1975.
Cormier, R. *The chocolate war.* Pantheon, 1974. Dell, 1975.
Crompton, A. E. *A woman's place.* Little, Brown, 1978. Ballantine, 1980.
Eaton, R. *The cheetah, nature's fastest racer.* Dodd, Mead, 1981.
Eyerly, J. *Bonnie Jo, go home.* Lippincott, 1972. Bantam, 1978.
George, J. C. *Julie of the wolves.* Harper & Row, 1972.
Graham, R., and L. T. Derek. *Dove.* Harper & Row, 1972. Bantam, 1974.
Gunther, J. *Death be not proud: A memoir.* Harper & Row, 1949. Pyramid, 1979.
Hemingway, E. *For whom the bell tolls.* Scribner's, 1940.
————. *The old man and the sea.* Scribner's, 1952, 1968.
Kerr, M. E. *Dinky Hocker shoots smack!* Harper & Row, 1972. Dell, 1978.
————. *Gentlehands.* Harper & Row, 1978.
————. *The son of someone famous.* Harper & Row, 1974. Ballantine, 1975.
Kübler-Ross, E. *On death and dying.* Macmillan, 1969, 1979.
Little, J. *One to grow on.* Archway, 1974.
Mazer, H. *The last mission.* Delacorte, 1979. Dell, 1981.
Ney, J. *Ox: The story of a kid at the top.* Little, Brown, 1970. Bantam, 1971.
————. *Ox goes north: More trouble for a kid at the top.* Harper & Row, 1973. Bantam, 1973.
————. *Ox under pressure.* Lippincott, 1976. Bantam, 1977.
Peck, R. *Representing super doll.* Viking, 1974. Avon, 1974.
Peyton, K. M. *The Beethoven medal.* Crowell, 1971. (Scholastic, 1974, as *If I ever marry.*)
————. *Flambards.* World, 1967. Penguin, 1980.
————. *Flambards in summer.* Penguin, 1980.
Rivera, G. *A special kind of courage: Profiles of young Americans.* Simon & Schuster, 1976. Bantam, 1977.
Tolkien, J. R. R. *The Hobbit, or there and back again.* Houghton Mifflin, 1957. Revised in 1965. Ballantine, 1973.
Townsend, J. R. *The summer people.* Lippincott, 1972. Dell, 1976.
Trease, G. *Message to Hadrian: An adventure story of ancient Rome.* Vanguard, 1955.

Suggested Readings

Blackburn, J. E., and W. C. Powell. *One at a time, all at once: The creative teacher's guide to individualized instruction without anarchy.* Goodyear, 1976.

Culliton, T. E. Techniques for developing reading interests and attitudes. In G. G. Duffy (ed.), *Reading in the middle school.* IRA, 1974, 183–96.

Early, M. Stages in growth in literary appreciation. *English Journal,* March 1960, pp. 161–67.

Fader, D., and E. B. McNeil. *Hooked on books: Program and proof.* Berkeley, 1966.

Gentile, L. M., and M. M. McMillan. Why won't teenagers read? *Journal of Reading,* May 1977, pp. 649–54.

Gill, N. T. Comparison of high school student interests across three grade and ability levels. *High School Journal,* January 1980, pp. 160–66.

Jackson, D. Books in the Bronx: A personal look at how literature shapes our lives. *Media and Methods,* March 1980, pp. 14–17.

McLaughlin, F. Place of fiction in the development of values. *Media and Methods,* March 1980, pp. 18–21.

Maslow, A. *Motivation and personality,* 2nd edition. Harper & Row, 1970.

Ritt, S. I. Journeys: Another look at the junior novel. *Journal of Reading,* May 1976, pp. 627–34.

Shores, J. H. Reading interests and informational needs of high school students. *The Reading Teacher,* April 1964, pp. 536–44.

Smith, M. L., and I. V. Eno. What do they really want to read? *English Journal,* May 1961, pp. 343–45.

Stanchfield, J. M. The reading interests of eighth-grade boys. *Journal of Developmental Reading,* Summer 1962, pp. 256–65.

————. *Sex differences in learning to read.* Phi Delta Kappa, 1973.

———— and S. R. Fraim. Follow-up study on the reading interests of boys. *Journal of Reading,* May 1979, pp. 748–52.

Tunis, J. What is a juvenile book? *Horn Book,* June 1969, pp. 307–10.

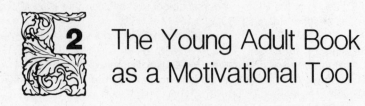

2 The Young Adult Book as a Motivational Tool

The Young Adult Book Motivates All Teenage Readers

One of the easiest and most enjoyable ways to motivate young adults to read is to introduce them to the wide world of young adult literature. The best thing about this reading world is that it has something for everyone.

THE POOR READER. The ninth-grade boy who has experienced great difficulty in gaining reading skills can be led to books that are written on low reading levels but are especially interesting to him. Educational publishers call these books high-low books, easy-to-read books, or high-interest–easy-reading books.[1] Their great value is that they address the needs of the adolescent in an interesting way without patronizing or insulting the reader. For example, this young reader might be attracted to stories that he can complete in one short sitting. Books like Michael Avallone's *Five-minute mysteries* or Alvin Schwartz's *Scary stories to tell in the dark* are likely to fill the bill for the young reader who enjoys television suspense shows. If these short tales whet the teenage reader's appetite, he can be directed to longer mystery-suspense tales that are part of

[1]There are many excellent guides for easy-to-read, high-interest books for adolescents. The National Council of Teachers of English publishes *High interest–easy reading*, edited by Hugh Agee. The Young Adult Services of the New York Public Library prints a new edition of *Easy-to-read books for teenagers* each year.

the easy-reading fare, such as Jay Bennett's *The birthday murderer,* which is written on a fifth-grade reading level but has the ability to hold the interest of most teenage readers. This type of progression from short tales to longer, easy-to-read novels can be accomplished no matter what the reader's interest—animals, cars, sports, science fiction, romance, humor, and so on.

THE RELUCTANT READER. Many young adults may fall into the category of "reluctant readers." These readers possess the skills necessary to read on grade level, or even well above grade level, but for some reason have become nonreaders. For these students there are thousands of young adult titles that will challenge their skills and keep them turning the pages. One of the characteristics of most young adult books is a fast-paced start. By the end of the first chapter of Lois Duncan's *Killing Mr. Griffin* we know that "Griffin's the sort of guy you'd like to kill." When the end of each chapter leaves the reader hanging, as in Robert Cormier's *After the first death,* putting the book down may be more difficult than punching the off button on the television set.

> ☐ *A lot of teachers complain that their students aren't motivated to read. That is like complaining that the students aren't motivated to walk or talk or run or dance or play.*
> HERBERT KOHL
> Reading, how to*

THE CAPABLE READER. Even young adults who are capable, avid readers can profitably be introduced to titles written for adolescents. One of the characteristics of all mature readers is that they are able to read a variety of books, at the same time, for a variety of different purposes. If you think about the books you are currently reading, you will probably see this characteristic in your own selections. It is rare, for example, for me to be reading fewer than four books at one time. Right now I am reading five books: *Forged in fury* by Evan Rhodes, for simple pleasure; Katherine Paterson's *Gates of excellence: On reading and writing books for children,* for professional and personal enjoyment; Nancy Larrick's newest edition of *A parent's guide to children's reading,* to help keep me aware of the newest books for young children; Maya Angelou's *The heart of a woman,* to give me a few moments for introspection; and Norma Fox Mazer's short-story collection for young adults, *Summer girls, love boys.* Of course, this reading variety is important for the mature reader's personal and professional development.

By introducing young, capable readers to the wonderful world of young adult titles that challenge them, meet their needs, and appeal to their interests, we are encouraging them to develop reading versatility at an early age. We can also begin to teach them the difference between those books that are read for

---

The mature, capable reader selects a variety of books. When given a stigma-free environment, she or he will choose to read age-related books more often than any others.

pleasure, those read for personal development, and those read for educational or professional reasons. We can begin to help these young readers understand that each type of reading serves a purpose and helps in the reader's development. Similarly, we can show young readers that not all books are read at the same rate for the same reason.

> ☐ *... The things young people want to read are related to their chronological age regardless of the level of their reading ability. Even if they have one foot in the world of adult literature, one foot will remain in the literature of childhood. I remember that one of my daughters, the summer before she reached sixteen, read not only* War and Peace—*at that time I had not read it—but also Maureen Daley's* Seventeen.
>
> JEANNETTE H. EYERLY
> *author of* Drop out / *in* The Alan Review / *Winter 1981*

There is an ever growing number of challenging books in the young adult classification. Younger and older adolescent readers will enjoy the thought-provoking books of Madeleine L'Engle, which can be read and reread on a variety of levels. Wonderful believable fantasies such as *A wrinkle in time, A ring of endless light,* and *The arm of the starfish* will delight the "intelligent" young reader for whom L'Engle writes. Students who are not fantasy fans but who enjoy challenging books may be intrigued by Katherine Paterson's *Jacob have I loved* or Robert Cormier's *The chocolate war.* The list of thought-provoking pleasure books for maturing readers is endless. The teacher who introduces the student to such thought-provoking books, as well as to textbooks and other books of the content area, will be helping them develop skills and attitudes that will allow them to become life-long readers.

☐ *Katherine Paterson discussed Ursula LeGuin's* The tombs of Atuan *with her former college professor:*

He began to speak about the powerful range of emotion that the book had evoked in him and wondered aloud if it was really suitable for children. . . . What I said to him rather inarticulately is the point I'm still fumbling to make. It was that what he had experienced in reading that book was not simply what the genius of the writer had put there (and I do not underestimate the genius), but the whole emotional history of a beautiful sixty-year-old life responding to that story. His creative genius had made a powerful book even more powerful.
KATHERINE PATERSON

Gates of excellence: On reading and writing books for children, *pp. 24–25* *

Amount of Reading Activity, Motivation to Read, and Reading Achievement Are Interrelated

In 1973 I surveyed 250 high school students as the beginning step in the development of an elective English program[2] that was being designed to improve the students' reading and communication skills. Through the survey I learned that the vast majority of the surveyed teenagers were not confident about their reading abilities. Many of them "hated" to read and read only when a course

---

*Copyright © 1981 by Katherine Paterson. Reprinted by permission of the publisher, E. P. Dutton, Inc.

[2] Elective English programs allow students to select from a variety of different English courses, often a quarter or semester in length, to fulfill English graduation requirements. The literature courses are organized in several different ways: (1) historically (American Literature I), (2) by genre (Science Fiction), (3) thematically (Literature of Love), (4) by author (Shakespeare).

■ ■ ■ **An Anthological Aside**

What His Mind Had No Words for His Body Understood Entirely and with Ease, and Praised

URSULA K. LE GUIN

When at last he sat up he did not feel that he had been asleep but still it was like waking, like waking from deep sleep in quietness, when the self belongs wholly to the self and nothing can move it, until one wakens further. At the root of the quietness was the music of the water. Under his hand sand slid over rock. As he sat up he felt the air come easily into his lungs, a cool air smelling of earth and rotten leaves and growing leaves, all the different kinds of weeds and grass and bushes and trees, the cold scent of dirt, a sweet tang that was familiar though he could not name it, all the odors mixed and yet distinct like the threads in a piece of cloth, proving the olfactory part of the brain to be alive and immense, with room though no name for every scent, aroma, perfume, and stink that made up this vast, dark, profoundly strange and familiar smell of a stream bank in late evening in summer in the country.

For he was in the country. He had no idea how far he had run, having no clear idea of how long a mile was, but he knew he had run clear out of streets, out of houses, off the edge of the paved world, onto dirt. Dark, slightly damp, uneven, complex again, complex beyond belief—moving one finger he touched grains of sand and soil, decayed leaves, pebbles, a larger rock half buried, roots. He had lain with his face against that dirt, on it, in it. His head swam a little. He drew a long breath, and pressed his open hands against the earth.

It was not dark yet. His eyes had grown accustomed, and he could see clearly, though the darker colors and all shadowed places were near the verge of night. The sky between the black, distinct branches overhead was colorless and without variation of brightness to show where the sun had set. There were no stars yet. The stream, twenty or thirty feet wide and full of boulders, was like a livelier piece of the sky, flashing and glimmering around its rocks. The open, sandy banks on both sides were light; only downstream where the trees grew thicker did the dusk gather heavy, blurring details.

He rubbed sand and dead leaf and spiderweb off his face and hair, feeling the light sting of a branch-cut under his eye. He leaned forward on his elbow, intent, and touched the water of the stream with the fingers of his left hand: very lightly at first, his hand flat, as if touching the skin of an animal; then he put his hand into the water and felt the musculature of the currents press against his palm. Presently he leaned forward farther, bent his head down, and, with both hands in the shallows at the sand's edge, drank.

The water was cold and tasted of the sky.

Hugh crouched there on the muddy sand, his head still bowed, with the taste that is no taste on his lips and in his mouth. He straightened his back slowly then until he was kneeling with head erect, his hands on his knees, motionless. What his mind had no words for his body understood entirely and with ease, and praised.

When that intensity which he understood as prayer lessened, ebbed, and resolved again into alert and manifold pleasure, he sat back on his heels, looking about him more keenly and methodically than at first.

Where north was, no telling, beneath the even, colorless sky; but he was certain that the suburbs, the freeway, the city all were directly behind him. The path he had been on came out there, between a big pine with reddish bark and a mass of high, large-leaved shrubs. Behind them the path went up steep and was lost to sight in the thick dusk under the trees.

The stream ran directly across the axis of that path, from right to left. He could see for a long way upstream along the farther bank as it wound among trees and boulders and finally began to shelve higher above the water. Downstream the woods dropped away in increasing darkness broken by the slipping glimmer of the stream. Above the shore on both sides of the water, close by, the banks rose and then leveled into a clearing free of trees, a glade, almost a little meadow, grassy and much interrupted by bushes and shrubs.

The familiar smell he could not put a name to had grown stronger, his hand smelled of it—mint, that was it. The path of weeds at the water's edge where he had put his hands down must be wild mint. He picked off a leaf and smelled it, then bit it, expecting it to be sweet like mint candy. It was pungent, slightly hairy, earthy, cold.

This is a good place, Hugh thought. And I got here. I finally got somewhere. I made it.

Behind his back the dinner in the oven, timer set, television gabbling to an empty room. The front door unlocked. Maybe not even shut. How long?

Mother coming home at ten.

Where were you, Hugh? Out for a walk But you weren't *home* when I got *home* you know how I Yes it got later than I thought I'm sorry But you weren't *home*—

He was on his feet already. But the mint leaf was in his mouth, his hands were wet, his shirt and jeans were a mess of leaves and muddy sand, and his heart was not troubled. I found the place, so I can come back to it, he said to himself.

He stood a minute longer listening to the water on the stones and watching the stillness of the branches against the evening sky; then set off back the way he had come, up the path between the high bushes and the pine.

The way was steep and dark at first, then leveled out among sparse woods. It was easy to follow, though the thorny arms of blackberry creepers tripped him up a couple of times in the fast-increasing dusk. An old ditch, grass-overgrown, not much more than a dip or wrinkle in the ground, was the boundary of the wood; across it he faced open fields. Clear across them in the distance was the queer shifting passing flicker of carlights on the freeway. There were stationary lights to the right. He headed towards them, across the fields of dry grass and hard ridged dirt, coming at last to a rise or bank at the top of which ran a gravel road. There was a big building, floodlit, off to the left near the freeway; down the road the other direction was what looked like a couple of farmhouses. One of them also had a light rigged in the front yard, and he headed for that, feeling certain that was how he should go: down this road between the farmhouses. Past their auto graveyards and barking dogs there was a dark stretch of trees in rows, and then the first streetlight, the end of Chelsea Gardens Place, leading to Chelsea Gardens Avenue, and on into the heart of a housing development. He followed a memory unavailable to consciousness of how he had come when he was running, and street by street unerringly brought himself back to Kensington Heights, onto Pine View Place, onto Oak Valley Road, and to the front door of 14067½-C Oak Valley Road: which was shut.

The televison set was vibrating with canned laughter. He turned it off, then heard the kitchen timer buzzing and hurried to turn it off. The kitchen clock said five to nine. The turkey dinner was withered in its little aluminum coffin. He tried to eat it but it was stone. He drank a quart of milk and ate four slices of bread and butter, a pint of blueberry yogurt, and two apples; he got the bag of peanuts from the living room floor and shelled and ate them, sitting at the dinette table in the kitchen, thinking. It had been a long walk home. He had not looked at his watch, but it must have taken pretty near an hour. And surely he had spent an hour or more by the stream, and it had taken him a while to get there; even if he had been running, he wasn't any four-minute miler. He would have sworn it was ten o'clock or even eleven, if the clock and his watch did not unanimously contradict him.

Never much of a one for argument, he gave it up. He finished the peanuts, moved into the living room, turned off the light, turned on the television, instantly turned it off again, and sat down in the armchair. The chair shook and creaked, but this time he was more aware of its inadequacy as an armchair than of his own clumsy weight. He felt good, after his run. He felt sorry for the poor sleazy, shoddy chair, instead of disgusted with himself. Why had he run? Well, no need to go over that. He had never done anything else all his life. Run-and-hide Rogers. But to have run and got somewhere, that was new. He had never got anywhere before, no place to hide, no place to be. And then to fall over his own feet onto his face into a place like that, a wild, secret place. As if all the suburbs, the duplex development motorhome supermarket parking lot used cars carport swingseat white rocks juniper imitation bacon bits special gum wrappers where in five different states he had lived the last seven years, as if all that was unimportant after all, not permanent, not the way life had to be, since just outside it, just past the edge of it, there was silence, loneliness, water running in twilight, the taste of mint.

You shouldn't have drunk the water. Sewage. Typhoid. Cholera . . . No! That was the first clean water I ever drank. I'll go back there and drink it any damned time I want.

The creek. Stream, they would call it in the states where he had been in high school, but the word "creek" came to him from farther back in the darkness of remembrance, a twilight word to suit the twilight water, the racing shift and glimmer that filled his mind. The walls of the room he sat in resonated faintly to the noises of a television program in the apartment overhead, and were streaked with light from the streetlamp through lace curtains and sometimes the dim wheeling of the headlights of a passing car. Within, beneath that restless, unsilent half-light was the quiet place, the creek. From thinking of it his mind drifted on to old currents of thought: If I went where I want to go, if I went out to the college here and talked to people, there might be student loans for library school, or if I save enough and got started maybe a scholarship—and from this further, like a boat drifting past the islands within sight of shore, moving into a remoter future dreamed of earlier, a building with wide and much-frequented steps, stairways within and grand rooms and high windows, people quiet, at work quietly, as much at home among the endless shelves of books as the thoughts in a mind are at home, the City Library on a fifth-grade school trip to celebrate National Book Week and the home and harbor of his longing.

"What are you doing sitting in the dark? Without the TV on? And the front door not locked! Why aren't the lights on? I thought nobody was here." And when that had been talked about she found the turkey dinner, which he had not jammed far enough down into the garbage pail under the sink. "What did you eat? What on earth was wrong with it? Can't you read the directions? You must be taking the flu, you'd better take some aspirin. Really, Hugh, you just can't seem to look after yourself at all, you cannot manage the simplest thing. How can I be comfortable about going out after work to have a little time with my friends when you're so irresponsible? Where's the bag of peanuts I bought to take to Durbina's tomorrow?" And though at first he saw her, like the armchair, as simply inadequate, trying hard to do a job she wasn't up to, he could not keep seeing her from the quiet place but was drawn back, roped in, till all he could do was not listen, and say, "All right," and, after she had turned on the last commercial of the movie she had wanted to watch, "Good night, mother." And run and hide in bed.

■ ■ ■

required it, and not even then, if it could be avoided. More than 75 percent of the students indicated a strong dislike for reading and claimed they saw no purpose to it. Standardized test scores confirmed the students' dislike for reading. They had good reason for their distaste; they were, for the most part, poor readers. The test scores should have been no surprise. As early as second grade a 60 to 70 percent variance in reading achievement is accountable by the amount of reading activity (Yap 1977). And, as the high school students in the 1973 informal survey indicated, they did not read. A nonreading cycle can develop very early, maybe as early as kindergarten. If not broken, the cycle can lead to poor reading-test scores, justifiable lack of confidence in reading ability, and dislike of reading. The greater the dislike of reading, the greater the likelihood the child will become a nonreader, standardized test scores will be poor, self-confidence will decline, and reading dislike will grow. The cycle will continue!

Reading is a skill, and like any other skill it needs practice. No one would suggest that an outstanding pianist, football player, or ballet dancer achieves success without practice. The same is true of the outstanding reader. The more readers practice the skill of reading, the more likely they are to become proficient at it.

In one high school, a student teacher began reading *A tale of two cities* aloud to a group of unmotivated seniors. When it became apparent that they were bored, frustrated, and not listening, she closed the book and borrowed multiple copies of five different titles from the high school library. With *The hard life of the teenager,* a nonfiction portrayal of teenage anxiety by James L. Collier, *The chocolate war* (Cormier), *If I love you, am I trapped forever?* (Kerr), *Of love and death and other journeys* (Holland), and *I heard a scream in the street: Poetry by young people in the city* (Larrick, ed.) she created a unit on teenage alienation. The unmotivated students not only read the books but enjoyed them. Another student teacher in the same high school had similar results when she created a unit on love and friendship for sophomore English classes using S. E. Hinton's first three books: *The outsiders, That was then, this is now,* and *Rumble fish.* One young man told her, after he had finished reading all three titles in two weeks, "These are the first books I've read all the way through!" He was as proud of his accomplishment as she was of hers. She should have been proud; she had broken the nonreading cycle.

One of the interesting discoveries made by these student teachers was that once the students completed reading a book, they demanded "another one just like the other one." The more they read, the more they wanted to read. Motivation to read was increasing in exact proportion to the amount of reading activity.

Fader and McNeil (1966) clearly, enthusiastically, have shown what the "saturation-diffusion" technique of teaching literature and encouraging reading through paperbacks can do for unmotivated students. Consider this quotation from a reading coordinator's report:

Student response has been overwhelming. Never have I seen such interest shown in reading since my arrival here at Northwestern four years ago. . . . Students are seen reading everywhere—on hall duty, in lunch-rooms, in study halls, and even in classrooms (undercover). The status symbol is the paperback.

    At least half a dozen or more students have asked if they could serve as librarians. Boys seem to outnumber the girls in attendance. One teacher commented, "This is the best thing that's happened to North-western since I've been here." (Fader and McNeil 1966, p. 102)

I have experienced similar results in other schools. In 1973 the unmotivated, poor readers I surveyed rarely read. By 1974, after the adoption of a saturation-diffusion elective English curriculum, the students were reading a minimum of five paperbacks during every nine-week period. They were reading so much that it was difficult to keep enough books in the classroom libraries to satisfy their needs.

Not only were students selecting paperbacks written for young adults, but they were demanding the teaching of the "classics." In an elective course enti-tled The Literature of Love, the students developed bibliographies from the classroom library, the school library, and the literature anthology. They were allowed to indicate whether any of the literary works should be required reading for the entire class. While skimming the literature anthology, the students dis-covered *Romeo and Juliet;* they requested that it be read by everyone in the class. The instructor, playing devil's advocate, objected, saying that not all stu-dents would be interested in reading the play. The students argued that they could not study the literature of love without studying Shakespeare. They took a vote and unanimously agreed to read *Romeo and Juliet,* as well as some of Shakespeare's love sonnets. (I was the instructor. I loved arguing that we should not read Shakespeare and having the students take the other side; it was as if our roles had been reversed from my early teaching years, when I had argued in favor of Shakespeare. I remember the teaching of *Romeo and Juliet* as one of my truly enjoyable defeats.) The students read *Romeo and Juliet* in record time, without the usual agony. They loved it! So much so that more than half the class decided to continue to study Shakespeare's love plays by reading *Antony and Cleopatra.* This newfound interest required the development of two new elective courses: one in Shakespeare's comedies and the other in his tragedies.

The students were reading. Book sales in the local drugstore, the only pur-veyor of books, skyrocketed. Library circulation soared. Standardized reading test scores increased dramatically. Student writing improved. The percentage of the senior class electing to attend college increased from 4 percent to over 40 percent in three years. Discipline problems were practically nonexistent in the English classroom. The introduction of the young adult book into the curric-ulum was turning nonreaders into avid readers.

Middle school students sift through a pile of newly obtained paperbacks.

□ *I think this [saturation-diffusion] program in our school may do for the teaching of reading what Sputnik did for the teaching of science.*
ENGLISH TEACHER
quoted in Fader and McNeil 1966, p. 102

The Teacher's Role in Motivating Students to Read

BECOMING FAMILIAR WITH YOUNG ADULT BOOKS. One of the easiest ways to motivate students to read is to introduce them to young adult books that are likely to whet their appetites for more and more books. In order to do this, the teacher must become familiar with the world of young adult literature. This is not an easy task; the number of offerings in the young adult category is growing at a rapid pace.

There are several ways the teacher can begin to gain an understanding of this vast literary world. One means, of course, is reading this textbook or one of several other useful texts that are devoted to or include chapters on young adult books. Obviously, this must be done in conjunction with reading a variety of young adult titles. But where to begin?

The best place to begin is with your students' interests, needs, and abilities. Conduct an interest inventory in your class (like the one suggested in Chapter 1). From these inventories you can develop a list of your students' interests. For example, Gradetta Hinson used the inventory form in Chapter 1 and found the following: the favorite television programs of her tenth-grade social studies students included "Dallas," "General Hospital," and "Dynasty." All are soap operas, of course, but they have another characteristic in common as well: all deal with relationships, primarily family relationships. This became one beginning point for her reading.

Since she knew her students very well, she was familiar with many of their needs and problems. She understood that a large percentage of her tenth-graders came from single-parent homes. Others had been alienated from their parents. One 16-year-old was living alone as an "emancipated minor." This knowledge gave further direction to the types of family relationships she would begin reading about.

Similarly, Ms. Hinson was aware of the reading ability of her students. She knew that most of the students in this particular class were above average ability but exhibited a distaste for reading. Therefore, she would search for books that were both highly motivational and at an appropriate reading level for these students.

She made a trip to the local public library, which, she knew, had recently hired a specialist in adolescent literature. She asked the librarian to suggest titles that were appropriate to her students' interests, needs, and abilities, and could be introduced into the social studies classroom. The librarian agreed to prepare a bibliography for Ms. Hinson that also could be used with the students. Each book Ms. Hinson read led her to another book, often by the same author or on a similar theme. Within a month she felt that she had gained enough information about young adult books dealing with family relationships to introduce some of them to her students.

BRINGING STUDENTS AND BOOKS TOGETHER. Ms. Hinson first read *Tex* by S. E. Hinton aloud to the class. As she hoped, the fast-paced, simple story about two boys who spend most of their lives apart from their parents quickly captured the students.

It wasn't long before the students were asking for additional books by S. E. Hinton. Therefore, Ms. Hinson decided to check out enough library books on the topic of family relationships so that each student could read his or her own book. She asked the librarian to come to the class and discuss several of the books with the students. After this brief introduction to the books, each student selected one book for personal reading.

At first Ms. Hinson hoped to keep the books in the classroom, but the enthusiastic response encouraged her to allow them to circulate. The day after the books left the classroom she overheard several of her students discussing the books they had selected. Suddenly, it seemed important to allow these discussions to continue in an organized fashion in the classroom. The question was, how? The thirty students in her class were reading twenty-four different titles.

She decided to divide the students randomly into groups of five or six, give them a list of questions that would direct the discussion toward similar content-related points made in each book, and allow the students to share their books with their peers. She was afraid chaos would prevail. However, the students' enthusiasm not only encouraged discussion on the questions Ms. Hinson had prepared, but also led them in many interesting, unexpected directions. The end result of the discussions was the swapping of books among the students. Ms. Hinson knew that somehow she needed to use this motivation to teach the skills she hoped to emphasize in her social studies curriculum.

THE YOUNG ADULT BOOK IN THE CURRICULUM. Ms. Hinson decided to design a unit on family relationships (see the following pages) that would incorporate the young adult books the students were reading, selections from the textbook and other traditional sources, and several of the social studies skills she hoped to teach during the year.

The first step in designing her two-week unit was to limit the topic so that it could be accomplished in the allotted time period. Therefore, she decided to deal with one of the most important issues in family relationships: divorce.

Having selected the topic, she visited the public library, the school library, and a bookstore in an effort to obtain multiple copies of several young adult books. She was able to get three copies of each of ten different young adult titles that deal with the family and divorce. The students could select from these ten titles and work with other students in two different grouping patterns. The first pattern called for groups of three students, each reading a different book. As part of the final miniproject each student was to be regrouped with two other students who had read the same book. These two grouping patterns allowed the students to share views as presented in different books as well as discuss with their peers the books they had read in common.

After the books were obtained, Ms. Hinson determined the objectives she hoped to reach during the two-week unit. She wanted the students to examine stereotypical attitudes toward divorce, statistics about divorce in the United States, their own attitudes about divorce, factors that contribute to divorce, personal adjustments that follow a divorce, and emotional effects of divorce on all the people involved. Apart from her primary objectives, she also wanted the students to become familiar with divorce laws, professionals who deal with divorce, current sources of information about divorce, and groups that assist family members in coping with divorce. The course outline was quite simple to design once the objectives were determined.

Sources, other than the young adult books, had to be obtained and made available to students. These sources included current journal and newspaper articles about divorce, television programs and advertisements about or directed toward divorced people, and guest speakers.

Finally, the assignments the students were to complete during the unit and the evaluation of these assignements had to be determined. Reading the young adult book and answering questions about it were to be two of the primary assignments. In addition, the students were to complete several individual and group writing assignments that integrated the book read, material covered in class, and additional resources. The final project for the unit was to be a group presentation of the book read in common by group members. This presentation

■ ■ Sample Social Studies Unit

Subject: Social Studies—
       Contemporary
       Issues
Topic: Divorce—Issue and
      Answers
Duration: 2 weeks
Grade: 10

INTRODUCTION

Statistics show that 1 out of 2.5 marriages in our society will end in divorce. However, when divorce occurs, not only are marriages dissolved but basic family units as well. Young people who find themselves in a one-parent home soon learn that many adjustments are necessary. How do we cope with these changes? Is there a "best" way to deal with the transition? Is it "off limits" to find out the reasons for the divorce? Young adults, who are nearing an age when they may consider marriage, need to learn how to nourish relationships so that they may avoid the trauma of divorce in their future marriage. A deeper study of the issue may help children of divorce gain a better understanding of their parents' adjustments, behavior, and needs—as well as their own.

In this study, a mini journal will be kept by each student. It will include all assignments, articles, group work, and evaluations. A grade will be assigned to the completed journal, based on its content, order, and neatness.

A major source for the topic is a young adult book, selected by the students. There are a sufficient number of titles to allow

Designed by Gradetta Hinson, Adolescent Literature Class, University of North Carolina at Asheville, 1982.

for three students to read the
same book. Students will form
groups consisting of three members. No two in the group will
read the same book. Group members will serve as resources for
each other as well as for evaluating each other's work. Young
adult books offered for this
topic are:

Arundel, Honor. A family
failing. Elsevier-Nelson,
1972.

Bradbury, Bianca. The blue
year. Ives Washburn, 1967.

Cleaver, Vera, and Bill
Cleaver. Ellen Grae. Lippin-
cott, 1967. New American
Library, 1978.

——. Me, too. Lippincott,
1973. New American Library,
1975.

Greene, Constance. A girl
called Al. Viking, 1969.
Dell, 1977.

Holland, Isabelle, Heads you
win, tails I lose. Lippincott, 1973. Dell, 1979.

Klein, Norma. Taking sides.
Pantheon, 1974. Avon, 1982.

——. Mom, the wolf man and me.
Random House, 1972. Avon,
1977.

Mendonca, Susan. Tough
choices. Dial, 1980.

Platt, Kin. The boy who could
make himself disappear.
Chilton, 1968. Dell, 1972.

Objectives	Content outline	Strategies	Materials	Resources	Assignments	Evaluation

The students will:
(1) examine aspects of divorce; stereotypes.
	I. Aspects of Divorce
	A. Age group of most divorced couples.
	B. Point in marriage where most divorces occur.
	C. Number of divorce cases handled each year in U.S.
	  1. Nationwide
	  2. Statewide
	  3. Countrywide
	D. Divorce rates among various ethnic groups.
	  1. Blacks
	  2. Orientals
	  3. Jews
	  4. Mexican-Americans
	  5. Native Americans
	E. American stereotypes of divorce
	  1. Always negative
		—discussion
		—lecture
		—allow time to group students and select books to read
			—Guide sheet for YA books (See Figure 2.1)	—county, state, national statistics
				—YA books
				—report from a divorce lawyer
					—begin reading YA book (3 chapters)	30 students will be grouped for this unit. The book list allows for 3 students to read the same book. Each group will consist of 3 students reading 3 different books. A guide sheet will accompany each book describing the purpose for reading it and what to look for. Each student will keep a booklet or mini-journal of the information, essays, assignments, and contributions to the class (posters, articles, etc.)

Objectives	Content outline	Strategies	Materials	Resources	Assignments	Evaluation
(2) Consider and describe their individual attitudes toward divorce.	2. Wealthy divorce more often 3. Easy to get one II. Personal attitudes toward divorce A. Relationships with divorced people. 1. Parents 2. Friends 3. Acquaintances B. Is divorce negative, neutral, or positive? 1. Negative Aspects 2. Neutral Aspects 3. Positive Aspects C. Famous divorced people D. Famous married couples	-discussion -list aspects -allow time to read at least one chapter of YA book in class	-posterboard to list aspects -photos of famous people	"Branded or barefaced." Time (special supplement May 17, 1976).	-Watch two TV shows that involve divorce. -Find two commercials or ads aimed at divorced people. Answer questions: • How are divorces presented? • What characteristics do they portray? • Are they accepted, respected, ignored, etc., by the rest of society? • Are the results of the divorce	-class participation (The next lesson will review the findings of the assignment.)

(3) recognize factors contributing to divorce.

III. Factors contributing to divorce.
A. Extra marital relationship
B. Incompatability
C. Death of a child
D. Religious difference
E. Career stress
F. Illness/Disease
G. Immaturity
H. Others

—discussion
—brainstorming the factors
—Guest speaker (marriage/family) counselor

—poster-board (Review guest speaker's talk by listing the common reasons for divorce)

marriage counselor
—survey research material that focuses on marriage and divorce (see attached bibliography)

negative, neutral, or positive?
—Begin collecting any advertisements, pictures, etc., that depict or speak to the divorced person's situation.
—Read YA book (3 chapters)

—Read YA book (2 chapters) and begin answering questions on the guide sheet.
—Write a "Dear Abby" letter. Choose one of the factors discussed today and create a credible situation con-

Students will share their assignments with group members at beginning of next class. Each paper should have comments of the other two members attached to the original letter. Evaluating members will offer solutions in their com-

Objectives	Content outline	Strategies	Materials	Resources	Assignments	Evaluation
	H. Immaturity I. Others				cerning divorce. (These will be evaluated by group members, who will role-play "Abby.") Help with a solution.	ments. The teacher will award 3 grades based on the presentation of the situation and supportive data to the solutions of group members' letter.

(4) determine the personal adjustments that follow a divorce.	IV. Physical Adjustments of Divorce
	A. The Home
	  1. Duties and responsibilities
	  2. Financial budget
	  3. Dividing property
	B. Scheduling
	  1. Activities
	  2. Visiting Rights
	  3. Holidays & vacations
		—discussion
		—readings in magazines and other materials
		—draw from examples in YA books
		—(reading time)
			—poster for main outline of this section of unit. (Outline as the class discusses.)	—Single Parents Organization material
				—Senior Scholastic magazine
				—YA books
					—Read YA book (3 chapters)
					—Be ready to discuss emotional effects/changes brought about by divorce, using examples from your YA book.	

(5) assess the emotional	V. Emotional Effects of Divorce A. On parents 1. Singleness	—in-class readings of magazine arti-	—poster with main outline for this sec-	—Home Life magazine —YA books —"Dear Abby"	—Write one paragraph (½ page) as a group depict-	—peer evaluation through comments (groups

effects
of
divorce
on par-
ents,
chil-
dren,
and
friends.

2. Added
responsi-
bilities
3. Concern for
children
4. New roles
B. On children
1. Transition
2. Guilt
3. Shame/embar-
rassment
4. Rebellion
5. Confusion/
hate
6. New roles
C. On friends

cles
—"Dear
Abby" col-
umn (read
and dis-
cuss)
—discus-
sion
—(reading
time)

tion of
unit (Out-
line as the
class dis-
cusses).

columns

ing a divorce
situation.
Each group
member will
then write an
additional
paragraph,
one viewing
the situation
from the par-
ents' per-
spective, one
from the
child's per-
spective, and
one from a
friend's per-
spective.
(You may
choose your
perspective
within the
group.) The
perspective
paragraph
should
include feel-
ings, atti-
tudes, etc.,
concerning
the situa-
tion.
Finish YA
book and
guide sheet.

exchange their
paragraphs
with other
groups)
—class partici-
pation

BIBLIOGRAPHY

Gardner, R. The boys and girls books about divorce. Aronson, 1970. Bantam, 1971.

Gettleman, S., and J. Markowitz. The courage to divorce. Simon and Schuster, 1974. Ballantine, 1975.

Kessler, S. The American way of divorce. Nelson-Hall, 1975.

Krantzler, M. Creative divorce. M. Evans, 1973. New American Library, 1975.

Rheinstein, M. Marriage stability, divorce, and the law. University of Chicago Press, 1972.

Richards, A., and I. Willis. How to get together when your parents are coming apart. McKay, 1976. Bantam, 1977.

could use one of several suggested formats, such as a dramatic production, panel discussion, taped radio show, or debate. The most important criterion for evaluating the miniproject, in addition to the quality of the presentation, was to be the inclusion of the divorce situation as depicted in the book.

Ms. Hinson understood that one of her most important tasks was the designing of the guide sheet (see Figure 2.1) to be used during the discussion of the three different young adult books in the first grouping pattern. The completed guide sheet would also be extremely important in determining the success of the final miniproject to be completed by the second grouping of students. This single activity would guide the students' discussion of books, tie the fictional books to the factual information to be studied in class, help the students relate to the problems faced by the characters in the books, assist the students in understanding the various viewpoints of all the characters involved in the divorce situation, and help the students understand the content of the book.

Motivating the students to read the material covered in the unit was not difficult. They had already begun to develop an interest in the topic of family relationships during Ms. Hinson's oral reading of *Tex*. This interest continued as they selected their own young adult book to read after the librarian's visit to the classroom. Ms. Hinson capitalized on their interest in the topic and their motivation to read about the topic by developing a unit that not only furthered this interest and continued the high level of motivation, but gave the students factual information about divorce, encouraged them to examine the effects of divorce on all people involved, helped them explore their own attitudes, and taught them important reading and research skills of the social scientist and historian.

The success of the unit was built on several important building blocks. Ms. Hinson's knowledge of her students' interests, needs, and abilities gave her the beginning point for her investigation of young adult literature and the topic for the unit. Her individual exploration of literature written for young adults helped her locate materials that would be motivational and interesting to reluctant readers. Her slow, methodical incorporation of that literature into the classroom sparked her students' interest and motivated them to read related books. Using

Figure 2.1 Guide Sheet to Be Used in Discussing Young Adult Books Dealing with Divorce

---

GUIDE SHEET FOR READING YOUR YOUNG ADULT BOOK

Young adult books are written from the perspective of a young person who, just like you, faces many problems, pressures, inconsistencies, and needs in life. Perhaps in reading your selection you will find that you are not alone in your feelings. Sometimes the problems presented are similar to yours, but are dealt with in a different manner. Let's consider the young adult in your book and see the relationship of divorce to his or her world. As you read, consider the following questions and answer them as thoughtfully as you can. We will discuss your book at the end of our unit study.

1. What characteristics do you notice about the divorced/separated parents?
2. How are the parents viewed by the young adult(s)?
3. What sort of outlook on life do the divorced/separated parents and the young adult(s) seem to have?
4. Has the divorce/separation harmed the young adult(s) in any way?
5. What conflicts does the young adult face?
6. What specific problems created by the divorce does the young adult encounter?
7. Are any of the problems resolved?
8. How does the young adult view the divorce?
9. What factors/issues are involved in the divorce/separation?
10. Has the young adult changed in any way at the book's conclusion? Does the young adult notice the changes?
11. What sorts of relationships does the young adult have with his/her parents?
12. Do you have any other comments about the book?

In addition to completing this guide sheet, please include the title of your book, the author, the publisher, the date, and a *brief* summary of the story.

Source: Designed by Gradetta Hinson
Adolescent Literature Class / University of North Carolina at Asheville / 1982

this enthusiasm, she developed a unit that was based on their newly discovered curiosity about books and on their expressed interest in family relationships. Then she added her knowledge of the skills and concepts important in her content area and her expertise in developing methodology to teach them successfully. Young adult books were the tools for motivating her students to read. Those tools made teaching and learning the skills and concepts more enjoyable and educational for Ms. Hinson and her students.

Anthological Aside in Chapter 2

LeGuin, U. K. *The beginning place.* Harper & Row, 1980. Bantam, 1981.

Titles Mentioned in Chapter 2

Angelou, M. *The heart of a woman.* Random House, 1981. Bantam, 1982.
Avallone, M. *Five-minute mysteries: Cases from the files of Ed Noon, private detective.* Scholastic, 1978.

Bennett, J. *The birthday murderer.* Delacorte, 1977. Dell, 1979.

Collier, J. L. *The hard life of the teenager.* Four Winds, 1972.

Cormier, R. *After the first death.* Pantheon, 1979. Avon, 1980.

————. *The chocolate war.* Pantheon, 1974. Dell, 1975.

Duncan, L. *Killing Mr. Griffin.* Little, Brown, 1978. Dell, 1979.

Eyerly, J. *Drop out.* Lippincott, 1963. Berkley, 1969.

Hinton, S. E. *The outsiders.* Viking, 1967. Dell, 1980.

————. *Rumble fish.* Delacorte, 1975. Dell, 1976.

————. *Tex.* Delacorte, 1979. Dell, 1980.

————. *That was then, this is now.* Viking, 1971. Dell, 1980.

Holland, I. *Of love and death and other journeys.* Lippincott, 1975. Dell, 1977.

Kerr, M. E. *If I love you, am I trapped forever?* Harper & Row, 1973. Dell, 1975.

Larrick, N., ed. *I heard a scream in the street: Poetry by young people in the city.* Evans, 1970. Dell, 1974.

L'Engle, M. *The arm of the starfish.* Farrar, Straus & Giroux, 1968.

————. *A ring of endless light.* Farrar, Straus & Giroux, 1980. Dell, 1981.

————. *A wrinkle in time.* Farrar, Straus & Giroux, 1962. Dell, 1976.

Mazer, N. F. *Summer girls, love boys, and other short stories.* Delacorte, 1982.

Paterson, K. *Jacob have I loved.* Crowell, 1980. Avon, 1981.

Rhodes, E. H. *Forged in fury.* Berkley, 1982.

Schwartz, A. *Scary stories to tell in the dark.* Lippincott, 1981.

Suggested Readings

Agee, H., ed. *High interest–easy reading: For junior and senior high school students,* 4th ed. National Council of Teachers of English, 1984.

Burton, D. L. *Literature study in the high schools,* 3rd ed. Holt, Rinehart & Winston, 1970.

Carlsen, G. R. *Books and the teenage reader.* 2nd rev. ed. Harper & Row, 1980. Bantam, 1980.

Donelson, K. L., and A. P. Nilsen. *Literature for today's young adults.* Scott, Foresman, 1980.

Eyerly, J. H. Writing for today's youth. *The ALAN Review,* Winter 1981, pp. 1–3.

Fader, D., and E. B. McNeil. *Hooked on books: Program and proof.* Berkley, 1966.

Fader, D., et al. *The new hooked on books.* Berkley, 1976, 1981.

Kohl, H. *Reading, how to.* Dutton, 1973. Bantam, 1974.

Larrick, N. *A parent's guide to children's reading.* 5th rev. ed. Bantam, 1982.

New York Public Library, Office of Young Adult Services. *Easy-to-read books for teenagers.* Published annually.

Paterson, K. *Gates of excellence: On reading and writing books for children.* Elsevier/Nelson, 1981.

Yap, K. O. Relationships between amount of reading activity and reading achievement. *Reading World,* October 1977, pp. 23–29.

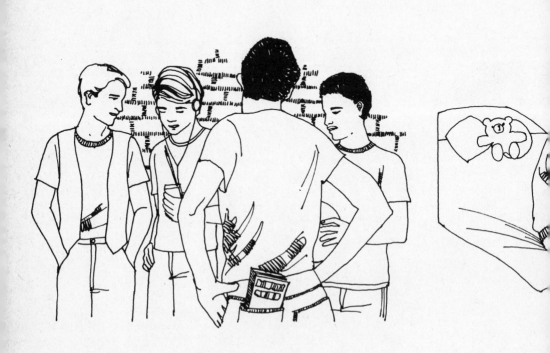

Part Two
Literature for Young Adults

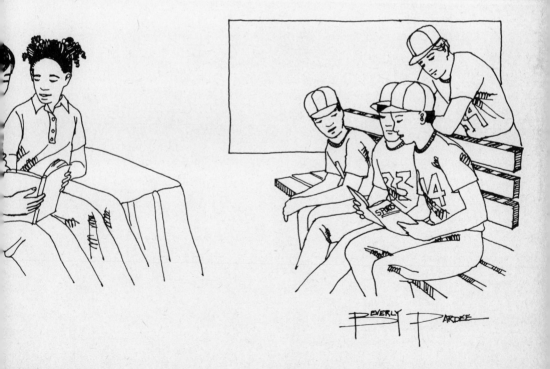

3 The Young Adult Book: Unreality Masked as Realism

What Is Young Adult Literature?

Young adult literature can be most simply defined as "literature which adolescents read" (Carlsen 1980, p. 1). It includes books written specifically for adolescents and books written for children, adults, or a general audience that relate to the young adult's needs and interests. The common characteristics of books selected by young adults are simplicity, characters who are young or experience situations of the young, and modern themes that relate to the life of today's young adults.

This definition of young adult literature makes little distinction among books written for children, adults, or young adults. Most of the books mentioned in this text are written for the young adult audience. However, many are written for children, adults, or a general audience. The reason for the inclusion of books written and distributed to readers other than adolescents is that the young adult makes no distinction. The distinction is made by the publishing houses who market the books for a specified audience. The young adult readers' only distinction is between books they like and books they dislike.

> ☐ *These books are not just for kids. They're for everybody!*
> PAULA DANZIGER
> *author of* There's a bat in bunk five / *in a phone conversation with UNC–Asheville Adolescent Literature Class / 1979*

Limiting a discussion of young adult literature to books specifically marketed for the young adult audience would drastically reduce the world of reading possibilities for teenagers. Fay Blostein (1980), author of the wonderfully creative guide for librarians *Invitations, celebrations,* agrees.

> *I find it difficult to observe what often seems to me an arbitrary line of demarcation.... Admittedly, senior students are less self-conscious about reading a "young-looking" book than 12–14-year-olds, and readers of fantasy cross all age barriers. Yet a book talk for Grade 12 on the quest for meaning and identity should include any one of the following: Julia Cunningham's* Dorp dead *and* Come to the edge; *William Mayne's* A game of dark *and* The incline. *No talk on allegory would be complete without allusion to Penelope Farmer's* A castle of bone, *or Leon Garfield's* The ghost downstairs. *Enrich a discussion on heroism with Jaap ter Haar's* Boris. *Alan Garner's fascination with time in* Red shift *and* The owl service *deserves the attention of older readers. And Mollie Hunter's work is possibly the best example of storytelling whose craftmanship defies age categorization. (p. 174)*

☐ *Our goal as writers for the very young is of course to make them inveterate, chronic readers whose tastes will keep pace with their maturity.*
RICHARD PECK
author of Don't look and it won't hurt / News from ALAN / *September–October 1975*

As G. Robert Carlsen points out, "A book has a writer and reader within. Most writers in telling a story are telling it to someone; usually, they have an exact image of the audience they hope to reach...." (1980, 2). However, the author's image and the audience to which the book is marketed are not always the same. Sue Ellen Bridgers, for example, does not consider herself an author of young adult books. She believes her books, which have been successfully marketed to young adults, should have a wide appeal for a general audience. Unfortunately, because they have been labeled "young adult," very few adults are introduced to them.

Apparently most adolescents, and probably most adults, are willing to select a book for themselves that is written for people older than they are, but not younger. Similarly, most young readers are not likely to be caught in the stacks of the children's room of the library, even though many libraries still house the young adult books in the children's section. It is likely that this reluctance to read books for younger readers has little to do with the book, but rather is caused by the label given it by libraries, bookstores, or publishers. Such labeling of books is unfortunate. Many books appropriate for young adults are in the children's stacks, just as many are in the adult reading room.

It is interesting to note that when given a stigma-free opportunity, young adults are likely to select and enjoy books written for younger and older audiences. A course on children's literature taught to high school juniors and seniors has a record enrollment. The course that examines literature from picture books for infants to books for young adolescents attracts the intellectually superior student as well as the academically slow student. All of the students indicate not only that they enjoy reading the books, but also that they are learning things from them. Several of the students in the class are reading complete books for the first time in their lives. Others are able to use their mature reading ability to give new meaning to books like *Charlotte's web* (White) and *Where the wild things are* (Sendak).

Similarly, books written for adults in other generations are of interest to teenagers of this generation. Books such as *Gone with the wind* and *Catcher in the rye* have huge teenage audiences when they are placed on the bookshelves frequented by young adults.

There is little reason to doubt that children's books and adult books when written on themes of interest to young adults will be read by them if available in a stigma-free environment. G. Robert Carlsen points out in his revised *Books and the teenage reader* that most adolescent novels (those written for and distributed to adolescents) are read by twelve- to fifteen-year-olds. Only about 25 percent of the books read by high school seniors fall into the adolescent literature category. However, "there is some evidence that if the adolescent novel were more readily available to the late teenager, if teachers and librarians were more knowledgeable about the development of reading tastes, [the adolescent novel] would be more widely read by this older group" (p. 3). The B. Dalton bookstore chain's experience tends to support this view. In 1980 the stores clustered some young adult titles in prominent positions, and sales increased 65 percent.

According to Carlsen, it has been well documented that reading interest peaks between the ages of twelve and fourteen. During this time young adults are interested in finding out about themselves and the world. However, young teenagers are usually unable to discover the world through direct experiences. They are limited by lack of transportation, money, and freedom. Therefore, many young adults read and read and read to learn more about themselves and the world. As mobility and freedom increase and money becomes more available, adolescents are not so likely to experience vicariously through books. Therefore, older adolescents read fewer books.

Adolescents' interest in books changes as they mature. Until the age of sixteen, most of the books selected by teenagers relate to their intense interest in self and how they relate to the world. After sixteen, adolescents are more likely to turn to books of greater variety.

☐ *... The land of the young is the land of energy, enthusiasm, confusion, hope, despair, love, optimism, faith, and belief....*
NORMA FOX MAZER
author of Saturday, the twelfth of October

For the young adult, books are a way to experience "adventure and excitement, or to feel tenderness and caring, to enjoy imaginative wanderings, to know the feeling of self-sufficiency without adult domination, to experience life in various historical periods and cultural patterns, to feel the frustrations and despairs of the psychological deviate. Reading makes possible the living of thousands of lives instead of only one" (Carlsen 1980).[1] Young adult literature contains all these things and more.

Problem Novels

According to Richard Peck, author of many books for young adults, the young adult novel is "unreality masked as realism" (1975, p. 5). The setting, plot, and dialogue, says Peck, must reflect a world familiar to the adolescent. However, the protagonist usually must be about to do something the adolescent reader cannot do.

Young adult readers may want their books to take them out of themselves, but they also want their books to speak to them of the problems they are experiencing. Problem novels have become one of the major categories within the field of young adult literature. The problems addressed in the novels range from physical characteristics of puberty to sexuality, from pregnancy to parenthood, from rape to drugs. The list of problems examined in adolescent literature is as endless as the list of problems experienced by the adolescent.

Being too fat or too tall, having acne, developing too quickly or not quickly enough, are all physical problems faced by the adolescent. Novels written for young adults deal with these problems in honest, realistic, often humorous ways. In the end the protagonist usually survives the problem and learns to deal with it in a human way. Being too fat is dealt with in such novels as Robert Lipsyte's *One fat summer,* Paula Danziger's *The cat ate my gymsuit,* and M. E. Kerr's *Dinky Hocker shoots smack!* Judy Blume helps boys understand the problems of approaching puberty in *Then again, maybe I won't;* she does the same for girls in *Deenie* and *Are you there, God? It's me, Margaret.* The central character in *C. C. Poindexter* by Carolyn Meyer has to face the problems of being sixteen, over six feet tall, and a girl. Being thirteen is very difficult for many girls, and they can share their problems with the protagonist in Betty Miles's *The trouble with thirteen.* Fifteen and a half may not be much better for some girls. The reader can respond to the experiences of the protagonist in Richard Peck's *Don't look and it won't hurt.* Acne, or at the least "zits," is a traumatic, often-not-spoken-of problem for many teenagers. *I was a ninety-eight-pound duckling* by Jean Van Leeuwen and *Do black patent leather shoes really reflect up?* by John R. Powers show that acne need not ruin a life. Stuttering, though not as common as acne, is a difficult problem for many teenagers. Tuck Faraday in

[1]Copyright © 1967, 1971, 1980 by G. Robert Carlsen. Reprinted by permission of Harper & Row, Publishers, Inc.

Mildred Lee's *The skating rink* stutters and withdraws into his own shell. Some days he dislikes himself so much that he walks a long distance home from school rather than take the bus and face his peers. When a skating rink is built near his home, he discovers that even though he stutters, he can be a likable person.

SEXUALITY. Emerging adults must discover and nurture the development of their sexuality. Sex has only recently become a topic of novels for young adults. Books that deal explicitly with teenage sex are quite controversial and often banned from schools and libraries. However, these are some of the most popular books with young adult readers, perhaps because there has been a dearth of books that honestly deal with sex in the teen years available to young readers. Probably the most popular and controversial book in this category is Judy Blume's *Forever,* an honest narrative about a first love that will last "forever," and a first sexual encounter experienced during stolen moments in stolen places. *Forever,* told from the point of view of Katherine, ends like most first loves—at a new beginning. Katherine begins college and a new romance; "forever" does not last forever.

Emerging sexuality is interesting not only to adolescent females, but to adolescent males as well. A book that is told from both the male and female viewpoints is *Up in Seth's room* by Norma Fox Mazer. This popular book for older teens centers on the first serious romance of fifteen-year-old Finn. Seth, who is nineteen, is ready for a sexual relationship, but Finn is not. The playing out of the relationship, Finn's feelings about Seth and her virginity, and Finn's parents' objections about her dating Seth, an older male, are the major conflicts in the narrative.

Many other young adult books deal with developing sexuality from the male viewpoint. Some are more explicit than others. All give the teenage male the opportunity to explore his sexual identity. Books such as *The sum and total of now* (Robertson), *The terrible love life of Dudley Cornflower* (Platt), *Summer of '42* (Raucher), *The running back* (McKay), *Hard feelings* (Bredes), *Very far away from anywhere else* (LeGuin), *Stop-time* (Conroy), *Jim Tweed* (Parr), *Vision quest* (Davis), and *If I love you, am I trapped forever?* (Kerr) give the young adult male reader the opportunity to examine his sexual/love relationships through the characters and situations presented in the novels.

Developing sexuality is described from the female viewpoint in books such as *Morning is a long time coming* (Greene), *Home before dark* (Bridgers), *It's O.K. if you don't love me* (Klein), *A matter of feeling* (Boissard), *Love is like peanuts* (Bates), *Loveletters* (Shreve), *Dear Bill, remember me?* (short stories by Mazer), *Cruisin' for a bruisin'* (Rosen), *A little demonstration of affection* (Winthrop), *Love is one of the choices* (Klein), *Growing up guilty* (Schwartz), *The green of me* (Gauch), *Hello, good-bye* (Klamkin), and *A love, or a season* (Stolz). *Marcia* (Steptoe) is told from the perspective of a fourteen-year-old black girl who talks to her best girlfriend, her boyfriend, the reader, and, finally, her mother about the confusion she is feeling about her emerging womanhood.

The conversation with her mother about her boyfriend, her fears, babies, love, abortion, contraception, economics, and self-respect is frank and sensitive.

Fay Blostein in *Invitations, celebrations* suggests to health education and English teachers that students can explore the developing sexuality of themselves and of a character in a book by designing a personal atlas, as done by Maggie Clarke in Barbara Corcoran's *Me and you and a dog named Blue.*

Young adult literature also provides students with narratives about homosexuality. Most of these accounts are handled sensitively and honestly. Isabelle Holland's *Man without a face* is the story of a teenage boy who feels rejected by his family and inferior to his bright, beautiful sister. While studying for entrance exams for a prep school he meets the "man without a face." The disfigured, lonely man tutors Chuck and they become friends. The two lonely, rejected people are naturally attracted to each other. The attraction leads to a brief, sensitive homosexual encounter. The book, however, ends not with the encounter, but rather with Chuck's developing understanding of the meaning of love and affection.

Other books dealing with homosexuality from the male point of view include *Good times/bad times* (Kirkwood), *Trying hard to hear you* (Scoppettone), *I'll get there. It better be worth the trip* (Donovan), *Sticks and stones* (Hall), and *Cages* (Covert). Books that deal with homosexuality from the female viewpoint include *Hey, Dollface* (Hautzig), *Happy endings are all alike* (Scoppettone), and *Ruby* (Guy).

PREGNANCY, ABORTION, AND PARENTHOOD. The problems of teenage pregnancy, abortion, and parenthood are dealt with in a number of young adult novels. Teenage pregnancy is discussed in *Too bad about the Haines girl* (Sherburne), *It could happen to anyone* (Craig), *You would if you loved me* (Stirling), *A girl like me* (Eyerly), *Phoebe* (Dizenzo), *Arriving at a place you never left* (Ruby), and *Growing up in a hurry* (Madison). The struggle to keep and support an illegitimate child is examined in *The girls of Huntington House* (Elfman), *A house for Jonnie O.* (Elfman), and *Diving for roses* (Windsor). The alternative of abortion is raised in young adult novels such as *My darling, my hamburger* (Zindel), *Bonnie Jo, go home* (Eyerly), *It's not what you expect* (Klein), *Love is one of the choices* (Klein), and *Mia alone* (Beckman). Teenage parenthood is the topic of *Mr. and Mrs. Bo Jo Jones* (Head). It's the rare book that deals with the male's perspective in cases of teenage pregnancy, abortion, and parenthood. In *He's my baby now* by Jeannette Eyerly, however, Charles, after his casual affair, discovers he has surprising feelings for the baby and objects to the mother's insistence on putting the baby up for adoption.

RAPE. Rape has been a central theme in several recent young adult books. Janet, in Sandra Scoppettone's *Happy endings are all alike,* is raped by a disturbed boy. The rape leads to the discovery of her lesbian relationship with Peggy. Other books that deal with rape in a more traditional manner are *Why me? The Story of Jenny* (Dizenzo) and *Are you in the house alone?* (Peck).

TEENAGE PROSTITUTION. The topic of *Steffie can't come out to play* by Fran Arrick, who writes books for younger teens under the name Judie Angell, is teenage prostitution. Steffie is a fourteen-year-old runaway who dreams of becoming a model. However, her dreams are shattered when she meets Favor and becomes one of his prostitutes.

DRUGS AND ALCOHOL. Drugs and drug addiction are the topics of *Go ask Alice* (anonymous), *Richie* (Thompson), *That was then, this is now* (Hinton), *A hero ain't nothin' but a sandwich* (Childress), *The angel dust blues* (Strasser), *Cool cat* (Bonham), *Tuned out* (Wojciechowska), and many others.

One interesting young adult book that deals with drug dependence in an unusual way is Isabelle Holland's *Heads you win, tails I lose.* Caught in the middle of her parents' fighting, fifteen-year-old Melissa feels fat and ugly. When her drama coach suggests she try out for a play, she steals diet pills from her "beautiful" mother. She loses weight, gets a part in the play, and in the process nearly loses her life. Her experience with the pills and the knowledge of her mother's pill and alcohol dependence bring her closer to her father. In the end Mel doesn't lose. She overcomes her problems, gains a new friendship with her father, and develops an understanding for her mother.

Alcoholism is also a topic developed in young adult literature. Books like *Sarah T.—Portrait of a teenage alcoholic* (Wagner), *The boy who drank too much* (Greene), *The late great me* (Scoppettone), and *I can stop anytime I want* (Trivers and Davis) frankly discuss a problem that has become epidemic among teenagers. The books clearly show that both popular and lonely teenagers become alcoholics. In Linnea A. Due's *High and outside* the star pitcher of the girl's softball team, Niki, has a drinking problem she won't admit.

Realistic Heroes and Unrealistic Tasks

Young adult readers want books to be realistic. They also want them to move a step beyond what can be done in life. As a result, young adult novels are filled with "realistic" heroes who accomplish unreal tasks or surmount unbelievable obstacles. In young adult literature the hero is usually someone who is just like the reader, even if he or she lives in another era. The hero, however, is confronted with tasks greater than the reader's and can accomplish them with greater ease.

☐ *Helplessness is a basic ingredient of every child's life.... Children's literature can help overcome the helplessness.*

JOAN AIKEN

author of The wolves of Willoughby Chase / *in a speech to the National Council of Teachers of English* / *November 1981*

HEROES OF SPORTS. Both fictional and nonfictional heroes of sports are popular in young adult books. For years, fiction and nonfiction written for teenage males have centered on athletes. The athlete remains an important figure in books for today's reader. Unfortunately, sports books of past decades often were trite, with protagonists showing superhuman characteristics. The change in sports literature for young adults can be seen in *The contender* by Robert Lipsyte, a cutting-edge book of the late 1960s. The protagonist is a young boxer who is not perfect. Alfred fights the odds to become the champion. He never becomes one, but learns in the process that being the contender is just as important.

Heroes of sports in fiction for today's teens include a handicapped hero, in *Winning* (Brancato); an athlete hero who lives with his girlfriend, in *Vision quest* (Davis); a hero who does not always come in first, in *Brogg's brain* (Platt); a hero with an alcohol problem, in *The boy who drank too much* (Greene); a hero just out of reform school, in *The running back* (McKay); a hero who fulfills his father's dream, in *Football dreams* (Guy); a hero who plays all life as a game, in *The game player* (Yglesias); and heroes who are not great athletes, in *Quarterback walk-on* (Dygard). These characters are not superhuman, not beyond reproach. Today's hero of sports faces real problems and real frustrations, but the problems are usually resolved and the hero emerges a "winner," if not a champion.

Nonfiction sports accounts are popular with young adults when they are realistic and well written. Four popular nonfiction sports books written primarily for teenage males are *Life on the run* (Bradley), *Free to be Muhammad Ali* (Lipsyte), *Joe Dimaggio: A biography* (Schorr), and *Breakout: From prison to the big leagues* (LeFlore and Hawkins).

The protagonists of many young adult books for females are involved in sports. Nancy Drew, for example, is a good athlete. Katherine, in Judy Blume's *Forever,* is a champion tennis player. However, the woman athlete only recently has become the central character in books that focus on sports and the personal development of the athlete. Unfortunately, the characters in these novels do not match the characters in sports books for males. Consequently, the books are often one-dimensional and interesting only to younger and less sophisticated readers. It is hoped the development of women athletes as multidimensional characters in young adult books will parallel the development of women in athletics. Two recent novels may show a trend toward more mature sports fiction for female readers. *High and outside* by Linnea A. Due portrays a female softball star with a drinking problem. *When no one was looking* by Rosemary Wells centers on a champion tennis player who thrives on pressure until the death, and possible murder, of a competitor. Her reexamination of the sport, her values, and her motives provides an interesting view into competitive athletics among women. Probably the best-known writer of sport books for girls is R. R. Knudson, whose books include *Zanballer, Zanbanger, Zanboomer,* and *Fox running.* These books are particularly enjoyable to younger teens who are themselves interested in athletics for women.

THE HANDICAPPED HERO. The handicapped are often heroes who serve as examples to young adult readers. They include people who were born with a handicap or became handicapped at a young age, and those who develop the handicap during the teen years.

The retarded and their relationship to other teens play a part in young adult literature. *A boy called hopeless* (Melton) is about a boy with brain damage. *Hey, Dummy* (Platt), *Yesterday's child* (Brown), *All together now* (Bridgers), *Melissa comes home* (Krentel), *Tim* (McCullough), *But I'm ready to go* (Albert), and *The war on Villa Street* (Mazer) discuss mental retardation. Emotional and mental illness of teens is handled in *Passing through* (Gerson) and *Ordinary people* (Guest). Both of these books deal with the emotional and mental stress experienced after the death of a sibling. The protagonist of *The best little girl in the world* (Levenkron) is a victim of anorexia nervosa, an emotional disorder related to excessive dieting and weight loss. The title character of *Sudina* (Schell) retreats into her own world after the death of her grandmother. Hannah Green (who also writes under the name Joanne Greenberg) depicted recovery from mental illness in *I never promised you a rose garden,* which has become a classic young adult book.

Other young adult books deal with the physical handicaps that begin at birth or during childhood. *On the move* (Savitz) is about wheelchair patients and sports. *Only love* (Sallis) recounts the moving love story of two handicapped people confined to wheelchairs. Two books, *Karen* and *With love from Karen,* by Marie Killilea tell the true story of Karen's paralysis and her family's reaction to it. William is the dwarf hero of *In Neuva York* by Nicholasa Mohr. Another book about growing up as a little person is M. E. Kerr's *Little Little.* Deafness is examined in *A single light* (Wojciechowska) and *In this sign* (Greenberg). In *Change of heart* (Mandel) Sharlie has a congenital heart defect. Her love for a young lawyer encourages her to undergo a heart transplant, which is her last hope for a normal life.

Physical disability does not always occur early in life; at times it happens when least expected. A high school athlete in Robin Brancato's *Winning* is completely paralyzed during the first game of the season. With the help of a teacher, his girlfriend, a friend he didn't know was a friend, and other victims, he gains the courage to face life in a wheelchair. Ben, who is blinded in an accident, in *The world of Ben Lightheart* (Haar), must fight himself and his family to begin a new life. *Head over wheels* (Kingman) is the story of twins, one of whom is paralyzed in a car accident.

True-life accounts of people overcoming handicaps include *The story of Stevie Wonder* (Haskins), *The story of my life* (Keller), *Joni* (Eareckson), and *The other side of the mountain* (Valens).

Realistic Heroes in Times of Extreme Trial

The hero who faces incredible hardship is a common character in adolescent literature. At times the trial is a handicap; at other times it is a personal crisis, the environment, prejudice, a terrifying interpersonal relationship, or even death.

YOUNG ADULT HEROES IN CONFLICT WITH ADULTS. In *The great Gilly Hopkins* (Paterson), Gilly is a rebellious foster child who has been moved from home to home. Two other stories of foster homes are *Toby lived here* (Wolitzer) and *Broken promise* (Hayes and Lazzarino). Buddy in *Gentlehands* (Kerr) discovers that his beloved grandfather is a Nazi war criminal. In *The 290* (O'Dell) sixteen-year-old Jim discovers that his father is involved in slave trading. In *The masquerade* (Shreve), seventeen-year-old Rebecca's father is arrested for embezzlement and her mother suffers a nervous breakdown. In *Taking Terri Mueller* (Mazer), Terri believes her mother is dead. However, when she learns that she was kidnapped by her father after her parents' divorce, she begins a search for her missing mother and her family roots.

YOUNG ADULT HEROES IN UNANTICIPATED ROLES. In several young adult books the protagonist is a child totally in charge of other children. Books that place young adult characters in charge of siblings or other children are *Where the lilies bloom* and *Trial Valley* (Cleaver and Cleaver), *Mountain laurel* (Emery), *Fike's point* (Britton), *The night swimmers* (Byars), and *Edith Jackson* (Guy). All these protagonists fight for their independence; some are successful, some not. In Isabelle Holland's *Alan and the animal kingdom,* Alan is left alone to care for his animals and the house. He keeps his lonely situation a secret in an attempt to remain independent.

YOUNG ADULT HEROES BATTLING PREJUDICE. In *Iggie's house* (Blume), Iggie is from the only black family on the block. Other books that deal with black teens facing prejudice include *Jazz country* (Hentoff) and *Words by heart* (Sebestyen). Ludell fights the segregated South of the 1950s and 1960s in two books, *Ludell* and *Ludell and Willie* (Wilkinson). In *Ludell's New York Time,* he learns that prejudice in the North might be more subtle, but just as demeaning. *Roll of thunder, hear my cry* (Taylor) is about the Logan family of rural Mississippi during one year of the Depression. The 1930s South is the setting for *In a bluebird's eye* (Kornfeld), which examines the secret friendship between a white girl and a black woman.

☐   *I'm not black or white. I'm me. I'm gray!*
OUIDA SEBESTYEN

author of Words by heart / *in a speech to the National Council of Teachers of
English* / *November 1980*

At times a young hero might fight his or her own prejudice. In *Choice of straws*
(Braithwaite), a white boy who has hated blacks all his life falls in love with a
black girl.

Not all prejudice is leveled at black characters. *Carlota* (O'Dell) narrates the
story of a Spanish girl in Anglo-dominated California of gold rush days. Tom in
When the legends die (Borland) is an Indian who must survive in a white man's
culture after his parents are killed. A Protestant in a camp for Jewish children
experiences prejudice in *The summer ends too soon* (Grossman). In *Jemmy*
(Massler) a half-Indian boy grows up in Minnesota. *Sing down the moon* (O'Dell)
describes the Navajos' forced march from Canyon de Chelly to Fort Sumner in
1864. *No-no boy* (Okada) is about growing up Japanese in America. *It's crazy
to stay Chinese in Minnesota* (Telemaque) is another book about growing up in
a foreign culture.

YOUNG ADULT HEROES AGAINST THE ENVIRONMENT. Young adults facing the
cruelty of nature are found in such books as *Canyon winter* (Morey), *Snow
bound* (Mazer), *Eagle fur* (Peck), *Cold river* (Judson), *Deborah: A wilderness
narrative* (Roberts), *The hall of the mountain king* (Snyder), *And I alone survived*
(Elder and Streshinsky), *The cay* (Taylor), and *The mountain of my fear*
(Roberts).

Other teens fight hostile environments created by humankind. In *Child of fire*
(O'Dell), *Rumble fish* and *That was then, this is now* (Hinton), *City cool* (deJongh
and Cleveland), and *Take the A train* (Blankfort), the young adult protagonists
must overcome problems encountered in an urban environment. A very unusual,
masterful book in which the hero fights an environment made by man is Robert
Cormier's *The bumblebee flies anyway.* Barney Snow, the teenage hero of the
book, is confined in the Complex, an experimental hospital. Barney fights "the
merchandise" prescribed by "the Handyman," Dr. Lakendorp, the aloneness of
his compartment, the bitterness of Mazzo, and, in the end, learns that "the bumblebee flies anyway."

YOUNG ADULTS FACING INTERPERSONAL CONFLICT. In several young adult
novels the hero faces terrifying interpersonal conflicts. Books that deal with the
relationship between a kidnapper and a young adult victim are *After the first
death* (Cormier), *Catch a killer* (Wood), *Five were missing* (Duncan), *Taking
Gary Feldman* (Cohen), *A child is missing* (Paul), *Kidnapping Mr. Tubbs* (Schellie), *The solid gold kid* (Mazer and Mazer), and *Soul catcher* (Herbert). In *The
kidnapping of Christina Lattimore* (Nixon), the victim is accused, after her rescue, of having conspired with her abductors.

Some young adult heroes are alone, or almost alone, against a stronger adversary. *Are you in the house alone?* (Peck) is a story of rape. In *A stranger is watching* (Clark), a murderer stalks a boy who witnessed his mother's murder. *Hitchhike* (Holland) is about the abduction of young female hitchhikers. In *The pied piper* (Paier), Lee Criley single-handedly stops the torturing and killing of young boys.

Some young adult heroes battle pressures from peers. In *The chocolate war* by Robert Cormier, Jerry conducts a one-man campaign against the school chocolate sale and refuses to seek admittance to the school's "secret society." Jerry is at first a hero to his peers. Then he becomes a victim, but as the victim he is a hero to the readers. In *Very far away from anywhere else* (LeGuin), two gifted young people, a scientist and a musician, decide to pay the price for being different and seek comfort in each other. In spite of pressure from his peers, Alfred, in Robert Lipsyte's *The contender,* continues his boxing training. It may not be popular to date a younger boy, but the teenage protagonist of *Can you sue your parents for malpractice?* (Danziger) decides to take the risk. In *The friends* (Guy), two outcasts become friends despite pressures from peers and family.

HEROES WHO FACE IMMINENT DEATH. The death faced by the teenage hero may be caused by external events or by terminal illness. In *I am fifteen and I don't want to die* (Arnothy), Christine faces her own death. She is a Hungarian living in Budapest while war rages outside her basement apartment. Christine confronts her fear of death with the help of others who live with her.

The classic narration of a teenager facing terminal disease is John Gunther's *Death be not proud: A memoir,* based on the final year of the life of his son Johnny. The nonfictional accounts *Brian Piccolo, a short season* (Morris) and *Brian's song* (Blinn) both center on the life and death from cancer of professional football player Brian Piccolo. Another book with Brian as a hero, told from the perspective of his professional roommate, Gale Sayers, is *I am third.* Another young nonfiction hero dying of cancer is remembered in *Eric* (Lund). At seventeen, Eric discovered he has leukemia. The story of his last years, told by his mother, show Eric in college, playing soccer, and suffering great pain. Eric is a hero who shows that life can be lived even when death is imminent.

Three fictional accounts of the imminent death of a young person are *Sunshine* (Klein), which developed from a television movie about the death from cancer of a young wife and mother, and *Admission to the feast* (Beckman), about a sixteen-year-old Swedish girl who, upon learning of her terminal disease, leaves her fiancé and family and goes off to a summer cottage to write a long, poignant letter to a friend. Alice Bach's *Waiting for Johnny Miracle* is the story of twin sisters, one with bone cancer and the other healthy. The story deals with the girls' efforts to come to terms with this difference in their twinness. The narrative is more than a story about facing cancer; it is a tale of the emotional impact on the family, life in the pediatric cancer ward, and the desperate attempt to keep life as normal as possible.

■ ■ ■ **An Anthological Aside**

I'm Learning to Do What I Think Is Best for Me

PAULA DANZIGER

It's absolutely disgusting being fourteen. You've got no rights whatsoever. Your parents get to make all the decisions: Who gets the single bedroom. How much allowance is enough. What time you must come in. Who is a proper friend. What your report card is supposed to look like. And what your parents don't tell you to do, the school does. What section you're in. What's good literature. What courses you have to take to fulfill their requirements. The worst thing is that the more I realize what I want to do, the stricter everyone becomes.

Linda lies down in her bed and stares at the ceiling. "John Pollack asked Judy out. He's in the sixth grade."

Judy again.

"Linda, do you really care about going out because you want to or because other people in the class are starting to go out?"

She signs.

"Well?"

"I don't know. A little of both, I think."

"Don't you think you should just relax a little and then do what you really want to do?"

She looks at me. "What about you? Is that what you do?"

Wham. She's got me. That's not what I do. At least I don't think I do. I mean I can't even decide what I want with Zack and Bobby. And I am letting other people make the decision for me. I think that's what I'm doing. I really don't even know anymore. I go downstairs to wait for Bobby.

. . . I wonder why it's taking Bobby so long to get here. He's a half hour late. He used to do that all the time. I'd forgotten about that.

Finally I hear the horn honk. He's not even coming up to the door. He did that after we'd been going out for a while. I would have thought he'd come up to the door this time to show that things would be different. I guess he's pretty sure of himself.

I go out. He's sitting behind the wheel. I get in on the other side. He smiles at me. He's wearing a football varsity jacket.

"Hi," I say.

He keeps smiling and says, "Let's go for a soda and hamburger. We can talk there."

I nod.

Neither of us says much for most of the ride.

As we pull up into Stewart's, Bobby says, "I've missed you. I'm glad we're getting back together."

I shake my head. "I didn't say that we were. I just said we'd talk about it."

He says, "But I know we will. Remember all the fun we used to have? You know you like hanging around with the high-school crowd. Being driven places. And you know I'm just crazy about you."

He pulls into a parking space, turns off the engine, and leans back, looking very sure of himself.

I take a good look at him. He's very attractive, tall, kind of strong-looking, the kind of guy that most of the kids who have been teasing me would love to go out with.

I say, "If you are so crazy about me, why'd you break up with me?"

He frowns. "I just got tired of your being such a scared kid about sex, and I knew Sandy wasn't."

I say, "Well, what makes you think I'm any different, that things will be different?"

He says, "Well, you're getting older, and I'm sure that you've got to be getting bored with that little kid you've been hanging around with."

He looks so sure of himself. I debate telling him that Zack turns me on more than he ever did, and that I really don't think he should be so sure of himself, that maybe he should go back to Sandy.

I don't say anything yet.

We order from the guy who comes out.

It is nice being able to go out with someone who has a driver's license. Zack won't have one for almost four years.

Bobby says, "There's a party at Marty's on Friday. I'll pick you up at eight."

For a second I'm tempted to say yes; then I realize there was no question.

"How can you assume I'm going with you?" I ask him. "You don't even ask, you just tell."

He says, "I know you want to go out with me again. Remember how upset you were when you found out about me and Sandy, when I told you it was over? And now I'm telling you I was wrong. Doesn't that make you happy?"

I wait until the guy bringing the order puts it on the window and leaves.

"Bobby, you're unbelievable. You walk out and then expect to come back as if nothing had ever happened."

He looks at me. "But I told you I'm sorry."

I look at him. He seems so sure of himself in his varsity jacket, with his driver's license, being seventeen. I think of Zack. He's smarter, nicer, more fun. I think of what I told Linda about doing what she wants to, not what others think she should do. Next I think of how the kids act to me in the hall. I don't even like them. Why do I have to worry about what they think of me? I wouldn't want them as friends anyway.

Bobby says, "Look, I'm giving you the chance to go out with me again. If you don't want to, just tell me. There are a lot of girls who would love the chance."

I almost laugh. When they handed out egos and conceit, Bobby must have gotten a double dose.

First I bite into my hamburger. Then I say, "I think maybe you should give one of them the pleasure of your company. I don't think I want to go out with you. In fact I know I don't."

He looks stunned. "But I thought ... I mean, you were so upset when ..."

"I was. But I'm not now. Look, Bobby, I don't think you know me anymore. You didn't even ask me what's new or anything. I don't want to be with someone who doesn't look at me and really see me."

"But I do."

"No." I realize it's true. "You don't and you never did. Everything's always the way you want it."

He says, "Well, if that's the way you feel, there's no reason for us even to stay together any longer tonight." He turns on the engine.

"Don't you think you should honk so the guy gets the tray before you drive off?" I ask him.

He frowns. Bobby never likes to be told that he's goofed, considers it a sin. He honks. We drive back in silence.

When I get out of the car, I say, "It would have been nice if we could have ended up friends even without going out. But that's not possible because I don't think we've ever been friends."

He just frowns.

Linda is still lying on her bed when I enter the room. "Everything OK?" she asks.

I nod and smile.

"No Bobby?"

"No Bobby."

"Good." She grins back. "Zack's a better audience for my jokes. And I like him better."

"Me, too." I say.

I lie down on my bed to think about it. There are still going to be nasty remarks at school from some of the kids. My life's not going to drastically change. It hardly ever does when you're a kid. My parents certainly aren't going to change that much. It doesn't look like Melissa's going to be allowed to visit soon. I don't think I'm going to turn into a bio brain, like Erik Marks. I'm not even sure whether Zack and I will end up winning the pool, staying together for twenty-two years.

What I am sure of is that I finally did something for myself, that I'm learning to do what I think is best for me.

Maybe suing my parents for malpractice isn't as important as making sure that I don't do malpractice on myself. For the next newsletter, I'm going to write an article about that. I'll even sign it.

In the meantime, I'm calling Zack. We owe each other six and a half minutes.

■ ■ ■

Heroes of Other Times

One of the exciting aspects of young adult fiction is its ability to make history come to life for today's young readers. The heroes of young adult historical fiction have needs and interests that are similar to the readers'. As a result, today's young adult can identify with the young characters of bygone days and understand the world in which they lived.

YOUNG HEROES IN WARTIME. The World War II era is full of young heroes who defy great odds to survive. Some heroes remain at home, as in *Don't sit under the apple tree* (Brancato) and *Summer of my German soldier* (Greene). Others fight in battle, as in *The Exeter blitz* (Rees) and *The last mission* (Mazer). The young in Europe fight for their survival and the survival of others in *Chase me, catch nobody!* (Haugaard), *The upstairs room* (Reiss), *Bright candles: A novel of the Danish resistance* (Benchley), *Ceremony of innocence* (Forman), *A bag of marbles* (Joffo), and *Friedrich* (Richter). The fifteen-year-old hero of Brian Garfield's exciting tale *The paladin* is a personal secret agent of Winston Churchill. He is involved in murder, assassination, and sabotage on both sides of the World War II front lines.

Books about young adults in World War I include: *How many miles to Babylon?* (Johnson), *Johnny got his gun* (Trumbo), and *Company K* (March).

Other U.S. wars have provided heroes for young adult books. *My brother Sam is dead* (Collier and Collier) is the story of a young man who joins the Minutemen against his family's objections. *The Hessian* (Fast) tells of a drummer boy who is hidden by a Quaker family until he is discovered by the authorities. Howard Fast depicts a young hero of the Revolutionary War in *April morning*. A classic young adult novel is *Johnny Tremain* (Forbes), about a young pre–Revolutionary War hero in Boston. The title character of Patricia Clapp's *I'm Deborah Sampson: A soldier in the War of the Revolution* is a heroine who appeals to female readers. Robert Newton Peck's *Fawn,* set during the French and Indian Wars, is the story of Fawn, whose father is a French Jesuit and whose mother is an outcast Mohawk. *Across five Aprils* (Hunt) is about a family torn apart by the Civil War. In *Rifles for Watie* (Keith), a Union soldier, befriended by the rebel soldiers on whom he has been spying, sees the horrors of the war from the other side. *The dunderhead war* (Baker) is a novel about a young man and his German immigrant uncle, who travel on a wagon train from Missouri into Mexican territory and become involved in the early stages of the war with Mexico. The wars between white settlers and American Indians have been the subject of several adolescent novels. *The life and death of Yellow Bird* (Forman) chronicles the life of an Indian seer from the battles of Little Bighorn to Wounded Knee. In *Save Queen of Sheba* (Moeri), two children are the only survivors of an Indian attack on a wagon train.

SLAVERY AND THE YOUNG ADULT. In Joan Blos's Newbery Medal book, *A gathering of days: A New England girl's journal,* a girl helps a slave escape. *I, Juan de Pareja* (deTrevino), another Newbery award winner, is about a seventeenth-century slave of the painter Velázquez who eventually wins his freedom and becomes an artist in his own right. Gabriel, a slave, leads a revolt on an 1800 Richmond plantation in *Black thunder* (Bontemps). *Amos Fortune, free man* (Yates), *Long journey home: Stories from black history* (Lester), *To Ravensrigg* (Burton), and *First of midnight* (Darke) are four more books about slavery and young heroes.

TEENAGE HEROES AND THE EARLY DAYS OF THE UNITED STATES. The story of an adolescent boy who survives the destruction of the Roanoke settlement is recounted in *Roanoke* (Levitin). *Sarah Bishop* (O'Dell) is set in the pre–Revolutionary War period. *The witch of Blackbird Pond* (Speare) is the story of Kit, a young islander, who is accused of witchcraft. A young settler is the heroine of *Constance: A story of early Plymouth* (Clapp). Esther Forbes' *A mirror for witches* tells of the New England witch hunts. The westward movement is catalogued in *The snowbird* (Calvert). The *Little House* books by Laura Ingalls Wilder depict the life of a family on the unsettled plains. The westward migration of the Sager family along the Oregon Trail is told in *Stout-hearted seven* (Frazier). *The people therein* (Lee) is a love story that takes place in late-nineteenth-century Appalachia. The tale unites two unlikely lovers: Janthy, who is crippled and resigned to a life without marriage, and Drew, a botanist who comes from Boston to overcome his alcoholism.

HEROES OF OTHER COUNTRIES AND ERAS. Soaring Hawk is a seventeen-year-old pre-Columbian Cherokee hero in *Long Man's song* (Rockwood). *The king's fifth* (O'Dell) is the tale of a young Spanish mapmaker who travels with Coronado and the conquistadors to find the cities of Cibola. *The clan of the cave bear* (Auel) is the story of a Cro-Magnon girl adopted by a Neanderthal tribe. Her struggle to maintain her identity in a male-dominated society is very modern despite the story's prehistoric setting. The young hero in *The trumpeter of Krakow* (Kelly) lives in Poland in the 1400s. In Elizabeth Speare's *The bronze bow,* the hero, who lives in the time of Jesus, is obsessed with hatred for the Romans and a desire for revenge, until he meets the rabbi Jesus. *Young Fu of the upper*

Yangtze (Lewis) is a young hero of early-twentieth-century China. In *The dancing bear* (Dickinson), set in the sixth century, a young Greek slave and his dancing bear journey with an old holy man to rescue Lady Ariadne.

Heroes of Japan appear in two young adult books by Katherine Paterson. Twelfth-century Japan is the setting for *Of nightingales that weep.* During the Keike-Genji civil wars, Takiko, the daughter of a famous samurai killed in the wars, becomes the personal servant of a musician. In *The master puppeteer,* Jiro is the son of a starving puppetmaker in eighteenth-century Japan. He runs away from home and becomes an apprentice to the master of the Nanza puppet theater.

Rosemary Sutcliff's heroes live in the early days of British history. *The eagle of the ninth* takes place in A.D. 125 in Roman England as Marcus sets out to trace the lost Ninth Hispana Legion. Two other Roman Britain novels by Sutcliff are *The silver branch* and *The lantern bearers.* Her other books, *The Capricorn bracelet, The mark of the horse lord, Warrior scarlet, Song for a dark queen, Knight's fee, Simon,* and *Rider on a white horse,* are historical novels set in England from the days of Roman occupation to the English Civil War and Cromwell. Fans of the romantic heroes of Arthurian legend will particularly enjoy Sutcliff's *Sword at sunset.*

Many other young adult books are set in Great Britain. Gunnar, the young

A selection of books dealing with heroes of bygone eras from a classroom paperback library.

hero of Nathaniel Benchley's *Beyond the mists,* is the sole survivor of a Viking raid on Britain. Gunnar meets Leif Ericson, who takes him on his next journey. *The Maude Reed tale* (Lofts) is set in fifteenth-century Britain. Maude's problem is that she doesn't want to learn to be a lady; instead, she wants to manage the family's wool business.

Leon Garfield's books are set in eighteenth-century England. The young hero of *Jack Holborn* searches for his home. A second novel, *The sound of coaches,* is in the tradition of Henry Fielding's *The history of Tom Jones.* It tells the story of Sam, who is cared for by passengers on a coach who witness the death of his mother in childbirth. Part of the book talks of his early years and his desire to become a coachman. The next two parts of the narrative center on his journey to London, his apprenticeship, and his search for his father.

Cross-Cultural Heroes

THE MELTING POT. In these books, immigrant or minority teenagers become part of the mainstream U.S. culture despite hardships and prejudice. The heroes of Chaim Potok's *The chosen* and *My name is Asher Lev* are boys who were born and raised as Hasidic Jews. Two books depict the internment of Japanese-Americans in the United States during World War II: *Farewell to Manzanar* (Houston and Houston) is about a community that was created in the Sierras to house thousands of Japanese-Americans. In this true story Jeanne Wakatuski Houston recalls the fears and frustrations she experienced in the internment camp. *The moved-outers* (Means) is the tale of a Japanese family prior to and during their relocation.

Fifth Chinese daughter (Wong) is an account of an American-born Chinese girl in San Francisco, her family, her education, and her budding career as an artist. The Chinese immigrant experience is further catalogued in *Dragonwings* (Yep), which tells of eleven-year-old Moon Shadow and his experiences in San Francisco's Chinatown in the early twentieth century. *Year walk* (Clark) is the story of Basque sheepherders in Idaho in the early 1900s. Growing up as an Irish Catholic boy in Pittsburgh in the 1930s is the theme of *Duffy's rocks* (Fenton). *Lonesome whistle: The story of the first transcontinental railroad,* a recent adaptation of the longer adult book by Dee Brown, depicts the unsung heroes of the western expansion by rail. In *Viva Chicano* (Bonham), Joaquín "Keeny" Durán struggles to rise above the problems of the Mexican-American ghetto in which he lives. Life as a Mexican-American girl is dealt with in *Go up the road* (Lampman).

THE BLACK HERO. A wealth of books explore the world of the young black hero. In *The second stone* (Brown), fifteen-year-old Henry Wilson is struggling between loyalty to his family and acceptance by his friends. In *Cornbread, Earl, and me* (Fair), Earl and Wilford ("me" of the title) witness the murder of their hero, Cornbread, by a policeman. The two boys eventually gain an understanding of the circumstances that allow the black community to accept the political corruption that resulted in Cornbread's death.

The masterfully written books of Virginia Hamilton, *M. C. Higgins, the great, The planet of Junior Brown, The house of Dies Drear, Zeely,* and *Arilla Sun Down,* are about young blacks in a variety of environments. The plots, themes, and genres are varied, but the literary style is always of highest quality.

Three books by Rosa Guy, *The friends, Ruby,* and *The disappearance,* and *Fast Sam, Cool Clyde, and Stuff* by Walter Dean Myers examine city life. *Roll of thunder, hear my cry* and *Song of the trees,* both by Mildred Taylor, take place in rural Mississippi.

Other notable authors of young adult books about black people include Alice Childress *(A hero ain't nothin' but a sandwich),* Kristin Hunter *(The soul brothers and Sister Lou),* June Jordan *(His own where),* and Sharon Bell Mathis *(Listen for the fig tree* and *Teacup full of roses).*

Two biographies by Virginia Hamilton provide real-life black models for young readers: *Paul Robeson: The life and times of a free black man* and *W. E. B. Dubois: A biography.*

NATIVE AMERICAN HEROES. *Creek Mary's blood* (Brown) is the epic story of an Indian and her descendants. *To spoil the sun* (Rockwood) tells of a girl growing up in an Indian tribe during the first white settlement. In *Waterless Mountain* (Armer) a young Navaho boy who wants to become a medicine man must learn of his culture to achieve his goal. Hidden Poe in *We are Mesquakie, we are one* (Irwin) grows to maturity among the Mesquakie.

Several books tell of white children who learn the ways of their Indian captors. In *Ghost Fox* (Houston) sixteen-year-old Sarah is kidnapped by the Abnaki Indians. She gradually adopts their ways and must choose between being an Indian or returning to her earlier culture. In the classic young adult novel *Light in the forest* (Richter), True Son, a white boy, is captured and raised by the Delaware Indians but is later forced to return to his white family, which no longer loves or understands him.

REALISTIC HEROES FROM OTHER CULTURES. *The blanket word* (Arundel) presents the story of a young woman who comes home from the University of Edinburgh to be at her dying mother's side in Wales. Another timeless story about life in Wales is Richard Llewellyn's *How green was my valley,* a family chronicle, much of which concentrates on the mines and their destruction of the land.

Australia is the setting for the novel *The Min-Min* (Clark), in which Sylvia finds life in the outback devastating. Family problems make this modern adolescent novel an interesting companion piece for the popular adult novel *The thorn birds* (McCullough).

Young Eskimos are the heroes of several young adult novels. In *The white dawn* (Houston) a band of Eskimos discover three survivors of a boat wreck and restore them to health. An Eskimo family in *Back to the top of the world*

(Ruesch) find the ways of the white man strange but amusing. The book allows the reader to see the world through the eyes of the Eskimo. *A hunter comes home* (Turner) is the story of an Eskimo boy. The heroine of *Julie of the wolves* (George) is a teenager torn between two cultures. She runs away from her young, mentally retarded husband and goes to her father's home. Her father has accepted white culture, which she rejects, but she soon learns that she cannot return to the culture of the Tundra.

Canada is the setting for *Mrs. Mike* (Freedman and Freedman). Mrs. Mike is a sixteen-year-old Bostonian who marries a member of the Royal Canadian Mounted Police. The rugged life of the Canadian North causes many heartbreaks for the young heroine.

Fourteen-year-old Lesley in *One more river* (Banks) leaves her comfortable life in Canada to live in Israel. Her experiences there can be contrasted to life on a kibbutz as described in *Elsewhere, perhaps* (Oz). *My enemy, my brother* (Foreman) chronicles the early days of the Israeli state from the viewpoint of a Jewish boy who has just been released from a Nazi concentration camp. The power of this novel comes from the protagonist's relationship with a young Arab.

Modern-day Belfast is the setting for *Across the barricades* (Lingard), in which a Protestant girl and a Catholic boy fall in love despite family opposition. *Don't cry for me* (Jarunkava) is a problem novel in which a Czech teenager attempts to find a place among her peers and revolts against adult values. *The shadow of a bull* (Wojciechowska) is the tale of a teenager who lives in the shadow of his famous bullfighter father. Even though he wants to become a doctor, he must accept his legacy and follow his father as Spain's greatest toreador. *A matter of feeling* (Boissard) is a family-oriented love story set in France. The book centers on Pauline's first real romance, with an artist nearly twice her age.

Mystery and Suspense Books

Young adult characters in mystery and suspense literature share many traits with young adult readers, but the situations in which the characters are placed are often unrealistic. The protagonists of these novels are usually young, between the ages of twelve and twenty-five, and act like most young adults, but by chance or design find themselves embroiled in a suspenseful plot.

MYSTERIES. Mysteries have always been a popular genre for the young adult reader, and the Nancy Drew formula mysteries maintain their popular appeal today. Young adult readers often enjoy mysteries written primarily for adults. The simplicity of plot and characterization of these books makes it possible for immature readers to read and enjoy them.

In the last decade, authors of young adult literature have increasingly supplied the teenage reader with well-written, critically acclaimed mysteries. Jay Bennett, author of *The birthday murderer, Deathman, do not follow me, The exe-*

cutioner, The killing tree, The pigeon, and other mysteries for young adult readers, won the Edgar Allan Poe award for Best Juvenile Mystery for two successive years. In 1978 the prestigious Newbery Medal was given to Ellen Raskin for her intriguing puzzle mystery *The westing game.* Joan Aiken, author of *Nightfall,* has become a popular author of mystery and adventure stories for young adults. Most of Lois Duncan's books written during the past decade are macabre mysteries that combine suspense and the occult. *I know what you did last summer* is about four teenagers attempting to conceal their hit-and-run accident while being pursued by a mysterious person seeking revenge. Robbie Branscum, the author of wonderful southern regional narratives including *Me and Jim Luke, Johnny May, Toby, Granny and George,* and *The murder of hound dog Bates,* often turns to mystery as a plot tool to help develop her characters.

Other popular authors of young adult literature have tried their hand at mystery writing. Paul Zindel often combines a bit of mystery in his narratives. *The undertaker's gone bananas* is a humorous whodunit. Richard Peck unites the supernatural with mystery in *The ghost belonged to me* and *Ghosts I have been.* In *Dreamland Lake,* Peck's two young protagonists find a body in the woods near an amusement park. *Jane-Emily* by Patricia Clapp is a suspenseful tale of mystery and the occult, featuring a very unusual girl. Isabelle Holland writes Gothic mysteries, marketed to adults but very popular with young readers.

Madeleine L'Engle has written several mysteries, including *The arm of the starfish, Dragons in the water,* and *The young unicorns,* in which she uses her amazing ability to combine fantasy, suspense, science, music, and theology.

Virginia Hamilton's critically acclaimed *The house of Dies Drear* unravels a mystery against the historical backdrop of the Civil War and the Underground Railroad. Walter Dean Myers, an author of urban fiction for young adolescents, has written the humorous mystery *Mojo and the Russians.* Lynn Hall's successful mysteries for young adults include *The secret of stonehouse.* M. E. Kerr entered the mystery genre with her book *Gentlehands.* Elaine Konigsburg's *From the mixed-up files of Mrs. Basil E. Frankweiler* is a humorous mystery for young adolescent readers. Those readers also enjoy Dorothy Francis's *Mystery of the forgotten map,* about two young sleuths who attempt to prove their grandfather is not a thief by using an old map, and *Golden girl,* about a girl who may be forced out of a pageant by being murdered. Georgess McMargue's *Funny bananas: the mystery in the museum* is also a funny mystery for young adolescent readers. A romance mystery by Barbara Michaels, *Wait for what will come,* is very popular with young adult female readers. The book is about a young American who inherits an ancient, crumbling mansion in Cornwall, England—and the mysterious legend that goes with it.

Leon Garfield is a master of the mystery genre. In *Footsteps,* Garfield sets the scene in eighteenth-century England. Young William sets out to quiet his father's ghost by finding the old partner his father had swindled. In the narrative the reader is introduced to colorful characters such as Shot-in-the-Head, a gangster who makes his living by "snick-and-lurk" and even contemplates stealing the gold on the dome of St. Paul's Cathedral. The story, which begins and ends in William's father's bedroom, is full of humor, suspense, figures of speech, and amusing characters who will delight and intrigue the young reader.

The seance by Joan Lowery Nixon is another exciting mystery that introduces a touch of the supernatural. Lauren must welcome Sara Martin, a ward of the court, into her aunt Melvamay's household. From the beginning there is something strange about Sara, and when she invites Lauren to a seance, Lauren agrees to go because she fears the taunts of Sara more than the seance. During the seance Sara disappears, and later her body is discovered in a swamp. Another teenager is murdered before the tragic and frightening conclusion of the mystery.

SUSPENSE NOVELS. Suspense novels for young adults have gained popularity in recent years. Many such stories written for adults are also popular with adolescents, but the length and complexity of plot line often make them difficult for the immature reader. Therefore, many young adult authors have used their skills to compose suspense stories for young readers. Joan Aiken's *Died on a rainy Sunday* is a good example of the genre. In the story a four-year-old child is instinctively terrified, with just cause, by a new baby-sitter. Jay Bennett has written the suspenseful young adult books *Say hello to the hit man* and *The long black coat,* about Phil, who discovers why two of his dead brother's army buddies are after him. In Robbie Branscum's *Me and Jim Luke,* the boys find a murdered man while hunting possums. The entrance of the Ku Klux Klan into the story creates the suspense. Barbara Corcoran's *The clown* is a narrative of a young girl attempting to smuggle a Jewish circus clown out of Moscow. Lois Duncan's *Down a dark hall* is a mystery suspense about a very strange girls' boarding school and its even stranger headmistress. James Forman tries his hand at suspense in *So ends this day,* a tale about sea voyagers in search of whales, a ship, and a murderer. Robert Cormier's terrifying *After the first death* is about a hijacked bus, terrorism, and family relationships. Lois Duncan's *Five were missing* is also about a bus hijacking. Richard Peck's *Are you in the house alone?* and *Through a brief darkness* are two suspenseful stories about young female protagonists and terror. The first deals with rape, the second with kidnapping. Frances Miller's *The truth trap* is the tale of a fifteen-year-old who runs away to Los Angeles with his nine-year-old deaf sister and finds himself unjustly accused of murder. John Rowe Townsend's *The intruder* is the eerie tale of a sinister stranger who claims to be a close blood relative of the young protagonist's friend, a shopkeeper. In Patricia Windsor's *Something's waiting for you, Baker D.,* Mary the Hulk wants to protect Baker D. from something, but she is not sure what.

Survival books are a popular subgenre of the suspense novel. In Scott O'Dell's *Island of the blue dolphins,* a girl survives eighteen years alone on an island. Theodore Taylor's *The cay* is the tale of a shipwrecked blind boy who first lives with a black islander and a cat, but later manages by himself on his deserted island home. In J. Allan Bosworth's *White water, still water,* Chris and his homemade raft survive the Canadian wilderness as Chris attempts to find his way back to civilization before the winter. In Mavis Clark's *Wildfire,* five young characters are united in a desperate struggle to escape a raging forest fire in Australia. *Incidents at Hawk's Hill* by Allan Eckert is the strange tale of endurance of a young child who lives for weeks in the hole of a fierce badger. In John Ives's *Fear in a handful of dust,* four kidnapped psychiatrists, including one woman, endure the horrors of the desert after being abandoned to die by a psychotic killer. In the historical novel by Sonia Levitin, *Roanoke: A novel of the lost colony,* sixteen-year-old William tells of the hardships and struggles in the ill-fated colony. In *Canyon Winter* by Walt Morey, a fifteen-year-old boy lives through a plane crash and now must survive the northwest wilderness. Harry Mazer's *Snow bound* is about Tony, who has run away from home, and Cindy, the hitchhiker he picks up, stranded near the Canadian border, where they must make it through a raging blizzard. *Pilot down, presumed dead* by Marjorie Phleger is about the survivor of a plane crash and a coyote companion on an uninhabited island off the coast of Baja California. In Joan Aiken's *The wolves of Willoughby Chase,* winner of the Lewis Carroll Shelf Award, two cousins are left in the care of an evil governess. The girls are chased by wolves, and their parents are lost at sea. They escape the evil governess and now must travel four hundred miles to London with their friend Simon and his geese. In this narrative the young protagonists must struggle against both natural hardships and human malice.

The recent popularity of suspense and mystery novels with young adult readers is obvious in G. Robert Carlsen's "Books for Young Adults" poll, in which young adult readers select "the most popular books" of the year. Of the approximately ninety titles selected in a three-year period no fewer than 25, or 28 percent, fall into the mystery and suspense categories. Young adult paperback publishers, Dell and Bantam, are capitalizing on the interests of the young adult audience. Dell is reissuing the mystery and suspense novels of Joan Aiken, and Bantam is publishing a series called "Choose Your Own Adventure," in which the reader answers a series of multiple-choice questions in the text and is then directed to different pages in the book that change the plot.

Survival stories seem to be particularly popular with young adults. In the three years of the poll, at least ten survival stories were selected as the most popular books. In 1979 the young adult readers selected Barnaby Conrad and Niels Mortensen's *Endangered,* about a photographer who inadvertently photographs a murder and then must flee the murderers. Robert Newton Peck's adventure *Eagle fur* was another favorite. A story of the Canadian frontier of 1754, it presents sixteen-year-old Abbot Coe, who must survive the frontier of the fur trader. Linda Weintraub's *Runaway!* is the story of three runaways, two from a juvenile detention home and one from the home of unloving parents. In 1980 three additional survival books were selected by teen readers. *Winterkill* by Xavier Jefferson is the tale of how various people in a winter resort react to blizzard warnings. Oliver McNab's *Horror story* is a narrative of a young couple and their five-year-old daughter who are lost in the New Hampshire woods and become captives of a community led by a man seeking revenge against society. This book features the suspense of survival against natural and human environments. Mara Rostov's *Night hunt* is about a military hero who volunteers for a war game. He doesn't realize that the commander of the games really wants him dead. The games turn into a fight for survival. In the 1981 poll, young readers selected *Crooked tree* by Robert C. Wilson, which combines the suspense of bears stalking humans with supernatural events and Indian legend. *Free fall* by J. D. Reed involves the identification and tracking of a former Green Beret who parachutes into Pinchot National Forest with $750,000 in ransom money.

BOOKS THAT COMBINE SUSPENSE AND THE OCCULT. In Charles Crawford's *Bad fall,* everyone is charmed by the new boy in school. However, what they do not know about him is terrifying. Almost all of Lois Duncan's suspense stories combine an aspect of the occult. Mark in *Killing Mr. Griffin* possesses a strange, unexplainable power over his young friends; the headmistress in *Down a dark hall* has unusual, terrifying talents. In Barbara Michaels's *Witch,* Ellen purchases a house that formerly belonged to a witch. When Ellen moves into the house she is labeled a witch and bizarre things begin to happen. In Stephen King's occult suspense tale *Firestarter,* Charlie, a young girl, can set things on fire just by looking at them. She must decide whether she will use her power against the secret government agency pursuing her and her father. A collection of horror stories by Stephen King, *Night shift,* includes vampires, bogeymen, rats, and a fatal can of beer. In Dora Polk's *The Linnet estate,* an English girl visits a California widow who is interested in the occult. The girl becomes the object of what appears to be a supernatural campaign to drive her away. In Otfried Preussler's *The satanic mill,* a tale of seventeenth-century Germany, a boy attempts to escape from a master of necromancy, a conjurer of spirits from the dead.

Recent polls of young adult reading tastes also show an interest in books about the occult or macabre. In Carsen's 1979 poll, the young adult readers selected books such as Thomas Cullinan's *The bedeviled,* in which a family moves to a quiet farmhouse in Ohio and Dugg, the adolescent son, appears to become possessed by the spirit of his evil great-great-grandfather. In 1980 the student readers selected, among other suspense books, Edward Levy's *Came a spider,* about a giant mutated spider that lays eggs in Lee's bloodstream as he hunts in the California hills. *The mirror* by Marlys Millhiser, another selection of the young adults, is the story of Shay, who, as she looks at the image of her grandmother in a strange mirror, sees their bodies switched. She continually attempts to return to the twentieth century through the mirror. *The totem* by David Morrell is about a mysterious disease, spread by biting, that invades a small valley in the western mountains. In 1981 the young adult readers selected *Haunted* by Judith St. George, a tale of murder, suicide, and unexplainable incidents.

Another type of suspense novel that is particularly intriguing to young adult readers is the story of the search. Ian Cameron's *The lost ones* and *The mountains at the bottom of the world* are both based on the search plot. In *The lost ones* a father seeks his son, lost during the son's hunt for whales in the Arctic. A dead man's diary is the cause of a quest in remote Chile for a tribe of primitive men and an active volcano in *The mountains at the bottom of the world.* Danny of Walter Edmond's *Wolf hunt* attempts to track down the "stump-toed wolf." In Hal Evarts' *Bigfoot,* the abominable snowman is the object of the search. In M. Ray's *The ides of April,* a historical novel, a seventeen-year-old boy looks for the killer of the Roman senator Caius Pomponius. In 1979 three books incorporating searches in their plots were chosen by young adults in Carlsen's poll. *A stranger is watching* by Mary Higgins Clark is about a murderer who stalks the victim's son, who witnessed the murder. *The snake* by John Godey is about the hunt for a dangerous reptile that has escaped from the Central Park Zoo. Charlotte Paul's *A child is missing* is about the kidnapping of a couple's eldest son. The surprise ending of the book, which suggests a solution to the Lindbergh case, is fast paced and suspenseful. The 1981 Carlsen poll added two search books to the list of adolescent favorites: *Free fall* (Reed) and *The cradle will fall* (Clark). In Clark's book, a young lawyer sees a woman's body being placed in a car outside a hospital. The lawyer's investigation leads her to discover that a medical professional is murdering his patients.

Fantasy and Science Fiction

Like mystery and suspense, fantasy and science fiction books usually have not been specifically written for a young adult audience. Even so, young adults read large numbers of these stories, perhaps because the protagonists are usually young, the plots often simple, and the literary techniques predictable. Therefore, many young readers are able to read and enjoy science fiction and fantasy written for an adult audience. Unfortunately, some young adult readers turn away from adult science fiction and fantasy books because of their length. However, recent trends in young adult publishing indicate that a growing number of writers who write for young readers are entering the genres of fantasy and science fiction.

COMBINING REALISM WITH FANTASY. A recent useful trend in young adult fantasy writing has been the joining of realism and fantasy in a single narrative. These books may assist the young reader in developing a taste for the fantasy. Bruno Bettelheim pointed out in his book *The uses of enchantment: The meaning and importance of fairy tales* that the fairy tale is an important aspect of the young child's life, that it teaches children, through simplification, that they can master fears and overcome obstacles. However, many young adult readers find fantasy confusing, unrealistic, and hard to follow. We often assume that fantasy should appeal to the young, so it is hard to understand why many adolescents lack interest in fantasy. Perhaps it is that young adults, in putting away their childish things, have also put away their imagination, the desire to fantasize, the

Author Katherine Paterson brings her books to life for a group of ten-year-olds in a school library.

need to leave the real world and enter a world in which they can be victorious. It is possible that the adults in their lives have encouraged teenagers to grow up and stop playing with the toys of childhood, to stop imagining. This is unfortunate indeed. The lessons to be learned in fantasy and fairy tales are important, and teachers and parents should encourage young adults to develop an interest in these genres.

> *This is exactly the message that fairy tales get across to the child in manifold form: that a struggle against severe difficulties in life is unavoidable, is an intrinsic part of human existence—but that if one does not shy away, but steadfastly meets unexpected and often unjust hardships, one masters all obstacles and at the end emerges victorious.... The child needs most particularly to be given suggestions in symbolic form about how he may deal with these issues and grow safely into maturity. "Safe" stories mention neither death nor aging, the limits of our existence, nor the wish for eternal life. The fairy tale, by contrast, confronts the child squarely with the basic human predicaments. (Bettelheim 1976, p. 8)*

Books that join realism with fantasy can act as a bridge to the world of the fantasy. Teachers and parents who discover that the adolescent is reluctant to or refuses to read fantasy can use books that join realistic characters and situations with fantastic situations and characters to bridge the gap.

In the world of fantasy, the hero must strive to overcome evil through a quest in which a multitude of problems must be solved. The protagonist need not conform to the natural laws as we know them, but can use fantastic means to reach his or her goal. At the end of the fantasy the hero has achieved something. What has been achieved is not necessarily what the hero expected to accomplish. Evil is not destroyed, but it is temporarily defeated; it will return to be conquered again.

Often in the fantasy, a new world is created that may be totally different from the real world. Animals may speak or a new language may be developed. People may be unnaturally small or large. Mythological beasts may roam the landscape. It may be a world that looks nothing like the world in which the reader lives—under the sea, upside-down, total darkness, or total light. But always, in the world of fantasy and fairy tale, characters must struggle and accept the consequences of their actions. Through steadfast struggles they conquer the odds. Temporarily victorious, the hero knows that the struggle will not end.

□ *Heroes are the gathering of all characteristics of people. The hero in the epic is the people—to have a hero you must have a community of people.*
WALTER WANGERIN, JR.

author of The book of the dun cow / *in a speech to the National Council of Teachers of English* / *November 1980*

When the realistic world is joined with the fantastic, the young realistic hero, who is like the reader in almost every way, is involved in a fantastic situation among fantastic people. In *Hangin' out with Cici* (Pascal), young Victoria is plagued by problems in her relationship with her mother that are typical of difficulties experienced by many young adults. Their arguments are continual. One day the young heroine is taken back in time to an unfamiliar era. In her search for the familiar in this new world, she meets Cici. After many unusual experiences she realizes that Cici is her mother as a teenager. She and Cici become great friends. When she returns to her real world, she is able to conquer the problems she has with her mother through the new understandings she has gained. *Saturday, the twelfth of October* (Mazer) uses a similar technique to transport an unhappy girl into a fantastic situation and return her, a changed person, to the real world. In Richard Parker's *A time to choose,* Stephen and Mary move back and forth between their own world and a parallel world in which they live in a utopian commune. They must finally choose in which world they will remain. Katherine Paterson in *Bridge to Terabithia* never allows Jesse and Leslie to exit their real world totally; but the imaginary world they create in Terabithia helps Jesse transcend his limitations and learn to accept himself and the life he is living with increased maturity and understanding. In a recent book by Ursula LeGuin, *The beginning place,* Irena and Hugh follow each other to the fantasy world of Tembreabrezi, where they struggle to save their friends and find a place for themselves in the real world.

The Harper Hall trilogy by Anne McCaffrey introduces the reader to a real girl, with real problems, in an unreal world on a fantastic planet. In the first book, *Dragonsong,* Menolly, ordered by her father to stop "tunemaking," runs away from home and develops a friendship with the fire lizard, whom she teaches to sing. In *Dragonsinger,* Menolly arrives at Harper Hall to continue her music studies. During her stay she learns about the extraordinary role she must play in the future of her planet. The final book of the trilogy, *Dragondrums,* tells the story of Piemur, a mischievous boy introduced in *Dragonsinger.* Piemur grows from a restless troublemaker to a self-sufficient young man while endeavoring to quell the political unrest in Pern during the perilous Threadfall. The realistic characters in McCaffrey's stories meet the unrealistic trials of the quest to conquer evil in real and unreal ways.

Madeleine L'Engle's three time books, *A wrinkle in time, A wind in the door,* and *A swiftly tilting planet,* transports a girl, her somewhat unusual brother, and their mother through time and place from their real world into several fantastic worlds. It all begins in the kitchen one stormy night where Meg meets her brother, Charles, who seems to anticipate her arrival in a superhuman way. The appearance of an unearthly visitor changes their lives in *A wrinkle in time.* In *A wind in the door* the children fight the forces of evil to save Charles's life. Charles, now fifteen, in *A swiftly tilting planet* attempts to save the world with the unicorn Gaudior. This fascinating novel is based on the legend of Madoc of Wales. The combination of human characters, fantastic situations, science, and theology makes L'Engle's books a joy for even the reluctant reader of fantasy.

THE FANTASTIC QUEST. A good fantasy must communicate truths of human existence if it is to be understandable to the reader. The quest in the fantasy is often improbable, and the actions of the hero are unlikely; but through the author's skill, the quest and the hero become acceptable and believable. Many quest fantasies are appropriate for young readers.

If the quest is accomplished in a series, each book can stand alone; however, the quest, usually against evil, is never complete. The Prydain Cycle by Lloyd Alexander is an excellent fantasy quest series that can be read by young readers as early as nine or ten years of age, and enjoyed, on a more advanced level, by older readers. The cycle, based on Welsh legend and myth, is about Taran and his search for his true identity. The cycle includes *The black cauldron, The book of three, The castle of Llyr, The high king,* and *Taran wanderer.* The Children of Green Knowe series by Lucy Boston consists of four books, *An enemy at Green Knowe, The treasure of Green Knowe, The river at Green Knowe,* and *Stranger at Green Knowe,* appropriate for young adolescent readers. Susan Cooper's The Dark Is Rising series is about Will Stanton, last of the Old Ones, or immortals, and his dedicated fight against evil. The series includes *Over sea, under stone, The dark is rising, Greenwitch, The grey king,* and *Silver on the tree.* Sparrowhawk in Ursula LeGuin's Earthsea trilogy, which includes *The wizard of Earthsea, The tombs of Atuan, The farthest shore,* grows from boyhood to old age. Throughout his life he attempts to overcome the evil force he released when he misused his gift of magic. In old age he must use his hard-won wisdom to fight the forces that attempt to destroy his gift. Patricia McKillip's *The riddle-master of Hed* and *Heir of sea and fire* are the stories of Morgan, prince of Hed, and his betrothed, Raederle. The two are linked in the fate that awaits Morgan as they search for his true identity. Roger Zelazny's Amber series, including *Nine princes in Amber, The guns of Avalon, Sign of the unicorn,* and *The hand of Oberon,* takes place in a strange world of purple cloud and Kentucky fried chicken. The saga is of the royal family of Amber and their attempt to control the powers of evil that threaten their world and all the worlds of Shadow. The stories contain a quest, as well as sword-and-scorcery, mystery, suspense, and humor. Though not written specifically for young adults, J.R.R. Tolkien's Lord of the Rings trilogy has many young adult fans. The trilogy— *The fellowship of the ring, The two towers,* and *The return of the king*— is an epic account of the defeat of the Dark Lord through the destruction of the One Ring of power.

Other fantasies that have the search and the conquest of evil as their themes are of interest to young adult readers. L. Frank Baum's *Ozma of Oz* is a tale of good versus evil that is easy reading for many young adolescents. Jay Williams's *The hero from otherwhere,* another good fantasy for younger readers, tells about two boys who are called in to save a world that is a mirror to our own. In Poul Anderson and Gordon Dickson's *Star Prince Charlie,* a boy, accompanied by his tutor, Charlie Stewart, travels to Talyina, where he discovers and fulfills an ancient prophecy. In *A spell for chameleon* by Anthony Piers, Bink must search to find his magic talent or be exiled and lose Sabrina. In Joyce Ballou Gregorian's *The broken citadel* and *Castledown,* Prince Leron goes on a quest to free Princess Dastra from her glass prison. Valentine of *Lord Valentine's castle* by Robert Silverberg joins a troupe of jugglers and gathers a motley party of supporters as he journeys across Majipoor to regain his rightful throne.

FANTASY WITH MAGICAL ELEMENTS. Some fantasies enjoyed by young adult readers catapult the character from one world to another by magical means. In Norton Juster's *The phantom tollbooth,* Milo passes through a magical tollbooth into a land where the mathemagician rules the world of numbers and King Dictionopolis rules the kingdom of words. This humorous book contains many plays on words, idioms, and unusual phrases. In Marvin Kaye's *The incredible umbrella,* the umbrella transports the hero to another universe. An ancient Scottish tower becomes a door to the fifteenth century for children of the twenty-second century in Margaret Anderson's *In the keep of time.*

Heroes of these books may employ fantastic means to reach their goals. In *The butterfly kid* by Chester Anderson, blue pills are distributed to make fantasies become real. In *The dragon and the George* by Gordon R. Dickson, Jim goes into a time machine a man and comes out a dragon.

Wizards are common in fantasies, and in Lloyd Alexander's *The wizard in the tree,* a kitchen maid learns the secret of magic from a rusty, humorous, and heartwarming wizard.

DRAGONS AND OTHER MYTHOLOGICAL BEASTS. Valgard is a changeling, half elf, half troll, in *The broken sword* by Poul Anderson. In Peter Beagle's *The last unicorn,* the beautiful unicorn, knowing she is the last of her species, is told to be brave and she will find others. *Unicorns in the rain* by Barbara Cohen is a tale of violence, pollution, and overcrowding. One family builds a large ship and, when it begins to rain, fills it with animals. Dragons are also common in fantasy, as *The dragon and the George,* mentioned in the preceding section illustrates. In *The forgotten beast of Eld,* Patricia McKillip introduces the readers to a wonderful world of strange, magical animals. In the seven books of the Narnia series by C. W. Lewis (including *The lion, the witch, and the wardrobe*), the mythological animals are ruled by a wise lion, Aslan.

A recent nonfiction book by Peter Dickinson, *The flight of dragons* (illustrated by Wayne Anderson), is an interesting companion work to the study of mythological creatures in fantasy. In the book Dickinson contends that dragons did exist, and he presents his theory of why no physical evidence of them is left except in artwork and mythology.

FANTASY THAT CREATES A NEW WORLD. A fantasy world may be inhabited by talking animals, such as the lovable rabbits in Richard Adams' *Watership Down* or the talking barnyard animals in Walter Wangerin's *The book of the dun cow.* Arthur is turned into a stray dog by an African schoolmate he has ridiculed in *The dog days of Arthur Cane* by T. Ernesto Bethancourt. However, he learns a great deal about life and love, good and evil, and human and canine natures. In Russell Hoban's book for young adolescents, *The mouse and his child,* a toy wind-up mouse searches for his first home and family. Kenneth Grahame's classic children's book *The wind in the willows*, loved by people of all ages, is about the adventures of mole, badger, rat, and toad. The lizards in Manus Pinkwater's *Lizard music* not only talk, but sing.

The fantastic world of Tolkien is explored in *The atlas of Middle-Earth* by Karen Wynn Fonstad, a geographer whose knowledge of her subject makes this intriguing book seem very realistic. The maps include topography, trails, highways, territories, cities, forts, castles, cave works, battles, and even troop positions. This book will fascinate the sophisticated young reader with a taste for Tolkien.

FANTASY LANGUAGES. Many fantasies create new languages. The language of the rabbits in *Watership Down* is so complex that it requires a lexicon at the end of the book. Tolkienese has practically become incorporated into the

English language. Many of his readers use the language in his books to name stores or restaurants or children.

SCIENCE FICTION. Science fiction, like fantasy, allows the reader to enter a realm of limitless possibility. The world of science fiction usually has realistic characters attempting superhuman tasks. Unlike the world of fantasy, the world of science fiction is described according to natural laws. Usually, the world is one of an advanced scientific state; however, it may be a world of the present or the past that examines scientific possibilities. While fantasy is as old as humankind, science fiction is a relatively new genre. Depending on the historic source, the earliest science fiction work is considered to be either Mary Shelley's *Frankenstein,* written in 1818 (recently updated for young readers by Bantam), or Jules Verne's *Journey to the center of the earth,* written in 1864 (a version for junior and senior high school students is currently available from Scholastic). According to James Gunn, editor of the Road to Science Fiction series:

> *Science fiction is the branch of literature that deals with the effects of change on people in the real world as it can be projected into the past, the future, or to distant places. It often concerns itself with scientific or technological change, and it usually involves matters whose importance is greater than the individual or the community; often civilization or the race itself is in danger. (1978, p. 1)*

THE PAST. Projection into the past is explored in Lester del Rey's *Tunnel through time,* in which Pete and Bob are the only ones who can save Pete's father from a perilous fate after his jammed time machine strands him in the Mesozoic era. When time travel in Jack Finney's *Time and again* takes Simon Morley back to New York of the 1880s, he experiences the difficulty of being out of step with the times. An outstanding recent book that involves time travel is Joan Aiken's *The shadow guests.* Cosmo Curtoys discovers from his cousin Eunice, an Oxford mathematics professor, that his family line carries a deadly curse that has infiltrated every generation since the Roman occupation of Britain. Cosmo sets out to discover and break the curse. Traveling through time, he encounters three of his ancestors just before they become victims of the curse. Aiken combines Einstein's theory of relativity, parapsychology, and mysticism to create a believable tale.

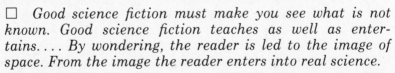

□ *Good science fiction must make you see what is not known. Good science fiction teaches as well as entertains.... By wondering, the reader is led to the image of space. From the image the reader enters into real science.*
H. M. HOOVER

author of The lost star */ in a speech at the IRA Convention / Atlanta, Ga. / April 1979*

THE PRESENT OR NEAR FUTURE. In some science fiction books the effects of new technological advancements are examined and often taken to the farthest extremes of possibility. In Phyllis Gotlieb's *O master Caliban!* the possibility of human genetic mutation is taken to its extreme limit, resulting in disaster. In *The boys from Brazil* (Levin) and *The paper dolls* (Davies), scientists face serious ethical issues in their research into genetics. The possible dangers of computers are considered in *The god machine* (Caidin) and *The tale of the big computer* (Johannesson). What would happen if a child had a twin robot he could send to school in his place? Mildred Ames's *Is there life on a plastic plant?* examines the problem. Will technology take us too far? Will the machines become our masters? Ten science fiction writers explore these questions in *Men and machines*, edited by Robert Silverberg. Ecological disaster is a common theme of science fiction set in the present or the near future. In John Brunner's *The sheep look up,* an ecologist battles to alert the world to ecological disaster and impending doom. What are some of the likely results of a nuclear attack? The possibilities are investigated in such books as D. C. Halacy's *Return from Luna,* Ruth Hooker's *Kennaquhair,* H. M. Hoover's *Treasures of Morrow,* Walter M. Miller's *A canticle for Leibowitz,* and Robert O'Brien's *Z for Zachariah.* John Rowe Townsend's *Noah's castle* is set ten years from now in a world suffering from a shortage of food. However, some families have stockpiled large quantities of food and attempt to hide it from neighbors. Is it possible that our great scientific advancements are increasing the chances for a new ice age? Ray Kytle in *Fire and ice* explores what happens when the ice age threatens. Daniel Keyes's narrative *Flowers for Algernon* examines unchecked scientific experimentation. Charlie, a young retarded man, lives for a short time with superior intelligence. The loss of his intelligence is heartbreaking to him and to the people around him. In *House of stairs* by William Sleater, five teenagers find themselves in an experiment in which they are conditioned to become robots.

ALIEN BEINGS. In Alexander Key's *The forgotten door,* Little Jon can read people's minds, communicate with animals, and run like the wind. Sirius, the Dog Star, is falsely accused of losing the Zoi in *Dogsbody* by Diane Jones. As a punishment he must roam the earth in search of it. Lucinda, in Jean Karl's *Beloved Benjamin,* meets an alien mentor in a deserted house on the grounds of a cemetery after she is abandoned by her parents. Martin comes to earth as a spaceman in *Down to earth* by Patricia Wrightson. In John Towe Townsend's *The visitors,* sixteen-year-old John is baffled by the unconventional behavior of three visitors from the future. An excellent novelization of the movie script *Close encounters of the third kind* by Steven Spielberg tells of the earth's first encounter with aliens from outer space. In Robert Heinlein's *Stranger in a strange land,* an earthling, raised by Martians, returns to Earth and upsets society. Though not written only for young readers, this book is often a favorite, even with teenagers who have not yet discovered science fiction.

THE FAR DISTANT FUTURE. Isaac Asimov is the editor of *Tomorrow's children,* a collection of stories about children of a hundred, a thousand, a million years from now. *Children of infinity,* edited by Roger Elwood, is a collection of original science fiction stories for young readers. Though not written for young adults, Asimov's Foundation trilogy, including *Foundation, Foundation and empire,* and *The second foundation,* is a favorite with teenage science fiction fans. Hari Seldon creates the Foundations to preserve human culture during the dark ages after the collapse of the first galactic empire; the development of the Foundations is followed throughout the trilogy. In Gregory Benford's *Jupiter project,* a living laboratory is orbiting Jupiter, and Matt must prove himself or be returned to a hostile Earth. *Cities in flight* by James Blish is another set of novels not written specifically for teens but enjoyed by those who are already science fiction fans. The tale centers on the "spindizzy" drive that the Earth's cities use to leave Earth, escaping its repression for an existence in space. *Star Trek* and *The Star Trek reader* by Blish are pure entertainment for teenage devotees of the "Star Trek" reruns on television. The books, based on compilations of the characters and plot lines of the television show, enjoy the almost cultlike following of the TV series. The Earth of the future looks rather bleak in Ben Bova's *City of darkness,* in which Ron Morgan explores life in the isolated dome that once was New York City. World War IV in Leigh Brackett's *The long tomorrow* has brought an end to the technological age. Len Colter must decide whether to join a group of dissident scientists who want to restore science. An earth that is controlled by superior beings is explored in John Christopher's *The city of gold and lead, The pool of fire,* and *The white mountains,* as well as in Arthur C. Clarke's *Childhood's end.* Six teenagers in John Neufeld's *Sleep two, three, four!* are running away from the totalitarian police state of the future. In Kurt Vonnegut's *Cat's cradle,* the end of the world is satirized. Although this book is too difficult for many young readers, mature adolescent readers who enjoy science fiction usually find it interesting and humorous.

ROBOTS, MECHANICAL BEINGS, AND CYBORGS. In Martin Caidin's *Cyborg,* an air force test pilot becomes the first cyborg. This book became the basis for television's "Six Million Dollar Man" series. Ron Goulart's *What's become of screwloose?* is a series of stories about mechanical devices gone wild and man's problems in coming to terms with the cyborgs he has created. In Arthur Clark's *2001: A space odyssey* we meet a computer gone crazy. David Gerrold's *When Harlie was one* is about a computer that thinks it's human. The robots in *The unsleeping eye* by David Guy Compton and *The humanoids* by Jack Williamson can see. The 1981 poll surveying books for young adults added a recent robot science fiction book to the list of teenage favorites, Walter Tevis' *Mockingbird.* In this book robots and clones have replaced most of the human population; reading and writing are no longer useful; and human lives are without purpose. The book ends with hope, however, as two humans find the lost emotion of love.

THE SEA. The future and the sea are part of the science fiction genre. In Carl Biemiller's *The hydronauts,* 80 percent of Earth is covered by water; its inhabitants live in hive cities, commmunicate with dolphins, and listen to songs with titles like "Amoeba Though I Am, Nothing Can Divide Me." The underwater world in Karel Čapek's *The war with the newts* supports a giant race of intelligent newts that are discovered and enlisted to do people's work under the sea. They dig harbors and canals, and learn human ways. Eventually, they turn against their masters.

NEW PLACES AND STRANGE SOCIETIES. *The Martian chronicles* by Ray Bradbury, though not written specifically for young adults, is about the colonization of Mars by Earth in the late twentieth century. Possibly because of its near-time proximity, even students who are not particular fans of science fiction usually enjoy this book. Another book about Mars is Gordon R. Dickson's *The far call.* Some science fiction narratives take place on spaceships or space stations somewhere in space. Jeffrey Carver's *Star riggerr's way* is about an apprentice starship pilot who drifts into the Flux, a strange area of space that carries vehicles at speeds faster than sound. Interstellar warfare is the backdrop for Gordon Dickson's *Dorsai!* Robert Heinlein's *Rocketship Galileo,* an early narrative about the flight to the moon, is good for immature readers. The story of the flight is particularly interesting in comparison with the actual moon voyages. In Leonard Wibberley's *Encounter near Venus,* four young people take a cruise on their uncle's custom-built flying saucer. *Splinter of the mind's eye* by Alan Dean Foster is a sequel to the film *Star Wars* in which the ship on a diplomatic mission crashes on Mimban.

Societies in imaginative worlds and galaxies are important to science fiction writers. H. M. Hoover, a science fiction writer of books for young readers, has created new worlds in *The Delikon* and *The rains of Eridan.* In Lester del Rey's *Prisoners of space,* the maze of tunnels beneath the lunar surface holds the secrets to life in space. In *Enchantress from the stars* and *The far side of evil,* Sylvia Engdahl tells of the adventures of Elana, whose mission is to aid developing civilizations without interfering with their natural evolution. In *This star shall abide* and *Beyond the Tomorrow Mountains,* Engdahl depicts the coming of age of young Noren, a rebel against the establishment in his faraway world. Ursula LeGuin in *The dispossessed: An ambiguous utopia* explores the differences between anarchy in Anarres and capitalism in Urras. Neither of the systems, taken to extremes, provides an atmosphere in which people can work creatively in freedom. In *The left hand of darkness* she explores the relationship of Genry, an envoy from the technologically advanced world of the galaxy, and Estraven, from the underdeveloped winter kingdom of Karhide. LeGuin explores another side of humankind in the far-off world of the planet Athshe in *The word for world is forest.* The human invaders of the planet enslave the natives and despoil the forest of Athshe. The Athsheans, who have learned to kill from the humans, turn the tables on their captors.

THE JOINING OF SCIENCE FICTION AND REALITY. Not all young adult readers are attracted to the world of science fiction. However, the joining of science fiction and reality in many novels helps bridge the gap between the real world, as the adolescent knows it, and the extrapolative world of the science fiction writer. In *Stardance* by Spider Robinson and Jeanne Robinson, Shara Drummond wants to become a professional dancer but is unable to. However, the zero-gravity environment of the orbiting Skyfac gives her the chance. Shara is an Earth child with earthlike dreams, but she achieves her dreams in space. In Jean Karl's *Beloved Benjamin is waiting,* a realistically portrayed girl who has been abandoned by her parents meets a fantastic mentor, an alien from another galaxy. The narrative takes place in a deserted house in a cemetery. In T. W. Hard's *Sum VII,* a well-preserved Egyptian mummy at a state university is resuscitated by a team of medical students. He turns out to be a visitor from outer space. In *Mastodonia* by Clifford Simak, a dog returns home with an ancient spear in his side and meat on the bones of a 10,000-year-old dinosaur. The dog's owner soon learns the secret of traveling to the Pleistocene era. The people of the Earth exploit the secret as big-game hunters plan safaris into Mastodonia and the government finds a solution to the world's overpopulation problem. *The hunters* by Burt Wetanson and Thomas Hoobler takes place in the normal, everyday town of Bear Paw, Montana. However, when a strange couple walk down Main Street and promise the residents a journey into a better world, peculiar things begin to happen. The young reader who judged this book one of the best of 1979, according to Carlsen's readers' poll, said, "I felt like I was really there." This joining of real people and real places to unreal events and unreal places makes the science fiction narrative believable to the adolescent. Young readers can see themselves in the story.

The writer of good science fiction, as well as the writer of good fantasy, must make the unreal seem real. The characters must possess believable human traits, even if they are unicorns. Their problems must have the essence of reality, even if they are experienced on a flying saucer. Good science fiction and fantasy must be plausible to the reader. Concomitantly, the reader must be removed from the real world and must feel invincible. Good fantasy and science fiction is unreality masked as realism, and it is realism masked as unreality.

Folklore, Legend, Myth, and Religion

For many years, folklore, legend, myth, and religion have been fertile sources for children's books. Unfortunately, the same has not been true for most young adult literature. In recent years, however, we are increasingly seeing new works enter the marketplace that use these sources. Perhaps this is a sign that young adult literature is indeed coming of age.

Welsh legend is the source for several interesting young adult books. Alan Garner's *The owl service* is based on the legend of the *Mabinogion.* In this interesting tale three children find an old set of dishes in an attic. They discover that an ancient Welsh myth involving love, hatred, and jealousy is tied in some symbolic way to the pattern of these dishes. The story describes their attempt to determine the hold the old myth has on their dreams and actions of themselves and those of their parents. The third book of Madeleine L'Engle's time trilogy, *A swiftly tilting planet,* is based on the legend of Madoc of Wales. The seven Narnia tales by C. S. Lewis are also based on ancient Welsh legend. Likewise, the Prydain chronicles of Lloyd Alexander are drawn from Welsh legend and the entire world of mythology.

Other young adult books use Greek or Roman mythology. Leon Garfield and Edward Blishen's *The god beneath the sea,* which is divided into three parts, is the story of Hephaestus, first son of Zeus. Patrick Skene Catling's *The chocolate touch* is a retelling of the Midas myth.

Epic folktales are a source for some young adult books. *A song for Gilgamesh* (Hodges) is an interesting retelling of the ancient epic. *Beowulf* by Rosemary Sutcliff retells the Old English epic.

Several young adult books begin with the Arthurian legend. Constance Hieatt's *The minstrel knight* is the story of Sir Orfeo, a traveling knight who comes to King Arthur's court. This tale is interesting in that it is also based on the Orpheus tale of Greek legend. The two combine to provide romance and excitement. *Here abide monsters* by Andre Norton is about a boy, a girl, and a dog who are transported through time to Avalon of Arthurian legend. T. H. White's *The sword in the stone* retells the tale of the boy Wart who becomes King Arthur. Rosemary Sutcliff's three-book Arthurian cycle is an excellent "bridge" to Sir Thomas Malory's *La mort d'Arthur* and can be used as an introduction to Arthurian legend and values. *The light beyond the forest* is a retelling of the quest for the Holy Grail. The second book in the cycle, *The sword and the circle,* is a tale of King Arthur's knights and the round table. The final book, *The road to Camlann,* is the story of the death of King Arthur.

The French legend of Charlemagne is the basis for Norton's *Huon of the horn.* The story is about Huon, betrayed in Charlemagne's court, who must complete an almost impossible task to return to France.

The medieval Child Waters ballad provides the foundation for Katie Letcher Lyle's beautiful, believable *Fair day, and another step begun.* The story is about sixteen-year-old Ellen Burd, who loves John Waters and is pregnant with his child. She is convinced that someday she and John will be united, even though he seems indifferent to her.

Christianity is a source of many beautiful books for young adult readers. The most notable of these works are the books of Madeleine L'Engle, who ties Christian theology into many of her stories. Though only a few of her books deal directly with Christian themes, most of them possess the symbols of her faith. In *A wind in the door,* for example, the Christian concept of naming is a central aspect of the book. The title of *A ring of endless light* alludes to the concept of immortality. The works of other authors also use Christianity as a basis. C. S. Lewis, a well-known theologian as well as an author of books for young readers, used Christian symbolism throughout his Narnia books. Walter Wangerin, author of *The book of the dun cow,* is a Lutheran minister who has incorporated much theology into his book about talking animals.

Judaism is a theme of many young adult books. Yuri Suhl's *The merrymaker* is based on the customs and folkore of Eastern European Jews, for example. Much of the literature of the Holocaust incorporates significant references to Jewish tradition. Books such as *The upstairs room* (Reiss), *A bag of marbles* (Joffo), and *The devil in Vienna* (Orgel) tell of Jewish young people who strengthen their religious conviction as they attempt to survive the Holocaust.

Hermann Hesse's *Siddhartha* is the story of a soul-searcher who meets Buddha. In an attempt to find the ultimate good, he abandons his friends and family, rejecting their values, and travels to the city to learn the life of man.

Young readers can find an ever-growing number of books that rely on folklore, legend, myth, and religion. These books can spark the storytelling and creative writing talents of young adults. Comparing the actual myth to a story based on it may provide many young writers with the creative seed they need to begin their own story. Examining folklore and legends of the area in which the students live may encourage them to begin gathering legend and lore in the tradition of the students in Rabun Gap, Georgia, who have compiled and written the remarkable *Foxfire* books under the tutelage of Eliot Wigginton.

Anthological Aside in Chapter 3

Danziger, P. *Can you sue your parents for malpractice?* Delacorte, 1979. Dell, 1980.

Titles Mentioned in Chapter 3

Aiken, J. *The wolves of Willoughby Chase.* Doubleday, 1962. Dell, 1968.
Danziger, P. *There's a bat in bunk five.* Delacorte, 1980. Dell, 1982.
Mitchell, M. *Gone with the wind* (1936). Avon, 1976.
Peck, R. *Don't look and it won't hurt.* Holt, Rinehart & Winston, 1972. Avon, 1973.
Salinger, J. D. *Catcher in the rye.* Little, Brown, 1951. New American Library, 1962.
Sendak, M. *Where the wild things are.* Harper & Row, 1963.
White, E. B. *Charlotte's web.* Harper & Row, 1952.

Quest for Meaning and Identity

Cunningham, J. *Come to the edge.* Pantheon, 1977. Avon, 1978.
————. *Dorp dead.* Pantheon, 1965. Avon, 1974.
Farmer, P. *A castle of bone.* Antheneum, 1972. Penguin, 1974.
Garfield, L. *The ghost downstairs.* Pantheon, 1972.
Garner, A. *The owl service.* Walck, 1967. Ballantine, 1981.
————. *Red shift.* Macmillan, 1973.
Haar, J. ter. *Boris.* Delacorte, 1970. Dell, 1971.

Problems of Adolescence

Anonymous. *Go ask Alice.* Prentice-Hall, 1971. Avon, 1972.

Arrick, F. *Steffie can't come out to play.* Bradbury, 1978. Dell, 1979.

Bates, B. *Love is like peanuts.* Holiday, 1980. Pocket Books, 1981.

Beckman, G. *Mia alone.* Viking, 1975. Dell, 1978.

Blume, J. *Are you there, God? It's me, Margaret.* Bradbury, 1970. Dell, 1980.

————. *Deenie.* Bradbury, 1973. Dell, 1979.

————. *Forever.* Bradbury, 1976. Pocket Books, 1975.

————. *Then again, maybe I won't.* Bradbury, 1971. Dell, 1976.

Boissard, J. *A matter of feeling.* Translated by E. Walter. Little, Brown, 1979. Fawcett, 1981.

Bonham, F. *Cool cat.* Dutton, 1971. Dell, 1972.

Bredes, D. *Hard feelings.* Atheneum, 1977.

Bridgers, S. E. *Home before dark.* Knopf, 1976. Bantam, 1977.

Childress, A. *A hero ain't nothin' but a sandwich.* Coward, McCann & Geoghegan, 1973. Avon, 1974.

Conroy, F. *Stop-time.* Viking, 1967. Penguin, 1977.

Corcoran, B. *Me and you and a dog named Blue.* Atheneum, 1979.

Covert, P. *Cages.* Liveright, 1971.

Craig, M. M. *It could happen to anyone.* Crowell, 1961. Berkley, 1973.

Danziger, P. *The cat ate my gymsuit.* Delacorte, 1974. Dell, 1978.

Davis, T. *Vision quest.* Viking, 1979. Bantam, 1981.

Dizenzo, P. *Phoebe.* McGraw-Hill, 1970. Bantam, 1975.

————. *Why me? The story of Jenny.* Avon, 1977.

Donovan, J. *I'll get there. It better be worth the trip.* Harper & Row, 1969. Dell, 1973.

Due, L. A. *High and outside.* Harper & Row, 1980.

Elfman, B. *A house for Jonnie O.* Houghton Mifflin, 1976. Bantam, 1978.

————. *The girls of Huntington House.* Houghton Mifflin, 1972. Bantam, 1973.

Eyerly, J. *A girl like me.* Lippincott, 1966. Berkley, 1970.

————. *Bonnie Jo, go home.* Lippincott, 1972. Bantam, 1978.

————. *He's my baby now.* Lippincott, 1977. Pocket Books, 1978.

Gauch, P. *The green of me.* Putnam, 1978.

Greene, B. *Morning is a long time coming.* Dial, 1978. Pocket Books, 1979.

Greene, S. *The boy who drank too much.* Viking, 1979. Dell, 1980.

Guy, R. *Ruby.* Viking, 1976. Bantam, 1979.

Hall, L. *Sticks and stones.* Follett, 1972. Dell, 1972.

Hautzig, D. *Hey, dollface.* Greenwillow, 1978. Bantam, 1980.

Head, A. *Mr. and Mrs. Bo Jo Jones.* Putnam, 1967. New American Library, 1968.

Hinton, S. E. *That was then, this is now.* Viking, 1971. Dell, 1980.

Holland, I. *Heads you win, tails I lose.* Lippincott, 1973. Dell, 1979.

————. *Man without a face.* Lippincott, 1972. Dell, 1980.

Kerr, M. E. *Dinky Hocker shoots smack!* Harper & Row, 1972. Dell, 1978.

————. *If I love you, am I trapped forever?* Harper & Row, 1973. Dell, 1975.

Kirkwood, J. *Good times/bad times.* Fawcett, 1968. Penguin, 1975.

Klamkin, L. *Hello, good-bye.* Dodd, Mead, 1973.

Klein, N. *It's O.K. if you don't love me.* Dial, 1977. Fawcett, 1977.

————. *It's not what you expect.* Random House, 1973. Avon, 1974.

————. *Love is one of the choices.* Dial, 1978. Fawcett, 1979.

Lee, M. *The skating rink.* Seabury, 1969. Dell, 1972.
LeGuin, U. K. *Very far away from anywhere else.* Atheneum, 1976. Bantam, 1978.
Lipsyte, R. *One fat summer.* Harper & Row, 1977. Bantam, 1978.
McKay, R. *The running back.* Harcourt Brace Jovanovich, 1979.
Madison, W. *Growing up in a hurry.* Little, Brown, 1973. Pocket Books, 1975.
Mazer, N. F. *Dear Bill, remember me? And other stories.* Delacorte, 1976. Dell, 1978.
————. *Up in Seth's room.* Delacorte, 1979. Dell, 1981.
Meyer, C. *C. C. Poindexter.* Atheneum, 1978.
Miles, B. *The trouble with thirteen.* Knopf, 1979. Avon, 1980.
Parr, J. L. *Tim Tweed.* Queenston House, 1977.
Peck, R. *Are you in the house alone?* Viking, 1976. Dell, 1978.
————. *Don't look and it won't hurt.* Holt, Rinehart & Winston, 1972. Avon, 1973.
Platt, K. *The terrible love life of Dudley Cornflower.* Bradbury, 1976.
Powers, J. R. *Do black patent leather shoes really reflect up?* Regnery, 1975. Popular
  Library, 1976.
Raucher, H. *Summer of '42.* Putnam, 1971. Dell, 1978.
Robertson, D. *The sum and total of now.* Putnam, 1966.
Rosen, W. *Cruisin' for a bruisin'.* Knopf, 1976. Dell, 1977.
Ruby, L. *Arriving at a place you never left.* Dial, 1977. Dell, 1980.
Schwartz, S. *Growing up guilty.* Pantheon, 1978.
Scoppettone, S. *Happy endings are all alike.* Harper & Row, 1978. Dell, 1979.
————. *The late great me.* Putnam, 1976. Bantam, 1977.
————. *Trying hard to hear you.* Harper & Row, 1974. Bantam, 1976.
Sherburne, Z. *Too bad about the Haines girl.* Morrow, 1967.
Shreve, S. *Loveletters.* Knopf, 1978. Bantam, 1981.
Steptoe, J. *Marcia.* Viking, 1976.
Stirling, N. *You would if you loved me.* M. Evans, 1969. Avon, 1982.
Stolz, M. S. *A love, or a season.* Harper & Row, 1964.
Strasser, T. *The angel dust blues.* Coward, McCann & Geoghegan, 1979. Dell, 1981.
Thompson, T. *Richie.* Saturday Review Press, 1973. Dell, 1981.
Trivers, J., and A. Davis. *I can stop anytime I want.* Prentice Hall, 1974. Dell, 1977.
Van Leeuwen, J. *I was a ninety-eight-pound duckling.* Dial, 1972. Dell, 1979.
Wagner, R. *Sarah T.—Portrait of a teen-age alcoholic.* Ballantine, 1975.
Windsor, P. *Diving for roses.* Harper & Row, 1974.
Winthrop, E. *A little demonstration of affection.* Harper & Row, 1975. Dell, 1977.
Wojciechowska, M. *Tuned out.* Harper & Row, 1968. Dell, 1972.
Zindel, P. *My darling, my hamburger.* Harper & Row, 1969. Bantam, 1971.

Realistic Heroes in Sports

Bradley, W. *Life on the run.* Quadrangle, 1976. Bantam, 1977.
Brancato, R. *Winning.* Knopf, 1977. Bantam, 1979.
Davis, T. *Vision quest.* Viking, 1979. Bantam, 1981.
Due, L. A. *High and outside.* Harper & Row, 1980.
Dygard, T. J. *Quarterback walk-on.* Morrow, 1982.
Greene, S. *The boy who drank too much.* Viking, 1979. Dell, 1980.
Guy, D. *Football dreams.* Seaview, 1980. New American Library, 1982.

Knudson, R. R. *Fox running.* Harper & Row, 1975. Avon, 1977.
———. *Zanballer.* Delacorte, 1972. Dell, 1980.
———. *Zanbanger.* Harper & Row, 1977. Dell, 1979.
———. *Zanboomer.* Harper & Row, 1978. Dell, 1978.
LeFlore, R., and J. Hawkins. *Breakout: From prison to the big leagues.* Harper & Row, 1978.
Lipsyte, R. *The contender.* Harper & Row, 1967. Bantam, 1979.
———. *Free to be Muhammad Ali.* Harper & Row, 1978. Bantam, 1980.
McKay, R. *The running back.* Harcourt Brace Jovanovich, 1979.
Platt, K. *Brogg's brain.* Lippincott, 1981.
Schorr, G. *Joe Dimaggio: A biography.* Doubleday, 1980.
Wells, R. *When no one was looking.* Dial, 1980. Fawcett, 1981.
Yglesias, R. *The game player.* Doubleday, 1978.

Realistic Heroes with Handicaps

Albert, L. *But I'm ready to go.* Bradbury, 1976. Dell, 1978.
Brancato, R. *Winning.* Knopf, 1977. Bantam, 1979.
Bridgers, S. E. *All together now.* Knopf, 1977. Bantam, 1980.
Brown, H. *Yesterday's child.* Evans, 1976. New American Library, 1977.
Eareckson, J., and J. Musser. *Joni.* Zondervan, 1976. Bantam, 1978.
Gerson, C. *Passing through.* Dial, 1978. Dell, 1978.
Green, H. (Greenberg, J.) *I never promised you a rose garden.* Holt, Rinehart & Winston, 1964. New American Library, 1964.
Greenberg, J. (Green, H.) *In this sign.* Holt, Rinehart & Winston, 1970. Avon, 1972.
Guest, J. *Ordinary people.* Viking, 1976. Ballantine, 1980.
Guy, R. *Edith Jackson.* Viking, 1978. Bantam, 1978.
Haar, J. ter. *The world of Ben Lighthart.* Delacorte, 1977.
Haskins, J. *The story of Stevie Wonder.* Lothrop, Lee & Shepard, 1976. Dell, 1979.
Keller, H. *The story of my life* (1903). Doubleday, 1954.
Kerr, M. E. *Little Little.* Harper & Row, 1981.
Killilea, M. *Karen.* Prentice-Hall, 1952. Dell, 1983.
———. *With love from Karen.* Prentice-Hall, 1963. Dell, 1963.
Kingman, L. *Head over wheels.* Houghton Mifflin, 1978. Dell, 1981.
Krentel, M. *Melissa comes home.* Moody Press, 1972. Popular Library, 1972.
Levenkron, S. *The best little girl in the world.* Contemporary Books, 1978. Warner, 1979.
McCullough, C. *Tim.* Harper & Row, 1974.
Mandel, S. *Change of heart.* Delacorte, 1979. Dell, 1981.
Mazer, H. *The war on Villa Street.* Delacorte, 1978. Dell, 1979.
Melton, D. *A boy called hopeless.* Independence Press, 1976. Scholastic, 1977.
Mohr, N. *In Neuva York.* Dial, 1977. Dell, 1979.
Platt, K. *Hey, Dummy.* Chilton, 1971. Dell, 1973.
Sallis, S. *Only love.* Harper & Row, 1980. Dell, 1982.
Savitz, H. M. *On the move.* Day, 1973. Avon, 1979.
Schell, J. *Sudina.* Avon, 1967.
Valens, E. G. *The other side of the mountain.* Warner Books, 1975.
Wojciechowska, M. *A single light.* Harper & Row, 1968. Bantam, 1971.

Realistic Heroes in Times of Extreme Trial

Arnothy, C. *I am fifteen and I don't want to die.* E. P. Dutton, 1956.

Bach, A. *Waiting for Johnny Miracle.* Harper & Row, 1980. Bantam, 1982.

Beckman, G. *Admission to the feast* (1971). Holt, Rinehart & Winston, 1972. Dell, 1978.

Blankfort, M. *Take the A train.* Dutton, 1978.

Blinn, W. *Brian's song* (screenplay). Bantam, 1972.

Blume, J. *Iggie's house.* Bradbury, 1970. Dell, 1976.

Borland, H. *When the legends die.* Lippincott, 1963. Bantam, 1976.

Braithwaite, E. R. *Choice of straws* (1965). Bobbs-Merrill, 1967. Pyramid, 1972.

Britton, A. *Fike's point* (1977). Coward, McCann & Geoghegan, 1979.

Byars, B. *The night swimmers.* Delacorte, 1980. Dell, 1980.

Clark, A. N. *Year walk.* Viking, 1975.

Clark, M. H. *A stranger is watching.* Simon & Schuster, 1977. Dell, 1979.

Cleaver, V., and B. Cleaver. *Trial Valley.* Lippincott, 1977. Bantam, 1978.

———. *Where the lilies bloom.* Lippincott, 1969. New American Library, 1974.

Cohen, S. *Taking Gary Feldman.* Putnam, 1970.

Cormier, R. *After the first death.* Pantheon, 1979. Avon, 1980.

———. *The bumblebee flies anyway.* Pantheon, 1983.

———. *The chocolate war.* Pantheon, 1974. Dell, 1975.

———. *I am the cheese.* Pantheon, 1977. Dell, 1978.

Danziger, P. *Can you sue your parents for malpractice?* Delacorte, 1979. Dell, 1980.

deJongh, J., and C. Cleveland. *City cool.* Random House, 1978.

Duncan, L. *Five were missing.* Signet, 1966. New American Library, 1972.

Elder, L., and S. Streshinsky. *And I alone survived.* Dutton, 1978. Fawcett, 1978.

Emery, A. *Mountain laurel.* Putnam, 1948. Scholastic, 1961.

Greene, S. *The boy who drank too much.* Viking, 1979. Dell, 1980.

Grossman, M. *The summer ends too soon.* Westminster, 1975.

Gunther, J. *Death be not proud: A memoir.* Harper & Row, 1949. Pyramid, 1979.

Guy, R. *Edith Jackson,* Viking, 1978. Bantam, 1978.

———. *The friends.* Holt, Rinehart & Winston, 1973. Bantam, 1974.

Hamilton, V. *M. C. Higgins the great.* Macmillan, 1974. Dell, 1976.

Hassler, J. *Jemmy.* Atheneum, 1980.

Hayes, E. K., and A. Lazzarino. *Broken promise.* Putnam, 1978. Fawcett, 1978.

Hentoff, N. *Jazz country.* Harper & Row, 1965. Dell, 1967.

Herbert, F. *Soul catcher.* Putnam, 1972. Berkley, 1979.

Hinton, S. E. *Rumble fish.* Delacorte, 1975. Dell, 1976.

———. *That was then, this is now.* Viking, 1971. Dell, 1980.

Holland, I. *Alan and the animal kingdom.* Lippincott, 1977. Dell, 1979.

———. *Hitchhike.* Lippincott, 1977. Dell, 1979.

Judson, W. *Cold river.* Mason & Lipscomb, 1974. New American Library, 1976.

Kerr, M. E. *Gentlehands.* Harper & Row, 1978.

Killilea, M. *Karen.* Prentice-Hall, 1952. Dell, 1983.

———. *With love from Karen.* Prentice-Hall, 1963. Dell, 1963.

Klein, N. *Sunshine.* Avon, 1974.

Kornfeld, A. *In a bluebird's eye.* Holt, Rinehart & Winston, 1975. Avon, 1976.

LeGuin, U. K. *Very far away from anywhere else.* Atheneum, 1976. Bantam, 1978.

Lipsyte, R. *The contender.* Harper & Row, 1967. Bantam, 1979.

Lund, D. *Eric*. Lippincott, 1974. Dell, 1979.

Messler, J. *Jimmy*. Atheneum, 1980.

Mazer, H. *Snow bound*. Delacorte, 1973. Dell, 1973.

Mazer, N. F. *Taking Terri Mueller*. Avon, 1981.

——, and H. Mazer. *The solid gold kid*. Delacorte, 1977. Dell, 1978.

Morey, W. *Canyon winter*. Dutton, 1972.

Morris, J. *Brian Piccolo, a short season*. Rand McNally, 1971. Dell, 1972.

Nixon, J. L. *The kidnapping of Christina Lattimore*. Harcourt Brace Jovanovich, 1979. Dell, 1980.

O'Dell, S. *Carlota*. Houghton Mifflin, 1977. Dell, 1980.

——. *Child of fire*. Houghton Mifflin, 1974. Dell, 1978.

——. *Sing down the moon*. Houghton Mifflin, 1970. Dell, 1970.

——. *The 290*. Houghton Mifflin, 1976. Dell, 1979.

Okada, J. *No-no boy*. Combined Asian American Resources Project, 1976. University of Washington Press, 1981.

Paier, R. *The pied piper*. McGraw-Hill, 1979.

Paul, C. *A child is missing*. Putnam, 1970. Berkley, 1978.

Paterson, K. *The great Gilly Hopkins*. Crowell, 1978. Avon, 1979.

Peck, R. *Are you in the house alone?* Viking, 1976. Dell, 1978.

Peck, R. N. *Eagle fur*. Knopf, 1978. Avon, 1979.

Roberts, D. *Deborah: A wilderness narrative*. Vanguard, 1970.

——. *The mountain of my fear*. Vanguard, 1968.

Sallis, S. *Only love*. Harper & Row, 1980.

Sayers, G. and A. Silverman. *I am third*. Viking, 1970. Bantam, 1972.

Schellie, D. *Kidnapping Mr. Tubbs*. Four Winds, 1978. Scholastic, 1978.

Sebestyen, O. *Words by heart*. Little, Brown, 1979. Bantam, 1981.

Shreve, S. *The masquerade*. Knopf, 1980. Dell, 1981.

Snyder, H. *The hall of the mountain king*. Scribner's, 1973.

Taylor, M. *Roll of thunder, hear my cry*. Dial, 1976. Bantam, 1978.

Taylor, T. *The cay*. Doubleday, 1969. Avon, 1970.

Telemaque, E. W. *It's crazy to stay Chinese in Minnesota*. Nelson, 1978.

Wilkinson, B. *Ludell*. Harper & Row, 1975. Bantam, 1980.

——. *Ludell and Willie*. Harper & Row, 1977. Bantam, 1981.

——. *Ludell's New York time*. Harper & Row, 1980.

Wolitzer, H. *Toby lived here*. Farrar, Straus & Giroux, 1978. Bantam, 1980.

Wood, G. A. *Catch a killer*. Harper & Row, 1972. Dell, 1973.

Realistic Heroes of Other Times

Auel, J. *The clan of the cave bear*. Crown, 1980. Bantam, 1981.

Baker, B. *The dunderhead war*. Harper & Row, 1967.

Benchley, N. *Beyond the mists*. Harper & Row, 1975.

——. *Bright candles: A novel of the Danish resistance*. Harper & Row, 1974.

Blos, J. *A gathering of days: A New England girl's journal*. Scribner's, 1979.

Bontemps, A. *Black thunder*. Beacon Press, 1968.

Borland, H. *When the legends die*. Lippincott, 1963. Bantam, 1976.

Braithwaite, E. R. *Choice of straws* (1966). Bobbs-Merrill, 1967. Pyramid, 1972.

Brancato, R. *Don't sit under the apple tree*. Knopf, 1975. Bantam, 1980.

Burton, H. *To ravensrigg* (1976). Crowell, 1977.

Calvert, P. *The snowbird.* Scribner's, 1980. New American Library, 1982.

Clapp, P. *Constance: A story of early Plymouth.* Lothrop, Lee & Shepard, 1968. Dell, 1975.

————. *I'm Deborah Sampson: A soldier in the War of the Revolution.* Lothrop, Lee & Shepard, 1977.

Collier, J. L., and C. Collier. *My brother Sam is dead.* Four Winds, 1974. Scholastic, 1974.

Darke, M. *First of midnight* (1977). Seabury, 1978.

deTrevino, E. B. *I, Juan de Pareja.* Farrar, Straus & Giroux, 1965. Dell, 1978.

Dickinson, P. *The dancing bear.* Little, Brown, 1972.

Fast, H. *April morning.* Crown, 1961. Bantam, 1970.

————. *The Hessian.* Morrow, 1972. Dell, 1980.

Forbes, E. *A mirror for witches.* Dell, 1956, 1971.

————. *Johnny Tremain.* Houghton Mifflin, 1945. Dell, 1969.

Forman, J. *Ceremony of innocence.* Hawthorn, 1970. Dell, 1977.

————. *The life and death of Yellow Bird.* Farrar, Straus & Giroux, 1973.

Frazier, N. L. *Stout-hearted seven.* Harcourt Brace Jovanovich, 1973.

Garfield, B. *The Paladin.* Simon and Schuster, 1979. Bantam, 1981.

Garfield, L. *Jack Holborn.* Random House, 1965.

————. *The sound of coaches.* Viking, 1974.

Greene, B. *Summer of my German soldier.* Dial, 1973. Bantam, 1974.

Haugaard, E. C. *Chase me, catch nobody!* Houghton Mifflin, 1980.

Hunt, I. *Across five Aprils.* Follett, 1964. Grosset & Dunlap, 1964.

Joffo, J. *A bag of marbles.* Houghton Mifflin, 1974. Bantam, 1977.

Johnson, J. *How many miles to Babylon?* Doubleday, 1974. Avon, 1975.

Keith, H. *Rifles for Watie.* Crowell, 1957.

Kelly, E. P. *The trumpeter of Krakow.* Macmillan, 1928, 1966.

Lee, M. *The people therein.* Houghton Mifflin, 1980.

Lester, J. *Long journey home: Stories from black history.* Dial, 1972. Dell, 1975.

Levitin, S. *Roanoke: A novel of the lost colony.* Atheneum, 1973.

Lewis, E. *Young Fu of the Upper Yangtze.* Winston, 1932. Dell, 1973.

Lofts, N. *The Maude Reed tale.* Nelson, 1972. Dell, 1974.

March, W. *Company K.* Hill & Wang, 1957.

Mazer, H. *The last mission.* Delacorte, 1979. Dell, 1981.

Moeri, L. *Save Queen of Sheba.* Dutton, 1981. Avon, 1982.

O'Dell, S. *The king's fifth.* Houghton Mifflin, 1966. Dell, 1978.

————. *Sarah Bishop.* Houghton Mifflin, 1980.

Oz, A. *Elsewhere, perhaps.* Translated by N. DeLange. Harcourt Brace Jovanovich, 1973. Bantam, 1974.

Paterson, K. *Of nightingales that weep.* Crowell, 1974. Avon, 1980.

————. *The master puppeteer.* Crowell, 1975. Avon, 1981.

Peck, R. N. *Fawn: A novel.* Little, Brown, 1975. Dell, 1979.

Rees, D. *The Exeter blitz* (1978). Nelson, 1980.

Reiss, J. *The upstairs room.* Crowell, 1972. Bantam, 1973.

Richter, H. P. *Friedrich.* Holt, Rinehart & Winston, 1980. Dell, 1973.

Rockwood, J. *Long Man's song.* Holt, Rinehart & Winston, 1975. Dell, 1978.

Speare, E. *The bronze bow.* Houghton Mifflin, 1961.

————. *The witch of Blackbird Pond.* Houghton Mifflin, 1958. Dell, 1975.

Sutcliff, R. *The Capricorn bracelet.* Walck, 1973.

———. *The eagle of the ninth.* Walck, 1954, 1961.

———. *Knight's fee.* Walck, 1961.

———. *The lantern bearers.* Walck, 1959.

———. *The mark of the horse lord.* Walck, 1965.

———. *Rider on a white horse.* Coward, McCann & Geoghegan, 1959.

———. *The silver branch.* Walck, 1958. Dell, 1966.

———. *Simon.* Oxford University Press, 1953.

———. *Song for a dark queen.* Crowell, 1979.

———. *Sword at sunset.* Coward, McCann & Geoghegan, 1963.

———. *Warrior scarlet.* Walck, 1958.

Trumbo, D. *Johnny got his gun.* Lippincott, 1939. Bantam, 1970.

Turner, A. *A hunter comes home.* Crown, 1980.

Wilder, L. I. *The little house books,* 9 vols. Harper & Row, 1953.

Yates, E. *Amos Fortune, free man.* E. P. Dutton, 1950, 1968.

Yates, E. *Amos Fortune, free man.* E. P. Dutton, 1950, 1968.

Cross-Cultural Heroes

Armer, L. A. *Waterless mountain.* McKay, Longmans, Green, 1931.

Bonham, F. *Viva Chicano.* Dutton, 1970. Dell, 1971.

Brown, D. *Lonesome whistle: The story of the first transcontinental railroad.* Holt, Rinehart & Winston, 1980.

———. *Creek Mary's blood.* Franklin Library, 1980. Pocket Books, 1981.

Brown, M. W. *The second stone.* Putnam, 1974.

Clark, A. N. *Year Walk.* Viking, 1975.

Childress, A. *A hero ain't nothin' but a sandwich.* Coward, McCann & Geoghegan, 1973. Avon, 1974.

Fair, R. L. *Cornbread, Earl, and me.* Bantam, 1975. Previously published as *Hog butcher* (1966). Bantam, 1975.

Fenton, E. *Duffy's rocks.* E. P. Dutton, 1974.

Guy, R. *The disappearance.* Delacorte, 1979. Dell, 1980.

———. *The friends.* Holt, Rinehart & Winston, 1973. Bantam, 1974.

———. *Ruby.* Viking, 1976. Bantam, 1979.

Hamilton, V. *Arilla Sun Down.* Greenwillow, 1976. Dell, 1979.

———. *The house of Dies Drear.* Macmillan, 1968. Dell, 1978.

———. *M. C. Higgins, the great.* Macmillan, 1974. Dell, 1976.

———. *Paul Robeson: The life and times of a free black man.* Harper & Row, 1974. Dell, 1979.

———. *The planet of Junior Brown.* Macmillan, 1971. Dell, 1978.

———. *W. E. B. DuBois: A biography.* Crowell, 1972.

———. *Zeely.* Macmillan, 1967. Dell, 1978.

Houston, J. W., and J. D. Houston. *Farewell to Manzanar.* Houghton Mifflin, 1973. Bantam, 1974.

Houston, J. *Ghost Fox.* Harcourt Brace Jovanovich, 1977. Avon, 1978.

Hunter, K. *The soul brothers and Sister Lou.* Scribner's, 1968. Avon, 1970.

Irwin, H. *We are Mesquakie, we are one.* Feminist Press, 1980.

Jordan, J. *His own where.* Crowell, 1971. Dell, 1973.

Lampman, E. S. *Go up the road.* Atheneum, 1972.

Mathis, S. B. *Listen for the fig tree.* Viking, 1974. Avon, 1974.

———. *Teacup full of roses.* Viking, 1972. Avon, 1973.

Means, F. C. *The moved-outers.* Houghton Mifflin, 1945, 1972.
Myers, W. D. *Fast Sam, Cool Clyde, and Stuff.* Viking, 1975. Avon, 1978.
Potok, C. *The chosen.* Simon and Schuster, 1967. Fawcett, 1968.
————. *My name is Asher Lev.* Knopf, 1972. Fawcett, 1972.
Richter, C. *Light in the forest.* Knopf, 1953. Bantam, 1971.
Rockwood, J. *To spoil the sun.* Holt, Rinehart & Winston, 1976. Dell, 1979.
Taylor, M. *Roll of thunder, hear my cry.* Dial, 1976. Bantam, 1978.
————. *Song of the trees.* Dial, 1975. Bantam, 1978.
Wong, J. S. *Fifth Chinese daughter.* Harper & Row, 1950.
Yep, L. *Dragonwings.* Harper & Row, 1975.

Realistic Heroes from Other Cultures

Arundel, H. *The blanket word.* Nelson, 1973. Dell, 1975.
Banks, L. R. *One more river.* Simon & Schuster, 1973.
Boissard, J. *A matter of feeling.* Translated by E. Walter. Little, Brown, 1979. Fawcett, 1981.
Clark, M. T. *The min-min.* Macmillan, 1978.
Forman, J. *My enemy, my brother.* Meredith, 1969. Nelson, 1981.
Freedman, B., and N. Freedman. *Mrs. Mike.* Coward, McCann & Geoghegan, 1947. Berkley, 1968.
George, J. C. *Julie of the wolves.* Harper & Row, 1972. Harper, 1975.
Houston, J. *The white dawn: An Eskimo saga.* Harcourt Brace Jovanovich, 1971, 1983.
Jarunkova, K. *Don't cry for me.* Four Winds, 1968. Scholastic, 1969.
Lingard, J. *Across the barricades.* Nelson, 1973. Penguin, 1973.
Llewellyn, R. *How green was my valley.* Macmillan, 1940.
McCullough, C. *The thorn birds.* Harper & Row, 1977. Avon, 1978.
Oz, A. *Elsewhere, perhaps.* Harcourt Brace Jovanovich, 1973. Penguin, 1979.
Ruesch, H. *Back to the top of the world.* Scribner's, 1973. Ballantine, 1974.
Turner, A. *A hunter comes home.* Crown, 1980.
Wojciechowska, M. *The shadow of a bull.* Atheneum, 1964.

Mystery and Suspense

Aiken, J. *Died on a rainy Sunday.* Holt, Rinehart & Winston, 1972.
————. *Nightfall.* Holt, Rinehart & Winston, 1969.
————. *The wolves of Willoughby Chase.* Doubleday, 1972. Dell, 1968.
Bennett, J. *The birthday murderer.* Delacorte, 1977. Dell, 1979.
————. *Deathman, do not follow me.* Meredith Press, 1968. Scholastic, 1968.
————. *The executioner.* Avon, 1982.
————. *The killing tree.* Watts, 1972. Avon, 1979.
————. *The long black coat.* Delacorte, 1973.
————. *The pigeon.* Methuen, 1980. Avon, 1981.
————. *Say hello to the hit man.* Delacorte, 1976. Dell, 1977.
Bosworth, J. A. *White water, still water.* Doubleday, 1966. Pocket Books, 1969.
Branscum, R. *Johnny May.* Doubleday, 1975. Avon, 1976.
————. *Toby, Granny, and George.* Doubleday, 1976. Avon, 1977.
————. *Me and Jim Luke.* Doubleday, 1971. Avon, 1975.
————. *The murder of hounddog Bates.* Viking, 1982.

Cameron, I. *The island at the top of the world*. Elmfield Press, 1961. Also published as *The lost ones*. Morrow, 1968. Avon, 1978.

———. *The lost ones*. Morrow, 1968. Avon, 1974.

———. *The mountains at the bottom of the world*. Morrow, 1972. Avon, 1974.

Clapp, P. *Jane-Emily*. Lothrop, Lee & Shepard, 1969. Dell, 1978.

Clark, M. H. *A stranger is watching*. Simon & Schuster, 1977. Dell, 1979.

———. *The cradle will fall*. Simon & Schuster, 1980. Dell, 1981.

Clark, M. T. *Wildfire* (1973). Macmillan, 1974.

Conrad, B., and N. Mortensen. *Endangered*. Putnam, 1978. Berkley, 1980.

Corcoran, B. *The clown*. Atheneum, 1975.

Cormier, R. *After the first death*. Pantheon, 1979. Avon, 1980.

Crawford, C. *Bad fall*. Harper & Row, 1972. Bantam, 1973.

Cullinan, T. *The bedeviled*. Putnam, 1978. Avon, 1979.

Duncan, L. *I know what you did last summer*. Little, Brown, 1973. Pocket Books, 1975.

———. *Down a dark hall*. Little, Brown, 1974. Pocket Books, 1975.

———. *Five were missing*. Signet, 1966. New American Library, 1972.

———. *Killing Mr. Griffin*. Little, Brown, 1978. Dell, 1979.

Eckert, A. W. *Incident at Hawk's Hill*. Little, Brown, 1971. Dell, 1972.

Edmond, W. D. *Wolf hunt*. Little, Brown, 1970.

Evarts, H. *Bigfoot*. Scribner's, 1973. Atheneum, 1981.

Forman, J. *So ends this day*. Farrar, Straus & Giroux, 1970.

Francis, D. B. *Golden Girl*. Scholastic, 1974.

———. *Mystery of the forgotten map*. Follett, 1968.

Garfield, L. *Footsteps*. Delacorte, 1980.

Godey, J. *The snake*. Putnam, 1978. Berkley, 1979.

Hall, L. *The secret of stone house*. Follett, 1968.

Hamilton, V. *The house of Dies Drear*. Macmillan, 1968. Dell, 1978.

Ives, J. *Fear in a handful of dust*. Dutton, 1978. Jove, 1979.

Jefferson, X. *Winterkill*. Ashley Books, 1978.

Kerr, M. E. *Gentlehands*. Harper & Row, 1978.

King, S. *Carrie*. Doubleday, 1974. New American Library, 1976.

———. *Firestarter*. Viking, 1980. New American Library, 1981.

———. *Night shift*. Doubleday, 1978. New American Library, 1979.

Konigsburg, E. L. *From the mixed-up files of Mrs. Basil E. Frankweiler*. Atheneum, 1967. Dell, 1977.

L'Engle, M. *The arm of the starfish*. Farrar, Straus & Giroux, 1965. Dell, 1980.

———. *Dragons in the water*. Farrar, Straus & Giroux, 1976.

———. *The young unicorns*. Farrar, Straus & Giroux, 1968. Dell, 1980.

Levitin, S. *Roanoke: A novel of a lost colony*. Atheneum, 1973.

Levy, E. *Came a spider*. Arbor House, 1978. Berkley, 1980.

McHargue, G. *Funny bananas: The mystery in the museum*. Holt, Rinehart & Winston, 1975. Dell, 1976.

McNab, O. *Horror story*. Houghton Mifflin, 1979.

Mazer, H. *Snow bound*. Delacorte, 1973. Dell, 1973.

Michaels, B. *Wait for what will come*. Dodd, Mead, 1978. Fawcett, 1979.

———. *Witch*. Dodd, Mead, 1973. Fawcett, 1973.

Miller, F. A. *The truth trap*. Dutton, 1980.

Millhiser, M. *The mirror*. Putnam, 1978. Fawcett, 1980.

Morey, W. *Canyon winter*. Dutton, 1972.

Morrell, D. *The totem*. Evans, 1979. Fawcett, 1980.

Myers, W. D. *Mojo and the Russians*. Viking, 1977. Avon, 1977.

Nixon, J. L. *The seance*. Harcourt Brace Jovanovich, 1980. Dell, 1981.

O'Dell, S. *Island of the blue dolphins*. Houghton Mifflin, 1960. Dell, 1975.

Paul, C. *A child is missing*. Putnam, 1978. Berkley, 1978.

Peck, R. *Are you in the house alone?* Viking, 1976. Dell, 1978.

————. *Dreamland Lake*. Holt, Rinehart & Winston, 1973. Avon, 1973.

————. *The ghost belonged to me*. Viking, 1975. Avon, 1976.

————. *Ghosts I have been*. Viking, 1977. Dell, 1979.

————. *Through a brief darkness*. Viking, 1973.

Peck, R. N. *Eagle fur*. Knopf, 1978. Avon, 1979.

Phleger, M. *Pilot down, presumed dead*. Harper & Row, 1963.

Polk, D. *The Linnet estate*. McKay, 1973.

Preussler, O. *The satanic mill*. Translated by A. Bell. Macmillan, 1973.

Raskin, E. *The westing game*. Dutton, 1978. Avon, 1980.

Ray, M. *The ides of April* (1974). Farrar, Straus & Giroux, 1975.

Reed, J. D. *Free fall*. Delacorte, 1980. Dell, 1981.

Rostov, M. *Night hunt*. Putnam, 1979.

St. George, J. *Haunted*. Putnam, 1980. Bantam, 1982.

Taylor, T. *The cay*. Doubleday, 1969. Avon, 1970.

Townsend, J. R. *The intruder* (1969). Lippincott, 1970. Dell, 1977.

Weintraub, L. *Runaway!* Ballantine, 1978.

Wilson, R. C. *Crooked tree*. Putnam, 1980. Berkley, 1981.

Windsor, P. *Something's waiting for you, Baker D*. Harper & Row, 1974.

Zindel, P. *The undertaker's gone bananas*. Harper & Row, 1978. Bantam, 1979.

Fantasy

Adams, R. *Watership down*. Macmillan, 1972. Avon, 1975.

Alexander, L. *The black cauldron*. Holt, Rinehart and Winston, 1965. Dell, 1980.

————. *The book of three*. Holt, Rinehart and Winston, 1964. Dell, 1980.

————. *The castle of Llyr*. Holt, Rinehart and Winston, 1966. Dell, 1980.

————. *The high king*. Holt, Rinehart and Winston, 1968. Dell, 1980.

————. *Taran wanderer*. Holt, Rinehart and Winston, 1967. Dell, 1980.

————. *The wizard in the tree*. Dutton, 1975. Dell, 1981.

Anderson, C. *The butterfly kid*. Gregg, 1967. Pyramid, 1967.

Anderson, M. *In the keep of time*. Knopf, 1977. Scholastic, 1978.

Anderson, P. *The broken sword*. Abelard-Shumen, 1954. Ballantine, 1971.

————, and G. Dickson. *Star prince Charlie*. Putnam's, 1975. Berkley, 1975.

Baum, L. F. *Ozma of Oz*. Reilly & Britton, 1907. Ballantine, 1979.

Beagle, P. *The last unicorn*. Viking, 1968. Ballantine, 1978.

Bethancourt, T. E. *The dog days of Arthur Cane*. Holiday, 1976. Bantam, 1981.

Boston, L. *An enemy at Green Knowe*. Harcourt, Brace & World, 1964. Voyager, 1979.

————. *The river at Green Knowe*. Harcourt, 1959. Voyager, 1979.

————. *Stranger at Green Knowe*. Harcourt, 1961. Voyager, 1979.

————. *The treasure of Green Knowe*. Harcourt, 1958. Voyager, 1978.

Cohen, B. *Unicorns in the rain*. Atheneum, 1980.

Cooper, S. *Over sea, under stone*. Harcourt, 1965. Penguin, 1978.

————. *The dark is rising.* Atheneum, 1973.

————. *Greenwitch.* Atheneum, 1974. Puffin Books, 1980.

————. *The grey king.* Atheneum, 1975.

————. *Silver on the tree.* Atheneum, 1977.

Dickson, G. R. *The dragon and the George.* Doubleday, 1976. Ballantine, 1980.

Dickinson, P. *The flight of dragons.* Harper & Row, 1979.

Fonstad, K. W. *The atlas of Middle-Earth.* Houghton Mifflin, 1981.

Grahame, K. *The wind in the willows.* Scribner's, 1908.

Gregorian, J. B. *The broken citadel.* Atheneum, 1975.

————. *Castledown.* Atheneum, 1977.

Hoban, R. *The mouse and his child.* Harper & Row, 1967. Avon, 1974.

Juster, N. *The phantom tollbooth.* Random House, 1961.

Kaye, M. *The incredible umbrella.* Doubleday, 1979.

LeGuin, U. K. *The wizard of earthsea.* Parnassus, 1968. Bantam, 1975.

————. *The tombs of Atuan.* Atheneum, 1971. Bantam, 1975.

————. *The farthest shore.* Atheneum, 1972. Bantam, 1975.

————. *The beginning place.* Harper & Row, 1980. Bantam, 1981.

L'Engle, M. *A wrinkle in time.* Farrar, Straus & Giroux, 1962. Dell, 1976.

————. *A wind in the door.* Farrar, Straus & Giroux, 1973. Dell, 1981.

————. *A swiftly tilting planet.* Farrar, Straus & Giroux, 1978. Dell, 1981.

Lewis, C. S. *The lion, the witch, and the wardrobe.* Macmillan, 1950.

McCaffrey, A. *Dragonsong.* Atheneum, 1976. Bantam, 1978.

————. *Dragonsinger.* Atheneum, 1977. Bantam, 1978.

————. *Dragondrums.* Atheneum, 1979. Bantam, 1980.

McKillip, P. *The riddle-master of Hed.* Atheneum, 1976. Ballantine, 1978.

————. *Heir of sea and fire.* Atheneum, 1977. Ballantine, 1978.

————. *The forgotten beat of Eld.* Atheneum, 1974. Avon, 1975.

Mazer, N. F. *Saturday, the twelfth of October.* Delacorte, 1975. Dell, 1976.

Parker, R. *A time to choose.* Harper & Row, 1974.

Pascal, F. *Hangin' out with Cici.* Viking, 1977. Pocket Books, 1978.

Paterson, K. *Bridge to Terabithia.* Crowell, 1977. Avon, 1979.

Piers, A. *A spell for chameleon.* Ballantine, 1977.

Pinkwater, M. *Lizard music.* Dodd, Mead, 1976. Dell, 1979.

Silverberg, R. *Lord Valentine's castle.* Harper & Row, 1980. Bantam, 1981.

Tolkien, J. R. R. *The fellowship of the ring.* Allen & Unwin, 1954. Ballantine, 1965.

————. *The two towers.* Allen & Unwin, 1954. Ballantine, 1965.

————. *The return of the king.* Allen & Unwin, 1954. Ballantine, 1965.

Wangerin, W. *The book of the dun cow.* Harper & Row, 1978. Pocket Books, 1979.

Williams, J. *The hero from otherwhere.* Walck, 1972. Dell, 1973.

Zelazny, R. *Nine princes in Amber.* Doubleday, 1970. Avon, 1973.

————. *The guns of Avalon.* Doubleday, 1972. Avon, 1974.

————. *Sign of the unicorn.* Doubleday, 1975. Avon, 1976.

————. *The hand of Oberon.* Doubleday, 1976. Avon, 1977.

Science Fiction

Aiken, J. *The shadow guests.* Delacorte, 1980.

Ames, M. *Is there life on a plastic planet?* Dutton, 1975.

Asimov, I. *Foundation.* Gnome, 1951.

————. *Foundation and empire*. Gnome, 1952. Avon, 1974.

————. *The second foundation*. Doubleday, 1953. Avon, 1974.

————, ed. *Tomorrow's children*. Doubleday, 1966.

Benford, G. *Jupiter project*. Nelson, 1975. Berkley, 1980.

Biemiller, C. *The hydronauts*. Doubleday, 1970.

Blish, J. *Cities in flight*. Doubleday, 1970. Avon, 1971.

————. *Star Trek*. Bantam, 1967–1978.

————. *The Star Trek reader*. Dutton, 1976–1978.

Bova, B. *City of darkness*. Scribner's, 1976.

Brackett, L. *The long tomorrow*. Doubleday, 1955. Ballantine, 1974.

Bradbury, R. *The Martian chronicles*. Doubleday, 1946. Bantam, 1979.

Brunner, J. *The sheep look up*. Harper & Row, 1972. Ballantine, 1973.

Caidin, M. *Cyborg*. Arbor House, 1972. Ballantine, 1978.

————. *The god machine*. Dutton, 1968. Bantam, 1969.

Čapek, K. *The war with the newts*. Translated by M. Weatherall and R. Weatherall. Putnam, 1937. Berkley, 1976.

Carver, J. *Star riggerr's way*. Doubleday, 1978. Dell, 1978.

Christopher, J. *The city of gold and lead*. Macmillan, 1967. Collier, 1970.

————. *The pool of fire*. Macmillan, 1968. Collier, 1970.

————. *The white mountains*. Macmillan, 1967. Collier, 1967.

Clarke, A. C. *2001: A space odyssey*. New American Library, 1968.

————. *Childhood's end*. Harcourt Brace Jovanovich, 1953.

Compton, D. G. *The unsleeping eye*. DAW Books, 1974. Pocket Books, 1980.

Davies, L. P. *The paper dolls*. New American Library, 1965.

del Rey, L. *Prisoners of space*. Westminster, 1967.

————. *Tunnel through time*. Westminster, 1966. Scholastic, 1966.

Dickson, G. R. *The far call*. Dial, 1978. Dell, 1978.

————. *Dorsai!* DAW Books, 1960. Ace, 1980.

Elwood, R., ed. *Children of infinity: Original science fiction stories for young readers*. Franklin Watts, 1973.

Engdahl, S. *Beyond the Tomorrow Mountains*. Atheneum, 1973.

————. *Enchantress from the stars*. Atheneum, 1970.

————. *The far side of evil*. Atheneum, 1971.

————. *This star shall abide*. Atheneum, 1972.

Finney, J. *Time and again*. Simon & Schuster, 1970. Warner, 1974.

Foster, A. D. *Splinter of the mind's eye*. Ballantine, 1978.

Gerrold, D. *When Harlie was one*. Doubleday, 1972. Ballantine, 1972.

Gotlieb, P. *O master Caliban!* Harper & Row, 1976.

Goulart, R. *What's become of screwloose?* Scribner's, 1971. DAW Books, 1973.

Halacy, D. C. *Return from Luna*. Norton, 1969.

Hard, T. W. *Sum VII*. Harper & Row, 1979. Ballantine, 1980.

Heinlein, R. *Rocketship Galileo*. Scribner's, 1947. Ballantine, 1977.

————. *Stranger in a strange land*. Putnam, 1961. Berkley, 1971.

Hooker, R. *Kennaquhair*. Abingdon, 1976.

Hoover, H. M. *The Delikon*. Viking, 1977. Avon, 1978.

————. *The lost star*. Viking, 1979. Avon, 1980.

————. *The rains of Eridan*. Viking, 1977. Avon, 1979.

————. *Treasures of Morrow*. Four Winds, 1976.

Johannesson, O. *The tale of the big computer*. Coward, McCann & Geoghegan, 1968.
Jones, D. W. *Dogsbody*. Greenwillow, 1975. Dell, 1979.
Karl, J. E. *Beloved Benjamin is waiting*. E. P. Dutton, 1978. Dell, 1980.
Key, A. *The forgotten door*. Westminster, 1965. Scholastic, 1968.
Keyes, D. *Flowers for Algernon*. Harcourt Brace Jovanovich, 1966. Bantam, 1978.
Kytle, R. *Fire and ice*. Mckay, 1975.
LeGuin, U. K. *The dispossessed: An ambiguous utopia*. Harper & Row, 1974. Avon, 1975.
———. *The left hand of darkness*. Walker, 1969. Ace Books, 1976.
———. *The word for world is forest*. Berkley, 1972, 1976.
Levin, I. *The boys from Brazil*. Random House, 1976. Dell, 1977.
Miller, W. M. *A canticle for Leibowitz*. Lippincott, 1959. Bantam, 1980.
Neufeld, J. *Sleep two, three, four!* Harper & Row, 1971. Avon, 1972.
O'Brien, R. *Z for Zachariah*. Atheneum, 1975. Dell, 1977.
Robinson, S., and J. Robinson. *Stardance*. Dial, 1979. Dell, 1980.
Shelley, M. *Frankenstein* (cartoons and caricatures). Bantam, 1978.
Simak, C. D. *Mastodonia*. Ballantine, 1978.
Silverberg, R., ed. *Men and machines*. Hawthorn, 1968.
Sleater, W. *House of stairs*. E. P. Dutton, 1974. Avon, 1975.
Spielberg, S. *Close encounters of the third kind*. Delacorte, 1977. Dell, 1977.
Townsend, J. R. *Noah's castle*. Lippincott, 1976. Dell, 1978.
———. *The visitors*. Lippincott, 1977.
Tevis, W. *Mockingbird*. Doubleday, 1980. Bantam, 1981.
Verne, J. *Journey to the center of the earth*. Grade 7–12. Scholastic, 1973.
Vonnegut, K. *Cat's cradle*. Holt, Rinehart and Winston, 1963. Dell, 1979.
Williamson, J. *The humanoids*. Lancer, 1949. Avon, 1975.
Wetanson, B., and T. Hoobler. *The hunters*. Doubleday, 1978.
Wibberley, L. *Encounter near Venus*. Farrar, Straus & Giroux, 1967.
Wrightson, P. *Down to earth*. Harcourt Brace Jovanovich, 1965.

Folklore, Legend, Myth, and Religion

Catling, P. S. *The chocolate touch*. Morrow, 1952. Bantam, 1981.
Garfield, L., and E. Blishen. *The god beneath the sea*. Pantheon, 1971.
Garner, A. *The owl service*. Philomel, 1967. Ballantine, 1981.
Hesse, H. *Siddhartha*. Translated by H. Rosner. New Directions, 1951.
Hieatt, C. *The minstrel knight*. Crowell, 1974.
Hodges, E. J. *A song for Gilgamesh*. Atheneum, 1971.
L'Engle, M. *A ring of endless light*. Farrar, Straus & Giroux, 1980. Dell, 1981.
———. *A swiftly tilting planet*. Farrar, Straus & Giroux, 1978. Dell, 1981.
———. *A wind in the door*. Farrar, Straus & Giroux, 1973. Dell, 1981.
Lyle, K. L. *Fair day, and another step begun*. Lippincott, 1974. Dell, 1975.
Norton, A. *Here abide monsters*. Atheneum, 1973. Daw, 1974.
———. *Huon of the horn*. Harcourt Brace, 1951. Fawcett Crest, 1980.
Suhl, Y. *The merrymaker*. Four Winds, 1975.
Sutcliff, R. *Beowulf*. Dutton, 1961.
———. *The light beyond the forest: The quest for the Holy Grail* (1979). Dutton, 1980.
———. *The road to Camlann: The death of King Arthur* (1981). Dutton, 1982.

―――. *The sword and the circle: King Arthur and the Knights of the Round Table* (1981). Dutton, 1981.

Wangerin, W. *The book of the dun cow.* Harper & Row, 1978. Pocket Books, 1979.

White, T. H. *The sword in the stone.* Putnam, 1939. Berkley, 1966.

Wigginton, E., *Foxfire.* Doubleday, 1972.

Suggested Readings

Bettelheim, B. *The uses of enchantment: The meaning and importance of fairy tales.* Knopf, 1976.

Blostein, F. *Invitations, celebrations: A handbook of ideas and techniques for promoting reading in junior and senior high schools.* Ontario Library Association, 1980.

Calabro, M. A special report: Trends and topics in YA books. *Media and Methods,* April 1980, pp. 24–31+.

Carlsen, G. R. *Books and the teenage reader.* 2nd rev. ed. Harper & Row, 1980. Bantam, 1980.

Denham, A., ed. Adolescent literature. *Texas Tech Journal of Education,* 1980.

Donelson, K. L., and A. P. Nilsen. *Literature for today's young adults.* Scott, Foresman, 1980.

Grossberg, K. Literature of adolescence: The inevitable battle ground. *Journal of Reading,* October 1977, pp. 76–80.

Gunn, J., ed. *The road to science fiction.* 3 vols. New American Library, 1978–1979.

Haley, B. The fractured family in adolescent literature. *English Journal,* February 1974, pp. 70–72.

Peck, R. Some thoughts on adolescent literature. *News from ALAN,* September–October 1975, pp. 4–7.

Reasoner, C. F. *A teacher's guide to the novels of Joan Aiken.* Dell, 1982.

―――. *A teacher's guide to the Prydain Chronicles by Lloyd Alexander.* Dell, 1982.

Shadow, L. The challenge of Alan Garner's fiction. In Gallo, D., ed., *Connecticut English Journal,* Fall 1980, pp. 151–54.

Stanford, B. D., and K. Amin. *Black literature for high school students.* National Council of Teachers of English, 1978.

Tway, E., ed. *Reading ladders for human relations.* 6th ed. American Council on Education, 1981.

4 The Emotional Emphasis Of Young Adult Literature

The young adult novel, according to the author Richard Peck, provides an emotional outlet for the reader. The emotional emphasis of these novels often centers on the variety of feelings experienced by young adults in their relationships with other teenagers, with siblings, with parents, and with nonfamily adults.

Humor is an important emotional element of this literature. According to Peck, incorporating humor into the young adult novel is not easy "because like all people who laugh a lot, [young adults] are essentially humorless" (1975, p. 6).

Sentimentality is another emotional aspect of many narratives. "To oversimplify, after a reassuring outcome in a story, I suspect . . . [the young adults] like best a good cry" (Peck 1975, p. 6).

The "Good Cry" Novel

Many young adult novels provide the reader with a good cry. The themes of death, broken relationships, handicaps, and young adults "making it" despite the odds against them appeal to the sentimentality of the young adult reader. The teacher who gives a book talk on the theme of "attitudes toward death" by reading sections of the books *Bridge to Terabithia* (Paterson), *A ring of endless light* (L'Engle), *The magic moth* (Lee), *Our Eddie* (Ish-kishor), and *The edge of next year* (Stoltz) will need to have a box of tissues on hand for all the students in the class, even the least sentimental.

A RELATIONSHIP ENDS. The ending of relationships, through death, war, departure, or family opposition, is touching to the young adult, who is spending a large amount of energy building relationships. Saying good-bye to a loved one who is about to die is a tear-producing episode in a number of young adult books. *Love story* (Segal), though not written as a young adult book, was read by an entire generation of young adult women. I remember sitting at a pool one hot summer afternoon and watching girl after girl being reduced to tears while reading Erich Segal's narrative. In Patricia Windsor's *The summer before,* the young protagonist must put her life back together again after the death of her love, Bradley, the summer before.

Many young adults face the departure of a young love to a distant college campus or the military. Not many young adults in this generation have sent their lovers into the unknown world of war. However, all young adults sympathize with the great loss experienced by Patty in *Summer of my German soldier* (Greene) when she sends her German soldier off to his likely capture. And when word of his death is received by Patty, all young adult female readers understand her torment.

> ☐ *We are obligated to write about what makes us break out into tears or into song.*
> BETTE GREENE
> *author of* Them that glitter and them that don't *(Knopf, 1983) and* I've already forgotten your name, Philip Hall *(Knopf, 1984)* / *in an address at the IRA Convention* / *Atlanta, Ga.* / *April 1979*

Having to choose between family ties and the love of another young person is not unusual for young adults. In *The Beethoven medal* (Peyton), Ruth becomes infatuated with Pat, a truck driver who is always in trouble. Her mother attempts to force a breakup. Ruth, however, learns that Pat is an accomplished musician. Unfortunately, he is also sentenced to nine months in jail for his criminal acts. Ruth, unsure of her feelings, does not know whether to succumb to her emotions and wait for his return, or to use her common sense and leave him.

Friendships that endure despite all the reasons for ending them provide many sentimental moments in young adult novels. In *First of midnight* (Darke), Jess, an auctioned white chattel, befriends Midnight, a black boxer. Their relationship, set against a backdrop of slavery, continues to grow despite their differences. Young adult literature of today often features the ''star-crossed lovers'' theme. In *Kathleen, please come home* (O'Dell), Kathleen's love for a deported alien, Ramón, leads her to a life in Mexico with Ramón's family, a pregnancy and miscarriage, a car accident, and, finally, a return to a home owned by strangers. *Circle of love* (Leahy) is the story of Anton and Anna, who fall in love while bicycling through Germany in search of Anna's parents after World War II. They are separated after each emigrates to America, but eventually their tale has a happy ending. *Across the barricades* (Lingard) is the story of two lovers torn by war, one a Belfast Protestant, the other a Catholic. *Masks: A love story* (Bennett) illustrates the Romeo and Juliet theme with a twist. Peter Yeng, a college freshman, falls in love with sixteen-year-old Jennifer. Peter, the son of a Chinese immigrant, resents his father for not having accompanied his mother to China, where she died. However, when Peter's father forbids him to see Jennifer, he complies despite his love for her. He would rather leave Jennifer than destroy his relationship with his father.

RELATIONSHIPS WITH HANDICAPPED YOUNG ADULTS. The portrayal of relationships between young adults who are handicapped and young adults who are not is less sugar-coated in today's young adult fiction than in the young adult novel of the past. *The war on Villa Street* (Mazer) is the story of thirteen-year-old Willis, who escapes from an unhappy home life and meets and coaches a retarded boy in athletics. The relationship begins as a business venture, and Willis resents the time he must spend coaching Richard. Both boys, however, experience satisfaction when Richard makes his best jump at Field Day. In *It's too late for sorry* (Hanlon), Kenny becomes friends with Harold, a mentally handicapped teenager. When Phil, Kenny's friend, bullies Harold, Kenny tries to compensate by being more than nice to Harold. However, the unusual friendship takes on a more egocentric twist when Kenny meets Rachel, who has a retarded sister. He attempts to use his friendship with Harold to impress Rachel. When he senses that his friendship with Harold is infringing on his relationship with Rachel, however, he begins mistreating Harold. Later he is remorseful and tries to patch up the friendship, but finds that "it's too late for sorry."

The difficulty of maintaining relationships with friends who become handicapped is vividly portrayed in Robin Brancato's *Winning.* When Gary is paralyzed, his best friend visits him in the hospital, but Gary notices that their usual comfortable banter is missing. The friendship ends as the visits become less and less frequent. However, Gary discovers new relationships, with a black teammate, a teacher, and other handicapped young adults.

MAKING IT DESPITE THE ODDS. Young adult characters who "make it" despite the great odds against them appeal to teenagers' emotions. In *Tell me that you love me, Junie Moon* (Kellogg), three grotesquely injured people live together as normally as possible by defying the regulations of the normal society. Sentimental young adults will be moved to tears by *Only love* (Sallis), in which two young people conduct a love affair despite their confinement to wheelchairs and their knowledge that one of them will die soon.

Poverty cannot keep some young adults from triumph. A family of orphaned children survive the difficult life of Appalachia by wildcrafting in Vera Cleaver and Bill Cleaver's *Where the lilies bloom* and *Trial valley.* Other children cling together to fight the juvenile court system in *Broken promise* (Hayes and Lazzarina). The five children in the book, abandoned by their parents, spend many months struggling to stay together. Another book about children fighting to remain together is Adrienne Jones's *So nothing is forever,* the story of children of an interracial marriage who are suddenly orphaned.

"Good cry" novels appear in a variety of genres. In the autobiographical fiction narrative *A sound of chariots* (Hunter), for example, a Scottish girl overcomes poverty and a series of family tragedies to accomplish her dream of becoming a writer.

Developing Relationships

Relationships are of prime importance to young adults. The emotional impact of relationships is portrayed in almost all young adult literature. Friendships between young adults, sibling relationships, parent-teenage relationships, the changing family circle, the ending of relationships, and the friendships between teenagers and nonparental adults are all important themes in the young adult novel.

BEST FRIEND NOVELS. Seemingly the most important developing relationships are between two young adults. The best friend plays an essential role in the life of the teenager and, consequently, in young adult fiction. The development of friendship is important in all literary genres read by young adults. In the historical novel *The witch of Blackbird Pond* (Speare), for example, the friendships between Kit and Mercy, Kit and Hannah, and Kit and Prudence are central to the development of plot and theme. In the genre of fantasy the relationship of the young adult to other young adults is equally important. In *Hangin' out with Cici* (Pascal) thirteen-year-old Victoria goes back in time and becomes best friends with Cici, who turns out to be Victoria's mother as a teenager. The mystery also provides many best-friend relationships. How would Nancy Drew ever make her discoveries without her friend George? The strange friendship between Mark and the other teenagers provides much of the action in Lois Duncan's *Killing Mr. Griffin.* The friendships in *The friends* (Guy), *Bridge to Terabithia* (Paterson), *Moon and me* (Irwin), *Something left to lose* (Brancato), *Ronnie and Rosey* (Angell), *Can you sue your parents for malpractice?* (Danziger), and many other young adult novels are important to the development of the plot and theme of the narrative.

> ☐   *I feel the novels must work first as stories with real people who have meaning for the reader. Otherwise, the novel would be an empty tract. So I emphasize story and character, knowing if they work, the themes will emerge as strong and forceful.*
> ROBERT CORMIER
> *author of* I am the cheese / *in a letter to the author* / July 1979

Developing friendships is not always easy, however. The extreme pain that can be involved in attempting to be accepted is best exemplified by Robert Cormier's classic young adult novel *The chocolate war*. This book examines how the need for peer approval can be very destructive to the young adult. Jerry refuses to sell the fifty boxes of candy required by Brother Leon for Trinity High School. For the first several days of the candy campaign, he follows the orders of the Vigils, the powerful school "fraternity," in an attempt to gain recognition and membership. However, when their requests become too demanding and demeaning, Jerry balks and refuses to implement them. Because of his refusal to participate, Jerry becomes a hero to his peers, but his hero status threatens Archie, the leader of the Vigils, and Archie uses his power to turn the school against Jerry. The book ends with an arranged boxing match between Jerry and a bully who is trying to be accepted by the Vigils. Jerry learns of the pain, both emotional and physical, that can result from trying to become a member of a peer group. He tells his friend Goober at the end of the novel: "They don't want you to do your thing, not unless it happens to be their thing, too. It's a laugh, Goober, a fake. Don't disturb the universe, no matter what the posters say."

Since acceptance into the "in group" is very important to many teens, a large number of young adult books address this issue. In Sol Stein's *The magician,* sixteen-year-old Ed is the magician who provides entertainment for a school dance. Like Archie in Cormier's book, the gang leader Urek is jealous of Ed's success. This book, however, ends with the murder of Urek by Ed and the ironic hiring of the unethical lawyer who defended Urek at the beginning of the novel to defend Ed. Other books that deal with the teenager's desire to be part of the gang include *Child of fire* (O'Dell), *The outsiders* and *Rumble fish* (Hinton), *City cool* (deJongh and Cleveland), *Headman* (Platt), and *Durango Street* (Bonham).

SIBLING RELATIONSHIPS. Characters in young adult literature reflect the difficult nature of changing sibling relationships. In some young adult novels this relationship is the central aspect of the narrative. In *And you give me a pain, Elaine* (Pevsner), thirteen-year-old Andrea resents her older sister, whose behavior is tearing the family apart. In Judy Blume's *Tales of a fourth grade nothing,* Peter is convinced he must be a "nothing" because his baby brother Fudge gets all the family attention. The central character in *The loner* (Bradbury) is twelve-year-old Jay Sharp. His brother, the "Great Mal," who is fourteen, seems to have everything Jay lacks: Mal is good-looking, athletic, popular, and ougoing. The resolution of Jay's resentment is the topic of the narrative. In another book about a difficult sibling relationship, the flashback technique is used to relate the story of eighteen-year-old Rion and his older brother, Doug. In *Count me gone* (Johnson), Rion tells his story to a sympathetic lawyer after he has been seriously injured and charged with assaulting an officer and resisting arrest. Everyone, including his parents, believes Rion is mentally unstable, but Rion reveals how the difficult relationship with his brother, the unasked-for advice, and the bizarre behavior of Doug's fiancée caused his problems. In *Jacob have I loved*

(Paterson), Louise grows up on a small island in the Chesapeake Bay with her parents, grandmother, and twin sister. Louise resents her sister Caroline's talent and beauty, and the extra attention Caroline seems to receive because of her fragile health. The antagonism between the sisters deepens when Call, Louise's best friend and crabbing companion, marries Caroline, and Louise learns that her dream of becoming a doctor is impossible. Instead, she becomes a nurse, moves to a remote valley in western Virginia as a midwife, marries, and presides over the difficult delivery of twins. Through this delivery she learns much about her feelings toward Caroline and accepts her birthright as the ''stronger'' of the twins.

Even though most of the sibling relationships portrayed in young adult books have difficult moments, they are often beneficial to the young protagonists of young adult fiction. The siblings in S. E. Hinton's *The outsiders* and *Tex* are left on their own most of the time. As children alone, they experience many problems, but through their relationship life is made bearable. Eleven-year-old Claudia and her nine-year-old brother, Jamie, run away from home in Elaine Konigsburg's *From the mixed-up files of Mrs. Basil E. Frankweiler*. They make a home in the Metropolitan Museum of Art and develop methods for eluding the guards and museum workers. During the escapade, which ends when the children agree to return home in exchange for the name of the sculptor of a ''mystery statue,'' Jamie and Claudia become friends. The attempt of a boy to save the life of his brother is a central part of the action in Sharon Mathis's *Teacup full of roses*. This stark story is a narrative about three brothers attempting to sur-

A mother and son discuss the unusual parent/child relationship in Robert Cormier's I am the cheese.

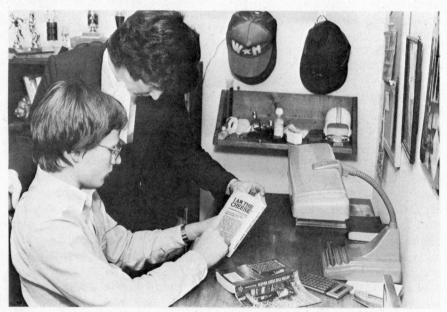

vive life in the ghetto. One escapes through drugs, one uses his academic talents, and the other joins the navy and helps his younger brother reach his dream.

THE PARENT AND THE YOUNG ADULT. Many relationships, other than those with young people, are important in the young adult's life. The bond that exists between parents and young adults is a changing one. Young adults moving toward independence seek to redefine their dependent relationship with their parents. Often this redefinition causes pain for both child and parent.

The mother-daughter relationship plays an important role in young adult books. In *Mom, the Wolfman, and me* (Klein), Brett has enjoyed her closeness with her mother, who has never married, wears jeans, and works odd hours. Then the Wolfman enters their lives, proposes marriage to her mother, and threatens to change Brett's relationship with her mother. In *Anne Frank: The diary of a young girl,* Anne describes her mother as always criticizing, as liking her older sister better, and as condemning her friendship with Peter. Even in the extreme, life-threatening situation of this Jewish family hiding from the Nazis, the difficulties of the mother-daughter relationship retain their poignancy. In the teen years, many girls are just beginning to realize that their mothers are not perfect, that they, too, have problems. Iris in *A midsummer night's death* (Peyton) believes her mother lacks the "prerequisite of ninety-nine percent of the mother race: a natural concern for its young." Susan's mother in *Growing up guilty* (Schwartz) appears cold, overcritical, and petty. Dinky's mother in *Dinky Hocker shoots smack!* (Kerr) seems to be more interested in social work than in her own overweight, frustrated daughter. Jenny of *The green of me* (Gauch) reflects upon the overconcern of her mother.

In *The sister act* (Elfman), Molly is torn between making her own life or staying home with her neurotic mother to help support the family. In *Beloved Benjamin is waiting* (Karl), Cherry's mother cares about her children, but has so many of her own problems that she "had to keep running to stay ahead of them and didn't have time for much else." The changing relationship between mother and daughter is exemplified by Rachel and her mother in *Hey, that's my soul you're stomping on* (Corcoran):

> *When her mother wasn't throwing an emotional tantrum or trying to possess her family's lives, she was nice and she was fun. As a little girl Rachel had thought she had the best mother in the world. But when you got to be sixteen and your mother expected to know not only everything you did, but everything you thought and felt, that was more than a person could stand. Rachel knew exactly how her father felt. Smothered. Her mother was like a big, squashy quilt that came down over your head and smothered you.*

The relationship between father and son can also be difficult for the young adult. In Barbara Wersba's *Run softly, go fast,* Dave and his father have a love-

■ ■ ■ An Anthological Aside

What Is Left of This Girl?

ANNE FRANK

Tuesday, 7 March, 1944

Dear Kitty,

If I think now of my life in 1942, it all seems too unreal. It was quite a different Anne who enjoyed that heavenly existence from the Anne who has grown wise within these walls. Yes, it was a heavenly life. Boy friends at every turn, about twenty friends and acquaintances of my own age, the darling of nearly all the teachers, spoiled from top to toe by Mummy and Daddy, lots of sweets, enough pocket money, what more could one want?

You will certainly wonder by what means I got around all these people. Peter's word "attractiveness" is not altogether true. All the teachers were entertained by my cute answers, my amusing remarks, my smiling face, and my questioning looks. That is all I was—a terrible flirt, coquettish and amusing. I had one or two advantages, which kept me rather in favor. I was industrious, honest, and frank. I would never have dreamed of cribbing from anyone else. I shared my sweets generously, and I wasn't conceited.

Wouldn't I have become rather forward with so much admiration? It was a good thing that in the midst of, at the height of, all this gaiety, I suddenly had to face reality, and it took me at least a year to get used to the fact that there was no more admiration forthcoming.

How did I appear at school? The one who thought of new jokes and pranks, always "king of the castle," never in a bad mood, never a crybaby. No wonder everyone liked to cycle with me, and I got their attentions.

Now I look back at that Anne as an amusing, but very superficial girl, who has nothing to do with the Anne of today. Peter said quite rightly about me: "If ever I saw you, you were always surrounded by two or more boys and a whole troupe of girls. You were always laughing and always the center of everything!"

What is left of this girl? Oh, don't worry, I haven't forgotten how to laugh or to answer back readily. I'm just as good, if not better, at criticizing people, and I can still flirt if . . . I wish. That's not it, though I'd like that sort of life again for an evening, a few days, or even a week; the life which seems so carefree and gay. But at the end of that week, I should be dead beat and I would be only too thankful to listen to anyone who began to talk about something sensible. I don't want followers, but friends, admirers who fall not for a flattering smile but for what one does and for one's character.

I know quite well that the circle around me would be much smaller. But what does that matter, as long as one still keeps a few sincere friends?

Yet I wasn't entirely happy in 1942 in spite of everything; I often felt deserted, but because I was on the go the whole day long, I didn't think about it and enjoyed myself as much as I could. Consciously or unconsciously, I tried to drive away the emptiness I felt with jokes and pranks. Now I think seriously about life and what I have to do. One period of my life is over forever. The carefree schooldays are gone, never to return.

I don't even long for them any more; I have outgrown them, I can't just only enjoy myself as my serious side is always there.

I look upon my life up till the New Year, as it were, through a powerful magnifying glass. The sunny life at home, then coming here in 1942, the sudden change, the quarrels, the bickerings. I couldn't understand it, I was taken by surprise, and the only way I could keep up some bearing was by being impertinent.

The first half of 1943: my fits of crying, the loneliness, how I slowly began to see all my faults and shortcomings, which are so great and which seemed much greater then. During the day I deliberately talked about anything and everything that was farthest from my thoughts, tried to draw Pim to me; but couldn't. Alone I had to face the difficult task of changing myself, to stop the everlasting reproaches, which were so oppressive and which reduced me to such terrible despondency.

Things improved slightly in the second half of the year. I became a young woman and was treated more like a grownup. I started to think, and write stories, and came to the conclusion that the others no longer had the right to throw me about like an india-rubber ball. I wanted to change in accordance with my own desires. But one thing that struck me even more was when I realized that even Daddy would never become my confidant over everything. I didn't want to trust anyone but myself any more.

At the beginning of the New Year: the second great change, my dream.... And with it I discovered my longing, not for a girl friend, but for a boy friend. I also discovered my inward happiness and my defensive armor of superficiality and gaiety. In due time I quieted down and discovered my boundless desire for all that is beautiful and good.

And in the evening, when I lie in bed and end my prayers with the words, "I thank you, God, for all that is good and dear and beautiful," I am filled with joy. Then I think about "the good" of going into hiding, of my health and with my whole being of the "dearness" of Peter, of that which is still embryonic and impressionable and which we neither of us dare to name or touch, of that which will come sometime; love, the future, happiness and of "the beauty" which exists in the world; the world, nature, beauty and all, all that is exquisite and fine.

I don't think then of all the misery, but of the beauty that still remains. This is one of the things that Mummy and I are so entirely different about. Her counsel when one feels melancholy is: "Think of all the misery in the world and be thankful that you are not sharing in it!" My advice is: "Go outside, to the fields, enjoy nature and the sunshine, go out and try to recapture happiness in yourself and in God. Think of all the beauty that's still left in and around you and be happy!"

I don't see how Mummy's idea can be right, because then how are you supposed to behave if you go through the misery yourself? Then you are lost. On the contrary, I've found that there is always some beauty left—in nature, sunshine, freedom, in yourself; these can all help you. Look at these things, then you find yourself again, and God, and then you regain your balance.

And whoever is happy will make others happy too. He who has courage and faith will never perish in misery!

Yours,
Anne

■ ■ ■

hate relationship. The death of his father forces Dave to reexamine this relationship, his own life, his values, and his beliefs. The poignant book *Richie* (Thompson) considers the changing relationship of a father and his son, Richie. Richie's personality changes dramatically, often because of his drug use. In *The boy who could make himself disappear* (Platt), Roger's father is so wrapped up in his career that he has little time for his son. Roger is so consumed by his speech impediment that he withdraws into schizophrenia. In *Father figure* (Peck), seventeen-year-old Jim accepts the role of surrogate father for his younger brother, Byron, after his parent's breakup. His role is threatened when Byron and Jim are forced to move in with their father.

Relationships between fathers and daughters and between sons and mothers also are important in young adult literature. In Isabelle Holland's *Of love and death and other journeys,* Peg must learn to accept her long-absent father after the death of her beloved mother. In Lee Bennett Hopkins' *Mama,* a mother loves her two sons a great deal, but they are disconcerted when they learn that she steals to buy them things.

□   *. . . It is that struggle between the child and the adult in the creating of that self-portrait, that often preoccupies my writing. The lucky children are the ones who are taught to believe, as they go through life, that, whatever their faults, they themselves are lovable and estimable human*

beings. Most parents do not mean to convey a different message, but they often do. And if my books are about wounds given in that message, they are also about the healing that can take place, given the right adult at the right time.
ISABELLE HOLLAND
author of Man without a face

Not all relationships between parents and children in young adult literature are consumed by problems. Even in *Mama* the boys learn to accept their mother and her love. In *Bridge to Terabithia* (Paterson), Jesse is embarrassed by his parents' lack of education. He believes that because he is the oldest, and a boy, he must do too many things around the house. On the other hand, he is jealous and envious of the good relationship Leslie has with her parents. However, after Leslie's death, the concern and support he receives from his father show him the power of his father's love. Rob in *A day no pigs would die* (Peck) does not always understand his father, but he always respects him. Papa is poor, but he is proud and works hard for his family. Rob learns of his father's humanity and gains his own manhood when he is forced to slaughter his pet pig. The pig is sterile and the family must have food.

> *"Oh, Papa. My heart's broke."*
>
> *"So is mine," said Papa. "But I'm thankful you're a man."*
>
> *I just broke down, and Papa let me cry it all out. I just sobbed and sobbed with my head up toward the sky and my eyes closed, hoping God would hear it.*
>
> *"That's what being a man is all about, boy. It's just doing what's got to be done."*

In *Home before dark* (Bridgers), Stella must form a new relationship with her father after her mother's death. At first the relationship is strained. However, he gives her space and time, and at the end of the novel the continuing relationship between father and daughter is ensured.

RELATIONSHIPS WITH GRANDPARENTS. Touching relationships between young adults and their grandparents or great-grandparents are popular in the young adult novel. Salty in Ouida Sebestyen's *Far from home* searches for his long-lost father. He finds, instead, the love and friendship of family with his elderly grandmother in the Buckley Arms Hotel. Other relationships with grandparents are found in Madeleine L'Engle's *The summer of the great grandmother* and M. E. Kerr's *Gentlehands*. An extremely difficult relationship with a grandparent is experienced by the twins Caroline and Louise in Katherine Paterson's *Jacob have I loved*. In Hadley Irwin's book *What about Grandma?* the relationships between mother, daughter, and grandmother are interestingly contrasted.

Changing Family Relationships

Changes in familial relationships are the basis for many young adult novels. The family who learns it is not what it thought it was is the theme of Susan Shreve's *The masquerade.* Seventeen-year-old Rebecca must face the changes in her family after her father is arrested for embezzlement and her mother suffers a nervous breakdown.

SEPARATION AND DIVORCE. The family that changes from a two-parent household to a one-parent household because of separation or divorce faces many problems. The changing relationship between the young adult and the parent can produce tension between them and feelings of isolation for the teenager. In Bianca Bradbury's *The blue year,* seventeen-year-old Jill stays with the family of her friend while her mother is in Nevada getting a divorce. Jill is convinced she is the cause of the divorce, although she does not know what she has done. When her mother returns, she becomes dependent on Jill. Jill attempts to reunite her parents, but learns that her father, whom she sees once a week, is dating another woman. Jill has no one to talk to and is very confused. Like Jill, Katie in Hadley Irwin's *Bring to a boil and separate* has no one to talk to about her parent's divorce. Her younger brother refuses to talk about it, and her best friend is away at camp until the end of the summer. The feeling of aloneness after the separation of a family is also experienced by Jimmie in *Leap before you look* (Stolz). Jimmie, at fourteen, feels alienated from her mother and can't talk to her father about the physical and emotional changes she is facing. Joanna Douglas lives through a crisis in *A family failing* (Arundel) when her father loses his job and must rely on her mother for support of the family. When Jonathan, Joanna's father, finds a temporary job he encourages his family to move with him. Mark, Joanna's brother, who has withdrawn from the family since the start of the crisis, refuses. Joanna's mother, Elspeth, says she has too many business responsibilities. Joanna agrees to go, but spends most of her time traveling between one family member and another. She, like many young adults, hopes that the family will be reunited. The crisis begins to resolve itself for Joanna when she understands that reunion is impossible and she must live her own life.

In Norma Klein's *Taking sides,* Nell feels she must choose sides in her parents' divorce. When she is living with her mother she believes she wants to be with her father, but when she is with him she is distressed by his relationship with another woman and the fact that she and her young brother must share a room. Like Joanna, Nell begins to understand that the divorce is final and nothing will be the same again. Finally, she realizes that she need not choose between her parents, but can love and be loved by both of them. In *Guy Lenny* (Mazer), Guy has enjoyed his life with his father. However, things start to change when his father begins to date Emily. Guy's mother asks him to move in with her and her new husband. Guy, who resents his mother for leaving, refuses. However, he learns that his father has asked his mother to take him. He runs away but eventually returns to face both parents.

Some family divorces result in the total separation of the young adult from the parents. In Vera Cleaver and Bill Cleaver's *Ellen Grae,* for example, Ellen Grae is sent to Florida to live with Mr. and Mrs. McGruder. In the sequel, *Lady Ellen Grae,* Ellen Grae is again sent away, this time to Seattle to live with her aunt Eleanor, who is to teach her to be a lady. In *This is a recording* (Corcoran), Marianne lives with her grandmother while her parents travel in Europe. She does not know that the trip will end in divorce. When word of the divorce reaches Marianne, she begs to stay with her grandmother, convinced that she is a burden on her parents and the cause of their problems. In *Notes for another life* (Bridgers), Wren and Kevin attempt to understand why their mother chose to leave them with their grandparents while she pursues a career. The stress caused by the mental illness of their father, who is institutionalized through much of the book, the divorce of their parents, and their mother's move to a faraway city leads Kevin to a suicide attempt. Through the teenagers' love for music and for each other, the book ends on an upbeat note: "He took a deep breath and croaked out a little noise. It sounded better than he'd expected. And so they went the distance, covering the miles between themselves and Tom, singing as they went."

The problems arising when one parent gains custody of the child, and the way the custody affects the child's relationship with the other parent, are discussed in Judy Blume's *It's not the end of the world* and John Neufeld's *Sunday father.*

Relationships between parents and teenagers are complicated when two families become one through remarriage. In Betty Bates's *Bugs in your ears,* Carrie objects to her mother's remarriage. She believes that no one is listening to or hearing her. Even her new brothers and sisters pay no attention to her. When her stepfather wants to adopt her, she rebels and causes an unpleasant scene in the courtroom. Chloris of *Chloris and the creeps* (Platt) attempts to turn her eight-year-old sister Jenny against their mother's new husband, Fidel. When he offers to adopt the girls, Chloris refuses. Fidel accepts her decision, hoping that she will eventually change her mind. Chloris, like Carrie, unrealistically glamorizes her real father. The saga of Chloris and Jenny continues in two sequels, *Chloris and the freaks* and *Chloris and the weirdos,* which catalogue the divorce of Fidel and their mother and the effects this divorce has on Jenny, who begins to wonder if all adults act irrationally, particularly after Fidel defines "mature behavior": "It means to have a genuine concern for other individuals, and very little concern for oneself."

ILLNESS AND DEATH IN THE FAMILY. Familial relationships change for young adults when a parent becomes critically ill or dies. The death of a father can change the role of the young adult in the family. In *Swift water* (Annixter), Bucky has a good relationship with Cam, his father. They share the dream of setting up a wildlife sanctuary in northern Maine. Cam, an idealist, is killed on a hunting trip while trying to stop the duck hunters from shooting at geese. Grief-stricken, Bucky believes the dream of the sanctuary is lost after Cam's death. However, he takes his new role as developer of the sanctuary seriously, and word of the dream spreads through the publicity gained when a newsman investigates the story. In *Big Doc's girl* (Medearis) an adolescent must assume responsibility for the family after the death of her father and the institutionalization of her mother. In *Red sky at morning* (Bradford), Josh's father leaves in 1944 to enlist in the navy; and Josh and his mother move to New Mexico. Josh adjusts quite well to his new life, but his overprotected mother has many difficulties. He learns he must accept responsibility for the family. This new role is reinforced after his father is killed and his mother suffers a nervous breakdown. In *Ronnie and Rosey* (Angell), Ronnie plays a new role as companion to her mother after her father's death. At first she resents her mother's dependence upon her, but she learns to adapt to their new relationship.

The grief, guilt, and sense of loss experienced by young adults at the death or serious illness of a father is exemplified in *The ups and downs of Jorie Jenkins* (Bates). Jorie has always been close to her handsome, strong father. When he suffers a heart attack, she feels he has let her down. He is not the man he used to be, and she can no longer relate to him in the same way. In *Run softly, go fast* (Wersba), nineteen-year-old David Marks returns from his father's funeral and begins writing a journal about their realtionship. At first he catalogues the hate he feels for his father. However, as the journal unfolds he realizes he has made an error in his recollections of his father, and he reexamines them. When Birdie McShane is told of her father's death in *A sound of chariots* (Hunter), she automatically carries on with her life as usual. Soon she is devastated by grief as she pedals through the village on her paper route. Plagued by nightmares of death, Birdie continues to grieve for her father. Several years later her teacher tells her she cannot come to terms with his death by continuing her grief; she must begin to live her own life to the fullest. In *Fog* (Lee), Luke suffers two tragedies: the death of his father and the death of a friend in a fire for which Luke assumes responsibility. Throughout the book Luke experiences feelings of grief and guilt, and a sense of great loss.

The changing roles within the family after the death of the mother is central to *The rock and the willow* (Lee). Enie has always taken on the helping role in her poor household, but she has sustained herself with her love of learning and the knowledge that one day she will go to college. Her mother has shared her dream. However, the dream appears to be shattered after her mother's death when Enie is needed at home to maintain the household. Ingrid in *The pigeon pair* (Ogilvie) must take on the responsibility of homemaker after the death of her pregnant mother and the withdrawal of her father. Barbara Girion's *A tangle of roots* deals with Beth's reaction to her mother's sudden death. She must adjust to the fact that her assumption that her parents would always be there is untrue. In *The night swimmers* (Byars), Retta must care for her siblings after their mother's death. Their father, a country singer, is never home. The children are resourceful and cope with their problem successfully. The title comes from the recreation the children find for themselves by swimming in the neighborhood pools as the neighbors sleep. In *The blanket word* (Arundel), Jan feels grief over the death of her mother even though she did not love her. Through her friendship with Thomas she explores her feelings about love and comes to terms with her mother's death. Grover knows his mother is ill in *Grover* (Cleaver and Cleaver), but he assumes all will be well when she returns from the hospital. Once she is home he notices that she wants to talk to him more than usual. One day while Grover is outside playing, she commits suicide. Grover feels all alone after his mother's death because his father withdraws and he has no one to confide in. In *A matter of time* (Schotter), Lisl witnesses her mother's slow deterioration from cancer. Through her mother's illness and death Lisl struggles to find the meaning of her own life.

The death of both parents often leads to the breakup of a family or the struggle to keep it together. The relationship of all the siblings and their roles within the family change dramatically. In *Break a leg, Betsy Maybe!* (Kingman), Betsy ends up living in the suburbs with her rich aunt and uncle. Throughout the book she is desperately seeking a role for herself in her new life. In *Where the lilies bloom* and its sequel, *Trial Valley,* by Bill Cleaver and Vera Cleaver fourteen-year-old Mary desperately attempts to keep the family together as a promise to her dead father. To do so she must conceal his death from the authorities, who will attempt to send the children to the county home.

The death of a grandparent can greatly change the role of the young adult within the family unit. In *A figure of speech* (Mazer), Jenny's grandfather has lived with her family since she was an infant. Jenny does not communicate with her parents but she does develop a special relationship with Grandpa. When she learns her family plans to move him to a nursing home, she tries to help Grandpa move back to his boyhood farm. They stay in the unoccupied farmhouse. One night Jenny "dreams" she hears Grandpa say, "No use, Jenny." The next morning he is dead. Jenny returns home, but knows life will not be the same. Other books that center on a young adult's relationship with a grandparent and the teenager's changing role after the death of the grandparent are *Toby alone* (Branscum), *Duffy's rocks* (Fenton), *The loners* (Garden), and *The changes* (Rabin).

A ring of endless light by Madeleine L'Engle is a beautiful book in which the author relates the thoughts and feelings of sixteen-year-old Vicky Austin as she deals with the death of a family friend and her beloved grandfather. Throughout the narrative Vicky struggles with the questions of mortality. The book is not about fearing death, but living with it. Vicky comes to terms with the death of her grandfather and family friend, as well as that of a small girl who dies in her arms, by remembering the light that her grandfather had urged her to seek: "You have to give the darkness permission. It cannot take over otherwise. . . . You are to be a lightbearer. You are to choose the light."

The death of a sibling is sensitively portrayed in many young adult books.

Pudge in *Uncle Mike's boy* (Brooks) blames himself for his sister's death. Pudge turns to Uncle Mike, who is a steadying influence on the grief-stricken, guilt-ridden boy. *The year of the three-legged deer* (Clifford) is a story of guilt, responsibility, and prejudice. Takawsu, who is fourteen, and his younger sister, Chilili, live with their white father and Indian mother. When Chilili's pet deer escapes and Chilili is killed in the search for it, the family's life changes drastically. Takawsu feels guilty because he didn't help his sister look for the deer, his father takes responsibility for not fixing the pen, and his mother takes Takawsu and moves back to her tribe, which is forced to move farther west. No character is more influenced by the death of a sibling than Karana in *Island of the blue dolphins* (O'Dell). After most of the men in the village are killed, a boat comes to rescue the women and children of the island. When Karana realizes her brother Ramo is not aboard, she leaves the boat to search for him. The boat leaves the children on the island. Ramo is killed the next morning by a pack of wild dogs. Karana survives on her own until a boat finally comes to the island eighteen years later. *The magic moth* (Lee) is a book written for younger readers, but its sensitivity makes it appropriate for all ages. Maryanne, who has incurable heart disease, is one of five children in the Foss family. The beautiful story depicts the confusion all of the family members feel as they stand by the deathbed of Maryanne and watch a moth emerge from a cocoon Maryanne has kept through the winter. Just as the life leaves Maryanne's body, the moth "flutters to life."

ADOPTION. The adoption of a new family member provides confusion in relationships. *Edgar Allan* (Neufeld) is the story of a white family's love for and rejection of the three-year-old black child they have adopted. When Edgar Allan enters nursery school in the all-white community, the family experiences prejudice for the first time. When a cross is burned on the family's lawn, sixteen-year-old Mary Nell delivers an ultimatum: " . . . if he stays . . . I'll just leave." The family succumbs to the pressure and fear for the lives of the other children and returns Edgar Allan to the adoption agency. The two youngest children are shaken when their little brother is "given away." Michael, who is telling the story, and Mother feel the injustice done to Edgar Allan. In the end the rest of the community turns on the family for giving way under pressure. Other books tell of the recently publicized phenomenon of adopted children searching for their natural parents. In *Tell me no lies* (Colman), an adolescent searches for her real parents. In *Find a stranger, say goodbye* (Lowry), Natalie is planning a medical career, but before she can pursue it she feels compelled to find her biological parents. Although her home life has been happy and her adoptive parents disapprove, she begins her search.

TEENAGE AND NONFAMILY ADULT RELATIONSHIPS. Numerous young adult novels deal with the relationship between the teenager and the nonfamily adult. One of the best-known narratives is *The Pigman* (Zindel), in which John and

Lorraine befriend an eccentric old man called the Pigman. However, they take advantage of the friendship. While the Pigman is in the hospital they use his house for a party and invade his privacy by removing his dead wife's clothes from the closet where he has kept them for years. *The Pigman's Legacy* is the sequel. John and Lorraine befriend another old man who has been hiding from the Internal Revenue Service in the Pigman's house. They share many poignant experiences with him, and through these experiences discover the legacy the Pigman left for them. In *Better than laughter* (Aaron), a similar theme is expressed as two boys befriend an eccentric junkman. In *Lilith summer* (Irwin), a young girl is hired to take care of elderly Lilith, or so she thinks. Lilith, for her part, believes she has been hired to baby-sit for the girl. Even though the deception is discovered, a relationship grows. In *Remove the protective coating a little at a time* (Donovan), fourteen-year-old Harry, who has a difficult home life, meets Amelia, an elderly beggar.

> ☐ *We respect this audience of young adults and try to write with honesty, humor, and understanding. Ann says it helps to have raised four children. Lee says it helps to have survived one's own adolescence.*
> LEE HADLEY AND ANN IRWIN
> from a biographical sketch of the authors, under the pseudonym Hadley Irwin, of Moon and me

Most of the relationships between adolescents and adults are built on mutual need and caring. This is particularly true in Isabelle Holland's *Man without a face* and Frankcina Glass's *Marvin and Tige.* Tige is an orphaned street-wise black boy who meets Marvin, a white, alcoholic, dropout executive. A friendship is established based on their mutual need.

In Theodore Taylor's *The cay* the need is much more pronounced. Here the boy is white and prejudiced and the old man is black.

> *I was thinking that it was very strange for me, a boy from Virginia, to be lying beside this giant Negro out on the ocean. And I guess maybe Timothy was thinking the same thing.*
> *Once, our bodies touched. We both drew back, but I drew back faster. In Virginia, I knew they'd always lived in their sections of town, and us in ours.*

Phillip, a survivor of a shipwreck, is rescued by Timothy, a kind West Indian. Injured in the wreck, Phillip goes blind and must rely totally on Timothy. Timothy encourages Phillip by telling him the blindness will go away: "Once, ovah 'round Barbados, a mahn 'ad an outrageous crack on d'ead when a sailin' boom shift. Dis mahn was blin' too. Tree whole day 'e saw d'night. Den it true went away." But Phillip's blindness does not go away. However, the older man teaches the boy so well that even after Timothy's death Phillip is able to survive on the island by remembering the things Timothy told him. Finally he is rescued from the island, discovers his parents are alive, and after several operations regains his sight. He vows to return to the cay:

> *Someday, I'll charter a schooner out of Panama and explore the Evil's Mouth. I hope to find the lonely little island where Timothy is buried.*
>
> *Maybe I won't know it by sight, but when I go ashore and close my eyes, I'll know this was our own cay. I'll walk along east beach and out to the reef. I'll go up the hill to the row of palm trees and stand by his grave.*
>
> *I'll say, "Dis b'dat outrageous cay, eh, Timothy?"*

Humor

All people need to laugh. Paula Danziger, author of several funny books for young adults, says, "Laughter helps us with being invincible. As long as we can laugh, we can survive."

LAUGHING AT ONESELF. Paula Danziger has written several books that young adults, particularly young teens, find very funny. She has discovered what makes young adults laugh by remembering what made her laugh as an adolescent, by discussing humor with young adults, by observing them, and by collecting "clean, good jokes" told by and laughed at by teenagers.

> ☐ *Did you hear about the rodent who almost drowned and his brother had to give him mouse-to-mouse resuscitation?*
>
> *Did you hear the one about the guy who only works on Saturdays and Sundays because he's a candle trimmer and they only work on wick ends?*
>
> PAULA DANZIGER
>
> Can you sue your parents for malpractice?

Teenagers never fail to laugh at Danziger's books. Her characters undergo the everyday experiences of young adults at school, at home, at the library. In *The cat ate my gymsuit,* for example, Marcy believes she's "too fat and ugly" to get into a gymsuit. She has hundreds of excuses for not taking gym, from "I had been mugged on the way to school by a syndicate specializing in stolen gymsuits" to "My little brother had misplaced his security blanket and was using my gymsuit instead" to "The cat ate my gymsuit." When Ms. Finney, the kids' favorite teacher, is fired, Marcy and her friends decide upon twenty-three ways to show everyone how they feel about the firing: "Clog up the faculty-room toilets with *The New York Times* school supplements, . . . steal all the chalk in the entire school, . . . go to the guidance counselors and ask for guidance, . . . steal the faculty room coffee pot, . . . call all the major TV networks and have them cover the story, . . . cut school and then forge notes saying that we were absent because of cases of acute acne." Such incidents are familiar in the lives of the teenager. The readers can see themselves in the situations. Laughing with and at Marcy is like laughing at the teenager in each of us. Another Danziger title, *There's a bat in bunk five,* finds Marcy at summer camp with Ms. Finney as counselor.

The laughing-at-ourselves theme is found in many other humorous books for young adult readers. One example is Judie Angell's *In summertime it's Tuffy,* whose main character is reminiscent of Marcy in *The cat ate my gymsuit.* Tuffy is in summer camp, where she meets many comical bunkmates and participates in a variety of hilarious adventures. The book is particularly funny to young adults who have been to camp.

HUMOR WITH A MESSAGE. Many young adult humorous books have a message beyond the laughter, including three by Judie Angell. *Dear Lola or how to build your own family* is the story of six refugees from an orphanage who band together to form their own very humorous family. *Secret selves* is the warm story of two teenagers who are too shy to show their interest in each other. Finally, Julie calls Rusty on the phone under the pretense that she is trying to locate someone else. Rusty begins to play a similar game. The two become telephone friends, but remain aloof from each other during the school day. In *A word from our sponsor or my friend Alfred,* a boy discovers that a drinking mug is made of poisonous materials. He decides to alert consumers to the problem. In the process he must challenge his father's advertising agency. The story allows the reader to laugh and at the same time consider the serious problem of integrity.

Judy Blume has written many amusing and meaningful books for young adolescents. Margaret of *Are you there, God? It's me, Margaret* is the new girl in town. It's bad enough to be new in town, but to be experiencing the onset of puberty at the same time can be agonizing. The story is told with great sensitivity and humor that allow the young reader who is experiencing the same problems to laugh at them along with Margaret and her friends. The heroine of *Blubber* is fifth-grader Jill Brenner, whose classmates harass her. When another girl begins to show sympathy for Jill the students persecute her as well. Like most Judy Blume books, *Blubber* is funny, but hidden behind the humor is a moral message.

OUTWITTING ADULTS. Outwitting adults is a favorite humorous theme in young adult books. *From the mixed-up files of Mrs. Basil E. Frankweiler* (Konigsburg), a Newbery Medal book, is about a brother and a sister who run away from home and hide out in New York's Metropolitan Museum of Art. Their escapades in avoiding guards and employees and the deal they make before they go home are very funny. *Secrets of the shopping mall* (Peck) has much of the same humor. Two teenagers take refuge in a huge shopping mall and outwit suburbia.

LAUGHING AT AN EARLIER SELF. Many books allow teenage readers to look back on the days when they were even younger. The Soup books by Robert Newton Peck are bad-boy stories that are particularly amusing to preteen or early teenage males. *How to eat fried worms* by Thomas Rockwell is also funny to the same age group. Beverly Cleary's *Ramona, the pest* is a laugh fest for young adolescent girls. Ramona is five, and the silly book recounts her first few months in kindergarten. James Thurber has said that "humor is emotional chaos remembered in tranquillity," and this book allows the young adult reader to reflect on the emotional chaos of the first days in kindergarten in the relative tranquillity of young adulthood. The problems of Ramona are far enough removed, but still close enough, that they can be laughed at and understood by the young reader.

Looking at school days is one of the favorite humorous occupations of adolescents. There are two hilarious books that examine life in the classroom. Stanley Kiesel's *The war between the pitiful teachers and the splendid kids* is about the war at Scratchland School. The students are led by Skinny Malinky and are clearly the "white hats" of the tale; the teachers are led by Mr. Foreclosure and have The Status Quo Solidifier on their side. Big Alice, the hyena girl, is the heroine of the students and the terror of the teachers—after all, she has eaten one of them! Another comical book about school days, which, unfortunately, is already somewhat dated, is Ellen Conford's *The Alfred G. Graebner Memorial High School Handbook of Rules and Regulations.* This narrative about a girl's first year in high school as she copes with the rules and regulations will tickle the funny bone of many high school students and teachers. *Oom-pah* by William B. Crane looks at school life in a slightly different way. The book is about a California high school band that is invaded by a very funny, very large tuba player from Texas. The reader can't help liking Fred, the tuba player, even though he is constantly teasing, playing practical jokes, arriving late to half-time, and getting other students in trouble. The author is a former high school band master who is able to catch the humor and fun of being in a high school band. A very funny how-to book that allows young readers to laugh at themselves is Delia Ephron's *Teenage romance: Or how to die of embarrassment.* From the book young readers can learn how to (or how not to) have a crush, hide a pimple, talk to your mother, among many other humorous, true-to-life incidents in teenage life.

BAD-BOY AND BAD-GIRL BOOKS. The books of Walter Dean Myers are the bad-boy books of Harlem.[1] In a review of *Fast Sam, Cool Clyde, and Stuff,* a *Horn Book* reviewer commented, "The humorous and ironic elements of the book

---

[1] An excellent guide for teaching Walter Dean Myers' novels, prepared by Lou Willett Stanek, is available from Avon Books, Education Department, 959 Eighth Ave., New York, NY 10019.

give it the flavor of a Harlem Tom Sawyer or Penrod.'' The novels, which are written in black dialect, depict life in modern Harlem. In *Mojo and the Russians* the action begins with a trumped-up bicycle accident in which Dean hits Drusilla: ''Stupid child amost knock me clear out of this world! I walking along, minding not a soul's business in this whole world but my own, and along comes this child like a bat out of a dark place and send me flying in the middle of the street.'' Dean's friends convince him that he is in big trouble. Willie, a janitor in the university at which classified research is being conducted, is visited by a group of Russians. The boys imagine the worst. From these two early incidents the amusing narrative, filled with hyperbole, puns, and irony, takes off. Two other humorous books by Myers are *It ain't all for nothin'* and *The young landlords.*

Another bad-boy book for young adolescents, *The best Christmas pageant ever* by Barbara Robinson, is one of the funniest Christmas books ever written. It is about children who set about to destroy the Christmas pageant, but instead make it the best one ever.

The bad-boy (and -girl) books of Samuel Clemens (Mark Twain) are still very popular with young readers. According to a survey conducted by Ted Hipple and Bruce Bartholomew (1982), *The adventures of Huckleberry Finn* (1884) is the book most widely read by today's college freshmen. The humorous misadventures of Huck and his raftmate, the slave Jim, still provide some of the best belly laughs in print. *The adventures of Tom Sawyer* (and Becky Thatcher) gives the young adult a look into the rural past and an understanding of the timeless nature of childhood antics. One of Mark Twain's funniest and shortest books is *Pudd'nhead Wilson.* Its length makes it particularly good for reluctant readers. The story revolves around two boys who are born on the same day in 1830, one to a prosperous landowner the other to his mulatto slave. In an attempt to advance her child, the slave arranges to switch the two infants. The witty story unravels from that point.

HUMOR IN SCIENCE FICTION AND FANTASY. D. Manus Pinkwater's books for young adolescents are extraordinarily funny fantasy/science fiction adventures. In *Lizard music* the author mixes puns and absurdities with the fantastic tale of a child who attempts to track reality in a media-crazy environment. *Alan Mendelsohn, the boy from Mars* is a pseudo-science-fiction fantasy about Leonard, who is short, fat, and wrinkled. Poor Leonard is doomed to a life as an outcast until he meets Alan Mendelsohn. The adventures they experience are wild and hilarious. The classic George Orwell book *Animal farm* is a satire that is enjoyed by many older adolescent readers. In the book the revolt of the farmyard animals leads to the fall of the human owners. In *The dog days of Arthur Cane* (Bethancourt), Arthur is magically turned into a stray dog who learns more about life than he has learned in his sixteen years as an upper-middle-class Long Islander. *Tune in yesterday* is a time-travel novel by Bethancourt which takes two teenage jazz fans back to the 1940s. This humorous novel allows the reader to see the jazz era from the vantage point of the 1970s. (Ernesto T. Bethancourt is the pseudonym of singer-guitarist Tom Paisley, whose knowledge of the music scene makes this novel informative as well as entertaining.) Another book in this genre is the satire *The kryptonite kid* by Joseph Torchia. Jerry Chariot is the kryptonite kid, who writes letters to his hero, Superman. The book tells Jerry's story through the letters he writes. He dreams of being just like his hero and of watching his classmates express jealousy and amazement at his wondrous feats.

HUMOR IN MYSTERY AND SUSPENSE. One of the funniest series to be published in some time is the Doris Fein series by Ernesto T. Bethancourt. Doris is a liberated Nancy Drew with a wonderful sense of humor. The series includes *Doris Fein: Superspy; Doris Fein: Quartz boyar; Doris Fein: The mad samurai; Doris Fein: Deadly Aphrodite,* and *Doris Fein: Phantom of the casino.* As Doris describes herself in *Doris Fein: The mad samurai:*

> . . . *I'm hardly a typical Southern Californian, even though I am a native. The standard of beauty here in SoCal is well known. The girls all look like Barbie dolls: tall, blond, beautiful and without ever having had a pimple in their lives. I, on the other hand, am five feet four inches tall and, depending on my discipline, a teensy bit, or a whole lot, overweight.*

Another humorous book in the mystery genre is by Alan Rune Pettersson's *Frankenstein's Aunt.* Hanna Frankenstein, very tall and smoking a cigar, arrives to restore the sinister castle of her nephew. Her hope is to clear the family's blackened name. The results of her endeavors are suspenseful and funny. Lovers of the Frankenstein legend will laugh uproariously at this book. *Favorite haunts* by Charles Addams is a collection of spooky, sinister cartoons for spine-tingler fans.

HUMOROUS COLLECTIONS. Woody Allen's books are usually enjoyed by older teenagers. Three of the funniest are *Getting even,* a collection of his hilarious essays; *Without feathers,* an assortment of absurd commentaries on love, death, and humanity; and *Side effects,* another collection of short comic pieces.

High school students who have read Shakespeare with tears will appreciate Richard Armour's *Twisted tales from Shakespeare.* Though written in 1957, these offbeat summaries of Shakespearean plays are enjoyed by each new generation of high school students.

Many good collections of humor are available for adolescent readers. Two anthologies dealing with life in the classroom, *Tales out of school* and *More tales out of school,* edited by Helen S. Weiss and M. Jerry Weiss, include the humorous writing of Erma Bombeck, Woody Allen, Sam Levenson, and many others. In *Isaac Asimov's treasury of humor,* the well-known writer has assembled his favorite jokes, anecdotes, and limericks. *The fireside book of humorous poetry,* edited by William Cole, includes the poems of McGinley, Updike, Nash, Carroll, and many others. Another book edited by William Cole, with drawings by Tomi Ungerer, is *Beastly boys and ghastly girls.* This anthology includes poems about the terrible things children do, by Silverstein, Ciardi, and others. A third collection edited by Cole is *Oh, what nonsense!* The 821 nonsense verses in this book appeal to children of all ages. Lillian Morrison has edited a collection of verses for the autograph book, entitled *Best wishes, amen.* An unusual collection, *Bible stories you can't forget,* has been put together by Marshall Efron and Alfa-Betty Olsen and illustrated by Ron Barrett. Its eight stories from the Old and New Testaments are told with a great deal of wit, wisdom, and humor in modern idiomatic language.

Joke books have always been popular with young adults. Two current favorites are *The original preppy jokebook* by D. J. Arneson and E. Richard Churchill's *The bionic banana* (with Linda R. Churchill, illustrated by Carol Nicklaus), a book of jokes about fruits and vegetables. William Cole has compiled several joke books, including *Knock knocks: The most ever* and *Knock knocks you've never heard before,* both illustrated by Mike Thaler. Thaler has published some of his own joke books, such as *Funny bones: Cartoon monster riddles,* with pun-filled cartoons about Dracula, Frankenstein, King Kong, and many other monsters. The Snoopy books by Charles M. Schultz and the Doonesbury books by Gary Trudeau seem to retain their popularity with young readers over the years.

FUNNY BOOKS THAT ARE NOT WRITTEN PRIMARILY TO BE FUNNY. Numerous young adult books are not written to be primarily humorous, but reading them produces many good laughs. Paul Zindel's books are a good example. There is nothing comical about being a misfit, but the story of fifteen-year-old Chris Boyd in *Confessions of a teenage baboon* is the source of many chuckles as he moves with his mother, a practical nurse, from one live-in job to another. In *The undertaker's gone bananas* Zindel's teenage character goes through hysterically funny incidents. Though it is difficult to regard *The pigman* as humorous, it does provide the reader with many good laughs.

Robbie Branscum's books are delightful. The plots are interesting, the problems often seem insurmountable, but the characters provide the teenage reader with heartwarming laughter. Toby in *Toby, Granny and George* goes from one mysteriously funny incident to another. Nell in *To the tune of the hickory stick* is an earthy adolescent who will make readers laugh. Every page in *Johnny May* produces a new and amusing surprise.

    □   *I love the things of childhood—slow moving rivers, woods, fields and fishing poles, tall tales and mystery, long summer days and slipping away from the adult world into the world of children where the lines are boldly drawn.*
ROBBIE BRANSCUM
author of To the tune of the hickory stick, *in a biographical sketch from Doubleday and Company*

One would not normally think of a book about a shoplifting mother as humorous. However, the mother of Lee Bennett Hopkins' book *Mama* is a very funny character. Her ability to bamboozle train conductors, relatives, and employers produces much laughter.

Madeleine L'Engle is not usually considered an author of humor. However, her books about the Austin family, particularly *Meet the Austins* and *The moon by night,* are often amusing. The books are not written primarily to evoke laughter, but the adventures of the family as they take in orphaned Maggy Hamilton and go on a cross-country camping trip provide much fun for the reader.

Books that offer social commentary can also be humorous. A recent example is Byrd Baylor's *Yes is better than no.* The story is about three groups of people in Tucson, Arizona. The Papago Indians are attempting to understand and survive the Anglo environment. The American social workers are trying to help them, but make little effort to understand the Indians. And a group of militant Indians are in opposition to all Anglos, but do not understand their own people or their customs. The well-intentioned but wrong-headed actions of these three groups produce a funny commentary on the failure of people to understand one another. When one of the Indians, Mrs. Domingo, wins a swimming pool, for example, she uses it as a dwelling place for herself and her mentally ill daughter. The empty pool also provides the address needed by a neighbor to collect welfare checks. With all good intentions, the community bands together to fill the pool. As the pool is filled, the home and the address are lost.

Conclusion

☐ *Not all readers cry at the same author's words as he/ she describes a tragic situation. Emotions, especially as roused by reading, are very personal. We never know what triggers a strong response. Interests, attitudes, experiences, values affect reading responses.*
M. JERRY WEISS

coeditor of Tales out of school / *in a letter to the author* / *February 1982*

Those things that make readers "break out into tears or into song," in Bette Greens words, come from the experiences of their own lives. We don't all laugh, or cry, at the same things. Therefore, it is the responsibility of the teacher, the librarian, and the parent of the young adult to find a variety of books that are likely to produce laughter and tears. For the adolescent these books can provide an emotional outlet at the most emotional time in the human life cycle. A good laugh and a good cry can be very important.

Anthological Aside in Chapter 4

Frank, A. *Anne Frank: The diary of a young girl.* Doubleday, 1946. Pocket Books, 1978.

Titles Mentioned in Chapter 4

"Good Cry" Novels

Bennett, J. *Masks: A love story.* Watts, 1971.

Brancato, R. *Winning.* Knopf, 1977. Bantam, 1979.

Cleaver, V., and B. Cleaver. *Where the lilies bloom.* Lippincott, 1969. New American Library, 1974.

————. *Trial valley.* Lippincott, 1977. Bantam, 1978.

Darke, M. *First of midnight.* Seabury, 1977.

Greene, B. *Philip Hall likes me. I reckon maybe.* Dial, 1974. Dell, 1978.

————. *Summer of my German soldier.* Dial, 1973. Bantam, 1974.

Hanlon, E. *It's too late for sorry.* Bradbury, 1978. Dell, 1981.

Hayes, K., and A. Lazzarina. *Broken promise.* Putnam, 1978. Fawcett, 1978.

Hunter, M. *A sound of chariots.* Harper & Row, 1972. Avon, 1972.

Irwin, H. *Moon and me.* Atheneum, 1981.

Ish-kishor, S. *Our Eddie.* Pantheon, 1969.

Jones, A. *So nothing is forever.* Houghton Mifflin, 1974.

Kellogg, M. *Tell me that you love me, Junie Moon.* Farrar, Straus & Giroux, 1968. Popular Library, 1968.

Kerr, M. E. *Gentlehands.* Harper & Row, 1978.

Leahy, S. R. *Circle of love.* Putnam, 1980.

Lee, V. *The magic moth.* Seabury, 1972.

L'Engle, M. *A ring of endless light.* Farrar, Straus & Giroux, 1980. Dell, 1981.

Lingard, J. *Across the barricades.* T. Nelson, 1973. Penguin, 1973.

Mazer, H. *The war on Villa Street.* Delacorte, 1978. Dell, 1979.

O'Dell, S. *Kathleen, please come home.* Houghton Mifflin, 1978. Dell, 1980.

Paterson, K. *Bridge to Terabithia.* Crowell, 1977. Avon, 1979.

Peyton, K. M. *The Beethoven medal.* Crowell, 1971. Scholastic, 1974.

Segal, E. *Love story.* Harper & Row, 1970. Avon, 1977.

Sallis, S. *Only love.* Harper & Row, 1980.

Stoltz, M. S. *The edge of next year.* Harper & Row, 1974. Dell, 1979.

Windsor, P. *The summer before.* Harper & Row, 1973. Dell, 1973.

Developing Relationships

Aaron, C. *Better than laughter.* Harcourt Brace Jovanovich, 1972. Dell, 1973.

Angell, J. *Ronnie and Rosey.* Bradbury, 1977. Dell, 1979.

Annixter, P. *Swift water.* A. A. Wyn, 1950. Paperback Library, 1965.

Arundel, H. *The blanket word.* T. Nelson, 1973. Dell, 1975.

————. *A family failing.* T. Nelson, 1972. Scholastic, 1972.

Bates, B. *Bugs in your ears.* Holiday, 1977. Pocket Books, 1979.

————. *The ups and downs of Jorie Jenkins.* Holiday, 1978. Pocket Books, 1981.

Blume, J. *It's not the end of the world.* Bradbury, 1972. Bantam, 1980.

———. *Tales of a fourth grade nothing.* Dutton, 1972. Dell, 1979.

Bonham, F. *Durango Street.* Dutton, 1965. Dell, 1972.

Bradbury, B. *The blue year.* Ives Washburn, 1967.

———. *The loner.* Houghton Mifflin, 1970.

Bradford, R. *Red sky at morning.* Lippincott, 1968. Pocket Books, 1969.

Brancato, R. *Something left to lose.* Knopf, 1976. Bantam, 1979.

Branscum, R. *Toby alone.* Doubleday, 1979. Avon, 1980.

Bridgers, S. E. *Home before dark.* Knopf, 1976. Bantam, 1977.

———. *Notes for another life.* Knopf, 1981.

Brooks, J. *Uncle Mike's boy.* Harper & Row, 1973.

Byars, B. *The night swimmers.* Delacorte, 1980. Dell, 1980.

Cleaver, V., and B. Cleaver. *Ellen Grae.* Lippincott, 1967. New American Library, 1978.

———. *Grover.* Lippincott, 1970. New American Library, 1975.

———. *Lady Ellen Grae.* Lippincott, 1968. New American Library, 1978.

———. *Trial Valley.* Lippincott, 1977. Bantam, 1978.

———. *Where the lilies bloom.* Lippincott, 1969. New American Library, 1974.

Clifford, E. R. *The year of the three-legged deer.* Houghton Mifflin, 1972. Dell, 1973.

Colman, N. *Tell me no lies.* Crown, 1978. Pocket Books, 1980.

Corcoran, B. *Hey, that's my soul you're stomping on.* Atheneum, 1978.

———. *This is a recording.* Atheneum, 1971.

Cormier, R. *The chocolate war.* Pantheon, 1974. Dell, 1975.

Danziger, P. *Can you sue your parents for malpractice?* Delacorte, 1979. Dell, 1980.

deJongh, J., and C. Cleveland. *City cool.* Random House, 1978.

Donovan, J. *Remove the protective coating a little at a time.* Harper & Row, 1973. Dell, 1975.

Duncan, L. *Killing Mr. Griffin.* Little, Brown, 1978. Dell, 1979.

Elfman, B. *The sister act.* Houghton Mifflin, 1978. Bantam, 1979.

Fenton, E. *Duffy's rocks.* Dutton, 1974.

Frank, A. *Anne Frank: The diary of a young girl.* Doubleday, 1952.

Garden, N. *The loners.* Viking, 1972. Avon, 1974.

Gauch, P. L. *The green of me.* Putnam, 1978.

Girion, B. *A tangle of roots.* Scribner's, 1979. Dell, 1981.

Glass, F. *Marvin and Tige.* St. Martin's, 1977. Fawcett, 1977.

Guy, R. *The friends.* Holt, Rinehart & Winston, 1973. Bantam, 1974.

Hinton, S. E. *The outsiders.* Viking, 1967. Dell, 1980.

———. *Rumble fish.* Delacorte, 1975. Dell, 1976.

———. *Tex.* Delacorte, 1979. Dell, 1980.

Holland, I. *Man without a face.* Lippincott, 1972. Dell, 1980.

———. *Of love and death and other journeys.* Lippincott, 1975. Dell, 1977.

Hopkins, L. B. *Mama.* Knopf, 1977. Dell, 1978.

Hunter, M. *A sound of chariots.* Harper & Row, 1972. Avon, 1972.

Irwin, H. *Bring to a boil and separate.* Atheneum, 1980.

———. *Lilith summer.* Feminist Press, 1979.

———. *Moon and me.* Atheneum, 1981.

———. *What about Grandma?* Atheneum, 1982.

Johnson, A. *Count me gone.* Simon and Schuster, 1968.

Karl, J. *Beloved Benjamin is waiting.* Dutton, 1978. Dell, 1980.

Kerr, M. E. *Dinky Hocker shoots smack!* Harper & Row, 1972. Dell, 1978.
———. *Gentlehands.* Harper & Row, 1978. Bantam, 1979.
Kingman, L. *Break a leg, Betsy Maybe!* Houghton Mifflin, 1976. Dell, 1979.
Klein, N. *Mom, the Wolfman, and me.* Pantheon, 1972. Avon, 1982.
———. *Taking sides.* Pantheon, 1974. Avon, 1982.
Konigsburg, E. L. *From the mixed-up files of Mrs. Basil E. Frankweiler.* Atheneum, 1967. Dell, 1977.
Lee, M. *Fog.* Houghton Mifflin, 1972. Dell, 1974.
———. *The rock and the willow.* Lothrop, 1963. Washington Square Press, 1970.
Lee, V. *The magic moth.* Houghton Miffin, 1972. Seabury, 1972.
L'Engle, M. *A ring of endless light.* Farrar, Straus & Giroux, 1980. Dell, 1981.
———. *Summer of the great grandmother.* Farrar, Straus, & Giroux, 1974. Seabury Press, 1979.
Lowry, L. *Find a stranger, say goodbye.* Houghton Mifflin, 1978. Pocket Books, 1978.
Mathis, S. B. *Teacup full of roses.* Viking, 1972. Avon, 1972.
Mazer, H. *Guy Lenny.* Delacorte, 1971. Dell, 1977.
Mazer, N. F. *A figure of speech.* DeLacorte, 1973. Dell, 1975.
Medearis, M. *Big Doc's girl.* Lippincott, 1942. Pyramid, 1974.
Neufeld, J. *Edgar Allan.* Phillips, 1968. New American Library, 1969.
———. *Sunday father.* New American Library, 1976.
O'Dell, S. *Child of fire.* Houghton Mifflin, 1974. Dell, 1978.
———. *Island of the blue dolphins.* Houghton Mifflin, 1960. Dell, 1975.
Ogilvie, E. *The pigeon pair.* McGraw-Hill, 1967.
Pascal, F. *Hangin' out with Cici.* Viking, 1977. Pocket Books, 1978.
Paterson, K. *Bridge to Terabithia.* Crowell, 1977. Avon, 1979.
———. *Jacob have I loved.* Crowell, 1980. Avon, 1981.
Peck, R. N. *A day no pigs would die.* Knopf, 1972. Dell, 1978.
Peck, R. *Father figure.* Viking, 1978. New American Library, 1979.
Pevsner, S. *And you give me a pain, Elaine.* Seabury, 1978. Pocket Books, 1981.
Peyton, K. M. *A midsummer night's death.* Philomel Books, 1979. Dell, 1981.
Platt, K. *The boy who could make himself disappear.* Chilton, 1968. Dell, 1972.
———. *Chloris and the creeps.* Chilton, 1973. Dell, 1974.
———. *Chloris and the freaks.* Bradbury, 1975. Bantam, 1976.
———. *Chloris and the weirdos.* Bradbury, 1978. Bantam, 1980.
———. *Headman.* Greenwillow, 1975. Dell, 1978.
Rabin, G. *The changes.* Harper & Row, 1973.
Schotter, R. *A matter of time.* Collins, 1979. Grosset & Dunlap, 1981.
Schwartz, S. *Growing up guilty.* Random House, 1978.
Sebestyen, O. *Far from home.* Little, Brown, 1980.
Shreve, S. *The masquerade.* Knopf, 1980.
Speare, E. *The witch of Blackbird Pond.* Houghton Mifflin, 1958. Dell, 1975.
Stein, S. *The magician.* Delacorte, 1971. Dell, 1972.
Stolz, M. S. *Leap before you look.* Harper & Row, 1972. Dell, 1972.
Taylor, T. *The cay.* Doubleday, 1969. Avon, 1970.
Thompson, T. *Richie.* Saturday Review Press, 1973. Dell, 1981.
Wersba, B. *Run softly, go fast.* Atheneum, 1970. Bantam, 1972.
Zindel, P. *The pigman.* Harper & Row, 1968. Bantam, 1978.
———. *The pigman's legacy.* Harper & Row, 1980. Bantam, 1981.

Humor

Addams, C. *Favorite haunts.* Simon & Schuster, 1976.

Allen, W. *Getting even.* Random House, 1971. Warner, 1976.

————. *Without feathers.* Random House, 1975. Warner, 1976.

————. *Side effects.* Random House, 1980. Ballantine, 1981.

Angell, J. *Dear Lola or how to build your own family: A tale.* Bradbury, 1980. Dell, 1982.

————. *In summertime it's Tuffy.* Bradbury, 1977. Dell, 1979.

————. *Secret selves.* Bradbury, 1979. Dell, 1981.

————. *A word from our sponsor or my friend Alfred.* Bradbury, 1979. Dell, 1981.

Arneson, D. J. *The original preppy jokebook.* Dell, 1982.

Armour, R. *Twisted tales from Shakespeare.* McGraw-Hill, 1957. New American Library, 1966.

Asimov, I. *Isaac Asimov's treasury of humor.* Houghton Mifflin, 1971, 1979.

Baylor, B. *Yes is better than no.* Scribner's, 1977. Avon, 1980.

Bethancourt, E. T. *Doris Fein: Deadly Aphrodite.* Holiday, 1982.

————. *Doris Fein: Superspy.* Holiday, 1980.

————. *Doris Fein: Quartz boyar.* Holiday, 1980.

————. *Doris Fein: Phantom of the casino.* Holiday, 1981.

————. *Doris Fein: The mad samurai.* Holiday, 1981.

————. *The dog days of Arthur Cane.* Holiday, 1976. Bantam, 1981.

————. *Tune in yesterday.* Holiday, 1978. Bantam, 1978.

Blume, J. *Are you there, God? It's me, Margaret.* Bradbury, 1970. Dell, 1980.

————. *Blubber.* Bradbury, 1974. Dell, 1979.

Branscum, R. *Johnny May.* Doubleday, 1975. Avon, 1976.

————. *Toby, Granny and George.* Doubleday, 1976. Avon, 1977.

————. *To the tune of the hickory stick.* Doubleday, 1978.

Churchill, E. R., and L. R. Churchill. *The bionic banana.* Illustrated by C. Nicklaus. Watts, 1979. Dell, 1981.

Cleary, B. *Ramona, the pest.* Morrow, 1968. Scholastic, 1968.

Clemens, S. *The adventures of Huckleberry Finn* (1884). Bantam, 1981.

————. *The adventures of Tom Sawyer* (1876). Bantam, 1981.

————. *Pudd'nhead Wilson* (1894). Bantam, 1981.

Cole, W. *Knock knock: The most ever.* Illustrated by M. Thaler. Watts, 1976. Dell, 1977.

————. *Knock knocks you've never heard before.* Illustrated by M. Thaler. Watts, 1974. Dell, 1977.

————, ed. *Beastly boys and ghastly girls.* Illustrated by T. Ungerer. Dell, 1977. World, 1964.

————, ed. *The fireside book of humorous poetry.* Simon & Schuster, 1959.

————, ed. *Oh, what nonsense!* Viking, 1966.

Conford, E. *The Alfred G. Graebner Memorial High School Handbook of Rules and Regulations.* Little, Brown, 1976. Pocket Books, 1977.

Crane, W. B. *Oom-pah.* Atheneum, 1981.

Danziger, P. *Can you sue your parents for malpractice?* Delacorte, 1979. Dell, 1980.

————. *The cat ate my gymsuit.* Delacorte, 1974. Dell, 1979.

————. *There's a bat in bunk five.* Delacorte, 1980. Dell, 1982.

Efron, M., and A. B. Olsen. *Bible stories you can't forget, no matter how hard you try.* Illustrated by R. Barrett. Dutton, 1976. Dell, 1979.

Ephron, D. *Teenage romance: Or how to die of embarrassment.* Viking, 1981.

Hopkins, L. B. *Mama.* Knopf, 1977. Dell, 1978.

Hotcher, A. E. *Looking for miracles: A memoir about loving.* Harper & Row, 1975.

Kiesel, S. *The war between the pitiful teachers and the splendid kids.* Dutton, 1980. Avon, 1982.

Konigsburg, E. L. *From the mixed-up file of Mrs. Basil E. Frankweiler.* Atheneum, 1967. Dell, 1977.

L'Engle, M. *Meet the Austins.* Vanguard, 1960. Dell, 1981.

————. *The moon by night.* Farrar, Straus & Giroux, 1963. Dell, 1981.

Morrison, L. *Best wishes, amen.* Crowell, 1974.

Myers, W. D. *Fast Sam, Cool Clyde, and Stuff.* Viking, 1975. Avon, 1978.

————. *Mojo and the Russians.* Viking, 1977. Avon, 1977.

————. *It ain't all for nothin'.* Viking, 1978. Avon, 1979.

————. *The young landlords.* Viking, 1979. Avon, 1980.

Orwell, G. *Animal farm* (1945). New American Library, 1974.

Peck, R. *Secrets of the shopping mall.* Delacorte, 1979. Dell, 1980.

————. *Soup.* Knopf, 1974. Dell, 1979.

————. *Soup and me.* Knopf, 1975. Dell, 1979.

Pettersson, A. R. *Frankenstein's aunt* (1978). Translated by J. Tate. Little Brown, 1980.

Pinkwater, D. M. *Alan Mendelsohn, the boy from Mars.* Dutton, 1979. Bantam, 1981.

————. *Lizard music.* Dodd, Mead, 1976. Dell, 1978.

Robinson, B. *The best Christmas pageant ever.* Illustrated by J. G. Brown. Harper & Row, 1972. Avon, 1979.

Rockwell, T. *How to eat fried worms.* Franklin Watts, 1973. Dell, 1980.

Thaler, M. *Funny bones: Cartoon monster riddles.* Watts, 1976. Dell, 1978.

Torchia, J. *The kryptonite kid.* Holt, Rinehart & Winston, 1979, 1980.

Weiss, H. S., and M. J. Weiss, eds. *Tales out of school.* Dell, 1967. Dell, 1978.

————. *More tales out of school.* Bantam, 1980.

Zindel, P. *Confessions of a teenage baboon.* Harper & Row, 1977. Bantam, 1978.

————. *The undertaker's gone bananas.* Harper & Row, 1978. Bantam, 1979.

————. *The pigman.* Harper & Row, 1968. Bantam, 1978.

Suggested Readings

Carlsen, G. R. *Books and the teenage reader,* 2nd rev. ed. Harper & Row, 1980. Bantam, 1980.

Donelson, K. L., and A. P. Nilsen. *Literature for today's young adults.* Scott Foresman, 1980.

Harada, V. H. A selective list of Japanese literature titles for high school readers. In Donelson (ed.), *Arizona English Bulletin,* April 1976, pp. 116–21.

Hipple, T., and B. Bartholomew. The novels college freshmen have read. *ALAN Review,* Winter 1982, pp. 8–10.

Hopkins, L. B. *The best of "Book Bonanza."* Holt, Rinehart & Winston, 1980.

Peck, R. Some thoughts on adolescent literature. *News from ALAN,* September–October 1975, pp. 4–7.

Weiss, M., ed. *From writers to students: The pleasures and pains of writing.* International Reading Association, 1979.

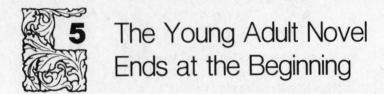

5 The Young Adult Novel Ends at the Beginning

The Rite of Passage

A distinguishing feature of the young adult novel, according to Richard Peck, is that "it needs to end at a beginning . . ." (1975, p. 6). The fifteen-year-old has not yet begun to live life; the best and worst still lie ahead. The events of the young adult novel, therefore, must prepare the reader and the book's protagonist for a life yet to be lived.

Adolescence is a period of transition from the usually carefree life of childhood to the increased responsibility of adulthood. During this phase young adults experiences isolation, socialization, confusion, and rebellion. They desire to return to dependence on the family and at the same time to forge ahead into the unknown. Teenagers seek the support of a peer group and at the same moment are fiercely individualistic and independent. In past civilizations this period in life was celebrated by an initiation or rite-of-passage ceremony. Today, in our society, the passage is unceremonious, often difficult for adolescents, and usually painful for parents. Even though the rite of passage is no longer celebrated, it is still categorized by three stages, outlined by Hugh Agee (1973): the separation from childhood, the transition, and the incorporation into the adult community. For the young adult these three stages denote an ending of one life and the beginning of a new life.

Literature is one means by which the adolescent can explore the passage

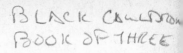

from childhood to adulthood. The characters in young adult books face many of the problems of transition and allow young adults to examine themselves using the book's protagonist as a model.

> ☐ *A [good young adult] book should speak to readers not only where they are . . . but where they will be.*
> LLOYD ALEXANDER
> *author of* The Kestrel / *in a speech to the National Council of Teachers of English /* November 1982

Separation from Childhood

The processes of physical and emotional development that mark the separation from childhood are common themes in novels written for preteens and young teens. The challenges boys face in growing up are dealt with in Judy Blume's *Then again, maybe I won't,* Ray Bradbury's *Dandelion wine,* Robert Lipsyte's *One fat summer,* and John Powers's *Do black patent leather shoes really reflect up?* These books deal with everything from wet dreams, first drinks, and girls to acne and overweight. All of them reflect on the emotional problems stemming from physical maturation.

In *Then again, maybe I won't,* Tony is thirteen and has moved to a new neighborhood. He is thrown together with the boy next door, Joel, who introduces him to pornographic books and booze. Tony is not sure what he thinks about his new friend. He worries about his new life and his physical maturation. He is concerned about the erections and wet dreams he cannot control. He likes to think about girls, but dislikes himself for looking into Joel's sister's window while she undresses. He is upset that his mother believes Joel is a gentleman because of his good manners. All these concerns result in Tony's "nervous stomach." When his brother decides to leave his teaching job to take a high-paying job with his father, Tony is upset. His stomach pains grow worse, and he finally ends up in the hospital. During his stay his physician recommends that he see a psychiatrist, who will help him understand and cope with his normal problems.

Problems girls face in dealing with physical maturation are far more common in young adult literature than problems boys face. Judy Blume has provided two frank, cutting-edge books in *Are you there, God? It's me, Margaret* and *Deenie.* The importance of beauty has always been emphasized for Deenie. Both she and her mother panic when they discover Deenie has a curvature of the spine and must wear a back brace. The book talks frankly about the fitting of the brace, the difficulty Deenie has adjusting to it, and her concern that she is no longer beautiful. Margaret's problems in *Are you there, God? It's me, Margaret* are not unusual for an eleven-year-old girl. She has just moved to a new neighborhood and is forced to deal with the onset of puberty while she is adjusting to new friends and a new school. Margaret's mixed-faith parents do not attend

Two preteenage girls share their enjoyment of Judy Blume's books.

church as her friends' parents do, and she wonders whether she is Christian or Jewish. Her parents want her to decide for herself, but Margeret finds she is torn between her two grandmothers. She, like all young adults, seeks independence and at the same time demands answers from the adults in her life. Throughout the book she talks to God about religion, menstruation, wearing a bra, and anything else that is troubling her.

Other books about girls facing the problems of their emerging maturity are *The trouble with thirteen* (Miles), *Don't look and it won't hurt* (Peck), *The long secret* (Fitzhugh), *I was a ninety-eight-pound duckling* (Van Leeuwen), and *Leap before you look* (Stolz).

The Transitional Phase

Once young adults have been separated from childhood, a lonely, frustrating transitional phase often begins. Now teenagers learn about themselves and how to fit into the adult society. This period is a time of continual testing. The teenager evaluates and questions long-held values and beliefs. The value system of the family must be meshed with that of the peer group. As the stage of transition progresses, the adolescent begins, more and more, to acquire the freedom and responsibility of adulthood.

■ ■ ■ **An Anthological Aside**

Let Me Be Like Everybody Else

JUDY BLUME

One week later Gretchen got it. We had a special PTS meeting that afternoon.

"I got it last night, Can you tell?" she asked us.

"Oh, Gretchen! You lucky!" Nancy shrieked. "I was sure I'd be first. I've got more than you!"

"Well, that doesn't mean much," Gretchen said, knowingly.

"How did it happen?" I asked.

"Well, I was sitting there eating my supper when I felt like something was dripping from me."

"Go on—go on," Nancy said.

"Well, I ran to the bathroom, and when I saw what it was I called my mother."

"And?" I asked.

"She yelled that she was eating."

"So—so—" Nancy prompted.

"So . . . uh . . . she came and I showed her," Gretchen said.

"Then what?" Janie asked.

"Well, she didn't have any stuff in the house. She uses Tampax herself—so she had to call the drugstore and order some pads."

"What'd you do in the meantime?" Janie asked.

"Kept a wash cloth in my pants," Gretchen said.

"Oh—you didn't!" Nancy said, laughing.

"Well, I had to," Gretchen said.

"Okay—so then what?" I asked.

"Well . . . in about an hour the stuff came from the drugstore."

"Then what?" Nancy asked.

"My mother showed me how to attach the pad to the belt. Oh . . . you know . . ."

Nancy was mad. "Look, Gretchen, did we or did we not make a deal to tell each other absolutely everything about getting it?"

"I'm telling you, aren't I?" Gretchen asked.

"Not enough," Nancy said. "What's it feel like?"

"Mostly I don't feel anything. Sometimes it feels like it's dripping. It doesn't hurt coming out—but I had some cramps last night."

From July Blume, *Are you there, God? It's me, Margaret* (New York: Bradbury Press, 1970), pp. 97–101, 132–133. Reprinted with permission of Bradbury Press, Inc. Copyright © 1970 by Judy Blume.

"Bad ones?" Janie asked.

"Not bad. Just different." Gretchen said. "Lower down, and across my back."

"Does it make you feel older?" I asked.

"Naturally," Gretchen answered. "My mother said now I'll really have to watch what I eat because I've gained too much weight this year. And she said to wash my face well from now on—with soap."

"And that's it?" Nancy said. "The whole story?"

"I'm sorry if I've disappointed you, Nancy, But really, that's all there is to tell. Oh, one thing I forgot. My mother said I may not get it every month yet. Sometimes it takes a while to get regular."

"Are you using that Private Lady stuff?" I asked.

"No, the drugstore sent *Teenage Softies*."

"Well, I guess I'll be next," Nancy said.

Janie and I looked at each other. We guessed so too.

When I went home I told my mother. "Gretchen Potter got her period."

"Did she really?" my mother asked.

"Yes," I said.

"I guess you'll begin soon too."

"How old were you Mom—when you got it?"

"Uh . . . I think I was fourteen."

"Fourteen! That's crazy. I'm not waiting until I'm fourteen."

"I'm afraid there's not much you can do about it, Margaret. Some girls menstruate earlier than others. I had a cousin who was sixteen before she started."

"Do you suppose that could happen to me? I'll die if it does!"

"If you don't start by the time you're fourteen I'll take you to the doctor. Now stop worrying!"

"How can I stop worrying when I don't know if I'm going to turn out normal?"

"I promise, you'll turn out normal."

ARE YOU THERE GOD? IT'S ME, MARGARET. GRETCHEN, MY FRIEND, GOT HER PERIOD. I'M SO JEALOUS GOD. I HATE MYSELF FOR BEING SO JEALOUS, BUT I AM. I WISH YOU'D HELP ME JUST A LITTLE. NANCY'S SURE SHE'S GOING TO GET IT SOON, TOO. AND IF I'M LAST I DON'T KNOW WHAT I'LL DO. OH PLEASE GOD. I JUST WANT TO BE NORMAL.

Nancy and her family went to Washington over Lincoln's birthday weekend. I got a postcard from her before she got back which means she must have mailed it the second she got there. It only had three words on it.

I GOT IT!!!

I ripped the card into tiny shreds and ran to my room. There was something wrong with me. I just knew it. And there wasn't a thing I could do about it. I flopped onto my bed and cried. Next week Nancy would want to tell me all about her period and about how grown up she was. Well, I didn't want to hear her good news!

ARE YOU THERE GOD? IT'S ME, MARGARET. LIFE IS GETTING WORSE EVERY DAY. I'M GOING TO BE THE ONLY ONE WHO DOESN'T GET IT. I KNOW IT GOD. JUST LIKE I'M THE ONLY ONE WITHOUT A RELIGION. WHY CAN'T YOU HELP ME? HAVEN'T I ALWAYS DONE WHAT YOU WANTED? PLEASE ... LET ME BE LIKE EVERYBODY ELSE ...

. . . . .

Then my mother excused herself to pay the lady in the kitchen, who signaled that her taxi was waiting out front. So my grandmother turned on me.

"Do you like school?" she asked.

"Most of the time," I said.

"Do you get good marks?"

"Pretty good," I said.

"How do you do in Sunday school?"

My mother came back into the den then and sat down next to me.

"I don't go to Sunday school," I said.

"You don't?"

"No."

"Father ..." (That's what Grandmother called Grandfather. He called her "Mother.")

"What is it, Mother?" Grandfather said.

"Margaret doesn't go to Sunday school." Grandmother shook her head and played with her cross.

"Look," my mother said, trying a smile. "You know we don't practice any religion."

Here it comes, I thought. I wanted to leave the room then but I felt like I was glued to my seat.

"We hoped by now you'd changed your minds about religion," Grandfather said.

"Especially for Margaret's sake," Grandmother added. "A person's got to have religion."

"Let's not get into a philosophical discussion," my father said, annoyed. He sent my mother a warning look across the room.

Grandfather laughed. "I'm not being a philosopher, Herb."

"Look," my mother explained, "we're letting Margaret choose her own religion when she's grown."

"If she wants to!" my father said, defiantly.

"Nonsense!" Grandmother said. "A person doesn't choose religion."

"A person's born to it!" Grandfather boomed.

Grandmother smiled at last and gave a small laugh. "So Margaret is Christian!" she announced, like we all should have known.

"Please . . ." my mother said. "Margaret could just as easily be Jewish. Don't you see—if you keep this up you're going to spoil everything."

"I don't mean to upset you, dear," Grandmother told my mother. "But a child is always the religion of the mother. And you, Barbara, were born Christian. You were baptized. It's that simple."

"Margaret is nothing!" my father stormed. "And I'll thank you for ending this discussion right now."

I didn't want to listen anymore. How could they talk that way in front of me! Didn't they know I was a real person—with feelings of my own!

■ ■ ■

THE TEENAGE BOY IN TRANSITION. Males have been much more common as protagonists in transitional literature than females, as in the two classic coming-of-age books *The catcher in the rye* (Salinger) and *A separate peace* (Knowles).

Literature about the teenage male in transition often involves the actual journey from one physical setting to another. This journey is symbolic of the passage from childhood to adulthood. In Kathryn Borland's and Helen Speicher's *Goodbye to Stony Crick,* Jeremy moves from Appalachia to Chicago. Josh in Richard Bradford's *Red sky at morning* moves from the South to a little town in New Mexico where he passes from childhood to adulthood as he and his mother wait out World War II. In *I'll get there. It better be worth the trip* by John Donovan, Davy moves to New York City after the death of a beloved grandmother. In Paula Fox's *The slave dancer,* Jessie is kidnapped and taken aboard a slave ship bound for Africa. Forced to play his fife so that the slaves will dance and not lose their physical condition, Jessie struggles with the conflicting emotions of compassion and hate. *Summer of '42* by Herman Raucher is spent on the beach. During summer vacation three adolescent boys play the games of children while learning the lessons of adulthood. Katherine Paterson's *Bridge to Terabithia* uses a vine and a bridge across a river to symbolize the passage beyond childhood. In *A solitary blue* by Cynthia Voigt two trips to visit his mother, who abandoned the family, symbolize Jeff's emergence. The solitary blue heron he sees near his mother's home becomes Jeff's symbol for himself.

☐ *And whatever adversity life may bring, the young person must cast off the bonds of fear and have courage. He must reach down in himself to find strength. . . .*
MARGARET A. EDWARDS

author of The fair garden and the swarm of beasts / *in* ALAN Newsletter / *Winter 1975*

Other narratives that center on the journey from boyhood to adulthood include Frank Bonham's *Durango Street*. Rufus, on probation for auto theft, is warned by his probation officer not to join a gang. Rufus knows, however, that he needs the gang for safety. When he is picked up by the police the night of his induction into the gang, he is not arrested. Instead, Alex Robbins, a special officer, is assigned to Rufus's gang to channel its energies into constructive activities. Rufus decides ultimately to cooperate with Alex, and in the process he learns lessons that lead to his emerging adulthood. *Hoops* by Walter Dean Myers deals with growing up on the streets of Harlem. Lonnie Jackson is seventeen and sees basketball as his way out of the ghetto. As in many coming-of-age novels, an adult, in this case a coach who is a frustrated basketball player, helps Lonnie see his dreams for what they are—dreams. Other young adult novels about male transition include *The chocolate war* (Cormier), *The owl's song* (Hale), *I'm really dragged but nothing gets me down* (Hentoff), *That was then, this is now* and *Tex* (Hinton), *Come alive at 505* (Brancato), *If I love you, am I trapped forever?* and *The son of someone famous* (Kerr), *Fog* (Lee), *No moccasins today* (Lockett), *A day no pigs would die* (Peck), *The chosen* (Potok), *Good night, Prof, dear* (Townsend), and *Confessions of a teenage baboon* (Zindel).

A recent transition book reminiscent of Knowles's *A separate peace* is *At the shores* by Thomas Rogers. It tells the story of Jerry Engles, a student in the Chicago Laboratory School of the 1940s. Jerry, like many boys who are approaching adulthood, finds women baffling and is not quite sure how to react to them or to his feelings. The book helps readers understand that the experiences of the young adult are universal, even though the time and the environment change. In the 1981 *Books for young adults* poll one young female respondent commented about this book, "Guys are still just like that." *Far from shore* by Kevin Major takes place in a small town in Newfoundland. The experiences of Chris and the reactions of Jennifer, Mother, Dad, and Reverend Wheaton to Chris's behavior prove that the pain of growing up is experienced in all cultures. Chris blames his problems on everyone and everything other than himself. Through the support of his friends and family, who never make excuses for his behavior, he learns to face the consequences of his actions and accept responsibility for his problems.

THE TEENAGE GIRL IN TRANSITION. Girls in transition are increasingly the protagonists of young adult novels. As with male protagonists, the female's journey often spans not only time but distance. In Jean Craighead George's *Julie of the wolves* thirteen-year-old Julie travels from the home of her Eskimo husband to the home of her father in search of herself. In *Mr. and Mrs. Bo Jo Jones* by Ann Head, two young adults move from their parents' homes to their own apartment and struggle to maintain a marriage as they continue to grow away from each other. In Isabelle Holland's *Of love and death and other journeys,* Peg must leave the home of the mother she has loved and move in with the father she has never known. Julie's journey in *Up a road slowly* by Irene Hunt begins when she is seven years old and ends when she is seventeen. During her journey to adulthood her mother dies and she is sent to live with her strict Aunt Cordelia. She visits her married sister to discover that their once close relationship has changed, and she travels on a train after the visit with her sister. On the train she meets a friendly conductor who helps her understand that she must think of making others happy before she can be truly happy herself. Julie's father remarries, and she visits with him and her stepmother, of whom she is fond. She contemplates moving in with them but realizes she is out of place. Discovering that she loves Aunt Cordelia, she makes her home with her while she works on her dream of becoming a writer.

☐ *They [adolescents] have left the Garden of Eden and seen their own nakedness, just as Adam and Eve in that parable of growing up.*
KATIE LETCHER LYLE
author of Finders weepers / *in* News from ALAN / *March–April 1975*

Another book that uses a trip as a symbol of a girl's transition to adulthood is *The green of me* by Patricia Lee Gauch. As Jenny travels to meet her sweetheart, she recalls the joys and pains of her growing-up years. In Bette Greene's *Morning is a long time coming,* Patty travels to Europe to find the parents of her German soldier. The search for the parents becomes a search for herself. In *The runaway's diary* by Marilyn Harris, sixteen-year-old Cat runs away from her parents, ends up in an accident on a Canadian highway, and in the process learns many things about herself. In Katie Lyle's *I will go barefoot all summer for you,* Jessie is lonely and lives with her cousin. Like many young adults, she dreams of becoming famous. When Toby comes to visit, she falls in love and decides to travel by cab to see him. In *The April age* by Lavinia Russ, Peakie is almost eighteen in 1925. She is full of dreams and fantasies about life and men and love. On a trip to Europe she meets a handsome British lord, and through this introduction she meets herself. The heroine of *Homecoming* and *Dicey's Song* (Voigt) travels with only her younger siblings in search of a new home. She finds that home with Gram in a run-down farm on Chesapeake Bay.

In the Newbery Medal winner *Jacob have I loved* (Paterson), Wheeze has a twin sister, Caroline, to whom she has always felt second. Through most of the book takes place on an island in the Chesapeake Bay, much of Wheeze's acceptance of herself occurs during or after journeys. She spends much of her growing-up time on a crabbing boat with Call, who later marries Caroline. Wheeze travels to the mainland to continue her education and learns it will be impossible for her to become a doctor as she has dreamed. Instead, she moves to remote western Virginia and serves as a midwife. It is after this journey that she reaches adulthood and an understanding of her own birthright as she delivers twins during a very difficult birth. Wheeze learns during the delivery that there is sometimes a reason to treat one child differently from another. Suddenly, she knows why she has always felt second. The settings of the narrative are important to her coming of age. In each setting she discovers something new about herself. The transfer from the isolation of the island to the isolation of an Appalachian valley helps Wheeze better understand her mother, her sister, and herself.

An actual journey is not always necessary for the female protagonist to learn about herself. Katherine of Judy Blume's *Forever* begins to grow up as she experiences her first love affair. Critics of the narrative have pointed out that at the end of the book Katherine is not yet a responsible adult. When asked what she wants to do with her life, she replies that she wants to be happy "and make other people happy too." Nor does it appear that she has learned the meaning of the word "forever." She leaves her "forever" love for a new boy on the college campus. Katherine, like many college freshmen, is still in the process of growing, and the narrative ends with her still in the transitional phase of adolescence. In Sue Ellen Bridgers's *Home before dark,* the very act of putting down roots, of finding a home after many years of migrant farming, causes Stella to grow up. Through her relationship with an aunt, an attraction to an egocentric young man, a growing friendship with another boy, the death of her mother, Mae, and the remarriage of her father, Stella learns much about herself. The contrast between Stella's growth because of the land and Mae's death because of the land is central to the theme of the narrative. Mae's life is ending on the day they pull the old car into the family homestead; Stella's life is just beginning.

Maureen Daly's *Seventeenth summer,* written in 1942, may be the first honest account of an adolescent female's coming of age. *Edith Jackson* by Rosa Guy centers upon the coming of age of a young black protagonist. Other coming-of-age books include *A girl called Al* (Greene), *The leaving* (Hall), the historical novel *The Maude Reed tale* (Lofts), *Heart-of-Snowbird* (Lorenzo), *Island of the blue dolphins* (O'Dell), *The changeling* (Snyder), *The girl who wanted a boy* (Zindel), *A star for the latecomer* (Zindel and Zindel), and *Working on it* (Oppenheimer).

Incorporation into the Adult Community

GIRLS ENTERING THE COMMUNITY. Many of the books that deal with a girl's transition from childhood to adulthood also discuss the protagonist's movement into the adult society.

> *The culminating ceremony of the initiation ritual is the incorporating of the novice into the adult community. This phase is very important, for without incorporation all previous ceremonies have been useless. The transition rites are endured in seclusion or in an unfamiliar environment, but incorporation rites in primitive initiation are generally witnessed by the entire community, signifying to all that the novice is now "a new one," a member. (Agee 1973, p. 134)*

In *Julie of the wolves* (George), Julie understands that she cannot return to her primitive ways. This understanding, symbolized by the death of the bird with whom she has traveled, leads to her reunion with her father and her entry into his adult world. In *Morning is a long time coming* (Greene), Patty's lonely search for her German soldier's parents has ended and she rejoins the world she has abandoned, but this time as an adult who has come to terms with herself. In *Jacob have I loved* (Paterson), Wheeze can live with herself by forgiving her sister and mother because of her new understanding of her own childhood. This new understanding allows her to enter the world as an adult who has come to terms with herself. July in *Mr. and Mrs. Bo Jo Jones* (Head), reaches a new level of maturation when her premature baby dies. Even though there is no reason to keep the marriage together, she and Bo Jo decide to rebuild their relationship from their mutual respect and enter the adult world with a new courage that allows them to accept the lasting quality of marriage. In *Island of the blue dolphins* (O'Dell), Karana moves into adult society as the entire community watches. After her lonely existence on the island for eighteen years, she is rescued by a ship and is ready to enter a new world and a new life. Tracy in Joan Oppenheimer's *Working on it* makes a conscious decision to change from a shy young girl to an adult who functions easily in society. To do this she signs up for a drama class taught by a sensitive, helpful teacher. With the help of the teacher, her drama partner, and her own determination, Tracy is able to break out of her shyness.

In Paul Zindel and Bonnie Zindel's novel *A star for the latecomer*, Brooke's mother is dying of cancer and her boyfriend, Brandon, is moving from the gentle romanticism of young love to the superficial narcissism of Hollywood stardom. Brooke's mother has always wanted to be a star, and she pushes her dreams onto her daughter. The mother's cancer parallels the "cancer" that is growing in Brandon as his life becomes more and more consumed with his star status. Coping with the problems of her mother and Brandon helps Brooke grow into adulthood while gaining an increased understanding of herself. After her mother's death, Brooke is able to let go of the dreams of stardom and her love for Brandon, who has responded to Brooke's desperate love letter in a cold, impersonal way.

□ *More than any other, I think, this present generation needs a sense that the future holds a great deal of promise for those who are free enough to face it.*
RICHARD PECK
in News from ALAN / *September–October 1974*

BOYS ENTERING THE COMMUNITY. The young male protagonist is welcomed into the adult community in many young adult novels. Nathaniel Benchley's *Only earth and sky last forever* centers on ancient primitive initiation rites. Dark Elk is an inexperienced brave at the beginning of the novel. He leaves childhood and enters the lonely transitional phase by trying desperately to prove himself in battle against white soldiers, and thereby gain the hand of the beautiful maiden Lashuka. At the end of the novel he is welcomed into adult society by Crazy Horse at Little Big Horn. In *Red sky at morning* by Richard Bradford, Josh is a young boy forced to move to a little town in New Mexico after his father leaves to fight in World War II. By the end of the story his father has died and he has moved into adulthood, assuming responsibility for his mentally disturbed mother. In Paula Fox's *Blowfish live in the sea,* eighteen-year-old Ben is a rebel. Deserted by his father when he was very young, he fights the values of his mother and stepfather by dropping out of school and refusing to look for work. When he receives an unexpected mesasge from his father, he agrees to meet him but is shocked by the alcoholic person he finds. This shock and the lies his father tells about successful business deals force him out of his rebellious stage and into adulthood. In making the decision to stay with his father and help him, Ben finds a new purpose to his life.

In *Undertow* by Finn Havrevold, Jorn passes through all the stages of the initiation rite. At age fifteen he leaves home, against the wishes of his parents, with seventeen-year-old Ulf. Jorn expects to spend the summer at Ulf's family's cabin but soon discovers that Ulf has other ideas. Jorn agrees to go sailing Norway's fjords with Ulf. Unaware that the vessel is stolen, he at first goes along with Ulf's journey. During the days aboard the ship Jorn discovers that Ulf does not know the difference between right and wrong. Although Jorn knows he can leave at any time, he decides to stay because he believes Ulf needs him. During a land layover Ulf steals money, and when they believe they are being chased, the boys head out to sea. A violent storm seizes them, and Ulf is drowned in the sinking of the ship. Jorn is rescued and reunited with his family. During the days between the rescue and the funeral, Jorn reevaluates the meaning of his friendship with Ulf and his relationship with his parents. Through finding the good and bad in others, Jorn discovers the good and bad in himself. He rejoins society at Ulf's funeral, this time as an adult.

Manolo Olivar in the *Shadow of a bull* (Wojciechowska) is the son of Spain's greatest bullfighter. Although afraid of the bull, Manolo is expected to follow in his father's footsteps. He goes into training on his twelth birthday. Manolo experiences great conflict between his fear of the bull and of failure and his desire to fulfill his father's dreams. When he must fight his first bull, he is terrified. However, once he enters the ring he realizes he can fight the bull. He has proved himself to himself, to his father, and to the community. Now that he is successful he can pursue his own dreams.

THE SEARCH FOR A CAREER. Many young adults are pressured to make early career choice decisions. A number of good nonfiction books have been written to help the adolescent in the choice. These books will be discussed in the next chapter.

In recent years young adult fiction dealing with the selection and pursuit of a career has become increasingly realistic. The career books of today usually show the difficulties and benefits of the career. In *Gift of gold* by Beverly Butler, a blind girl becomes a speech therapist for the mentally retarded. *The muskie hook* by Peter Cohen is about a boy's resistence to becoming a fishing guide like his father. However, when he is forced to guide a group of muskie fishermen, he catches the "muskie fever." *The tennis machine* by Helen Hull Jacobs is about the loneliness and hard work involved in becoming a champion. Robert Lipsyte's *The contender* shows that even though a hard-working aspiring athlete will probably not become a champion, being a contender "makes the man." In Elsa Pedersen's *Fisherman's choice,* a young man decides to become a fisherman against his parent's wishes. Bel Kaufman's *Up the down staircase* is about the life of an inner-city junior high school teacher. Max of *Max's wonderful delicatessen* by Winifred Madison pursues his dream of becoming a sculptor.

Biographies and autobiographies, which often combine fiction with fact, give the young adult guidance in career choice. In two nonfiction books, *A circle of children* and *Lovey—a very special child,* Mary McCracken tells about her work teaching the mentally retarded. *Friend within the gates* (Hogg) is about Edith Cavell, a World War I nurse. Rachel Baker's *The first woman doctor* is the story of Elizabeth Blackwell. Another biography about the medical profession is Richard Hardwick's *Charles Richard Drew: Pioneer in blood research.* Robert Maiorano's *Worlds apart: The autobiography of a dancer from Brooklyn* presents the first sixteen years of his life by contrasting the tough world of the streets with the demanding world of ballet. *Kurt Thomas on gymnastics* by Kurt Thomas and Kent Hannon portrays the world of men's gymnastics: the training, the dedication, and the life-style of a champion gymnast. *The education of an American soccer player* by Shep Messing and David Hirshey tells of Messing's life as a child in the Bronx, a student at Harvard, a participant in the Olympics, and a goalie for the New York Cosmos.

Conclusion

In a talk to the Assembly on Literature for Adolescents of the National Council of Teachers of English, author Joan Aiken said, "Helplessness is a basic ingredient of every child's life." Good literature written for and read by the young adult can help readers overcome, or at least understand, the feeling of helplessness as they progress through the often difficult years between childhood and adulthood. Teachers, librarians, and parents should help young readers locate books that deal with the conflicts and difficulties that arise in the transition between childhood and adulthood. According to Joan Aiken, one of the legitimate aims of literature for young people is to show the "tragic tension of life." In encountering this part of life through literature, the reader can better deal with the feeling of helplessness and better understand the tragedy that is part of the human condition. Young adult books that "end at a beginning" give young adult readers hope that they can survive life's tragic tension and move into adult life with confidence.

Anthological Aside in Chapter 5

Blume, J. *Are you there, God? It's me, Margaret.* Bradbury, 1970. Dell, 1980.

Titles Mentioned in Chapter 5

Separation from Childhood

Blume, J. *Are you there, God? It's me, Margaret.* Bradbury, 1970. Dell, 1980.
————. *Deenie.* Bradbury, 1973. Dell, 1979.
————. *Then again, maybe I won't.* Bradbury, 1971. Dell, 1976.
Bradbury, R. *Dandelion wine.* Doubleday, 1957. Bantam, 1976.
Fitzhugh, L. *The long secret.* Harper & Row, 1965. Dell, 1978.
Lipsyte, R. *One fat summer.* Harper & Row, 1977. Bantam, 1978.
Miles, B. *The trouble with thirteen.* Knopf, 1979. Avon, 1980.
Paterson, K. *Bridge to Terabithia.* Crowell, 1977. Avon, 1979.
Peck, R. *Don't look and it won't hurt.* Holt, Rinehart & Winston, 1972. Avon, 1973.
Powers, J. *Do black patent leather shoes really reflect up?* Regnery, 1975. Popular Library, 1976.
Stolz, M. S. *Leap before you look.* Harper & Row, 1972. Dell, 1972.
Van Leeuwen, J. *I was a ninety-eight-pound duckling.* Dial, 1972. Dell, 1979.

Transition from Childhood to Adulthood

Blume, J. *Forever.* Bradbury, 1976. Pocket Books, 1973.
Bonham, F. *Durango Street.* Dutton, 1965. Dell, 1972.
Borland, K., and H. Speicher. *Goodbye to Stony Crick.* McGraw-Hill, 1976.
Bradford, R. *Red sky at morning.* Lippincott, 1968. Pocket Books, 1969.
Brancato, R. *Come alive at 505.* Knopf, 1980, Bantam, 1981.
Bridgers, S. E. *Home before dark.* Knopf, 1976. Bantam, 1977.
Cormier, R. *The chocolate war.* Pantheon, 1974. Dell, 1975.
Daly, M. *Seventeenth summer.* Dodd, Mead, 1942. Scholastic, 1971.
Donovan, J. *I'll get there. It better be worth the trip.* Harper & Row, 1969. Dell, 1973.
Fox, P. *The slave dancer.* Bradbury, 1973. Dell, 1975.
Gauch, P. L. *The green of me.* Putnam, 1978.
George, J. C. *Julie of the wolves.* Harper & Row, 1972.
Greene, B. *Morning is a long time coming.* Dial, 1978. Pocket Books, 1979.
Greene, C. *A girl called Al.* Viking, 1969. Scholastic, 1971.
Guy, R. *Edith Jackson.* Viking, 1978. Bantam, 1978.
Hale, J. C. *The owl's song.* Doubleday, 1974. Avon, 1976.
Hall, L. *The leaving.* Scribner's, 1980.
Harris, M. *The runaway's diary.* Four Winds, 1971. Pocket Books, 1974.
Head, A. *Mr. and Mrs. Bo Jo Jones.* Putnam, 1967. New American Library, 1968.
Hentoff, N. *I'm really dragged but nothing gets me down.* Simon & Schuster, 1968. Dell, 1974.
Hinton, S. E. *That was then, this is now.* Viking, 1971. Dell, 1980.
————. *Tex.* Delacorte, 1979. Dell, 1980.
Holland, I. *Of love and death and other journeys.* Lippincott, 1975. Dell, 1977.

Hunt, I. *Up a road slowly.* Follett, 1966. Grosset, 1966.

Kerr, M. E. *If I love you, am I trapped forever?* Harper & Row, 1973. Dell, 1975.

————. *The son of someone famous.* Harper & Row, 1974. Ballantine, 1975.

Knowles, J. *A separate peace.* Macmillan, 1959. Bantam, 1976.

Lee, M. *Fog.* Houghton Mifflin, 1972. Dell, 1974.

Lockett, S. *No moccasins today.* T. Nelson, 1970.

Lofts, N. *The Maude Reed tale.* T. Nelson, 1972. Dell, 1974.

Lorenzo, C. L. *Heart-of-snowbird.* Harper & Row, 1975.

Lyle, K. L. *I will go barefoot all summer for you.* Lippincott, 1973. Dell, 1974.

Major, K. *Far from shore* (1980). Delacorte, 1981. Dell, 1983.

Myers, W. D. *Hoops.* Delacorte, 1981.

O'Dell, S. *Island of the blue dolphins.* Houghton Mifflin, 1960. Dell, 1975.

Oppenheimer, J. *Working on it.* Harcourt Brace Jovanovich, 1980.

Paterson, K. *Bridge to Terabithia.* Crowell, 1977, Avon, 1979.

————. *Jacob have I loved.* Crowell, 1980. Avon, 1981.

Peck, R. N. *A day no pigs would die.* Knopf, 1972. Dell, 1978.

Potok, C. *The chosen.* Simon & Schuster, 1967. Ballantine, 1982.

Raucher, H. *Summer of '42.* Putnam, 1971. Dell, 1978.

Rogers, T. *At the shores.* Simon & Schuster, 1980.

Russ, L. *The April age.* Atheneum, 1975.

Salinger, J. D. *The catcher in the rye.* Little, Brown, 1951. New American Library, 1962.

Snyder, Z. *The changeling.* Atheneum, 1970.

Townsend, J. R. *Good night, Prof, dear.* Lippincott, 1970. Dell, 1977.

Voigt, C. *Dicey's Song.* Atheneum, 1982.

————. *Homecoming.* Atheneum, 1981. Fawcett, 1982.

————. A solitary blue. Atheneum, 1983.

Zindel, P. *Confessions of a teenage baboon.* Harper & Row, 1977. Bantam, 1978.

————. *The girl who wanted a boy.* Harper & Row, 1981.

————, and B. Zindel. *A star for the latecomer.* Harper & Row, 1980. Bantam, 1981.

Incorporation into the Adult Community

Benchley, N. *Only earth and sky last forever.* Harper & Row, 1972.

Bradford, R. *Red sky at morning.* Lippincott, 1968. Pocket Books, 1969.

Fox, P. *Blowfish live in the sea.* Bradbury, 1970. Dell, 1975.

George, J. C. *Julie of the wolves.* Harper & Row, 1972.

Greene, B. *Morning is a long time coming.* Dial, 1978. Pocket Books, 1979.

Havrevold, F. *Undertow.* Translated by C. B. Curry. Atheneum, 1968.

Head, A. *Mr. and Mrs. Bo Jo Jones.* Putnam, 1967. New American Library, 1968.

O'Dell, S. *Island of the blue dolphins.* Houghton Mifflin, 1960. Dell, 1975.

Oppenheimer, J. *Working on it.* Harcourt Brace Jovanovich, 1980.

Paterson, K. *Jacob have I loved.* Crowell, 1980. Avon, 1981.

Wojciechowska, M. *Shadow of a bull.* Atheneum, 1964.

Zindel, P., and B. Zindel. *A star for the latecomer.* Harper & Row, 1980. Bantam, 1981.

Careers

Baker, R. *The first woman doctor: The story of Elizabeth Blackwell, M.D.* Julian Messner, 1944.

Butler, B. *Gift of gold.* Dodd, Mead, 1972. Pocket Books, 1973.

Cohen, P. Z. B. *The muskie hook.* Atheneum, 1969.

Hardwick, R. *Charles Richard Drew: Pioneer in blood research.* Scribner's, 1967.

Hogg, B. *Friend within the gates: The story of nurse Edith Cavell.* Houghton Mifflin, 1960. Dell, 1973.

Jacobs, H. H. *The tennis machine.* Scribner's, 1972.

Kaufman, B. *Up the down staircase.* Prentice-Hall, 1964. Avon, 1966.

Lipsyte, R. *The contender.* Harper & Row, 1967. Bantam, 1979.

McCracken, M. *A circle of children.* Lippincott, 1973. New American Library, 1975.

————. *Lovey—a very special child.* Lippincott, 1976. New American Library,

Madison, W. *Max's wonderful delicatessen.* Little, Brown, 1972 Dell, 1976.

Maiorano, R. *Worlds apart: The autobiography of a dancer from Brooklyn.* Coward, McCann & Geoghegan, 1980.

Messing, S., and D. Hirshey. *The education of an American soccer player.* Dodd, Mead, 1978. Bantam, 1979.

Pedersen, E. K. *Fisherman's choice.* Atheneum, 1964.

Thomas, K., and K. Hannon. *Kurt Thomas on gymnastics.* Simon & Schuster, 1980.

Suggested Readings

Agee, H. Adolescent initiation: A thematic study in the secondary schools. In R. Mead and R. Small, eds., *Literature for adolescents,* Merrill, 1973.

Edwards, M. A. *The fair garden and the swarm of beasts: The library and the young adult.* Hawthorn, 1974.

Peck, R. Some thoughts on adolescent literature. *News from ALAN,* September–October 1975, pp. 4–7.

Weiss, M., ed. *From writers to students: The pleasures and pains of writing.* International Reading Association, 1979.

Yoder, J. M. The rites of passage: A study of the adolescent girl. *ALAN Newsletter,* Fall 1976.

6 Nonfiction, Poetry, and Short Fiction

Although the primary literary form written for and read by young adults is the novel, other types of literature are of interest to many young readers. As indicated earlier, studies show that teenage boys particularly enjoy reading about suspense and adventure. A great deal of true-to-life suspense and adventure can be found in the growing world of nonfiction written for young readers.

Hooking young readers on poetry at a very early age is quite easy when they are introduced to the humorous verse of contemporary authors like Shel Silverstein and Judith Viorst. Keeping that reading interest alive as readers progress through their teens is made easier by contemporary poets who, like Nancy Willard, write for young readers, and anthologers, like Lee Bennett Hopkins, who compile poetry collections that span the ages of the reader.

An encouraging new trend in adolescent literature is the introduction of short stories written for the teen-age audience by well-known young adult novelists. These ''short-read'' books are attractive to the reluctant reader of longer fiction, as well as to the busy teen-ager who enjoys reading, but finds his/her schedule too busy for full-length books. Likewise, these wonderful short tales, by authors like Robert Cormier and Norma Fox Mazer, are excellent classroom tools for introducing students to the literary craft of the writers. Often short fiction can whet the student's reading appetite for longer works on a similar theme or by the same author.

Biography and Autobiography

G. Robert Carlsen writes: "Teens want the same qualities in biography as in fiction. They seek real-life stories about heroes and heroines who resemble the characters in their fiction. Boys prefer to read about men; girls about women. Both sexes want a fictionalized biography rather than a factual account. They enjoy undocumented dialogue, thoughts and feelings of the subject."[1]

The biographical and autobiographical works written for or enjoyed most by young adults are short in length (150 to 250 pages). Just as in the fiction enjoyed by teenagers, the subject of a biography must seem real, so that by the end of the book, the reader has a sense of knowing the person. The person should not be portrayed as so good or so bad as to seem unrealistic. The situations, though removed from the young adult's life, must appear to be true to life and not trumped up to make the person seem better than humanly possible. The writer of the young adult biography does not preach to the reader, sensationalize the accounting of events, or invent situations that are impossible given the person being described or the historical period of the account. Good biography for the young adult is like good fiction; it is readable and relates to the needs and interests of the reader.

G. Robert Carlsen (1980) identifies seven categories of biography: fictionalized, definitive, interpretive, objective, monumental, critical, and collected. Though it is often hard to place a biography or autobiography in a specific category (for example, an account that attempts to be objective or critical may also be fictionalized to some degree), these categories are useful in talking about biography and autobiography written for or particularly enjoyed by young adults.

FICTIONALIZED BIOGRAPHY. An account of a historical figure can seem real even when it is part of a fictionalized biography, as long as the fictionalization is consistent with the person's character development and the historical period of the narrative. Fictionalized biography includes events and dialogue that might have happened but cannot be backed by historical documentation. Many works about historical figures about which little or no primary source documentation is available are fictionalized. Even when primary source information is available, the author may chose to fictionalize to make a point about the person, describe the person's thoughts, or show the person's relationship to other historical figures. Rhoda Lerman's *Eleanor* is a good example of a fictionalized biography. It covers the life of Eleanor Roosevelt during the four years following her discovery that Franklin was having an affair with another woman. Though based on documented evidence, Gene Smith's *The horns of the moon: A short biog-*

---

[1]G. Robert Carlsen, *Books and the Teenage Reader,* 2nd rev. ed. (Harper & Row, 1980). Copyright © 1967, 1971, 1980 by G. Robert Carlsen. Reprinted by permission of Harper & Row, Publishers, Inc.

raphy of Adolf Hitler is also fictionalized. The book deals with Hitler's first love, his boyhood friends, and his fascination with astrology, and attempts to relate these experiences to what he later became.

DEFINITIVE BIOGRAPHY. Definitive biographies are usually long works based on all the known facts about the person. Such works are scholarly and well documented. Consequently, definitive biographies are enjoyed most by mature young adult readers. The four-volume *Henry James* by Leon Edel is too long and too involved for many young readers, but is often enjoyed by the mature young adult. The same is true of Carl Sandburg's six-volume *Abraham Lincoln* and Carlos Baker's *Ernest Hemingway*. Fawn Brodie's *Thomas Jefferson: An intimate history* is an interesting scholarly portrait of the man's attitudes and relationships. Because of its length, over 200 pages, it is likely to be overlooked by immature readers. The young reader who is fascinated by a particular historic figure, however, may be able to read and enjoy a definitive biography. One that is enjoyed by many young adults is Virginia Hamilton's *Paul Robeson: The life and times of a free black man*. Fewer than 250 pages, it is a well-researched account of the singer's life, including the disruption of his career in the United States, owing to his political sympathy for the Soviet Union. Another definitive biography young aduts enjoy, not for its reading ease but for its subject, is *Buried alive: The biography of Janis Joplin* (Friedman). This book portrays the rock idol of the 1960s as a troubled young woman who thought herself ugly and attempted to dull her pain through drugs and alcohol.

INTERPRETIVE BIOGRAPHY AND AUTOBIOGRAPHY. Interpretive biographies attempt to find patterns in a person's life that cause him or her to behave in a particular way. The interpretive biographer may purposely omit evidence that does not support the portrait being drawn. Many autobiographies enjoyed by young adults can be placed in this category. One good example is Eldridge Cleaver's *Soul on ice*. Cleaver's prison recollections are short, spiritual, and intellectual. The book may be difficult for some young adults, but, many teenagers who read it find it illuminating.

There are many other more easily read interpretive biographes and autobiographies, such as Maya Angelou's *I know why the caged bird sings*. It and its three sequels—*Gather together in my name, Singin' and swingin' and gettin' merry like Christmas,* and *The heart of a woman*—tell the life story of this gifted black writer, poet, and actress who grew up in the Depression-era South. Another interpretive autobiography set in the Deep South is Anne Moody's *Coming of age in Mississippi*. Jimmy Carter in *Why not the best?* interprets his own life from his Depression-era childhood to his nomination as president. *Farewell to Manzanar* by Jeanne Wakatsuki Houston and James D. Houston is told through the eyes of five-year-old Jeanne as a child in an internment camp for Japanese-Americans during World War II. Gayle Sayers with Al Silverman in *I am third* interprets his own life from his youth in a black ghetto to his professional football career and the death of his close friend and teammate Brian Pic-

Three high school students find fun, frustration, and fear in Maya Angelou's works of poetry and prose.

colo. Tim O'Brien's account of his experience in the Vietnam War in *If I die in a combat zone*, is a powerful interpretive autobiographical account. Robert Maiorano in *Worlds apart: The autobiography of a dancer from Brooklyn* is an interpretive account of a soloist with the New York City Ballet, contrasting the worlds of his youth and of the dance studio. In *Birthmark,* Lorraine Dusky writes of her experiences having a child out of wedlock, putting her up for adoption, and later searching unsuccessfully to find her. In *Breakout: From prison to the big leagues,* Ron LeFlore with Jim Hawkins reflects on the events that led him from drug addiction and crime to the Detroit Tigers and the All-Star game. *Starring Sally J. Freeman as herself* is an interpretive autobiographical sketch of Judy Blume's young years. This humorous book is appropriate for younger adolescent readers. Two interpretive autobiographies by popular authors of young adult fiction which discuss becoming an author and growing into a writer are: Lois Duncan's *Chapters: My growth as a writer* and M. E. Kerr's *Me Me Me Me Me.*

Among the many other interpretive biographies of interest to young adult readers is *Anyone's daughter* by Shana Alexander. This sensitive account of the Patty Hearst case traces the events from her kidnapping to the trial. Robert Conot's *A streak of luck: The life and legend of Thomas Alva Edison* tells of the inventor's career and personal life. Conot's portrait paints Edison as a complex and contradictory man. William Bradford Huie's *A new life to live: Jimmy Putman's story* tells of the illegitimate son of Alabama's governor "Big Jim" Folsom. The book follows Jimmy through his troubled adolescence to his decision to devote his life to Christ. In *The right stuff,* Tom Wolfe portrays the ascent of astronauts from test pilots to the beginning of the space program to space flights. *Free to be Muhammad Ali* by Robert Lipsyte is an interpretive look into the life of the great boxing champion. The book examines the controversies that have surrounded Ali's career.

OBJECTIVE BIOGRAPHY. The objective, or factual, biography records documented facts about the subject's life, usually in chronological order. The author does not attempt to judge, criticize, or interpret. There is no attempt to show how incidents in the person's life developed his/her character. However, the work may or may not be definitive.

Being objective in an autobiography is more difficult than being objective in a biography. However, James Herriot's books about his life as a Yorkshire veterinary surgeon can be broadly placed in the objective autobiography category. The four books record the events of his life in the Yorkshire Downs from Herriot's first years as a vet to his life after World War II. The very humorous accounts never attempt to judge or criticize, only to report. Herriot does not attempt to show how one event leads to another. Each chapter can stand alone as a piece of writing in its own right. These books, though not written specifically for young adults, have been enjoyed by teenage readers. Their warm, simple, funny tales have won them many accolades, including the American Library Association Best of the Best Books for Young Adult Award for both *All creatures great and small* and *All things bright and beautiful.*

Another author who writes wonderfully funny books about the adventures and misadventures of his own life is Farley Mowat. *The dog who wouldn't be* is the tale of his boyhood adventures with Mutt. The story of his leaky old schooner, *Happy Adventure,* is told in *The boat who wouldn't float.* Mowat's books not only relate incidents in his own life, but paint an interesting picture of Canada.

BIOGRAPHICAL MONUMENTS AND ANTIMONUMENTS. Many biographers attempt to build monuments to the persons about whom they are writing. These biographies minimize the faults of the subject. In the past, young adult biographies leaned in this direction. However, today we are seeing more and more biographies using the opposite, or debunking, approach. Young adults today are increasingly interested in antimonument biographies that destroy rather than build monuments. The widely read *Mommie dearest,* the debunking of Joan Crawford by Christina Crawford, is an example of this phenomenon.

The teenage reader, however, also likes to read touching tales about real-life heroes, even if the hero may be too good to be true. Many books that deal with the handicapped or the recently deceased seem to attempt to deify the person. *The story of Stevie Wonder* (Haskins) and *Brian Piccolo, a short season* (Morris) seem to fit this category. *Elvis, we love you tender* by members of Presley's family as told to Martin Torgoff reviews his final, difficult years and his strict code of conduct. Like the Presley book, many titles give away the author's attempt to create a monument to the hero. *Cudjoe of Jamaica: Pioneer for black freedom in the new world* by Milton McFarlane tells the story of General Cudjoe, who led the fight against slavery in eighteenth-century Jamaica.

CRITICAL BIOGRAPHY. Critical biography looks at the subject in relationship to the times and attempts to assess the value of the person's contribution to society. This type of biography neither deifies nor debunks the person, but rather presents both strengths and weaknesses. The critical biography seems to be more predominant today than it was several years ago, when most biographies, particularly those written for the young, seemed to deify. *Scoundrel time* by Lillian Hellman is not just an autobiography but also a portrait of a historic period—the witch-hunting, blacklisting years of the Joseph McCarthy era. Because this book is short, it can act as an excellent companion to the textbook presentation of the 1950s in a U.S. history class. Another short biography that is enjoyable to many young adults, particularly those interested in a career in art, is Donald Walton's *A Rockwell portrait.* A book that became an Academy Award–winning film is Ladislas Farago's *Patton: Ordeal and triumph,* which portrays George S. Patton as a man, not as a hero. Though the book is over 400 pages, many students, particularly those who have seen the movie or are interested in the military, enjoy it. Phyllis Bentley's *The Brontës and their world* examines the Brontë sisters against the backdrop of the world in which they lived.

BIOGRAPHICAL COLLECTIONS. A collection of biographies contains short accounts of people's lives or descriptions of particular events in their lives that tie the people in the collection together. John F. Kennedy's *Profiles in courage,* an excellent example of this type of biography, tells the stories of several congressmen who took unpopular stands and risked their careers. Though this is a valuable book to help teenagers see another side of the political arena, many teenagers find it difficult and consequently boring. Assigning a few chapters of the book, reading several aloud to the class, and allowing students to elect to read the entire book or parts of it are preferable to requiring the entire class to read it.

Hettie Jones's *Big star fallin' Mama: Five women in black music* is an easy-to-read biography for young blues fans. Donald Bogle's *Brown sugar: Eight years of America's black female superstars* is another compilation that unites the biographical sketches by virtue of race and struggle. In *GirlSports!,* Karen Folger Jacobs has collected stories about fifteen young women athletes, ages nine to seventeen, some famous, others not. Steven Clark's *Fight against time: Five athletes—a legacy of courage* is the story of athletes faced with personal tragedy. *Glorious triumphs: Athletes who conquered adversity* by Vernon Pizer is a collection of thirteen interpretive biographies that center on feats of the body and the spirit. The stories tell of athletes who combat cancer, drug abuse, severe burns, and paralysis. Some of the athletes included in this book, first released in 1966 and revised in 1980, will be familiar to today's young adults; others will be new to them.

Recollections of people experiencing the same event or living the same life-style make interesting biographical collections. John Hersey's *Hiroshima,* about six survivors of the A-bomb, is an important example. *Hillbilly women,* compiled by Kathy Kahn, tells the stories of nineteen women, in their own words, who live in Appalachian coal mining and mill towns. This collection paints a vivid picture of the region and its people.

Other biography collections are loosely tied together. *Great modern American short biographies,* edited by Joseph Mersand, is a good example.

Though not too many biographies are written specifically for the young adult reader, there are many that appeal to their needs and interests.[2] Encouraging students to read biography, helping them select good biographies, and instructing them in the characteristics and value of each category of biography are useful tools in teaching about historical periods, particular people, and particular events.

HISTORY. For years enjoyable, entertaining, and illuminating historical accounts were the sole possession of the adult audience. The works of historians such as T. S. Morison or Dee Brown were too long and too difficult for most young adults. Fortunately, many authors are now writing enjoyable historical accounts for young adult readers.

The historian James Forman has written some excellent histories for young adults. His *Anarchism: Political innocence or social violence?* is a historical analysis that introduces young readers to the philosophies of Rosseau, Sorel, Spencer, Tolstoy, Thoreau, and others. His *Capitalism: Economic individualism to today's welfare state* follows capitalism from its origins through the changes brought about by industrialization, to the Depression and the big businesses of today. In *Communism: From Marx's Manifesto to twentieth-century reality,* Forman looks at Communism from its origins to its present influence in Eastern Europe, China, and the Third World. *Fascism: The meaning and experience of reactionary revolution* is an examination of fascism's roots and its future. *Nazism* is an informative history of the Nazi party, including the writings of Hitler and the social and political climate in which Nazism developed. *Socialism: Its theoretical roots and present-day development* examines the history of socialism and the differences between it and communism.[3] *The mad game* seeks to examine the question of why we have war. In this book Forman looks at peacemaking efforts that have been made as well as at ways to stop us from destroying the earth. He traces the history of war from the beginnings of human history to the

---

[2]An excellent bibliography of biographies that appeal to young adult readers can be found in G. Robert Carlsen's *Books and the teenage reader,* 2nd rev. ed. (1980).

[3]A teacher's guide to James Forman's books by Nancy E. Gross is available from Dell Publishing Co., 1 Dag Hammarskjold Plaza, New York, NY 10017.

Russian invasion of Afghanistan. This unique historical account would be an excellent textbook or resource book for a history class studying war. In addition to the study of war, Forman examines the history of pacifism from its roots in Eastern religions and Christianity. In this interesting counterpoint to his study of war he discusses the successes of pacifism in this century, focusing on the Quakers, Gandhi, and Martin Luther King, Jr. He points out how it requires the same courage, patriotism, and heroism as war. The book is readable rather than scholarly. However, many historical references are cited to support the author's views. The book includes a bibliography for further reading and an index. All of Forman's books are readable, interesting, and well documented, and they attempt to present a variety of viewpoints.

The historian Milton Meltzer has also written several appealing histories for the young adult reader. His best is probably *Never to forget: The Jews of the Holocaust.* This book is divided in three sections: History of hatred, Destruction of the Jews, and Spirit of resistance.[4] Other young adult histories by Meltzer include *Taking root: Jewish immigrants in America; World of our fathers: The Jews of Eastern Europe; In their own words: A history of the American Negro 1619–1965* (three volumes); *Bound for the Rio Grande: The Mexican struggle, 1846–1848;* and *Violins and shovels: The WPA arts projects.*

□ *When I went to work on* **Never to Forget,** *it was with the idea of trying to provide young people, particularly of junior and senior high school age, with a deeper understanding of the origins of the Holocaust. There had been a number of very good novels about the experience of the Holocaust written for young people, some based on personal experience and others purely imagined experience. But there has been almost nothing* nonfictional *trying to deal with the Holocaust.*

MILTON MELTZER

author of Underground man / *in Weiss (1979)*

An interesting recent trend is the adaptation of adult histories for young readers. The best current examples are the rewriting of Dee Brown's outstanding adult works. His *Hear the lonesome whistle blow,* which recounts the building of the transcontinental railroad, became a book for adolescents titled *Lonesome whistle: The story of the first transcontinental railroad.* His *Bury my heart at Wounded Knee* was modified for young readers and retitled *Wounded Knee.* If this trend continues, many adult histories that are difficult for young readers will become available to them.

Many other good histories are available for young adult readers. In *To be a slave,* a Newbery honor book by Julius Lester, slaves eloquently relate their

---

[4]An excellent teacher's guide to *Never to forget* by Max Nadel is available from Dell Publishing Co., 1 Dag Hammarskjold Plaza, New York, NY 10017.

stories. Burke Wilkinson has edited books for young adults including *Cry sabotage! True stories of twentieth century saboteurs.* Richard Deming's *Man and the world* is about the origins and development of international law. An excellent book for young readers about American Indian life is Forrest Carter's *The education of Little Tree.*

Current Social Issues

CONSTITUTIONAL RIGHTS. Many nonfiction books on issues of social importance are being written for the young adult audience. Alan Sussman's *The rights of young people: An American Civil Liberties Union handbook* is an up-to-date guide cataloguing the legal rights of young adults in all fifty states. It includes such topics as driving, drugs and alcohol, employment, search and seizure, rape, pornography, child abuse and child neglect, adoption, and more. *The first freedom: The tumultuous history of free speech in America* by Nat Hentoff also addresses the rights of teenagers.

TEENAGE SEX AND PREGNANCY. Janet Bode's *Kids having kids: The unwed teenage parent* discusses the sexual conduct of teenagers and the health risks associated with pregnancy and birth control. Options such as adoption, abortion, and keeping the child are frankly discussed. *Learning about sex* by Gary F. Kelly is a straightforward, nonjudgmental guide for teenagers. *Sex with love* by Eleanor Hamilton is also a guide for young adults. Sol Gordon's *You would if you loved me* examines the "lines" used by boys to entice girls into sex. Also included is a candid discussion of the difference between love and manipulation. John Langone's *Like, love, lust: A view of sex and sexuality* is an attempt to give young adults the facts they need to make informed decisions about sex. He gives information from scientific, historical, psychological, and sociological viewpoints. The informative and nonjudgmental nature of this work makes it a useful guide for teenagers. *The ambivalence of abortion* by Linda Bird Francke is a compilation of the feelings of adults and teenagers, both male and female, about abortion.

WOMEN'S ISSUES. Richard Deming's *Women: The new criminals* deals with the increase in women criminals in the past twenty years and discusses some reasons for it. *Heart songs: The intimate diaries of young girls,* edited by Laurel Holliday, is a collection of writings by ten young girls across several centuries. The diaries reflect the same joys and fears of approaching womanhood that young adults experience today. Carol Hymowitz and Michaele Weissman's *A history of women in America* spans the years from the colonial times to the present. This easy-to-read book presents many first-person accounts. *Growing up female in America,* edited by Eve Merriam, another easy-to-read book, is about ten American women from different times and places. Dell's Women of America paperback series, under the general editorship of Milton Meltzer, includes *Ida Tarbell: First of the muckrakers* and *The senator from Maine: Margaret Chase Smith* (Fleming), *The world of Mary Cassatt* (McKown), *Probing the unknown: The story of Dr. Florence Sabin* (Phelan), *Fanny Kemble's America* (Scott), and *Sea and earth: The life of Rachel Carson* (Sterling).[5]

A VARIETY OF SOCIAL ISSUES. Other social concerns of interest to teenagers are presented in nonfiction written for young adult readers. Drugs and alcohol are discussed in Robert deRopp's *Drugs and the mind,* Gregor Felsen's *Can you do it until you need glasses? The different drug book,* and *Worlds apart: Young people and drug programs,* edited by Dennis T. Jaffe and Ted Clark. *Alcohol: The delightful poison* by Alice Fleming traces the history of the discovery and use of alcohol. Involvement in religious cults is addressed in Christopher Edwards's firsthand account, *Crazy for God: The nightmare of cult life.* The issue of toxic chemicals is examined in Michael Brown's *Laying waste: The poisoning of America by toxic chemicals.* Ecological issues are discussed in Jonathan Schell's *The fate of the earth,* Laurence Pringle's *Lives at stake* and *What shall we do with the land? Choices for America,* and Betty Sue Cummings' *Let a river be.* Patricia Curtis's *Animal rights: Stories of people who defend the rights of animals* offers seven imaginary case studies that provide an interesting look at animal rights. Family problems are considered in Richard Gardner's *The boys and girls book about divorce* and Arlene Richards and Irene Willis's *How to get it together when your parents are coming apart.*

Two good books about money by economist John Kenneth Galbraith are useful to young adults. *Money: Whence it came and where it went* is a history of money from ancient times to the present. *Almost everyone's guide to economics* is a short, simple introduction to the world of supply-and-demand curves. Another good money book for older teens is Jane Bryant Quinn's *Everyone's money book.* It is filled with useful personal financial advice of particular interest to young adults, including handling college expenses, buying a car, and renting an apartment.

The nuclear arms race is discussed in many books. Two appropriate for young readers are: *The mad game* (Forman) and *The nuclear question* (Weiss).

Ethnic Literature

BLACK LITERATURE. In *Young and black in America,* edited by Rae Pace Alexander and Julius Lester, eight men and eight women tell of their experiences. *Growing up black,* edited by Jay David, is a compilation of the views of nineteen young people. *A pictorial history of black Americans* is edited by Langston Hughes, Milton Meltzer, and C. Eric Lincoln. June Jordan's *Dry victories* is the story of the Reconstruction and civil rights era told in photographs and dialogue

---

[5]An excellent study guide for this series by Nancy E. Gross is available from Dell Publishing Co., 1 Dag Hammarskjold Plaza, New York, NY 10017.

between two young black boys. She contrasts the two periods in black American history when "Black folks were supposed to win . . ." but "what we won was not nearly enough." *Selma, Lord, Selma: Girlhood memories of the civil rights days* by Sheyann Webb and Rachel West Nelson is a recollection of events from the 1965 Selma civil rights movement. In James Haskins' *Witchcraft, mysticism and magic in the black world,* the development of beliefs and their sources are traced from the West African slave-supplying regions.

NATIVE AMERICANS. Alvin M. Josephy's *The Indian heritage of America* is an archaeological, ethnological, and historical account of the tribes and cultures of the Indians of the Americas. *Ishi, last of his tribe* by Theodora Kroeber is an excellent account for young adolescents of the Yahi Indians of California. Mari Sandoz's *These were the Sioux* is an interesting history of the tribe. Vine Deloria's *Behind the trail of broken treaties: An Indian declaration of independence* makes a strong case for a federal policy defining the Indians' sovereign states.

OTHER ETHNIC GROUPS. Other nonfiction books with ethnic themes include *Rising voices,* edited by Al Martinez, containing brief biographies of fifty-two outstanding Chicanos. *Strangers in their own land* by Albert Prago is a history of Mexican-Americans. The Jews as part of the American melting pot are seen in books such as *Growing up Jewish,* edited by Jay David, *The Jewish family album,* edited by Franz Hubmann, and Meltzer's *Taking root.* Several books for young adults deal with the entire melting-pot experience of U.S. history. J. Joseph Huthmacher's *A nation of newcomers: Ethnic minority groups in American history* is a short, easy-to-read survey. A more difficult book, *Pride and protest: Ethnic roots in America,* presents the viewpoint of the immigrant. Edited by Jay Schulman, Aubrey Shatter, and Rosalie Ehrlich, it is a selection of essays, fiction, drama, and poetry that reflect the view of the diverse culture of the modern United States.

Selecting a Career

The selection of an appropriate career is very important to the young adult. Many books have been published to guide the teenager in the process. Studs Terkel's *Working: People talk about what they do all day and how they feel about what they do,* though not written specifically for young adults, is a resource guide to jobs—from gravedigger to piano tuner, from copy boy or girl to editors, and hundreds of jobs in between. The book can be used as an overview of the wide range of career opportunities. Another book that interviews workers is Sheila Cole's *Working kids on working.* The book shows the positive side of young adults in the work force. The young people interviewed are enthusiastic about the jobs they do, from washing dishes and busing tables to delivering newspapers. The book emphasizes the responsibility needed for and developed through a job. The interviews help young readers understand what can be obtained from a job besides the money earned.

To learn more about specific careers, young adults can turn to any of the hundreds of books written about individual fields. The best of these books describe a typical work schedule, the benefits and problems of the job, the training needed for the job, the possibility of advancement, and other information helpful to those pursuing a life-long career or a summer job. Most school and public libraries have these books listed in the subject card catalogues. Other books that give an overview of career choice and tell how to gain access to the profession include *The American almanac of jobs and salaries* (Wright); *I can be anything: Careers and colleges for young women, The men's career book: Work and life planning for a new age,* and *The work book: A guide to skilled jobs* (Mitchell); and *Getting into college* (Leana). *Conversations: Working women talk about doing a "man's job,"* edited by Terry Wetherby, presents twenty-two women who work in traditionally male-dominated fields as welders, carpenters, butchers, and chairpersons of the board. A book that is designed to help the reader identify skills and aspirations and set a realistic career target is Tom Jackson's *Guerrilla tactics in the job market.* All of these books are interesting to young adults and help them in pursuing, obtaining, and keeping a job.

How-To Books

How-to books tell readers how to do everything from losing weight to making a million dollars in the stock market. Assessing the value of these books is difficult. One misleading sentence can render a book useless. However, many of the how-to books help the reader gain useful skills. The *Foxfire* books are edited by Eliot Wigginton but written by high school students in Georgia as part of an experiential English program in which the students interview local people to report on the everyday life of Rabun Gap. The series teaches how to slaughter hogs, make moonshine, read weather signs, build furniture, hook rugs, and many other skills mastered by the self-sufficient mountain people.

Every bookstore and library has hundreds of self-help books for young and adult readers. Before purchasing a book, it is a good idea to check it out of the library to be sure it can be easily understood by the teenager, has easy-to-follow directions, is accurate, and does not present misleading or dangerous information. The readability can easily be determined by having a young adult read a section and try to follow the author's directions. If the directions are hard to follow, the book is not for teenagers.

The novice or the person who knows nothing about a topic cannot easily detect misinformation in a book. However, the following guidelines are useful in selecting an accurate, helpful how-to book. The book is likely to be accurate and helpful to the teenage reader if (1) the reviewers' comments printed on the book jacket are from reputable persons who know something about the topic;

(2) the publisher is well known for other how-to books in this field; (3) the author's biographical sketch indicates that he or she has the appropriate background to write the book; (4) the points the author makes in the first few pages seem logical and well thought out; (5) there are no physical, emotional, or financial reasons why teenagers should not do what this book suggests.

Science Books

An increasing number of easy-to-read, accurate science books are available for young readers.[6] Isaac Asimov is a prolific writer whose books are appropriate for many older teenage readers and span the entire world of scientific study. Some of his best books for teenage readers include *Asimov on astronomy, The nearest star* (astronomy), *Of time and space and other things* (astronomy), *The collapsing universe* (black holes in space), *The solar system and back, The universe: From flat earth to quasar* (astronomy), *From earth to heaven* (astronomy), *Life and energy* (physical and chemical bases of biology), *The neutrino* (atomic structure and conservation principles of physics), *The tragedy of the moon* (a collection dealing with cosmology and the physics of light and sound, microbiology, astronomy, and sociology), *The left hand of the electron* (discussion of problems of left and right, of numbers and lines, of history and population), and *The planet that wasn't* (Vulcan, astronomy, biology, chemistry, sociology, religion, and economics). All of his books are readable, many of them written at eighth-grade level or below.

Most other science writers emphasize one branch of science in their writings. Older adolescents are often interested in the works of Lewis Thomas on biology. *The lives of a cell: Notes of a biology watcher* won the National Book Award. The second biology-watcher diary, *The Medusa and the snail,* won the Christopher Award. Teenagers interested in biology will also enjoy David Carroll's *Wonders of the world,* a beautiful book of photographs of tundras, tidal waves, blue whales, polar lights, and more; Jacques-Yves Cousteau and Phillippe Diole's *Life and death in a coral sea;* James Hays's *Our changing climate;* Ronald Glasser's *The body is the hero,* an account of how the body protects itself from disease; the books of the Diagram Group entitled *Child's body, Man's body: An owner's manual,* and *Woman's body: An owner's manual;* Margaret Hyde's *Your brain: Master computer;* Paul Lewis and David Rubenstein's *The human body;* the script of the Educational Broadcasting Corporation's *VD Blues;* and Dorothy Hinshaw Patent's *Evolution goes on every day.*

Young students of physics and astronomy are often interested in Lincoln Bar-

---

[6]Two excellent sources for keeping current on the world of science books for young readers are *Appraisal: Science books for young people,* published three times a year by Boston University School of Education, 36 Cummington St., Boston, MA 02215, and *Science Books and Films,* American Association for the Advancement of Science, 1515 Massachusetts Ave., N.W., Washington, DC 20005.

nett's *The universe and Dr. Einstein,* which makes Einstein's theories understandable to a lay audience. *Cosmos* by Carl Sagan is based on the Public Broadcasting System's series. This beautifully illustrated catalogue of life includes history, physics, biology, astronomy, and philosophy. *A house in space* by Henry Cooper is about *Skylab's* daily working regimen. The student astronomer is likely to enjoy Sune Engelbrekston's *Stars, planets, and galaxies.*

Books for young experimenters include Magnus Pyke's *Butter side up! The delights of science,* which teaches many basic concepts and dispels many myths. John Gunter and his students put together the delightful book *The Gunter papers,* a do-it-yourself guide to experiments in biology, earth sciences, chemistry, and physics. It even contains a play, "A visit with the cold germ rancher." *The formula book* by Norman Stark is for teenagers who enjoy creating their own products. This simple guide to "consumer chemistry" shows the reader how to make personal, pet-care, and household products from easily acquired materials.

Mathematics and Puzzle Books

Even the world of mathematics has found a home in literature written for young adults. *Asimov on numbers* covers the uses of numbers, the meanings of symbols, and more. *Fantasia mathematica,* edited by Clifton Fadiman, presents the strange and unusual drawn from the world of mathematics. *Figuring: The joy of numbers* by Shakuntala Devi demonstrates puzzles, shortcuts, and mathematical tricks that make figuring fun.

Playing with numbers through games and puzzles can make mathematics enjoyable even for the reluctant student. Some interesting game books in mathematics include *Coin games and puzzles* by Maxey Brooke, *Fun with figures* by J. A. Hunter, *Mathematical magic* (tricks using numbers) by William Simon, *The mathematical magpie* (stories, rhymes, music, anecdotes, and epigrams) by Clifton Fadiman, *More posers* by Phillip Kaplan, *The Moscow puzzles* (359 mathematical recreations) by Boris A. Kordemsky, *100 geometric games* by Pierre Berloquin, *Perplexing puzzles and tantalizing teasers* (*including droodles for nimble noodles*) by Martin Gardner, *The Tokyo puzzles* by Kobon Fujimura, *We dare you to solve this!* by John Adams, *Your move* (100 decision problems) by David L. Silverman, *Mathematical carnival* and *Mathematical circus* by Martin Gardner, and *Pocket calculator game book* by Edwin Schlossberg and John Brockman.

Books about the history of mathematics and mathematicians can be appealing to adolescents, particularly those interested in mathematics. *The ages of mathematics: The modern ages* by Peter D. Cook presents the latest mathematical theories and the people behind them. This book is part of a four-volume set edited by Charles F. Linn which explores the complete history of mathematics in both East and West. A briefer history of mathematics is Lancelot Hogben's *Mathematics in the making.* Hogben's *The wonderful world of mathemat-*

ics seeks to show that the growth and development of civilization is also the growth and development of mathematics as a science. Julia Diggin's *String, straightedge and shadow* is the story of geometry. *Men of mathematics* by Eric Bell is a series of short biographies from Zeno to Poincaré. *Women in mathematics* by Lynn Osen tells of mathematicians from A.D. 370 to 1935. *Math and aftermath* by Robert Hooke and others shows how practicing mathematicians contribute to the community. Nathan Court's *Mathematics in fun and in earnest* explains how mathematicians think.

A textbook written for students who don't like mathematics—*Mathematics, a human endeavor: A textbook for those who think they don't like the subject* by Harold Jacobs—shows the beauty and symmetry of mathematics.

Poetry

Poetry is a part of our oral language heritage. We listen to it on records, tapes, radios, and jukeboxes. We sing it in the shower, in cars, at parties, at church. We recite it in playground jump-rope chants, in rhymes sung to babies in their cribs, in singing along with advertising jingles on television. Poetry is living language. It is the language of the street, the home, and the playground.

Poetry comes naturally to us when we are young children. As preschoolers we are chased away by other children with rhyme. ("Fat and skinny had a race all around the pillow case; fat fell down and broke his face, and skinny won the race.") We reply in rhyme. ("Sticks and stones can break my bones, but names can never hurt me.") We commit to memory words of advertising jingles before we read the first word on the printed page. We learn nursery rhymes and Bible verses as we sit on our parents' laps.

> ☐ *Poetry, beyond any other literary form, solicits participation from the listener or reader. Indeed, some people insist that a poem is not complete until there is a partner adding his own experiences and feelings to those of the poet.*
> NANCY LARRICK
> *Editor of* I heard a scream in the street: Poetry by young people in the city, *in her book* Somebody turned on a tap in these kids *(1971)*

For many young people, unfortunately, this natural love of rhythm and rhyme is lost between the playground and the classroom. What happens when the poetry on the radio and television is shut off? Why do teenagers then tune out the poetry on the printed page? Perhaps the turn-off comes about because students are made to study poetry as something removed from their lives. For the child, a poem has been an experience, a part of life; the child has lived the poem. When children are asked to divorce the poem from experience and read it, they resist. Rhyme and rhythm, chant and song are to be lived, committed to memory because they are loved and used. The poetry in the textbook is to be read, analyzed, memorized, and reproduced on a test. It is no longer alive; it is no longer loved; it is no longer experienced.

Nancy Larrick, in a book that grew out of a poetry festival at Lehigh University, reports that no textbooks are used in the poetry workshop she teaches. Instead, the workshop participants are encouraged to discover poetry in readings of their own selections, and by listening to the students they teach. The teachers who take the workshop learn to allow their students to experience poetry "as naturally as they talk." The teachers help their students "to see and dream and feel as a poet does" (Larrick 1971, p. 49).

In order to feel and dream like the poet, the student must become the poet. Fortunately, the student already is a poet. The child has been a poet since the discovery of two words that rhyme, since the singing of the first song, since the chanting of the first rhythmic phrase, since the first jumping of rope or bouncing of ball. To help students understand their natural poetic talents, the teacher begins with the poetry of the students themselves.

□ *Children have no need to have poetry explained to them, they don't need to know what it is; they need to be part of it. Poetry comes into the student's life as naturally as breathing.*
LEE BENNETT HOPKINS

author of Best of book bonanza / *in a speech to the National Council of Teachers of* English / November 1980

No textbooks or poetry anthologies are needed, then. The class creates its own. The teacher encourages the students to remember rhymes they chanted while playing as youngsters. The students begin an anthology of collected chants. Possibly the anthology can be posted on an empty classroom bulletin board. A student can ask his younger sibling to recite a jump-rope chant; another can ask her mother to recall the phrases to which she jumped rope; maybe even Grandmother remembers some. A visit to the elementary school playground at recess time on a spring day can produce a large variety of rhythm chants for the anthology.

Television and radio are wonderful sources of poems. Teachers should alert the students to listen for new jingles. Have them search their minds for ones of the past. Parents and other adults can be consulted for old advertising jingles they remember.

Billboards, newspaper and magazine advertisements, signs on store windows, even the names of businesses produce a variety of different rhymes and rhythms. All the students in the class can keep their eyes open for these bits of commercial poetry. Some may even report ones they have seen in their travels. Anyone who has traveled the heavily trafficked route down the East Coast from New England to Florida knows exactly what Pedro says, and says, and says, all the way to south of the border of South Carolina.

Greeting cards include bits of poetry that are familiar to all young adults. The

Rebecca Devet, the poetry lady in the Charlotte-Mecklenburg (NC) Schools, brings poetry to life for adolescents.

students can begin recording their favorites, or even the ones they think are trite or corny. To illustrate the shared poems of greeting cards, two anthologies are useful: *Postcard poems: A collection of poetry for sharing,* edited by Paul Janeczko, and *Best wishes, amen,* edited by Lillian Morrison.

Most teenagers listen to music continually. The words of the songs they listen to and sing can be written down from memory or from their album covers. These lyrics are added to the class anthology of poetry. Because of their interest in music, teenagers are likely to enjoy a poetry anthology entitled *Grandfather rock* edited by David Morse. This book compares rock lyrics with classic poetry. It is a lively resource for helping teenagers understand that poetry is a part of their lives.

One of the ways to keep poetry alive for young readers is to share with them poems that are written by their peers. Some good collections of teenage poetry include *It is the poem singing into your eyes* (ed. Adoff), *Almost grown, a book of photographs and poems* (ed. Szabo and Ziegler), *I heard a scream in the street: Poetry by young people in the city* (ed. Larrick), *I really want to feel good about myself* (ed. Hopkins and Rasch), and *Who I am* (ed. Lester and Gahr).

Other anthologists select poems written for adults that are appropriate for young adult readers and, therefore, particularly useful in the classroom. Some of these anthologies include *Sounds and silences* and *Pictures that storm inside my head* (ed. Peck), *Bring me all your dreams* (ed. Larrick), *A book of love poems* (ed. Cole), *Zero makes me hungry* (ed. Lueders and St. John), *Poems for pleasure* (ed. Ward), *A green place* (ed. Smith), and *Rainbows are made: Poems by Carl Sandburg* (ed. Hopkins).

Other poetry anthologies that are enjoyable to young readers are *Reflections on a gift of a watermelon pickle* and *Some haystacks don't even have any needles* (ed. Dunning), *Hosannah the home run! Poems about sports* (ed. Fleming), *Room for me and a mountain lion* (ed. Larrick), *My mane catches the wind* (ed. Hopkins), *Sprints and distances* and *The sidewalk racer and other poems of sports and motion* (ed. Morrison), and *Where the sidewalk ends: The poems and drawings of Shel Silverstein.* Paul Janeczko's *The crystal image* is a collection of poems selected for their clear and precise images. Two excellent anthologies of poetry that is rarely discovered by young readers are *A poison tree and other poems* (Mayer), which includes works by poets such as Langston Hughes, Eve Merriam, and Nikki Giovanni; and *Straight on till morning: poems of the imaginary world,* compiled by Helen Hill, Agnes Perkins, and Alethea Helbig, containing nearly one hundred poems by modern English and American poets, many of which appear in anthologies.

☐ *MY BEARD*

My beard grows to my toes,
I never wears no clothes,
I wrap my hair
Around my bare,
And down the road I goes.
SHEL SILVERSTEIN[7]

Some poetry uses a specialized form to deliver its message. The jingle is an example. Other examples include haiku, limerick, sonnet, and concrete poetry.

The teacher can share some of these forms with students in the anthologies *Haiku-vision* (Atwood), *A few flies and I* (ed. Merrill and Solbert), *Laughable limericks* (Brewton and Brewton), and Edna St. Vincent Millay's *Poems selected for young people,* which contains some of her best sonnets. Helen Plotz has collected sonnets and ballads in *The powerful rhyme: A book of sonnets* and *As I walked out one evening: A book of ballads.*

Poetry that looks like what it says is called concrete poetry. A very interesting anthology of poems, edited by Emmett Williams, illustrates the concrete poem for the students. The selections in *An anthology of concrete poetry* (Williams) demonstrate that poems are graphic and graphics can become poems. Young readers who have not yet discovered an interest in poetry often find it helpful to see not only the words of the poem but also the forms the words simulate. In Robert Froman's *Street poems,* for example, the poetry takes the shape of city objects: skyscrapers, a brick wall, a fire hydrant.

[7]From *Where the sidewalk ends: The poems and drawings of Shel Silverstein* (Harper & Row, 1974), p. 163. Copyright © 1974 by Shel Silverstein. Reprinted by permission of Harper & Row, Publishers, Inc.

☐ *NO PRETENDING*[8]

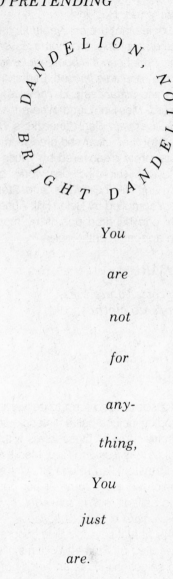

DANDELION, BRIGHT DANDELION

You

are

not

for

any-

thing,

You

just

are.

INCORPORATING POETRY INTO THE CURRICULUM. In the classroom, poetry should be incorporated into the regular curriculum. The students should continually share and discover poems. For example, poetry can become a part of the examination of the great themes of literature. Richard Peck's *Sounds and silences* groups poems under a variety of themes. Other thematic poetry anthologies for the classroom bookshelves include *To see the world afresh* by Lilian

[8]From Robert Froman, *Street poems* (New York: Dutton, 1971). Reprinted by permission of the author.

Moore and Judith Thurman; Adrienne Rich's collection exploring relationships, *The dream of a common language: Poems 1974–1977;* Terry Rowe's *To you with love;* Stephen Dunning's *Some haystacks don't even have any needles; A journey of poems,* edited by Richard Niebling; *The Malibu and other poems* by Myra Cohn Livingston; Timothy John's *The great song book: A collection of the best loved songs in the English language; Shrieks at midnight: Macabre poems, eerie and humorous* edited by Sara Brewton and John Brewton; *The evil image: Two centuries of gothic short fiction and poetry,* edited by Patricia L. Skarda and Nora Crow Jaffe; *Saturday's children: Poems of work,* edited by Helen Plotz.

Teaching a unit on black literature would not be complete without an examination of the powerful black poetry in words and songs.[9] These anthologies are useful: Arnold Adoff's *Celebrations, the poetry of black America: Anthology of the twentieth Century* and *Black out loud: An anthology of modern poems by black Americans;* Maya Angelou's *Just give me a cool drink of water 'fore I diiie, Oh pray my wings are gonna fit me well,* and *And still I rise;* Ntozake Shange's powerful autobiographical collection *Nappy edges; On our way,* edited by Lee Bennett Hopkins; Langston Hughes's *Selected poems;* Nancy Larrick's collection *On city streets; The black poets,* edited by Dudley Randall; and *Don't explain: A song of Billie Holiday,* an unusual book by Alexis De Vaux about the singer's life which is written in a free verse "song" that reflects her music. Two exceptionally valuable anthologies are *American Negro poetry* (ed. Bontemps) and *Black voices: An anthology of Afro-American literature* (ed. Chapman). Some of the writers included in these two anthologies are Claude McKay, Jean Toomer, Countee Cullen, Paul Laurence Dunbar, Phillis Wheatley, and Jupiter Hammon.

□ *There were few nonwhites in my school classes, and fewer in my social groups. Very little was studied and mentioned in black American history and literature in classrooms. But I was a student of history at an early age, and full of a young drive to find all answers immediately ... fit all the pieces of the great puzzle together. . . . If there were many thousands of black Americans all around me in this city, where was their history, their novels, their poetry, and so on? . . . Golden Slippers (and other collections by [Arna] Bontemps and Langston Hughes) gave me my first look at some of the missing pieces of the puzzle . . . some of the first tastes and smells of black American life as it was depicted by its artists.*

ARNOLD ADOFF

editor of Celebrations / *in Cullinan and Weiss (1980)*

[9]An excellent unit on black poetry can be found in Barbara Dodds Stanford and Karima Amin's *Black literature for high school students,* National Council of Teachers of English, 1978.

In a unit on women and literature, students can read poems by women collected in anthologies such as *Alone amid all this noise* (ed. Reit), *The other voice* (ed. Bankier et al.), *The world of Gwendolyn Brooks, No more masks!* (ed. Howe and Bass), Sylvia Plath's *Colossus and other poems; I became alone* (ed. Thurman) and *Emily Dickinson.*

In a unit on native Americans, anthologies such as William Brandon's *The magic world: American Indian songs and poems* and Terry Allen's *The whispering wind: Poetry by young American Indians* and *Arrows four: Prose and poetry by young American Indians* can be used.

Most young readers enjoy humorous poetry. *Fireside book of humorous poetry* (ed. Cole), e.e. cummings's *95 poems, Pocket book of Ogden Nash,* May Swenson's *Poems to solve,* Herman M. Ward's *Poems for pleasure,* and *Speak roughly to your little boy: A collection of parodies and burlesques* (ed. Livingston) are wonderful books to introduce in a unit on humor or to illustrate how much fun poetry can be. *The American way of laughing* (ed. Weiss and Weiss) contains not only poems but also fables, folktales, short stories, jokes, and all types of humor.

The works of Lewis Carroll should be included in a unit emphasizing humor. Myra Cohn Livingston has selected some of the best of Carroll's poetry in *Poems of Lewis Carroll,* a collection of poems from *Alice's adventures in Wonderland* and *Through the looking-glass.* When read aloud, "Jabberwocky" can be greatly enjoyed by young readers for its humorous, imaginative language. An excellent illustrated interpretation of the poem appears in *Jabberwocky,* illustrated in watercolors by Jane Breskin Zalben.

In mentioning "Jabberwocky" I feel compelled to repeat a warning voiced by Myra Cohn Livingston in protest of "assaults" by publishers of basal reading texts on her poem "Whispers." The "assaults" of which she speaks are changes made in her poem, inane questions asked of the children about it, and exercises suggested by the publishers.

> *. . . do not use it* [*the poem*] *to teach about rhyming words or punctuation, do not ask . . . inane and unanswerable questions. . . .*
>
> *Is it any wonder we lose children to poetry after the early grades? Is it any wonder we have lost many adults to poetry because they have long memories for the poetry and even the prose selections that were ripped apart and made whole again? (1983, pp. 143–144)*

Poetry must be read, listened to, and enjoyed by the young adult. Students must have the opportunity to develop their own images, to re-create the poem not as the poet wrote it, or the teacher taught it, but as the reader-listener imagined it.

The poetry of Edward Lear is also a must in a unit on humor. Two favorite collections are *The complete nonsense book* and *The nonsense book of Edward Lear.* Lear's poetry, influenced by his friendship with Alfred Lord Tennyson, includes limericks, nonsense verse, narrative poems, tongue twisters, and songs.

Other poets have written collections of humorous verse appropriate for young readers. N. M. Bodecker's poems are most often used with beginning readers; however, *Hurry, hurry, Mary dear* is appropriate for older students. The poems in this volume often tell a story. The title poem, for example, tells about poor Mary, who is continuously verbally harassed by a man who does nothing but sit in his rocking chair. Students enjoy the way the poet plays with words. In the poem "Bickering," Bodecker asserts, "I find it downright sickering!"

Nancy Willard's *A visit to William Blake's inn: Poems for innocent and experienced travelers* made history when it won the Newbery Award in 1982—the first book of poetry to do so. This book is appropriate in a unit on humor because of its cast of characters: two dragons who bake the bread and a rabbit who makes the bed. It is also useful as a bridge to the work of such classic poets as William Blake.

As mentioned earlier, the books of Shel Siverstein are particularly enjoyable for young readers. *A light in the attic* and *Where the sidewalk ends* are most useful in the middle and junior high school classroom.

John Ciardi's poetry is enjoyed by readers of all ages. His volume *Fast and slow,* which contains many satirical observations, is particularly appropriate for young adult readers.

Poetry about nature is important in helping students develop the ability to see the world in new and creative ways. There are many excellent poets as well as compilers of poetry who explore the natural world in words. Ann Atwood's collection *Fly with the wind, flow with the water* contains haiku verses that celebrate movement. Byrd Baylor's *The other way to listen* gives young readers the opportunity to hear, through words, cactus blooming or hills singing. *To look at any thing,* compiled by Lee Bennett Hopkins, combines the unusual nature photographs of John Earl with poetry that depicts haunting scenes of nature.

Another unusual way to look at things is presented by Arnold Adoff in *Under the early morning trees.* In this work he writes from the perspective of a young girl who goes out to explore a line of one hundred trees that protect her farmhouse from the weather. The girl finds ants working near a rock, beetles in dead wood, and a red bird in the branches. She hears the sounds of animals moving in the dry leaves and sees the farm animals beyond the line of trees. She feels secure in the newly discovered fact that the trees will still be there to protect her tomorrow.

Moments, also compiled by Hopkins, is a collection of poems about seasons which includes the work of David McCord, Langston Hughes, and Karla Kuskin. Another seasonal collection is *Sun through small leaves: Poems of spring,* which includes poems by Emily Dickinson, Gerard Manley Hopkins, Rudyard Kipling, and William Blake.

The value of poetry in language arts, English, and even social studies classes is clear. Less obvious is the fact that poetry can be of great value in science and mathematics classes. The anthology *Of quarks, quasars, and other quirks: Quizzical poems for the supersonic age,* compiled by Sara Brewton and John E. Brewton, introduces students to scientific concepts from the perspective of the poet. *Imagination's other place: Poems of science and mathematics,* compiled by Helen Plotz, introduces the poetry of many of the best-known poets to young science and math students. Through poetry students are introduced to new ways of examining the world of science and mathematics. The poems can be used to introduce new concepts or reinforce previously learned skills. The scientist and the poet have in common their ability to observe the world in detail. Students can be taught this skill by viewing slides of animals, by determining common characteristics of the various animals, by creating their own classification system, by reading poems about specific animals, by "developing" a new animal that fits into the classification system, and, finally, by writing their own poems about the animals they have invented.

Short Stories

Finding short stories written or compiled for young adult readers has not always been an easy task. Fortunately, an increasing number of short stories for young readers are now being published.

Some short story collections are written by a single author. Several of these collections have been written specifically for young readers. Norma Fox Mazer's *Dear Bill, remember me?* contains eight stories that deal with the maturation of a teenage girl. This Christopher Award–winning book is particularly enjoyable to the young female reader. A more recent Mazer book of stories, *Summer girls, love boys,* is an excellent addition for the classroom library. The maturation of the young black woman is explored in Kristin Hunter's short story collection *Guests in the Promised Land.* Likewise, Nicholasa Mohr's *In Nueva York* is a series of interrelated stories about growing up Puerto Rican in New York City's Lower East Side. The popular author Roald Dahl has compiled seven of his short stories for preteen and early teenage readers in *The wonderful story of Henry Sugar and six more.* The book is filled with exciting and suspenseful stories that are injected with Dahl's special sense of humor. *Arriving at a place you've never left* by Lois Ruby is a short story collection that was selected by the American Library Association as a Best Book for Young Adults. Its unifying theme is the stressful situation into which each of the young protagonists is placed: leaving a loved one to enlist in the army, being caught stealing, watching a parent go mad. Kurt Vonnegut's *Welcome to the monkey house* is a controversial collection of his short stories and essays that is often enjoyed by mature young adult readers. *A touch of chill* by Joan Aiken is a collection of fifteen tales that illustrate the storytelling quality of good short stories. The stories are fantastic, but never unreal. Everyday events become strange and terrifying, and the feeling of horror builds throughout the book. The macabre character of these stories attracts young readers, while their literary quality is sure to please the teacher. Robert Cormier has compiled his short stories in *Eight plus one.* All of these stories have been previously published in magazines, but never available for young readers. The book is particularly useful for students who wish to try their hand at writing their own short stories, because Cormier introduces each selection with information about the sources of the characters and plots, the difficulties he experienced writing the story, and other information about the story's creation. All the stories, except the "plus one," deal with the growing-up of young people. The stories take place either in the 1930s, the time of Cormier's youth, or today. Though the times are different, the young reader can see the similarities in the problems and their solutions.

Other short story collections of interest to young readers are anthologies of pieces by several authors, often within a single genre or theme. One of the best of these is *Authors' choice* (ed. Aiken). Eighteen writers selected their favorite short story for inclusion in this book. The authors include Joan Aiken, Vera Cleaver and Bill Cleaver, and Damon Runyon.

Good short story anthologies representing a single genre include *Fifty great ghost stories* and *Fifty great horror stories* (ed. Canning), *Great tales of action and adventure* (ed. Bennett), and *Dark imaginings* (ed. Boyer and Zahorski). These four books include selections by some of the great authors of horror and suspense fiction: Frank Usher, Sir Arthur Conan Doyle, Edgar Allan Poe, Arthur C. Clarke, Ursula K. LeGuin, Ray Bradbury, and others. *Dream's edge* (ed. Carr) is a science fiction anthology for young adult readers that includes stories by Larry Niven, Ursula K. LeGuin, Frank Herbert, Poul Anderson, and others.

Other anthologies address specific themes. Two edited by Robert Gold contain stories about growing up: *Point of departure: Nineteen stories of youth and discovery* and *Stepping stones: Seventeen powerful stories of growing up*. These two collection include stories with young protagonists by John Updike, Elizabeth Enright, William Saroyan, D. H. Lawrence, Grace Paley, and other well-known writers. An anthology of short stories that examines the futility of war is Georgess McHargue's *Little victories, big defeats: War as the ultimate pollution*. The collection includes stories by T. H. White, Kurt Vonnegut, Frank O'Connor, William Dean Howells, John Dos Passos, and others.

Some anthologies compile the works of authors of another generation or a different culture. *Giving birth to Thunder, sleeping with his daughter* (ed. Lopez) is a collection of sixty-eight stories from the oral tradition of more than forty tribes of American Indians. *Great Jewish short stories* (ed. Bellow) assembles twenty-nine short stories by authors such as Heinrich Heine, Sholom Aleichem, Philip Roth, and Grace Paley. *Long journey home: Stories from black history* and *Black folktales* (ed. Lester) intertwine black history, oral tradition, and literature. *Modern black stories* (ed. Mirer) is specifically for classroom use, with study aids that include "Questions for Discussion," "Building Vocabulary," and ideas for "Thinking and Writing." The collection includes stories by two black African authors as well as by well-known U.S. writers such as Arna Bontemps, Frank Yerby, Rudolph Fisher, Ralph Ellison, James Baldwin, and Richard Wright.

Some collections of well-known short story writers are of particular interest to young adult readers. *The complete short stories of Mark Twain* is humorous and thus enjoyable to many young adults. Edgar Allan Poe has been a favorite author of teenagers for generations. Some of his best and strangest short stories have been compiled for young readers in *Eighteen best stories by Edgar Allan Poe* (ed. Wilbur). An adaptation of the works of Arthur Conan Doyle for young teenagers is available for immature readers in four books entitled *The adventures of Sherlock Holmes* (ed. Sadler).

If the trend continues, many new short story collections will be published for young adult readers. The collections will include original works by authors of young adult novels, anthologies collected for young readers, and stories adapted for young teenagers and immature readers.

Conclusion

The books read and enjoyed by today's young adults cover the broad range of all literature. It is a rich and varied literature including all genres. It differs from the literature read and enjoyed by adults in its ability to meet adolescents' needs and speak to their interests. Some of the works read and enjoyed by adolescents are not written specifically for them, but speak to them nonetheless. Some, however, are written especially with the adolescent's needs, interests, and reading development in mind. Older adolescents who are developing the skills of the mature reader are likely to move easily from a book written specifically for them, to a book written for the general adult audience, to a book written many years ago and still read for its literary value. The developing reader begins adolescence reading the books of childhood and reaches the middle stages of adolescence reading the books of young adulthood as well as more adult works. The mature young adult reader exits adolescence reading everything—the wonderful literature written for children, popular current works, the literature of a profession, and the timeless works that will survive through the changing ages of humankind.

Titles Mentioned in Chapter 6

Biography and Autobiography

Alexander, S. *Anyone's daughter: The times and trials of Patty Hearst.* Viking, 1979. Bantam, 1980.

Angelou, M. *Gather together in my name.* Random House, 1974. Bantam, 1975.

———. *The heart of a woman.* Random House, 1981. Bantam, 1982.

———. *I know why the caged bird sings.* Random House, 1969. Bantam, 1971.

———. *Singin' and swingin' and gettin' merry like Christmas.* Random House, 1976. Bantam, 1977.

Baker, C. *Ernest Hemingway: A life story.* Scribner's, 1969. Avon, 1980.

Bentley, P. *The Brontës and their world.* Scribner's, 1969.

Blume, J. *Starring Sally J. Freeman as herself.* Bradbury, 1977. Dell, 1979.

Bogle, D. *Brown sugar: Eighty years of America's black female superstars.* Harmony, 1980.

Brodie, F. *Thomas Jefferson: An intimate history.* Norton, 1974. Bantam, 1975.

Brown, D. *Wounded knee: An Indian history of the American West.* Adapted by A. Ehrlich. Holt, Rinehart & Winston, 1974. Dell, 1975.

Carter, F. *The education of Little Tree.* Delacorte, 1976. Dell, 1981.

Carter, J. *Why not the best?* Broadman, 1975. Bantam, 1976.

Clark, S. *Fight against time: Five athletes—a legacy of courage.* Atheneum, 1979.

Cleaver, E. *Soul on ice.* McGraw-Hill, 1967. Dell, 1978.

Conot, R. *A streak of luck: The life and legend of Thomas Alva Edison.* Seaview Books, 1979. Bantam, 1980.

Crawford, C. *Mommie dearest.* Morrow, 1978. Berkley, 1981.

Duncan, L. *Chapters: My growth as a writer.* Little, Brown, 1982.

Dusky, L. *Birthmark.* Evans, 1979.

Edel, L. *Henry James.* Lippincott, 1953.

Farago, L. *Patton: Ordeal and triumph.* Astor-Honor, 1964. Dell, 1971.

Friedman, M. *Buried alive: The biography of Janis Joplin.* Morrow, 1973, 1975.

Hamilton, V. *Paul Robeson: The life and times of a free black man.* Harper & Row, 1974. Dell, 1979.

Haskins, J. *The story of Stevie Wonder.* Lothrop, Lee & Shepard, 1976. Dell, 1979.

Hellman, L. *Scoundrel time.* Little, Brown, 1976.

Herriot, J. *All creatures great and small.* St. Martin's, 1972. Bantam, 1978.

———. *All things bright and beautiful.* St. Martin's, 1974. Bantam, 1978.

Hersey, J. *Hiroshima.* Knopf, 1946, 1978. Bantam, 1975.

Houston, J. W., and J. D. Houston. *Farewell to Manzanar.* Houghton Mifflin, 1973. Bantam, 1974.

Huie, W. B. *A new life to live: Jimmy Putman's story.* Nelson, 1977. Bantam, 1980.

Jacobs, K. F. *GirlSports!* Bantam, 1978.

Jones, H. *Big star fallin' Mama: Five women in black music.* Viking, 1974. Dell, 1974.

Kahn, K. *Hillbilly women.* Doubleday, 1973. Avon, 1980.

Kennedy, J. F. *Profiles in courage.* Memorial ed. Harper & Row, 1964. Scholastic, 1964.

Kerr, M. E. *Me Me Me Me Me.* Harper & Row, 1983.

LeFlore, R., and J. Hawkins. *Breakout: From prison to the big leagues.* Harper & Row, 1978.

Lerman, R. *Eleanor.* Holt, Rinehart & Winston, 1979.

Lipsyte, R. *Free to be Muhammad Ali.* Harper & Row, 1978. Bantam, 1980.

McFarlane, M. C. *Cudjoe of Jamaica: Pioneer for black freedom in the new world.* Enslow, 1977.

Maiorano, R. *Worlds apart: The autobiography of a dancer from Brooklyn.* Coward, McCann & Geoghegan, 1980.

Mersand, J., ed. *Great modern American short biographies.* Dell, 1966.

Moody, A. *Coming of age in Mississippi.* Dial, 1968. Dell, 1980.

Morris, J. *Brian Piccolo: A short season.* Rand McNally, 1971. Dell, 1972.

Mowat, F. *The dog who wouldn't be.* Little, Brown, 1957. Bantam, 1981.

———. *The boat who wouldn't float.* Little, Brown, 1970. Bantam, 1981.

O'Brien, T. *If I die in a combat zone.* Delacorte, 1973. Dell, 1979.

Pizer, V. *Glorious triumphs: Athletes who conquered adversity.* Dodd, Mead, 1980.

Presley, P., et al. *Elvis, we love you tender.* Delacorte, 1980. Dell, 1981.

Sandburg, C. *Abraham Lincoln.* Scribner's, 1926–1939.

Sayers, G., and A. Silverman. *I am third.* Viking, 1970. Bantam, 1972.

Smith, G. *The horns of the moon: A short biography of Adolf Hitler.* Charterhouse, 1973. Dell, 1975.

Walton, D. *A Rockwell portrait: An intimate biography.* Andrews & McMell, 1978. Bantam, 1979.

Wolfe, T. *The right stuff.* Farrar, Straus & Giroux, 1979. Bantam, 1980.

History

Brown, D. *Lonesome whistle: The story of the first transcontinental railroad.* Adapted by L. Proctor from *Hear the lonesome whistle blow.* Holt, Rinehart & Winston, 1980.

———. *Wounded Knee.* Adapted by A. Ehrlich from *Bury my heart at Wounded Knee.* Holt, Rinehart & Winston, 1974. Dell, 1975.

Carter, F. *The education of Little Tree.* Delacorte, 1976. Dell, 1981.

Deming, R. *Man and the world: International law at work.* Hawthorn, 1974. Dell, 1975.

Forman, J. *Anarchism: Political innocence or social violence?* Franklin Watts, 1975. Dell, 1976.

———. *Capitalism: Economic individualism to today's welfare state.* Watts, 1972. Dell, 1976.

———. *Communism: From Marx's Manifesto to twentieth-century reality.* Watts, 1972. Dell, 1976.

———. *Fascism: The meaning and experience of reactionary revolution.* Watts, 1974. Dell, 1976.

———. *The mad game.* Scribner's, 1980.

———. *Nazism.* Watts, 1978. Dell, 1980.

———. *Socialism: Its theoretical roots and present-day development.* Watts, 1972. Dell, 1976.

Lester, J. *To be a slave.* Dial, 1968. Dell, 1978.

Meltzer, M. *Bound for the Rio Grande: The Mexican struggle, 1846–1848.* Knopf, 1974.

———. *In their own words: A history of the American Negro 1619–1965.* 3 vols. Crowell, 1964–1967.

———. *Never to forget: The Jews of the Holocaust.* Harper & Row, 1976. Dell, 1977.

———. *Taking root: Jewish immigrants in America.* Farrar, Straus & Giroux, 1976. Dell, 1977.

———. *Underground man.* Bradbury, 1972. Dell, 1974.

———. *Violins and shovels: The WPA arts projects.* Delacorte, 1976.

———. *World of our fathers: The Jews of Eastern Europe.* Farrar, Straus & Giroux, 1974. Dell, 1976.

Wilkinson, B., ed. *Cry sabotage! True stories of twentieth century saboteurs.* Bradbury, 1972. Dell, 1975.

Current Social Issues

Alexander, R. P., and J. Lester, eds. *Young and black in America.* Random House, 1970.

Bode, J. *Kids having kids: The unwed teenage parent.* Franklin Watts, 1980.

Brown, M. *Laying waste: The poisoning of America by toxic chemicals.* Pantheon, 1980. Pocket Books, 1981.

Cummings, B. S. *Let a river be.* Atheneum, 1978.

Curtis, P. *Animal rights: Stories of people who defend the rights of animals.* Four Winds, 1980.

David, J., ed. *Growing up black.* Morrow, 1968. Pocket Books, 1969.

————. *Growing up Jewish.* Morrow, 1969. Pocket Books, 1970.

Deloria, V. *Behind the trail of broken treaties: An Indian declaration of independence.* Delacorte, 1974. Dell, 1974.

Deming, R. *Man and the world: International law at work.* Hawthorn, 1974. Dell, 1975.

————. *Women: The new criminals.* Nelson, 1977. Dell, 1979.

deRopp, R. S. *Drugs and the mind.* St. Martin's, 1957. Rev. ed., Delacorte, 1976. Dell, 1976.

Edwards, C. *Crazy for God: The nightmare of cult life.* Prentice-Hall, 1979.

Felsen, H. G. *Can you do it until you need glasses? The different drug book.* Dodd, Mead, 1977.

Fleming, A. *Alcohol: The delightful poison: A history.* Delacorte, 1975. Dell, 1979.

————. *Ida Tarbell: First of the muckrakers.* Crowell, 1971. Dell, 1976.

————. *The senator from Maine: Margaret Chase Smith.* Crowell, 1969. Dell, 1976.

Forman, J. D. *The mad game.* Scribner's, 1980.

Francke, L. B. *The ambivalence of abortion.* Random House, 1978. Dell, 1979.

Galbraith, J. K. *Money: Whence it came from and where it went.* Houghton Mifflin, 1975. Bantam, 1976.

————, and N. Salinger. *Almost everyone's guide to economics.* Houghton Mifflin, 1978. Bantam, 1979.

Gardner, R. *The boys' and girls' book about divorce.* Aronson, 1970. Bantam, 1971.

Gordon, S. *You would if you loved me.* Bantam, 1978.

Hamilton, E. *Sex with love: A guide for young people.* Beacon, 1978.

Haskins, J. *Witchcraft, mysticism and magic in the black world.* Doubleday, 1974. Dell, 1976.

Hentoff, N. *The first freedom: The tumultuous history of free speech in America.* Delacorte, 1980. Dell, 1981.

Holliday, L., ed. *Heart songs: the Intimate diaries of young girls.* Bluestocking, 1978. Avon, 1981.

Hubmann, F. *The Jewish family album.* Little, Brown, 1975.

Hughes, L., M. Meltzer, and C. E. Lincoln, eds. *A pictorial history of black Americans.* Crown, 1956. Rev. ed., 1973.

Huthmacher, J. J. *A nation of newcomers: Ethnic minority groups in American history.* Delacorte, 1967. Dell, 1967.

Hymowitz, C., and M. Weissman. *A history of women in America.* Bantam, 1978.

Jaffe, D. T., and T. Clark, eds. *Worlds apart: Young people and drug programs.* Vintage, 1974.

Jordan, J. *Dry victories.* Holt, Rinehart & Winston, 1972. Avon, 1975.

Josephy, A. M. *The Indian heritage of America.* Knopf, 1968. Bantam, 1976.

Kelly, G. F. *Learning about sex: The contemporary guide for young adults.* Barron, 1976.

Kroeber, T. *Ishi, last of his tribe.* Parnassus, 1964.

Langone, J. *Like, love, lust: A view of sex and sexuality.* Little, Brown, 1980. Avon, 1981.

McKown, R. *The world of Mary Cassatt.* Crowell, 1972. Dell, 1976.

Martinez, A., ed. *Rising voices.* New American Library, 1974.

Meltzer, M. *Taking root: Jewish immigrants in America.* Farrar, Straus & Giroux, 1976. Dell, 1977.

Merriam, E., ed. *Growing up female in America.* Doubleday, 1971. Dell, 1973.

Phelan, M. K. *Probing the unknown: The story of Dr. Florence Sabin.* Crowell, 1969. Dell, 1976.

Prago, A. *Strangers in their own land: A history of Mexican-Americans.* Four Winds, 1973.

Pringle, L. *Lives at stake.* Macmillan, 1980.

———. *What shall we do with the land? Choices for America.* Crowell, 1981.

Quinn, J. B. *Everyone's money book.* Delacorte, 1979. Dell, 1980.

Richards, A., and I. Willis. *How to get together when your parents are coming apart.* Bantam, 1977.

Sandoz, M. *These were the Sioux.* Hastings, 1961. Dell, 1971.

Schell, J. *The fate of the earth.* Knopf, 1982.

Schulman, J., A. Shatter, and R. Ehrlich. *Pride and protest: Ethnic roots in America.* Dell, 1977.

Scott, J. A. *Fanny Kemble's America.* Crowell, 1973. Dell, 1975.

Sterling, P. *Sea and earth: The life of Rachel Carson.* Crowell, 1970. Dell, 1970.

Sussman, A. *The rights of young people: An American Civil Liberties Union handbook.* Avon, 1977.

Webb, S. and R. W. Nelson. *Selma, Lord, Selma: Girlhood memories of the civil rights days.* University of Alabama Press, 1980. Morrow, 1980.

Weiss, A. E. *The nuclear question.* Harcourt, 1981.

Jobs and Careers

Cole, S. *Working kids on working.* Lothrop, Lee & Shepard, 1980.

Jackson, T. *Guerrilla tactics in the job market.* Bantam, 1978.

Leana, F. *Getting into college.* Farrar, Straus & Giroux, 1980. Hill & Wang, 1980.

Mitchell, J. S. *I can be anything: Careers and colleges for young women.* Bantam, 1978. College Examination Board, 1975. Rev. ed., 1978.

———. *The men's career book: Work and life planning for a new age.* Bantam, 1979.

———. *The work book: A guide to skilled jobs.* Sterling, 1978. Bantam.

Terkel, S. *Working: People talk about what they do all day and how they feel about what they do.* Pantheon, 1974. Avon, 1975.

Wetherby, T., ed. *Conversations: Working women talk about doing a "man's job."* Les Femmes, 1977.

Wright, J. W. *The American almanac of jobs and salaries.* Avon, 1982.

Science

Asimov, I. *Asimov on astronomy.* Doubleday, 1974. Bonanza, 1979.

———. *The nearest star.* Lothrop, Lee and Shepard 1976.

———. *Of time and space and other things.* Doubleday, 1965. Avon, 1975.

———. *The collapsing universe.* Walker, 1977. Pocket Books, 1978.

———. *The solar system and back.* Doubleday, 1970. Avon, 1972.

———. *The universe: From flat earth to quasar.* Walker, 1966. Avon, 1968.

———. *From earth to heaven.* Doubleday, 1966. Avon, 1972.

———. *Life and energy.* Doubleday, 1962. Avon, 1972.

———. *The neutrino.* Doubleday, 1966. Avon, 1975.

————. *The tragedy of the moon.* Doubleday, 1973. Dell, 1978.

————. *The left hand of the electron.* Doubleday, 1972. Dell, 1976.

————. *The planet that wasn't.* Doubleday, 1976. Avon, 1977.

Barnett, L. *The universe and Dr. Einstein.* Harper & Row, 1948. Rev. ed., Bantam, 1974.

Carroll, D. *Wonders of the world.* Bantam, 1977.

Cooper, H. S. Jr. *A house in space.* Holt, Rinehart & Winston, 1976. Bantam, 1978.

Cousteau, J., and P. Diole. *Life and death in a coral sea.* Doubleday, 1971.

The Diagram Group. *Child's body.* Paddington, 1977. Bantam, 1979.

————. *Man's body: An owner's manual.* Paddington, 1976. Bantam, 1977.

————. *Woman's body: An owner's manual.* Paddington, 1977. Bantam, 1978.

Educational Broadcasting Corporation. *VD blues* (script). Avon, 1973.

Englebrekston, S. *Stars, planets, and galaxies.* Ridge Press, 1975. Bantam, 1975.

Glasser, R. J. *The body is the hero.* Random House, 1976. Bantam, 1979.

Gunter, J. *The Gunter papers.* Avon, 1975.

Hays, J. D. *Our changing climate.* Atheneum, 1977.

Hyde, M. *Your brain: Master computer.* McGraw-Hill, 1964.

Lewis, P., and D. Rubenstein. *The human body.* Grosset & Dunlap, 1971. Bantam, 1972.

Patent, D. H. *Evolution goes on every day.* Holiday, 1977.

Pyke, M. *Butter side up! The delights of science.* Sterling, 1977.

Sagan, C. *Cosmos.* Random House, 1980.

Stark, N. *The formula book.* Andrews & McMell, 1975, 1979. Avon, 1977.

Thomas, L. *The lives of a cell: Notes of a biology watcher.* Viking, 1974. Penguin, 1978.

————. *The Medusa and the snail: More notes of a biology watcher.* Viking, 1979. Bantam, 1980.

Mathematics

Adams, J. *We dare you to solve this!* Berkley, 1957.

Armstrong, J. M. *Women in mathematics.* Education Commission of the States, 1980.

Asimov, I. *Asimov on numbers.* Doubleday, 1977. Pocket Books, 1978.

Bell, E. *Men of mathematics.* Simon & Schuster, 1937, 1962.

Berloquin, P. *100 geometric games.* Scribner's, 1976, 1977.

Brooke, M. *Coin games and puzzles.* Dover, 1963, 1973.

Cook, P. D. *The ages of mathematics: The modern ages.* Doubleday, 1977.

Court, N. A. *Mathematics in fun and earnest.* Dial, 1958. New American Library, 1964.

Devi, S. *Figuring: The joy of numbers.* Barnes & Noble, 1977, 1981.

Diggin, J. *String, straight edge and shadow: The story of geometry.* Viking, 1965.

Fadiman, C. ed. *Fantasia mathematica.* Simon & Schuster, 1958, 1961.

————. *The mathematical magpie.* Simon & Schuster, 1962. Rev. ed., 1981.

Fujimura, K. *The Tokyo puzzles.* Scribner's, 1978.

Gardner, M. *Perplexing puzzles and tantalizing teasers.* Simon & Schuster, 1969. Pocket Books, 1971.

————. *Mathematical carnival.* Knopf, 1975. Viking, 1977.

————. *Mathematical circus.* Knopf, 1979. Vintage, 1981.

Hogben, L. *Mathematics in the making.* Doubleday, 1960.

————. *The wonderful world of mathematics.* Doubleday, 1955, 1968.

Hooke, R., et al. *Math and aftermath.* Walker, 1965.

Hunter, J. A. *Fun with figures.* Dover, 1965.

Jacobs, H. *Mathematics, a human endeavor: A textbook for those who think they don't like the subject.* Freeman, 1970, 1982.

Kaplan, P. *More posers.* Harper & Row, 1964.

Kordemsky, B. A. *The Moscow puzzles: 359 mathematical recreations.* Scribner's, 1972.

Linn, C. F., ed. *The ages of mathematics.* 4 vols. Doubleday, 1977.

Osen, L. *Women in mathematics.* MIT Press, 1974.

Schlossberg, E., and J. Brockman. *Pocket calculator game book.* Morrow, 1975. Bantam, 1976. *Book #2.* Morrow, 1977. Bantam, 1977.

Silverman, D. L. *Your move.* McGraw-Hill, 1971.

Simon, W. *Mathematical magic.* Scribner's, 1964.

Poetry

Adoff, A., ed. *It is the poem singing into your eyes.* Harper & Row, 1971, 1972.

———. *Celebrations: The poetry of black America.* Follett, 1977.

———. *Black out loud.* Macmillan, 1970. Dell, 1975.

———. *Under the early morning trees.* Illustrated by R. Himler. Dutton, 1978.

Allen, T. D., ed. *The whispering wind: Poetry by young American Indians.* Doubleday, 1972.

———. *Arrows four: Prose and poetry by young American Indians.* Washington Square Press, 1974.

Angelou, M. *And still I rise.* Random House, 1978. Bantam, 1980.

———. *Just give me a cool drink of water 'fore I diiie.* Random House, 1971. Bantam, 1979.

———. *Oh pray my wings are gonna fit me well.* Random House, 1975. Bantam, 1977.

Atwood, A. *Fly with the wind, flow with the water.* Scribner's, 1979.

———, ed. *Haiku-vision.* Scribner's, 1977. Filmstrip, Lyceum Productions.

Bankier, J., et al., eds. *The other voice.* Norton, 1976.

Baylor, B. *The other way to listen.* Illustrated by P. Parnall. Scribner's, 1978.

Bodecker, N. M. *Hurry, hurry, Mary dear.* Atheneum, 1976.

Bontemps, A., ed. *American Negro poetry.* Rev. ed. Hill & Wang, 1974.

Brandon, W., ed. *The magic world: American Indian songs and poems.* Morrow, 1971.

Brewton, J., and S. Brewton, eds. *Laughable limericks.* Crowell, 1965.

———. *Of quarks, quasars, and other quirks: Quizzical poems for the supersonic age.* Crowell, 1977.

———. *Shrieks at midnight: Macabre poems, eerie and humorous.* Crowell, 1969.

Brooks, G. *The world of Gwendolyn Brooks.* Harper & Row, 1971.

Carroll, L. *Poems of Lewis Carroll.* Selected by M. C. Livingston. Crowell, 1973.

———. *Jabberwocky.* Illustrated by J. B. Zalben. Warne, 1977.

Chapman, A., ed. *Black voices: An anthology of Afro-American Literature.* New American Library, 1968. St. Martin's, 1970.

Ciardi, J. *Fast and slow.* Illustrated by B. Gaver. Houghton Mifflin, 1975.

Cole, W., ed. *Fireside book of humorous poetry.* Simon & Schuster, 1959.

———. *A book of love poems.* Viking, 1965.

———. *The book of giggles.* World, 1970. Dell, 1980.

cummings, e. e. *Ninety-five poems.* Harcourt Brace Jovanovich, 1958, 1970.

DeVaux, A. *Don't explain: A song of Billie Holiday.* Harper & Row, 1980.

Dickinson, E. *Emily Dickinson.* Simon & Schuster, 1927. Dell, 1960.

Dunning, S., ed. *Reflection on a gift of watermelon pickle.* Lothrop, Lee and Shepard, 1966. Scholastic, 1967.

——. *Some haystacks don't even have any needles.* Lothrop, Lee & Shepard, 1969.

Fleming, A., ed. *Hosannah the home run! Poems about sports.* Little, Brown, 1972.

Froman, R. *Street poems.* McCall, 1971.

Hill, H., A. Perkins, and A. Helbig, eds. *Straight on till morning: Poems of the imaginary world.* Crowell, 1977.

Hopkins, L. B., and S. Rasch, eds. *I really want to feel good about myself: Poems by former drug addicts.* Nelson, 1974.

Hopkins, L. B., ed. *My mane catches the wind: Poems about horses.* Illustrated by S. Savitt. Harcourt Brace Jovanovich, 1979.

——. *Moments.* Illustrated by M. Hague. Harcourt Brace Jovanovich, 1980.

——. *On our way: Poems of pride and love.* Photographs by D. Parks. Knopf, 1974.

——. *Rainbows are made: Poems by Carl Sandburg.* Illustrated by F. Eichenberg. Harcourt Brace Jovanovich, 1952.

——. *To look at any thing.* Photographs by J. Earl. Harcourt Brace Jovanovich, 1978.

Howe, F., and E. Bass, eds. *No more masks: An anthology of poems by women.* Doubleday, 1973.

Hughes, L. *Selected poems of Langston Hughes.* Knopf, 1974–1979.

Janeczko, P., ed. *Postcard poems: Collection of poetry for sharing.* Bradbury, 1979.

——. *The crystal image.* Dell, 1977.

John, T., ed. *The great song book.* Doubleday, 1978.

Larrick, N., ed. *I heard a scream in the street: Poetry by young people in the city.* Evans, 1970. Dell, 1974.

——. *Bring me all your dreams.* Evans, 1980.

——. *On city streets.* Evans, 1968. Bantam, 1969.

——. *Room for me and a mountain lion.* Evans, 1974. Bantam, 1975.

Lear, E. *The complete nonsense book* (1912). Dodd, Mead, 1934, 1943. Includes *A book of nonsense,* originally published in 1846, and *Nonsense songs and stories,* originally published in 1871.

——. *The nonsense book of Edward Lear.* New American Library, 1964.

Lester, J., and D. Gahr. *Who I am.* Dial, 1974.

Livingston, M. C., ed. *The Malibu and other poems.* Atheneum, 1972.

——. *Speak roughly to your little boy: A collection of parodies and burlesques.* Harcourt Brace Jovanovich, 1971.

——. *What a wonderful bird the frog are.* Harcourt Brace Jovanovich, 1973.

Lueders, E., and P. St. John, eds. *Zero makes me hungry.* Lothrop, Lee & Shephard, 1976.

Mayer, M., ed. *A poison tree and other poems.* Scribner's, 1977.

Merrill, J., and R. Solbert, ed. *A few flies and I.* Pantheon, 1969.

Millay, E. S. V. *Poems selected for young people.* Harper & Row, 1951, 1979.

Moore, L., and J. Thurman. *To see the world afresh.* Atheneum, 1974.

Morrison, L., ed. *Best wishes, amen: A new collection of autograph verses.* Crowell, 1974.

—————. *The sidewalk racer and other poems of sports and motion.* Lothrop, Lee & Shepard, 1977.

—————. *Sprints and distances: Sports in poetry and the poetry in sport.* Crowell, 1965.

Morse, D., ed. *Grandfather rock.* Delacorte, 1972. Dell, 1974.

Nash, O. *Pocket book of Ogden Nash.* Pocket Books, 1954, 1962.

Niebling, R., ed. *A journey of poems.* Delacorte, 1964. Dell, 1964.

Peck, R., ed. *Sounds and silences.* Delacorte, 1970. Dell, 1970.

—————. *Pictures that storm inside my head.* Avon, 1976.

Plath, S. *Colossus and other poems.* Knopf, 1962. Vintage, 1968.

Plotz, H., ed. *As I walked out one evening: A book of ballads.* Greenwillow, 1976.

—————. *Imagination's other place: Poems of science and mathematics.* Crowell, 1955.

—————. *The powerful rhyme: A book of sonnets.* Greenwillow, 1979.

—————. *Saturday's children: Poems of work.* Greenwillow, 1982.

Randall, D., ed. *The black poets.* Bantam, 1971, 1976.

Reit, A. *Alone amid all this noise: A collection of women's poetry.* Four Winds, 1976.

Rich, A. *The dream of a common language: Poems 1974–1977.* Norton, 1978.

Rowe, T. *To you with love.* 2nd ed. Souvenir Press, 1977.

Shange, N. *Nappy edges.* St. Martin's, 1978. Bantam, 1980.

Silverstein, S. *A light in the attic.* Harper & Row, 1981.

—————. *Where the sidewalk ends.* Harper & Row, 1974.

Skarda, P. L., and N. C. Jaffe, eds. *The evil image: Two centuries of gothic short fiction and poetry.* New American Library, 1981.

Smith, W. J., ed. *A green place.* Delacorte, 1982.

Sun through small leaves: Poems of spring. Illustrated by S. Ichikawa. Collins, 1980.

Swenson, M. *Poems to solve.* Scribner's, 1966.

Szabo, J., and A. Ziegler, eds. *Almost grown.* Harmony, 1978.

Thurman, J., ed. *I became alone.* Atheneum, 1975.

Ward, H. M., ed. *Poems for pleasure.* Hill & Wang, 1963, 1966.

Weiss, H. S., and M. J. Weiss, eds. *The American way of laughing.* Bantam, 1977.

Willard, N. *A visit to William Blake's inn: Poems for innocent and experienced travelers.* Harcourt Brace Jovanovich, 1981.

Williams, E., ed. *An anthology of concrete poetry.* Something Else Press, 1967. Ultramarine, 1967.

Short Story Collections

Aiken, J. *A touch of chill.* Delacorte, 1980.

—————, ed. *Authors' choice 2.* Crowell, 1974.

Bellow, S., ed. *Great Jewish short stories.* Dell, 1963, 1978.

Bennett, G., ed. *Great tales of action and adventure.* Dell, 1959.

Boyer, R. H., and K. J. Zahorski, eds. *Dark imaginings.* Dell, 1978.

Canning, J., ed. *Fifty great ghost stories.* Taplinger, 1967. Bantam, 1973.

—————. *Fifty great horror stories.* Taplinger, 1969. Bantam, 1978.

Carr, T. *Dream's edge.* Sierra Club, 1980.

Cormier, R. *Eight plus one: Stories by Robert Cormier.* Pantheon, 1980.

Dahl, R. *The wonderful story of Henry Sugar and six more.* Knopf, 1977. Bantam.

Doyle, A. C. *The adventures of Sherlock Holmes.* Adapted by C. E. Sadler. Avon, 1981.

Gold, R., ed. *Point of departure: Nineteen stories of youth and discovery.* Dell, 1981.
———. *Stepping stones: Seventeen powerful stories of growing up.* Dell, 1981.
Hunter, K. *Guests in the Promised Land.* Scribner's, 1973. Avon, 1976.
Lester, J., ed. *Black folktales.* R. W. Baron, 1969. Grove, 1970.
———. *Long journey home: Stories from black history.* Dial, 1972. Dell, 1975.
Lopez, B. H. *Giving birth to thunder, sleeping with his daughter.* Andrews & McMell, 1977. Avon, 1981.
McHargue, G. *Little victories, big defeats: War as the ultimate pollution.* Delacorte, 1974. Dell, 1978.
Mazer, N. F. *Dear Bill, remember me?* Delacorte, 1976. Dell, 1978.
———. *Summer girls, love boys.* Delacorte, 1982.
Mirer, M., ed. *Modern black stories.* Barron, 1971.
Mohr, N. *In Nueva York.* Delacorte, 1977. Dell, 1979.
Poe, E. A. *Eighteen best stories by Edgar Allan Poe.* Edited by R. Wilbur. Dell, 1974.
Ruby, L. *Arriving at a place you've never left.* Dial, 1977. Dell, 1980.
Twain, M. *The complete short stories of Mark Twain.* Bantam, 1981.
Vonnegut, K. *Welcome to the monkey house.* Delacorte, 1968, 1974. Dell, 1970.

Suggested Readings

Alexander A. *The poet's eye: An introduction to poetry for young people.* Prentice-Hall, 1967.
Blostein, F. *Invitations, celebrations: A handbook of ideas and techniques for promoting reading in junior and senior high schools.* Ontario Library Association, 1980.
Carlsen, G. R. *Books and the teen-age reader.* 2nd rev. ed. Harper & Row, 1980. Bantam, 1980.
Cullinan, B., and M. J. Weiss, eds. *Books I read when I was young.* Avon, 1980.
Healy, M. P. *Teaching history through literature: A teacher's manual.* New American Library, 1983.
Hopkins, L. B. *The best of Book Bonanza.* Holt, Rinehart & Winston, 1980.
———. Poetry Place. *Instructor.* Monthly column.
Larrick, N., ed. *Somebody turned on a tap in these kids: Poetry and young people today.* Delacorte, 1971. Dell, 1971.
Livingston, M. C. An unreasonable excitement. *The Advocate,* Spring 1983, pp. 141–45.
Stanford, B. D., and K. Amin. *Black literature for high school students.* National Council of Teachers of English, 1978.
Weiss, M. J., ed. *From writers to students: The pleasures and pains of writing.* International Reading Association, 1979.

Part Three
Methodology for
Incorporating Young
Adult Literature
into the Secondary
School Classroom

BEVERLY PARDEE

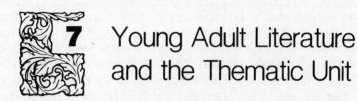

7 Young Adult Literature and the Thematic Unit

Reading Is Essential to Learning

Students must read if they are to learn the content of the subject matter. Without reading, they will be unable to apply the lessons of the subject to their lives; likewise, they will be unable to analyze the truth or falsehood of statements and to make judgments about right or wrong. Print, even in the electronic age, is the foundation of all learning in the schools. As adults, reading allows us to make decisions based on a vast array of information rather than on hearsay, gossip, or the media message. Reading helps us discover who we are, why we are here, and where we are going.

> ☐ *Literature is the exploration of the human dilemma. It has always asked the questions: What are we? Why are we? What are we doing here? What may we expect of ourselves?*
> VERA CLEAVER AND BILL CLEAVER
> *authors of Where the lilies bloom*

The best way to motivate teenagers to read is to allow them to read books based on their needs, interests, and abilities. Motivating young adults to read means letting them make their own choices from among a wide range of books available in the classroom or library. The difficulty for the teacher is in organizing

195

a curriculum that will help students learn necessary skills, concepts, and ideas while they are reading books based on their individual needs, interests, and abilities.

Clearly, in a classroom in which students select their own reading materials, not every student is reading the same book at the same time. Possibly no two students are reading the same book at the same time. Traditional teaching methods that require secondary school students to read a chapter in the text, answer the questions at the end of the chapter, discuss the commonly read material in class, and take a test on the skills, ideas, or concepts presented in the chapter will not work in the classroom in which students are reading self-selected materials. Similarly, the traditional method of teaching secondary school literature in which each student reads the same literary work, followed by an analysis of the work, activities based on the commonly read materials, and, finally, a test on the reading is inadequate in a classroom in which John is reading *Death be not proud* (Gunther), Sarah is reading *Eric* (Lund), Jane is reading *Questions and answers on death and dying* (Kübler-Ross), Sandy is reading *The loved one* (Waugh), Sam is reading *Death of a salesman* (Miller), and so on.

If every student is reading a different book, or even if small groups of six students each are reading a common book, with each of the five groups in the classroom reading different books, then the teacher must find a common thread that becomes "the cohesive strand running through all learning and teaching activities" (Kniep 1979, p. 388). This strand is often a common theme. For example, in the literature classroom mentioned above, the common theme of all the books being read by Sandy and Jane and the others might be Facing Death. This common theme becomes the building block of the curriculum for both planning and instruction.

Teaching Thematically

Thematic units join together the many concepts, ideas, and skills needed within a single discipline or across several disciplines. The fusion allows students to practice skills as they discover the concepts and ideas of the discipline(s). Similarly, thematic units enable teachers and students to use a wide variety of reading materials at various reading levels. Activities, discussions, projects, reports, tests, and the like relate to the common theme, rather than to the commonly read chapter. Through large-group, small-group, and individual activities, students are able to work simultaneously on a common concept or problem while using a wide range of materials and participating in a variety of activities in different interest areas and at different ability levels.

The thematic unit serves three functions: (1) it integrates the various areas of the discipline(s) by relating them all to one theme, (2) it allows the teacher to incorporate into the curriculum a wide variety of materials at different reading levels, including young adult literature, and (3) it assists the teacher in incorpo-

■ ■ ■ An Educational Aside

"Society must reaffirm the value of a balanced education." *Leaders of several professional organizations reached this conclusion in 1978. They circulated a statement on the essentials of education among a number of professional associations whose governing boards endorsed the statement and urged that it be called to the immediate attention of the entire education community, of policymakers and of the public at large.*

The statement that follows embodies the collective concern of the endorsing associations. It expresses their call for a renewed commitment to a more complete and more fulfilling education for all.

Public concern about basic knowledge and the basic skills in education is valid. Society should continually seek out, define, and then provide for every person those elements of education that are essential to a productive and meaningful life.

The basic elements of knowledge and skill are only a part of the essentials of education. In an era dominated by cries for going "back to the basics," for "minimal competencies," and for "survival skills," society should reject simplistic solutions and declare a commitment to the essentials of education.

A definition of the essentials of education should avoid three easy tendencies: to limit the essentials to "the three R's" in a society that is highly technological and complex; to define the essentials by what is tested at a time when tests are severely limited in what they can measure; and to reduce the essentials to a few "skills" when it is obvious that people use a combination of skills, knowledge, and feelings to come to terms with their world. By rejecting these simplistic tendencies, educators will avoid concentration on training in a few skills at the expense of preparing students for the changing world in which they must live.

Educators should resist pressures to concentrate solely upon easy-to-reach, easy-to-test bits of knowledge, and must go beyond short-term objectives of training for jobs or producing citizens who can perform routine tasks but cannot apply their knowledge or skills, cannot reason about their society, and cannot make informed judgments.

What Are the Essentials of Education?

Educators agree that the overarching goal of education is to develop informed, thinking citizens capable of participating in both domestic and world affairs. The development of such citizens depends not only upon education for citizenship, but also upon other essentials of education shared by all subjects.

The interdependence of skills and content is the central concept of the essentials of education. Skills and abilities do not grow in isolation from content. In all subjects, students develop skills in using language and other symbol systems; they develop the ability to reason; they undergo experiences that lead to emotional and social maturity. Students master these skills and abilities through observing, listening, reading, talking, and writing *about* science, mathematics, history and the social sciences, the arts, and other aspects of our intellectual, social and cultural heritage. As they learn about their world and its heritage they necessarily deepen their skills in language and reasoning and acquire the basis for emotional, aesthetic, and social growth. They also become aware of the world around them and develop an understanding and appreciation of the interdependence of the many facets of that world.

More specifically, the essentials of education include, among others, the ability to use language, to think, and to communicate effectively; to use mathematical knowledge and methods to solve problems; to reason logically; to use abstractions and symbols with power and ease; to apply and to understand scientific knowledge and methods; to make use of technology and to understand its limitations; to express oneself through the arts and to understand the artistic expressions of others; to understand other languages and cultures; to understand spatial relationships; to apply knowledge about health, nutrition, and physical activity; to acquire the capacity to meet unexpected challenges; to make informed value judgments; to recognize and to use one's full learning potential; and to prepare to go on learning for a lifetime.

Such a definition calls for a realization that all disciplines must join together and acknowledge their interdependence. Determining the essentials of education is a continuing process, far more demanding and significant than listing isolated skills assumed to be basic. Putting the essentials of education into practice requires instructional programs based on this new sense of interdependence.

Educators must also join with many segments of society to specify the essentials of education more fully. Among these segments are legislators, school boards, parents, students, workers' organizations, businesses, publishers, and other groups and individuals with an interest in education. All must now participate in a coordinated effort on behalf of society to confront this task. *Everyone* has a stake in the essentials of education.

Organizations for the Essentials of Education

American Alliance for Health, Physical Education, Recreation and Dance

American Council on the Teaching of Foreign Languages

American Federation of Teachers

American Theater Association

The Arts, Education, and Americas, Inc.

Association of American Publishers, Inc.

Association for Educational Communications and Technology

Association for Supervision and Curriculum Development

Council for Basic Education

Home Economics Education Association

International Reading Association

Modern Language Association

Music Educators National Conference

National Art Education Association

National Association of Elementary School Principals

National Association of Secondary School Principals

National Business Education Association

National Committee for Citizens in Education

National Council for the Social Studies

National Council of Teachers of English

National Council of Teachers of Mathematics

National Education Association

National Science Teachers Association

Speech Communication Association

■ ■ ■

rating a variety of grouping and individual instructional patterns that allow for individual needs, interests, and abilities.

The Single-Discipline Thematic Unit

The students in Mrs. Smith's English class are examining the theme Youth's Alienation from Adult Society. One group of six students is busily reading Paul Zindel's *The pigman.*[1] This novel is, in part, the story of two teenagers and their relationship to an elderly man. At the end of the book the old man dies. His death may, or may not, be the result of John and Lorraine's actions toward him. After the students finish reading the book, they will begin to work on a problem. Their assignment asks them to suppose that John and Lorraine have been arrested for the murder of Mr. Pignati. One student in the group will play the role of Lorraine, another will be John. Two other students will act as their defense attorneys. The remaining two students will act as the prosecution. The trial will take place in the classroom, with Mrs. Smith as the judge and six students, selected by the defense and the prosecution, as jurors. The students' assignments are to prepare the defense or prosecution based on the book and extrapolate additional evidence from the book. They must also investigate the legal procedures they will need to perform in the courtroom. During their group work, Mrs. Smith will help them by suggesting resources, asking them questions about the story that will lead to better understanding, quizzing them on legal vocabulary they will need during the trial, helping them write a legal brief, and introducing them to a real attorney to interview as a resource person. These students will use a variety of skills needed in the English classroom. They will be reading, writing, interviewing, learning vocabulary, role playing, doing research, and analyzing the book they have read.

---

[1]An excellent resource for developing group work is Gene Stanford, *Developing effective classroom groups: A practical guide for teachers* (Hart, 1977).

■ ■ ■ An Anthological Aside

The Oath

PAUL ZINDEL

Being of sound mind and body on this 15th day of April in our sophomore year at Franklin High School, let it be known that Lorraine Jensen and John Conlan have decided to record the facts, and only the facts, about our experiences with Mr. Angelo Pignati.

Miss Reillen, the Cricket, is watching us at every moment because she is the librarian at Franklin High and thinks we're using her typewriter to copy a book report for our retarded English teacher.

The truth and nothing but the truth, until this memorial epic is finished, So Help Us God! . . .

I stayed until the ambulance doctor gestured that the Pigman was dead. A whole crowd of people had gathered to crane their necks and watch them roll a dead man onto a stretcher. I don't know where they all came from so quickly. It must have been announced over the loudspeaker. Hey everybody! Come see the dead man in the monkey house. Step right up. Special feature today.

"Good-bye, Mr. Pignati," I said, hardly moving my lips. The police and attendants moved calmly, surely, as if they were performing a ritual and had forgotten the meaning of it. I don't think they ever *knew* the meaning of it. I thought of machinery—automatic, constant, unable to be stopped.

The sun had come out, and I had to cover my eyes. Finally I saw Lorraine sitting on a bench in the large center mall near the entrance of the zoo. There was a long pond that was heated in some way so the water wouldn't freeze and kill the fish, and she looked strange surrounded by the mist that rose from its surface.

"Here's your glasses."

She didn't answer at first—just kept looking at the ground. Then she struck out at me, as though trying to punch me.

"We murdered him," she screamed, and I turned away because I had been through just about all I could stand.

"Here's your glasses," I said again, almost hating her for a second. I wanted to yell at her, tell her he had no business fooling around with kids. I wanted to tell her he had no right going backward. When you grow up, you're not supposed to go back. Trespassing—that's what he had done.

I sat down next to her and lit up another cigarette. I couldn't help but look at the flashing light on top of the ambulance. They had driven it right up to the entrance of the monkey house, and it looked weird because it didn't belong. Right in the bright sunlight you could see the flashing dome going like crazy, pulsing like a heartbeat.

Then I saw this ridiculous sight running toward us from the other end of the mall—a great big fat man in a stupid-looking uniform, clutching a fistful of strings attached to helium balloons that bobbed in the air behind him. He was hobbling as fast as he could go, right toward the monkey house, with this sign around his neck: BUY YOUR FUNNY-FACE BAL-LOONS HERE!

Lorraine lifted her head slightly and watched him go by. Then she broke down crying again and turned away so she was facing the pond and didn't have to look at me. I noticed a whole school of goldfish practically sticking their noses out of the water because they thought someone was going to feed them. In the deep center a large carp flipped its tail and then disap-peared as quickly as it had surfaced.

"Let's go, Lorraine," I said softly, standing beside her. I lowered the sun-glasses, and she took them, almost dropping them again trying to get them on.

Her hand lingered near mine, and I took it gently. She seemed funny peering up at me over the thin metal rims. We looked at each other. There was no need to smile or tell a joke or run for roller skates. Without a word, I think we both understood.

We had trespassed too—been where we didn't belong, and we were being punished for it. Mr. Pignati had paid with his life. But when he died some-thing in us had died as well.

There was no one else to blame anymore. No Bores or Old Ladies or Nortons, or Assassins waiting at the bridge. And there was no place to hide—no place across any river for a boatman to take us.

Our life would be what we made of it—nothing more, nothing less.

Baboons.

Baboons.

They build their own cages, we could almost hear the Pigman whisper, as he took his children with him.

■ ■ ■

Through this thematic activity many of the skills needed for successful English study will be integrated into the curriculum. Not all students in the class are reading *The pigman*. There are five other groups working. Each group has a similar integrating assignment. These groups are reading *That was then, this is now* (Hinton), *The catcher in the rye* (Salinger), *The boy who could make himself disappear* (Platt), *Dinky Hocker shoots smack!* (Kerr), and *Hamlet*. One student, who elected not to participate in the groups, is reading *Alan and the animal kingdom* (Holland). Through their assignments the various elements of English language teaching have been integrated, serving the first function of the thematic unit. Second, the students have been allowed to select from a variety of different works at a variety of different reading levels tied together by a common theme, Youth's Alienation from Adult Society.

Finally, Mrs. Smith has been able to incorporate a variety of grouping and individual instructional patterns during the unit. Most of the students are working in groups of five or six students. One student is working alone. During the group work the students' assignments require them to divide into subgroups of two or three students. For example, the groups preparing for the trial will work in three pairs: Lorraine and her defense attorney, John and his defense attorney, and the two prosecutors.

Similarly, Mrs. Smith uses other grouping patterns during the unit. The entire class met as a group for an introductory activity, or turn-on event, which introduced the students to the theme and provided a common experience. The turn-on event in this unit on Youth's Alienation from Adult Society was the viewing of *Breaking Away.* While watching this film about a teenager's attempt to gain independence, symbolized by winning a bicycle race, the students were instructed to be particularly aware of the teenager's interaction with the adults in the film. A large-group discussion followed the viewing, its major thrust being the title of the film. Why was Dave breaking away? What was he breaking away from? Was he really breaking away? At the end of the film, was he more independent than at the beginning? In what other ways do teenagers attempt to break away? Is breaking away a necessary part of growing up?

Several interesting points were raised during the discussion. Mrs. Smith listed major areas of disagreement on the board. The following day the students divided into self-selected discussion groups based on the disagreements of the previous day. Mrs. Smith prepared a list of questions after reviewing a tape recording of the class discussion. The class period of fifty minutes was divided so that the first ten minutes were used for group selection and organization. Each student selected a first- and second-choice problem to discuss. Mrs. Smith quickly organized the groups based on the individual student's selection and her knowledge of her students' abilities to work in a group. Once the groups were formed, the students randomly drew from marked index cards for group leadership positions. One student acted as chairperson and fielded responses to the questions; another student acted as recorder and reported the results of the group discussion. The groups were told to try to come to an agreement on the issue being discussed. The questions Mrs. Smith had prepared were used for guidance, but were not used if the discussion was proceeding without them. The discussion lasted fifteen minutes. The group problems ranged from "Is the support of a peer group necessary for all teenagers?" to "Must teenagers rebel against their parents to become independent?" At the conclusion of the discussion, each of the six small groups was given a maximum of three minutes to summarize the results of their discussion. During the remaining several minutes of the period, Mrs. Smith synthesized, with the help of the students, the result of the discussions and gave the long-range unit assignment. The students were instructed to select one of the problems they had been discussing, to solve the problem in their own minds, and to seek support for their individual solutions in their reading. Several class periods were to be devoted to individual research, and a short paper or project was to be completed at the end of the unit. The purpose of this assignment was to tie together the various activities of the unit for each student.

During the eight-week unit, other grouping arrangements are used by Mrs. Smith. In each of Mrs. Smith's classes the students are required to keep a journal. They are asked to jot down in it any unfamiliar words they discover during their reading; they need not find dictionary definitions for these words. Every Friday, half the class period is devoted to a discussion of the words. Each student presents one or two unfamiliar words. All the words are listed on the board, and each is discussed. Mrs. Smith tries to help the students figure out the meanings of the words during this discussion. Words that are not understood by the majority of the students are listed on a piece of newsprint. No more than five words are listed each week. These words become the basis of the next week's intensive vocabulary study. On Monday the class is given a sentence based on the theme they are studying. For example, on one Monday the sentence was: "Larry despised everything his father stood for." Small groups of three to four students write a brief composition using as many of the vocabulary words from the previous week as possible. Fifteen minutes are given for this exercise. The words during that particular week were *determinate, exonerate, iconoclast, metamorphism,* and *ethos.*

The success of Mrs. Smith's vocabulary lessons became obvious to me one Monday morning in my homeroom. The students in her classes were busily discussing the words they would be using that day. Even though no weekend assignment had been given, they already knew the definition of each word. One Monday an announcement of an assembly came over the public address system. A groan went up from the dictionary perusers in my homeroom: "Not during third period, that's English class!"

During the week, Mrs. Smith's students complete individual activities based on the five vocabulary words. They do crossword puzzles, often designed by volunteers from Mrs. Smith's study hall. They try to use the words correctly in the writing they do during their small-group work (e.g., *the pigman* group). They search magazines and newspapers for the words, and an extra point of credit goes to the first person to find the word in a particular source (this encourages the students to read on their own time). Finally, when they feel they know the words sufficiently, they complete a mastery test on these words and on words randomly selected from lessons of weeks past. They may take the test as many times as they like, but must place the completed test in their folders by the end of their English class period each Friday.

The various activities in Mrs. Smith's unit are tied together by the theme Youth's Alienation from Adult Society. Essential language skills are incorporated into the unit work rather than taught in isolation. During the unit the students read, analyze literary works, learn vocabulary, do research, practice composition skills, role-play, discuss, prepare oral and written reports, and work together in groups. Similarly, Mrs. Smith incorporates a wide variety of literature at many different reading levels. The students not only read the books they use for their small-group projects, but also are required to read independently from three to five other books, depending on the grade they hope to receive for the unit's work. The activities Mrs. Smith selects allow for a variety of grouping and individual instructional patterns. The patterns may include individual conferences with Mrs. Smith on independent reading materials, small-group work based on a common book, discussions by the entire class, individual research, and so on.

The basic organizational pattern for Mrs. Smith's thematic unit is quite simple. (See Figure 7–1.)

In the planning of the thematic unit, Mrs. Smith, often with the help of her students, selects the theme and decides on the objectives to be reached through the teaching of the unit. The turn-on event is selected by Mrs. Smith to

Figure 7–1 Organization of a thematic unit

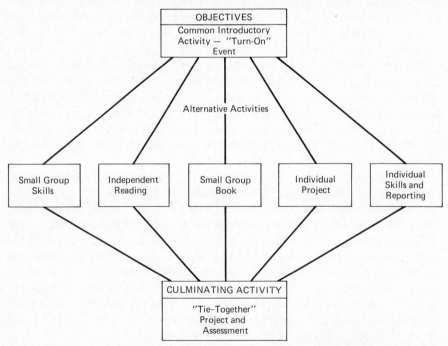

Based on Willard M. Kniep, Thematic units: Revitalizing a trusted tool. *Clearing House* 52, no. 8 (April 1979): 380–94, a publication of the Helen Dwight Reid Foundation. Used by permission.

give all of the students a common introduction to the unit, to set the tone for the unit, and to help fix the unit's objectives in the students' minds. The alternative activities are based on the objectives and stem from the turn-on event. For example, the individual project, as discussed above, is selected by the student based on the discussion following the viewing of the turn-on event film. The student chooses a book to be used during the completion of the small-group report based on information gained from the turn-on event and an annotated bibliography prepared by Mrs. Smith. Likewise, other reading materials are selected by the student in the course of working on the project. Usually these independent selections are related to needs and interests discovered during the project. The small-group skill work is developed following the discussion about the turn-on events, and language-related strengths and weaknesses are discovered through the reading, group work, and reporting. The individual skill and reporting activities are established as a result of needs uncovered during group work and individual work.

The culminating activity, which is designed to help the students and Mrs. Smith assess the extent to which they have reached the unit's objectives, is developed during the completion of the unit's alternative activities. In the case of the Youth's Alienation unit, the culminating activity was the group projects, such as the *Pigman* trial, based on the small-group book work. In other units Mrs. Smith and her students have developed culminating activities such as field trips to the opera, to a play, or to a funeral home. At times the culminating event has been a film, a panel discussion, a guest speaker, or a telephone hookup with an author. After each culminating activity, the class discusses how well the unit's objectives have been achieved.

The completion of the tie-together project on which the students have been working throughout the unit helps Mrs. Smith and the students assess the progress that has been made in understanding the unit's theme and reaching the unit's objectives. (The tie-together project in the Youth's Alienation unit involved the definition of a problem, research to help select an alternative solution to the problem, and a short individual paper or project presenting the problem and solution.) Other assessment techniques are used to evaluate student progress toward objectives. Vocabulary tests are completed each week. Students report on their individual reading in a variety of ways. Essay tests are given to help determine students' ability to analyze and synthesize the readings and activities completed during the thematic unit. Group and individual compositions and/or positions papers (e.g., the legal brief) are written throughout the unit. Group oral reports or projects are completed at the end of the unit.[2]

---

[2]For more information on developing a classroom organization similar to Mrs. Smith's, see Beach 1977, Blackburn and Powell 1976, Grambs and Carr 1979, and Chapters 8–11 of the present text.

■ ■ Sample Thematic English Unit

THE INDIVIDUAL VERSUS SOCIETY

OVERVIEW

This unit is designed to enable students to experience vicariously some situations in which the demands of society conflict with other individual values——artistic, intellectual, religious, or humanitarian. Having these vicarious experiences and responding to them may help students to have more empathy with individuals encountering similar situations, may help them to clarify some of their own attitudes and values, and perhaps will enable them to deal with comparable real-life situations.

GENERAL OBJECTIVES

As a result of this unit, the student:

1. Recognizes that social pressures exist in different forms in different situations;
2. Recognizes that different cultures favor different values with different priorities;
3. Recognizes that individuals may internalize conflicts between different ideal courses of action;
4. Is better able to empathize with an individual in conflict with social pressures;
5. Becomes more comfortable with discussion of values;
6. Examines and clarifies some of his/her own values;
7. Becomes more aware of the impact of slang and colloquial language on fiction;
8. Improves reading and viewing skills, especially sensitivity to expression of intangibles, of attitudes;
9. Improves oral and written communication skills.

EVALUATION

The student's progress toward these objectives may be evaluated by his/her:

1. Participation in a number of small- and large-group discussions;

From Nadine Shimer, Adolescent novels in thematic units: Bridging the gap, in K. Donelson (ed.), *Arizona English Bulletin,* April 1976. Reprinted by permission of the *Arizona English Bulletin.*

2. Short essay based on the conscription issue;
3. Short essay based on a short story;
4. Participation in oral presentation of a novel (or play);
5. Written response to a language research assignment;
6. Performance on a test, partly objective, largely essay.

MATERIALS

Films——"The Dehumanizing City . . . and Hymie Schultz"
        "The Man Who Had to Sing"
        "My Country Right or Wrong?"
        "The Violinist"

Novels——Robert Cormier's THE CHOCOLATE WAR
        Ken Kesey's ONE FLEW OVER THE CUCKOO'S NEST
        Harper Lee's TO KILL A MOCKINGBIRD
        Sinclair Lewis' MAIN STREET
        Robert McKay's THE TROUBLEMAKER
        Sandra Scoppettone's TRYING HARD TO HEAR YOU
        Mary Stoltz's PRAY LOVE, REMEMBER

Plays——Henrik Ibsen's AN ENEMY OF THE PEOPLE
       William Saroyan's THE MAN WITH HIS HEART IN THE
       HIGHLANDS

Poetry——W. H. Auden's "The Unknown Citizen"
        e. e. cummings' "i sing of olaf"
        Patricia Goedicke's "Jack and the Beanstalk"
        Phyllis McGinley's "The Angry Man"

Recording——Arlo Guthrie's "Alice's Restaurant"

Short Stories——Frank O'Connor's "The Idealist"
               John Updike's "The A&P"

LESSON PLANS AND ACTIVITIES

1. Have class see the film "The Dehumanizing City . . . and
    Hymie Schultz" and discuss Schultz's frustrations and
    his responses to them. Even though students recognize
    Schultz's efforts to break the red tape are often irra-
    tional, most of them will tend to identify and empathize
    with him.
2. Have class read aloud the short play "The Man With His
    Heart in the Highlands" and discuss the way the artist's
    relationship to society is presented. Many students are
    apt to identify with the storekeeper, Mr. Kosak, and

feel that, as a representative of society, he is victimized.

3. Have students, working in groups of 5 or 6, undertake the following values clarification exercise:

> Assume that you are the city council of a small city badly hit by economic problems. Your staff has determined that by instituting a rigid austerity program, you can continue to provide "essential services" (fire and police protection, hospitals, etc.) if you abolish one of these institutions or services: asylum for the mentally ill, institution for the citizens' center, or park and golf course. Decide which institution or service you would vote to do away with (underline it). After each member of the council has decided, try to reach a consensus as to which one the council will determine to abolish.

After all the groups complete their work, collect their reports, compare results, and ask them to describe any interesting features of their group deliberations. Try to elicit from group members who defended minority positions descriptions of how they felt as they did so.

4. Assign (or ask students to choose from among) the 7 novels and the play AN ENEMY OF THE PEOPLE. Arrange to have at least 3 students reading each major work. Give them some time to begin reading in class; estimate a date they should be finished reading them.

5. Read aloud in class the poem "The Unknown Citizen" and discuss the implications of it. Follow with readings of "Jack and the Beanstalk" and "The Angry Man." In discussion try to resolve the contrasting attitudes revealed in these two poems.

6. Have class see the film "My Country Right or Wrong?" and discuss it only to establish the plot—what they are to assume has actually happened. Then sketch in the historical context and basic situation of "Alice's Restaurant" and play Arlo Guthrie's recording of it. Finish by reading aloud "i sing of olaf."

7. Elicit in a brief discussion an identification of the issue of conscription and then ask each student to discuss the issue more fully in a short essay written in class.

8. Have students see the films "The Violinist" and "The Man Who Had to Sing" and discuss the attitudes revealed in them.

9. Distribute language assignment sheets which define the status labels used by many dictionaries, "slang" and "colloquial," and give several examples of each. The

assignment is to find and list several examples of "colloquial" language in the works in which it appears. These assignments should not be turned in until after all the novels have been completed, and then can be used as a basis for discussing the use of these kinds of language in works of fiction and its impact on them.

10. Have each group reading the same novel (or play) meet and construct a Johari window for a central character——Jerry Renault, Dr. Stockman, McMurphy, Atticus Finch, Carol Kennicott, Jesse Wade, Jeff Grathwohl, or Dody Jenks. (The Johari window is a technique I learned from Linda Shadiow of Bozeman, Montana. I regret that I don't know who originally devised it, but I think it was initially published in one of the Scholastic magazines.)*

The Johari window is a diagram used to show the many ways people see and don't see themselves, and the ways they are seen and not seen by others. There is often a wide gap between what a person seems to be and what he is. A Johari window is arranged like this:

	self-aware	self-blind
other-aware	things in a personality that both the person and others are aware of of--traits, habitual actions, etc.	things in a personality which others can observe but the person himself is not conscious of
other-blind	traits, facts, or intentions which the person deliberately withholds from others	facts or traits not known either to the person himself or to others (the sort of thing discovered by a psychologist)

11. Have students read either "The Idealist" or "The A&P" and write a short essay in response to this question: "Where did (the central character) get the values he determined to defend at such expense to himself?"

12. Lead students in discussions of the various responses to the question about the characters in the short stories.

*The Johari window was originally developed by Joseph Luft and Harry Ingham to aid in the analysis of interpersonal relationships.

13. Have students who have read the same novel (or play) meet and prepare to share that experience with the rest of the class. Each group should be given a work sheet designed for that book with a number of questions that elicit the ways in which the character(s) was in conflict with his/ her society, how pressures were manifested, and how the conflict was resolved. (I would suggest that each member of each group be required to participate in the oral presentation for full credit in this activity.) As much as 15 to 25 minutes could be allowed for each book, to permit the rest of the class to ask questions the presentation raises.

14. Each group shares its reading experiences with the rest of the class. (This should be a student-directed activity as much as possible, but if members of a given group don't see parallels between their book and other works studied in the unit, the teacher may want to lead them to discover these similarities.)

15. Lead the entire class in a discussion of the theme "individuals vs. societies" in order to help them perceive the entire scope of the unit and formulate some generalizations about issues. For example, students may not have observed that Carol Kennicott's dissatisfaction with her adopted home, Zenith, is paralleled by Dody Jenks' feelings about the town she was born and reared in. They may need guidance to realize that individuals' conflicts range from these subtle disaffections with cultural narrowness to the direct confrontations with powerful authorities in AN ENEMY OF THE PEOPLE and THE TROUBLEMAKER. Students can discover that multiple assaults on an individual's integrity can be provoked by such massive issues as white supremacy, as in TO KILL A MOCKINGBIRD, or by utter foolishness, as in THE CHOCO-LATE WAR. They can recognize that Camilla's distress with sexual mores is, in some measure, comparable with McMurphy's struggles with society's assessment of sickness and sanity. It is best to help students identify parallels and let them articulate generalizations rather than telling them anything.

16. Have students take a unit test. I would urge that the test consist of about ⅓ objective items--simple identification tasks to help fix titles, authors, well-known characters, and basic situations in the memory--and ⅔ essay items. The essay items might ask students to defend a choice of a character they know of who had to resolve the most pressing internal conflict and another character who had to display the greatest courage in defending his/her personal choice of a course of action.

Let me reiterate emphatically that any of these materials and activities are optional——there may be many other better suited to a given group of students. Teachers can select and devise the best strategies for their own classes. The same is true of the thematic unit and book titles that follow. I've simply identified some topics and books that have been useful for me with students I've known.

SUBJECT-CENTERED UNITS

"Puritan New England," Miller's THE CRUCIBLE, Speare's THE WITCH OF BLACKBIRD POND.

"What will the future bring?" Frank's ALAS, BABYLON, Levin's THIS PERFECT DAY, Neufeld's SLEEP TWO, THREE, FOUR, Orwell's 1984, Vonnegut's PLAYER PIANO.

"The Civil War," Crane's THE RED BADGE OF COURAGE, Gaines' THE AUTOBIOGRAPHY OF MISS JANE PITTMAN, Hunt's ACROSS FIVE APRILS, Mitchell's GONE WITH THE WIND, West's EXCEPT FOR THEE AND ME.

THEMATIC UNITS

"Search for identity through commitment to others," Byars' SUMMER OF THE SWANS, Cleavers' I WOULD RATHER BE A TURNIP, Donovan's REMOVE PROTECTIVE COATING A LITTLE AT A TIME, Malamud's THE ASSISTANT, McCullers' THE HEART IS A LONELY HUNTER, Saroyan's THE HUMAN COMEDY.

"Difficult decisions," Bradbury's FAHRENHEIT 451, Kerr's SON OF SOMEONE FAMOUS, Richard's PISTOL, Steinbeck's THE PEARL, Stewart's FIRE, Tunis' HIS ENEMY, HIS FRIEND, Wouk's THE CAINE MUTINY.

"The impulse to escape," Brautigan's A CONFEDERATE GENERAL AT BIG SUR, Hamilton's THE PLANET OF JUNIOR BROWN, Harris' THE RUNAWAY'S DIARY, Hemingway's A FAREWELL TO ARMS, Hinton's THE OUTSIDERS, McCarthy's BIRDS OF AMERICA.

"Learning through commitment," Fitzgerald's THE GREAT GATSBY, Holland's THE MAN WITHOUT A FACE, Kerr's IF I LOVE YOU, AM I TRAPPED FOREVER?, Knowles' A SEPARATE PEACE, Mather's ONE SUMMER IN BETWEEN, Steinbeck's OF MICE AND MEN, Zindel's THE PIGMAN.

"Loving and losing," Agee's A DEATH IN THE FAMILY, Brontë's WUTHERING HEIGHTS, Hemingway's A FAREWELL TO ARMS, Horgan's WHITEWATER, Kirkwood's GOOD TIMES, BAD TIMES, Peck's A DAY NO PIGS WOULD DIE, Stoltz's THE EDGE OF NEXT YEAR.

"On Self-Reliance," Cleavers' WHERE THE LILIES BLOOM, Crane's RED BADGE OF COURAGE, Defoe's ROBINSON CRUSOE, Donovan's WILD IN THE WORLD, Hemingway's FOR WHOM THE BELL TOLLS, O'Dell's ISLAND OF THE BLUE DOLPHINS.

THEMATIC UNIT BIBLIOGRAPHY

Cormier, R. The chocolate war. Pantheon, 1974. Dell, 1981.
Kesey, K. One flew over the cuckoo's nest. Viking, 1962. New American Library, 1975.
Ibsen, H. An enemy of the people.
Lee, H. To kill a mockingbird. Lippincott, 1960.
Lewis, S. Main Street. Grosset & Dunlap, 1920. New American Library, 1980.
McKay, R. The troublemaker. T. Nelson, 1971. Dell, 1972.
O'Connor, F. "The idealist."
Saroyan, W. "The man with his heart in the highlands."
Scoppettone, S. Trying hard to hear you. Harper & Row, 1974. Bantam, 1976.
Stoltz, M. Pray love, remember. Harper & Row, 1954.
Updike, J. "The A & P."

NONPRINT SOURCES

The dehumanizing city. Available from Learning Corporation of America.
Guthrie, A. "Alice's restaurant." Available from Reprise Records.
The man who had to sing. Available from Mass Media Associates.
My country right or wrong? Available from Learning Corporation of America.
The violinist. Available from Learning Corporation of America.

BIBLIOGRAPHY FOR OTHER SUGGESTED UNITS

Agee, J. A Death in the family. McDowell, Obolensky, 1957. Bantam, 1969.
Bradbury, R. Fahrenheit 451. Ballantine, 1953, 1970.
Brautigan, R. A confederate general at Big Sur. Ballantine, 1964, 1977.
Brontë, E. Wuthering Heights (1847). Bantam, 1981.
Byars, B. Summer of the swans. Viking Press, 1970. Avon, 1974.
Cleaver, B., and V. Cleaver. I would rather be a turnip. Lippincott, 1971. New American Library, 1976.
——. Where the lilies bloom. Lippincott, 1969. New American Library, 1974.
Crane, S. The red badge of courage (1894). Bantam, 1981.
Defoe, D. Robinson Crusoe (1719). Bantam, 1981.
Donovan, J. Remove the protective coating a little at a time. Harper & Row, 1973. Dell, 1975.

——. Wild in the world. Harper & Row, 1971. Avon, 1971.

Fitzgerald, F. S. The great Gatsby (1925). Scribner's, 1980.

Frank, P. Alas, Babylon. Lippincott, 1959, Bantam, 1960, 1979.

Gaines, E. The autobiography of Miss Jane Pittman. Dial, 1971. Bantam, 1972.

Hamilton, V. The planet of Junior Brown. Macmillan, 1971. Dell, 1978.

Harris, M. The runaway's diary. Four Winds, 1971. Pocket Books, 1974.

Hemingway, E. A farewell to arms (1929). Scribner's, 1977.

——. For whom the bell tolls (1940). Scribner's, 1968.

Hinton, S. E. The outsiders. Viking, 1967. Dell, 1982.

Holland, I. Man without a face. Lippincott, 1972. Dell, 1980.

Horgan, P. Whitewater. Farrar, 1970. Paperback Library, 1973.

Hunt, I. Across five Aprils. Follett, 1964.

Kerr, M. E. If I love you, am I trapped forever? Harper & Row, 1973. Dell, 1974.

——. Son of someone famous. Harper & Row, 1974. Ballantine, 1975.

Kirkwood, J. Good times, bad times. Simon & Schuster, 1968. Fawcett, 1968.

Knowles, J. A separate peace. Macmillan, 1959. Bantam, 1975.

Levin, I. This perfect day. Random House, 1970. Fawcett 1970.

McCarthy, M. Birds of America. Harcourt Brace Jovanovich, 1971. Avon, 1981.

McCullers, C. The heart is a lonely hunter. Houghton Mifflin, 1940.

Malamud, B. The assistant. Modern Library, 1952. Avon, 1980.

Mather, M. One summer in between. Harper & Row, 1967. Avon, 1968.

Miller, A. The crucible. Viking, 1953, 1973.

Mitchell, M. Gone with the wind. Macmillan, 1936.

Neufeld, J. Sleep two, three, four. Harper & Row, 1971. Avon, 1972.

O'Dell, S. Island of the blue dolphins. Houghton Mifflin, 1960. Dell, 1978.

Orwell, G. 1984 (1949). New American Library, 1981.

Peck, R. N. A day no pigs would die. Knopf, 1972. Dell, 1978.

Richard, A. Pistol. Little, Brown, 1969. Dell, 1970.

Saroyan, W. The human comedy. Harcourt, Brace & Co., 1943, 1971.

Speare, E. The witch of Blackbird Pond. Houghton Mifflin, 1958. Dell, 1975.

Steinbeck, W. Of mice and men (1937). Bantam, 1965.

——. The pearl (1947). Bantam, 1972.

Stewart, G. Fire (1948). Ballantine, 1974.

Stoltz, M. The edge of next year. Harper & Row, 1974. Dell, 1979.

Tunis, J. His enemy, his friend. Morrow, 1967. Avon, 1967.

Vonnegut, K. Player piano. Scribner's, 1952. Avon, 1966.

West, J. Except for thee and me. Harcourt, Brace & World, 1969. Avon, 1969.

Wouk, H. The Caine mutiny. Doubleday, 1951. Dell, 1965.
Zindel, P. The pigman. Harper & Row, 1968. Dell, 1978.

The Interdisciplinary Thematic Unit

A common concern, interest, or activity must provide the impetus for the development of an interdisciplinary thematic study. Several years ago I visited a high school in a suburban area that bordered on a large city. Many of the children in the area had contracted the same serious disease. The community was concerned that the illness was the result of air or water pollution possibly aggravated by industries in a bordering city. One of the biology teachers in the school brought up the problem at a departmental meeting. He suggested the development of a departmental unit investigating pollution, its causes and its results. One of the members of the department commented that the problem was as political as it was scientific. She suggested that the social studies department be brought into their discussions on the unit development. In the teachers' lounge the chairperson of the English department heard two social studies teachers discussing the unit and suggested that the English department might be interested in developing bibliographies of literature dealing with ecological issues. The interdisciplinary unit was born.

With the help of the school administration, members of the community were contacted and asked to join a curriculum committee to develop the unit. The student council was also involved in the curriculum development discussions. Each department developed activities, based on the theme, appropriate to their own discipline.

In English classes the students read books such as *Swiftwater* (Annixter), the story of a young man's attempt to develop a game preserve in Maine; *M. C. Higgins, the great* (Hamilton), about a boy who grows up in his attempt to rescue his family from an encroaching strip mine; *The lion's paw* (Sherman), about a young African who is caught in a conflict between efforts to protect the lion and the opposing views of white hunters; *Deathwatch* (White), an exciting novel about hunting, murder, survival, and escape; *The Martian chronicles* (Bradbury), a science fiction commentary on humankind's self-destructiveness; *Born free* (Adamson), a true story about the relationship of humans and animals; and *Cities in flight* (Blish), a science fiction work, actually four books, about people who are evacuating into space to escape an overpopulated earth.

In science classes the students examined the ecosystem of a local stream, analyzed the water contents, and investigated the materials being dumped into the stream by industries and municipalities. Wildlife in and around the stream was also studied. Other classes studied techniques for measuring the pollutants in the air, tested the air for specific chemicals, and analyzed industries' air pollution protection equipment and emissions. Other classes examined the emissions from cars, buses, and trucks, and sought to establish a pattern of high and low pollution periods.

Social studies classes examined federal, state, and local pollution guidelines and enforcement. Students visited city council meetings at which the pollution problem was discussed. They completed a case study on the pollution guideline enforcement in one highly polluting industry. Similarly, they examined the regulations in smaller municipalities upstream from their community.

Mathematics classes became involved in computation of some of the results of the scientific studies. They calculated the probability of the passage of stricter pollution regulations in the city council, and surveyed the community to establish the results of an antipollution referendum.

Journalism classes reported the results of the studies for the school newspaper. They interviewed officials of industry and government. They wrote feature articles on the families of sick children.

□ *I want to give you a glimpse of the choices you have before you, of the price that will be asked of you. . . . When you know what life has to sell, for how much, and what it can give away free, you will not live in darkness. I hope that in books you'll find your light, and that by this light you may cross from one shore of love to another, from your childhood into your adulthood. I hope that some of the light will come from my books and that, because of this light, life will lose its power to frighten you.*
MAIA WOJCIECHOWSKA
author of Shadow of a bull / *in her Newbery Award acceptance speech, reprinted in* Current Biography Yearbook / *September 1976*

The interdisciplinary unit[3] produced no conclusive results. However, the students became aware that there were no easy, or even right, answers. They learned that there were many sides to the issue. They developed their own opinions and supported them with evidence. They thought, they reasoned, they argued, they became involved citizens. And all the while, they were learning skills, concepts, and ideas central to the disciplines they were studying.

[3]Excellent interdisciplinary units that incorporate black literature appear in Barbara Dodd Stanford and Karima Amin's *Black literature for high school students,* National Council of Teachers of English, 1978.

■ ■ Sample Interdisciplinary Thematic Unit

Unit--Dealing with the Fear of Death
Duration--4 weeks
Subject(s)--Art, Math, English, Social Studies, and Music
Coordinator and Designer--Mark Finley

OBJECTIVES

Concepts

The student will:

(Eng./S.S.) (1) identify the different kinds of fears
that people have toward death.
(Eng./S.S.) (2) explore how some fears stem from a lack of
knowledge.
(S.S.) (3) explain how death can stimulate more than
one reaction/feeling at the same time.

Skills

The student will:

(Art) (1) do tombstome "rubbings" and create the
images
(Eng.) (2) read books dealing with the theme.
(Eng.) (3) compose a piece of writing that has a central
theme.
(Math) (4) learn how to compose statistical data.
(Math) (5) learn how to chart statistical data once it
is compiled.
(Music) (6) examine a variety of music used at funerals,
both modern and classic.
(Eng.) (7) identify new vocabulary words related to the
theme.
(S.S.) (8) learn about the occupations that deal
directly with death.
(Eng.) (9) compose a piece of writing that deals with
a hypothetical situation (e.g., obituary)
(Eng./S.S.) (10) use the newspaper to compile facts and
examine current events

Mark Finley is a teacher in the Hendersonville (N.C.) Schools.

Values

The student will:

(S.S.)   (1) express an understanding of the importance
              of dealing directly with a problem rather
              consequences.

(Music)   (2) express an appreciation of music and its
              purpose.

(S.S.)   (3) express an appreciation of those
              professional people who make dealing with
              death less of a burden for others.

(Eng.)   (4) read from a wide variety of literature.

(Math)   (5) derive answers mathematically to help to
              explain a trend.

CONTENT OUTLINE

I. Identification of the most feared deaths (other than death
   of self).
   A. death of a family member
   B. death of a close friend
   C. death of a classmate
   D. death of a teacher
   E. death of a neighbor
   F. death of an adult friend

II. Establishing a basis for the collection from the newspaper
    of statistical information concerning death.
    A. Using a data sheet to record the following information
       from obituaries for one week.
       1. name
       2. age
       3. sex
    B. Charting the findings on graphs
       1. Line graph: to show the relationship between the male
                      and the female death rate
       2. Bar graph: to show the average age of people who have
                     died each day during one week

III. Identification of people and methods that aid in dealing
     with the fear of death
     A. Examining the ways that music can help in dealing with
        death.
     B. Examining professional people who deal directly with
        death and help to ease our fears.
        1. coroner
        2. clergy
        3. funeral director

INSTRUCTIONAL STRATEGIES

I. Completion of an interest inventory (see Chart D).

II. Turn-on Event——visiting a graveyard.
   A. Examine the tombstones for different types of epitaphs. Do rubbings of the stones.
   B. Conduct a group search for the newest and the oldest graves and compute the difference. Attempt to determine how old the graveyard is.
   C. Examine the various types of grave markers.

III. Examination of different types of fears we have toward death.
   A. Brainstorm various feelings aroused after the visit to the graveyard.
      1. What were your personal feelings before, during, and after the visit?
      2. What emotions did you experience?
   B. Discuss the messages that the various epitaphs contained. How were they different or similar?
   C. Assignment. Create a tombstone that tells something special about you and write an epitaph on it as if it were on your own grave.

IV. Examination of how we deal with death
   A. List various situations in which death is most feared.
      1. death of a family member
      2. death of a close friend or classmate
      3. death of a teacher, a neighbor, or some other adult friend
   B. Conduct an informal survey to determine which is most feared by individual students.
   C. Place the students into small groups based on their fears.
   D. Assignment. Select one of the following books to read:
      1. A day no pigs would die (Peck)
      2. A ring of endless light (L'Engle)
      As you read the book, notice how the main characters deal with their feelings toward death. Are these feelings similar to the ones you have? Are there any differences?

V. Examination of various words that are commonly used in connection with death
   A. In your group discuss death-related terms with which you are familiar.
      1. One member should list words or phrases on newsprint.
      2. Share list with the class.
      3. Which words or phrases increase the fear of death? Why?

    4. <u>Assignment:</u> As you read your book, list all other words that create a feeling of fear toward death.

B. In your group discuss how the actions or words of the characters in the book help to overcome the fear of death.

    1. One member should list actions and words.

    2. Share this list with the class.

    3. How do the actions or words deal directly or indirectly with death?

    4. How do the characters' situations or life-styles alter their reactions or fears?

VI. Collect data from current newspapers concerning death.

A. Give each student the data sheet (Chart A).

B. Each day for one week keep the information required on the sheet.

C. Supply daily newspapers to the class.

VII. Chart compiled statistical data.

A. Using Charts B and C, draw conclusions from the data compiled.

B. Chart the findings.

VIII. Examine and discuss the various means by which people deal with death.

A. In your groups discuss the music used by different denominations during funerals. (Supply each group with a number of different hymnals and song books.)

    1. What do the lyrics indicate about fear or acceptance of death?

    2. Are there any major differences or similarities that you find in the lyrics?

    3. What mood do you feel while you read them?

    4. Which do you prefer? Why?

    5. Sing selected hymns as a class.

    6. As a class discuss

        (a) most familiar/frequent titles and themes.

        (b) hymns that make you feel sad.

        (c) hymns that give reassurance.

B. Identify classical music that deals with death.

    1. As a class, listen to either Verdi's or Brahms' <u>Requiem.</u>

        (a) What feelings do you experience while listening?

        (b) How do these compare to those that you experience when hearing and singing hymns that are used today?

        (c) List these feelings on the board.

    2. <u>In-Class Assignment.</u>
      Write a brief creative explanation as to why or why not you feel music helps to overcome the fear of

death. Support your view with examples from the
music that we have discussed.
C. In groups discuss the professional people who deal
directly with death.
1. One member should make a list.
2. Decide which professionals aid in overcoming fear
and which ones make death more fearful.
3. As a class discuss people in these professions from
the books read.
4. Assign each group one of the following professions
to research; eventually the groups will invite rep-
resentatives of the professions to the classroom
for a panel discussion.
(a) coroner
(b) clergy
(c) funeral director
(d) doctor
(e) psychologist
(f) social worker
D. Set up the panel discussion with four professionals who
deal directly with death.
1. Prior to discussion each group presents introductory material gathered from its research.
2. Class discusses each of the roles these people play
in dealing with death.
3. Class lists questions to be asked during the panel
discussion.
IX. "Tie-Together Event"
A. Four professionals meet in class with the students.
1. After the discussion, students examine reaction to
each professional.
2. What similarities or differences existed among
them?
3. Do you think they helped you to deal with your fear of
death?
4. Do they help others deal with the fear of death?
B. Assignment:
Complete any one of the following.
1. Write a letter of sympathy to a character of your
choosing from the book you read. Include methods
that you have learned from this unit that may be
helpful in that character's dealing with death.
2. Write a eulogy for any of the characters who died in
the book you read. How could you comfort the family
of the character by what you have to say about him or
her?
3. Write a creative paper on what you have gained from
this unit. Include any personal changes that have

occurred in your attitude toward death. Is the fear
that you expressed at the beginning still as great as
it was?

SUGGESTED READING LIST FOR THE UNIT

Angell, J. Ronnie and Rosey. Bradbury, 1977. Dell, 1979.

Bayly, J. The view from a hearse. Cook, 1973.

Bridgers, S. E. Home before dark. Knopf, 1976. Bantam, 1977.

Broughton, T. A. A family gathering. Dutton, 1977. Fawcett, 1977.

Cohen, B. The carp in the bathtub. Lothrop, Lee & Shepard, 1972.
Dell, 1975.

Cunningham, J. Come to the edge. Pantheon, 1977.

———. Far in the day. Pantheon, 1972. Dell, 1980.

Friedman, M. The story of Josh. Praeger, 1974. Ballantine, 1974.

Gackenbach, D. Do you love me? Seabury, 1975. Dell, 1978.

Greene, B. Summer of my German soldier. Dial, 1973.

Guest, J. Ordinary people. Viking, 1976. Ballantine, 1980.

Holland, I. Alan and the animal kingdom. Lippincott, 1977. Dell,
1979.

———. Of love and death and other journeys. Lippincott, 1975. Dell,
1977.

———. Man without a face. Lippincott, 1972. Dell, 1980.

Hall, L. Sticks and stones. Follett, 1972. Dell, 1972.

Jacot, M. The last butterfly. McClelland & Stewart, 1963. Ballantine, 1975.

L'Engle, M. A ring of endless light. Farrar, Straus & Giroux,
1980. Dell, 1981.

———. The summer of the great-grandmother. Farrar, Straus &
Giroux, 1974.

Mazer, N. A figure of speech. Delacorte, 1973 Dell, 1975.

Paterson, K. Bridge to Terabithia. Crowell, 1977. Avon, 1978.

Peck, R. N. A day no pigs would die. Knopf, 1972. Dell, 1978.

Rosenthal, T. How could I not be among you? Avon, 1973.

Sayers, G., and A. Silverman. I am third. Viking, 1970. Bantam,
1972.

Taylor, T. The cay. Doubleday, 1969. Avon, 1970.

Wojciechowska, M. A single light. Bantam, 1971.

Zindel, P. The pigman. Harper & Row, 1968. Deil, 1978.

Chart A

Record name, sex, and age of each person listed on the obituary column

MONDAY	1.				
	2.				
	3.				
	4.				
TUESDAY	1.				
	2.				
	3.				
	4.				
WEDNESDAY	1.				
	2.				
	3.				
	4.				
THURSDAY	1.				
	2.				
	3.				
	4.				
FRIDAY	1.				
	2.				
	3.				
	4.				
SATURDAY	1.				
	2.				
	3.				
	4.				
SUNDAY	1.				
	2.				
	3.				
	4.				

Student's Name: _____   Source of Information: _____

222

Daily Number of Deaths: Male and Female **Chart B**

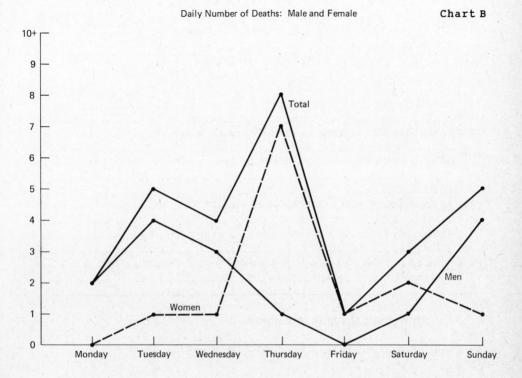

Average Ages of Daily Deaths **Chart C**

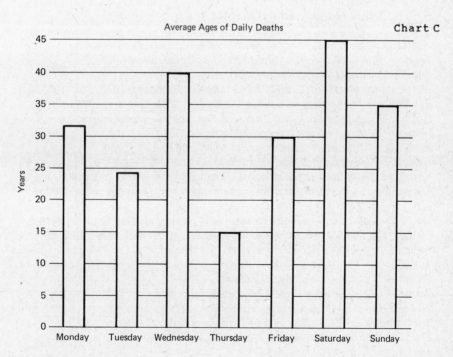

Chart D

Students' Name_____

INTEREST INVENTORY

1. What is your greatest fear? _____
   _____

2. Do you feel that others share this same fear? _____
   _____

3. Is there any way that you know to help overcome this fear? _____
   _____
   _____

4. To whom would you like to speak about this fear? _____
   _____

5. Does this fear involve only you or other people? _____
   _____

6. Does this fear create problems for you at home? _____
   in school? _____ with friends? _____

Anthological Aside in Chapter 7

Zindel, P. *The pigman.* Harper & Row, 1968. Bantam, 1978.

Titles Mentioned in Chapter 7

Adamson, J. *Born free.* Random House, 1974. Pantheon Books, 1960.
Annixter, P. *Swiftwater.* A. A. Wyn, 1950. Paperback Library, 1965.
Blish, J. *Cities in flight.* Doubleday, 1970. Avon, 1971.
Blume, J. *Are you there, God? It's me, Margaret.* Bradbury, 1970. Dell, 1980.
Bradbury, R. *The Martian chronicles.* Doubleday, 1946. Bantam, 1979.
Gunther, J. *Death be not proud.* Harper & Row, 1949. Pyramid, 1979.
Hamilton, V. *M. C. Higgins, the great.* Macmillan, 1974.
Hinton, S. E. *That was then, this is now.* Viking, 1971. Dell, 1980.
Holland, I. *Alan and the animal kingdom.* Lippincott, 1977. Dell, 1979.
Kerr, M. E. *Dinky Hocker shoots smack!* Harper & Row, 1972. Dell, 1978.
Kübler-Ross, E. *Questions and answers on death and dying.* Macmillan, 1974.
Lund, D. *Eric.* Lippincott, 1974. Dell, 1979.
Miller, A. *Death of a salesman.* Bantam, 1951. Dramatists Play Service, 1979.
Platt, K. *The boy who could make himself disappear.* Chilton, 1968. Dell, 1972.
Salinger, J. D. *The catcher in the rye.* Little, Brown, 1961. New American Library, 1962.
Sherman, D. R. *The lion's paw.* Doubleday, 1974.
Waugh, E. *The loved one.* Dell, 1948, 1966.
White, R. *Deathwatch.* Doubleday, 1972. Dell, 1973.
Wojciechowska, M. *Shadow of a bull.* Atheneum, 1964, 1970.
Zindel, P. *The pigman.* Harper & Row, 1968. Bantam, 1978.

Suggested Readings

Beach, D. M. *Reaching teenagers: Learning centers for the secondary classroom.* Goodyear, 1977. Scott, Foresman, 1981.

Blackburn, J. E., and W. C. Powell. *One at a time all at once: The creative teacher's guide to individualized instruction without anarchy.* Goodyear, 1976.

Grambs, J. D., and J. C. Carr. *Modern methods in secondary education.* 4th ed. Holt, Rinehart & Winston, 1979.

Kniep, W. M. Thematic units: Revitalizing a trusted tool. *Clearing House,* April 1979, pp. 388–94.

Stanford, B. D., and K. Amin. *Black literature for high school students.* National Council of Teachers of English, 1978.

Stanford, G. *Developing effective groups. A practical guide for teachers.* Hart, 1977.

Tanner, D., and L. N. Tanner. *Curriculum development: Theory into practice.* Macmillan, 1975, 1980.

Nonprint Sources

Breaking away. 20th Century–Fox, 1979. Available from Magnetic Video Corporation, Farmington Hills, Mich.

Roots. Available from Films Incorporated, 1144 Wilmette, Wilmette, IL 60091.

8 The English Classroom and the Young Adult Book

The Thematic Unit in the English Classroom

Teaching English involves helping students learn a myriad of language-related skills, developing in them an appreciation of great literature, and helping them gain a life-long reading pattern in which they critically read from a variety of authors, genres, and themes. Frances Erickson (1959) believes that the five aims of a high school program in language arts are:

1. To think clearly and logically
2. To communicate thought with clarity and with a degree of correctness acceptable to those with whom the student is communicating
3. To develop sensitivity to beauty and sensibility of the feelings of others by responding to imaginative literature
4. To develop independence in finding, using, and evaluating language materials
5. To become aware of the significance of language and one's responsibility in using it

The English teacher has an awesome responsibility. How can he or she accomplish all of Erickson's aims and still motivate students to read? One answer is to employ the thematic unit.

The goal of the thematic unit is not only to teach the theme, but also to use it as a vehicle for teaching English. The theme is the means by which the English teacher can encourage secondary school students to write, read, and speak. When writing, reading, and speaking are done in relationship to a meaningful theme, students are more likely to complete the tasks with enthusiasm.

SELECTING AN APPROPRIATE THEME. Selecting a theme that incorporates each of the skill areas of English, motivates students to read, helps them reach the aims of the high school English program, and is of interest to the large variety of students in the classroom can be a monumental task. Dwight Burton (1974) gives some helpful guidelines for selecting a theme. His guidelines are based only on the literature portion of the English classroom. The creative teacher, however, will incorporate the other skill areas into the unit. According to Burton, the content of a secondary school literature program is twofold: concepts and activities. The concepts to be taught within the literature portion of the program are based on some definition of the structure of literature. Burton proposes that the concepts should be based on the substance, mode, and form of the literary work.

Substance, according to Burton, deals with what the literary work is about. He claims that all literature is about human beings in four relationships: with their gods, with the natural world, with other humans,[1] and with themselves. The archetypal themes or central myths of all human experience, and therefore all literature, grow from these relationships. These myths, says Burton, could be used to develop thematic units on U.S. literature. He lists the following examples (p. 30):

1. The Puritan myth
2. The frontier myth
3. The myth of the significance of the individual's everyday life
4. The myth of importance of material success
5. The myth of youth's alienation from adult society

The same can be done when designing units for a British literature course. Basing the development of themes on the concept of substance can be very useful for the teacher who must teach U.S. literature to all juniors and British literature to all seniors. Dividing the year into themes can create the flexibility necessary for including a wide array of reading materials, for teaching all of the language arts skill areas, and for incorporating a variety of instructional and grouping strategies.

Mode, the second literary concept on which to base thematic units, is the general point of view of the author or the life experience that the literary work represents. Burton adapts the four literary modes, identified by Northrop Frye, to thematic teaching: romantic, comic, tragic, and ironic.

[1]See the sample thematic unit "The Individual versus Society" on pages 208–214 of this text.

> *Frye, in his book* Fables of Identity, *differentiates these modes in terms*
> *of the human condition which they frame: the nature and predicament*
> *of the hero or protagonist. If the hero is superior in degree to other men*
> *and to his environment, we have the typical romance and its literary affil-*
> *iates, the legend and folktale. If the protagonist is superior in degree to*
> *other men and is a leader but is not superior to his natural environment,*
> *we have the hero of most tragedies and epics. If the hero is superior to*
> *neither other men nor to his environment, we have the comic mode. If he*
> *is inferior in power or intelligence to ourselves so that we have a sense of*
> *looking down on a scene of frustration and absurdity, the protagonist*
> *belongs to the ironic mode. (Burton 1974, p. 30)*

The English teacher can develop units based on the modal approach to help the students understand how literature can be a study of the human condition.

A unit based on the tragic mode, for example, can highlight such young adult novels as *The contender* and *One fat summer* (Lipsyte), *Bridge to Terabithia* (Paterson), *Home before dark* (Bridgers), *Summer of my German soldier* (Greene), *Heads you win, tails I lose* (Holland), *Across five Aprils* (Hunt), *April morning* (Fast), *His enemy, his friend* (Tunis), *Very far away from anywhere else* (LeGuin), *Tunes for a small harmonica* (Wersba), *Pardon me, you're stepping on my eyeball* and *The pigman* (Zindel), and many others. Once the students are able to understand and relate to the tragic mode in these books, they can be directed with increased understanding to the more adult classics written in this mode. Allowing students to read about and relate to the tragedy of fifteen-year-old Adam Cooper in Howard Fast's *April morning*, who runs from the Continental Army at Lexington after his father is shot by British redcoats, is an excellent way of increasing student understanding and appreciation of Stephen Crane's *The red badge of courage.*

Form is the third literary concept that Burton suggests for use in the development of thematic units. "Form refers to the various genres of literature—fiction, drama, and poetry—and their subgenres, as well as to certain elements of structure—point of view, setting, dialogue, and the like—and to certain devices—metaphor and symbols. . . ." (p. 30). Burton says it is form that separates the teaching and study of literature from the study of other disciplines. Once having selected the genre or element of structure to emphasize, the teacher can develop a unit based on this literary form.

For example, in a unit entitled Location, Location, Location, the teacher might choose to emphasize young adult novels and classics in which the setting is of particular importance. In Peck's *A day no pigs would die* the plot would lose its meaning without the rural Vermont Shaker setting of the 1920s. The same, of course, is true in regional stories such as *Hawaii* and *Chesapeake* (Michener), *When the legends die* (Borland), and *Dust of the earth* (Cleaver and Cleaver). Often, historic events become settings that are essential to the plot. For example, the Nazi invasion of the Netherlands was the setting in which Anne Frank and her family fled to their attic hiding place. Similarly, the plight of poor black

Americans creates the setting and informs the plot of books like William Armstrong's *Sounder*. Teachers emphasizing the setting as an essential element of structure in the novel can also examine books like Lois Duncan's *Down a dark hall*, in which the remote Victorian house in which the private girls' school is located adds to the suspense created by the headmistress and her son. In Katherine Paterson's *Jacob have I loved*, the isolated island setting allows the characters and the plot to develop.

Literature and the Young Adult Book

Robert C. Small, Jr., in a fascinating article (1977a) on using the young adult novel to teach the art of literature, writes:

> *A study of most novels for adults, surely almost all the so-called "classics," puts students at a great disadvantage. The well-written junior novel, in contrast, invites, welcomes, students to meet it as equals. They can become real authorities on the literary craft of books like* Johnny May *(Branscum) or* A Hero ain't Nothin' but a Sandwich *(Childress). They can establish a critical relationship to* Fair Day, *and* Another Step Begun *(Lyle) and* Z for Zachariah *(O'Brien), similar to the critical relationship you or I have to our reading. As you can be a successful literary critic in relation to a* Peter Benchley *or a* John Hersey, *so students can apply with reasonable success a critical approach to* Virginia Hamilton *or* M. E. Kerr. *(p. 57)*

Small compares the English teacher's desire to plunge the students head first into the classics to attempting to teach a child how an automotive engine works by having him examine the engine of a 747 or an advanced modern racing car: "Their size, complexity, and refinement would make them poor starting places for the beginner" (p. 58). He suggests, instead, the use of working models. In the automotive engineering class the teacher would probably want to begin with a working model of a simple jet engine, a combustion engine with a single cylinder. In an English class the working model of a mature piece of literature, a "classic," according to Small, is the young adult novel. "Other subjects, mathematics and the sciences particularly, have made great use of the concept of the working model; but as literature teachers we have turned directly to the great and complex for examples of art and frequently experience not too surprising failure" (p. 58).

Most teenage students are developmentally prepared to read, enjoy, and analyze the young adult novel. Similarly, the vast majority of teenagers prefer young adult novels to the classics and are therefore more likely to be willing to discuss young adult books enthusiastically. The young adult book can act as a working model for studying the form of literature: plot, setting, characterization, dialogue, theme, and even metaphor and symbol. Once the student becomes an expert in the literary craft of the young adult novelist, the step to the classics is easier. The challenge of trying one's craft on new, more advanced objects is ever present.

> ☐ *Young adult literature is transitional literature. By its nature, it should move the reader closer to maturity not only by its subject matter and philosophy, but also by its inventiveness of style, its characterization, sensitivity and discovery, and most of all, by the commitment of its writers to do their best work.*
> SUE ELLEN BRIDGERS
> *author of* Home before dark

Much of the literature written for young adults is excellent. Using a working model is not using something that is inferior. For as Robert Small points out, "some of the most beautiful objects ever made by human hands have been working models—models of the solar system crafted of brass and walnut in the eighteenth century, models of ships built with perfect detail in the nineteenth century, models of steam engines and locomotives and automobiles constructed in our own time" (1977a, p. 58).

Some of the young adult literature may be superior in its literary craft to the classical works we want our students to read and understand. Of a young adult novel by Howard Fast, literary critic J. Donald Adams wrote:

> *Another kind of book of the same length might well have taken me longer, but this was one of compelling narrative power, of unflagging interest. It was Howard Fast's* April morning, *a story of the battle of Lexington as seen through the eyes of a 15-year-old boy who took part in it. When I had finished it, I said to myself, "This is an even better book than Crane's* The Red Badge of Courage." *I still think so. I readily wager that* April Morning *will some day reach the standing of an American classic.*[2]

Through the best of young adult literature the English teacher can simply and beautifully illustrate the author's technique in handling the many aspects of a literary work. For example, the plot and interrelated subplots of Robert Cormier's young adult novels *The chocolate war, I am the cheese,* and *After the first death* provide an excellent working model for the more involved and subtle plots of Conrad and Hardy. The characterization of Fielding, Faulkner, Thackeray, and Updike can be introduced through the character development in young adult novels such as *The great Gilly Hopkins* (Paterson), *A wind in the door* (L'Engle), and *Notes for another life* (Bridgers). The symbolism of the

---

[2] J. Donald Adams, "Speaking of Books," *New York Times Book Review,* April 23, 1961, p. 2. Copyright © 1961 by the New York Times Company. Reprinted by permission.

works of Hawthorne can be approached through a young adult book such as *The contender* (Lipsyte) and *A wrinkle in time* (L'Engle). The importance of the the settings in the classic works of Austen and Hemingway can be better understood after an examination of the settings in young adult books such as *Soul catcher* (Herbert), *Trial Valley* (Cleaver), and *Island of the blue dolphins* (O'Dell). The observant English teacher can find examples of metaphor and simile in almost every young adult novel. In M. E. Kerr's *Gentlehands,* we find this simple illustration of the simile: "Once I got to Beauregard, I always seemed able to put my own life out of my head, and just wallow in theirs, with Skye. Beauregard was like a drug; so was she." Metaphors are one of the most common forms of figurative language. Teenagers use them all the time (usually without recognizing them), and they are omnipresent in young adult literature. Often the epithets teenagers apply to peers and teachers are examples of metaphor. In Paul Zindel's *The pigman,* John and Lorraine call the librarian the Cricket. Similarly, John refers to his friends Dennis and Norton as "two amoebae." One of the most difficult literary concepts to teach teenagers is that of theme. Although the theme of Hawthorne's *The scarlet letter* might escape them, most teenagers can grasp the concept of theme in books such as *The outsiders* (Hinton), *The contender* (Lipsyte), and *Dinky Hocker shoots smack!* (Kerr).

The English teacher need not—in fact, should not—lecture on the literary art found in young adult novels. Rather, the teacher should develop activities that allow young adults to discover the literary form for themselves. Small suggests these activities "to focus meaningful attention on the major aspects of the novel while avoiding the abstractness of direct analysis":

> Plot: *Examining a sports event for the elements of a clear cause-effective plot as well as the relation of the plot to other literary elements such as setting and character; comparing the results to the stages in the plot of a novel like* Undertow *(Havrevold).*

> Characterization: *Selecting characters from television programs and describing the appearances and personalities of several of them, including one or more incidents to demonstrate those characteristics: using scenes and characters from a novel such as* Mom, the Wolfman, and me *to create a television series.*

> Setting: *Examining the settings in a number of different comic strips, looking for the ways artists create settings and how those settings suit the stories and characters, and considering the amount of detail each artist presents; comparing the presentation of settings in novels like* Where the red fern grows *to the visual settings in the comic strips in terms of detail, style, etc., and drawing several scenes in a style suitable to the book.*

> Theme: *Reading a passage which presents only facts about some topic and one from a junior novel about the same subject but containing opin-*

> *ions or emotions and comparing the two*—The Pigman, *with its several themes and numerous passages expressing the feelings and opinions of the two major characters, is especially effective. (1977a, p. 59)*

A film or videotape of a television show can be used to teach the concept of theme. The title of the show must relate to its theme. After watching the show, students discuss why the title was selected. Next, they refer to several books read in class. The students are asked why the author selected the title for the book. The criteria they suggest are listed on the chalkboard. The technique can be used with theme-related titles such as *The outsiders* (Hinton), *I never promised you a rose garden* (Green), *Morning is a long time coming* (Greene), *Home before dark* (Bridgers), *Man without a face* (Holland), *I am the cheese* (Cormier), and *Pardon me, you're stepping on my eyeball* (Zindel). Finally, a short story, poem, or chapter from a novel is read to the class. The title of the selection is not revealed, and the students are asked to decide on a title using the criteria they suggested. The students then reveal their titles and discuss the reasons for their selection.

An interesting twist can be added to this technique by using a novel, *Bugs in your ears* (Bates), and a television show, "Family of strangers," based on the novel. The questions can be asked: Is the change in the title a reflection of a change in the theme? Why was the title (and, perhaps, the theme) changed for television? What other changes were made in the plot, characters, or setting?

Language and the Young Adult Book

The study of language, its structure and its usage, is an important part of all secondary English studies. Students need to explore "items related to standard English as well as other varieties of English. They should explore language heritage, geographical and social dialect, semantics, and the silent language" (Bushman and Jones 1975, p. 56). Language can be studied through language-related units dealing with semantics, the media, communication, changes in language patterns, and advertising. It is also possible to study language in non-language-centered units. For example, in a thematic unit entitled Man against Man, the students can study differing dialects and social, geographic, and cultural language variations presented in books such as *Sounder* (Armstrong), a story set in the impoverished South, and *The chocolate war* (Cormier), a cruel tale of life in a wealthy New England private boys' school. Students can examine the difference between standard and nonstandard English as spoken by the characters in three books by Maya Angelou—*I know why the caged bird sings, Gather together in my name,* and *Singin' and swingin' and gettin' merry like Christmas.*

VOCABULARY. Vocabulary is much more than the memorization of lists of words to be regurgitated for the weekly test. The recognition of a vast array of words and the ability to use them correctly are valuable skills in our society. The lack of an adequate vocabulary can force students to learn far less than they are intellectually capable of learning. Without a good vocabulary, students cannot analyze what they read or verbalize their responses.

Since the goal of education is to prepare the student for the world beyond those that will ultimately lead students to become independent learners''
(Kaplan and Tuchman 1980, p. 33). By integrating the study of vocabulary with the study of the theme, the teacher is likely to produce students who independently use the vocabulary skills they have learned in their own identification and use of new words. To this end, there are a number of strategies using young adult books that can be incorporated into the thematic unit. The learning of the new vocabulary results not only in the identification and use of new words, but in the increased understanding of the concepts and ideas emphasized in the unit.

For example, in a unit entitled The Teenager in the Urban Environment, students select one of five young adult titles to read: *The outsiders* and *That was then, this is now* (Hinton), *Durango Street* (Bonham), *Mama* (Hopkins), and *A raisin in the sun* (Hansberry). Before reading their choices, students predict words they expect to encounter in the books. The teacher, Martha Wight, makes five columns on the chalkboard and lists the words the students identify.

To ensure that the students are able to use the words they have identified, Ms. Wight creates groups based on the students' book selections. Each group

Students in a middle school English class list words that describe the quail in the book That quail Robert *(Margaret Stranger) to later turn the words into a poem.*

copies the words on the board that relate to the book chosen and then writes a paragraph using ten of the words. The students are allowed to use the dictionary and change the forms of the words in constructing their sentences. At the end of the group work, the paragraphs are read aloud and the class agrees upon whether the words have been used correctly. Ms. Wight assigns one point for each word attempted and three points for each word used correctly. One group is declared the winner. The students understand the point system before they begin. The competition encourages them to use the words and to try to use them correctly.

Finally, the students record the words as a checklist to use during their reading. Each time one of the words appears in the book, the student checks the word and notes the page number on the list. Similarly, the students are told to keep lists of unfamiliar words found in their reading and page numbers on which the words appear. The students need not look up these words or define them. The words are used in future vocabulary study in the classroom.

It is important that students learn to identify the meaning of words from the context if they are to become independent learners. Therefore, Ms. Wight encourages students to predict the meaning of words from context. To do this the students use the lists of unfamiliar words they have been compiling from their reading. Each week Ms. Wight reviews each student's list and identifies generally unfamiliar words and the page numbers on which they were found. She develops a title for a chapter using one unfamiliar word and selects several sentences that give different clues to its meaning. Usually the sentences come from the students' reading. She places each on a transparency. Beginning with the title, she asks the students to write down the meaning of the word based on the title. She next flashes each of the sentence clues on the screen, asking the students to predict the word meaning. After having shown all the clues, she gives the meaning and asks each student to identify the clue that finally revealed the meaning of the word. She asks each student to tell how the particular clue helped to show the meaning. The students are learning to identify words in context. They are also developing additional information about the unit topic being studied from the words and sentences Ms. Wight selects.

Ms. Wight understands that words and skills learned and used in class need constant reinforcement. Therefore, she creates games, activities, and worksheets to reinforce vocabulary and skills. In a vocabulary learning center, students complete crossword puzzles, design games, play Password and Scrabble, and complete worksheets based on the words studied in class. Each center contains activities that pertain to each of the adolescent novels being read and deal with parts of speech, definitions, associations, synonyms or antonymns, and connotations (see Figure 8–1).

FIGURATIVE LANGUAGE. Teaching figurative language techniques, such as simile and metaphor, is often quite difficult. Jane Hyder has discovered a painless method using young adult literature. The students are given a picture of an easily described item, such as a fancy sports car. The students, in small groups,

Figure 8-1 Vocabulary Learning Center for *That was then, this is now* (Hinton)

Here are 20 words to be mastered from reading *That was then, this is now:*

1. delinquent	11. throwback
2. criminal	12. advised
3. drug	13. conviction
4. bond	14. freaks
5. drunken	15. guilty
6. pharmacy	16. knuckles
7. reformatory	17. hysterical
8. promoted	18. vengeful
9. juvenile	18. violence
10. authorities	20. celebrity

Activity 1

Copy these words on your own paper. Write the definition if you do not already know the meaning. Write a sentence using each word.

Example: criminal: Being a criminal means you have broken a law and possibly have gone to prison.

Activity 2

On the worksheets enclosed in this folder, fill out the necessary work.

Activity 3

Find pictures from magazines that illustrate the words. Select only five words.

SAMPLE VOCABULARY WORKSHEET

Some words describe, some words "work," and some name things. Place each word from the vocabulary list above in the correct column.

Descriptive words (adjectives)   Working words (verbs)   Naming words (nouns)

Words from words:
Make a list of words that are derived from or related to the vocabulary words.
Example:
    drug: druggist, drugstore, drugged
    celebrity: celebrate, celebration, celebrities

For each of the following words, write a synonym, or word that means the same.

Examples:
    criminal: prisoner, jailbird
    drug: medication, pill, medicine

1. delinquent:	6. promoted:
2. bond:	7. juvenile:
3. drunken:	8. authorities:
4. pharmacy:	9. throwback:
5. reformatory:	10. advised:

Source: Designed by Martha Wight, a secondary social studies teacher and former student in the Adolescent Literature class at the University of North Carolina at Asheville, 1980.

are allowed five minutes to write down every word they can think of that relates to the picture. When the five minutes are up, time is called and the class's words are listed on the board. The students are then given a picture of something that is totally unlike the described object, such as the school basketball team. The small groups must then attempt to match the words on the board with various aspects of the school team. Each group is given one point for every correct matching and two points if no other group has selected the pairing. Ms. Hyder gives a few examples before the groups begin the exercise. The students have discovered interesting similes and metaphors such as "Joe and Raymond are the headlights of the team"; "The team works together like a well-oiled engine"; "Coach Alan's heavily padded leather seat protects him during his fights with the official." After the points have been tabulated and the group winner announced, the students are told to begin reading or continue reading a young adult book. As they read the book, they keep a list of descriptive words or phrases that are paired with an unlike object. During the first five minutes of each class session for the next week, Ms. Hyder asks the students to report on the unusual word pairings they have found. Two lists of the discoveries are kept, one of metaphors and one of similes. At the end of the week the differences between each list are discussed by the class and Ms. Hyder places the correct heading on the list. These lists are displayed in the room for future reference.

Young adult literature can serve as a model for the careful development of language. Students can be taught to appreciate the sound of the English language through the reading of young adult literature. "To be exposed to trade books [books that are not part of a regular classroom textbook series] . . . in which development of plot, character, and setting is accomplished via such elements [as alliteration, onomatopoeia, rhyme, rhythm] is to provide an opportunity for the child to reflect upon language" (Burke 1978, p. 144–45). Reflection upon language should produce "richer, more original, more concise and precise use of words" (p. 145).

Many excellent young adult books provide young writers with the opportunity to reflect upon the careful development of language. Laura Ingalls Wilder in her book *Little house in the big woods* uses beautiful imagery and precise, carefully chosen words to evoke a feeling for the forest. Her language is deceptively simple, with short sentences and easily understood words, but the result is a rhythmical passage that is a very effective beginning for the book.

> *Once upon a time, sixty years ago, a little girl lived in the Big Woods of Wisconsin, in a little gray house made of logs.*
>
> *The great, dark trees of the Big Woods stood all around the house, and beyond them were other trees and beyond them were more trees. As far as a man could go to the north in a day, or a week, or a whole month, there was nothing but woods. There were no houses. There were no roads. There were no people. There were only trees and the wild animals who had their homes among them.*

Alvin Schwartz has collected humorous folklore from around the country and published it in a series of books that can be used in the classroom to integrate the teaching of language with a unit on U.S. folklore. The books are *A twister of twists, a tangler of tongues: Tongue twisters; Tomfoolery: Trickery and foolery with words; Witcracks: Jokes and jests from American folklore; Cross your fingers, spit in your hat: Superstitions and other beliefs;* and *Whoppers: Tall tales and other lies.* Each contains "Notes and Sources" that provide additional resource information about the material in the book. The collections not only provide students with wonderful examples of how alliteration, rhyme, and rhythm are used to develop humor and communicate ideas, but also give them an understanding of humor as a valuable part of the nation's history and culture. Students can use the tongue twisters, jokes, superstitions, and tall tales in these books as models for creating their own humorous twists, tomfoolery, "witcracks," and whoppers. Similarly, students can collect bits of local folklore that can be transcribed and sent to Alvin Schwartz in care of his publisher, J. B. Lippincott. Schwartz welcomes correspondence from both students and teachers.[3]

Onomatopoeic language is fun to reflect upon and to compose. Words that sound like what they denote are found throughout literature. Stories that evoke feelings of eeriness provide vocal imitations of sounds. The best ghost stories told around the campfire are terrifying because of the evocative language used. Edgar Allan Poe is of course the master of such onomatopoeic language, but other sources, particularly appealing to young adults, can be located. Three excellent sources for models to teach the use and composition of onomatopoeic language are *Some things strange and sinister,* edited by Joan Kahn, and two books compiled by Seon Manley and Gogo Lewis, *Masters of the macabre* and *Mistresses of mystery.*

Students can be encouraged to search for sounds and images in written language. Sam McKane has his eighth-grade students keep a journal of "fun" sounds and images they discover in their reading. His students are constantly playing with, sharing, and composing language that creates sounds and images. Consequently, they are conscious of the use of rhythm, tunes, rhyme, pattern, metaphor, simile, alliteration, onomatopoeia, interesting adjectives, and even unusual sentence structures. Mr. McKane uses the examples the students record as the basis for many writing lessons. One student, for example, copied this poem about television viewing from Roald Dahl's *Charlie and the chocolate factory:*

IT ROTS THE SENSES IN THE HEAD!
IT KILLS IMAGINATION DEAD!

---

[3]Lee Bennett Hopkins has written a teacher's guide for use in conjunction with Alvin Schwartz's books. It can be obtained by writing to J. B. Lippincott Co., Harper & Row, Publishers, Inc., 10 East 53 St., New York, NY 10022.

IT CLOGS AND CLUTTERS UP THE MIND!
IT MAKES A CHILD SO DULL AND BLIND
HE CAN NO LONGER UNDERSTAND
A FANTASY, A FAIRYLAND!
HIS BRAIN BECOMES AS SOFT AS CHEESE!
HE CANNOT THINK—HE ONLY SEES!

The poem provides many examples for teaching the "fun" sounds and images of language. The poem possesses rhythm and rhyme and is easily turned into a song. A good example of a simile is found in the line "His brain becomes as soft as cheese!" The poem includes alliteration ("clogs and clutters" and "a fantasy, a fairyland") and onomatopoeia ("clogs and clutters"). The poem's sentence structure adds to its rhythm: three short sentences, a long sentence, followed by two short sentences. The poem also provides the foundation for an interesting discussion about television viewing. Finally, the students use the poem as a model for composing their own poems on everyday subjects.

Examples of "fun" language usage abound in young adult literature. Even book titles are examples of imaginative usage. *A ring of endless light* (L'Engle), *Blinded by the light* (Brancato), *Heads you win, tails I lose* (Holland), *Bugs in your ears* (Bates), *The pigman* (Zindel), and *The outsiders* (Hinton) are sources for many lessons on the imaginative use of language.

THE STRUCTURE OF LANGUAGE. Understanding the basic structure of the English language is essential to understanding the meaning of the written word. Sentence structure, punctuation and capitalization, tense and mood, person, and the like can all alter the meaning or emphasis of a written passage. Subtleties of language are difficult to recognize, but students must understand them in order to become independent, critical readers.

Books written for the age level of the student are one means of encouraging the recognition and use of appropriate language patterns. A book that relates to the student's needs and interests and is well written serves as a good model for standard English usage. Teachers can select a book dealing with the theme being studied in the classroom to help the students learn concepts as well as language skills.

Cyrus Smith (1979) has developed an excellent way to guide students in learning the structure of the language as well as the structure and content of a book. The technique uses an exercise that Smith calls "read a book in an hour." The teacher selects a young adult book that is interesting to the students and easily understood by them. The teacher divides the book into chapters and distributes a section of the book to an individual or group of students for silent reading. The length of the sections assigned varies, depending on the individual student's reading ability and speed.

After completing the silent reading, each group or individual recounts the important events of the chapter to the class. The teacher structures the discussion of the important story events by writing several headings on the chalkboard. These categories can differ depending on the unit theme and might include setting, significant events, scientific discoveries, conflicts, characters, and important historic events. As the student retells the chapters, the teacher directs the discussion by asking open-ended questions that lead the student to not-to-be-missed information relating to the headings on the board.

After the individual or group has completed retelling the section of the story, the teacher summarizes and records the summary on the board beneath the appropriate heading. Students can refer to the headings as the story unfolds.

Once the book has been retold and the sections summarized, the teacher can use the technique to teach a variety of skills, such as sentence combining. The source for the combined sentences is the chapter summaries. Smith gives these examples from the first three chapters of Theodore Taylor's *The cay*.

> Chapter 1. *In February of 1942, twelve-year-old Philip Enright is growing up on the island of Curaçao. Curaçao lies off the coast of Venezuela, and its principal industry is an oil refinery. Philip's father is an engineer at the refinery.*
>
> Chapter 2. *Because of the threat of an attack on the refinery by a German submarine, Philip and his mother leave Curaçao for the mainland on a ship called the* Hato.
>
> Chapter 3. *The* Hato *is torpedoed on April 6th. In the confusion of the attack, Philip is separated from his mother and knocked unconscious by a piece of flying debris. Philip awakens on a raft with a West Indian named Timothy and a cat called Stew Cat.*

These summaries can be transformed into short, simple sentences by the teacher.

> 1. *Philip Enright is twelve years old.*
> 2. *He lives on the island of Curaçao.*
> 3. *Curaçao lies off the coast of Venezuela.*
> 4. *An oil refinery is on Curaçao.*
> 5. *The time is February 1942.*
> 6. *A German submarine threatens to attack the refinery.*
> 7. *Philip and his mother leave Curaçao.*
> 8. *They embark on the S.S.* Hato.

Working alone or in small groups, the students then combine these sentences. For example, they might write: Twelve-year-old Philip Enright lives on the island of Curaçao, off the coast of Venezuela.

The "read a book in an hour" technique allows the rapid reading of a book that relates to students' interests and to the theme being studied. The teacher, through the selection of headings for the summaries, manipulates the information gained from the book. The teacher creates simple sentences from the summaries that are important to the story and to the subject being studied. Finally, the students combine these into compound or complex sentences that require them to see the interrelationship of the sections of the book.

The sentence combining can be taken a step further by having the students turn the combined sentences into paragraphs. These paragraphs can be related to the unit being studied. For example, in a unit on World War II, students combine the information about *The cay* into sentences that are turned into newspaper accounts and radio news reports of the incident. Others students turn the sentences into a short play. Others combine the sentences with additional events from books about other World War II children to create a documentary about the children of the war. Each activity uses the "read a book in an hour" technique as the beginning point for examining and using language in experiences that relate to the unit being studied.

This technique helps the students understand the structure of the language by searching for the essential aspects of the author's writing. In an interview by Jean Greenlaw in M. Jerry Weiss's *From writers to students: The pleasures and pains of writing,* Mollie Hunter, an author of many historical fiction novels for young adults, responds to the question "How did you develop [your] appreciation of and ability to use language so well?"

> *... I had grasped the language simply as a result of the fact that every English lesson consisted partly, at least, of a passage which had to be analyzed. I had to analyze sentences so that I understood what the structure of language was. Then we had to do a passage which we called precis ... it was simply a long passage that had to be condensed, keeping the essential meaning of it. Now this meant that we were taught to understand the structure of language; we were taught to search for the words which had the strongest and most extensive meaning and to replace that whole sentence with that one word. (Weiss 1979, p. 47)*

The summarizing and sentence-combining technique gives the students some of the same training Mollie Hunter received in analyzing language in order to reduce it to its simplest form. In the sentence-combining technique, the students reduce the chapter to its essential elements, combine these elements to make sentences, and, perhaps, paragraphs.

BROADENING AN INTEREST IN LANGUAGE. The mature reader consciously attempts to discover new words or new meanings of familiar words. Similarly, the mature reader is interested in the structure and use of language.

Playing with words has always been a part of Alyce Cramer's classes. To encourage interest in words, their meanings and their use, Ms. Cramer creates a variety of language lessons based on the words in the books the students are reading.

Because in-depth understanding of a word and its use is essential in the study of literature, Ms. Cramer teaches a unit on language, propaganda, and persuasion. As part of the unit the students read young adult novels that illustrate how

■ ■ ■ An Anthological Aside

The Happiest Family

ROBIN BRANCATO

"Guess what, Gail?" he whispered. "I asked for you in my discussion group. We're calling ourselves The Happiest Family."

Gail cleared her throat. "I have a family," she said, feeling her palm grow moist as it touched his.

Michael smiled. "So now you're blessed with two! Hey, brothers and sisters," he said, "what do you think of this weekend so far?"

"Great!" Twenty-some people pounded their feet on the floor.

"Are we glad we're together?"

"Yes!"

In unison, as if they were cheering on a high school football team. Gail, backing away, felt Zora's arm encircle her waist.

"And what do we think of our guests?" Michael asked, holding Gail's hand up in the air. "What do we think of Bob and Marc and Gail?"

"Terrific!"

"Do we love them?"

"Yes!"

"Then let's show them how much," he said. "Let's overwhelm them with our love. Let's separate and join your family leaders, brothers and sisters. This is a time for really getting to know each other." He took Gail by the hand.

O.K., so she'd hang in for a few more minutes and slip out when she wouldn't attract so much attention.

"Welcome home," Michael said to them as they sat in a circle on the floor. "Zora—Dan—Charlie—Scott—Gail. Some of us have been brothers and sisters for a long time; others we hardly know at all. This is the time in our workshop when we tell who we are and how we came here. I'll begin, O.K.?"

Gail fixed her eyes on the space between his front teeth. He looked like a little kid. A lot of them did. As a group they were plain-looking, sickeningly cheerful, slightly grubby from living like kids at summer camp.

"I'm Michael Royerson," he said. "I come from Indiana. I started out studying accounting because that's what my dad wanted me to do. But my heart wasn't in it. Something was missing. I was empty. I was just going through the motions of practicing my parents' religion—they're Protestant. I was going along with their values without thinking.

"Anyway, I left college after two years and headed for California. Thought I'd like to try living in a commune. I did for a while, but things were terrible. Everybody argued—over money, over sharing the work, over women. I was more lost than ever—really turned off to people. So I left. I was just wandering aimlessly, at my wits' end . . ."

Zora's eyes were large as she listened. Dan studied his hands. Scott sprawled out on the carpet.

Michael looked up. "Then, one day in Berkeley, by accident, I met up with a girl who told me about a wonderful group of people who wanted to make the world a peaceful place. I told her, 'Yeah, I've heard that before!' I was skeptical—but I was curious. So I went to a meeting and then to a weekend like this. And I met some beautiful people. And that's how I first found the Light of the World, four years ago. Since then I've been all over the country."

"Were your parents behind you?" Dan asked.

"Well," Michael said, his cheeks glowing, "to tell you the truth—"

Scott smiled ironically. "They sent the Snuffer after you, didn't they?"

"They tried," Michael said. "That was one of his early attempts. He failed."

Snuffer? Gail looked from face to face.

"What did he do to you?" Scott asked.

"Kidnapped me as I was waiting for a bus to return from my grandmother's funeral. Wasn't that about as low as he could get? He got me all right. Tied me to a bed for about eight hours, tried to argue me out of my beliefs, but he couldn't keep me. When he let me go to the bathroom, I bolted out the window, borrowed a bicycle, and rode thirty miles back to the church."

"Michael!" Zora covered her mouth with her hands. "That's so amazing! You must have felt so betrayed by your parents, so alone."

"Yes, alone, until I got back here—to safety."

"I felt alone until I got here, too," she said, her voice subdued, "and do you know why that was so strange?"

"Why?"

Zora tilted her face. "Because I grew up in a family of fourteen."

"Fourteen? Really?"

"Yes, two parents and eleven brothers and sisters, and I still felt alone—can you believe that?"

Michael nodded. "Sometimes one family isn't enough, no matter how big it is. Tell us how you came, Zora."

"I'm from Ohio," she said. "From a little stick of a town. As far back as I can remember I wanted to get out of there. I often thought of running away, but I was scared to because I had no money. I couldn't afford college, so right after high school, last June, I went to Cleveland and got a job in an office, but the work was boring and I didn't know anybody.

"Then one night in summer, after I'd been in Cleveland a month, the Light of the World Sunbeam Chorale came to town. They sang for free in the park. I had always wanted to be a singer. I hung around afterward and tried out for the chorale. Well, I made it. I gave up my job and came here with the chorale. I've been a member of the Light of the World ever since."

"You're a different person now, aren't you, Zora?" Michael asked.

"Yes," she said. "I used to be so shy. Now I'm confident. I travel. I get to stay in beautiful places like this."

Gail watched her smoothing her skirt over her knees. "Do you miss your brothers and sisters at home?" Gail asked her.

"Sometimes," Zora said. "But I have my brothers and sisters here. And my Father is everywhere."

"That's right, Zora," Michael said. "You're very lucky. We all are. Dan, will you tell us about your life now?"

Dan, in a neat white sport shirt, fingered the dark rims of his glasses.

Gail, leaning back against the wall, listened to the overlapping voices as people around the room told their stories. Jim must have sat here once telling his. What had he said? "I'm from suburban New Jersey. I had what most guys want—nice house, decent parents, a sister who looked up to me—but that wasn't enough . . ."

"My name is Daniel Wong," Dan said, his speech precise, clipped. "I was born on the mainland of China. My family fled from the Communists. We came to California. We were very poor at first and were discriminated against. I went to school on the West Coast and studied political science in college. When I graduated I looked for a job for a full year. Nothing was open. I was prepared to devote myself completely to my work, but there was no work.

"Then one evening at a lecture, I met Mr. Brock, our East Coast director, who was then in California. I was impressed with his leadership. He introduced me to others, and I began to see a future for myself in the family of Father Adam. Since I became a member I've met a lot of important people and I've gained a lot of valuable experience."

"Wonderful, Dan," Michael said. He put his hand on Charlie's shoulder. "It's your turn, Charlie."

"I come from near Washington, D.C.," Charlie began, biting his lower lip. "I had an unhappy childhood. I was overweight and had almost no close friends in school. My older brother was an athlete and very popular, and I figured I couldn't ever match him so I might as well give up. I hated him then. Since I've found the Light of the World I don't hate anymore. Luckily I was good at science. I did pretty well in that, so I got accepted at Munro."

"Did things go better for you then?" Zora asked sympathetically.

"Not at first," Charlie said, "but at the end of my freshman year, I found this wonderful group where everybody was welcome—Protestant, Catholic,

Jew; black, white, brown, and yellow; old and young; male and female. It was a group called STIC—Students and Teachers for Improved Communications. And through it I came to the Light of the World."

Michael smiled. "Charlie's had a few interesting experiences since then, haven't you, Charlie?"

"Yes," he said ruefully. "My brother decides every once in a while I ought to be rescued."

Scott sat up. "Pity the poor Snuffer if he ever lays hands on Charles!"

"You know it!" Charlie said. "So far a Snuffer or two has trailed me, but I've never been captured. I have new courage since I found the Light."

"Oh, Charlie," Zora cried.

"He's an inspiration to all of us," Michael said. "How about it, Scott? How did you come to the church?"

"A hopeless wreck," Scott said, stretching languidly.

Gail watched him. Very expressive face. A talented musician. Generally sharp. Tense, though. Fingernails stubby from being bitten.

"I'm Scott Halloran. I'm originally from North Carolina, but I've been everywhere, including hell. I was the only child in a Catholic family. That's unique right there, isn't it? My father was a career officer in the U.S. Army and my mother played bridge a lot. They seldom remembered they had me, but I didn't care, because all I was interested in was music. I wanted to be a star!" he said in a tone of self-mockery.

"Well, I left home six years ago when I was seventeen, and I worked in New Orleans in a piano bar, where I got a taste of bourbon. I played guitar and dropped acid for a while in the Village in New York. Then I snorted coke in Paris, where I went to study and wound up being kept by an older woman. I wrote poetry and played music, but what I was producing got worse and worse, because I debauched myself by night and slept by day. You can't imagine how badly I wanted to get out of that scene, but I just couldn't do it by myself. Well, brothers and sisters," he said, pushing his hair off his forehead, "after six months of that—I could go into much more sordid details, but I'll spare you—I woke up one morning in Paris—didn't know who I was or where I was—and decided . . . enough. Enough. I'll kill myself."

He paused. "Now here you see the Father's wondrous ways. On the way to the Seine—I figured in Paris, if I was going to do myself in, it had to be the Seine—I happened to run into a beautiful brother singing like crazy right on the street. I ran up to him, blissed out at the thought that somebody could be that happy. He took me to a cafe and spoke to me about my music and my poetry, and he told me about a family that was so high on love they didn't need anything artificial, not even cigarettes. And he brought me back to America. And"—he bowed slightly—"that's the story of a lost soul who went off to drown in darkness and found instead the Light of the World!"

"Scott!" Zora sobbed.

Gail joined the others as they clapped.

"In spite of your expressions of appreciation," he said with a twisted smile, "I remain most humble and self-effacing. I live to serve others."

Gail watched him. Was the story for real? There was something studied about it—rehearsed, almost. Still, he was interesting. Did he know Jim? she wondered.

"Scott," Michael said, "you've been through a lot—more than the rest of us put together, maybe. In this world of evil and temptation, what do you fear the most?"

Scott, looking at his hands, thought for a minute. "Myself," he said.

Michael nodded knowingly. "Gail." His voice was gentle "It's your turn. Will you tell us who you are?"

She coughed, uncertain what he meant. Make up a last name. Not that they seemed to care what her name was. I'm—Gail—Gail Brown," she began, suddenly overpowered by an unpleasant odor. Feet, she realized, glancing around. Stockinged feet.

"Yes, Gail, go on," Michael said. "Tell us your story."

Brown—dumb choice of name. They were all looking at her. "I—I grew up in New York," she said. "I've lived there all my life. I came to Munro last year. There's nothing terrible in my life, really—"

"Everybody's got some problems, Gail," Zora said. "You can tell us."

"Do you have any brothers or sisters?" Michael asked.

His blue eyes were looking right through her. She blinked. "No—no, I'm an only child."

"Don't feel alone," Zora said. "We're your brothers and sisters now."

Michael was still watching her closely. "You live with your parents?"

"Yes."

"Where did you go to high school?"

"I—I went to a small private school. You probably never heard of it." She was glad suddenly that Doug wasn't here. She could never lie like this if he were.

"Are you happy, Gail?" Michael asked. "Do you get along with your parents?"

"Yes . . ."

"All the time?"

She shrugged. "Well, that's impossible—"

"So you disagree with them sometimes," Dan said.

"Yes—"

"About what?" Michael asked.

"Oh, they don't like me to do certain things."

"I know what you mean," Dan said. "They don't think you're old enough to make up your own mind, and you find that insulting."

"Yeah, that's it."

"And they probably don't always approve of your friends," Dan went on.

"That's true, they don't," she said. Why don't Ed and Frances appreciate me? Doug had asked her the other night at Pepe's, and she'd avoided the truth. Because they like people who're just like they are, she should've said. You're too different. You like art and films and talking about serious stuff, and you're sarcastic and frank and too liberal for them. And they don't like your moustache.

"It's tough when your parents try to alienate you from your friends," Michael said. "By the way, what do you think of all the different kinds of people here this weekend?" He waved his hand.

"Great," Gail said.

"Is that why you came to us, Gail?" Dan asked. "To expand your friendships?"

"Sort of," she said. Why were they giving her the third degree?

"I think you're looking for a place to let out your feelings, Gail," Zora beamed. "Here you can let everything out—you really can."

"I think I know why Gail's here," Michael said.

She met his eyes. Could it be that he'd known all along and was trying to torment her?

"She's looking for a person—to believe in. Is that it, Gail?"

"I don't know," she said impatiently.

"We can help you find whatever you're looking for," Zora said, hugging her. "Let us!"

■ ■ ■

words can be used to persuade. In *Blinded by the light* (Brancato), members of a religious cult attempt to twist the words of the new recruits to force them to join. After reading aloud a section of the book, Ms. Cramer discusses with the students the persuasive language techniques used by the cultists.

Composition and the Young Adult Book

The teaching of composition must be a central aspect of the thematic unit. "In a good thematic unit, emphasis is placed on frequent writing. The premise is that students have something to say and should be given ample opportunity to express themselves in writing" (Bushman and Jones 1975, p. 55). Within the thematic unit students are able to write about what interests them. Gone are the isolated writing assignments; gone are the lists of one hundred composition topics. Students write because they have something to say, to share, to defend, to criticize, not because they must complete an assignment. Students are taught writing skills as they write legal briefs about the guilt of Lorraine in *The pigman*. They learn how to convince their audience as they write letters to the editor about the abuse of pollution regulations in their city. They learn how to describe as they write descriptions of the defense system for a new galaxy in a *Star wars* unit. They write letters, advertisements, television and radio scripts, newspaper articles, legal briefs, plays, short stories, poems, and more. They write often, as often as every day, and they learn to write well because what they are writing is not just an English assignment, but meaningful writing.

Because writing and reading go hand in hand, it is essential that each unit emphasize and teach both writing and reading skills. A review of eighty-nine studies conducted betwen 1950 and 1978, compiled by Donald D. Hammill and Gaye McNutt (1980), found that there is a strong relationship between measures of written expressive language and reading. "This relationship may lend support to those who advocate teaching reading (and writing) through a combined reading and writing approach . . ." (p. 273).

If recent studies are correct and students learn to write more effecively when they are taught to write in conjunction with the reading being done, then teaching writing during units of work that require reading is a useful approach.

Published authors consistently tell students of writing that reading is the first step in learning how to write. This advice is confirmed in a collection of interviews with authors of young adult books (Weiss 1979), in which the authors were asked, "What advice do you give young authors?" S. E. Hinton, who wrote *The outsiders* when she was only sixteen, replied, " . . . first of all, they've got to read. Just read everything" (p. 36). Milton Meltzer, author of several nonfiction books for young adults, agreed: "First do a good deal of reading, read a great variety of writers . . ." (p. 71). Norma Klein, author of *Mom, the Wolfman, and me,* said, "I . . . read all the time, and I think you can be influenced by a writer that you really admire tremendously" (p. 57).

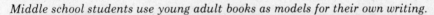

Middle school students use young adult books as models for their own writing.

STUDENTS REACTING DIRECTLY TO THE YOUNG ADULT BOOK AS A MEANS OF TEACHING WRITING.[4] One way the teacher can use young adult novels to teach composition skills is by encouraging the students to react directly in writing to the book they are reading. In this way the writing of the author becomes an impetus for the writing of the student. There are many ways in which students can react directly to books. Robert Small (1979, p. 76) and his adolescent literature students at Virginia Polytechnic Institute and State University describe sixteen ways:

1. *Choose the book you would most like to have with you if you were stranded on a desert island and explain why.*
2. *Write a letter to a friend recommending the book.*
3. *Put together a reader's support kit for the book* Nothing ever happens here *(York).*
4. *Write a nomination for the book for the School Book Award.*
5. *Discuss in writing reactions to the book. Did you enjoy reading it? Why?*
6. *Discuss the major character in the book in terms of whether or not you would like to know that person.*
7. *Discuss an important place where the book is set in terms of whether or not you would like to visit that place and how you would expect to feel about being there.*
8. *Discuss whether or not the book is believable.*
9. *Retell the story of the book.*
10. *Discuss a minor character in terms of whether or not you would like to meet that person.*
11. *Discuss one thing you think the book tells about people and their lives.*
12. *Discuss one new idea about people and their lives that you got from the book.*
13. *Disagree with one of the author's ideas or opinions.*
14. *Write something to go on a book jacket or in an ad.*
15. *Write a review of the book from some other person's viewpoint—an English teacher, a parent, a person of the opposite sex.*
16. *Write a letter to a character in the book in which you react to something that character said or did.*

Other ways for students to respond to a book in writing include these:

1. Write a letter to the author explaining why you liked the book and ask specific questions about how it was written.
2. Write a letter to the local public library asking the librarians to order the book and explain why it should be purchased.

---

[4]All subheadings in the section "Composition and the Young Adult Book" are based on ideas outlined by Robert Small, Jr., in "The Y.A. Novel in the Composition Program" (Part II), *English Journal,* October 1979, pp. 75–77.

3. If the book is controversial, defend it, in writing, to your parents, teacher, or another adult who might object to the book.
4. Explain why the scientific or historic "facts" discussed in the book are correct or incorrect.
5. Describe how a character's life-style would change if he or she lived in this community today.
6. Pretend you are the major character in the book and write a letter to a friend telling about some of the things that have happened to you recently.

YOUNG ADULT LITERATURE AS A MODEL FOR STUDENT WRITING (OR HOW MY STUDENTS CAN WRITE A NOVEL). Possibly the best reason for incorporating the young adult novel into the classroom curriculum is its qualities as a model for writing. Teenagers may find it difficult to study a so-called classic and use that book as a model for their own writing. Most mature works are too involved technically for teenagers to read critically. The young adult novel, however, allows students to meet it as an equal. As a result, readers can respond to it with some confidence and can use it as a model for their writing. The well-written young adult book can set a good example for student writing and may encourage the students to attempt the process of writing.

Before narrative writing begins, students must first study the elements of young adult books. Making the leap from understanding the elements to using them in writing appears to be difficult. However, it can be simplified by allowing the students to work in small groups on the development of setting, characters, plot, dialogue, and point of view. Working in small groups enables the young writers to share and test ideas. The process is fun as well as educational.

For example, studying the setting of a young adult novel helps students learn to develop a setting in their own writing. *Forever Island* (Smith) provides a good example of setting. The novel describes a Seminole Indian family living in the Big Cypress Swamp, north of the Florida Everglades. The family clings to the ways of its ancestors, refusing to be assimilated by the white culture. A large corporation purchases the land on which they live. After the silting of the streams and the poisoning of the marsh, the family is forced to move. Charlie, the young character in the novel, leaves his family as they search for the lost island of Seminole legend, Forever Island.

The student examines the importance of setting to the novel by completing one of these activities:

1. Rewrite one chapter of the novel. Pretend that the family is faced with the same problem, except that this time the story takes place in New York City. The building in which they live is bought by a large corporation and is being turned into condominiums. How would the story be different? How would it be the same? Would the family search for a Forever Island?
2. Rewrite a chapter of the book in play form, emphasizing the descriptive details of the swamp.

3. Assume that Charlie finds Forever Island. Describe in detail how the island appears to him. What readjustments will Charlie have to make? How will his new surroundings affect his life? Do you think he will survive? How?
4. Charlie's family moves to the community in which you live. Write a chapter describing how they deal with their new environment.

In these exercises the student has been encouraged to examine the setting and determine how the setting affects the mood and the action of the story. Many young adult novels provide excellent models for setting. Books such as *The war on Villa Street* (Mazer), *Johnny May* (Branscum), *Where the lilies bloom* (Cleaver and Cleaver), *Where the red fern grows* (Rawls), and *M. C. Higgins, the great* (Hamilton) would change dramatically in another setting. By placing the same characters and basic plot line in a new setting, the student can begin to understand how the setting is essential to the plot, the character development, the mood, and the theme of the novel.

To help students make the transition from the study of setting in the young adult novel to developing setting in their own writing, the teacher has them form small groups. Each group is told to select a mood (such as foreboding, fear, happiness, freedom) and to design a setting that evokes that mood. In designing their setting they draw a map or diagram, find pictures, or create a diorama before writing. Once the setting has been developed in pictures, each student describes it in writing. The group reviews each of the descriptions, and, by combining them, develops a written description that accurately depicts the setting and creates the mood.

Similar small-group writing experiences can be developed to help students learn the art of characterization. *The great Gilly Hopkins* (Paterson), *Mama and her boys* (Hopkins), *Man without a face* (Holland), *Killing Mr. Griffin* (Duncan), *Of love and death and other journeys* (Holland), *Tex* (Hinton), and *Is that you, Miss Blue?* (Kerr) are all excellent resource books to use as the students examine how to develop characters in their own writing.

☐ *I left my sister out of my first novel,* **Mama,** *because I didn't know how to write a book with four characters.*
LEE BENNETT HOPKINS
author of Mama and her boys / *in an interview with middle school students / Asheville, N.C. / April 1982*

The structuring of plot is essential in narrative writing. Because young adult books emphasize plot, they are excellent models for students to use in their own writing. Several years ago I heard young adult author Scott O'Dell ask a group of young readers if they would continue reading a book if the first page were not interesting. All of them shook their heads in unison. The point Mr. O'Dell was making to the adults in the audience was that the young adult book must hook readers early and keep them turning the pages. This requires a good plot.

A good plot, according to Robert Newton Peck in his book on writing, *Secrets of successful fiction,* is "two dogs and one bone." In other words, a good plot requires conflict. Many young adult books are exceptional models to use in helping young writers develop plot. Some of the best are *Fawn* (Peck), *Killing Mr. Griffin* (Duncan), the *Soup* books (Peck), *Home before dark* (Bridgers), *Blinded by the light* (Brancato), and *After the first death* (Cormier).

☐ *I think I usually start off with the idea of a relationship or an enmity, which becomes a relationship between two people....*
ISABELLE HOLLAND
author of Man without a face / *in Weiss (1979)*

Developing dialogue is difficult for novice writers. Again, students are helped through the examples in young adult novels. Effective use of dialogue reveals the characters and strengthens the plot. In Robbie Branscum's books, dialogue reveals the strengths and weaknesses of the characters. Books like *Johnny May, Toby, Granny and George, Toby and Johnny Joe,* and *Toby alone* are stories about characters who come to life for the readers through their dialogue. The dialogue in Branscum's books is colorful and consistent, and the characters take on those same qualities.

"Toby, do ye take Johnny Joe Treat to be yore wedded husband?"
    "Reckon so, Preacher, else I wouldn't be here." I didn't mean to snap the words so sharp, but truth to tell, I was a mite jumpy and all of a sudden it sorta seemed like I didn't know big ole Johnny Joe a'tall....
    "Toby, do ye promise to love and obey Johnny Joe?"
    My chin shot up and I said, "I promist to love him, Preacher, but I ain't gonna say I'll mind him, 'cause I ain't a-marryin' me a pa to obey."

One of the most difficult aspects of narrative writing is deciding upon and maintaining a consistent point of view. By the time the young writers have explored setting, characters, plot, and dialogue, they should be developing point of view. At the same time they have seen how professional authors of young adult books establish a point of view. However, moving from understanding point of view to actually writing it is difficult.

The students' understanding of point of view begins with examination of novels that present various points of view, both personal and omniscient. For example, *The cat ate my gymsuit* (Danziger) is a good example of a novel told from the personal point of view of the major character. The book is Marcy's story. Sometimes authors tell stories from more than one point of view. In Robin Brancato's *Winning,* most of the story is told by English teacher Ann Treer, but substantial parts of it are told by Gary Madden, and other parts by Diane. Since Brancato is working with the theme of how individuals relate to paralysis and death, she must present a variety of viewpoints. To do this she changes the chapter each time a different character's point of view is expressed.

The students can be helped to understand the point of view by rewriting a section of the book, changing it from one point of view to another. For example, after reading *Winning,* the students are instructed to work in small groups to change the chapter in which Gary examines his fears and frustrations about being strapped to a bed that allows him to be flipped over several times a day, to a chapter told from Ann's point of view as she sees Gary on the apparatus. Once the chapter has been rewritten, the class discusses how the change in point of view alters the development of the characters, the plot, and the author's message. Three excellent books for teaching point of view are Judith Guest's *Ordinary people* and Lynn Hall's *Sticks and stones* and *The leaving.* All are told from the personal point of view of two or more characters.

Since most young adult books address the development of young adult characters, very few are told from the omniscient, or all-knowing, point of view. Exceptions are memoirs such as *Death be not proud* (Gunther), biographies such as *The silent storm* (Brown and Crone), and nonfiction accounts such as *Never to forget: The Jews of the Holocaust* (Meltzer). Examining these books, or others like them, helps the students understand the all-knowing point of view that gives the writer the freedom to stand outside the narrative and enter the minds of the characters.

To better understand the omniscient point of view, students could examine a section of a book that uses an all-knowing technique and then rewrite it in the point of view of one of the characters. Following the writing, a discussion could stress the advantages and disadvantages of the two points of view and the difference between them.

USING YOUNG ADULT NOVELS AS RAW MATERIALS FOR WRITING. One of the biggest complaints of students in composition classes is, "I don't know what to write about." Teachers spend hours helping reluctant writers identify topics. Out of frustration, teachers assign topics. Books have been written for students listing hundreds of topics for essays. Consequently, teachers read and students write hundreds of boring essays that do nothing to help motivate the student to get into the writing habit. Young adult novels can act as raw materials to get students writing. Robert Small writes:

> *We teachers know that the basis for writing does not have to be exotic, but most students will not believe us. Efforts to appeal to students' own experiences are, therefore, not particularly successful, although many of us suspect that teenagers, in fact, lead more interesting lives than most of their teachers. Young adult novels can, however, provide the focused and intensified experiences the teacher must supply, experiences that are within the teenager's world, but not their own and thus devalued by them. (1979, p. 75)*

The intensified experience illuminated in the young adult novel is the beginning point for the student's writing. If the novel was selected based on the student's own interest, it is likely, with the help of the teacher, to provide many good ideas for writing. In a thematic unit entitled Heroes, one three-week subunit is based on realistic heroes placed in times of trial. Each student has elected to read one of seven books: *Canyon winter* (Morey), *A hero ain't nothin' but a sandwich* (Childress), *The edge of next year* (Stolz), *Toby lived here* (Wolitzer), *The girl who had no name* (Rabe), *The kidnapping of Christina Lattimore* (Nixon), and *Blinded by the light* (Brancato). Elaine McCraken decided to use these books to teach journalistic writing skills. The entire class was involved in putting out a newspaper and using the plots and characters in these books in the development of news and features. The procedure Ms. McCraken established was as follows.

1. Students examine copies of the local newspaper.
2. They compose a list of the sections (such as editorials, news, features) they plan to include in their class newspaper.
3. An editor and an assistant are chosen by the class.
4. Section assignments are made.
5. The sections of the newspaper are written.
6. Each article is checked by the editor, assistant editor, and teacher.
7. The material is printed for distribution. Copies are run off by the teacher and stapled by the students.
8. Copies are distributed to members of the class.

This procedure not only helps the students develop journalistic writing skills, but also helps them learn the various elements of the novel. In order to write about the characters, the students must understand their development. To relate the events of the tale involves the understanding of the plot.

☑ *Write every day, even if it's only your name. Get into the habit of writing.*
MOLLIE HUNTER
author of A sound of chariots / in Weiss (1979)

Using adolescent novels as raw materials for encouraging student writing need not entail an entire class project. Robert Small (1979, p. 77) and his students at Virginia Polytechnic Institute suggest nine ways to use young adult books to begin writing.

1. *Create a scene in which the main characters from two books meet—* Then again, maybe I won't *and* It's not the end of the world *(Blume).*
2. *Write a letter to Dear Abby as a person with the same problem as a character in the book. Write the answer for the column—*Are you there, God? It's me, Margaret *(Blume).*

3. *Write a newspaper editorial commenting on a problem dealt with in the book*—A figure of speech *(N. F. Mazer)*.
4. *Write the diary of the main character covering several crucial days*—Are you in the house alone? *(Peck)*.
5. *Write a biography of a minor character using what is in the book and inventing the rest consistent with the book*—The chocolate war *(Cormier)*.
6. *Write a description of a place in the book, using what the book provides and inventing other suitable details*—The pigman *(Zindel)*.
7. *Create fully a scene mentioned but not shown in the book*—Mr. and Mrs. Bo Jo Jones *(Head)*.
8. *Write a poem that the major character might have written in reaction to an incident or other character*—Iceberg hermit *(Roth)*.
9. *Interview a character for a TV talk show creating both questions to be asked and answers consistent with the book*—Are you in the house alone? *(Peck)*.

STIMULATING STUDENT WRITING THROUGH YOUNG ADULT BOOKS. A book often carries inspiration for writing, even when the student is not writing directly about the book or the characters in it. Something in the book makes the student want to sit down with pencil in hand and begin composing. Although this does not happen often, young adult novels that appeal to the students' own experiences help them understand that their own lives are a source for writing. After reading a young adult novel, the student is moved to write a poem, a song, or a narrative that is not a direct response to or a rewriting of the story, but is inspired by it.

Teachers help encourage students to see young adult literature as an inspirational source by leading discussions about how an event in the book relates to the life of the student. The heart attack of Jorey's father, for example, in *The ups and downs of Jorey Jenkins* (Bates) stimulates discussion, and perhaps writing, about relationships that change as a result of illness. Similarly, students are helped through discussion to identify an adult who is as important to them as Donatelli is to Alfred in *The contender* (Lipsyte). Likewise, the teenager describes a situation that he or she expected to be terrible, but turns out to be very valuable. *Lilith summer* (Irwin) provides a good example of a terrible but valuable situation. *The friends* (Guy) is likely to stimulate thought, discussion, and writing about friendship. The sibling relationships in *Can you sue your parents for malpractice?* (Danziger) provide motivation for the student to begin thinking and writing about relationships with brothers and sisters.

☐ *I write a lot of the child I was.*
JUDY BLUME
in Weiss (1979)

The young writers are encouraged to examine places they have lived and visited. The description of the home in *Home before dark* (Bridgers) provides the motivation needed to write about feelings of home. Discussing places of extreme importance to the young adult's life after reading books like *Where the red fern grows* (Rawls) and *The witch of Blackbird Pond* (Speare) is enough to influence at least one student to begin thinking about the special places associated with his or her life.

The reading of problem novels that relate to the problems of the adolescent may stimulate thought and writing. The student who feels like an outcast for refusing to become involved in the drug scene reads the novel *The contender* and is influenced to write about drug-related experiences. The teenager who is still coming to terms with the death of a parent relates to the difficulties discussed in *A season in between* (Greenberg), *The empty chair* (Kaplan), *Big Doc's girl* (Medearis), *Of love and death and other journeys* (Holland), *Break a leg, Betsy Maybe!* (Kingman), *Grover* (Cleaver and Cleaver), and *Ronnie and Rosey* (Angell). The reading of these books results in the composing of a poem a song, or a narrative based on the student's own experience.

> ☐ *More than anything else . . . keep on writing. . . . I cannot stress this enough—the habit of writing is the most important thing a writer can develop.*
> ISABELLE HOLLAND
> *author of* Heads you win, tails I lose / *in Weiss (1979)*

Individualized Reading

Individualized reading programs have many different names, such as free reading, uninterrupted silent sustained reading (USSR), free choice program, silent reading program, read it and like it, and paperback book program. No matter what such programs are called, they have three things in common: (1) the students select books, at times from a teacher-prepared bibliography, (2) the students read during class time, and (3) the programs are designed to encourage reading.

In many schools the individualized reading program is schoolwide. For example, in one Florida middle school I was sitting in the principal's office when a bell rang. The principal looked at me and asked, "Do you have something to read?" After examining my briefcase I found nothing that was particularly appealing, so he thrust a magazine in my hand, demanding that I read it. I sat there examining the magazine for fifteen minutes as the principal busily turned the pages of a popular novel. When another bell rang, he put down his book and explained that the schoolwide reading program required that everyone read. "Everyone" meant everyone, including the principal, the janitors, the kitchen help, everyone. Several students wandered the hall each day to enforce the reading rule. He explained that one day, to his great embarrassment, he was meeting with the superintendent of schools and had ignored the reading bell. One of the student enforcers visited his office, discovered that they were not reading, and sen-

■ ■ ■ **An Anthological Aside**

Can It Be Longer?

S. E. HINTON

I still didn't want to do my homework that night, though. I hunted around for a book to read, but I'd read everything in the house about fifty million times, even Darry's copy of *The Carpetbaggers,* though he'd told me I wasn't old enough to read it. I thought so too after I finished it. Finally I picked up *Gone with the Wind* and looked at it for a long time. I knew Johnny was dead. I had known it all the time, even while I was sick and pretending he wasn't. It was Johnny, not me, who had killed Bob—I knew that too. I had just thought that maybe if I played like Johnny wasn't dead it wouldn't hurt so much. The way Two-Bit, after the police had taken Dally's body away, had griped because he had lost his switchblade when they searched Dallas.

"Is that all that's bothering you, that switchblade?" a red-eyed Steve had snapped at him.

"No," Two-Bit had said with a quivering sigh, "but that's what I'm wishing was all that's bothering me."

But it still hurt anyway. You know a guy a long time, and I mean really know him, you don't get used to the idea that he's dead just overnight. Johnny was something more than a buddy to all of us. I guess he had listened to more beefs and more problems from more people than any of us. A guy that'll really listen to you, listen and care about what you're saying, is something rare. And I couldn't forget him telling me that he hadn't done enough, hadn't been out of our neighborhood all his life—and then it was too late. I took a deep breath and opened the book. A slip of paper fell out on the floor and I picked it up.

Ponyboy, I asked the nurse to give you this book so you could finish it. It was Johnny's handwriting. I went on reading, almost hearing Johnny's quiet voice. The doctor came in a while ago but I knew anyway. I keep getting tireder and tireder. Listen, I don't mind dying now. It's worth it. It's worth saving those kids. Their lives are worth more than mine, they have more to live for. Some of their parents came by to thank me and I know it was worth it. Tell Dally it's worth it. I'm just going to miss you guys. I've been thinking about it, and that poem, that guy that wrote it, he meant you're gold when you're a kid, like green. When you're a kid everything's new, dawn. It's just when you get used to everything that it's day. Like the way you dig sunsets, Pony. That's gold. Keep that way, it's a good way to be. I want you to tell Dally to look at one. He'll probaby think you're crazy, but ask for me. I don't think he's ever really seen a sunset. And don't be so bugged over being a greaser. You still have a lot of time to make yourself be what you want. There's still lots of good in the world. Tell Dally. I don't think he knows. Your buddy, Johnny.

Tell Dally. It was too late to tell Dally. Would he have listened? I doubted it. Suddenly it wasn't only a personal thing to me. I could picture hundreds and hundreds of boys living on the wrong sides of cities, boys with black eyes who jumped at their own shadows. Hundreds of boys who maybe watched sunsets and looked at stars and ached for something better. I could see boys going down under street lights because they were mean and tough and hated the world, and it was too late to tell them that there was still good in it, and they wouldn't believe you if you did. It was too vast a problem to be just a personal thing. There should be some help, someone should tell them before it was too late. Someone should tell their side of the story, and maybe people would understand then and wouldn't be so quick to judge a boy by the amount of hair oil he wore. It was important to me. I picked up the phone book and called my English teacher.

"Mr. Syme, this is Ponyboy. That theme—how long can it be?"

"Why, uh, not less than five pages." He sounded a little surprised. I'd forgotten that it was late at night.

"Can it be longer?"

"Certainly, Ponyboy, as long as you want it."

"Thanks," I said and hung up.

I sat down and picked up my pen and thought for a minute. Remembering. Remembering a handsome, dark boy with a reckless grin and a hot temper. A tough, towheaded boy with a cigarette in his mouth and a bitter grin on his hard face. Remembering—and this time it didn't hurt—a quiet, defeated-looking sixteen-year-old whose hair needed cutting badly and who had black eyes with a frightened expression to them. One week had taken all three of them. And I decided *I* could tell people, beginning with my English teacher. I wondered for a long time how to start that theme, how to start writing about something that was important to me. And I finally began like this: When I stepped out into the bright sunlight from the darkness of the movie house, I had only two things on my mind: Paul Newman and a ride home. . . .

■ ■ ■

tenced them both to reading detention hall for a half-hour that afternoon. Both he and the superintendent enjoyed a half-hour of enforced reading at 3:30 that very day.

In other schools the individualized reading program is a single course sometimes elected in place of a study hall or an English class. In still others the individualized reading program is fifteen minutes of every English class session, or thirty minutes twice a week, or some other time allotted for free reading.

Many individualized reading programs have been extremely successful. As early as 1936, Lou L. LaBrant in an evaluation of the free reading program at the Ohio State University High School found that the students who participated in the program acquired reading habits that they carried on into their adult lives. Margaret Willis, in a research report published by the Ohio State University in 1961, followed up on the group of students who had participated in the free reading program and found that they still read a variety of materials, read more than their peers, and read more to their children; and their children read more than their peers. Likewise, Bruce Appleby (1971) found that students who took elective individualized reading courses were more aware than their peers of how literature contributed to their lives. Similarly, they liked a wider variety of literature than students who did not elect the course.[5]

The success of these individualized reading programs makes a study of their common attributes important. English teachers should examine individualized reading as an alternative means for allowing students to read a wide range of literature at a variety of reading levels within the English classroom.

Barbara Blow (1976) has delineated the most common elements of successful free reading programs. She found that in the successful individualized reading programs: (1) The teachers read what the kids were reading—not every book, necessarily, but always the most popular. (2) A classroom paperback library was available to the students, containing many different titles and several copies of the most popular titles. (3) Records of student reading were kept so that additional copies of the most popular books could be purchased. The records also assisted the teachers in recommending popular titles to other students. Students, according to Blow, are more likely to take recommendations from other students than from the teacher. (4) Regular conferences were held between teachers and students to discuss the book(s). During the conference time the teacher suggested additional titles that might interest the student. (5) Librarians were involved in the program and often gave short book talks to stimulate interest. (6) Students were prepared for the book conferences. They were instructed to focus on a single aspect of the book, such as characterization, setting, or theme. They were also encouraged to examine the social theme of the book, such as friendship, growing up, or family relationship. Likewise, they were permitted to select and discuss books from specific genres, such as autobiography, sports, and science fiction. Before the conference the student selected the appropriate discussion topic for the book and planned the conference by answering teacher-prepared questions on the topic chosen. (7) Each student conference was scheduled for ten to fifteen minutes every two weeks. The students signed up for the conference at least a week in advance. (8) Students were provided with a reading record in which they entered each day the number of pages read during that class period. Students were able to use this

[5]The results of the Appleby study are reprinted by permission of Bantam Books and the author.

record to check progress in their reading speed. (9) An evaluation and grading system were set up prior to the course, and the students understood the system. It is possible to individualize the grading system by basing it on the improvement of reading speed based on the number of pages read during the first class session. Or the system might be based on the difficulty and the number of books read and discussed.

I have observed other attributes of successful individualized reading programs. One of the most interesting programs uses group as well as individual conference techniques. The titles of especially popular books are printed on sheets of newsprint posted near the classroom paperback library. When students check out one of these books, they enter their name and the date on the list. The teacher arranges a meeting of the students after each one has had time to complete the book. During this meeting the students select one or several topics to discuss with the teacher. After the initial meeting, a group conference of twenty to thirty minutes is scheduled with the teacher. This organization of the free reading reporting allows for a variety of group and individual conference techniques. In this same individualized reading classroom the students may select from a variety of reporting techniques that do not involve a conference with the teacher. For example, they may design a poster or write a skit on the book they have completed. (See pages 374–375 for a list of book-reporting techniques.) Since not all students elect the teacher-student conferencing technique, the teacher has time for scheduling more time-consuming reporting activities, such as a videotaping of parts of *The undertaker's gone bananas* (Zindel).

In another successful individualized reading program I observed, bibliography charts based on specific themes are posted around the room. When a student reads a book that fits into a specific theme, he or she writes the title and author of the book on the chart. The student then dates and signs an index card, writes on it a brief paragraph about the book, and files the card in a catalogue under the appropriate theme. Since students receive five points of credit in a hundred-point credit system for each new book placed in the annotated card catalogue, they are challenged to read books not being read by other students. A student may complete only one card on each book read. Therefore, it is possible that another student may place the book under another theme and receive credit for this annotation. The card catalogue serves a variety of purposes. It assists students in selecting books similar to ones they have just read. It helps students seek out other readers of the book. Finally, it is extremely useful to the teacher in the development of thematic unit bibliographies for the regular English classroom.

An individualized reading class activity that also encourages student writing is the journal technique, which was modified by Robert Garcia to give his students the opportunity to write about the books they were reading. Each day the student writes in a journal. The student can write anything that relates to the reading being done in class. The entry can be as simple as the copying of a passage from the book or as complex as the rewriting of a section of the book. The student can also use the journal to express feelings about the book, the author, the characters, or the setting. Mr. Garcia does not check the journal for content or grammatical structure. Rather, he skims through the journal with the student prior to the biweekly conference. He reads only the entries the student suggests, and he asks that he be allowed to read a minimum of two entries for each two-week period. Students may use their journal entries as the basis for their book discussion with Mr. Garcia. The journal technique serves several functions: (1) It encourages the student to write something every day. (2) It reinforces in the student's mind the content of the book and the student's evaluation of it, making the individual conference with the teacher easier. (3) It helps convince the student that what he or she has to say about the book is valid. (4) It allows the student to relate personally to the book without the constant supervision of the teacher. (5) It encourages the student to share his or her best work with the teacher. (6) It gives the teacher the opportunity to encourage additional writing activities.

Individualized reading can increase motivation to read, ability to read books critically, reading enjoyment, the likelihood of establishing recreational reading patterns, reading rates, and even reading achievement scores on standardized tests (the student who reads more is likely to read better). However, independent reading courses are no different from any other course in the school curriculum. Those that are successful have specific objectives and are well planned, carefully organized, and easily evaluated.

Anthological Asides in Chapter 8

Brancato, R. *Blinded by the light.* Knopf, 1978. Bantam, 1979.
Hinton, S. E. *The outsiders.* Viking, 1967. Dell, 1980.

Titles Mentioned in Chapter 8

Angell, J. *Ronnie and Rosey.* Bradbury, 1977. Dell, 1979.
Angelou, M. *Gather together in my name.* Random House, 1974. Bantam, 1975.
————. *I know why the caged bird sings.* Random House, 1969. Bantam, 1971.
————. *Singin' and swingin' and gettin' merry like Christmas.* Random House, 1976. Bantam, 1977.
Armstrong, W. *Sounder.* Harper & Row, 1969, 1972.
Bates, B. *The ups and downs of Jorey Jenkins.* Holiday, 1978. Pocket Books, 1981.
————. *Bugs in your ears.* Holiday, 1977. Pocket Books, 1979.
Beatty, P. *Wait for me, watch for me, Eula Bee.* Morrow, 1978.
Blume, J. *Are you there, God? It's me, Margaret.* Bradbury, 1970. Dell, 1980.
————. *Forever.* Bradbury, 1975. Pocket Books, 1975.
————. *It's not the end of the world.* Bradbury, 1972. Dell, 1982.
————. *Then again, maybe I won't.* Bradbury, 1971. Dell, 1976.
Bonham, F. *Durango Street.* Dutton, 1965. Dell, 1972.
Borland, H. *When the legends die.* Lippincott, 1963. Bantam, 1976.
Brancato, R. *Blinded by the light.* Knopf, 1978. Bantam, 1979.

————. *Winning.* Knopf, 1977. Bantam, 1979.

Branscum, R. *Johnny May.* Doubleday, 1975. Avon, 1976.

————. *Toby alone.* Doubleday, 1979. Avon, 1980.

————. *Toby, Granny and George.* Doubleday, 1976. Avon, 1977.

————. *Toby and Johnny Joe.* Doubleday, 1969. Avon, 1981.

Bridgers, S. E. *Home before dark.* Knopf, 1976. Bantam, 1977.

————. *Notes for another life.* Knopf, 1981.

Brown, M. M., and R. Crone. *The silent storm.* Abingdon Press, 1963.

Childress, A. *A hero ain't nothin' but a sandwich.* Coward, McCann & Geoghegan, 1973. Avon, 1974, 1982.

Cleaver, V., and B. Cleaver. *Dust of the earth.* Lippincott, 1975. New American Library, 1975.

————. *Trial Valley.* Lippincott, 1977. Bantam, 1978.

————. *Where the lilies bloom.* Lippincott, 1969. New American Library, 1964.

Cormier, R. *After the first death.* Pantheon, 1979. Avon, 1980.

————. *The chocolate war.* Pantheon, 1974. Dell, 1975.

————. *I am the cheese.* Pantheon, 1977. Dell, 1978.

Crane, S. *The red badge of courage.* Appleton, 1894. Peter Pauper Press, 1980.

Dahl, R. *Charlie and the chocolate factory.* Knopf, 1964, 1973.

Danziger, P. *Can you sue your parents for malpractice?* Delacorte, 1979. Dell, 1980.

————. *The cat ate my gymsuit.* Delacorte, 1974. Dell, 1979.

Duncan, L. *Down a dark hall.* Little, Brown, 1974. New American Library, 1975.

————. *Killing Mr. Griffin.* Little, Brown, 1978. Dell, 1979.

Fast, H. *April morning.* Crown, 1961. Bantam, 1970.

Green, H. *I never promised you a rose garden.* Holt, Rinehart & Winston, 1964. New American Library, 1964.

Greenberg, J. *A season in-between.* Farrar, Straus & Giroux, 1979. Dell, 1981.

Greene, B. *Summer of my German soldier.* Dial, 1973. Bantam, 1974.

————. *Morning is a long time coming.* Dial, 1978. Pocket Books, 1979.

Guest, J. *Ordinary people.* Viking, 1976. Ballantine, 1980.

Gunther, J. *Death be not proud.* Harper & Row, 1949. Pyramid, 1979.

Guy, R. *The friends.* Holt, Rinehart & Winston, 1973. Bantam, 1974.

Haley, A. *Roots.* Doubleday, 1976. Dell, 1977.

Hall, L. *The leaving.* Scribner's, 1980.

————. *Sticks and stones.* Follett, 1972. Dell, 1972.

Hamilton, V. *M. C. Higgins, the great.* Macmillan, 1974. Dell, 1978.

Hansberry, L. *A raisin in the sun.* New American Library, 1966.

Havrevold, F. *Undertow.* Atheneum, 1968.

Head, A. *Mr. and Mrs. Bo Jo Jones.* Putnam, 1967. New American Library, 1968.

Hemingway, E. *The old man and the sea.* Scribner's, 1952, 1968.

Herbert, F. *Soul catcher.* Putnam's, 1972. Berkley, 1979.

Hinton, S. E. *The outsiders.* Viking, 1967. Dell, 1980.

————. *That was then, this is now.* Viking, 1971. Dell, 1980.

————. *Tex.* Delacorte, 1979. Dell, 1980.

Holland, I. *Heads you win, tails I lose.* Lippincott, 1973. Dell, 1979.

————. *Man without a face.* Lippincott, 1972. Dell, 1980.

————. *Of love and death and other journeys.* Lippincott, 1975. Dell, 1977.

Hopkins, L. B. *Mama.* Knopf, 1977. Dell, 1978.

————. *Mama and her boys.* Knopf, 1981.

Hunt, I. *Across five Aprils.* Follett, 1964. Grosset & Dunlap, 1965.

Hunter, M. *A sound of chariots.* Harper & Row, 1972. Avon, 1975.

Irwin, H. *Lilith summer.* Feminist Press, 1979.

Kaplan, B. *The empty chair.* Harper & Row, 1975.

Kahn, J. *Some things strange and sinister.* Harper & Row, 1973. Avon, 1974.

Kerr, M. E. *Dinky Hocker shoots smack!* Harper & Row, 1972. Dell, 1978.

———. *Gentlehands.* Harper & Row, 1978.

———. *Is that you, Miss Blue?* Harper & Row, 1975. Dell, 1976.

Kingman, L. *Break a leg, Betsy Maybe!* Houghton Mifflin, 1976. Dell, 1979.

Klein, N. *Mom, the Wolfman, and me.* Pantheon, 1972. Avon, 1982.

Le Guin, U. *Very far away from anywhere else.* Atheneum, 1976. Bantam, 1978.

L'Engle, M. *A ring of endless light.* Farrar, Straus & Giroux, 1980. Dell, 1981.

———. *A wind in the door.* Farrar, Straus & Giroux, 1973. Dell, 1976.

———. *A wrinkle in time.* Farrar, Straus & Giroux, 1962. Dell, 1976.

Lewis, C. S. *Out of the silent planet.* Macmillan, 1943, 1977.

Lipsyte, R. *The contender.* Harper & Row, 1967. Bantam, 1979.

———. *One fat summer.* Harper & Row, 1977. Bantam, 1978.

Lyle, K. L. *Fair day, and another step begun.* Lippincott, 1974. Dell, 1975.

Manley, S., and G. Lewis. *Masters of macabre.* Doubleday, 1975.

———. *Mistresses of mystery: Two centuries of suspense. Stories by the gentle sex.* Lothrop, Lee & Shepard, 1973.

Mazer, H. *Snowbound.* Delacorte, 1973. Dell, 1973.

———. *The War on Villa Street.* Delacorte, 1978. Dell, 1979.

Mazer, N. F. *A figure of speech.* Delacorte, 1973. Dell, 1974.

Medearis, M. *Big Doc's girl.* Lippincott, 1974. Pyramid, 1974.

Meltzer, M. *Never to forget: The Jews of the Holocaust.* Harper & Row, 1976. Dell, 1977.

Michener, J. *Chesapeake.* Fawcett, 1978.

———. *Hawaii.* Random House, 1959. Fawcett, 1973.

Morey, W. *Canyon winter.* Dutton, 1972.

Nixon, J. L. *The kidnapping of Christina Lattimore.* Harcourt Brace Jovanovich, 1979. Dell, 1980.

O'Brien, R. C. *Z for Zacharia.* Atheneum, 1975. Dell, 1977.

O'Dell, S. *Island of the blue dolphins.* Houghton Mifflin, 1960. Dell, 1975.

Paterson, K. *Bridge to Terabithia.* Crowell, 1977. Avon, 1979.

———. *The great Gilly Hopkins.* Crowell, 1978. Avon, 1979.

———. *Jacob have I loved.* Crowell, 1980. Avon, 1981.

Peck. R. *Are you in the house alone?* Viking, 1976. Dell, 1978.

Peck, R. N. *A day no pigs would die.* Knopf, 1972. Dell, 1978.

———. *Fawn.* Little, Brown, 1975. Dell, 1977.

———. *Soup.* Knopf, 1974. Dell, 1979.

Rabe, B. *The girl who had no name.* Dutton, 1977. Bantam, 1979.

Rawls, W. *Where the red fern grows.* Doubleday, 1961. Bantam, 1979.

Rockwell. *How to eat fried worms.* Franklin Watts, 1973. Dell, 1980.

Roth, A. *The iceberg hermit.* Four Winds, 1974. Scholastic, 1974.

Schwartz, A. *Cross your fingers, spit in your hat: Superstitions and other beliefs.* Lippincott, 1974.

———. *Tomfoolery: Trickery and foolery with words.* Lippincott, 1973. Bantam, 1976.

———. *A twister of twists, a tangler of tongues: Tongue twisters.* Lippincott, 1972. Bantam, 1977.

———. *Whoppers: Tall tales and other lies.* Lippincott, 1975.

———. *Witcracks: Jokes and jests from American folklore.* Lippincott, 1973. Bantam, 1977.

Smith, P. *Forever Island.* Norton, 1973. Dell, 1974.

Speare, L. *The witch of Blackbird Pond.* Houghton Mifflin, 1951. Dell, 1975.

Stolz, M. *The edge of next year.* Harper & Row, 1974. Dell, 1979.

Taylor, T. *The cay.* Doubleday, 1969. Avon, 1970.

Tunis, J. R. *His enemy, his friend.* Morrow, 1967. Avon, 1967.

Wersba, B. *Tunes for a small harmonica.* Harper & Row, 1976. Dell, 1977.

Wilder, L. I. *Little house in the big woods.* Harper & Row, 1932, 1971.

York, C. B. *Nothing ever happens here.* Hawthorn, 1970. New American Library, 1975.

Wolitzer, H. *Toby lived here.* Farrar, Straus & Giroux, 1978. Bantam, 1980.

Zindel, P. *Pardon me, you're stepping on my eyeball!* Harper & Row, 1976. Bantam, 1977.

———. *The pigman.* Harper & Row, 1968. Bantam, 1978.

———. *The undertaker's gone bananas.* Harper & Row, 1978. Bantam, 1979.

Suggested Readings

Andrews, L. Responses to literature: Enlarging the range. *English Journal,* February 1977, pp. 60–62.

Andrews, L. Responses to literature: In tennis the serve is crucial. *English Journal,* February 1974, pp. 44–46.

Appleby, B. C. Individualized reading as environment for the literary experience. In W. Evans, ed., *The creative teacher.* Bantam, 1971, pp. 1–10.

Beach, R. *Writing about ourselves and others.* National Institute of Education, 1977.

Bernstein, J. E. *Fiddle with a riddle: Write your own riddles.* Dutton, 1979.

Blow, B. Individualized reading. In K. Donelson, ed., *Arizona English Bulletin,* April 1976, pp. 151–53.

Brown, R., ed. *The whole word catalogue.* Teachers and Writers Collaborative, 1972, 1978.

Burke, E. M. Using trade books to intrigue children with words. *Reading Teacher,* November 1978, pp. 144–48.

Burton, D. L. Well, where are we in teaching literature? *English Journal,* February 1974, pp. 28–33.

Bushman, J. H., and S. K. Jones. Getting it all together . . . thematically. *English Journal,* May 1975, pp. 54–60.

Carlson, R. K. *Sparkling words: Three hundred and fifteen practical and creative writing ideas.* National Council of Teachers of English, 1979.

Cassedy, S. *In your own words: A beginner's guide to writing.* Doubleday, 1979.

Donelson, K., ed. *Non-print media and the teaching of English. Arizona English Bulletin,* October 1975.

Donelson, K. L., and A. P. Nilsen. *Literature for today's young adults.* Scott, Foresman, 1980.

Erickson, F. What are we trying to do in high school English? *English Journal,* September 1959, pp. 304–8.

Forrell, E. R., and M. H. Workman. The "novel" approach to reading and writing. *Reading Teacher,* October 1979, pp. 18–22.

Foster, H. M. *The new literacy: The language of film and television.* National Council of Teachers of English, 1970.

Gallo, R., ed. *A gaggle of gimmicks.* National Council of Teachers of English, 1978.

Glaus, M. *From thoughts to words.* National Council of Teachers of English, 1965.

Hammill, D. D., and G. McNutt. Language abilities and readings: A review of literature and their relationship. *Elementary School Journal,* May 1980, pp. 269–77.

Hawkins, T. *Group inquiry techniques for teaching writing.* ERIC Clearinghouse, 1976.

Heins, P. Johnny Tremain's Boston. *The Calendar.* March–October 1981.

Hillocks, G. *Observing and writing.* National Council of Teachers of English, 1975.

———. Toward a hierarchy of skills in the comprehension of literature. *English Journal,* March 1980, pp. 54–59.

Hopkins, L. B. *The best of book bonanza.* Holt, Rinehart & Winston, 1980.

Hubert, K. M. *Teaching and writing popular fiction: Horror, adventure, mystery and romance in the American classroom.* Teachers and Writers Collaborative, 1976.

Judy, S., and S. Judy. *Gifts of writing: Creative projects with words and art.* Scribner's, 1980.

Kaplan, E. M., and A. Tuchman. Vocabulary strategies belong in the hands of learners. *Journal of Reading,* October 1980, pp. 32–34.

LaBrant, L. L. *An evaluation of the free reading program in grades 10, 11, and 12.* Columbus: Ohio State University Press, 1936.

Landrum, R. L. *A day dream I had at night and other stories: Teaching children how to make their own readers.* Teachers and Writers Collaborative, 1971, 1974.

Long, L. *Writing exercises from exercise exchange.* National Council of Teachers of English, 1976.

Peck, R. N. *Secrets of successful fiction.* Writer's Digest Books, 1980.

Readence, J. E., and L. W. Searfoss. Teaching strategies for vocabulary development. *English Journal,* October 1980, pp. 43–46.

Sarkissian, A. *Children's authors and illustrators,* 3rd ed. Gale Research Co., 1981.

———. *Writers for young adults: Biographies master index.* 1st ed. Gale Research Co., 1979.

Shachter J. Videotaped authors advise student writers. *English Journal,* March 1980, pp. 85–86.

Shimer, N. Adolescent novels in thematic units: Bridging the gap. In K. Donelson, ed., *Arizona English Bulletin,* April 1976, pp. 209–15.

Small, R. C. Teaching the junior novel. *English Journal,* February 1972, pp. 222–29.

———. The junior novel and the art of literature. *English Journal,* October 1977a, pp. 55–59.

———. The adolescent novel as a working model. *ALAN Newsletter,* Winter 1977b.

Smith, C. F. Jr. Read a book in an hour: Variations to develop composition and comprehension skills. *Journal of Reading,* October 1979, pp. 25–29.

Spann, S., and M. B. Culp, eds. *Thematic units in teaching English and the humanities.* National Council of Teachers of English, 1975, 1977, 1980.

Weiss, M. J., ed. *From writers to students: The pleasures and pains of writing.* International Reading Association, 1979.

The Y. A. novel in the composition program (Part II). *English Journal,* October 1979, pp. 75–77.

Nonprint Sources

Death be not proud. Film based on Gunther's book. Available from Learning Corporation of America, 1350 Ave. of the Americas, New York, NY 10019.

Dinky Hocker. Film based on Kerr's *Dinky Hocker shoots smack!* Available from Learning Corporation of America.

Family of strangers. Film based on Bates's *Bugs in your ears.* Available from Learning Corporation of America.

The great Gilly Hopkins. Filmstrip based on Paterson's book. Available from Miller-Brody, Inc. 342 Madison Ave., New York, NY 10017.

A hero ain't nothin' but a sandwich. Record & cassette of original motion picture soundtrack, based on Childress's book. Available from Columbia Records.

I know why the caged bird sings. Film based on Angelou's book. Available from Learning Corporation of America.

Ordinary people. Film based on Guest's book. Available from Paramount Home Video, Hollywood, Calif.

Roald Dahl reads his "Charlie and the chocolate factory." Available from Caedmon, 1995 Broadway, New York, NY 10023.

Snowbound. Film based on Mazer's book. Available from Learning Corporation of America.

Sounder. Audiovisual unit based on Armstrong's book. Available from Educational Reading Services, Audiovisual Division, Mahwah, NJ.

Star Wars. Available from Films Incorporated, Wilmette, Ill.

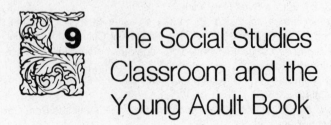

9 The Social Studies Classroom and the Young Adult Book

The Thematic Unit

It is not unusual to discover that the single textbook adopted for and used in the social studies classroom is inappropriate for many of the students. For many students it is too difficult to read with understanding; for others it is too easy and boring. Likewise, numerous students are dissatisfied with history courses as they are taught and consequently develop a lasting distaste for the subject. Similarly, teachers are frustrated by the lack of content in the text, coupled with student reading problems and apparent lack of motivation.

The solution to these problems involves the use of a myriad of interesting classroom reading materials at a variety of reading levels in a curriculum that is not preoccupied with facts, creates a sense of historical continuity, gives attention to cause-effect relationships, allows the students to ask questions, and creates a high level of interest. This type of curriculum can be developed by using the thematic approach to teaching social studies.

In social studies, as in English, the goal of the thematic unit is not only to teach the theme, but also to use the theme as a vehicle for teaching history, sociology, geography, political science, and economics. The theme is a means through which the secondary school social studies teacher can help students gain access to the discipline's major organizers and assist them in using these organizational skills to gain a better understanding of the world.

SELECTING AN APPROPRIATE THEME. According to Willard M. Kniep (1979), the four major organizers of social studies are (1) processes of inquiry, (2) concepts as building blocks, (3) certain phenomena that delimit the field, and (4) persistent problems. Kniep suggests that these four organizers can become the sources for the selections of thematic units for the social studies classroom (See Table 9–1 for an illustrative list of organizing themes for social studies.) And, if a balance is achieved in the study of units based on these four organizers, the students will gain skills, concepts, and ideas necessary for successful understanding of social studies.

For example, a thematic unit based on a process theme will focus instruction on the discovery process often employed by the social scientist. These processes can assist the student in developing an ability to make decisions, solve problems, and generate knowledge. Units that deal with themes in this area are skill-development units. It is essential that students develop these skills in order

Table 9–1 Organizing Themes for Thematic Units

Processes (skills)	Concepts	Phenomena (natural and man-made)	Persistent problems
Observing	Cause/Effect	Art	Communication
Questioning	Change	Banks	Conflict
Predicting	Cooperation	Cities	Crime
Hypothesizing	Community	Communities	Cultural
Gathering data	Conflict	Consumers	change
Quantifying	Culture	Cultural groups	Energy needs
Comparing	Evolution	Dress	Inflation
Classifying	Family	Economic Systems	Overcrowding
Measuring	Group	Elections	Pollution
Interpreting data	Human Being	Exploration	Poverty
Making	Interaction	Families	Powerlessness
inferences	Interdependence	Feelings	Racism
Communicating	Land-use	Governments	Scarcity
Making models	Motivation	Groups	Sexism
	Nation	Land forms	Technological
	Opportunity cost	Literature	displacement
	Population	Markets	Unemployment
	Power	Media	Urban decline
	Resources	Mythologies	War
	Producer and Consumer	Oceans	
	Roles	People	
	Rules	Political Organizations	
	Scarcity	Producers	
	Self	Religions	
	Specialization	Rural areas	
	Supply and Demand	Schools	
	System	Small towns	
	Technology	Technology	
	Time/Space	Wars	
	Tools		
	Values		

Source: Willard M. Kniep, Thematic units, *Clearing House,* April 1979, p. 390.

to function effectively within the other three organizational units of the social sciences.

A unit based on concepts will give students the structure needed to understand and describe the world in which they live. For instance, a unit developed around the theme of conflict will enable the student to study the various types of conflict and examine the components of each. Thereby, the student will be able to identify conflict-causing events in new situations and determine whether they are likely to develop into open confrontation. George Hemmingson developed an interesting social studies unit on conflict. The unit began with a study of conflicts beween parents and teenagers. Various young adult books, fiction and nonfiction, on different reading levels were employed. His bibliography included *Mom, the Wolfman, and me* (Klein), *Mama* (Hopkins), *Of love and death and other journeys* (Holland), *Summer of my German soldier* (Greene), *Dinky Hocker shoots smack!* and *Is that you, Miss Blue?* (Kerr), *The boy who could make himself disappear* (Platt), *Richie* (Thompson), *It's not the end of the world* and *Deenie* (Blume), *Run softly, go fast* (Wersba), *Anne Frank: The diary of a young girl*, *The cat ate my gymsuit* and *Can you sue your parents for malpractice?* (Danziger), *Ronnie and Rosey* (Angell), *I know why the caged bird sings* (Angelou), and *Mommie dearest* (Crawford). Each student, after reading one book, was asked to identify the major conflict between the parent and the young adult. Once the conflict was identified, the student was instructed to search the book to determine the events that led to the development of the conflict. The conflict-producing events were assigned to one or more of three categories: situations attributable to the teenager, situations that stem out of actions or lack of actions of the parent, and situations that arise from neither the teenager nor the parent. Next the student was asked to examine each situation and determine its cause—for example, lack of communication between the teenager and the parent. After the causes were identified, the students met in small groups to develop a list of the apparent causes of conflict between teenagers and parents. A final class list was developed and much discussion ensued. During the next class session the students saw a film of the events leading up to the Watts riots. Afterward, they formed small discussion groups and examined the events of the film, identifying the probable causes of each event. These causes were then compared with the list the class had developed after reading about and discussing teenage-parent conflict. Similarities and differences were discussed by the class. Mr. Hemmingson suggested that it might be interesting to look at the current city council discussions about the annexation of a new subdivision to determine whether open conflict was likely to develop around this local issue. The students examined the newspaper for information about the annexation, interviewed local residents, invited city council members to attend their class, and interviewed members of the local broadcast media. They concluded that open conflict was likely to develop, basing that conclusion on the fact that all the major causes they had identified in the parent-teenager conflict and in the Watts film were present in the annexation issue. The students were right; open confrontation arose at the next meeting of the city council.

Thematic units based on man-made and natural phenomena have the goal of assisting students in gaining a better understanding of the world in which they live. Within these units, often through actual experience, the students study events, places, structures, and organizations. During a presidential election year, for example, several high school classes became actively involved in the election process. In late 1983 the history department of a high school decided that the best way to teach the democratic election process was to involve students in the process from the start. Therefore, about three months before the primaries, students began seeking information about the announced candidates. Small groups of students developed files of information on each candidate. From these files oral reports were prepared and delivered to each of the history classes. Next, the students sought and obtained information about the presidential primary in their state. Similarly, they collected data about how to register and vote in the primary election. A videotape of a mock television interview show on registration and voting was made and shown to an assembly of the school. Afterward, the students conducted a register-to-vote campaign among the student body and school community. During this time the students were continuing to seek information about each candidate and review the data in each candidate's file. Several weeks prior to the primary election, the students wrote editorials supporting particular candidates and defending their choices by citing the candidates' qualifications. The editorials, without identification of the candidate, were copied and distributed. Small groups of students were assigned to examine the editorials for incorrect or biased information. Each group reported the results of its study to the class. Finally, the students were asked to select a candidate to support. Based on their decisions, the students were placed in groups and developed a campaign for each candidate. The campaign included posters, articles in the school paper, announcements over the intercom, and speeches to other classes. On primary day, a mock schoolwide election was held and the votes were counted. Also on primary day, the students assisted in getting the local population to the polls. A similar thematic unit was developed before the presidential election in November. The bibliography for this unit included many titles for young adults: *Politics from precinct to presidency* (Liston), *Facts about the presidents* (Kane), *We elect a president* (Weingast), *The nature of politics* (Curtis), *Lies, damn lies, and statistics* (Wheeler), *Defender of the Constitution: Andrew Johnson* (Green), *Young man in the White House: John Fitzgerald Kennedy* (Levine), *President from Missouri: Harry S. Truman* (Martin), *Those who love* (a historical novel about John and Abigail Adams by Irving Stone), *Breach of faith: The fall of Richard Nixon* (White), and *They also ran* (Stone).[1] The reading and maturity level of this bibliography was widely varied so that all the students in the class could participate in the study of the politics of the American presidency.

Using persistent problems as organizers for thematic units will help students understand and develop an explanation for the causes of these problems. A

[1] The excellent *Teacher's manual: The American presidency* is free upon request from New American Library, 1633 Broadway, New York, NY 10019.

unit based on problems allows students to use the skills developed in the units on processes and concepts. Thus, students will gain increased skill in analyzing and problem solving.

For example, in a unit on aging, the students in one high school examined the problems of growing old in our society, developed solutions, and examined the consequences of their solutions. This unit allowed the students to develop skills such as observing, questioning, and predicting. It also required them to examine cause-effect, change, cooperation, community and family, and culture.

In developing units on phenomena and persistent problems, the social studies teacher can incorporate the processes (skills) and concepts essential for effective study of social studies. The unit on aging is a good example. Similarly, the unit on elections uses skills such as observing, questioning, gathering data, comparing, interpreting data, and communicating. Likewise, the unit teaches the concepts of cooperation, community, interaction, interdependence, nation, and rules. The social studies teacher who is aware of the processes and concepts to be taught at each grade level will be able to incorporate all these skills and concepts within units on phenomena and problems.

> ☐ *The art of living cannot be taught or learned by rote, so I believe we should encourage our children to make inquiry and seek answers, directly, with honesty, through reading and open discussion in the home as well as at school.*
> ALICE CHILDRESS
> *author of* A hero ain't nothin' but a sandwich

The actual selection of a theme that incorporates the skills and concepts necessary for the successful understanding of social studies is a difficult task. It is particularly demanding in the social studies classroom, which requires the teaching of a specific body of knowledge, such as U.S. history, civics, or European history. However, it is even more essential that interesting themes be developed in these classrooms to avoid the students' accusations that segments of history do not seem to interrelate, that the study of history usually ends before 1920, and that history study is preoccupied with fact.

Selection of a theme that incorporates the concepts and skills of the social scientist requires that teachers establish in their own minds a series of key themes (phenomena or problems) that summarize the essence of the discipline or culture being studied. A list of key constructs for designing thematic units in U.S. history which synthesize the national ideal was established in 1957 by the National Council for the Social Studies. Robert Waller (1978) has further outlined these constructs for the history teacher. According to Waller, "By identifying select themes recurring throughout the nation's history, the instructor can provide an interpretive framework within which to develop a meaningful exposure to this nation's heritage of ideas and ideals" (p. 202). The following key constructs may serve as a useful example for social studies teachers attempting to develop themes for their courses.

■ ■ Sample Social Studies Unit

Grade: 10-12
Instructor: A. J. S. Reed
Course/Subject: Problems in Democracy/Social Studies

Unit: Aging
  Duration: Two weeks

I. Brief Introduction

The main concept to be covered by the unit is that aging is part of the natural life cycle and we must learn to deal with old age as part of our life and the lives of others. The problems involved in doing this, however, are complex.

The unit utilizes the process of inquiry. Since inquiry is a social process, the students interact with other students to solve a puzzling problem. By comparing their actions with others', the students are better able to understand themselves.

The student will be working at the highest levels of the cognitive domain: analysis, synthesis, and evaluation. Similarly, the student will develop high-level affective skills through the defense of the hypothetical solution. Defending the solution will require the organization of new values.

II. Objectives

A. The student will formulate a problem statement given limited information.

B. The student will use the library to investigate the problem statement(s).

C. The student will help organize a group to investigate problems and to locate and formulate solutions.

D. The student will locate, read, and comprehend articles in journals and books related to the problem statement.

E. Given information gathered, the student will formulate, with other group members, a solution hypothesis.

F. With the group the student will identify problem solutions, defend them, and discuss possible consequences of them.

G. The student will listen to and show respect for problem solutions of other groups.

H. The student will express in writing his/her contributions to the group's investigation of the problem.

III. Content Outlines

Day 1—A. Puzzling situation is presented (film: <u>Peege</u>).

B. Student writes his/her reactions to the film on a small piece of paper.

C. Student selects one book from attached bibliography.

Day 2—D. Reactions to the film are presented orally and key words are listed on the board.

E. Key words are analyzed and synthesized into categories. Some might include:

1. Differing reactions to old age.
2. Care systems for the elderly.
3. Family support systems.
4. Societal attitudes.
5. Historical aspects of aging.
6. Medical aspects of aging.

F. Each student selects three categories he or she finds interesting and lists them in order of preference.

Day 3—G. As a class, the students develop a problem statement for one of the categories not selected.

H. Groups are assigned based on student choice.

I. Each group develops a problem statement for its category.

Day 4—J. The students visit the library and discover the resources available to them in the areas of concern. The class develops a local resource list.

K. The assignment is given: Your task is to solve the problem and present to the class a hypothetical solution. The solution must be defensible given the research you do.

Days 5-8—L. Class time is used for research and design of hypothetical solution. Teacher acts as resource person.

M. A final evaluation instrument for the oral reports is designed by the class. The discussion will include the function of the report, what the other students need to know, and how best to present the information.

Days 9-10— N. Hypothetical solutions are presented and defended.

IV. Instructional Strategies

A. Turn-on Event (film: Peege)

B. Technique

The primary technique is group inquiry. The first element is the identification of problem statements. Since successful group process is the key to completion of this lesson, the groups will be expected to keep a daily (or more frequent) log of assignments, objectives, and progress. Similarly, they will be required to designate each person's responsibility on a group plan handout provided during the first small group session. Five minutes before the end of each session, the groups will be given an assessment form to complete. At the end of each week, the students will be given a progress report to complete.

C. Closing the Lesson

Each group will orally present a hypothetical solution. The day before the presentation they will hand in a one-page summary of their solution. These summaries will be duplicated and silently read by the other students in the class. Questions will be written, to be asked after the presentation. Each presentation will last 10-15 minutes, and a 15-minute question period will follow.

V. Instructional Aids and Resources

A. Film: Peege

B. Library facilities handout

C. A community resource list will be developed by the teacher, in consultation with the students during the visit to the library.

VI. Evaluation

Each group will develop a problem statement and a group plan for defending their solution. The solution and its defense will be presented during class time. The presentation will be evaluated by the other students in the class, using an instrument developed by the class. The instructor will evaluate the presentation, using a similar instrument.

Each student will read one book from the accompanying bibliography. A brief report on the problems faced by the elderly character will be required.

Each student will keep an individual journal, recording contributions to the group work. Five minutes before the end of each session, an individual evaluation will be completed by all students and collected by the instructor. These will be returned to the students for recording in the journal. The journal will be handed in after the oral presentation.

Each day a group meeting assessment form will be completed by all group members. At the end of each week, a group progress report will be completed.

VII. A Bibliography of Young Adult Books

Aaron, C. Better than laughter. Harcourt Brace Jovanovich, 1972. Dell, 1973.

Branscum, R. Toby, Granny, and George. Doubleday, 1976. Avon, 1977.

Bridgers, S. E. Notes for another life. Knopf, 1981.

Glass, F. Marvin and Tige. St. Martin's, 1977. Fawcett, 1977.

Holland, I. Man without a face. Lippincott, 1972. Dell, 1980.

Irwin, H. Lilith summer. Feminist Press, 1979.

Kerr, M. E. Gentlehands. Harper & Row, 1978.

L'Engle, M. A ring of endless light. Farrar, Straus & Giroux, 1980. Dell, 1981.

——. The summer of the great grandmother. Farrar, Straus & Giroux, 1974. Seabury, 1979.

Mazer, N. F. A figure of speech. Delacorte, 1973. Dell, 1975.

Paterson, K. Jacob have I loved. Crowell, 1980, Avon, 1981.

Taylor, T. The cay. Doubleday, 1969. Avon, 1970.

Zindel, P. The pigman. Harper & Row, 1968. Bantam, 1978.

——. The pigman's legacy. Harper & Row, 1980. Bantam, 1981.

1. *Economic opportunity* is a theme that is "readily apparent in American history from colonization efforts through contemporary society" (Waller 1978, p. 204). The theme is concerned with the high value placed on the utilization of scarce resources in order to attain the best for all citizens. According to Waller, teaching the theme can be approached through an examination of one's home state as a "frontier environment," through the labor movement as a collective drive toward prosperity, the Puritan work ethic, and the country's contrasting identification with equal opportunity and crass materialism.

2. *Wide participation in politics* is associated with U.S. economic development. An understanding of this theme, government of, by, and for the people, can be gained through the twin concepts of the theme "consent of the governed and the importance of public opinion in decision-making" (p. 205). The teacher can help students understand the wide participation of U.S. citizens in government by studying the two-party system. An examination of the Progressive movement, the home rule provisions, referendum, and constitutional amendments that have provided an expanded electorate would be helpful in understanding the theme.

3. *A belief in reform,* in evolution rather than revolution, is the third key theme. Teachers, according to Waller, should help students understand the delicate "balance between social stability and social change" (p. 205). An understanding of this theme is essential if students are to appreciate the "revolutionary heritage from which the United States originated and to perceive the dichotomies inherent in the Jeffersonian tradition of civil disobedience" (p. 205). Students should become familiar with the reforms of the Progressive era, the system of checks and balances that has been devised to encourage cooperation and yet allow for dissension, and the missionary zeal with which our nation has attempted to export its ideals to the rest of the world.

4. *Population mobility* is an excellent theme for helping students develop a sense of historic continuity in the study of the nation's development. The theme includes social mobility, economic mobility, and personal freedom. The movement westward is an example of geographic mobility. "The concept of the city and its place within society deserves special consideration in this category" (p. 206). The study of the growth of the middle class is an excellent way to approach this theme.

5. The *status of women* is a theme that ties together two centuries of this nation's development. A study of the history of the women's movement can shed light on this theme. An examination of women's changing roles in the family, the job market, and politics parallels the country's economic development. "Study of this theme enables one to draw some definitional distinctions between women's rights, women's emancipation, feminism, and women's liberation in order to illustrate the complexity of the issue in past as well as present time" (p. 206). Waller suggests that a study of the change in clothing styles can shed light on the movement toward suffrage. The relationship of women to the male culture may be an interesting study for some perceptive high school students.

6. *Widespread educational opportunity* is a theme that is rarely discussed in an institution that is built upon it. Students should understand how the concept of democracy is inherent in the public school system. The goal of universal, free public education can be traced. A study of the school as a socializing agent within the society can be of interest. Is the school an institution devoted to maintaining or evolving the values of society? Do all students have access to equal educational opportunity?

7. *A concern for the welfare of others* is an interesting consideration in the development of this nation, populated by people "hard-headed about making money but soft-hearted about spending it" (p. 207). A study of U.S. philanthropic concerns can shed light on this theme. The twentieth-century phenomenon of social welfare is a fascinating study. Similar studies of foreign aid as a humanitarian concern will interest students.

8. The *toleration of differences* is a concern that allows high school history students to examine how various groups have been assimilated, or not assimilated, into U.S. culture. An examination of immigration from the first days of the nation to the present in conjunction with intolerance toward groups of people (Know-Nothingism, Klanism, and McCarthyism) can help students understand the complexities of the issues involved.

9. A *respect for the rights and abilities of individuals* is the flip side of the same coin. An examination of individualism as the foundation of this nation is an interesting study to develop, from the Bill of Rights and the Four Freedoms to slavery, to emancipation, to the American Indian, to internment of Japanese-Americans, to civil rights, and so on. An examination of school integration from the 1954 *Brown* decision of the Supreme Court to the present can show students how respect for individual rights is interpreted by the courts and legislatures. The part played by violence and the threat of violence in the rights of the individual cannot be ignored in the study of this theme.

10. *Worldwide responsibility* is the final theme. A development of our country's sense of world responsibility can be examined. An understanding of the interdependence of the world's nations, a twentieth-century phenomenon, should be studied. A comparison of isolationism and internationalism is an interesting study. Each president's personality and conduct of foreign policy could also be studied. "The emergence of this nation as a world power is a theme

with significant implication for comprehending domestic politics as well as understanding the character of Americans'' (p. 208).[2]

Units based on subthemes of these ten key themes of U.S. history can employ the use of young adult literature in many different ways. A unit on population mobility, entitled Movement, Migration, and Mobility, can develop a bibliography of literature of the westward migration. Though much of this literature is not specifically written for young adults, its major characters are usually young, adventuresome, and exciting. Therefore, the literature of the West fits the definition of young adult literature and deserves mention in this text. The *Little house* books (Wilder), *The snowbird* (Calvert), *The massacre at Fall Creek* (West), *The Virginian* (Wister), *The log of a cowboy* (Adams), *Laughing boy* and *The enemy gods* (LaFarge), *The way west* (Guthrie), *The man who killed the deer* (Waters), *The taste of time* (Egan), *Down the long hills* and *The quick and the dead* (L'Amour), *The brave cowboy* (Abbey), *The spirit is willing* (Baker), *A woman of the people* (Capps), *My Antonia* (Cather), *The West of the Texas Kid, 1881–1910* (Crawford), *To be a man* (Decker), *The adventures of the Negro cowboys* (Durham and Jones), *The Chisholm Trail* (Gard), *To the last man* (Grey), *You bet your boots I can* (Hosford), *Home below Hell's Canyon* (Jordan), *Jim Bridger, mountain man* (Vestal), *The Missouri* (Vestal), *Once in the saddle: The cowboy's frontier 1866–1896* (Seidman), and others add interest at a wide variety of reading levels to a unit on westward expansion. The history teacher can have each student select one title and then join a work group of students whose book choices are based on a similar historic event, geographic location, or character. Activities that integrate these novels into the theme of the unit can be completed by the groups and presented to the class. In this way all the students can share from the information presented in all of the books.

If multiple copies of several titles are available, the teacher can give book talks on each of four or five titles and allow the students to select from among them. The students can be grouped according to the titles selected, and activities can be planned for each group. This allows the teacher to preselect the best titles for meeting the unit's objectives, while the students still have the opportunity to work in groups within their areas of interest.

Bibliographies of young adult titles can be developed on most of the subthemes suggested by Waller. John Ney's *Ox* books, about a boy growing up in wealthy Palm Beach society, are excellent choices for a unit on prosperity and materialism. Stories of poor families struggling to survive in the midst of a prosperous community, such as Sue Ellen Bridgers's *Home before dark* and Lee Bennett Hopkins's *Mama*, will add much food for thought to units dealing with equality of economic opportunity. The importance of public opinion can be seen in a personal sense in books such as Isabelle Holland's *Heads you win, tails I*

---

[2]Recurring themes have been paraphrased and quoted from Robert Waller, ''Thematic Approach to Teaching U.S. History,'' *The History Teacher*, February 1978, pp. 201–210. Reprinted courtesy of *The History Teacher*.

lose and S. E. Hinton's tales of teenage peer relationships, *The outsiders, That was then, this is now,* and *Rumble fish.*

The need to find a balance between social stability and social change can be found in many books dealing with the minority experience in the United States. Books such as *It's crazy to stay Chinese in Minnesota* (Telemaque); *The education of Little Tree* (Carter); *Sing down the moon* (O'Dell); *The autobiography of Miss Jane Pitmann* (Gaines); *Roll of thunder, hear my cry,* and *Let the circle be unbroken* (Taylor); *I know why the caged bird sings* (Angelou); *Bury my heart at Wounded Knee* (Brown); *Manchild in the promised land* (Brown); and *Ludell, Ludell and Willie* and *Ludell's New York time* (Wilkinson) help students view life from the perspective of people seeking to claim their fair share of the society, as well as from that of the society painfully attempting to adjust to new demands.

The status of women can be studied through an examination of women's roles as seen through the literature of the period. Anne Eliot Crompton's *A woman's place,* told in five sections (1750, 1800, 1850, 1900, and 1950), is a good place for young adults to begin their study. Other useful sources include *I speak for my slave sister: The life of Abbey Kelley Foster* (Bacon), *Born female* (Bird), *Never jam today* (Bolton), *First woman editor: Sarah J. Hale* (Burt), *Silent voices: The Southern Negro woman today* (Carson), *A minority of members: Women in the U.S. Congress* (Chamberlin), *Bloomers and ballots: Elizabeth Cady Stanton and women's rights* (Clarke), *Women of crisis: Lines of struggle and hope* and *Women of crisis II: Lives of work and dreams* (Coles and Coles), *An American*

Social studies students read historical fiction to learn about the Far East.

girl (Dizenzo), *Women out of history: A herstory anthology* (Forfreedom), *The ladies of Seneca Falls* (Gurko), *The lady is a jock* (Haney), *Claws of a young century* (Hunt), *Jeannette Rankin: First lady in Congress* (Josephson), *Zanballer* (Knudson), *Margaret Sanger: Pioneer of birth control* (Lader and Meltzer), *Jane Addams: Pioneer for social justice* (Meigs), *Growing up female in America: Ten lives* (Merriam), *That crazy April* (Perl), *Dorothy Thompson* (Sanders), *Indian women of the western morning: Their life in early America* (Terrell and Terrell), and many others.[3]

A unit on immigrants' impact on and contribution to U.S. culture can use books like *My name is Asher Lev* and *The chosen* (Potok), about the life of young Hasidic Jews. An excellent nonfiction account of Jewish-American life is *How we lived* (Howe and Libo). A subsection of the unit on immigration might include a study of intolerance as seen through such movements as Know-Nothingism, Klanism, and McCarthyism. The experiences of non-Anglo Saxon citizens in the United States can be better understood in young adult books such as *It's crazy to stay Chinese in Minnesota* (Telemaque), *Year walk* (Clark), and *Farewell to Manzanar* (Houston and Houston). Two recent nonfiction books for young adults are particularly useful in teaching this theme: *Coming to America: Immigrants from the Far East* (Perrin) and *Coming to America: Immigrants from the British Isles* (Blumenthal and Ozer).[4] (Other books useful in teaching about the melting pot are mentioned in Chapters 3 and 6.)

History textbooks tend to lump people into groups, to talk of the Japanese or the blacks or the American Indians. Good books, including good young adult books, allow students to examine people as individuals. Therefore, literature is exceedingly important in a unit on the rights and abilities of the individual. Scott O'Dell's *Sing down the moon,* for example, examines the impact of the Navajo's forced march from Canyon de Chelly to Fort Summer, New Mexico, on individuals, rather than on the group. Through Ann Nolan Clark's *Year walk,* young adults can examine the life of a single immigrant to the United States, in this case a Basque sheepherder, rather than the faceless groups that appear in history texts. An understanding of the individual is important in the 1980s, a decade in which the nation expects greater immigration than at any time in its history.

Thematic approaches in the social studies classroom allow the teacher to teach the skills and concepts necessary to the social scientist, to encourage all students to learn by providing a vast array of materials on all interest and reading levels, to create a sense of historic continuity, and to give attention to cause-effect relationships. Studying a theme allows students to ask questions. And basing the units on the students' conception of the world helps motivate them toward a study of the social sciences.

[3] *A teacher's guide to women's studies* by Andrea Berens Karls is available from Dell Publishing, Educational Sales Department, 245 East 47 St., New York, NY 10017.

[4] A teacher's guide, *The coming to America series: The roots of our immigrant past* by Paula McGuire, is available from Dell Publishing, Educational Sales Department, 245 East 47th St., New York, NY 10017.

Individualized Reading

An individualized reading program is as important in the social studies class-room as it is in the English classroom. In such a program, the student chooses from a variety of books, regularly reads highly motivating books in addition to the textbook, individually or in small groups reports on the reading to the teacher, writes about the reading at regular intervals, uses the books to increase understanding of the subject, and reads books that are written on his or her reading level. Similarly, individualized reading allows the student to become per-sonally involved with the study of history, geography, sociology, economics, and so on, through individual selection of reading materials. Literature can help the study of history come alive for the student.

> *Reading can help make events in history or concepts on topics such as prejudice come alive and be unforgettable for the student. We are talking about incorporating literature, biographies, and other personal accounts of events into the curriculum, integrating all types of reading material into the content, and encouraging reading as a lifetime habit: one that gives pleasure, expands the experience of the individual and creates an atmosphere of a historical era in a memorable way. (Cline and Taylor 1978, p. 27)*

An individualized reading program in a social studies classroom allows the student to select from an array of books suggested by the teacher. Usually, the books relate to the subject being studied. They are likely to include biographies such as *Josh Gibson: A life in the Negro leagues* (Brashler), autobiographies such as *The autobiography of Malcolm X,* historical fiction such as *The distant summer* (Patterson), personal accounts such as *First blood* (Morrell), nonfiction adventure such as *The "Ra" expeditions* (Heyerdahl), dissent literature such as *Soul on ice* (Cleaver), nonfiction reporting such as *Anyone's daughter: The times and trials of Patty Hearst* (Alexander), social problem books such as *Sarah T.—Portrait of a teenage alcoholic* (Wagnen), fictional books on religion and culture such as *Beyond the mists* (Benchley), nonfiction on religion and cul-ture such as *Gypsies* (Greenfeld), fiction dealing with changing roles and stan-dards such as *Mom, the Wolfman and me* (Klein), nonfiction accounts of chang-ing roles and cultures such as *A woman's place* (Crompton), books on the theme of human conflict such as *Deathwatch* (White), books on the struggle against natural forces such as *Snow bound* (Mazer), accounts of historic events such as *Battle in the Arctic Seas* (Taylor), and stories of sports figures such as *Life on the run* (Bradley).

If the students are studying the minority experience in U.S. culture, all of the books may relate to that theme. Similarly, if the unit deals with a historical period such as World War II, all of the individualized reading selections may relate to the various aspects of that period. Some may deal with battles, some with the

Holocaust, some with Nazism, some with the civilians involved, some with military figures, some with specific non-battle-related aspects of the war, and some with life on the home front. The following sample annotated bibliography lists young adult books related to World War II. (It is reprinted from *Study guide for use in conjunction with* The diary of Anne Frank. University of North Carolina at Asheville, 1980.)

If a concept such as conflict is being studied, all of the books may deal with various types of conflict: interpersonal, group, political, or international. If a phenomenon such as oceans is being examined, the books may deal with conquests on the high seas, explorations, sea journeys, or sea battles. During the study of a persistent problem such as the scarcity of natural resources and ecology, the individual selection of books may include fictional and nonfictional examples of the problem, solutions to the problem, and problems created by the solutions.

An individualized reading program in the social studies classroom should be well organized, carefully planned, and a regular part of the classroom activities. The essential elements of a successful program for social studies are the same as those for the English classroom. (See pages 000–000 for a description of the common elements in successful individualized reading programs.)

An individualized reading program in the social studies classroom increases the students' motivation to read books, personalizes the study of the subject area, gives a student the opportunity to view problems from many different vantage points, helps the student understand that there are often many right answers to any given question (and that there is often no right answer), increases the likelihood of the student's developing a lifelong reading habit, allows the student to select material that he or she can read, and helps further the student's motivation in the study of the subject area.

Biography and Autobiography

For many students the study of history is a very impersonal experience. The pages of the secondary school history textbook do not reveal the feelings, concerns, abilities, and weaknesses of the real people behind the events. Teenagers cannot see themselves as a part of the history of their country, nor can they imagine parents, grandparents, or friends on the pages of the textbook. The impersonal approach to teaching history may result in the student's inability to understand things as important to our national heritage as Jeffersonian democracy. Learning theorists have carefully researched and documented the learner's need to relate all new learning to past experiences and already acquired knowledge; learning must be personalized.

Recent studies, unfortunately, have shown that U.S. high school graduates are ignorant of basic U.S. history. A *New York Times* education questionnaire on U.S. history given to 1,856 college freshmen indicated that the respondents

■ ■ Sample Annotated Bibliography

An Annotated Bibliography of Young Adult Books
on World War II

Titles appropriate for younger readers are preceded by an asterisk.

Arnold-Forster, Mark. The world at war. New American Library, 1973. Accounts of campaigns beginning with the Nazi buildup and concluding with the fall of the Axis powers. Nonfiction.

Bauer, Yehuda. Flight and rescue. Random House, 1970. A fully documented, detailed history of the mass rescue of almost 300,000 Jews by underground organizations. Nonfiction.

*Benchley, Nathaniel. Bright candles: A novel of the Danish resistance. Harper & Row, 1974. Sixteen-year-old Jens is involved in dangerous sabotage work, helping fellow Danes resist the Nazi occupation in 1940. Fiction.

*Bonnell, Dorothy. Passport to freedom. Messner, 1967. Sally Schmidt is an American college student who has lost her passport and therefore cannot be evacuated to the U.S. when the Nazis march into Paris in 1940. Fiction.

Boom, Corrie ten (with John and Elizabeth Sherrill). The hiding place. Bantam, 1974. The author was arrested for protecting Jews and sent to a German concentration camp. Religion became her solace. Nonfiction.

Bor, Josef. Terezin requiem. Knopf, 1963. A conductor succeeds in putting on a performance of Verdi's Requiem amid the horrors of a concentration camp. Fiction.

Calvocoressi, Peter, and Guy Wint. Total war: The story of World War II. 2 vols. Ballantine, 1972. A detailed history. Nonfiction.

Chaneles, Sol. Three children of the Holocaust. Avon, 1974. The story of three young survivors adopted by wealthy American Jews. Fiction.

*Dank, Milton. The dangerous game. Lippincott, 1977. The story of a sixteen-year-old French boy and the French Resistance. Fiction.

Davidowicz, Lucy S. The war against the Jews, 1933-1945. Holt, Rinehart & Winston, 1975. The author attempts to answer three questions: Why did Germany allow the murder of the Jews? Why did the Jews allow this to happen to themselves? Why did the world allow this to happen? Mature nonfiction.

*Degens, T. Transport 7-41-R. Viking, 1974. A thirteen-year-old German girl discovers in the aftermath of the German defeat the importance of helping others. Fiction.

*Flender, Harold. Rescue in Denmark. Macfadden, 1964. An account of the heroism of the Danish people in saving Jews from the Nazis. Nonfiction.

*Flinker, Moshe. Young Moshe's diary: The spiritual torment of a Jewish boy in Nazi Europe. New York: Board of Jewish Education, 1965. A devoutly religious Dutch boy grapples with the problems of suffering and divine justice. Nonfiction.

*Forman, James. Horses of anger. Farrar, Straus & Giroux, 1967. A novel, set in Germany, based on the true story of brother and sister idealists who produced anti-Nazi pamphlets and were guillotined. Fiction.

——. The traitors. Farrar, Straus & Giroux, 1968. A novel about two half brothers. One becomes a Nazi; the other helps their father, a pastor, try to save a Jewish friend. Fiction.

——. Nazism. Dell. A history of the Nazi party that looks at Hitler's life and writings. Nonfiction.

*Frank, Anne. Anne Frank: The diary of a young girl. Doubleday, 1952. The story of Anne, her family, and four other Jews who hid from the Nazis for two years in an attic in Holland. Nonfiction.

*Glemser, Bernard. Radar commandos. Pocket Books, 1953. Fifteen-year-old Paul spies on a farmhouse that is a Nazi base for a new detecting device. The British destroy the base with Paul's help. Fiction.

*Greene, Bette. Summer of my German soldier. Dial, 1973. The oldest child of a Jewish family living in a small Arkansas town during the war aids a German prisoner of war. Her actions shock her parents and the town, and result in her arrest. Fiction.

*Grunberger, Richard. Hitler's SS. Dell, 1972. A sketch of the Nazi Schutzstaffel from the 1920s through World War II. Nonfiction.

——. Twelve-year Reich: A social history of Nazi Germany, 1933-1945. Holt, Rinehart & Winston, 1969. Covers such topics as education, sports, the arts, family life, and humor in the Nazi era. Nonfiction.

*Grunfeld, Frederic V. The Hitler file: A social history of Germany and the Nazis, 1918-45. Random House, 1974. A pictorial review including posters, cartoons, and photos. Nonfiction.

Jacot, Michael. The last butterfly. Bobbs-Merrill, 1974. A professional clown finds himself in a concentration camp together with a group of Polish children whose parents have been murdered. Fiction.

*Joffo, Joseph. A bag of marbles. Houghton Mifflin, 1974. The adventures of two young brothers fleeing the Gestapo in France. Fiction.

Kantor, Alfred. The book of Alfred Kantor. McGraw-Hill, 1971. The personal story of an inmate of Terezin, with 127 sketches depicting camp life. Nonfiction.

*Koehn, Ilse. Mischling, second degree. William Morrow, 1977. The author's account of her adolescence in Nazi Germany. She was a mischling, the "mixed" offspring of a union between a non-Jew and a Jew. Nonfiction.

Korczak, Janusz. Ghetto diary. Schocken, 1978. The author was director of an orphanage in the Warsaw ghetto. He refused offers of personal rescue and insisted on accompanying his 200 orphans to Treblinka, where they were eventually murdered. Nonfiction.

Levi, Primo. Survival in Auschwitz: The Nazi assault on humanity. Macmillan, 1961. The account of an Italian Jew captured by the Fascist militia and turned over to the Nazis. Nonfiction.

Levin, Jane Whitehead. Star of danger. Harcourt, 1966. The story of two teenage boys who flee Nazi Germany to Denmark. When the Nazis take over Denmark, they are helped by Danish friends to escape. Fiction.

Lind, Jakov. Counting my steps. Macmillan, 1969. The Austrian-Jewish writer recounts his years of hiding and fleeing from the Nazis. Nonfiction.

Lustig, Arnost. A prayer for Katerina Horovitzova. Avon, 1975. An American Jewish businessmen and a young girl are caught in a game of self-deception directed by the Nazis. Fiction.

——. Darkness casts no shadow. Avon, 1977. Two boys escape from a German death train and try to survive in the forest. Fiction.

——. Night and hope. Avon. Seven short stories, many about teen-agers, about life in Terezin concentration camp. Fiction.

*McKown, Robin. Patriot of the underground. Putnam, 1964. A story of teenagers who try to aid the French Resistance. Fiction.

Manvell, Roger, Films and the Second World War. Barnes, 1974. Dell, 1976. A study of film as propaganda, providing a compar-ison of what was happening and what was covered on film. Nonfiction.

Mayer, Milton. They thought they were free: The Germans 1933–45. University of Chicago Press, 1955. The stories of ten German citizens who become supporters of Hitler. Nonfiction.

*Meltzer, Milton. Never to forget: The Jews of the Holocaust. Harper & Row, 1976. Three sections: the first about the history of the Jews and the Nazis; the second about the destruction of the Jews; and the third about the hope of the Jews. Nonfiction.

Moskin, Marietta. I am Rosemarie. John Day, 1972. A Jewish girl grows up despite the overwhelming hardships of four years in a concentration camp. Fiction.

Mosse, George L., ed. Nazi culture: Intellectual, cultural, and social life in the Third Reich. Grosset & Dunlap, 1966. An anthology. Nonfiction.

*Murray, Michele. The Crystal Nights. Seabury, 1973. A German-Jewish family escapes from Germany and comes to a U.S. farm to live with relatives. Fiction.

*Orgel, Doris. The Devil in Vienna. Dial, 1978. A member of the Hitler Youth is friends with a Jew. Fiction.

Rabinowitz, Dorothy. New lives: Survivors of the Holocaust liv-ing in America. Knopf, 1976. Nonfiction.

*Reiss, Johanna. The upstairs room. Crowell, 1972. The story of two sisters hidden by a Christian family in Holland. Nonfiction.

*Richter, Hans Peter. Friedrich. Holt, Rinehart & Winston, 1970. A first-person account of a German boy whose best friend is a Jew. Fiction.

*——. I was there. Dell. Explores the reasons why children joined the Hitler youth. Fiction.

*Sachs, Marilyn. A pocket full of seeds. Doubleday, 1973. An account of a young girl who is separated from her parents during the Nazi invasion of France. Fiction.

Schaeffer, Susan Fromberg. Anya. Macmillan, 1974. The story of the Holocaust as experienced by a Polish woman survivor. Fiction.

Schoenberner, Gerhard. The yellow star: The persecution of the Jews in Europe, 1933–1945. Bantam, 1973. A photographic documentation of the Holocaust. Mature nonfiction.

Schwartz-Bart, André. The last of the just. Atheneum, 1960. A historical novel beginning with medieval English Jewry and ending with the Holocaust. Fiction.

*Smith, Gene. The horns of the moon: A short biography of Adolf Hitler. Charterhouse, 1973. Dell, 1975.

*Stadtler, Bea. The Holocaust: A history of courage and resistance. Anti-Defamation League/Behrman House, 1974. About the main events of the Holocaust and the heroes and heroines of the resistance. Nonfiction.

Suhl, Yuri. On the other side of the gate. Watts, 1975. Schocken, 1975. The story of a young Polish couple's struggle for survival. Fiction.

——. They fought back: The story of the Jewish resistance in Nazi Europe. Schocken, 1975. Thirty-three stories and documents describing organizers and heroes of the Jewish underground. Nonfiction.

Tunis, John R. His enemy, his friend. William Morrow, 1967. A German soldier who has a good relationship with a French village is ordered to shoot some hostages. Years later, as a member of a soccer team, he meets the son of one of the murdered hostages. Fiction.

Uris, Leon. Mila 18. Bantam, 1970. The story of the Jewish forces in the Warsaw Ghetto. Fiction.

Vogt, Hannah. The burden of guilt: A short history of Germany, 1914–1945. Oxford University Press, 1964. Translated from a text written for high school students in Germany today. Nonfiction.

*Volavkova, H., ed. I never saw another butterfly. McGraw-Hill, 1964. Drawings and poetry by children in the Terezin concentration camp. Nonfiction.

Wiesel, Elie. The gates of the forest. Holt, Rinehart & Winston, 1966. The resistance activities of a group of Jews hiding in the forests are described. Fiction.

——. Night, Dawn, The accident. Hill & Wang, 1972. Avon, 1972. The tale of the author's life in a death camp is three short novels in one volume. Nonfiction.

Wilhelm, Maria. For the glory of France: The story of the French Resistance. Messner, 1968. The French Resistance from 1940 until the liberation. Nonfiction.

*Wojciechowska, Maia. Till the break of day. Harcourt Brace Jovanovich, 1972. The story of how the author and her family fled Poland. Nonfiction.

Zassenhause, Hiltgunt. Walls: Resisting the Third Reich. One woman's story. Beacon Press, 1974. The story of a young woman who worked secretly with the Swedish Red Cross to smuggle food into German prisons. Nonfiction.

*Ziemian, Joseph. The cigarette sellers of Three Crosses Square. Lerner, 1975. The story of the children who survived the Warsaw Ghetto and of the members of the Jewish underground who aided them. Nonfiction.

had limited knowledge of the colonial period, that two-thirds had no idea what Jacksonian democracy means, and that less than half know that Woodrow Wilson was president during World War I (Wellington 1977, p. 528).

This ignorance may be the result of a distaste for the study of history exemplified by Janie, an intelligent woman with a major administrative position in state government. Janie lacked one course for completion of her undergraduate degree. Though she had been able to obtain major professional advancements without the degree, she was constantly worried that she would be denied a promotion in the future. However, she continued to procrastinate and failed to complete the single course she needed. The course was a sophomore-level history course. When I asked her why she didn't just take the course, she replied, "I hate to study history." To Janie, and to many other students, history is the study of a series of wars, with endless lists of dates and names to memorize. On the other hand, Janie loves historical fiction. She has read the entire John Jakes bicentennial series; her favorite book is *The thornbirds* (McCullough), a historical novel about a family in the Australian back country. Finally, after a bit of persuasion, she decided to see what it would take to complete this single degree requirement. She called a history professor at her undergraduate school and arranged an individualized reading program. The program required her to read a series of six books. The first book, *From these beginnings* (Nash), was a biographical presentation of many historic figures. It served the purpose of synthesizing all of her reading. Janie loved the course, and she continually discussed historical trends, personalities, and events. The difference between this study of history and her previous experience in the history classroom was the manner of presenting the material. It was offered in a personalized way; the character of each historical figure was revealed; she became part of the history she was studying.

Secondary history teachers can make the study of their subject come alive for their students by including the reading of biography and autobiography in the curriculum. The accounts need not be about famous people; they can be about everyday people with whom the students can identify. In this way teenagers will be able to personalize the study of history.

Biography and autobiography can provide the jumping-off point, the organizational "coat rack," the introductory turn-on event, or the synthesizing tie-together for much secondary school history study. "It is often stated that history is biography and biography is history" (Adejunmobi 1979, p. 349). Biography is a history, or a written account, of a person's life.

> *Good biography is sensitive reportage. Biography is writing that captures the heart and spirit of a man, his zest for life, his passion to know, to explore and discover, to reveal. . . . Over two centuries ago Samuel Johnson said that the first purpose of literature is to teach the art of living. Herein lies the relevance of biography. Good biography does teach living. (Osterlind 1976, p. 176)[5]*

Through the study of good biography and autobiography, the student is better able to understand the real person, gain increased knowledge of the events surrounding that person's life, develop a sense of people as individuals, begin examining groups as being made up of many individuals, and gain self-knowledge through an increased understanding of others. In this manner the study of history relates to the life of the teenager. This is particularly true since most good biography and autobiography depict the person from childhood, through the teenage years, into adulthood. As teenage students read about the person as a young adult, they can often see themselves in that person. The need for teenagers to personalize reading is essential to the development of adult reading skills as well as to the understanding of the book. Seeing themselves in the living character revealed through the writing of the biographer personalizes the

---

[5]Reprinted by permission of the *Arizona English Bulletin*.

study of history, an essential starting point for gaining new knowledge in the field.

Many good biographies and autobiographies are available at different reading levels. The secondary school history teacher can begin a study of biographies and autobiographies by reading those written for young adults. They should judge these biographies by criteria similar to those developed by Ken Donelson and Alleen Pace Nilsen (1980). A good biography, according to these authors, usually has these elements:

> *A subject of interest with whom the author and, therefore, the readers feel intimately acquainted.*
>
> *Documentation of sources and suggestions for further reading—both done inconspicuously so as not to interfere with the story.*
>
> *New and/or unusual sources of original information.*
>
> *Accurate facts about setting and characters.*
>
> *A central theme or a focal point that has been honestly developed from the author's research.*
>
> *In-depth development of the character so that readers understand the way in which the subject shaped his or her own life. Things did not just happen to the person.*
>
> *Use of language that is appropriate to the historical period and the literary style of the book.*
>
> *Information showing how the subject was thought about by contemporaries. (p. 289)*

The use of biographies and autobiographies in the history classroom can help personalize the study of history, increase the student's understanding of historic events and personalities, develop student interest in history, and provide the student with an essential advanced organizer for the understanding of new concepts, phenomena, and problems. (See Chapter 6 for a list of biographies and autobiographies.)

Historical Fiction

Teachers are rarely surprised to learn that their students would rather read fiction than nonfiction. History teachers can capitalize on this preference by using historical fiction to interest teenagers in historical fact.

For example, after Alex Haley's *Roots* was shown on television, many teachers incorporated a study of students' heritage into the classroom curriculum. Chris Knox added a new dimension to history study in his classroom. He divided the students into six small work groups, based on each student's selection of a segment of the *Roots* story. Each group's task was to read a specific section; take notes on all of the personalities, locations, and events cited; investigate the actual locations, events, and personalities using material available in the class-room, the school library, the public library, and a nearby university library; and defend or refute Haley's interpretation of history in the book. This challenging assignment led to many serious discussions about the difference between fact and fiction, a fiction writer's right to color an event to fit the plot or theme of the story, and the facts surrounding slavery in this country.

Good historical fiction should be realistic. Yet, no matter how good the novel, the author must take certain liberties to make a point. In many historical novels, for example, the main characters are not real people. However, in order to develop the historical nature of the novel, the author must create situations in which the characters meet real people. The situations during which the meetings occur are always fictional. At times the famous figure never visited the location of the contrived meeting, but usually, in good historical fiction, the situation could have taken place at the time and place the author suggests. These fic-tional encounters allow the teenage history student the opportunity to play the role of detective. Could the meeting have taken place? Is it likely to have taken place when and where the author suggests? The contrast between fact and fiction, and the often convincing nature of the fiction, provide the students with a chance to practice many of the skills (processes) required of the historian: observing, questioning, predicting, hypothesizing, gathering data, comparing, interpreting data, and making inferences.

Young adult literature has many excellent authors of historical fiction. Rose-mary Sutcliff deals with the period of Roman occupation in England. Her books, such as *The Capricorn bracelet,* allow the teenager to view the period from the perspective of the people living through it. Like most authors of good historical fiction, Sutcliff is a historian who cares about bringing history alive for young readers.

Leon Garfield's historical novels for young adults, including *Jack Holborn* and *The sound of coaches,* portray life in eighteenth-century England. The novels, using orphans searching for a home as the main characters and plot, show much of the unpleasant side of British life during this period.

The creative history teacher can develop units based on specific historical periods and season them with a wide array of good historical fiction for young adults. *Johnny Tremain,* written in 1943 by historian and Pulitzer Prize winner Esther Forbes, has become a classic tale of the pre–Revolutionary War period in America. Told by fourteen-year-old Johnny, it introduces students to Samuel Adams, John Hancock, and Paul Revere. Another excellent young adult histor-ical novel about the Revolutionary War is *April morning* by Howard Fast. This story of a young boy fleeing from battle rivals Stephen Crane's *The red badge of courage* in its account of the hardships of war. Another Revolutionary War tale is *I'm Deborah Sampson* by Patricia Clapp, based on the true story of a girl who, disguised as a boy, fights bravely in battle.

Other Revolutionary War books particularly appropriate in the middle and junior high school classrooms include the humorous biographical series by Jean Fritz: *And then what happened, Paul Revere?, What's the big idea, Ben Frank-*

lin?, Where was Patrick Henry on the twenty-ninth of May?, Why don't you get a horse, Sam Adams?, and Will you sign here, John Hancock? Each of these books is short and easy to read, and reveals interesting, little-known facts about these famous men. An excellent book to use in conjunction with Fritz's biographical works for preteen readers is Mr. Revere and I by Robert Lawson. This is the story of Paul Revere's famous ride told from the perspective of his horse Scheherazade. The book is beautifully illustrated with engravings by the author. (Because of the quality of this work I would recommend it to history students of all ages. It is a wonderful work to share with the entire family.) Poetry can be incorporated into this study of history with Henry Wadsworth Longfellow's well-known poem, which has been beautifully illustrated in the book Paul Revere's ride by Paul Galdone.

When studying Ben Franklin, young readers are likely to enjoy Robert Lawson's Ben and me. Amos the mouse is the "me" of the title. He is Mr. Franklin's friend, and his perceptive, warm, humorous narrative provides much insight into the historical figure.

Wars have provided much material for great literature. This is as true in the field of young adult literature as it is in adult literature. The period during and surrounding World War II has provided a wealth of young adult literature. James Forman stands out as one of the best authors of young adult literature about the period. In Ceremony of innocence, based on an actual incident, a brother and sister produce anti-Nazi literature in spite of the certainty of their capture and execution. Several of Forman's other books revolve around the theme of young people fighting or questioning Nazism. Many other writers have made the Holocaust come alive for young adult readers.

An interesting and frightening recent book that could be a useful addition to a bibliography of Holocaust readings is Morton Rhue's The wave. (Morton Rhue is a pseudonym of Todd Strasser.) It is factually based fiction that first appeared as an ABC television movie about a 1969 high school history class studying Nazism. The students ask, "If all the Germans weren't Nazis, why did they let the horrors happen?" The teacher answers with the Wave, a system of discipline in which students must sit straight in their seats and spring to attention when answering a question. The system has a membership card and special salute. The Wave moves beyond the classroom; other students want to become involved. As the momentum for the Wave grows, an anti-Wave movement begins to form. Anti-Wave students are threatened and beaten. The experiment gets out of hand, and the teacher is told to put a stop to it. At an assembly of Wave members the teacher stops a movie on a frame of Hitler and his followers and says to the students, "Yes, you all would have made good Nazis. Fascism isn't something those other people did, it is right here in all of us."

Other wars have provided grist for the authors' mills. Forman writes about the civil wars in Greece during the 1940s in Ring the Judas bell, about Israel in My enemy, my brother, and about Northern Ireland in A fine, soft day. Theodore Taylor's Battle in the Arctic seas is based on naval records and a personal diary. Across five Aprils by Irene Hunt is a fictional tale about maturing during

■ ■ ■ **An Anthological Aside**

I Remembered Thee

SCOTT O'DELL

When I showed Mrs. Thorpe, the cook, that I could bake good bread, she took me on as a helper. Sometimes I had to carry trays into the tavern and set them on the serving table. I always hurried in and out and never looked at anyone or spoke.

I worked six days. With the shillings I earned I went across the street to Morton and Son's store. Young Mr. Morton waited on me. I thought he would recognize me, but he didn't seem to, and I acted as if I hadn't seen him peering at me over the pile of boxes the first time I had visited the store.

I bought gunpowder and shot, a jug of molasses, salt, and a package of tea. I would have bought more, but I lacked the money. When I asked for the tea, Mr. Morton set out three boxes.

"Just today we had a shipment from New York," he said. "It's the first in a long time. Now that the British are winning the war, we'll have tea regularly. What kind does thee wish? We have these three brands, all from Ceylon."

I chose the least expensive and after he had wrapped it up and taken my money, he walked to the door with me. He held out his hand to say good-bye. It was pale, like his face. He had blue eyes and lanky, hay-colored hair, which he wore tied in a string knot. I still was sure that he hadn't recognized me.

"What is thy name?" he asked.

"Sarah Bishop," I nearly blurted out. Then I caught myself in time and said, "Travers. Amy Travers." Amy was my cousin in Midhurst, England.

"Pretty name," he said. "Thee was in the store last year late. Thee bought an ax, powder and ball, flour, and salt. Thee wanted three or four blankets but had money only for two."

"You have a good memory," I said. "But you forgot that I bought sweetening, too."

Mr. Morton smiled a little. Then he was serious again.

"Thee may think me rude," he said, "but I am not. There was a notice in the tavern. It was there before Christmas. It was signed by a Captain Cunningham and offered a reward for the return of a girl named Sarah Bishop, accused of starting a fire in New York City. It had a description of the girl. As I remember, it said she was tall yet slight of build and had blue eyes and freckles."

Mr. Morton looked at me as if he were certain that I was Sarah Bishop. As if all he need do was to march me down to the constable and collect Captain Cunningham's reward. I thought to flee out the door but he was standing against it.

"I don't know," he said, "whether thee is Sarah Bishop or not, though I am certain that if thee is not, then thee has a sister and her name is Sarah Bishop."

He smiled in a superior way at what he must have felt was a joke.

"But this is of little consequence," he said. "What I wish to say is that I remembered thee from the time thee first visited the store. And being most disturbed that thee was the Sarah Bishop responsible for the fire, I went to the tavern the next day after I saw the notice and took it down and destroyed it."

"Thank you," I managed to stammer. "That was kind."

He was looking at the musket I had under my arm.

"Why does thee carry that around with thee?"he said.

I knew well why I carried the musket, but I did not tell him.

He opened the door. Chill air rushed in, and he closed the door and stood with his back against it.

"My father waited on thee," young Mr. Morton said, "I heard thee tell him that thee wasn't settling around here, but going northward."

"Yes, something like that."

He was looking close at me, yet not unfriendly.

"I take it thee never went."

"What business is it of yours?" I had a mind to say, but I said nothing and edged toward the door. "And how do you know that I didn't go north?" I thought.

"Sam Goshen was in here a week ago to sell furs," Mr. Morton said. "He told us that there was a girl living up on Long Pond and described thee. I decided that thee must be the girl he was talking about."

It made me uneasy when he brought all this up. "I have a way to go," I said. "I'd better start."

Young Mr. Morton put out a hand to hold me back.

"My great-grandfather," he said, "was banished from Massachusetts Colony because he broke the law by appearing in the street without a musket. But there's no law now that compels thee to carry one. What is thee afraid of?"

"Most things," I said, "and all people."

"Fear is something that encourages people to harm thee. Fear causes hatred."

"You sound like a Quaker," I said.

"I am a Quaker," he replied.

Mr. Morton was dressed in a plain dark brown jacket and plain trousers bound at the knee. He wore a black hat with a wide brim that turned up at the sides and had earflaps. He looked like a Quaker. My father had always disliked the Quakers, their "thees" and "thys," and somber clothes. He couldn't stand the silence of their prideful ways.

"Is that why you are not off to the war?" I asked him, thinking of Chad. "Because you are one?"

"For that reason," Mr. Morton said.

He opened the door. Out of a gray sky it was beginning to snow.

■ ■ ■

the Civil War period. The Vietnam War is the subject of some young adult books. Two of the best accounts, which combine fiction and nonfiction, are a memoir, *If I die in a combat zone, box me up and ship me home* (O'Brien), and *First blood* (Morrell), a tale of a veteran's return home and his conflict with a small-town sheriff.

Social Problem Novels

Social problems are among the prominent themes of young adult literature. The treatment of native Americans by Americans of European heritage is presented in *The massacre at Fall Creek* (West), *Only earth and sky last forever* (Benchley), *Yellow Leaf* (Capps), *The life and death of Yellow Bird* and *People of the dream* (Forman), *The valley of the shadow* (Hickman), *White crow* (Quimby), and *Betrayed* (Sneve). (See Chapter 6 for a more complete list of books about native Americans.)

Teachers developing units on black Americans will find a wealth of young adult literature, both fiction and nonfiction, addressing the subject. One possible approach to a historical understanding of the place of black people in the culture is an examination of black characters in young adult novels from 1950 to 1980. In the 1950s Hope Newell wrote two career books, *A cap for Mary Ellis* and *Mary Ellis, student nurse,* in which a black heroine is presented in integrated student nursing situations. Mary Ellis is the only black in an all-white nursing school, but her color in no way affects the plot, and the problems she faces are the same as those of white student nurses. She lives in Harlem in a rather atypical tree-shaded apartment. Nicknamed "Tater" by her classmates, she is snubbed by only one girl, who is from the South. Mary Ellis is capped as a student nurse, and the Southern belle flunks out. Other books of the period are equally unrealistic. Most have the theme that everything will work out in time. In *Hold fast to your dreams* by Catherine Blanton, a black teenager works to become a ballet dancer.

In *South Town* (Graham), the white racist is reformed and a white doctor states that "progress is being made all the time. . . . In spite of what happened last week, things are better now than they were; in some places, I understand, you might be very comfortable, and the children could grow up to forget this.'' Thus, the message for blacks in these novels tends to be ''pull yourself up by the bootstraps'' and whites will grant acceptance; for whites the moral is to treat people as individuals and learn that ''they're as good as we are'' (Kraus 1976, p. 156).

Of books published prior to 1960, there are very few that openly deal with racial integration. A rare exception is *Call me Charley* by Jesse Jackson. This story about a black boy whose family moves to an all-white neighborhood and encounters racial discrimination is one of the few in which a black main character faces the real world, rather than the ''wouldn't it be nice if we could all live together in peace and harmony'' world of Mary Ellis. Another fairly realistic book of the 1950s is *Hard to tackle* by Gilbert Douglas. Clint, a black football player, moves to an all-white neighborhood, meets Jeff Washington, who persuades him to join the team, is helped by his team members when his house is damaged by hostile whites, and is accepted into the community after his house is burned. In this book Clint talks of the prejudice he faces; however, his acceptance into the community is not totally realistic.

The civil rights movement of the 1960s increased the number of realistic social problem novels with black characters. Books like *The Soul Brothers and Sister Lou* (Hunter), *Daddy was a number runner* (Meriwether), *A hero ain't nothin' but a sandwich* (Childress), *The friends* (Guy), *Sounder* (Armstrong), *Ludell* and *Ludell and Willie* (Wilkinson), *The contender* (Lipsyte), *Cool cat* (Bonham), *Manchild in a promised land* (Brown), *Five smooth stones* (Fairbairn), *The autobiography of Miss Jane Pittman* (Gaines), and *The learning tree* (Parks) paint a more realistic picture of young blacks in U.S. society. A study of these novels published from 1950 to the late 1970s in conjunction with a study of the history of black civil rights during this thirty-year period could reveal some interesting parallels between the novels and the civil rights struggle. (See page 77 and pages 167–168 for more complete lists.)

Social problems related to the place of women in our society are the theme of many good young adult novels. (See pages 166–167 for a partial list of novels dealing with women's rights.) A study of the history of women characters in young adult literature from 1950 to the present in conjunction with an examination of the factual history of the period would yield interesting parallels.

Drugs, alcohol, aging, institutionalization, the handicapped, abortion, ecology, homosexuality, rape, religious cults, and changing roles and values are other social issues dealt with in young adult literature. (A list of fiction books dealing with these problems appears in Chapter 3; a list of nonfiction titles is in Chapter 6.)

☐ *Truth will not stand still ... the young are indifferent to old truths ... and they are indifferent to future truths.*
PAUL ZINDEL
author of The pigman / *in a speech to the National Council of Teachers of English* / *November 1981*

SCIENCE FICTION AND SOCIAL PROBLEMS. The use of science fiction about the future can be useful in the social studies classroom for examining a number of social problems. Science fiction, though rarely written exclusively for young adults, contains many of the attributes of young adult novels: a young protagonist, frank discussion of real-life concerns, and adventure and excitement. Science fiction can be effectively used in the secondary school social studies classroom when examining themes such as ecology, other cultures, overpopulation, technology and its abuses, revolt against conformity, and theology and religion.

In an American history thematic unit entitled Technology: From the Industrial Revolution to the Third Wave, Stephen Sapp incorporates many science fiction books. He uses the books to attempt to help students deal with the question "What if industrialization continues at the same pace for the next generation?" The unit begins with the reading aloud of several short sections from the book *Future shock* (Toffler) and a viewing of the film based on it. The bibliography includes books such as *The god machine* (Caidin) and *The tale of the big computer* (Johannesson), about computer technology gone wild; *The fourth "R"* (Smith), about the terrifying possibilities of technological advancement in the classroom; *I sing the body electric* (Bradbury), nine short stories of mechanical grandmothers, four-dimensional babies, and humanoid heroes; *Is there life on a plastic planet?* (Ames), about a child robot; *Noah's castle* (Townsend), about the stockpiling of food; *Fire and ice* (Kytle), which presents the possibility that technological advancements are hastening the advent of a new ice age; and *Flowers for Algernon* (Keyes), the sad story about what happens to humans when scientific experimentation proceeds unchecked. The unit ends with the oral reading of several sections from Alvin Toffler's *The third wave,* and with the question "What can we do to ensure that technological advancements will help rather than hinder society?" (See Chapter 3 for other science fiction titles to use in the classroom in a variety of social studies thematic units.)

Anthological Aside in Chapter 9

O'Dell, S. *Sarah Bishop*. Houghton Mifflin, 1980. Scholastic, 1980.

Titles Mentioned in Chapter 9

Abbey, E. *The brave cowboy*. Dodd, Mead, 1956. University of New Mexico Press, 1980.

Adams, A. *The log of a cowboy: A narrative of the old trail days*. Leisure Books, 1976. University of Nebraska Press, 1964. Original Houghton Mifflin edition published in 1903.

Alexander, S. *Anyone's daughter: The times and trials of Patty Hearst*. Viking, 1979. Bantam Books, 1980.

Ames, M. *Is there life on a plastic planet?* Dutton, 1975.

Angell, J. *Ronnie and Rosey.* Bradbury, 1977. Dell, 1979.

Angelou, M. *I know why the caged bird sings.* Random House, 1969. Bantam, 1971.

Armstrong, W. *Sounder.* Harper & Row, 1969, 1972.

Bacon, M. H. *I speak for my slave sister: The life of Abbey Kelley Foster.* Crowell, 1974.

Baker, B. *The spirit is willing.* Macmillan, 1974.

Benchley, N. *Beyond the mists.* Harper & Row, 1975.

————. *Only earth and sky last forever.* Harper & Row, 1972.

Bird, C. *Born female: The high cost of keeping women down.* Pocket Books, 1971. McKay, 1968.

Blanton, C. *Hold fast to your dreams.* Messner, 1955. Archway, 1968.

Blume, J. *Deenie.* Bradbury, 1973. Dell, 1979.

————. *It's not the end of the world.* Bradbury, 1972. Bantam, 1980.

Blumenthal, S., and J. S. Ozer. *Coming to America: Immigrants from the British Isles.* Dell, 1981.

Bolton, C. *Never jam today.* Atheneum, 1971.

Bonham, F., ed. *Cool cat.* Dutton, 1971. Dell, 1972.

Bradbury, R. *I sing the body electric.* Knopf, 1969, 1978. Bantam, 1971.

Bradley, W. *Life on the run.* Quadrangle, 1976.

Brashler, W. *Josh Gibson: Life in the Negro league.* Harper & Row, 1978.

Brown, C. *Manchild in the promised land.* Macmillan, 1965. New American Library, 1965.

Brown, D. *Bury my heart at Wounded Knee: An Indian history of the American West.* Holt, Rinehart and Wisnton, 1971. Bantam, 1972.

Burt, O. W. *First woman editor: Sarah J. Hale.* Messner, 1960.

Caidin, M. *The god machine.* Dutton, 1968. Bantam, 1969.

Calvert, P. *The snowbird.* Scribner's, 1980.

Capps, B. *A woman of the people.* Duell, 1966. Fawcett, 1966.

Capps, M. J. *Yellow Leaf.* Concordia, 1974.

Carson, J. *Silent voices: The Southern Negro woman today.* Delacorte, 1969. Dell, 1971.

Carter, F. *The education of Little Tree.* Delacorte, 1976. Dell, 1981.

Cather, W. *My Antonia* (1918). Sentry, 1961.

Chamberlin, H. *A minority of members: Women in the U.S. Congress.* Mentor, 1974. Praeger, 1973.

Childress, A. *A hero ain't nothin' but a sandwich.* Coward, McCann & Geoghegan, 1973. Avon, 1974.

Clapp, P. *I'm Deborah Sampson.* Lothrop, Lee & Shepard, 1977.

Clark, A. N. *Year walk.* Viking, 1975.

Clarke, M. S. *Bloomers and ballots: Elizabeth Cady Stanton and women's rights.* Viking, 1972.

Cleaver, E. *Soul on ice.* McGraw-Hill, 1967. Dell, 1978.

Coles, R., and J. H. Coles. *Women in crisis: Lives of struggle and hope.* Delacorte, 1978. Dell, 1979.

————. *Women in crisis II: Lives of work and dreams.* Delacorte, 1980. Dell, 1980.

Crawford, C. *Mommie dearest.* Morrow, 1978. Berkley, 1981.

Crawford, T. E. *The West of the Texas Kid, 1881–1910.* University of Oklahoma Press, 1962.

Crompton, E. *A woman's place.* Little, Brown, 1978. Ballantine, 1980.

Curtis, M., ed. *The nature of politics.* Avon, 1962.

Danziger, P. *Can you sue your parents for malpractice?* Delacorte, 1979. Dell, 1980.

Decker, W. *To be a man.* Little, Brown, 1967. Pocket Books, 1975.

Dizenzo, P. *An American girl.* Holt, Rinehart & Winston, 1971. Avon, 1976.

Douglas, G. *Hard to tackle.* Crowell, 1956. Dell, 1967.

Durham, P., and E. L. Jones. *The adventures of the Negro cowboys.* Dodd, Mead, 1966. Bantam, 1969.

Egan, F. *The taste of time.* McGraw-Hill, 1977.

Fairbairn, A. *Five smooth stones.* Crown, 1966. Bantam, 1968.

Fast, H. *April morning.* Crown, 1961. Bantam, 1970.

Forbes, E. *Johnny Tremain.* Houghton Mifflin, 1945. Dell, 1969.

Forfreedom, A., ed. *Women out of history: A herstory anthology.* Ann Forfreedom, 1975.

Forman, J. *A fine, soft day.* Farrar, Straus & Giroux, 1978.

———. *Ceremony of innocence.* Hawthorn, 1970. Dell, 1977.

———. *My enemy, my brother.* Hawthorn, 1969. Scholastic, 1979.

———. *People of the dream.* Farrar, Straus & Giroux, 1972. Dell, 1974.

———. *Ring the Judas bell.* Farrar, Straus & Giroux, 1965. Dell 1977.

———. *The life and death of Yellow Bird.* Farrar, Straus & Giroux, 1973.

Frank, A. *Anne Frank: The diary of a young girl.* Doubleday, 1952. Pocket Books, 1978.

Frank, P. *Alas, Babylon.* Bantam, 1979.

Fritz, J. *And then what happened, Paul Revere?* Coward, McCann & Geoghegan, 1973. Scholastic, 1974.

———. *What's the big idea, Ben Franklin?* Coward, McCann & Geoghegan, 1976, 1982.

———. *Where was Patrick Henry on the twenty-ninth of May?* Coward, McCann & Geoghegan, 1975, 1982.

———. *Why don't you get a horse, Sam Adams?* Coward, McCann & Geoghegan, 1974, 1982.

———. *Will you sign here, John Hancock?* Coward, McCann & Geoghegan, 1976.

Gaines, E. *The autobiography of Miss Jane Pittman.* Dial, 1971. Bantam, 1972.

Gard, W. *The Chisholm Trail* (1954). University of Oklahoma Press, 1969.

Garfield, L. *Jack Holborn.* Pantheon, 1965.

———. *Sound of the coaches.* Viking, 1974.

Goodrich, F., and A. Hackett. *The diary of Anne Frank.* Dramatization of the book *Anne Frank: The diary of a young girl.* Dramatists Play Service, Inc., 1958.

Graham, L. *South Town.* Follett, 1958. New American Library, 1958.

Green, M. *Defender of the Constitution: Andrew Johnson.* Messner, 1962.

Greene, B. *Summer of my German soldier.* Dial, 1973. Bantam, 1974.

Greenfeld, H. *Gypsies.* Crown, 1977.

Grey, Z. *To the last man.* Harper & Brothers, 1921. Pocket Books, 1976.

Gurko, M. *The ladies of Seneca Falls.* Macmillan, 1974.

Guthrie, A. B. Jr. *The way west.* Houghton Mifflin, 1949. Bantam, 1979.

Guy, R. *The friends.* Holt, Rinehart & Winston, 1973. Bantam, 1974.

Haley, A. *Roots.* Doubleday, 1976. Dell, 1977.

Haney, L. *The lady is a jock.* Dodd, Mead, 1973.

Heyerdahl, T. *The "Ra" expeditions.* Doubleday, 1971. New American Library, 1972.

Hickman, J. *The valley of the shadow.* Macmillan, 1974.

Hinton, S. E. *Rumble fish.* Delacorte, 1975. Dell, 1976.

————. *Tex.* Delacorte, 1979. Dell, 1980.

————. *That was then, this is now.* Viking, 1971. Dell, 1980.

————. *The outsiders.* Viking, 1967. Dell, 1980.

Holland, I. *Heads you win, tails I lose.* Lippincott, 1973. Dell, 1979.

————. *Of love and death and other journeys.* Lippincott, 1975. Dell, 1977.

Hopkins, L. B. *Mama.* Knopf, 1977. Dell, 1978.

Hosford, J. *You bet your boots I can.* Nelson, 1971.

Houston, J. W., and J. D. Houston. *Farewell to Manzanar.* Houghton Mifflin, 1973. Bantam, 1974.

Howe, I., and K. Libo, eds. *How we lived: A documentary history of immigrant Jews in America, 1880–1930.* Marek, 1979. New American Library, 1981.

Hunt, I. *Across five Aprils.* Follett, 1964. Grossett & Dunlap, 1964.

————. *Claws of a young century.* Scribner's, 1980.

Hunter, K. *The Soul Brothers and Sister Lou.* Scribner's, 1968. Avon, 1970.

Jackson, J. *Call me Charley.* Harper & Row, 1945. Dell, 1970.

Johannesson, O. *The tale of the big computer.* Coward, McCann & Geoghegan, 1968.

Jordan, G. *Home below Hell's Canyon.* Crowell, 1954. University of Nebraska Press, 1962.

Josephson, H. *Jeannette Rankin: First lady in Congress.* Bobbs-Merrill, 1974.

Kane, J. N. *Facts about the presidents.* 3rd ed. Ace, 1976.

Kerr, M. E. *Dinky Hocker shoots smack!* Harper & Row, 1972. Dell, 1978.

————. *Is that you, Miss Blue?* Harper & Row, 1975. Dell, 1976.

Keyes, D. *Flowers for Algernon.* Harcourt Brace Jovanovich, 1966. Bantam, 1978.

Klein, N. *Mom, the Wolfman, and me.* Pantheon, 1972. Avon, 1982.

Knudson, R. R. *Zanballer.* Delacorte, 1972. Dell, 1980.

Kytle, R. *Fire and ice.* McKay, 1975.

Lader, L., and M. Meltzer. *Margaret Sanger: Pioneer of birth control.* Doubleday, 1955. Dell, 1974.

LaFarge, O. *The enemy gods.* Houghton Mifflin, 1937.

————. *Laughing boy.* Houghton Mifflin, 1929. New American Library, 1971.

L'Amour, L. *Down the long hills.* Bantam, 1968, 1975.

————. *The quick and the dead.* Bantam, 1973, 1979.

Lawson, R. *Ben and me.* Little, Brown, 1939, 1951. Dell, 1975.

————. *Mr. Revere and I.* Little, Brown, 1953. Dell, 1976.

Levine, I. E. *Young man in the White House: John Fitzgerald Kennedy.* Messner, 1964.

Lipsyte, R. *The contender.* Harper & Row, 1967. Bantam, 1979.

Liston, R. *Politics from precinct to presidency.* Delacorte, 1968. Dell, 1970.

Longfellow, H. W. *Paul Revere's ride.* Illustrated by P. Galdone. Crowell, 1969.

McCullough, C. *The thornbirds.* Harper & Row, 1977. Avon, 1978.

Malcolm X and A. Haley. *The autobiography of Malcolm X.* Grove, 1965. Ballantine, 1973.

Martin, R. G. *President from Missouri: Harry S. Truman.* Messner, 1973.

Mazer, H. *Snow bound.* Delacorte, 1973. Dell, 1973.

————. *The war on Villa Street.* Delacorte, 1978. Dell, 1979.

Meigs, C. *Jane Addams: Pioneer for social justice.* Little, Brown, 1970.

Meriwether, L. *Daddy was a number runner.* Prentice-Hall, 1970. Pyramid, 1974.

Merriam, E., ed. *Growing up female in America: Ten lives.* Doubleday, 1971. Dell, 1973.

Morrell, D. *First blood.* Evans, 1972.

Nash, R. *From these beginnings.* Harper & Row, 1973.

Newell, H. *A cap for Mary Ellis.* Harper, 1953. Berkley, 1969.

————. *Mary Ellis, student nurse.* Harper & Row, 1958. Berkley, 1966.

Ney, J. *Ox, the story of a kid at the top.* Little, Brown, 1970. Bantam, 1971.

O'Brien, T. *If I die in a combat zone, box me up and ship me home.* Delacorte, 1973. Dell, 1979.

O'Dell, S. *Sing down the moon.* Houghton Mifflin, 1970. Dell, 1970.

Parks, G. *The learning tree.* Harper & Row, 1963. Fawcett World, 1970.

Patterson, S. *The distant summer.* Simon & Schuster, 1976. Pocket Books, 1977.

Perl, L. *That crazy April.* Seabury, 1974. Houghton Mifflin, 1980.

Perrin, L. *Coming to America: Immigrants from the Far East.* Delacorte, 1980. Dell, 1981.

Platt, K. *The boy who could make himself disappear.* Chilton, 1968. Dell, 1972.

Potok, C. *My name is Asher Lev.* Knopf, 1972. Fawcett, 1972.

————. *The chosen.* Simon & Schuster, 1967. Ballantine, 1982.

Quimby, M. *White Crow.* Criterion, 1970.

Rhue, M. *The wave.* Delacorte, 1981. Dell, 1981.

Seidman, L. *Once in the saddle: The cowboy's frontier 1866–1896.* Knopf, 1973. New American Library, 1977.

Smith, G. O. *The fourth "R."* Ballantine, 1959. Dell, 1979.

Sneve, V. D. H. *Betrayed.* Holiday House, 1974.

Stone, I. *They also ran.* Pyramid, 1964. New American Library, 1968.

————. *Those who love.* Doubleday, 1965. New American Library, 1967.

Sutcliff, R. *The capricorn bracelet.* Walck, 1973.

Taylor, M. *Let the circle be unbroken.* Dial, 1981.

————. *Roll of thunder, hear my cry.* Dial, 1976. Bantam, 1978.

Taylor, T. *Battle in the Arctic seas.* Crowell, 1976.

Telemaque, E. W. *It's crazy to stay Chinese in Minnesota.* Nelson, 1978.

Terrell, J. U., and D. M. Terrell. *Indian women of the western morning: Their life in early America.* Dial, 1974. Anchor, 1976.

Thompson, T. *Richie.* Saturday Review Press, 1973. Dell, 1981.

Toffler, A. *Future shock.* Random House, 1970. Bantam, 1971.

————. *The third wave.* Morrow, 1980. Bantam, 1981.

Townsend, J. R. *Noah's castle.* Lippincott, 1976. Dell, 1978.

Vestal, S. *Jim Bridger, mountain man.* Morrow, 1946. University of Nebraska Press, 1970.

————. *The Missouri* (1945). University of Nebraska Press, 1964.

Wagnen, R. *Sarah T.—Portrait of a teenage alcoholic.* Ballantine, 1975.

Waters, F. *The man who killed the deer,* Farrar & Rinehart, 1942. Pocket Books, 1971.

Weingast, D. E. *We elect a president.* Rev. ed. Messner, 1977.

Wersba, B. *Run softly, go fast.* Atheneum, 1970. Bantam, 1972.

West, J. *The massacre at Fall Creek.* Harcourt Brace Jovanovich, 1975. Fawcett, 1976.

Wheeler, M. *Lies, damn lies, and statistics: The manipulation of public opinion in America.* Liveright, 1976. Dell, 1977.

White, R. *Deathwatch.* Doubleday, 1972. Dell, 1973.

White, T. *Breach of faith: The fall of Richard Nixon.* Atheneum, 1975. Dell, 1976.

Wilder, L. I. *Little house.* 9 vols. Harper & Row. Complete set, 1971.

Wilkinson, B. *Ludell.* Harper & Row, 1975. Bantam, 1980.

————. *Ludell and Willie.* Harper & Row, 1977.

————. *Ludell's New York time.* Harper & Row, 1980.

Wister, O. *The Virginian: A horseman of the plains.* Grossett & Dunlap, 1902. New American Library, 1979.

Suggested Readings

Adejunmobi, S. A. The biographical approach to the teaching of history. *History Teacher,* May 1979, pp. 349–57.

Cline, R. K. J., and B. L. Taylor. Integrating literature and "free reading" into the social studies program. *Social Education,* January 1978, pp. 27–31.

Committee on concepts and values. *A guide to content in the social studies.* National Council for the Social Studies, 1957.

Donelson, K. L., and A. P. Nilsen. *Literature for today's young adults.* Scott, Foresman, 1980.

Gross, N. E. *A teacher's guide to the paperback editions of "The women of America" Series.* Dell, 1977.

Kraus, W. K. From Steppin Stebbins to soul brothers: Racial strife in adolescent fiction. In K. Donelson, ed., *Arizona English Bulletin,* April 1976, pp. 154–60.

Kraus, W. K., ed. *Murder, mischief and mayhem: A process for creative research papers.* National Council of Teachers of English, 1978.

Nadel, M. *A teacher's guide to the paperback edition of "Never to forget: Jews of the Holocaust."* Dell, 1978.

Osterlind, S. J. Autobiographies and biographies for young people. In K. Donelson, ed., *Arizona English Bulletin,* April 1976, pp. 176–78.

Waller, R. A. Thematic approach to teaching U.S. history. *History Teacher,* February 1978, pp. 201–10.

Wellington, J. K. American education: Its failure and its future. *Phi Delta Kappan,* March 1977, pp. 527–30.

Nonprint Sources

Future shock. Film based on Toffler's book. Available from Metromedia Producers Corporation, McGraw-Hill.

The autobiography of Miss Jane Pittman. Film based on Gaines's book. Available from Learning Corporation of America, 1350 Ave. of the Americas, New York, NY 10019.

Peege. Available from Phoenix Films, 470 Park Ave. South, New York, NY 10016.

Richie. Film based on Thompson's book. Available from Learning Corporation of America.

Summer of my German soldier. Film based on Greene's book. Available from Learning Corporation of America.

The third wave. Spoken recording based on Toffler's book. Morrow. Available from National Library Service, 729 Alexander Rd., Princeton, NJ 08540.

Victory at sea. Available as a film with the original Rodgers score from Films Incorporated, 1144 Wilmette, Wilmette, IL 60091.

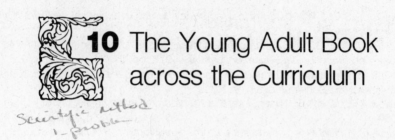

10 The Young Adult Book across the Curriculum

Scientific method
1 - proble—

Young adult literature can be incorporated into almost any subject area in the secondary school. One of the most effective science teachers I've ever visited uses science fiction to teach scientific fact. A creative student teacher in art found some helpful young adult literature for a male art student who was convinced it was not masculine to be an artist. Reading teachers who encourage their students to read books that are on the students' reading level find that constant reading improves reading ability more than any other instructional technique. A basketball coach I know uses young adult sports novels to help motivate his players.

The Science Classroom

SCIENCE FICTION LITERATURE. Most good science fiction is based on scientific fact. Robert Heinlein, a major science fiction author, calls science fiction "speculative fiction in which the author takes as his first postulate the real world as we know it, including all established facts and natural laws" (1953, p. 1188). He further contends that science fiction must be based on a thorough understanding of the scientific method (1969, p. 22). Paul Cook points out that in 1937, when John W. Campbell became editor of *Astounding Stories* (now *Ana-*

log Science Fiction), he sought "technically minded stories of speculative fiction, wherein the science as well as the characterization was believable" (1975, p. 87).

According to L. David Allen, editor of *The Ballantine teachers' guide to science fiction,* science has four basic functions in science fiction: (1) Science fiction "explores a situation which is in some way different from conditions as we now know them. In many cases, the science involved provides the basic element of change. . ." (p. 12). (2) Science provides "the basis for the exploration and interpretation of a new and different situation. . ." (p. 12). (3) The use of the scientific method is another facet of the use of science in the science fiction story. (4) Science in science fiction provides a "sense of possibility and of plausibility to a situation which might otherwise be strange and unbelievable" (p. 12).

The science teacher who wants to use science fiction in the classroom can determine the scientific authenticity of a book by learning about the author. Many authors of hard-science science fiction are scientists. Heinlein, a scientist himself, points out that the world-famous astronomer who writes under the pen name of Philip Latham would be a good source for science fiction literature about space travel.

□ *Good science fiction can be a teaching aid on many levels.*
ANNE McCAFFREY
author of Dragondrums

The teacher who attempts to use science fiction to help students better understand scientific fact should be familiar with the categories of science fiction. The including chemistry, physics, biology, astronomy, geology, and mathematics. A HARD good example of the use of mathematics in hard-science fiction appears in Isaac Asimov's *Foundation* trilogy, which probes the question whether science can and should pinpoint the future of the universe. The action of the trilogy begins when a character works out a series of equations that predict the empire's fall.

In soft-science fiction the major impetus for action is one of the soft sciences: sociology, psychology, anthropology, political science, historiography, theology, linguistics, and sometimes myth. Novels in these categories, such as the works of C. S. Lewis, are more appropriate in the social studies or English classroom.

The category known as science fantasy assumes "an orderly universe with regular and discoverable natural laws" and proposes that "the natural laws are different from those we derive from our current sciences" (Allen 1975, p. 20). This category, including works by Madeleine L'Engle and Ursula LeGuin, can be used in the science classroom in a comparison of natural laws with the fictional

High school biology students use fiction as a beginning place for their research on the dangers of genetic engineering.

"new natural laws" created by the author. Students reading this science fiction can be encouraged to invent their own fictional societies, each with its own "natural laws."

Science can be seen in science fiction through several literary techniques. The first, and most common, is the setting. According to Sheila Schwartz, the *"setting is never unimportant"* in science fiction (emphasis added). The setting includes the initial situation as well as the time and space involved. Though the science of a novel's setting is less pure than science in a textbook, it must be understood *"in relation to how things really are on earth"* (Schwartz 1975, p. 121). If the setting is to be examined in relation to things on earth, scientific accuracy is essential. Students in science classes can examine the setting of science fiction novels and try to discover the natural laws on which they are based.

According to scientist and science fiction author Isaac Asimov, the comparison of the science fiction world and the natural world can be a motivator for the young science student:

> *A law of nature ignored or distorted can rouse more interest sometimes than a law of nature explained. Are the events of the story possible? If not, why not? And in tracking that down, the student may sometimes learn more about science than from any number of correct classroom demonstrations." (quoted in Pell 1977)*

304

The plot also involves the use of science. The science fiction plot has its foundation in extrapolation. The plot extrapolates on the basis of what is known and creates new situations by inferring how things would be "if . . . ." Through extrapolation, technological possibility becomes one of the major characteristics of the plot. The short story "Caught in the organ draft" (Silverberg) starts with present knowledge of organ transplants and develops a society in which the young are drafted to give up their organs to the "splendid seniors." Current knowledge makes the transplanting of organs from one living human being to another a technological possibility. Through extrapolation Silverberg creates a fictional "new scientific fact." However, readers will understand the extrapolation only if they are familiar with the ideas, events, and technology of the scientific reality. The science teacher can pose the questions to the students: On what scientific reality has the author based his extrapolation? Is the extrapolation a technological possibility? How far in the future? What things must occur before this extrapolation becomes fact? Do we want science to continue moving in this direction? If not, how can we prevent science from moving in this direction?

Robert Heinlein relates science fiction plot to speculation. The student is able to relate current scientific knowledge to future possibilities by posing the question "What if. . . ?" The science fiction writer answers this question. Often the answer can lead to new human problems. "In the speculative science fiction story, accepted science and established facts are extrapolated to produce a new situation, a new framework for human action. As a result of this new situation, new *human* problems are created—and our story is about how human beings cope with these new problems" (Heinlein 1964, p. 17). According to Heinlein, the principles for the science fiction plot are:

1. *The conditions must be, in some respect, different from here-and-now, although the difference may lie only in an invention made in the course of the story.*
2. *The new conditions must be an essential part of the story.*
3. *The problem itself—the "plot"—must be a* human *problem.*
4. *The human problem must be one which is created by, or indispensably affected by, the new conditions.*
5. *And lastly, no established fact shall be violated, and furthermore, when the story requires that a theory contrary to present accepted theory be used, the new theory should be rendered reasonably plausible and it must include and explain established facts as satisfactorily as the one the author saw fit to junk. (1964, p. 17)*

The science teacher can use these principles in developing science units based on science fiction. The student can examine the conditions presented in the novel and compare them with the "here-and-now" of science. The student can examine why these conditions are essential to the story and determine whether the story could occur if no new conditions were created. Using the scientific method and knowledge of scientific fact, the student can attempt to solve

305

the problem presented in the story. Similarly, the student can determine which new conditions were essential for the problem to have developed, and discuss what would have occurred had this new condition not been present. Finally, the student can examine each theory presented in the story to determine its scientific plausibility.

Of course, the works of Heinlein and Asimov are particularly notable in their use of scientific fact extrapolated to form science fiction. However, many immature readers will find these authors too sophisticated for their reading interest and skill. Fortunately, an increasing number of science fiction authors write for young readers and are knowledgeable about the hard sciences. Two of the best among the field of good hard-science fiction authors for young adults are Madeleine L'Engle and H. M. Hoover.

L'Engle's books are difficult to categorize. The theme of good against evil often places them in the fantasy genre. However, the scientific concepts place them among the best of science fiction novels for young adults. In L'Engle's time trilogy, *A wrinkle in time, A wind in the door,* and *A swiftly tilting planet,* the son of two scientists is a genius who has trouble relating to his elementary school peers because he reveals his real interests on the first day of school. How many first-graders are interested in mitochondria? *A wrinkle in time* deals with the physics principle of the tesseract; *A wind in the door* examines cellular biology. Science plays a predominant role in several other books by L'Engle. *The arm of the starfish* examines the concept of regeneration and *A ring of endless light* looks at the life and death of stars, starfish, and dolphins. L'Engle's books present the concepts of the hard sciences and examine their relationship to theology, values, and family life. Therefore, her work can be placed in all three categories of science fiction: hard-science, soft-science, and science fantasy.

H. M. Hoover is another author who combines all of the best elements of science fiction and hard science in books for young adults. A recent book of hers is *Another heaven, another earth.* The story takes place on the planet Xilan, which was colonized and then forgotten by Earth. In spite of Earth's neglect, the colony endures but changes as the colonists adapt to the alien environment. New tools and technological skills are devised to repair broken-down equipment. When a new exploratory expedition arrives from Earth, intellectual, emotional, and biological problems arise. Some of Hoover's other useful books for the science classroom include *The Delikon, The rains of Eridan, The lost star,* and *Treasures of Morrow.*[1] (See Chapter 3 for other science fiction titles useful in the science classroom.)

Using science fiction in the science classroom may help students understand the difference between scientific fact and science fiction. Likewise, by reading these books, students will gain a better understanding of cause-effect relationships. Value judgments, based on the understanding of these relationships, can

---

[1]*A study guide to the novels of H. M. Hoover* by M. Jean Greenlaw is available from Avon Books, Education Department, Room 329, 959 Eighth Ave., New York, N.Y. 10019.

be discussed. The use of good science fiction will give students the opportunity to apply scientific knowledge vicariously, read materials written on their own reading levels, reinforce new learnings, analyze a myriad of possibilities, and gain new appreciation for the science's potential.

BOOKS ABOUT NATURE BY JEAN CRAIGHEAD GEORGE.[2] Jean Craighead George writes books with a style and clarity of purpose that come only with a solid scientific background and a love of the subject matter. George is the daughter of an entomologist and has twin brothers who work as wildlife ecologists. Her brothers, she says, "took me with them on hunting and camping trips, to the tops of cliffs to look for falcons, down the white water rivers to fish and swim, and over the forest floors in search of mice, birds, wildflowers, trees, fish, salamanders, and mammals. So absorbing and carefree were these excursions that my childhood in retrospect seems like one leaping, laughing adventure into the mysteries and joys of the earth" (quoted in Hopkins 1973, p. 1049). Perhaps it is because of these childhood experiences that she writes so graphically of life on this planet.

George's work is characterized by a concern with ecology and an uncommon respect for the delicate checks and balances of nature. The scientific accuracy demonstrated in both her fiction and nonfiction works is a result of research, study, and consultations with scientists in many fields. In order to sharpen her senses and develop her powers of observation, she literally lives with and draws every animal character, with the exception of bears and mountain lions, about which she writes.

Jean Craighead George has written prolifically (over forty books); many of her books have been award winners. *My side of the mountain* was a Newbery Honor Book as well as being included in the Hans Christian Andersen International Honor List. *Hold zero!* and *Spring comes to the ocean* were on the American Library Association's Notable Children's Books list. *Julie of the wolves* was winner of the Newbery Award in 1973.

If the science teacher is to justify the use of George's fiction in the classroom, he or she must be prepared to show that it is scientifically accurate and fits the criteria established for adopting scientific material for classroom use. Millicent Selsam defines good science books as follows:

> *By good science books . . . I mean those that show the methods of science at work, that elucidate basic principles of science and are not a mere assembly of facts, that convey something of the beauty and excitement of science, and that interest young people in thinking up good questions for new young scientists to test by experiment. (1967, p. 99)*

[2]This section about the writings of Jean Craighead George was written by Carol Burnette, a science teacher and a student in the Adolescent Literature class at the University of North Carolina at Asheville, 1981.

Mary K. Eakin, in a statement regarding science and the social sciences, indicates the need for a social conscience:

> *When children's books of science are written with an awareness of the responsibility of science for its contribution not only to technological progress but also for the social problems that technology creates; when books of social studies are written with an awareness of mankind's responsibility for insuring the wisest use of science's discoveries, then we can truly say that children's books are meeting the challenge of a changing world. (1973, p. 322)*

The idea of a social consciousness is reiterated by Selsam. "Good science books should help young people understand that in these days of atomic power and earth satellites, it is *necessary* that they know something of science if they want to be responsible citizens in this scientific age" (1980, p. 84).[3]

Another writer, Alice F. Randall, encourages teachers to "see science as a method of discovery, and to make judgments that can be translated into social, political, and personal action" (1979, p. 19). "Teachers must be committed to portraying science as a human endeavor, with a philosophy and history closely tied to societal issues. In order to do this, however, we must give our students the chance to read *beyond* the science text" (p. 18). Jean George takes her readers beyond the textbook and leads them directly to the scientist's greatest laboratory, the world of nature.

Probably no other book by George does a better job of showing the scientific method at work than *Who really killed Cock Robin?,* an ecological mystery that proves that scientists must use imagination, that their work is not error-free, and that some scientists are concerned about the effects of their work on society. In the book, Tony and his friends become involved in the investigation of the mysterious deaths of a family of robins whose eggs were laid in an old Stetson hat belonging to the mayor of the town of Saddleboro. Mayor Joe, delighted over having the robins' nest in his hat, decides to use them as a new symbol for his Clean Environment Party and begins radio broadcasts of their nesting habits. Their untimely deaths cast a shadow of doubt over the cleanliness of the town's environment and over the mayor's campaign for reelection. At this point the author skillfully incorporates scientific investigative techniques and an awareness of the balance of the ecosystem into the storyline. All possible causes of the deaths are explored, including sewage disposal, dumping of aniline dyes into the river, use of DDT and fungicides, and weather and wind patterns. Reader involvement peaks as the mystery is finally solved. This book, although basically a study of ecology, meets our scientific criteria and has a place in the chemistry and earth science classrooms as well as in the biology classroom.

Another of George's books, *Gull number 737,* is an excellent example of how

---

[3]This and the subsequent statement by Selsam from *Children's Literature in Education* quoted by permission of Agathon Press, Inc., New York.

pure scientific research may be used to solve practical problems. Luke Rivers's father, an ornithologist, has spent five summers observing and testing birds in an isolated area of Black Island. Just as Dr. Rivers is about to give up his study of the gulls, it becomes the key to solving a national crisis. An air crash in the Boston area, caused by gulls and starlings, propels him into the forefront of the action.

> *The telephone rang. It was the governor of the state.*
>
> *"Of course you can help. We need a committee of the best men in the country; not only ornithologists, but radar experts, chemists, physicists and sociologists. Get Dr. James Reeves of Illinois; he's a starling expert. We need him. The best man on shore birds is Carl Sprinter in Washington. And get Frank Allard at Northeast Harbor in Maine—he's the authority on animal behavior. . . ."*
>
> *The world of birds was bringing the outside world to Luke. He was astonished. "I didn't know you knew so much about civilization," he said. "I thought you only studied the tapping of gulls and little things like that." (pp. 134–135)*

Beautifully written and filled with interesting observations about the gulls, this book also includes the story of a father and son whose relationship is bonded by their common interest.

In her award-winning novel *Julie of the wolves,* George again shows her expertise in writing about animal behavior. Julie is Miyax, an Eskimo girl, lost on the Alaskan tundra. She is able to survive only through the kindness of a pack of wolves and her ability to finely tune her senses to the ways of nature, carefully observing the animal life around her.

Julie of the wolves was the result of an expedition Jean George and her son, Luke, made to Alaska. While there, they consulted with scientists such as Edgar Folk and Michael Fox, who were studying the characteristics of the alpha wolves. During this time she and her son learned how a pack communicates and began to "talk" with them. The genesis of Julie's story came for George when Dr. Fox "opened the door of this wolf's pen and stepped inside. Gently Dr. Fox bit him on the top of his nose. The alpha sat down before his 'leader,' and the two conversed in soft whimpers" (1973, p. 342). Such careful, scientific observations are reflected in Miyax's story as she confronts Jello, a renegade wolf.

> *"No!" she screamed. He snarled and came toward her. There was nothing to do but assert her authority. She rose to her feet and tapped the top of his nose with her man's knife. With that, he stuck his tail between his legs and slunk swiftly away. . . .*

Jean George is able to write about animals in such a way that they come alive on the pages, while carefully avoiding the pitfall of anthropomorphism. *Julie of the wolves* has practical application in both the sociology and science classrooms.

My side of the mountain and *River Rats, Inc.,* are both stories of the human ability to survive in the wild by being attuned to the environment. They are adventure stories filled with accurate and fascinating descriptions of wildlife and plants.

Although basically stories of survival, *Julie of the wolves, My side of the mountain,* and *River Rats, Inc.,* involve self-discovery on the part of the main characters, a process that helps the characters organize their reality and determine how they must respond to it. Thus, these three books in particular may aid some students of science to reach for the possibilities of growth and self-discovery available to them (Wright 1979).

Hold zero! is a George book that will tempt students who are interested in physics, rocketry, and mechanics. After months of work on an ingenious three-stage rocket, four adolescent boys must await community approval before launching their creation. Fortunately, a perceptive and sympathetic science teacher comes to the rescue by offering to supervise the blast-off as part of a class project. This book does a good job communicating the excitement and thrill of scientific accomplishments. According to Selsam, "Science books can give young people a basic idea of what an experiment is, and why it is so essential to the scientific method. They can learn the kind of thought that goes into the formulation of a problem, the need for a control, the necessity for careful observation, and the drawing of proper conclusions from what is observed (1980, p. 84). *Hold zero!* certainly does exactly that.

The works of Jean George span a period of over twenty years. During this time, she has consistently written fiction that is exciting, involves her characters in various phases of problem solving by the scientific method, presents accurate and scientific observations of nature and animal behavior, and develops within her readers a keen sense of awareness of their obligations and responsibilities toward the life of our planet. Her work stimulates the imagination and causes her readers to be intrigued by the unsolved mysteries of science.

BOOKS ABOUT SCIENTISTS AND CAREERS IN SCIENCE. Many librarians report that students ask for books about science. "Students want to know how scientific discoveries are made. They need to identify with men and women working in science to see that they, too, can become scientists, an idea they often do not believe. High school students are trying to discover where their interests lie and they are troubled about career choices" (Guerra and Payne 1981, p. 583).

Using books about scientific discovery, scientists, and careers in the science classroom can help students see the practical side of the sciences and make decisions about their own career options. Some useful books that deal with these concepts include Farley Mowat's *Never cry wolf,* about a scientist's adventure in the Arctic as he attempts to discover how wolves live. Jean Craighead George's books also shed light on scientists and careers in the sciences.

■ ■ Sample Thematic Science Unit

THE EXPLOITATION OF WILDLIFE

by Joanne Gentry Bartsch*

INTRODUCTION

The purpose of this unit is to introduce students to the variety of ways in which people exploit the environment, in particular, wildlife. Literature is used throughout the unit. Initially, it is the motivating activity upon which the unit is based: A whale for the killing is both a movie and a book. Passages are read from Amory's Mankind? and a variety of other books. Students may choose, from a wide reading list, a book based on their interests and abilities. The information gained from their reading is used in several ways throughout the unit. On the content outline, sections IIIB, IIIC, and IV relate to questions raised during the course of individual reading. Both fiction and nonfiction titles are on the reading list. Students are likely to select fiction at first and read the nonfiction as the unit progresses and more information is required.

The unit could be developed into an interdisciplinary study. This particular outline considers the biological aspects of wildlife exploitation. However, there are several points along the outline at which other disciplines could be incorporated. Also, there are several places at which other biological facts could be studied.

The first deviation could occur at I.B on the outline. Mankind? is an interesting book that explores the humane side of the wildlife issue. However, the author is overemotional at times in his appeal to the public. The people who argue the other side of this issue are often guilty of the same. Persuasion in Literature/Propaganda is an appropriate English unit to be taught in conjunction with this science unit. Where does the objectivity stop? What are the pros and cons of using persuasive writing? Where else is it used? Likewise, these concepts could be taught in a communications class, a speech class, or a psychology class.

Section II.B opens an avenue for the study of people's relationship to animals; adolescent novels could be used extensively here. The naked ape by Desmond Morris also investigates this topic in some detail. What things do we like to see in animals? What features do we not like to see? What is anthropomorphism? What is our relationship to pets?

*Joanne Gentry Bartsch is a secondary science teacher at Asheville (N.C.) Country Day School.

If a unit on ecology has not already been completed, then section III.B offers a good springboard. In particular, 1 and 3 would
be good points at which to discuss community dynamics. At III.B a
discussion of dinosaurs could be initiated. What are some of the
more up-to-date theories about dinosaurs? Were they cold-
blooded? Why did they disappear? An excellent short story to
introduce here would be ""Our Lady of the Sauropods,'' found in
the September 1980 issue of <u>Omni</u> magazine.

Natural history is mentioned in section III. C. If it has not
already been discussed in class, it can be at this point. However,
to teach this topic effectively requires examining it in great
detail.

Section IV.F could be discussed in conjunction with a political
science or history class studying governmental operations, in
particular lobbying. What are some groups that lobby in favor of
wildlife legislation? Which groups lobby against it? How do they
work? A class studying Congress could follow the passage of the
Marine Mammals Act. Who introduced it? Who supported it? What
does it say? What doesn't it say?

This unit leaves many unanswered questions that could be used as
a starting point for another unit. For example, what efforts are
being made to protect wildlife? What are game refuges and
reserves? What special problems are faced when we try to protect
wildlife? This question could lead to a unit on animal migration.
Should we keep wild animals in zoos? What efforts are being made
to breed rare species in zoos? Off we go with that question into a
study of genetics and genetic engineering. Will extinct animals
ever return? Evolution. Is there such a thing as an endangered
plant? Botany. A class could probably go on a whole year from this
one unit.

UNIT OBJECTIVES

1. The student will describe several ways in which wildlife is
   exploited by people.

2. The student will know five extinct or endangered species of
   animals and be able to describe the natural events and/or
   human actions that caused these animals to become extinct or
   endangered.

3. The student will understand the ecological interrelation-
   ships of all animals within an ecosystem, or natural community, and will be able to predict the impact upon the community
   if a species becomes extinct.

4. The student will become aware of the efforts being made on
   behalf of wildlife.

5. The student will be able to present accurately both sides of a modern wildlife issue and will be able to defend his or her position on that issue.

CONTENT OUTLINE

I. Turn-on Event

   A. Show movie A whale for the killing.

   B. Read passages from Cleveland Amory's Mankind?

   C. Class discussion of movie.

      1. What does exploitation mean?

      2. Where have you heard the word exploitation used before?

      3. In what way was the whale in this movie exploited?

      4. What are some other animals that you believe are being exploited, or have been exploited, in the same or different ways?

II. Group Reading

   A. Class reading list (attached)

      1. The teacher reads aloud bits and pieces from a few books.

      2. The student selects a book he or she would like to read.

   B. Individuals read books, answering the following questions.

      1. What animals are being exploited in this book?

      2. What are some ways in which they are being exploited?

      3. What are the reasons given for the actions being taken against wildlife?

      4. What actions are being taken to oppose this exploitation?

      5. What are the reasons given for the actions in (4)?

C. Teacher groups students randomly to discuss findings from individual readings.

D. Groups synthesize individual findings and report to class.

E. Class synthesizes and discusses group findings.

III. Extinction

A. Definition

1. What is extinction?

2. What animals are now extinct?

B. Compare natural with unnatural extinction.

1. Discuss reasons for extinction of prehistoric animals.

a. Competition

b. Climactic change

c. Failure to adapt

2. Discuss reasons for modern-day extinction (see II.B).

a. Progress

b. Hunting and trapping

c. Other

3. Discuss consequences of unnatural extinction.

a. Niche filling

b. Aesthetic losses

c. Examples

C. Investigation of Endangered Species List

1. Description and explanation of list

2. Individual project concerning list

   a. Students choose one species from list to investigate.

   b. Student answers questions on species.

      (1) What is the natural history of the animal?

      (2) Why has this animal been placed on the list?

      (3) What are the statistics concerning the survival of this animal?

      (4) What is being done to protect this animal from extinction?

      (5) What are some possible consequences of the loss of this animal?

3. Students may refer to reading list, periodicals, and other sources for information.

4. Students write a report and share their findings with other members of the class.

IV. Culminating Activity

A. Class chooses one "wildlife versus special interest" controversy.

B. Class members choose a side of the controversy to defend.

C. Opposing sides thoroughly investigate the issue, taking into account the questions raised and discussed in class.

D. Resources available to the student include the reading list, information from other students, pamphlets from special-interest groups that represent each side of the issue, books, periodicals, interviews.

E. Debate between opposing sides

F. Follow-up class discussion after the debate

1. Was the issue resolved?

2. Was either side right?

3. What particular problems are faced when we consider wildlife legislation?

4. On which side of the fence do you sit? Has your position changed as a result of the discussion or debate?

SUGGESTED READING LIST

Amory, Cleveland, Mankind? Our incredible war on wildlife. Harper & Row, 1974. Dell, 1974.

Brooks, Paul. The pursuit of wilderness. Houghton Mifflin, 1971.

Brown, Philip. Uncle Whiskers. Little, Brown, 1974.

Caras, Roger. The forest. Holt, Rinehart and Winston, 1979.

Clarke, James Mitchell. The life and adventures of John Muir. Illustrated by John Muir. Word Shop, 1979. Sierra Club, 1980.

Cummings, Betty Sue. Let a river be. Atheneum, 1978.

Curtis, Patricia. Animal rights. Four Winds, 1980.

Davis, J. A. Samaki: The story of an otter in Africa. Dutton, 1979.

Diole, Philippe. The errant ark. Translated by J. F. Bernard. Putnam, 1974.

Domalain, Jean-Yves. The animal connection. Translated by M. Barnett. Morrow, 1977.

Donovan, John. Family. Harper & Row, 1976. Dell, 1978.

East, Ben. The last eagle. Crown, 1974.

Ehrlich, Paul. Extinction. Random House, 1981.

George, Jean Craighead. Gull number 737. Crowell, 1964.

——. Hold zero! Crowell, 1966.

——. Julie of the wolves. Harper & Row, 1972.

——. My side of the mountain. Dutton, 1969. Grosset & Dunlap, 1969.

——. River Rats, Inc. Dutton, 1979.

——. Spring comes to the ocean. Crowell, 1965.

——. Who really killed Cock Robin? Dutton, 1971. Young Readers Press, 1973.

Herriot, James. All creatures great and small. St. Martin's, 1972. Bantam, 1978.

——. All things bright and beautiful. St. Martin's, 1974. Bantam, 1978.

——. All things wise and wonderful. St. Martin's, 1977, Bantam, 1978.

Humphrey, William. My Moby Dick. Doubleday, 1978. Penguin, 1979.

Jenkins, Alan. Wildlife in danger (1970). St. Martin's, 1973.

Kevles, Bettyann. Thinking gorillas: Testing and teaching the greatest ape. Dutton, 1980.

Kohl, Judith, and Herbert Kohl. The view from the oak. Illustrated by Roger Bayless. Sierra Club, 1977.

Lawrence, R. D. Secret go the wolves. Holt, Rinehart and Winston, 1980.

——. The zoo that never was. Holt, Rinehart and Winston, 1981.

L'Engle, Madeleine. A ring of endless light. Farrar, Straus & Giroux, 1980. Dell, 1980.

Linnaeus, Carl. Travels. Edited by D. Black. Scribner's, 1979.

Lopez, Barry Holstun. Of wolves and men. Scribner's, 1978.

Maclean, Norman. A river runs through it. University of Chicago Press, 1976, 1983.

McClung, Robert M. America's endangered birds: Programs and people working to save them. Morrow, 1979.

McPhee, John. Encounters with the Archdruid. Farrar, Straus & Giroux, 1971. Ballantine, 1972.

Moser, Don. A heart to the hawks. Atheneum, 1975.

Mowat, Farley. Never cry wolf. Little, Brown, 1963. Bantam, 1979.

——. A whale for killing. Little, Brown, 1972. Bantam, 1981.

O'Dell, Scott. Island of the blue dolphins. Houghton Mifflin, 1960. Dell, 1978.

Rawls, Wilson. Summer of the monkeys. Doubleday, 1976. Dell, 1979.

——. Where the red fern grows. Macmillan, 1961. Bantam, 1981.

Ryden, Hope. America's last wild horses. Dutton, 1970. Rev. ed., 1978.

——. God's dog. Coward, McCann & Geoghegan, 1975. Viking, 1979.

——. Mustangs: A return to the wild. Viking, 1972.

Samson, John G. The pond. Knopf, 1979.

Stoutenburg, Adrien. Out there. Viking, 1971. Dell, 1971.

Swarthout, Glendon. Bless the beasts and the children. Doubleday, 1970. Pocket Books, 1973.

Wallace, David Rains. The dark range: A naturalist's night notebook. Illustrated by Roger Bayless. Sierra Club, 1978.

——. Idle weeds: The life of a sandstone ridge. Illustrated by Jennifer Dewey. Sierra Club, 1980.

Walton, Bryce. Harpoon gunner. Crowell, 1968.

Warner, William W. Beautiful swimmers. Illustrated by Consuelo Hanks. Little, Brown, 1976. Penguin, 1977. This book about the Chesapeake Bay may be read in conjunction with one of two other books about the area: James Michener, Chesapeake (Random House, 1978), or Katherine Paterson, Jacob have I loved (Crowell, 1980; Avon, 1981).

The making of a surgeon by William Nolen relates the day-to-day events in the hospital life of a doctor. *Kon Tiki* by Thor Heyerdahl is an adventure story about a group of scientists who cross the ocean on a raft; *Aku-Aku* by Heyerdahl is the tale of a scientific expedition that led to the discovery of a lost civilization. *Sea and earth: The life of Rachel Carson* by Philip Sterling is a biography of the famous biologist and writer. *Woodswoman* is an autobiography by Anne LaBastille, who lived by herself in the mountains. In *Doctors for the people: Profiles of six who serve* by Elizabeth Levy and Mara Miller, six doctors discuss their careers. *Marie Curie* by Robert Reid is the biography of one of the most remarkable scientists of all time. James Herriot's books *All creatures great and small, All things bright and beautiful,* and *All things wise and wonderful* tell of the humorous adventures of a country veterinarian. Lewis Thomas's *The lives of a cell: Notes of a biology watcher* and *The medusa and the snail* are entertaining essays by a scientist who is fascinated by nature, science, life, and death. All of these books and many more give the student a personal glimpse at the world of the scientist.

ADVICE FROM SCIENCE TEACHERS ON INCORPORATING LITERATURE INTO THE SCIENCE CLASSROOM. Incorporating young adult literature into the science classroom may sound like a good idea to the teacher who watches the blank looks on the faces of students who cannot read the text or who find it boring and irrelevant.

> *Many students (and adults) enjoy reading short paperback books, and many students both want and need to read material beyond the class curriculum. Even more importantly, these books can provide needed background for science concepts covered in class, and they can help relate these concepts to students' everyday lives." (Dole and Johnson 1981, p. 579)*

But the curriculum in the typical junior and senior high school classroom is already overflowing with concepts and skills that must be taught if the student is to succeed in the next course in the sequence and in college. How can the teacher incorporate one more thing into the overcrowded curriculum?

Cathy L. Guerra, a biology teacher at Bolton High School in Alexandria, Louisiana, in collaboration with DeLores B. Payne suggests that before the science teacher incorporates nontextbooks in the classroom, the students must be encouraged to read course-related material outside the class. They propose that the teacher develop a regular, changing bulletin-board display that emphasizes appropriate books and authors. Similarly, the display can lead students to general topics that they might enjoy learning about. According to Guerra and Payne, "Interests develop naturally out of discussions about the material on the bulletin board." In addition, they suggest that the teacher read passages aloud from books related to the content being studied or books that relate to the interests of the students. This oral reading should be done regularly to acquaint students with the variety of science books that are available to them. Concomitantly, a reading center should be organized in a corner of the classroom, stocked with books that relate to the topic being studied and the students' interests within the subject. The center should also include magazines such as *National Geographic, Science World, Science News, Science Digest, Science, Scientific American,* and others related to the content of the course. As in the social studies and English classrooms, independent, free reading time should be set aside to allow the students to sample the reading material.

Once the students have developed an interest in the outside reading, according to Guerra and Payne, the teacher should begin to consider ways in which course-related young adult books can be assigned and class time set aside for activities dealing with the books. They suggest that small groups be formed based on the common book the group members are reading. The groups can report the course-related concepts they have discovered in the book to the rest of the class. Similarly, panel discussions about the books might prove valuable. These discussions can center on scientific issues and problems, as well as moral and ethical dilemmas that are discussed in the books. If science fiction is being read, the panel might discuss how the fiction of the book relates to scientific fact. Another way to involve the entire class in the reading of a nontext science book is to read one aloud to the class daily. After each reading, the class can note scientific facts and events, discuss the book's plausibility based on the concepts being learned in the class, and argue the substantiation (or lack of it) of information presented in the book. These discussions can lead to a research project in which students attempt to prove or disprove theories presented in the book.

Incorporating literature that deals with scientific concepts and scientists need not take away from time used for demonstrations, lectures, films, or lab work. Rather, it can supplement these activities and help personalize the study of science for the student.

The Reading Classroom

The only way to improve reading skill is by reading. Reading, like any other skill, takes practice. The star quarterback does not make it to the major leagues without practice. The concert pianist does not solo with the symphony without practice. So it is with every skill: the way to improve one's ability is to practice. Unfortunately, many young people do not have the opportunity to improve their reading skill. Once reading instruction ends in about the fifth grade, reading ends. Many students never read for pleasure; they do not think of reading as a skill that needs practice; and, consequently, their reading skill does not improve.

In the spring of 1980 I made this same point to a small group of junior and senior high school Title I (Chapter 1) reading parents. It was a warm evening, the flowers were in bloom, a Little League game was in progress outside the classroom window, and very few parents attended. However, right in front of me sat a teenager who seemed to scowl at every word I said. After the meeting was over I received this note from her reading teacher:

> *The one student in the whole [high school reading] program who has been most reluctant to read anything was seated directly in front of you. She said after the meeting that she felt like you were talking directly to her throughout the speech. She has since selected a book on her own and begun reading (a very positive step for her). She is also considering*

enrolling for the reading program next year. This may have been one of those times when who attended was more important than how many.

I began my presentation by telling the parents, "There is no great mystery in learning how to read, even though many of us who teach reading would like you to believe that what we do is somehow miraculous. The key to learning to read is in reading. The more a child reads, the greater the likelihood that he or she will be a good reader." I was encouraging the parents to help their sons and daughters get started on a reading habit. I gave them many suggestions for accomplishing the task: reading out loud as a family, discussing articles from the newspaper, going to the library together, visiting free museums and exhibits around the community and reading about them afterward, reading about television shows the family watches together, reading magazines, perusing cookbooks to find interesting recipes, and, probably most important, letting their children see them reading.

The same is true in the reading classroom. The most effective way to improve a student's reading ability is by allowing and encouraging the student to read. Of course, in every secondary school reading classroom there are students who need remedial or developmental reading help to learn reading-related skills, but all of the students also need practice reading. Most of the students in secondary school reading classes have the basic skills needed to read; what they lack is reading practice. Most of the students in secondary school reading classrooms are nonreaders, not because they cannot read, but because they do not read. Consequently, they are convinced they cannot read. And, like all reasoning people, they find every way possible to avoid doing what they cannot do well. If we are convinced we are "all thumbs," we are unlikely to take up needlepoint. If we believe we cannot hit a ball, we will not play softball (unless we are forced). If we do not swim well, we will not enter the pool when a dozen of our friends are sitting around watching. Students who are convinced that they do not read well will do anything in order not to read. The task of the reading teacher is to break down those inhibitions, to get the students into books, without throwing them in head first or forcing them to read aloud. The reading teacher who truly performs miracles is the one who can undo years of frustration, fear, misbehavior, bad grades, lost privileges, and flash cards, and persuade students that they can read if they do read.

To do this, the teacher must get students into reading materials. We need to learn a lesson from the successful bookstores. Being a book lover, I frequent bookstores whenever possible. Some stores always seem to be full of people; others have few customers. Why? Surely, there are many variables—location, price, friendliness of sales personnel. The major difference, however, seems to be in the outward appearance of the store. My favorite bookstore is a feast for the eyes. Colorful, easy-to-find books, magazines, and records cover the walls, the tables, the counter, and, in the children's section, even the floor. The books are displayed for the reader. The young adult book section of that store is always crowded with teenagers reading jacket covers, paperback front covers, and the books themselves. The other day when I was in the store I noticed that one young man was reading Lipsyte's *The contender;* he was on page 102. He didn't hear me approach, but as he saw me out of the corner of his eye, he quickly closed the book. I said, "Please don't stop. I'm glad to see you enjoying that book. It's one of my favorites, too." I continued by asking him if he'd gotten to Alfred's first fight yet. When he sheepishly replied that he had, we began discussing the story. After several minutes I asked him where he had begun reading the book. "Here," he said. "I come every day after school and read." I suggested that he might see if the school or community library had a copy. He looked at me with a smile and replied, "I'd rather read here. I like it better."

This young man is as captivated with the bookstore as I am. Apparently, according to the bookstore manager, he is not alone. "We've got dozens of kids who come in here to read. Some of our books get so rabbit-eared that we can't sell them. But we don't stop the kids; someday they'll be our best customers."

The reading teacher can learn from the popular bookstores. What is it about those stores that makes the passer-by walk in? What is it that makes the teenager stay and read an entire book? The store is not quiet like the library; it is not well ordered like the classroom; it is not comfortable like a living room. The bookstore is a feast for the eyes.

Students in this reading classroom can select from a wide range of young adult paperbacks.

Daniel Fader in *Hooked on books* relates the tale of the first day the paper-back books arrived in the school. The students were so excited that they did not want to give the teacher time to check the shipment. Many of us have experienced similar excitement. I remember the day our book distributor gave me a bookstore-type rolling book rack. There were so many students gathered around the rack that they could barely see the books. Every student left with a paperback in a pocket or purse. The paperbacks were not new to the class-room; they had been on the regular shelf for a month or more. However, the new display made the difference. The students could see the front covers of the books, and, like children in a toy store, they were captivated. Merchandising is an important part of reading instruction.

Additional activities to encourage teenagers to read should be developed: (1) Have students keep a list of books they look at and write down the number of pages they read (completing the book is not important). (2) Have students "sell" the book to other students in an informal small or large group situation. (3) Set aside time for in-class free reading. (4) Read aloud from one of the books to the class or to small groups. (5) Develop motivational activities based on one of the books (e.g., seeing the film *Summer of my German soldier* to get the kids interested in the book). (6) Relax the rules; allow the students to be accountable only to themselves for book titles and number of pages listed.

☐ *What turns kids off to reading are teachers who don't read and kill the story by asking a thousand picky questions.*
PAULA DANZIGER
author of The cat ate my gymsuit / *in a phone conversation with the author's class* / *November 1979*

Getting secondary school students into motivational reading materials is the best way to increase reading ability. Through practice, reading skills will improve, motivation to read will increase, and confidence in ability to read will grow. Therefore, the student is more likely to be willing to read in the subject-area classroom. The reading teacher must create a classroom environment that displays books and encourages reading. Books, particularly young adult books, magazines, and newspapers must be available on many different reading levels.[4] Motivational activities to get the students into the books must be designed. The teacher must exhibit a love of reading. Similarly, students must be helped to feel good about their ability as readers. They must be convinced that they can read and must be shown that reading need not be punishing, but can be enjoyable. The reading teacher who gets students into books will be far more successful than the reading teacher who teaches reading skills but never motivates the students to practice them.

---

[4]An excellent guide to easy-to-read books for reluctant readers is Hugh Agee, ed., *High interest, easy reading for junior and senior high school students*, NCTE, 1984.

The Non-Reading-Oriented Classroom

When university physical education majors who plan to teach are told they must take a class in teaching reading in the content areas, they are greatly puzzled. "That's a dumb rule! Why do I need a course in reading?" Many state departments of education are committed to the belief that every teacher, including those who traditionally do not incorporate reading into their classes, must become teachers of reading. The hope is that if all teachers encourage reading, students will be more likely to read and therefore will be more likely to improve their reading skills.

Coaches, art teachers, and music teachers who have taken my class on teaching reading in the content areas affirm that reading is essential. They also agree that many students flock to their subject areas because they have difficulty in reading. Similarly, they know that many students look up to them. They also agree that no teacher is more likely to motivate students to read than the teacher who commands the most respect from nonreaders.

THE PHYSICAL EDUCATION CLASSROOM. Several years ago a young man entered my reading education classroom with a frown on his face. By the end of the first class session, I knew why. He was a coach; he saw no reason to take this class, which took time away from his major concern, his losing basketball team. I made a deal with the coach. "If you'll give this class a chance, I'll try to give you some ideas to help you motivate your team, as well as help them become better readers." He agreed. I gave him an individual assignment and freed him from some of the usual course requirements. His assignment was to search young adult literature for motivational sports books to (1) read to his students for a few minutes before practice and (2) encourage them to read. He began his task unenthusiastically. However, by the end of the second week of class he had read John Tunis, James Summers, and Robert Lipsyte. One day he came to class with a big smile on his face. "Did you know that Robert Lipsyte is a sports reporter for the *New York Times*? I was reading the paper this Sunday and I saw his name on several articles. I made a poster of some of the articles and read sections of some of them to the team. Next week I'm going to begin reading *The contender* to them." His enthusiasm for the books he was discovering continued. After reading *Zanballer* (Knudson), he sent the girls' basketball coach to me to get some additional books. He began passing out copies of the books to members of the team. They came back and asked for more. Bill Bradley's *Life on the run* provided some real inspiration, he reported. By the end of the university class, he was convinced. Reading is important even in physical education. He wrote me a note, "You were right! If the brain is not being exercised properly, how can the rest of the body work? My team's record has not improved much, but we are a much closer group, we are much more optimistic, we practice better together, we don't feel so down about our losses, and we're really excited about next year. Thanks."

■ ■ Sample Physical Education Unit

USING YOUNG ADULT LITERATURE IN THE PHYSICAL EDUCATION
CLASSROOM

Jean Pettyjohn Chesnut*

Topic: Track and Running for Fun

Duration: 4 weeks   50-minute classes

INTRODUCTION TO UNIT PLAN

Track and Running for Fun is offered for one four-week period in
the fall and another four-week period in the spring. Track is a
sport that can be competitive or noncompetitive, a sport that can
be enjoyed for life. The purpose of introducing individual sports
is to kindle a love for feeling fit, to develop the cardiovascular
system, and to have a sport in which to participate at ages 30, 40,
or 50. Too many young women get out of high school with no desire
to exercise, no understanding of why their bodies need to stay
supple, and with such poor posture that they are adversely
affected throughout life.

Many children have physical and mental conditions that prevent
them from normal participation in a physical education class. The
most important information for a teacher to have is an accurate
report on each child and his or her physical condition. The teacher's goal must be to help each child develop to the fullest in
order to participate successfully in life.

To understand all students is difficult, but the physical education teacher is in a less formal teaching situation and can, in
many cases, develop a closer relationship with students. An individual sport unit is an opportunity for the teacher to reach more
children and understand their feelings, hopes, and problems.

* Jean Pettyjohn Chesnut received a B.S. in physical education from Auburn University and taught
high school physical education.

BASIC SKILLS (to be covered in unit)

Locomotor skills—walking, running, jumping, hopping, skipping.
Nonlocomotor skills—bending, stretching, rocking, balancing, reaching.

SPECIAL SPORTS SKILLS

Rhythmic skills
Fitness skills
Safety skills

OBJECTIVES

To demonstrate skills in running, jogging, long and high jump
To have intraclass competition
To become more familiar with vocabulary associated with running and jogging
To work within groups and to check one another on skills
To complete a weekly critique of each member of the group and to discuss skill improvement
To participate in a voluntary 5-mile walk at the end of two weeks and then a 10-mile walk after four weeks
To increase self-control
To develop cooperation and better understanding among class members
To solve problems in a reasonable way
To read in the content area
To improve reading and writing skills
To become familiar with sports literature
To understand differences between winning the game and winning for oneself

INSTRUCTIONAL AIDS AND RESOURCES

Examine students' cumulative records, checking specifically for any physical or reading disability.
There is no textbook, but a variety of books from the department and school library is available.
Read aloud to the class each day a section of Winning by Robin Brancato.

Films

The Bonnie Bell Mini Marathon. Wombat Productions.
There's genius in the average man. Bob Richards.

Filmstrip

Nutrition and exercise. Sunburst Communication, 1980.

Magazines

Archery World
Bassmaster magazine (freshwater fishing and boating)
Bike-world
Camping Journal
Co-ed (school-homemaking)
Dirt Bike
Football Digest (pro football)
Golf Digest
Seventeen
Skateboarder magazine
Skiing
Sporting News
Sports Afield (outdoor sports)
Sports Illustrated (all sports)
Stock Car Racing
Teen (beauty, health, fiction)
Tiger Beat (teenage)

Books

Aaron, Hank, Stan Baldwin, and Jerry Jenkins. Bad Henry. Chilton, 1974.

Blume, Judy. Deenie. Dell, 1973, 1979.

——. Are you there, God? It's me, Margaret. Bradbury, 1970. Dell, 1980.

——. Then again maybe I won't. Bradbury, 1971. Dell, 1976.

Brancato, Robin. Winning. Knopf, 1977. Bantam, 1979.

Bryant, Paul W. (with John Underwood). Bear. Little, Brown, 1974. Bantam, 1975.

Cleary, Beverly. Jean and Johnny. Morrow, 1959. Dell, 1981.

Crawford, Charles. Three-legged race. Harper & Row, 1974. Dell, 1977.

Danziger, Paula. The cat ate my gymsuit. Delacorte, 1974. Dell, 1979.

Davis, Mac. Sports shorts. Grosset & Dunlap, 1959. Bantam, 1963.

Gilbert, Nan. Champions don't cry. Harper & Row, 1960. Scholastic, 1979.

Greene, Constance. Beat the turtle drum. Viking, 1976. Dell, 1979.

Harris, Mark. Bang the drum slowly. Knopf, 1956. Dell, 1974.

Knudson, R. R. Zanballer. Delacorte, 1972. Dell, 1979.

——. Zanboomer. Harper & Row, 1978. Dell, 1978.

——. Zanbanger. Harper & Row, 1977. Dell, 1979.

Lipsyte, Robert. One fat summer. Harper & Row, 1977. Bantam, 1978.

——. Free to be Mohammad Ali. Harper & Row, 1978. Bantam, 1980.

Lopez, Nancy, and Peter Schwed. The education of a woman golfer. Simon & Schuster, 1979.

Madden, Betsy. The all-American co-eds. Criterion, 1971.

Mitchell, Joyce Slayton. Other choices for becoming a woman. Know, 1974. Dell, 1975.

Parlin, John. Amelia Earhart (1962). Dell, 1976.

Pomeroy, Wardell B. Girls and sex. Delacorte, 1970. Dell, 1981.

Price, Charles. World of golf. Random House, 1962.

Sabin, Francene. Women who win. Random House, 1975. Dell, 1977.

Sabin, Louis. Run faster, jump higher, throw farther: How to win at track and field. McKay, 1980.

Sanderlin, Owenita. Tennis rebel. Dell, 1978.

Sheehan, George. Running and being. Simon & Schuster, 1978.

Trent, George. Gentle art of walking. Random House, 1971.

Valens, E. G. The other side of the mountain. Warner Books, 1975.

Wojciechowska, Maia. Shadow of a bull. Atheneum, 1964.

Teacher References

Clarke, Louise. Can't read, can't write, can't talk too good either. Walker, 1973.

Dauer, Victor, and Robert P. Pangrazi. Dynamic physical education for elementary school children. 16th ed. Burgess, 1979.

Fader, Daniel. Hooked on books. Berkley, 1976.

Geri, Frank H. Illustrated game manual. Ernie Rose, 1950.

Hopkins, Lee Bennett. The best of book bonanza. Holt, Rinehart & Winston, 1980.

Maring, Gerald H., and Robert Ritson. Reading improvement in the gymnasium. Journal of Reading, October 1980, pp. 27-31.

Olson, Arthur V., and Wilbur S. Ames. Reading in the content areas. Interest Education Publications, 1972.

Prudden, Bonnie. Bonnie Prudden's quick Rx for fitness. Grosset & Dunlap, 1965.

Purdy, Robert L. The successful high school athletic program. Parker Publications, 1973.

Reed, A. J. S. Teaching reading in the subject area. Unpublished ms.

Resnick, Abraham. 350 ideas for teachers. Macmillan, 1973.

Shepherd, David L. Comprehensive high school reading methods. 3rd ed. Merrill, 1982.

Thomas, Ellen Lamar, and H. Alan Robinson. Improving reading in every class. 3rd ed. Allyn & Bacon, 1982.

COURSE OUTLINE AND INSTRUCTIONAL STRATEGY*

First Week:

1. Students orally give opinions on why the unit on track and running is offered. These opinions are recorded on flip chart for future reference.

2. Terms related to the unit are listed on the flip chart (examples: sprint, meter, scratch, relay).

*Included in the instructional strategies are more ideas than can be used in a four-week plan, but the unit may be expanded or selected activities may be chosen. Some of the activities listed in week 1 (discussion groups, activity groups, folders, demonstrations, and quizzes) continue throughout the unit. After the small discussion groups meet, a representative from each group reports its discussion to the entire class.

3. The class is divided into discussion groups (4 or 5 students in each group). These are permanent groups that will meet throughout the unit. The newly formed groups work to define and discuss several of the listed words. Definitions are recorded on the flip chart.

4. Students complete an interest inventory.

5. Activity groups are formed (at least three activity groups are needed). A team leader selected from each group acts as the warm-up leader for all physical activities. Warm-up leaders are recorded by name on the group folder. Different grouping patterns are used for the activity groups. This enables each student to work closely with several classmates.

6. Folders are given out to each student in which to keep personal records (weight, height, posture, track times, skills completed, paper work, quizzes, comments to the teacher, book reviews).

7. After jogging (or any other skill) is demonstrated, handouts are passed around with a description of how to perform the skill. This assists the student in learning to read and follow written instructions. This is an essential skill in physical education classes.

8. A quiz, based on the handout, is given several days after students are introduced to the skill. This need not be a quiz given for a grade, but should help students understand how to describe a particular physical skill in writing. The quiz assists the teacher in understanding each student's knowledge of the skill.

9. In discussion groups students critique the skill development of each group member and record it on each individual's folder.

10. Each student tells the discussion group about a book in a unique manner. For example:

    a. make a collage about a book.
    b. make a puppet that tells an interesting part of the book.
    c. tell about the book as if you were the protagonist.
    d. compose a telegram to the publisher telling in 100 words or less what you thought of the book.

Second Week:

1. Filmstrips on nutrition are shown. Discussion groups meet after each of the sections of the filmstrip to discuss specific teacher-designed questions. Each group relates to the class new information gained from the filmstrip and the discussion.

2. Each student writes instructions for completing a three-minute exercise that can be understood and followed by anyone in the class (stick-figure drawings may also be used). Written exercises are exchanged and instructions followed. Revisions are made based on problems students have in following written directions.

3. Posture learning center. The posture of each student is checked and recorded in the folder. Proper exercises are prescribed based on weaknesses discovered. Each student works with a partner. When posture exercises are completed, the partner records results in the folder. Follow-up posture checks are done several times during the unit and compared to the original record in each student's folder. Progress is recorded.

4. Sections from Robin Brancato's Winning are read aloud to the class each day.

5. The film There's genius in the average man is shown. Before the film is viewed, a class discussion on the following is held:

   a. What does winning mean?
   b. Does winning mean the same to everyone?
   c. Is winning to Gary Madden the same after his accident as it was before?
   d. What does winning mean in sports?
   e. Suppose you never "win" a game of tennis; can you still be a "winner"?
   f. How do personal goals relate to winning?
   g. What is a genius?

   After the film is shown, ask these questions:

   a. What is a genius?
   b. What must you do to become a genius?

6. Two voluntary "walk days" are organized for two Saturday mornings. (These walks are to help build endurance as well

as to help stimulate closer relationships among students.) The following class day students who participated
in the walk share with the class what was meaningful to
them, what was fun, and what was not fun.

7. Discussion groups meet to research and present a new game.
   The game may be quiet or active. The following guidelines
   are given to the group:

   a. Research a game with which you are not familiar,
      e.g., an old game, one from a foreign country, or one
      someone has told you about.
   b. Tell something about the history of the game, where
      it is played, the rules, and any tune, words, or
      motions that are used in it.
   c. Demonstrate the game alone or with the number of peo-
      ple required to play the game.
   d. Explain the importance of the game.
   e. Record on a single sheet of paper the information you
      find about the game and the reaction the class has to
      the game. Be sure to indicate what you learn from this
      experience.

The following books as well as books you find on your own may be
used:

Opie, Iona, and Peter Opie. Children's games in street and
playground. Oxford, 1979.

Gallagher, Rachel. Games in the street. Four Winds, 1976.

Rockwell, Anne. Games (and how to play them). Crowell, 1973.

Third Week:

1. Individual project. The following two examples can be used
   as requirements for the unit, as a final, or as extra
   credit. Other projects can be listed or proposed by
   students.

   a. Photo or cutout montage (do this on a sport you partic-
      ularly like)

      (1) Find several poems you like that relate to the
          sport, or write a poem.

      (2) Try to understand all you can about the poem and the
          poet. Why was the poem written?

(3) Set up a table display (either in the main hall, outside the office, or in the gym lobby) with pictures, the book, a copy of the poem(s), and any decorative pieces that will add to the display.

(4) The following are books of poems relating to sports. These may be used as well as any you find on your own:

Morrison, Lillian. Sprints and distances: Sports in poetry and the poetry in sports. Crowell, 1965.

Knudson, R. R., and P. K. Elbert, eds. Sports poems. Dell, 1971.

Hopkins, Lee Bennett, and Misha Arenstein, eds. Faces and places: Poems for you. Scholastic, 1971.

Fleming, Alice, ed. Hosannah, the home run! Poems about sports. Little, Brown, 1972.

Morrison, Lillian. The sidewalk racer and other poems of sports and motion. Lothrop, Lee & Shepard, 1977.

b. Research a favorite sport

Do a bulletin board in the gym after researching a favorite sport. Use one or more of the following methods or choose one of your own.

(1) Record any frivolous facts about the sport or persons who participate in the sport.*

(2) Research newspapers and magazines.

(3) Use clippings from magazines or newspapers about current sports events.

(4) Write a feature article or use one from the school paper.

(5) Interview a class sports personality.

---

*Lee Bennett Hopkins, *The best of book bonanza*. Holt, Rinehart and Winston, 1980.

(6) Work with the math teacher. Make a graph using various scoring techniques, percentages, and averages, related to popular teams and players. (One based on a school team would be interesting.)

(7) Interview a local retired sports personality.

(8) Interview a physical education teacher or coach.

(9) The following books may be used:

Seulig, Barbara. The last legal spitball and other little-known facts about sports. Doubleday, 1975.

McWhirter, Norris, ed. Guinness book of world records. Bantam.

2. An intraclass track meet is planned and held to see how well skills have been developed. After the meet, discuss and record in discussion groups: "I liked the class meet because ..." "I didn't like the class meet because ..." "I wish the class meet had included ..." These reactions are shared by each group with the entire class.

3. Posture check. Every student is given the name of someone in class to watch for good or bad posture. Posture skills will be checked when studying, walking, playing, and relaxing. At the end of the week the student places the record in the observed student's folder to be shared the next week. The skills are then recorded in the folder in the posture learning center.

Fourth Week:

1. Book telling. Each student selects one of several ways to tell about a book.

a. The student takes on the role of a salesperson. The student works for a large publishing house; the commission for selling this book is 80%. The students work only on commission, and the business is very competitive. A partner is chosen to be the (silent) buyer for a large chain of bookstores. The salesperson tries to convince the buyer that this book is the one book that should be featured in the bookstores for the next month.

b. In pantomime:

    (1) select a famous character and tell about his or her sport.

    (2) tell about that athlete's personality and attitude toward sports.

    (3) tell how he or she relates to other members of the team or to the profession.

    (4) explain the athlete's goals.

c. Select one to three passages from a book you are reading.

    (1) The passage(s) should explain the personal goals that the character is trying to achieve or has achieved. Examples: winning a tournament, making X dollars, learning to walk again, holding a team together, making X number of goals or points, teaching a child a skill, competing with oneself.

    (2) Read the passage(s) to the group.

    (3) Orally answer these questions:

        (a) What satisfaction does the character hope to attain?

        (b) How would you feel if this were the goal you were trying to achieve?

        (c) Would this achievement help you to feel better than anyone else?

        (d) According to the film we saw, would you be a genius if you reached this goal? Why?

2. Culminating activities (to be used in conjunction with the movie There's genius in the average man)

a. Individual activities

    (1) List several goals that you personally would like to achieve:

        (a) by the end of the year

        (b) by the time you graduate

        (c) in ten years

        (2) What steps will you take to achieve them?

        (3) How will you benefit after having achieved these goals?

        (4) Are these goals realistic?

    b. Small-group activities

        (1) Choose the five most popular goals (after compiling information from individual lists).

        (2) Decide how these goals can be reached (record on newsprint).

        (3) How will the individuals benefit from reaching these goals?

        (4) Are these goals realistic?

    c. Record results and present to class.

  3. <u>Evaluation of discussion and activity</u>

  4. <u>Personal evaluation</u>

  5. <u>Assessment of program.</u>

THE ART CLASSROOM. At the start of each class in reading in the content areas, I read a chapter from a young adult novel. One semester two art teachers were in the class. Therefore, I decided to read *Bridge to Terabithia* (Paterson). In the book Jesse is a budding artist, but he is convinced he must hide his interest from the world. His father laughs at him, his teachers yell at him because he is drawing instead of paying attention, his mother gets annoyed because drawing keeps him from his chores. Leslie, the girl who becomes his friend, convinces him that his talent is important. Through his friendship with Leslie he acknowledges his ability and openly begins to practice his skill.

A young art major was taking the class in the evening after he had student-taught all day. He was frustrated by the fact that many of his students had the potential to be quite good in art but were unwilling to acknowledge their creative abilities, particularly the boys. He decided to borrow the book I had been reading aloud to the university students and read it to his junior high school art students. He reported that the results were almost immediate. The students were totally attentive as he read; they began asking if he had other books they could read, and he noticed a marked improvement in their willingness to use their talents.

High school art students read books as the first step toward jacket design and illustration.

I suggested other titles that would be appropriate in his art classroom. Max in *Max's wonderful delicatessen* (Madison) dreams of being a sculptor of junk metal. However, the practical problem of making enough money to live on intrudes on his dream. The climax of the book comes when Max accidentally wrecks a $10,000 car and finds that creating something beautiful out of junk is indeed practical. Five of David Macaulay's wonderful books are particularly appropriate in the art classroom: *Cathedral: The story of its construction; Castle; City: A story of Roman planning and construction; Pyramid;* and *Great moments in architecture,* a tongue-in-cheek guide to what could have happened if. . . . *Art cop* (Adams) is a good book for boys who want to become artists but are afraid that being an artist is not masculine. Since the protagonist of the book is both an artist and a ''cop,'' he is assigned to the Art Squad, a unit that attempts to solve thefts from museums and galleries and art frauds and forgeries. The stealing of art treasures is the theme of Milton Esterow's *The art stealers.* This nonfiction book tells of various art thieves, from Vincenzo Perugia, who in 1911 stole the *Mona Lisa,* to modern art plunderers. Another book about the problem of protecting great works of art is John FitzMaurice Mills's *Treasure keepers.*

Biographies and autobiographies of famous artists are good additions to the reading corner in the art classroom. The great art scholar Kenneth Clark frankly tells of his early life and his growing appreciation for art in *Another part of the wood.* This is another good book for reluctant students of art. Biographies of

artists who were scorned, criticized, and often ignored can be inspirational reading for young readers. Sylvia Horwitz's *Toulouse-Lautrec: His world* demonstrates the possibility of success despite handicaps. The life of Mary Cassatt,
who was scorned by her father, is told in *American painter in Paris* (Wilson).
Other biographical accounts of artists show a variety of struggles. *Paintbox on
the frontier: The life and times of George Caleb Bingham* (Constant) and *Indian
gallery: The story of George Catlin* (Haverstock) are stories of two artists who
sought to record the events of the early American western frontier. *The double
adventure of John Singleton Copley* (Flexner) discusses the early life of Copley,
who grew up in colonial Boston without the opportunity to see the world's great
art. Consequently, he devised a style of his own and became a major artist.

A series of art history books by Christine Price is particularly useful for young
readers. It includes *Made in ancient Egypt, Made in ancient Greece; Made in
the Middle Ages; Made in the Renaissance: Arts and crafts of the Age of Exploration; Made in West Africa;* and *The story of Moslem art.*

THE MATHEMATICS CLASSROOM. Young adult books also have their place in
the mathematics classroom. The world of literature can open up new possibilities for the student who is turned off by math or bored by the repetition of problems first computed two years ago.

Puzzle books can help make mathematics fun and challenging. How about
this riddle-poem from *The mathematical mapgie* (Fadiman)?

> *Make three-fourths of a cross,*
> *and a circle complete,*
> *And let two semi-circles*
> *on a perpendicular meet;*
> *Next add a triangle*
> *that stands on two feet;*
> *Next two semi-circles and a circle complete.*

Do you know the solution to this riddle-poem? It's the word *tobacco.* (Other
mathematical puzzle, game, and fun books are listed in Chapter 6.)

Books about mathematicians and careers in mathematics are useful additions
to the reading shelf in the math classroom. Victor Boesen's *William P. Lear:
From high school dropout to space age inventor* tells the life story of the mathematical, business, and scientific genius who invented the Lear jet, among other
things. *Charles Babbage: Father of the computer* (Halacy) tells of a pioneer of
the modern technological age.

Books and magazines that contain statistical data are useful in the mathematics classroom. Books about sports, major sports magazines, and sports
pages of the daily newspaper may be the most valuable resources in this category. There are unmotivated math students who can compute the batting average of all the major league baseball players. Many books about individual sports
stars such as *The home run kings: Babe Ruth/Hank Aaron* (Gault and Gault)

can be included on the shelf. Other books such as *Basketball's fastest hands* (Sahandi) and *The great NFL fun book* give a variety of statistical information. Other compilations of statistics are worthwhile additions to the math classroom. A current almanac gives information that can be included in many interesting math lessons. Any book that compiles statistical data, such as Guinness book of world records (N. McWhirter), whether on sports, weather, superhuman tasks, or politics, is a good beginning place for reluctant math students or mathematical geniuses who desire a broader understanding of the world of numbers.

Other recent additions to the literary marketplace, such as books about computer games, puzzles for hand calculators, and instructions for solving Rubik's Cube, can be incorporated into the math classroom. Today's world is filled with technology that is familiar and fun to our students. Much of this technological advancement is possible because of our knowledge of mathematics. Teachers of math should not ignore this world but should incorporate it into the classroom to teach the basic skills and concepts of mathematics.

□   *We can't shelter our youth in books from words and situations they will hear and see in their own lives and at school and on TV. There is no one answer to anything, sometimes there are no answers at all, but the books young people read should at least raise the problems they are living with, instead of pretending they don't exist. And if . . . behind each book there is a thinking moral person, no matter what subject is being dealt with, the child will have new points of view rather than confusion to go forward with.*
CHARLOTTE ZOLOTOW
vice president and associate publisher
Harper Junior Books

■ ■ Sample Mathematics Unit

Grade: 7 or 8   Subject: Mathematics   Teacher: Glenda Burgin*
Topic: Statistics   Duration: Approximately 10 classes, 1 hour
each

I. INTRODUCTION

Statistics is the science of choosing samples and of collecting, organizing, analyzing, and interpreting data.
This topic is pertinent in practically every subject as a
means of drawing, explaining, and displaying conclusions.
Statistics should be learned as a skill for manipulating and
interpreting items and events in our world. Each student in
this unit will collect sample data, organize and display
them, and analyze them for the rest of the class.

II. OBJECTIVES

The student will

A. Collect sample data and organize them by one of the
prescribed methods, such as rankings, tallies, or
frequencies

B. Exhibit a vocabulary for describing the data, using the
mode, mean, median, range, and interpretation

C. Display and read data in one or several different manners
as appropriate for the particular data, such as bar
graphs, pictographs, circle graphs, and line graphs

D. Analyze his or her own data, interpreting and analyzing
patterns or items selected to be significant and of
interest

III. INSTRUCTIONAL AIDS OR RESOURCES

A. Textbook: <u>Mathematics for Mastery</u> by LeBlanc, Vogeli,
Moredock, and Prevost (Silver Burdett), chap. 13, pp.
337-67

---

*Glenda Burgin is an experienced computer programmer and a teacher of mathematics.

B. Guinness book of world records (McWhirter) for as many years as can be collected

C. Any other paperbacks of records and statistics: Great moments in sports (Gelman), All pro football stars, Basketball, All-time basketball stars, Basketball's fastest hands (Sahandi), Amazing sports facts (Sullivan), The baseball life of Sandy Koufax (Vecsey), Bill Walton: Star of the Blazers (Robinson), The great NFL fun book, and Great quarterbacks of pro football (Gelman). (All are available from Scholastic Book Services, 904 Sylvan Ave., Englewood Cliffs, NJ 07632.)

D. Newspapers and magazines, some already in the classroom and others brought in by students.

E. Electrocardiograms--copies secured from hospital.

F. Computer graph printouts from computer installation.

G. Statistical information such as maps, populations, elevations, temperatures, and other geographical facts from local weather station, camping/hiking supply store, and Chamber of Commerce.

H. Slide projector with prepared slides of data and also blank slides for use by students.

IV. CONTENT (CURRICULUM) OUTLINE

A. Organizing Data

1. Key words for this topic are data, statistics, samples, frequency, and rank order.
   a. Definitions of these words will be established first, using classroom discussion and some lecture, always emphasizing the relation to the unit definition of statistics. (As the unit progresses, a primary theme will be to show the importance of every component in the area of statistics.)

   b. From newspapers brought in by students or from resources in the classroom, students will find examples of data. They will then choose a sample to rank. Frequencies will then be reported, using tally marks and dot diagrams. Approximately 20 minutes.

2. Each student will start a folder in which all data collections will be saved.

    a. A log of the number of hours each student watches TV and the number of hours spent in recreational activities and/or reading per day will be kept for one week.

    b. The folder will be updated, turned in daily, and returned to students during the next class.

B. Describing Data

1. Key words for this topic are mode, median, mean, and range.

    a. Definitions from the textbook will be read and discussed. Comparisons with dictionary definitions will be made.

    b. The students will be divided into small groups and gather data about members of the group--age, hair color, height, eye color, number of siblings--and then report mode, median, mean, and range to rest of class. Approximately 30 minutes.

2. From the samples collected previously in A.1.b. the students will find the mode, median, mean, and range.

C. Displaying Data

1. The key word for this topic is interpretation.

    a. Examples of various displays of data will be exhibited and distributed to students.

    b. Each application for displaying statistics of data will be explained in terms of usefulness and appropriateness for a particular type of data.

        (1) Bar graphs--useful for showing frequencies such as population growth, individual baskets scored in basketball games.

        (2) Pictographs--useful for distinguishing subsets of data, such as months in which different vegetables can be grown in the state, numbers of persons in households in U.S.

342

(3) Circle graphs--useful for showing percentage of whole, such as budget costs.

(4) Line graphs--useful for showing changes, such as electrocardiograms, growth rate of children.

c. The student will define <u>interpretation</u> of data by reading various displays and distinguishing which measure of the data is being used in certain written descriptions.

2. From the A.1.b. samples and measurements, the students will display the data in the appropriate manner for that data type. Approximately 15-20 minutes.

3. From resources in the classroom the student will find two more collections of data that can be displayed in two different (from 2 above) methods, and will do so.

4. A group of selected statements that interpret data will be distributed to students, who will explain the statement using words other than the key words. Approximately 20 minutes each.

5. The students will be divided into five or six groups. They will make a group line graph showing each member's TV watching and recreation/reading time for one week. Poster paper with different colors or designated places on a wall mural can be used. Approximately one class period.

   a. Each individual member will compare his or her data with those of group members.

   b. Groups will compare with other groups.

   c. Each student will write an interpretation of the data as presented, including individual and group findings.

D. Individual Project

1. Each student is responsible for collecting data, which are to be organized, described, displayed, and interpreted in a manner that can be explained to class.

  a. This project is to be announced at beginning of
     unit.

  b. Data sample must be approved by teacher, but can be
     of any sort and category that are approved.

  c. As unit progresses, work on the project should
     progress and requirements will be made clear as
     each new topic is introduced.

  2. The projects will be presented in class. The two- to
     five-minute presentation will include:

  a. Reason for choosing to collect these data and
     resulting significance and interpretation of
     data.

  b. Visual displays as well as oral presentation;
     emphasis on either is an individual preference.

V. EVALUATION

   The success of the unit will be evaluated based on the
accomplishment of the students in demonstrating a knowledge of statistics by completing the objectives and finishing the project.

   If students can apply the skills of statistics to manipu-
late data of their choice and can present the results to fellow students, showing reasons for choice, findings of significance, and interpretation of findings, then both
affective and cognitive knowledge will be demonstrated.

   Participation in class discussion and/or activities will
show how well students are responding to the unit. The
folder contains material prepared by teacher and material
chosen by students--both requiring responses. This is an
ongoing measure of the progressive understanding of the
unit.

   Because of the various methods available to students to
express the mastery of this unit--verbal, written, hands-
on activities, visual displays, class presentations--each
student will have the opportunity to demonstrate knowledge. The right to choose one's own data should act to promote interest and make the project more pertinent to the
individual.

Titles Mentioned in Chapter 10

Adams, L. *Art cop Robert Volpe, art crime detective*. Dodd, Mead, 1974.

Asimov, I. *Foundation*. Gnome Press, 1951. Avon, 1974.

Boesen, V. *William P. Lear: From high school dropout to space age inventor*. Hawthorn, 1974.

Bradley, W. *Life on the run*. Quadrangle, 1976. Bantam, 1977.

Carson, R. *The sea around us*. Children's edition. Golden Press, 1958.

Clark, K. *Another part of the wood*. Harper & Row, 1975. Ballantine, 1976.

Constant, A. W. *Paintbox on the frontier: The life and times of George Caleb Bingham*. Crowell, 1975.

Danziger, P. *The cat ate my gymsuit*. Delacorte, 1974. Dell, 1979.

Esterow, M. *The art stealers*. Rev. ed. Macmillan, 1973.

Fadiman, C., ed. *The mathematical magpie*. Rev. ed. Simon & Schuster, 1981.

Flexner, J. T. *The double adventure of John Singleton Copley*. Little, Brown, 1969.

Gault, F., and C. Gault. *The home run kings: Babe Ruth/Hank Aaron*. Walker, 1974. Scholastic, 1974.

Gelman, M. *Great quarterbacks of pro football*. Scholastic, 1982.

Gelman, R. G. *Great moments in sports*. Scholastic, 1980.

George, J. C. *Gull number 737*. Crowell, 1954.

———. *Hold zero!* Crowell, 1966.

———. *Julie of the wolves*. Harper & Row, 1972.

———. *My side of the mountain*. Dutton, 1969. Grosset & Dunlap, 1969.

———. *River Rats, Inc*. Dutton, 1979.

———. *Spring comes to the ocean*. Crowell, 1965.

———. *Who really killed Cock Robin?* Dutton, 1971. Young Readers Press, 1973.

Halacy, D. S. *Charles Babbage: Father of the computer*. Crowell-Collier, 1970.

Haverstock, M. S. *Indian gallery: The story of George Catlin*. Four Winds, 1973.

Herriot, J. *All creatures great and small*. St. Martin's, 1972. Bantam, 1978.

———. *All things bright and beautiful*. St. Martin's, 1974. Bantam, 1978.

———. *All things wise and wonderful*. St. Martin's, 1977. Bantam, 1978.

Heyerdahl, T. *Aku-Aku*. International Collectors' Library, 1958. Ballantine, 1974.

———. *Kon Tiki*. Children's edition. Rand McNally, 1960.

Horwitz, S. L. *Toulouse-Lautrec: His world*. Harper & Row, 1973.

Hoover, H. M. *Another heaven, another earth*. Viking, 1981.

———. *The Delikon*. Viking, 1977. Avon, 1978.

———. *The lost star*. Viking, 1979. Avon, 1980.

———. *The rains of Eridan*. Viking, 1977. Avon, 1979.

———. *Treasures of Morrow*. Four Winds, 1976. Avon, 1980.

Knudson, R. R. *Zanballer*. Delacorte, 1972. Dell, 1980.

LaBastille, A. *Woodswoman*. Dutton, 1976, 1978.

L'Engle, M. *A swiftly tilting planet*. Farrar, Straus & Giroux, 1978. Dell, 1981.

———. *The arm of the starfish*. Farrar, Straus & Giroux, 1965. Dell, 1980.

———. *A ring of endless light*. Farrar, Straus, & Giroux, 1980. Dell, 1981.

———. *A wind in the door*. Farrar, Straus, Giroux, 1973. Dell, 1981.

———. *A wrinkle in time*. Farrar, Straus & Giroux, 1962. Dell, 1976.

Levy, E., and M. Miller. *Doctors for the people: Profiles of six who serve*. Knopf, 1977. Dell, 1979.

Lipsyte, R. *The contender.* Harper & Row, 1967. Bantam, 1979.

Macaulay, D. *Castle.* Houghton Mifflin, 1975.

———. *Cathedral: The story of its construction.* Houghton Mifflin, 1973, 1981.

———. *City: A story of Roman planning and construction.* Houghton Mifflin, 1974.

———. *Great moments in architecture.* Houghton Mifflin, 1978.

———. *Pyramid.* Houghton Mifflin, 1975, 1982.

McCaffrey, A. *Dragondrums.* Atheneum, 1979. Bantam, 1980.

McWhirter, N. *Guinness book of world records.* Bantam, 1982.

Madison, W. *Max's wonderful delicatessen.* Little, Brown, 1972. Dell, 1976.

Mills, J. F. *Treasure keepers.* Doubleday, 1973.

Mowat, F. *Never cry wolf.* Watts, 1963. Bantam, 1979.

National Football League. *The great NFL fun book.* Scholastic, 1981.

Nolen, W. *The making of a surgeon.* Random House, 1970. Dell, 1980.

Paterson, K. *Bridge to Terabithia.* Crowell, 1977. Avon, 1979.

Price, C. *Made in ancient Egypt.* Dutton, 1970.

———. *Made in ancient Greece.* Dutton, 1967.

———. *Made in the Middle Ages.* Dutton, 1961.

———. *Made in the Renaissance: Arts and crafts of the Age of Exploration.* Dutton, 1963.

———. *Made in West Africa.* Dutton, 1975.

———. *The story of Moslem art.* Dutton, 1964.

Reid, R. *Marie Curie.* New American Library, 1974, 1978.

Robinson, B. *Bill Walton: Star of the Blazers.* Scholastic, 1978.

Sahandi, L. *All-time basketball stars.* Scholastic, 1979.

———. *Basketball's fastest hands.* Scholastic, 1977.

Silverberg, R. Caught in the organ draft. In R. Elwood, ed., *And walk now gently through the fire . . . and other science fiction stories.* Chilton, 1972.

Sterling, P. *Sea and earth: The life of Rachel Carson.* Crowell, 1970. Dell, 1970.

Sullivan, G. *Amazing sports facts.* Scholastic, 1978.

Thomas, L. *The lives of a cell: Notes of a biology watcher.* Viking, 1974. Bantam, 1975.

———. *The medusa and the snail.* Viking, 1979. Bantam 1980.

Vecsey, G. *The baseball life of Sandy Koufax.* Scholastic, 1968, 1972.

Wilson, E. *American painter in Paris: A life of Mary Cassatt.* Farrar, Straus & Giroux, 1971.

Suggested Readings

Allen, L. D., ed. *The Ballantine teachers' guide to science fiction.* Ballantine Books, 1975.

Cook, P. H. Teaching proper science fiction. In K. Donelson, ed., *Arizona English Bulletin,* April 1975, pp. 86–89.

Dole, J. A., and V. R. Johnson. Beyond the textbook: Science literature for young people. *Journal of Reading,* April 1981, pp. 569–82.

Eakin, M. K. The changing world of science and the social studies. In V. Haviland, ed., *Children and literature, views and reviews.* Scott, Foresman, 1973. Lothrop, Lee & Shepard, 1974.

Fader, D. N., and E. B. McNeil. *Hooked on books: Program and proof.* Berkley, 1966.

George, J. C. Newbery Award acceptance. *Horn book,* August 1973, pp. 337–47.

Guerra, C. L., and D. B. Payne. Using popular books and magazines to interest students in general science. *Journal of reading,* April 1981, pp. 583–86.

Heinlein, R. A. On the writing of speculative fiction. In L. A. Eschback, ed., *Of worlds beyond.* Advent, 1964.

———. Ray guns and rocket ships. *Library Journal,* July 1953, pp. 1188–91.

———. Science fiction: Its nature, faults and virtues. In B. Davenport, ed., *The science fiction novel: Imagination and social criticism.* 3rd ed. Advent, 1969.

Hopkins, L. B. Jean Craighead George. *Elementary English,* October 1973, pp. 1049–53.

Lerner, F. Science magazines for young adults. *Voice of Youth Advocates,* April 1983, pp. 24–28.

Melvin, H. Jean Craighead George. *Horn Book,* August 1973, pp. 348–51.

Pell, S. J. Asimov in the classroom. *Journal of Reading,* December 1977, pp. 258–61.

Randall, A. F. Scientific writing beyond the textbook. *Science Teacher,* May 1979, pp. 18–21.

Schwartz, S. Choosing science fiction for the secondary school. In K. Donelson, ed., *Arizona English Bulletin,* April 1975, pp. 119–26.

Selsam, M. E. Science books: Reflections of a science writer. *Children's literature in education,* Summer 1980, pp. 82–84.

———. Writing about science for children. In S. Fenwick, ed., *A critical approach to children's literature.* University of Chicago Press, 1967, pp. 96–99.

Wright, J. L. The novel as a device for motivating junior high science students. *American Biology Teacher,* November 1979, pp. 502–4.

Nonprint Sources

Love to kill. Film based on Swarthout's book *Bless the beasts and the children.* Available from Learning Corporation of America, 1350 Ave. of the Americas, New York, NY 10019.

The orphan lions. Film based on Adamson's book *Born free.* Available from Learning Corporation of America.

Phillip and the white colt. Film based on Rook's book *Run wild, run free.* Available from Learning Corporation of America.

The ugly little boy. Film based on Asimov's short story. Available from Learning Corporation of America.

The white heron. Film based on Jewett's short story. Available from Learning Corporation of America.

11 Experiencing and Sharing Young Adult Books in All Subject Areas

How to Experience Books

In order for students to be exposed to the accumulated knowledge of human-kind, it is essential that they become involved with the concepts and ideas expressed on the pages of a variety of books by a variety of authors of all times. Unfortunately, many things seem to get in the way of book learning. It is junior prom week and the students are so excited that it is impossible to keep their minds on the discussion of the *Scarlet letter.* Snow just started to fall outside the classroom window. John is growing so much that he seems to be growing as he sits in his chair; he just can't seem to sit still. The secretary in the school office is having a wonderful time playing with the new public address system. How can these distractions be kept from ruining a well-planned lesson? How can the teacher keep the attention of the class with so many interruptions?

In order to minimize the effect of the interruptions that occur daily in the classroom, in order to keep the student's mind on the lesson, the student must be made to feel more involved in what is going on in the classroom than in what is happening outside the window, in the hallway, or in the office. To be involved in the lesson, students must participate in and experience the ideas and concepts being studied. Edgar Dale in his well-known ''cone of experience'' (Figure 11–1) shows that the experiences that schools provide to students vary from the direct to the very abstract. As the cone illustrates, the best starting point for meaningful learning is the lesson based on direct, purposeful experiences. Since creating direct, purposeful experiences is very difficult in most classrooms, the next best alternative is a lesson using contrived experiences.

According to Dale, the most difficult way to learn is through visual and verbal symbols. Therefore, the teacher must find ways to convert the visual and verbal symbols that come through reading and discussion into direct, contrived, or dramatized experiences. Dale is not saying that symbolic learning is unimportant. On the contrary, he is saying that symbolic learning is essential in our society. However, to be understood, symbolic abstractions must be based in the reality of the learner's life.

Figure 11–1 Cone of Experience

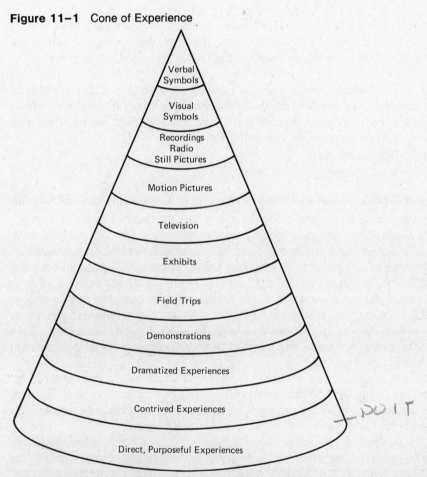

Source: Edgar Dale, *Audiovisual methods in teaching,* 3rd ed. (Holt, Rinehart and Winston, 1969). Copyright 1946, 1954, 1969 by Holt, Rinehart and Winston, CBS College Publishing.

There are many ways that the teacher can make the abstract visual symbols in a book come alive for the student. A book that comes to life for students is the book from which they will learn new ideas and concepts. A book that students are able to experience is a book that relates to their needs and interests. For teenage readers, this book is often a young adult novel.

AN AUTHOR HOOKUP. Creating a direct, purposeful experience in the classroom is difficult, and the results of the attempt can never be guaranteed. The only way an experience can be direct and purposeful is if it touches the life of the student in a meaningful way. An experience can be meaningful for one student and not meaningful for another. However, there are several ways in which the teacher can create direct experiences for learners that relate to the books they are reading or being encouraged to read.

One of these ways is the direct author hookup—either a classroom visit by an author or a phone conversation with an author. The first, of course, is the more desirable, but it is also the most expensive and difficult to achieve.

> ☐ *What really knocks me out is a book that when you're all done reading it, you wish the author that wrote it was a terrific friend of yours and you could call him up on the phone whenever you felt like it.*
> HOLDEN CAUFIELD
> *in J. D. Salinger's* Catcher in the rye

Most schools cannot pay much in the way of travel expenses and fees for authors to visit classrooms. However, there are several ways to arrange author visits even without extensive funding. Recent editions of *Contemporary authors: A bio-bibliographical guide to current authors and their works* (Locher) have current addresses of authors. By checking the addresses of favorite authors, the teacher may discover that one of them lives nearby. A phone call or a letter to that author may result in a visit at a nominal cost or possibly no cost at all.

Librarians can also be a great help in locating authors. Do the librarians know of any authors who live in your area and are willing to visit classrooms? Does the library have an author visit planned? Can you get your students involved in the already planned visit?

Local bookstores are another good source for information about author visits. At times bookstores sponsor autograph parties for local authors or for authors who are publicizing recent books. If an author is visiting your area, would it be possible for that person to visit your school or classroom?

If the address of the author is unattainable, if you cannot locate any authors who live in your area, if your local library or bookstore has no plans to bring an author to town, try the publicity department at the author's publishing house. Are there any authors who plan to visit your area in the near future? Would it be possible for them to visit your classroom?

If you cannot attract an author to your classroom, and cannot afford to pay for an author's honorarium and travel, you may be able to encourage teachers from other schools to join you in sponsoring an author visit. Civic organizations or professional education organizations might be interested in cosponsoring an author visit to your community.

An author visit to your classroom is worth the time you spend arranging it. The students have the opportunity to meet a real, live author, to talk to the author about his or her life, books, writing style, motivation for writing, place and time of writing, and the like. I remember the comment of a middle school friend of mine after she met Paula Danziger. "She's an author, but she's a real, live person. It was so neat! I can't wait to start writing a book!" What better way can there possibly be to bring a book to life than introducing the reader to the book's creator?

If you cannot arrange to have an author visit your classroom, you can do the next best thing. Call the author on the telephone and allow the entire class to participate in the conversation.[1] Many publishers' publicity departments, particularly those of publishers that specialize in or have large departments of children's and young adult books, are willing to set up author phone hookups for you. Call the publicity department and ask which authors are currently available for phone conversations with classes. Don't limit your request to one author. It is not necessary for your students to talk to their "favorite" author. The phone conversation will give them the opportunity to learn about a new author and his or her books. It is likely that the new author will rapidly become the class favorite.

Conference phone equipment can be used to allow all the students to talk to and hear the author. At times this equipment is available from media centers in the school or central office or from the local phone company. If the equipment is not already available and you cannot borrow it, suggest to your audiovisual department that they budget for it during the next budget year. The equipment is not very expensive (usually less so than a slide projector), it hooks up to any standard phone line, it allows you to tape the conversation by connecting a tape recorder, and it opens up many new experiences for your students. The equipment can be used to conduct phone conversations with anyone who has a phone and is willing to take the time. Think of the possibilities in all subject areas! Once you own the equipment, the only expense is the phone call.

Before, during, and after the author visit or the phone hookup, there are several things the teacher must do:

1. If a classroom visit is planned, be sure that you have provided for the guest's needs: give the author a tour of school facilities (restroom, teachers' lounge, office phone, library, cafeteria); introduce the author to the principal and other school officials; arrange for someone to meet the author and bring him or

---

[1] *Dial-an-author* by Pat Scales is an excellent guide to developing a reader-writer interview program. It is available free of charge from Bantam Books, 666 Fifth Ave., New York, NY 10103.

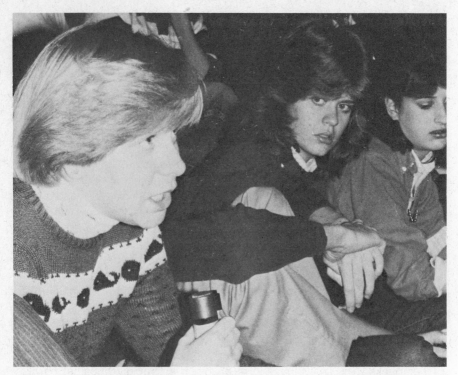

A phone hook-up helps to bring the author's books to life for adolescents.

her to the site of the interview; provide a comfortable place to sit and a glass of water; arrange the students' seats so that they and the author can see and hear one another; arrange for a meal or snack for the author; and have someone escort the author to his or her next appointment.

2. If you are planning a phone hookup, be sure to check the equipment beforehand. It is a good idea to call the author before the hookup to check the equipment, confirm the time, explain the format and a bit about your students, and allow the author an opportunity to ask you questions.

3. Before the interview with the author, be sure each student has read one or more of the author's books (if possible, all of the author's books should be read by the class). This cannot be overemphasized. The visit will be useless to the students and insulting to the author if the books have not been read by the students in attendance. Make book reading a requirement of participation. If the phone hookup or visit is planned well in advance, sample paperback copies of the author's books may be attainable from the publisher's publicity department. Be sure you have notified local and school libraries of the author's visit so that they can make available extra copies of books for students to read. Also, notify local bookstores so they can have on hand copies of the author's books for students to buy. Do not conduct an author interview unless there are

enough copies of the author's books available for every student to read at least one book in the time between the announcement of the interview and the actual interview. There is one exception to this rule. Nonreaders should be included in author visits. In this case the author's book should be read aloud to the students prior to the visit.

4. A chance for the students to share ideas and questions about the author before the interview is essential. Information about the author should be sought. School and local libraries are likely to have information about the author in *The junior book of authors* series (deMontreville and Hill), *Contemporary authors* (Locher), or the fifteen-volume *Something about the author* (Commire). Students can also be helped to find information about the author in journals such as *The ALAN Review, The Calendar* of the Children's Book Council, *English Journal, Library Journal, Children's Literature in Education, Horn Book, Language Arts*, and *The WEB*. (See Chapter 12 for additional information about these publications.) Several books, available in many libraries, may inform students about the author: *Books are by people* and *More books by more people* (Hopkins), *From writers to students: The pleasures and pains of writing* (Weiss), and *Books I read when I was young* (Cullinan and Weiss). The publisher's publicity department will probably send some limited information about the author at your request. Similarly, catalogues from the author's publishers and information sent by book clubs are likely to yield some information. Once the students have had ample time to find information about the author, all of it should be shared in a discussion session with the entire class. As questions are raised about the author's life and/or work, they should be recorded for future reference.

5. An opportunity to share ideas and questions about the author's books before the interview is essential. Many book-sharing techniques can be used to motivate students to read and discuss the books. Storytelling or reading-aloud techniques can be used for books that are not available in duplicate copies. Not all students need to read every book by the author, but every student must read at least one (or hear it read aloud), and every student must have limited knowledge about each of the author's books. Reading the book(s) and discussing them before the visit encourages involvement in the interview. As questions about the books arise, they should be listed for later use.

6. After the books have been discussed and information about the author shared, specific interview questions should be planned. The most gregarious group of eighth-graders can become mute in an interview situation. Each student should be armed with at least one question that he or she would like to ask the author. However, students should be encouraged to think of additional questions they would like to ask during the interview.

7. If the interview is to take place over the phone, be sure to explain the idiosyncrasies of the conference phone equipment to the students. Only one person can talk at a time. You cannot interrupt when the author is speaking. You must speak loudly and distinctly. It might be a good idea to have an advance dry run using the equipment with the class on a local, prearranged phone conversation. Once the students are familiar with the equipment, they

■ ■ ■

Eddie

KATHERINE PATERSON

Last spring I had been asked to speak in a junior high school, and I gave those in charge my usual little speech about what I would do and what I expected them to do. For example: I do not sing, dance or do card tricks, therefore, I will not attempt to entertain an auditorium full of bored children. I will speak to a classroom-sized group of students who have read something that I have written and who want to talk with me about it. I don't care a bit if they liked what they read or not, simply that it aroused sufficient interest to make them want to discuss it.

When I was actually in the car on the way to the school, one of the ladies in charge of my appearance began to explain to me that they uh hadn't uh exactly been able to follow out my wishes and uh they hoped I wouldn't be too upset. Their original plan had been for me to speak to the gifted-and-talented program, which was made up of about fifty seventh, eighth, and ninth graders. (I gasped.) But they'd gotten fouled up. It seems that the special reading teacher had read *The Great Gilly Hopkins* out loud to her class and, when she heard that I was going to be at the school, had simply demanded that her class be allowed to horn in on the gifted-and-talented's special event. So there I was with about seventy junior high students to enthrall. Much to my surprise, not to say relief, the session went all right. I wasn't sure who was from the gifted program and who was from the special reading class, the questions were more or less of the ordinary variety. But I did notice a boy in a red sweat shirt sitting several feet away from everyone else in the room who was giving me more than ordinary attention. After the program was over, he came up and hung around until the other students had left, and then he began to ask me about Gilly. Who was she? Where was she? Then he wanted to know all the other stories—the things that had happened that somehow hadn't gotten into the book. It was one of those times when you know the real question is not being voiced, but I didn't understand what it was. Finally, a teacher persuaded the boy that he must return to class, and besides, she explained, I had to catch a plane shortly. When he had gone, the librarian told me that Eddie was a member of the special reading class who had heard Gilly read. Like Gilly, he was battling his way through a world of trouble. He has never shown any particular positive interest in books or school until his teacher had read Gilly to the class. And suddenly he had a passion. He was wild about a book—

one of those reluctant readers, or even nonreaders, who had to this point seen words, not to mention books, as the deadliest of enemies.

I thought about Eddie for days. Here was a real-live Gilly who not only approved of but actually liked my fictional one. It was better than having a Japanese like *The Master Puppeteer*. Well, I decided, I'll just send him a copy. Even if he won't ever read it. At least he will own a book he likes. And that will be one for our side, now won't it?

Just before Gilly won the National Book Award, I got a letter from Eddie, and as some of you may remember, I read his letter with, I hasten to assure you, his permission, as part of my acceptance speech. But it feels so good to hear it that I'm going to repeat it.

> *Dear Mrs. Paterson,*
>
> *Thank you for the book "The Great Gilly Hopkins." I love the book. I am on page 16.*
>
> > *Your friend*
> > *Always*
> > *Eddie Young*

And Eddie didn't stop on page 16. He's read the book four times. He's also read *Bridge to Terabithia,* and in his last letter he said he was starting on *The Master Puppeteer*. I rushed off a "Now don't be discouraged by all those long Japanese names" letter to him. I don't know as I write this if he finished it, or even if he's read any other books since he learned that books are not fearsome enemies. I hope he has. I believe he will.

■ ■ ■

will be able to give their full attention to the interview rather than to the unusual nature of the equipment.

8. During the interview the teacher should field the questions. If the interview begins to drag, the teacher can ask a specific student to ask a question: "Sandy, didn't you have a question you wanted to ask?" Once the interview gets moving, it is likely that it will carry itself.

9. Esther Fusco, who has developed and coordinated an authors' week at Shoreham–Wading River Middle School in Shoreham, New York, suggests that students get involved in the visit in as many ways as possible. Before the visit they can write and distribute literature about the visit to the community and the school. During the visit the students can act as hosts by guiding the author through the school and introducing him or her to the class. Students can also be involved by preparing and/or participating in luncheons or receptions for the author. One very successful author visit in which I participated involved the students in a skit they wrote and directed based on one of the author's books. The students and the author had a wonderful time.

10. Publicity material about the author should be displayed in prominent places around the school. Similarly, articles should appear in the school and local newspapers about the author. Students should be involved in completing these pre–author visit responsibilities.

11. Ms. Fusco warns, and I confirm, that the number of students participating in each author interview should be small. There is a great temptation to involve every student in the school during the author visit. The visit will be neither enjoyable nor valuable if the group is larger than thirty students. Similarly, it is important that you do not try to squeeze too much into the author's brief visit. Hour sessions with small groups of students are far more effective than fifteen-minute or half-hour sessions.

> *In retrospect . . . the morning was probably too full. A more leisurely pace would have been less demanding for their visitor and would have allowed a built-in time for autographing. (Everyone was surprised by the number of girls who appeared at the last minute with books of their own to be signed.) Still, it was an exciting, wonderful morning. Madeleine [L'Engle] said afterwards that she felt she was conversing with the children, and the students reported the same kind of reaction. They hadn't been "talked at" by someone new to them; they had talked with a person they had already met through her books. (Parker and Hickman 1981)[2]*

To avoid a very rushed day it may be wise to plan for the author to spend some time in the school library during lunch or after school. At that time students who have been unable to meet the author in their regular classes can come for a leisurely chat in the library.[3]

12. After the author visit or phone hookup, follow up the event by encouraging students to continue reading the author's books. Suggest other books by authors who write on similar topics or in the same genre. Have students write *original* thank-you notes to the author. Suggest that they attempt to take one of the author's books and turn it into a script. In small groups have students write new chapters for the author's book as they think the author would write them. Develop a research project based on one of the author's books: on the topic, the theme, the period, or one of the characters.

An author hookup provides a direct opportunity for students to meet an author. As the author speaks, the books come to life for the students. Students have an opportunity to compare their ideas about the books with the author's ideas about the books. A sense of kinship with the author develops for them.

[2]Reprinted by permission.

[3]Before the visit it is a good idea to consult one of the following reports of author visits to schools: Paula Danziger, I followed the sweet potato, *Voice of Youth Advocates,* June 1979; Esther Fusco, Authors' week in a middle school, *Journal of Reading,* May 1981; Betty Miles, When authors visit schools: A symposium, *Children's Literature in Education,* Autumn 1980; Marilyn Parker, A visit from a poet, *Language Arts,* April 1981; and Teacher feature: An author is coming to school! *The WEB,* spring 1981.

They know something about the author that very few readers know. This direct, purposeful experience can be the impetus for a great deal of learning.

A CONTRIVED EXPERIENCE. When a direct experience is impossible for the teacher to arrange, contrived experiences to motivate the students to read or to encourage them to learn more about what they have been reading can be developed. A contrived experience is one in which the students participate, but which is organized and orchestrated by the teacher.

A good example of a contrived experience (Figure 11–2) uses characters from six young adult books: *Gently touch the milkweed* (Hall), *The pigman* (Zindel), *Swiftwater* (Annixter), *Teacup full of roses* (Mathis), *After the first death* (Cormier), and *Winning* (Brancato).

This particular contrived experience, designed by Guy Ellis, encourages students to read the novels carefully, to understand the characters thoroughly, and to reexamine the books for additional information about each character. Should we save Gary Madden, the quadriplegic with a good mind, or John Conlan, the

Figure 11–2   Contrived Experience

WHO SHOULD SURVIVE?

Following a worldwide nuclear disaster, a few survivors gathered. The only available shelter from the effects of radiation has enough supplies to support only ten people. A slow death will be the likely fate of the others.

From the list of characters below, choose the ones that you believe should survive. Have one or more reasons for each of your decisions. Then compare your list of survivors with other members of your group, trying to agree on a single list of ten.

Think clearly and carefully. Your choices reflect much about you and may shape the world's future.

1. Janet Borofen	15. Ma Calloway
2. Vesta Borofen	16. Joe Brooks
3. Willard Borofen	17. Paul Brooks
4. Mel Makinich	18. Matti Brooks
5. Mary Pat Makinick	19. Ellie
6. Jay Zupin	20. Davey Brooks
7. Mr. Conlan	21. Miro
8. Mr. Pignati	22. Artkin
9. Lorrain Jensen	23. General Marchand
10. Mrs. Jensen	24. Ben Marchand
11. John Conlan	25. Kate Forrester
12. Bucky Calloway	26. Gary Madden
13. Bridie Mellott	27. Diane
14. Cam Calloway	28. Anne Treer

Key: 1–6, *Gently touch the milkweed;* 7–11, *The pigman;* 12–15, *Swiftwater;* 16–20, *Teacup full of roses;* 21–25, *After the first death;* 26–28, *Winning*

Source: Designed by W. Geiger Ellis, University of Georgia.

healthy teenager who appears to be egocentric, or Cam Calloway, the kind-hearted dreamer? On what will we base our decision? Can we reach a consensus? A contrived experience can introduce a thematic unit, can conclude a study of the works of a particular author, can act as an introduction to a concept, can illuminate a discussion topic, and can encourage students to read books with new enthusiasm. A contrived experience such as "Who Should Survive?" makes books come alive for the reader.

DRAMATIZED EXPERIENCES. Viewing or participating in live dramatic performances is a good way to make learning come to life for students. Most communities have some access to amateur or professional theater productions. Viewing live theater is a great foundation for many units. Local college presentations of *The diary of Anne Frank, Romeo and Juliet, West Side story,* and *Of mice and men* have been used as turn-on events for units in my classroom. *The diary of Anne Frank* was an excellent beginning for an interdisciplinary unit on the Holocaust. *Romeo and Juliet* and *West Side story* were both used as jump-off points for a unit on love. *Of mice and men* was an unusual beginning for a unit on violence. All of these productions helped the students become involved in the theme before any reading assignments were made or any discussions conducted. The teacher who keeps abreast of future theater productions has a wealth of dramatic experience on which to build a unit for many subject areas.

Students can become involved in dramatic experiences in their own classrooms. Teachers can incorporate the teaching of reading, writing, and speaking into the classroom drama. After the reading of the young adult novel *The night swimmers* (Byars), Creighton Linder divides his eighth-grade English class into small groups to turn the chapters into a script that the class will produce. Mr. Linder uses the writing and producing techniques as the basis for much of the teaching of abstract language skills. The students read the book and carefully analyze its plot, theme, characters, and setting. Then they write and revise the play. During the revision they use many of the grammatical rules they have been studying and often consult grammar books, a thesaurus, and dictionaries. Each student participates in the oral reading during the initial readers' theater presentation of the script. In producing the play, the students consult many texts and manuals on staging, costuming, lighting, and directing a stage production. Throughout the unit all of the students are reading, writing, and speaking.

> ☐ *Jung knew a single alien letter from an unknown alphabet was enough to trigger endless thoughts in the human mind. Imagine the power of a whole book in the hands of a teacher and a class.*
> PAUL ZINDEL
> *author of* The pigman

The selection of an exceptionally well-written adolescent novel is particularly important in this unit. The students are able to relate to the story of Roy, Retta, and Johnny because they are young adults facing typical adolescent problems. On the other hand, the problems they deal with in their parentless home situation are far enough removed from the lives of Mr. Linder's students that they are able to act in the play without feeling they are revealing too much of themselves. The novel is also a good choice for teaching the literary techniques of plot, theme, character, and setting. It acts as an excellent model for some of the more mature literature the students study later in the year. Similarly, the language patterns of the characters in the book are easy for the eighth-graders to turn into dialogue because they are similar to the English spoken in Mr. Linder's class.

DEMONSTRATION EXPERIENCES. Demonstration, resulting from the reading of a book or held prior to the reading, can make the book seem more real to the students. In Bill Cleaver and Vera Cleaver's book *Where the lilies bloom,* fourteen-year-old Mary Call Luther and her brother and sisters are able to support themselves after the death of their father by "wildcrafting." In spite of the Cleavers' description of this picking and digging of medicinal plants, the students in a tenth-grade sociology class studying Appalachian life were unable to understand "wildcrafting." Their teacher, Christina Derrough, invited an Appalachian native who grew up with wildcrafting to her class. The guest, Ms. Chestnut, demonstrated the craft to the students. She brought with her many samples of plants, explained why roots were sometimes more valuable than flowers, showed some of the products made from the plants, and discussed the local uses for wildcrafted medicines. The students were fascinated and asked Ms. Derrough for more information. She contacted a local agriculture extension agent, who provided the class with several booklets on the topic. Early in the spring it was agreed that Ms. Chestnut would return and she and the students would go wildcrafting on the school nature trail.

The demonstration of the craft, initiated by the reading of this young adult novel, brought about much learning in Ms. Derrough's class. The students developed a better understanding of Appalachian culture, gained an appreciation of the resourcefulness of the mountain people, and learned a valuable new skill.

FIELD TRIP EXPERIENCES. Field trips are usually great fun and if well planned can be an educational beginning for much new learning.

The students in Henry Frame's history class have been studying America during the period before colonization. As part of the unit the students are examining the life of the American Indian. Mr. Frame has been reading aloud from Joyce Rockwood's books *To spoil the sun* and *Long Man's song.* These young adult historical novels are about a Cherokee girl and the impact the European settlers had on her life and on the Cherokee nation, and a Cherokee apprentice medicine man who attempts to save his sister's life. Early in the unit Mr. Frame plans a trip to Cherokee, North Carolina, to visit the Oconoluftee Indian Village and the Museum of the Cherokee. Before the trip he arranges for a Cherokee historian employed by the museum to meet with the students to discuss the Cherokee of the precolonization period and how the European settlers affected them. The day before the field trip the students prepare a series of questions to ask the historian, primarily based on the books Mr. Frame has been reading. Since Mr. Frame has previously visited the field trip locale, he prepares a hand-out for the students that requires them to answer a series of questions about the Cherokee. He also allows the students to choose from a list of assignments to be completed while in Cherokee. The assignments include these activities: sketch the Cherokee "houses" as they developed through the ages and are displayed in the village; briefly explain how the Cherokee hunted with the blow gun; sketch or make a typical ceremonial outfit worn by the Cherokee; explain why the Indians at most of the commercial establishments in the town of Cherokee are not wearing Cherokee clothing; assume that you experienced the Trail of Tears and write a letter to a friend who remains in North Carolina telling him or her about it; describe the Cherokee craft of basket weaving or try to make a basket using the technique; interview a Cherokee about life on the reservation today.

☐ *Among the most satisfying letters I received from people who had read* Long Man's Song *were those from seasoned anthropologists who had spent many years doing fieldwork among living Indans. . . . "Reading of the Deer Clan took me back to a winter visit once to Will West Long when I was searching for southeastern parallels of the eagle dance."*
JOYCE ROCKWOOD
Can novelists portray other cultures faithfully? / The Advocate / *Fall 1982*

After the field trip, the visit to Cherokee is carefully discussed in the class-room, beginning with the answering of the questions assigned prior to the trip. During this discussion Mr. Frame and the students make a time line of the history of the Cherokee with plenty of space to add new information throughout the year. Other activities integrate the trip, the books, and the historic periods. One group of students makes a time line of what is happening in Europe during the periods examined in the books. Another group creates a diorama of a Cherokee town (houses, grounds, meeting place) during the historical periods discussed in *To spoil the sun* and *Long Man's song*. A third group outlines a typical day in the life of a Cherokee girl in the sixteenth century, an American-European girl of the sixteenth century, and an aristocratic girl living in Europe during the same period. Another group of students outlines the life of fifteenth- and sixteenth-century Cherokee girls and compares them to a Cherokee girl during the period of time of the Trail of Tears and a Cherokee girl of today living on the Qualla reservation.

The field trip becomes the basis for an effective unit of study in Mr. Frame's class. In addition it provides the impetus for a year-long study of the Cherokee Indian throughout U.S. history. By the end of the school year the time line begun the day after the field trip has expanded to a time line that reaches two-thirds of the way around the room and encompasses events from around the globe.

EXHIBIT EXPERIENCES. An exhibit based on a book or an exhibit of books can be an excellent beginning step for getting students involved in a book or a topic being studied. The more students are involved in setting up the exhibit, the more likely they are to become involved in the book or the topic.

Many of the book-telling techniques described later (pp. 384–385) can be used in setting up an exhibit about books for the classroom. For example, students are encouraged to select a visual way to tell about a book they have just completed. During a unit on alcoholism and drug addiction in Karen Lang's tenth-grade health class, one of the students elects to sketch two important scenes from Frank Bonham's *Cool cat.* Another student shares a book by designing a jacket cover for Sandra Scoppetone's *The late great me.* John Donovan's *I'll get there. It better be worth the trip* is the source for a poster "advertising" the book. Costumes for the characters are sketched by one student for a dramatic presentation of Alice Childress's *A hero ain't nothin' but a sandwich.* Another student writes a poem and mounts it for the display based on *That was then, this is now* by S. E. Hinton. Using the anthology of poems compiled by Lee Bennett Hopkins and Sunna Rasch, *I really want to feel good about myself: Poems by former drug addicts,* a student elects to make a chart of facts learned from the poems in the book. Another student constructs a diorama of one of the scenes in Robert Lipsyte's *The contender.* After the projects have been completed, Ms. Lang sets aside a table and bulletin board in the room to display the projects as an exhibit about books on drug addiction and alcoholism. Next to the exhibit she places the book rack with the paperback books that relate to the exhibit. After examining the books and projects displayed, the students are encouraged to select a book of their choice to read as they continue their unit of work.

Exhibits that take very little time to create can encourage students to get into books. The teacher who takes the lead from bookstore managers who display books for browsing and buying is likely to have students who are constantly borrowing and reading. Simple display techniques—such as carousel book racks, which allow books to be displayed with their jackets showing, or racks that are constructed from peg board and small metal display shelves that place books in easy reach—increase the number of circulations from the classroom library. Changing exhibits of sales posters or jacket covers, often available free from publishers, will attract students to the new books on the classroom display rack.

In each of Janice Williams's eighth-grade English classes two students per month are in charge of the reading corner. As part of their responsibility they unpack and catalogue the new paperbacks that arrive, watch the mail for new posters, display information about books that have recently appeared on the shelves, distribute material that comes from the book club to which the class belongs, and select and display student projects related to the books. Ms. Williams's classroom is a constantly changing exhibit about books and authors. It is a rare student in Ms. Williams's class who walks the halls without carrying a paperback.

TELEVISION EXPERIENCES. Many teachers complain that television is one of the causes of students' inability to get involved in the learning process. According to many researchers, television encourages passive viewing rather than active participation. The classroom teacher, however, can use television to make books and authors come to life for students.

There is no doubt that children watch a great deal of television. A. C. Neilsen, the TV rating group, found that the average child of elementary school age watches approximately 24½ hours of television per week or 3½ hours per day. This means that upon entering high school, a student will have spent approximatly 11,000 hours in the classroom and 15,000 in front of the television set.

Many young people, according to Dorothy G. Singer, codirector of Family Television Research and Consultation Center, Yale University, "believe they must be knowledgeable about a variety of TV characters and able to imitate their sayings, gestures, hair styles, clothing and habits." She goes on to say that teachers and librarians can capitalize on this involvement and use television to encourage students to read more. To do this, however, teachers "will have to overcome their bias against television and learn how to make television 'work' for them" (1979, pp. 51–52).[4]

Harlan Hamilton, in a landmark study of television and reading, found that when junior high school students were given a choice of reading books connected with television programs, or books not connected with TV, over two-thirds selected television-related books. A similar study, conducted in 1978 in Virginia, found that 89 percent of the students surveyed were influenced to read a book by at least one television program. Other studies have found that television's potential for increasing reading of books related to television programs proved more effective than motivation from teachers, parents, or peers.

The television and publishing industries have begun to capitalize on the information gained from these studies. "Tie-ins" is a new term used to describe books related to television shows. The tie-ins take several different forms: television shows or movies based on books, books based on television scripts, books about celebrities or special programs, books about the development of a television series, books about the subjects treated in television programming, and the actual scripts of the television shows.

All three major networks are involved in book-television tie-in programs.[5] ABC

---

[4]Reprinted with permission from R. R. Bowker Company/A Xerox Corporation.

[5]For information about network tie-ins, write to ABC Community Relations, ABC-TV, 1330 Avenue of the Americas, New York, NY 10019; The CBS Television Reading Program, 51 West 52nd St., New York, NY 10019; NBC Parent Participation Workshops, Teachers' Guide to Television, 699 Madison Ave., New York, NY 10021.

is attempting to use television to channel children's interest toward learning. It provides educational materials to teachers for use in conjunction with many special programs. Viewing guides contain background information, program synopsis, suggested activities, and resource lists. The after-school and weekend specials presented on ABC are often based on young adult books. Librarians receive information on these programs and teacher guides are provided.

A CBS/Library of Congress television reading project, "Read More About It," has a star from the television program appear at the end of the presentation to mention books related to the topic of the program. Often the programs are based on a particular book; the kickoff show of the project in the spring of 1977 was "A circle of children," based on a book by Mary McCracken.

NBC funds Parent Participation Workshops. The program shows parents how to lead children from television to reading to active participation in life. In addition NBC promotes tie-ins during its "Special Treat" series. At the end of the book-based programs, stars from the show talk briefly about the book.

In addition to the programs prepared specifically for students, all of the networks present prime-time programming based on books appropriate for young readers. Programs and series based on *Summer of my German soldier* (Greene), *Roots* (Haley), *Friendly fire* (Bryan), *I know why the caged bird sings* (Angelou), *Joni* (Eareckson), *Blinded by the light* (Brancato), and many others have been aired in prime time on the three networks.

The Public Broadcasting System also presents single shows and television series based on a book or books. PBS has presented a series based on two books of James Herriott, *All things bright and beautiful* and *All creatures great and small.* The PBS series "Once upon a classic" re-creates classic novels. "Masterpiece theatre" has shown award-winning television drama for over a decade. Many of the shows are based on classic novels such as Austen's *Pride and prejudice,* Dostoevsky's *Crime and punishment,* and Tolstoy's *Anna Karenina.* Series that have dramatized twentieth-century works include "Danger UXB," based on the book *Unexploded bomb* by Major Bill Hartley, and *Testament of youth,* based on the autobiography of Vera Britton. Teachers can receive study guides for these and other prime-time programs through a variety of free or inexpensive subscription services.[6] Many publishing companies prepare, free for teachers, lists of their titles that will be made into television specials. In addition, some companies prepare study guides for the teachers to use along with the program and the book.

The Agency for Instructional Television produces several shows that use books as their foundation. AITV programs are aired on cable and closed-circuit systems and are available for broadcast through Public Broadcasting outlets. Some book-related television shows available in many parts of the United States

[6]Resources and study guides can be obtained from Action for Children's Television, 46 Austin St., Newtonville, MA 02160; Parent-Teachers' Association, 700 North Rush St., Chicago, IL 60611; Prime-time, 120 S. LaSalle St., Chicago, IL 60603; Scholastic Book Services, 904 Sylvan Ave., Englewood Cliffs, NJ 07632.

and Canada include "Storybound" (sixth-grade level), "Matter of Fact" and "Matter of Fiction" (junior and senior high), "The Short Story" (junior and senior high), "Cover to Cover" (fifth and sixth grade), and "Sixteen Stories Tall" (fifth grade). All of these shows, hosted by John Robbins, combine the story with illustrations completed by Mr. Robbins during the fifteen-minute program.[7]

Television, when used in conjunction with classroom learning, can motivate students to read, can improve attitudes toward reading, and can improve reading abilities. Teachers can make television viewing an active rather than a passive activity if they help the students understand how to become more involved television viewers.

One way to encourage active participation is to create a bulletin board on which notices of future television shows of educational value are posted. Next to the bulletin board, reading material related to the show can be displayed on a "TV tie-in table." Books related to television or news media events such as major elections, royal weddings, the Olympics, or other major sports or news events can be placed on the table. In science and social studies classrooms, teachers can place books that relate to shows such as "Nova," "Connections," "Cosmos," Jacques Cousteau specials, "Holocaust," "Marco Polo," and "The Third Reich." Science fiction literature related to television shows can be appropriately displayed in science, English, and reading classrooms. Books about television and television personalities (including sports figures) can be part of the display.

EXPERIENCING FILMS, FILMSTRIPS, SLIDE SHOWS, CASSETTES, AND RECORDINGS. Motion pictures can be experienced in much the same way as television programs. Good films that relate to the unit being studied can bring concepts, books, and abstract ideas to life. A film is particularly useful when the teacher encourages students to participate actively in the viewing of the film through creative activities before and after the film showing. These activities must involve the student with the subject of the film.

Thousands of good films are available for classroom use in all subject areas. Most schools have access to free film-lending libraries. School librarians can help teachers locate these sources and obtain the films. Unfortunately, most films must be ordered several months in advance to ensure show dates that correspond to units of work. Even with the difficulties in ordering and other problems—such as failure of films to arrive on expected dates, arrival and return dates that do not permit teacher preview (a very dangerous situation), and equipment failure—films are an excellent way to assist students in the understanding of difficult concepts and ideas.

It is impossible to mention all of the films that are particularly useful in units that use adolescent literature; however, some deserve particular attention. As mentioned earlier, most of the ABC after-school and weekend specials are

---

[7]Study guides can be obtained from Agency for Instructional Television, Box A, Bloomington, IN 47402.

available on film. Large numbers of these are based on young adult novels and can be used effectively in conjunction with them. Similarly, many commercial and prime-time films are based on literature written primarily for young adults or particularly appreciated by them. One recent well-known example of this phenomenon is the Academy Award–winning film *Ordinary people,* based on an ALA Best Books for Young Adults novel by Judith Guest. This film is available for classroom use through rental or lending libraries. Four other examples that are or will be available are Hinton's *The outsiders, Rumble fish,* and *Tex,* and Cormier's *I am the cheese.* Movies made for prime-time television are often available for classroom use. A lending library in my locale, for example, has Alex Haley's *Roots* series; *The autobiography of Miss Jane Pittman* by Ernest J. Gaines; *Sunshine,* which was first a television movie and later a young adult novel by Norma Klein; *The wave,* which like *Sunshine* was a television movie and later a novel by Morton Rhue; and many others.

Many educational film companies sell or rent films that incorporate a wide variety of young adult books. The *ALAN Review,* published by the Assembly on Literature for Adolescents–National Council of Teachers of English, has included a nonprint media section since the fall of 1976.[8] It includes information about films and other media based on young adult literature and about authors or films of particular merit for classrooms using young adult literature.

Every year the Young Adults Committee of the Young Adult Services Division of the American Library Association selects films to recommend for use in "programs planned to be of interest to young adults" (*Selected films for young adults,* 1981 edition, ALA). The committee's pamphlet contains annotations on the content of the film, information about the film's producer, and listings of the distributors and price.[9]

A discussion of the use of films in the classroom cannot ignore the technological revolution of the video disk. Many feature-length films, both modern and classic, are available for limited cost on video disks, packaged much like a record, for use on home television sets equipped wtih special players. Many communities are establishing lending libraries of these disks, both formally through a public library and informally through individually organized exchange groups. This could become a great resource for the future use of feature-length films in the classroom. However, teachers are warned that a large investment in video-disk films is unwise because they may not be legal for classroom use after a number of current court cases are decided.

Other nonprint media can motivate students to read, introduce them to authors and books, or bring books to life. Video cassettes of author interviews,

---

[8] *The ALAN Review* is published three times a year. A subscription and membership in the Assembly on Literature for Adolescents is $10 per year. Membership applications should be sent to NCTE, 1111 Kenyon Road, Urbana, IL 61801.

[9] *Selected films for young adults* is available from American Library Association, Young Adult Services Division, 50 Huron St., Chicago, IL 60611, for 20 cents per copy. Copies of previous yearly listings are available for the same price.

for example, are available in Temple University's "Profiles in Literature" series. The series features many young adult authors such as Katherine Paterson, Scott O'Dell, Madeleine L'Engle, Kristin Hunter *(The Soul Brothers and Sister Lou),* Beverly Cleary, Judy Blume, Ann Petry *(Harriet Tubman, conductor on the underground railroad),* and Jean Craighead George. Through this series students meet the authors and hear them discuss their books, their lives, and their writing.

Another series that helps students learn more about authors and their books is Miller-Brody's filmstrip and audio cassette series, "Meet the Newbery Author." The filmstrips show pictures of the authors and the cassettes feature the authors speaking about themselves, their books, and the art of writing. Also included in this series are audio cassettes and filmstrips depicting key action sequences from Newbery Award–winning books. Teacher guides and still pictures are included along with copies of the books. Teachers can use this series in many different ways and incorporate a variety of different reading, writing, and literature activities. The series can be incorporated successfully into units dealing with the authors and their books, or into learning centers and book nooks for individual listening.

Other companies emphasize young adult literature in their multimedia products. The Center for the Humanities produces sound slide shows. Many of the productions use young adult literature, poetry, and music. *I couldn't put it down: Hooked on reading* is designed to encourage reluctant readers to get into books and is based on six adolescent novels. Another production, *The poetry of rock,* uses young adult music as a turn-on for teaching poetry. Excellent teachers' guides and scripts are included with each program. Guidance Associates, which is affiliated with the Center for the Humanities, distributes sound filmstrip shows on the same and similar topics.

There are many good sources for media that use young adult literature as a basis for productions. Weston Woods is known for films, recordings, filmstrips, cassettes, and other multimedia items. Caedmon produces records of readings of young adult books, classic children's books, and modern and classic literature. Some of the young adult authors available on Caedmon records are Norma Klein, Roald Dahl, Jean Craighead George, C. S. Lewis, Isaac Asimov, Ursula LeGuin, and Anne McCaffrey. Many of the ABC and NBC network young adult specials as well as feature-length films of young adult novels are available for rent or purchase from Learning Corporation of America. Films based on books by authors such as Betty Bates, M. E. Kerr, Francine Pascal, Marion Dane Bauer, Harry Mazer, Mildred Lee, Maia Wojciechowska, Louise Fitzhugh, Thomas Thompson, and others are available in thirty-minute segments. Feature-length films from books by Gale Sayers, Ernest J. Gaines, John Gunther, Thomas Thompson, Margaret Craven, Maya Angelou, Mildred Taylor, Bette Greene, and others are also available for classroom use.

☐ *Writing for children is more fun than writing for adults and more rewarding. Children have the ability, which most*

adults have lost, the knack to be someone else, of living through stories the lives of other people. . . . If children like your book they respond for a long time, by thousands of letters. It is this response, this concern and act of friendship, that makes the task of writing worth the doing.
SCOTT O'DELL
author of The feathered serpent[10]

Sharing Books

READING ALOUD. One excellent way to involve all your students in the reading, learning, and thinking process is by reading aloud to them. Many people think that reading aloud is only for small children, that the elementary classroom is the last place in which books can be legitimately read aloud. This is a very unfortunate attitude.

Reading aloud is an art that has been lost with the advent of television. For centuries families used the evening hours as a time to gather together and read aloud together. The shared experience was entertaining, educational, motivational, and therapeutic.

Reading aloud continues to be wonderful entertainment. The age of the audience doesn't matter; all listeners can be captivated by the spoken word. Each listener pictures the story as he or she pleases. Each story fulfills a different need for each individual. A fantasy takes the listener to new and strange worlds. A mystery keeps students on the edge of their seats, groaning at the end of each day's chapter, begging the teacher to continue reading, and happily anticipating the reading time during the next class. Historical fiction brings the period being studied to life. As the teacher reads *The witch of Blackbird Pond* by Elizabeth George Speare, the students question the motives of the New England Puritans. They wonder why the citizens of Wethersfield, Connecticut, are so unaccepting of Hannah, the ''witch.'' They fear for the welfare of Kit, the niece from Barbados. And they begin to question their own motives and lack of acceptance of others different from themselves.

Reading humorous books aloud produces outbursts of laughter and anticipation of the next insane episode, as in *How to eat fried worms* by Thomas Rockwell. Sad books bring students together as each relates to the character's plight. The slow, agonizing death of Johnny Gunther in *Death be not proud,* a memoir by a proud father, brings tears to the eyes of the strongest, hardest boy in the class. Good literature allows every individual to react in his or her own way. Reading aloud gives students and teacher the opportunity to share reactions even if they are never discussed. Reading aloud is superb, shared entertainment.

Reading aloud is educational. Reading aloud enables the teacher who loves reading to share this love with the students. In some instances the teacher

[10]Reprinted from a publicity pamphlet by permission of Houghton Mifflin Company.

■ ■ ■ An Anthological Aside

The Words Take on New Meanings

ELIZABETH GEORGE SPEARE

Reverend Gershom Bulkeley laid down his linen napkin, pushed back his heavy chair from the table, and expanded his straining waistcoat in a satisfied sigh.

"A very excellent dinner, Mistress Wood. I warrant there's not a housewife in the colonies can duplicate your apple tarts."

He had just better compliment that dinner, thought Kit. The preparation of it had taken the better part of four days. Every inch of the great kitchen had been turned inside out. The floor had been fresh-sanded, the hearthstone polished, the pewter scoured. The brick oven had been heated for two nights in a row, and the whole family had gone without sugar since Sunday to make sure that the minister's notorious sweet tooth would be satisfied.

Well, Dr. Bulkeley had been pleased, but had anyone else? Matthew Wood had eaten little and spoken scarcely a word. He sat now with his lips pressed tight together. Rachel looked tired and flustered, and even Mercy seemed unusually quiet. Only Judith had blossomed. In the candlelight she looked bewitching, and Reverend Bulkeley smiled whenever he looked at her. But the greatest part of his condescension he had bestowed on Kit, once he had understood that her grandfather had been Sir Francis Tyler. He himself had visited Antigua in the West Indies, he had told her, and he was acquainted with some of the plantation owners there. He went back to the subject now for the third time.

"So, young lady, your grandfather was knighted for loyalty by King Charles, you say? A great honor, a very great honor indeed. And I take it he was a loyal subject of our good King James as well?"

"Why, of course, sir."

"And you yourself? You are a loyal subject also?"

"How could I be otherwise, sir?" Kit was puzzled.

"There are some who seem to find it possible," remarked the minister, staring meaningfully at a ceiling beam. "See that you keep your allegiance."

With an abrupt scrape of wood Matthew pushed back his chair. "Her allegiance is in no danger in this house," he announced angrily. "What are you implying, Gershom?"

"I meant nothing to offend you, Matthew," said the older man.

"Then watch your words. May I remind you I am a selectman in this town? I am no traitor!"

"I said no such thing, nor did I mean it. Mistaken, Matthew, I hold to that, but not a traitor—yet."

"I am mistaken," Matthew Wood challenged him, "because I do not favor knuckling under to this new King's governor?"

"Governor Andros was appointed by King James. Massachusetts has recognized that."

"Well, we here in Connecticut will never recognize it—never! Do you think we have labored and sacrificed all these years to build up a free government only to hand it over now without a murmur?"

"I say you are mistaken!" growled Gershom Bulkeley. "Mark my words, Matthew. If you do not live to see the evil results, your children or their children will suffer. Call it what you will, this stubbornness can lead only to revolution."

Matthew's eyes flashed. "There are worse things than revolution!"

"I know more about that than you. I was surgeon in the Fort fight with the Indians. War is an evil, Matthew. Believe me, there can no good thing come of bloodshed."

"Who is asking for bloodshed? We ask only to keep the rights that have already been granted to us in the charter."

The two men sat glaring at each other across the table. Tears sprang to Rachel's eyes. Then Mercy spoke from the shadows.

"I had looked forward to hearing Reverend Bulkeley read to us this evening," she said gently.

Dr. Bulkeley sent her a gracious smile and considered. "I have to coddle this throat of mine," he decided. "But my young pupil here is a very exceptional reader. I shall pass the honor on to him."

Grudgingly Matthew Wood lifted the heavy Bible and placed it in John Holbrook's hand, and Rachel moved a pewter candlestick nearer to his elbow. John had been respectfully silent all the evening. Indeed, he had had little opportunity to be anything else, and he now seemed pleased out of all proportion at this slight notice from his master. Kit felt suddenly provoked at him. One week in Wethersfield seemed to have changed the dignified young man she had known on shipboard. Tonight he appeared to be a shadow, hanging on every word from this pompous opinionated man. Even now he dared not assert himself but held the Bible uncertainly in his hands and asked, "What would you have me read, sir?"

"I would suggest Proverbs, 24th Chapter, 21st verse," said the old minister, with a canny gleam in his eye which Kit understood as John began to read.

"My son, fear the Lord and the King, and meddle not with them that are given to change, For their calamity shall rise suddenly, and who knoweth the ruin of them both?"

There was a harsh sound from Matthew, checked in response to his wife's pleading eyes. John continued reading.

As he read on, Kit forgot the meaning of the words and felt a stir of pleasure at the sound. John's voice was low-pitched but very clear, and the words fell with a musical cadence that was a delight. Every evening since she had come here she had sat waiting with impatience for her uncle's monotonous voice to cease. Tonight, for the first time, she caught the beauty of the ancient Hebrew verses.

When the reading was finished, family and guests bowed their heads and Reverend Bulkeley began the evening prayer. A little sigh escaped Kit. Her uncle's terse petitions were hard enough to endure; this prayer, she knew, would be a lengthy masterpiece. As the husky voice scraped inexorably on, she ventured to raise her head a little, and was gratified to see that Judith too was peeking. But Judith's attention was not wandering. She was studying, with deliberate appraisal, John Holbrook's bent head and the delicate chiseled line of his profile against the firelight.

A phrase of Dr. Bulkeley's prayer caught Kit's attention again. "And bless our sister in her weakness and affliction." Whom did he mean? Heavens, was he talking about Mercy? Had the man no perception at all? How Mercy must be shriveling at the fulsome words. After a few days in this household Kit had ceased to be aware of Mercy's lameness. No one in the family ever referred to it. Mercy certainly did not consider herself afflicted. She did a full day's work and more. Moreover, Kit had soon discovered that Mercy was the pivot about whom the whole household moved. She coaxed her father out of his bitter moods, upheld her timorous and anxious mother, gently restrained her rebellious sister and had reached to draw an uncertain alien into the circle. Mercy weak! Why, the man could not even use his eyes!

When the prayer was ended, the thanks repeated and the goodnights said, Rachel saw her guests to the door. She held out her hand to John Holbrook.

"I hope you will come again," she said kindly. "We would like you to feel welcome in our house."

John looked back to where Judith stood behind Mercy's chair. "Thank you, ma'am," he answered, "If I may, I would be very happy to come again."

■ ■ ■

shares with the class books of high literary quality that the students are unable to read on their own. In this way, they have the opportunity to participate in a great work as only a reader can. Similarly, the student hears the language of the author. The language may be very different from that heard at home, on the streets, and even in the classroom. Students can experience and be captivated by the beauty of carefully wrought written English.

Reading and writing skills are improved through reading aloud. As students listen to a book, they must comprehend the story line of the novel, not only that which is read today, but also that which was read yesterday, or the day before spring vacation. The teacher helps develop this comprehension by reviewing the story line with students prior to each day's reading. A teacher who hopes to use the oral reading to reinforce the concept of plot can list the main events of the story on a piece of newsprint for easy reference. This technique allows the student who misses a day of reading to keep up with the story. A similar technique is used to reinforce the concept of character development. The teacher keeps a running list of attributes learned about each of the main characters. This is a particularly useful exercise in a puzzle mystery such as *The Westing game* by Ellen Raskin. The list encourages students to comprehend not only the simple events of the novel, but also the subtleties of the characterization that finally add up to the solution of the puzzle. This same simple listing technique also allows the teacher to reinforce the literary device of setting.

Writing skills are improved as a result of the reading-aloud sessions. Students are asked to write about what has been read, to describe scenes or characters as they see them, to discuss what they believe is likely to happen next and why, to write a subsequent chapter, to describe how one of the characters would act in a situation described by the teacher. If the class contains several students who are reluctant to write, these activities can be accomplished in small groups of three to five students.

Reading aloud improves students' listening skills. Teachers often complain that students are not good listeners or that their attention span is very short. One way to lengthen the attention span is by reading a book with a lot of action, suspense, or humor. The teacher begins by reading only a few pages to the students on the first day of oral reading. It is necessary to find a book in which the plot begins on the first few pages and to end the reading shortly after the students' attention has been caught. Ending when the students are begging to hear more is a good way to ensure that their attention will be on the book when the reading begins during the next session. During the second reading-aloud period the teacher reads a section that is slightly longer than the first but, like the first, ends at a point of extreme action or humor. The teacher continues in this way until the students are willing and able to sit through the oral reading of a chapter or more, even if the excitement is waning.

Thinking skills are improved by reading aloud. When a book is read aloud to older students, they must picture the action and the characters. The pictures are not drawn in the text, except through the words of the author. Teachers encourage the imagination that students use in listening to the book by having them describe the scene as they see it in writing, orally, or in picture form. Comparison of different presentations of the same scene produces some interesting discussion. How did student A's presentation of the scene differ from student B's? Was one more accurate than the other? Did one more closely follow the book?

☐   *If you watch a television set for six hours a day for five years you may know a lot, but what you haven't done during*

that time is manufacture your own images. What you haven't done is exercise that imagination which is your bridge into the world.
DANIEL FADER
in a lecture at the University of North Carolina at Asheville / October 1981

Reading aloud encourages thinking by requiring the listeners to think ahead to what is likely to happen next. The television generation has become accustomed to stories completed in thirty-, sixty-, or ninety-minute segments. Reading an entire book aloud may take several weeks. The students must retain the story from each reading session and must come to their own conclusions about what is likely to occur. Reading aloud is particularly educational when used as an integral part of the day's lesson.

Reading aloud is motivational. The teacher who reads aloud to students is a model who embodies the fact that reading can be fun. The teacher who reads, and obviously enjoys reading, is more likely to improve the students' attitude toward reading than the teacher who does not read. For some students the experience of hearing a book read aloud may be the first time they have "read" an entire book. Even though they have not read it on their own, they have developed a sense of accomplishment in sitting through the reading of an entire book. For other students it may be the first time they have enjoyed a suspenseful book

Reading aloud brings to life The best Christmas pageant *(Barbara Robinson) for these middle school students.*

or a fantasy or a work of science fiction. It is not unusual to find avid young readers who are willing to tackle only one type of book. Reading aloud can expand a student's reading horizons. Reading aloud can motivate a student to read an entire book alone, can give a student a new reading interest, and can reverse a negative attitude toward reading and books.

□ *If I could convince youngsters that reading is as much fun as turning on a television, I would be doing them a service.*
LOIS DUNCAN

author of Daughters of Eve, *and other books / in a speech to the IRA Convention / Atlanta, Ga. / April 1979*

Reading aloud is therapeutic for the class, for the teacher, and for the individual student. Reading aloud pulled Eunice Hendrick's class out of the doldrums. It was February, and for the last six weeks the eleventh-grade English class had been studying grammar; both students and teacher were bored. Beginning each class with a suspenseful, motivating novel brought this class to life. Ms. Hendrick selected *The chocolate war* (Cormier). Each day she read one chapter of this young adult classic. Now the students had something to look forward to during each class session.

Reading aloud can provide therapy for the socially divided class. Margo Jones, an eighth-grade English teacher, told me about a class of hers in which the students seemed to be constantly at war with each other. She had tried everything she knew to create a community spirit: small-group work, field trips, special projects, learning centers, movies. One day, when she was at her wits' end, she decided to read a book aloud to her class. She chose the novel *The undertaker's gone bananas* (Zindel). She believed her students would respond well to the title and relate favorably to the humor. She was right. They not only listened but at the end of the first reading session begged her to continue. And, without prompting, they began discussing the book. The students began to share their feelings about the characters. Soon they were finding themselves agreeing with each other. A community spirit was developing.

Reading aloud can be therapeutic for the individual students in the class. Students who have not formed friendships with their peers are able to form friendships with the characters in the books. Students who are having difficulties dealing with problems common to adolescents may find solutions, or at least ways of dealing with the problem, through the book. A few years ago a teacher told me about a member of a ninth-grade class who had been paralyzed in a fall from the balance beam during a high school gymnastic competition. She was a popular student and a good gymnast. The other students were shocked and unable to deal with their frustration and fear. Likewise, the teacher was experiencing difficulty accepting the injury of one of her outstanding students. While glancing through a journal one day, she found a book review of the novel *Winning* by Robin Brancato. The novel is about a football hero who is paralyzed during a game, and how he, his family, his friends, and his teacher contend with the realization that he will never walk again. She bought the novel, read it, was moved by it, and decided to read it to her class. The experience of sharing her concern with the class through Robin Brancato's book was valuable to her, to the class, to the friends of the injured girl, and, indirectly, to the injured girl.

DEVELOPING A READING-ALOUD PROGRAM. Reading aloud can be a daily event at any grade level. It allows the teacher to share exceptional books with students. It gives the students something to anticipate each day. It helps develop a sense of community. It sets a comfortable atmosphere for learning. It allows students to hear well-written English. It encourages equal participation. It motivates the students to read more books by the same author or on the same theme. And it can be the basis for the day's lesson.

The teacher who plans to institute a reading-aloud program should look at the reading as a vital part of the daily lesson. The book selected can be one that fits the subject being studied. For example, students studying the early settlement of this country begin each day with a reading section from *Constance* by Patricia Clapp. Students studying our reliance on nature begin each day with a chapter from a book by Jean George. Or the book may be one that introduces the wide world of literature. For instance, a book like Richard Peck's *Ghosts I have been* can be used as an introduction to the world of mystery and fantasy.

Similarly, the book should be one that will interest the students and hold their attention. Most young people are attracted to books with action, suspense, and a lot of dialogue. Therefore, the teacher may want to begin reading aloud to the students from a suspenseful novel. However, as the students gain listening skills, a variety of moods and genres can be incorporated. Each book fills a different need for the students. Fantasy and science fiction stretch their imagination. Humor gives the class an opportunity to share laughter. Sad books give them a chance to share emotions that are rarely revealed in public.

Here are several helpful hints for the teacher who plans to read aloud to a class:

1. Select a book that appeals to you, not a book selected by a friend or a colleague. Be sure the book can be divided into easily read daily sections.

☐ *Don't read stories that you don't enjoy yourself. Your dislike will show in the reading, and that defeats your purpose.*
JIM TRELEASE
The read-aloud handbook

2. Be thoroughly familiar with the book. Look up the pronunciation and definition of unfamiliar words.
3. Practice reading aloud. Be aware of phrasing. Practice ending each sen-

tence without raising or dropping your voice. Practice looking up from time to time, and looking at a different person each time.

4. Never change words to simplify the text. However, dropping the "he said" and "she said" in long segments of conversation may improve the movement of the dialogue. Similarly, editing "objectionable" words may be appropriate in the classroom.

5. Try to create a symbol that indicates that the reading is about to begin. For example, pull an easy chair or stool to the front of the room and invite the students to gather their chairs around you.

6. Be sure the students are comfortable and can see and be seen by you, the reader. It is best to sit with a blank wall or curtain behind you; sitting in front of a window causes a glare.

7. Try to minimize classroom interruptions. Do not read at the end of class if announcements are always given at that time. Put a sign on the door that announces, "Reading aloud—do not interrupt."

8. Set aside a time each day for reading aloud. However, do not confine reading to this time. Read as often as is possible and practical.

9. When possible, duplicate sections of the book for take-home reading, or have available other books by the same author or on the same theme.

STORYTELLING. Storytelling has many of the same attributes as reading aloud and several additional benefits. Like reading aloud, storytelling is entertaining, educational, motivational, and therapeutic. Storytelling is an event enjoyed by people of all ages. In some parts of the country, like the mountains of North Carolina and Tennessee, storytelling continues to be a means of entertainment, a way to communicate knowledge and folklore, and a colorful, oral literary tradition that has been passed down from generation to generation. In such sections of the country storytelling has never died. In other places, however, it has been replaced by television and motion pictures. But in recent years the art form is experiencing a rebirth and gaining a new, active following.[11]

The benefits to the listener at a storytelling session are great. The story selected by the storyteller can be from the great oral literary tradition of the section of the country in which the story is being told (in recent years many of these tales have been collected and made into anthologies that are usually available in local libraries), a children's book, a poem, a song, or a section of a young adult book. One of the great benefits of storytelling is that any story can be told to any age group. A storyteller need not limit the audience to the age group for which the book is written. Recently, for example, I attended a

[11]The National Association for the Preservation and Perpetuation of Storytelling is in Jonesborough, Tennessee. Each year the association presents a storytelling conference in June and sponsors a storytelling festival in October. The association also maintains a National Storytelling Resource Center, which contains a resource library and an archive of storytelling audio and video recordings. For more information about the association and the art of storytelling, write to NAPPS in Jonesborough, Tenn. 37659.

Table 11-1   Good Books to Read Aloud

Author	Title	Comment	Appropriate age
Judie Angell	*Ronnie and Rosey*	Death of a parent; friendship	12+
	In summertime it's Tuffy	A 10-year-old girl at summer camp	10+
William Armstrong	*Sounder*	Man's cruelty to man; a dog's loyalty to its master	10+
Sue Ellen Bridgers	*All together now*	A girl's friendship with a retarded man	12+
	Home before dark	A family's search for a new home	12+
Roald Dahl	*Charlie and the chocolate factory*	A poor boy's relationship to his family and a dream come true	8+
Paula Danziger	*Can you sue your parents for malpractice?*	⎫ Humor that should appeal to the entire family	10+
	The cat ate my gymsuit	⎬	10+
	The pistachio prescription	⎭	10+
Lois Duncan	*Down a dark hall*	⎱ Mystery, supernatural fantasy, excitement, all with a message	12+
	A gift of magic	⎰	12+
	Killing Mr. Griffin		12+
Paula Fox	*The slave dancer*	A 13-year-old boy is kidnapped onto a slave ship and forced to play a fife while the slaves exercise	12+
Bette Greene	*Summer of my German soldier*	A young girl in Arkansas protects a German soldier; love; friendship	12+
Isabelle Holland	*Alan and the animal kingdom*	Death in a family; friendship with animals and an adult	10+
	Of love and death and other journeys	A girl's mother dies and she moves in with a father she does not know	14+
Lee Bennett Hopkins	*Mama*	Family relationships	10+
M. E. Kerr	*Is that you Miss Blue?*	A new girl at a private school; learning how to tolerate differences	12+
Madeleine L'Engle	*A wrinkle in time*	⎫ Exciting fantasy that incorporates science, theology, and music	10+
	A wind in the door	⎬	
	A swiftly tilting planet	⎭	
C. S. Lewis	*The lion, the witch, and the wardrobe*	Fantasy, kingdom of Narnia (Tolkien on a small scale)	10+
Scott O'Dell	*Island of the blue dolphins*	A girl lives alone on a Pacific island	12+
Katherine Paterson	*The great Gilly Hopkins*	An orphaned girl tries to find a stable home	10+

Table 11–1 (*continued*)

Author	Title	Comment	Appropriate age
	Bridge to Terabithia	Coming of age. Learning to live with sorrow.	10+
Robert Newton Peck	*A day no pigs would die*	A boy grows up on a Vermont farm	12+

Source: Compiled by Adolescent Literature Class, University of North Carolina at Asheville, 1980.

storytelling session given for 120 adults by Barbara Freeman and Connie Regan (The Folktellers), two well-known storytellers who work in tandem. They told the story of Maurice Sendak's *Where the wild things are.* Even though the book was written for very young readers, it had great appeal to the adult audience when related orally, using only the storyteller's words as pictures. Listeners have the distinct advantage of being able to enjoy a variety of different stories that they are unlikely to discover or enjoy in any other medium.

The listener becomes an active participant in the story. Often the storyteller actually involves the audience in the tale by asking them to repeat a refrain or make a sound that creates a special effect for the story. At other times, however, the listener is involved through sitting and imagining. The storyteller brings the listener into the story through hand gestures, the creation of pictures through the sound of the voice, and eye contact.

Being able to maintain eye contact is one of the advantages of storytelling over reading aloud. The storyteller in this way involves each individual in the experience whether the group is ten students or an audience of five hundred. As the storyteller's eyes meet the eyes of the listener, the listener becomes a part of the story.

LEARNING TO TELL A STORY IN THE CLASSROOM. Many people are afraid to attempt to tell a story without using the book as a crutch. It is true that telling a story is more difficult than reading orally from a book, but the personal rewards and the benefit gained by the listeners and the teller make it worthwhile. Telling a story well, like reading a book well, involves practice. Caroline Feller Bauer, in her *Handbook for storytellers,* says that in her experience as a teacher of storytelling, "almost everyone who takes the time to learn [a story] can become a competent storyteller" (1977, p. 48).

The key to learning to tell a story competently is taking the time to learn the story. However, the time invested need not be great if the novice storyteller does not worry about creating a large repertoire. As Barbara Freeman and Connie Regan remarked in a storytelling workshop, "If you learn only one story a year, think how many you will know by the time you are eighty."

Learning a story well is not very difficult; it just takes a little time each day.

1. Select a story you would like to learn. Read several stories, wait for several days or a week, and choose the story that keeps coming to mind. As Ruth Sawyer points out in *The way of the storyteller,* be sure that you really love the story you plan to learn. It is probably a good idea to buy the book from which you plan to learn a story so that you can truly make that story your own.

2. Divide the story into units of action. Identify separate sequences of action into which the plot can be divided. (When I am learning a new story, I actually list each bit of action on separate note cards that I use as I learn the story.) Learn these segments of action in order. You do not need to memorize the story, but rather learn the sequence of the story as it moves through the author's plot. (Some stories, however, may need to be completely memorized lest the beauty of the language, the rhythm, or the rhyme be lost.) Practice saying what needs to be said in the first unit of action to move the listener to the next action sequence, and so on.

3. Identify sections of the story that must be memorized. These sections include segments in which the author's words contribute to the mood of the story, are beautiful, rhyme, have rhythm, repeat a refrain, or simply need to be shared just as they are written. Memorize these sections. For the novice storyteller, choosing a story with only a few passages for memorization is probably best.

4. Practice telling the story. Incorporate the memorized sections into the action sequence you have already practiced. Rehearse the story aloud in a place in which you feel comfortable so that you become accustomed to the sound of your own voice. Try to tell the story at least twice a day until you are able to do it without error. If you confuse the sequence or forget the lines you have memorized, stop your practice and come back to it later. Try to avoid becoming frustrated. The experience should be fun. Connie Regan and Barbara Freeman say that "a gift you can give to your listeners is knowing the story so well that you are comfortable telling it." You can't be comfortable telling a story if you are not enjoying the process.

5. Record your progress. After you feel secure telling the story, put it on tape. Don't listen to it immediately because you will be too involved in the process to evaluate the performance. John Warren Stewig (1978, pp. 341–342) suggests that you ask these questions as you listen to the tape: (a) What parts of the story need more practice to achieve greater fluency? (b) What parts of the story need to be changed to make them more effective? (c) Would different words better evoke the mood set by the author? (d) Should I change my pitch, stress, pauses or tempo for greater effectiveness?

Once you have learned the story, you can prepare to tell it to an audience. The first thing to do is to be sure that the location in which the story is to be told is comfortable for you and your listeners. As in oral reading, it is important that the storyteller can see and be seen by the audience. Choose a location away from windows and doors. The best backdrop is a solid wall or curtain. If possible, the entrance should be behind the audience so that they will not be disturbed if someone enters the room. As in reading aloud, placing a sign on the door—"Storytelling in Progress—Do Not Disturb"—is a good idea. Before the storytelling session the storyteller should sit where the audience will sit to test the room. Telling a story outdoors may seem romantic; however, it can be disastrous, particularly for the beginning storyteller. All teachers know what the appearance of a bee can do to the attention of a class. Imagine what will happen if a neighborhood dog decides to join the group.

It is a good idea to establish a symbolic action to show that the storytelling is about to begin. The symbol may be the same one you use for oral reading because you may want to incorporate periods of storytelling into your reading session. The effect on the students when you begin by reading a section from the book and suddenly put it down and begin telling it is dramatic. Some good symbolic openings include the lighting of a candle (perhaps too dramatic in a high school classroom), the pulling forward of a special chair, or the playing of an instrument.

It is important that the storyteller set the mood for the story. "The introduction to a single story or program as a whole often sets the mood of the entire period. A question such as 'How many of you like to laugh, raise your hands?' suggests that the story will be funny, and in effect, you have set the mood that will elicit a humorous response to whatever you tell" (Bauer 1977, p. 35). An introduction to a story also gives the listeners an opportunity to get in tune with your voice. Therefore, your introduction should serve three purposes: setting the mood, getting the audience involved, and helping the listeners get used to listening to you.

When you begin the story you can help gain the attention of the audience by developing a one-to-one relationship through eye contact, by holding out your hand(s) toward the audience and slowly pulling them back in toward your body, and by using your voice to command the listeners' presence.

Props can enhance your story if they are used judiciously. A single prop to represent a single character or refrain that occurs throughout the story can be effective. Props can be good transitional tools to use with younger students. A prop helps build a bridge between a story told without pictures and a story told with pictures. Many students are not used to listening without visual cues; therefore, the props may be necessary. The teacher should be cautioned that if props are used they should be carefully incorporated during the practice sessions. They are as important to the story as the correct action sequence.

The storyteller does not act out the story, but rather tells it. When you tell a story you are yourself, not an actor playing the role of a character in the story.

After the story has been told, be sure to show the listeners the book from which it is taken. This is a particularly good way to encourage students to read the complete book or find other books by the same author or on the same theme. Therefore, it is wise to make available to the students copies of the book from which you are telling the story or other books by the same author or on the same theme. It is very important that you acknowledge the author and, possibly, mention some other books by the same author after you have told the story.

The storytelling program, whether it is one or several stories long, should end

Table 11–2 A Sampling of Young Adult Books That
Have Worked Well in Storytelling Sessions*

Book	Author
Watership down	Richard Adams
The wolves of Willoughby Chase	Joan Aiken
Bugs in your ears	Betty Bates
Freckle juice	Judy Blume
Superfudge	
Tales of a fourth grade nothing	
Blinded by the light	Robin Brancato
Toby, Granny and George	Robbie Branscum
Toby alone	
Toby and Johnny Joe	
Beezus and Ramona	Beverly Cleary
Ramona the pest	
Henry and the clubhouse	
Henry and the paper route	
The dark is rising	Susan Cooper
Charlie and the chocolate factory	Roald Dahl
The cat ate my gymsuit	Paula Danziger
Down a dark hall	Lois Duncan
Killing Mr. Griffin	
Incident at Hawk's Hill	Allan Eckert
Julie of the wolves	Jean Craighead George
The planet of Junior Brown	Virginia Hamilton
Mama	Lee Bennett Hopkins
Moon and Me	Hadley Irwin
We are Mesquakie; we are one	
A wrinkle in time	Madeleine L'Engle
One fat summer	Robert Lipsyte
Ox: The story of a kid at the top	John Ney
The black pearl	Scott O'Dell
Bridge to Terabithia	Katherine Paterson
The great Gilly Hopkins	
The ghost belonged to me	Richard Peck
Soup	Robert Newton Peck
Soup and me	
The resident witch	Marian T. Place
How to eat fried worms	Thomas Rockwell
Words by heart	Ouida Sebestyen
The cay	Theodore Taylor
The loner	Ester Wier

*Owing to their subject matter, not all of the books are appropriate for all ages. However, any attempt to limit any book to a single age group would defeat one of the major delights of storytelling. Putting down the book allows the storyteller to tell a variety of different types of stories to any age group. The teacher is cautioned to know the maturity level of the students before selecting any book for storytelling.
Source: Compiled and tested by the Adolescent Literature Classes of the University of North Carolina, Asheville.

with a symbol linked to the one chosen at the beginning: the blowing out of the candle, the return of the chair, or a final chord on the guitar.

According to Caroline Feller Bauer, several common faults of the beginning storyteller can easily be corrected when identified. She suggests that the storyteller have a friend listen to the story for these faults: speaking too rapidly or too slowly, speaking too softly, speaking with too high a pitch, failing to make eye contact, and using distracting gestures. Once these faults have been identified, the storyteller's practice sessions can be directed toward correcting them.

GIVING A BOOK TALK. An interesting storytelling technique that combines reading aloud and telling stories is the book talk. A book talk is a talk usually based on four or five books that have a common theme or author. This technique is particularly useful in the secondary classroom in which the teacher wants to emphasize a theme or an author and wants to encourage the students to read one or more books with the same theme or author.

In Barbara Soileau's English classroom, for example, the students are investigating the theme "Love and Infatuation: Discovering the Difference." She does a book talk using the books *Gentlehands* (Kerr), *Love is like peanuts* (Bates), *The great Gatsby* (Fitzgerald), *Summer of my German soldier* (Greene), and *Toby and Johnny Joe* (Branscum). Her book talk includes short segments from each of the books. Part of the book talk is read and part of it is told in a storytelling format. After the book talk, the students are told to select the book that is most interesting to them. They are given five minutes to begin reading the book. Then they have the opportunity to exchange the book they originally selected for another book. This process continues until each student has settled on a book he or she is interested in reading.

INVOLVING STUDENTS IN THE STORYTELLING. Students can be involved in the storytelling process by learning how to tell a story or by learning how to give a book talk. Teaching students to tell stories is an excellent motivator for reading and writing.

> ☐ *I'll tell you how I began writing stories. . . . I was the smallest person in my class and I was very clumsy. I couldn't walk down the hall without tripping over my own feet. Consequently, the kids in my class didn't want to play with me at recess time because I was so clumsy I ruined the games; so I sat by myself. Then one day I was very sick and tired of sitting by myself. There was a boy who wasn't playing either, and I said, "Come on; I'll tell you a story." And I began to tell a story that I made up as I went along. Before I was finished with the story, all the rest of the class had come to listen. It made me feel good and I figured, this is the way I'm going to have company every recess.*
> SUE ALEXANDER
> *author of* Small plays for you and a friend / *In Weiss (1979)*

Older students can give their reading a purpose by preparing and telling stories to younger children. In the early stages of learning the storytelling technique, the student is taught to read aloud a passage or an entire book to young children. This is a painless way of practicing oral reading and speaking skills. Having become proficient in reading aloud to an audience, the student is encouraged to read part of the story from the book, put the book down, and tell part of the story without the book. The same techniques the teacher uses to learn a story are taught to the student. Later the student is encouraged to learn an entire story to tell to the children.

It is essential that students have the opportunity to practice their skills. Therefore, it is necessary for the teacher to arrange for students to tell their stories in an elementary school or preschool classroom. It is important that the students know before they select a story the age group with which they will be working.

STUDENTS SHARING BOOKS WITH OTHER STUDENTS. An unfortunate aspect of the traditional book report technique is that the book read is shared only with the teacher. One of the most effective ways to motivate a student to read is to get a peer to do the motivating. Students motivate other students to read a book by sharing it with them in a way that makes the book seem interesting to students of similar interests.

The teacher motivates students to read by sharing books through reading aloud, storytelling, and book talks. How can the teacher encourage students to do the same sharing?

One way is to make sharing a common event in the classroom. Gloria Deaton, an English teacher, conducts a "book-sharing discussion" every Wednesday. On that day the students share what they have been reading. Since her class is designed thematically, most of the books discussed revolve around a common theme. Ms. Deaton believes that literature is exciting to students when they respond to it and become involved in it. She thus deems it essential that the teacher help students choose books that relate to their interests and are on their reading level. If the book does not interest the student, or if it is too hard or too easy to read, the student will have difficulty responding in a meaningful way. Therefore, Ms. Deaton incorporates many young adult books into her curriculum. It is not unusual in her class to find one student reading both a young adult and a classic at the same time. Ms. Deaton claims that reading begets reading, and that the adolescent who reads is likely to read a wide variety of books. If students have been allowed to choose their own books, they are usually willing and able to share them with other students.

The students in Ms. Deaton's class work in small groups based on the common title of the book they have selected. There may be five to seven books being read at any one time. The students are told to begin their small-group discussions with general impressions about the plot and the characters. One of the students in each group acts as a recorder and writes down a few key words in each of the students' responses. After approximately ten minutes of general, superficial responses, the recorder summarizes briefly what each student has said. The group members are instructed to look for disagreement in their responses and examine them for a cumulative change of attitude about the book. For example, does one student's response seem to influence the response of the next student? The students are then asked to elaborate on the initial response they had to the book by defending their opinions based on the book itself. Students with divergent opinions are asked to examine their differing feelings closely. After about fifteen minutes of discussion, Ms. Deaton instructs the group members to restate their opinions about the book, this time in writing. They are told to be careful to cite examples from the book to exemplify each opinion. After the students complete the written exercise, the recorder reads each original opinion as the student examines the essay to determine how his or her opinion has changed. A class discussion about how and why initial reactions to the book changed completes the lesson.

Through this exercise the students have the opportunity to share their reactions to the book. All reactions are valued. However, through the course of the discussion, opinions begin to change, just as initial superficial reactions change in any conversation. This book-sharing exercise not only enables students to react to the book they are reading, but prepares them for looking at the literary attributes of the book by helping them get beyond first impressions. Likewise, it gives members of the class who have not yet read the book a limited understanding of it through the final class discussion. Often the comments made during this discussion motivate other students to read the book being shared.

There are many other ways for students to share the books they are reading. Some are very simple and require little or no student or teacher preparation. One such way makes use of three-by-five-inch file cards and the envelope attached to the inside back cover, which usually holds a checkout card. After finishing a book, the student fills out a blank file card with the date, a brief response to the book, and signature. The card is then placed in the book checkout envelope. This technique encourages students to respond to the book in their own way, to value their responses, and to share them with other students.

Other book-sharing techniques are more formalized and require student preparation. If the student is allowed to select the book-telling technique to share the book he/she has read, the student is more likely to enjoy reading the book, enjoy telling about the book, and motivate other students to read the book.

SHARING BOOKS IN AN INTERDISCIPLINARY SCHOOLWIDE PROGRAM. At Shoreham–Wading River Middle School in Shoreham, New York, three teachers have developed a program that involves the entire school. The project, "Booktalks: An Innovative Approach to Reading," is a regular part of the English curriculum for all eighth-grade students. A Booktalk, as defined by project directors Diane Burkhardt, Ross Burkhardt, and Esther Fusco, is "a discussion of a book read by a group of up to ten students under the direction of a Booktalk discussion leader." The objectives of the book talks are to "(a) encourage independent reading, (b) stimulate interest in reading, (c) provide a selection of book titles that will appeal to students of diverse interests and reading abilities, and

Table 11–3 Sixty Ways to Tell about Books

1. Hold a panel discussion among several students who have read the same book or a group of similar ones.
2. Organize a pro-and-con panel made up of some students who liked a book and some who did not. Let one person represent the author. Try to have an impartial chairman.
3. Dramatize an incident or an important character. The student may relate an incident in the first person.
4. Prepare and deliver radio announcements to advertise books.
5. Have individual conferences in which students talk about favorite books with the teacher.
6. Appoint a committee of pupils who are avid readers to conduct peer discussions and seminars about books.
7. Hold a mock trial permitting the defendant to tell the story of a book of his choosing. The class renders a decision on its merits.
8. Reproduce illustrators' interpretations of important scenes for the whole class to enjoy.
9. Give brief oral talks, limited to five minutes each.
10. Get the plot down to a succinct nugget. It takes practice to do this in one paragraph.
11. Conduct dialogues between several students to reveal the style and story of the book.
12. Design book jackets that express the kind of book being illustrated as well as the story.
13. Write a précis—but don't do this too often. It can be dry as dust.
14. Compose a telegram, trying to give the essence of a book in fifteen words. Then expand it into a hundred-word "overnight telegram."
15. Compose a publisher's "blurb" to sell the book.
16. Read orally an interesting part, stopping at a strategic point.
17. Give a sales talk, pretending your audience is composed of clerks in a bookstore and you want them to promote a new book.
18. Have questions from the audience, or let three pupils be challengers.
19. Make comparisons with the movie and television versions of the same book.
20. Create a poster advertising the book and maybe others by the same author.
21. Build a miniature stage setting for part of the story.
22. Design costumes for characters, in miniature or life size.
23. Make a rebus of a short story and try it on your friends.
24. Write a book review for a newspaper or magazine, and really send it in for possible publication.
25. Write a movie script to sell to Hollywood.
26. For a how-to book, bring something you made according to the directions.
27. Prepare a travel lecture based on a travel book.
28. Write an original poem after studying a book of poetry for both style and choice of subjects.
29. After reading a book of poems, learn a verse to recite to the class, or read one aloud.
30. Tell a friend why you did or did not like a book.
31. Explain how the book could be used in social studies or science.
32. Make sketches of some of the action sequences.
33. Describe an interesting character, trying to make him or her come alive to your audience.
34. Write or tell a different ending to the story.

Table 11–3 (*continued*)

35. Write or tell the most humorous, most exciting, or the most interesting incident in the book, or the part you liked best.
36. Select a descriptive passage and read it aloud to the class.
37. List interesting new words and expressions to add to your vocabulary.
38. Describe a scene to orient your audience; then show it in pantomime.
39. Write a letter recommending the book to a friend.
40. Deliver an oral synopsis of the story, but don't give away the climax.
41. Make a scrapbook suggested by information in the book.
42. Construct puppets and present a show of an interesting part of the story.
43. Make a map that shows information gathered from a geographical book.
44. Have a friend who has read the story try to stump you with questions.
45. Make a list of facts you learned from reading a factual story.
46. Write questions you think everyone should be able to answer after reading the book; then try them on other readers.
47. Dress as one of the characters and act out the part you play.
48. Broadcast a book review on your school public address system.
49. Write a note to the school librarian explaining why the library ought to recommend the book to other students.
50. Review the book you read for another class.
51. Research the author's career and tell about his or her other books.
52. Make a clay, soap, or wood model to illustrate a phase of the story.
53. Construct a diorama or table exhibit to illustrate a phase of the story.
54. Make a bulletin-board exhibit.
55. Prepare a chalk talk or use an overhead projector.
56. Paint or draw an illustration of the story.
57. Make a mural to illustrate the book; get others who have read it to help.
58. Rewrite an incident in the book, simplifying vocabulary for a lower grade.
59. For a science book, plan a demonstration of what you learned.
60. For a historical book, make a time line, listing events in sequence.

Source: Based on a list of book-telling techniques I received at a conference around 1972. No name appeared on the original handout, so I cannot credit the originator. Though I have seen many similar lists since 1972, I have found this one to be the most helpful. Reports of books range from the casual to the formal, but their primary use should not be to check up on students or to give them a mark. Instead, the goal is to get them to talk about books as a natural part of their day-to-day conversation.

(d) provide an opportunity for students to discuss books on several different levels."

During the school year each eighth-grader participates in at least nine book talks, conducted on nine Booktalk Days scattered throughout the school year. Discussion leaders for the book talks include all eighth-grade teachers, the principal and assistant principal, the librarian, art teachers, teaching assistants, and teaching aides—"in short, all staff members are encouraged to lead a Booktalk."

On Booktalk Registration Day, approximately three and one half weeks prior to each Booktalk Day, the students select a book (they may participate in two talks by selecting two titles) from a list of twenty-five or thirty titles. Each student indicates five selections on the registration form in order of preference. Every

■ ■ Book-Talk Selection Form

Name _____

English Teacher _____

The first eighth-grade Booktalk is scheduled for Wednesday, October 1. Your Booktalk will be either period 2 or period 4. You will attend a large-group program during the period when you do not have a Booktalk. If you wish to sign up for two Booktalks, please do! (If you do two Booktalks, you will not be able to see the large-group program.)

The large-group program will be "The Beatles—1956-70."

Do you want to have two Booktalks? (Circle your answer.) YES NO

My five choices in order of preference are:

1. _____ 2. _____ 3. _____ 4. _____ 5. _____
(Fill in the book's code number from the list below. If you have more than one first choice please indicate that by putting more than one code number in space #1.)

SELECTIONS FOR OCTOBER 1 BOOKTALK. Please look at the books carefully before making your selections.

   1. THE ANDROMEDA STRAIN
   3. THE OUTSIDERS
   4. THAT WAS THEN, THIS IS NOW
   5. RUMBLE FISH
   6. BAD FALL
  11. OF MICE AND MEN
  14. WHEN MICHAEL CALLS
  19. THE EFFECT OF GAMMA RAYS ON MAN-IN-THE-MOON MARIGOLDS
  27. THE PIGMAN
  37. THE CHOCOLATE WAR
  38. CHILDHOOD'S END
  43. DINKY HOCKER SHOOTS SMACK!
  46. THE SUMMER OF MY GERMAN SOLDIER
  48. ERIC
  66. RENDEZVOUS WITH RAMA
  72. A SPECIAL KIND OF COURAGE
  74. SUMMER OF FEAR
  78. ON COURAGE
  85. I KNOW WHAT YOU DID LAST SUMMER

```
 86.  THE YEAR OF THE JEEP
 97.  THE LONG BLACK COAT
 98.  INTO THE ROAD
100.  ONE FAT SUMMER
103.  NO PLACE TO RUN
104.  HANGIN' OUT WITH CICI
108.  A SEPARATE PEACE
109.  KILLING MR. GRIFFIN
123.  A FIVE-COLOR BUICK AND A BLUE-EYED CAT
113.  THE WAR ON VILLA STREET
125.  COLLISION COURSE
```

effort is made to give students their first choices. However, no more than ten students may participate in each Booktalk group.

The Booktalks take place during two class periods on Booktalk Day. Approximately twelve Booktalks meet during each period. Students who do not have a Booktalk scheduled during that period attend a large-group program.

Booktalk leaders evaluate the students by using the BookTalk Evaluation Form. (See page 388.) Similarly, Booktalk leaders are given a list of sample general questions to help them plan their talks. For example: Does the book answer any questions or solve any problems you have faced? Which ones? How? At what point in the book does a very slight incident alter an entire life? A suggested format also is given to the leaders. The format for the Booktalk includes an objective quiz, word associations, interpretive questions, evaluative questions, and factual questions. Each Booktalk leader gives a member of the English staff a copy of the format used in the Booktalk, including the questions asked and handouts provided to the students.

The success of this program is the result of several important factors. All of the students are involved. All staff members are encouraged to participate. Students are allowed to select books from a limited list of titles that cover a wide range of interests and reading levels; staff members are allowed to select the books (as much as possible) that they will discuss. No more than ten students participate in a single Booktalk. The Booktalk format and questions are left up to the leader; however, significant guidance is given. The leaders evaluate the participants by means of a common evaluation form. Students who are not involved in a Booktalk can participate in a motivational large-group program.[12]

☐ *I myself can't separate reading, writing, and speaking.*
PEGGY BROGAN
author of The Sounds Books *with Bill Martin / at a Young Authors' Project Workshop /*
The University of North Carolina at Asheville / March 1981

---

[12]For additional information see: Esther Fusco, *Everybody reads: A step-by-step guide to establishing a book discussion group program in your school,* Dell, 1983.

■ ■ Book-Talk Evaluation Form

Name _____

Book # _____ Returned _____ Book Title _____

Booktalk Leader _____ English Teacher _____

Booktalk Checklist	Yes	No	In Part	Objective Quiz
Completed book				1.
Understood book				2.
Offered insights				3.
Asked questions				4.
Actively participated				5.
Participated by listening				6.
Distracted others				7.
				8.
				9.
				10.

Comment _____

_____

_____

_____

_____

Grade (Please circle one.)

A   B   C   N

Note: Please return evaluation forms to the English teacher as
soon as possible after your Booktalk.

Anthological Aside in Chapter 11

Speare, E. G. *The witch of Blackbird Pond.* Houghton Mifflin, 1958. Dell, 1975.

Titles Mentioned in Chapter 11

Adams, R. *Watership down.* Macmillan, 1972. Avon, 1975.
Aiken, J. *The wolves of Willoughby Chase.* Doubleday, 1962. Dell, 1968.
Alexander, S. *Small plays for you and a friend.* Houghton Mifflin, 1973.
Angell, J. *Ronnie and Rosey.* Bradbury, 1977. Dell, 1979.
———. *In summertime it's Tuffy.* Bradbury, 1977. Dell, 1979.
Angelou, M. *I know why the caged bird sings.* Random House, 1969. Bantam, 1971.
Annixter, P. *Swiftwater.* A. A. Wyn, 1950. Paperback Library, 1965.
Armstrong, W. *Sounder.* Harper & Row, 1969, 1972.
Bates, B. *Bugs in your ears.* Holiday, 1977. Pocket Books, 1979.
———. *Love is like peanuts.* Holiday, 1980. Pocket Books, 1981.
Blume, J. *Freckle juice.* Four Winds Press, 1971. Dell, 1979.
———. *Superfudge.* Dutton, 1980. Dell, 1981.
———. *Tales of a fourth grade nothing.* Dutton, 1972. Dell, 1979.
Bonham, F. *Cool cat.* Dutton, 1971. Dell, 1972.
Brancato, R. *Blinded by the light.* Knopf, 1978. Bantam, 1979.
———. *Winning.* Knopf, 1977. Bantam, 1979.
Branscum, R. *Toby alone.* Doubleday, 1979. Avon, 1980.
———. *Toby, Granny and George.* Doubleday, 1976. Avon, 1977.
———. *Toby and Johnny Joe.* Doubleday, 1979. Avon, 1981.
Bridgers, S. E. *All together now.* Knopf, 1979. Bantam, 1980.
———. *Home before dark.* Knopf, 1976. Bantam, 1977.
Britton, V. *Testament of youth* (1935). Seaview, 1980.
Bryan, C. D. B. *Friendly fire.* Putnam, 1976. Bantam, 1977.
Byars, B. *The night swimmers.* Delacorte, 1980. Dell, 1981.
Childress, A. *A hero ain't nothin' but a sandwich.* Coward, McCann & Geoghegan, 1973. Avon, 1974.
Clapp, P. *Constance: A story of early Plymouth.* Lothrop, Lee & Shepard, 1968. Dell, 1975.
Cleary, B. *Beezus and Ramona.* Morrow, 1955. Dell, 1980.
———. *Ramona the pest.* Morrow, 1968. Scholastic, 1968.
———. *Henry and the clubhouse.* Morrow, 1962. Dell, 1979.
———. *Henry and the paper route.* Morrow, 1957. Dell, 1980.
Cleaver, V., and B. Cleaver. *Where the lilies bloom.* Lippincott, 1969. New American Library, 1964.
Cooper, S. *The dark is rising.* Atheneum, 1973.
Cormier, R. *After the first death.* Pantheon, 1979. Avon, 1980.
———. *The chocolate war.* Pantheon, 1974. Dell, 1975.
———. *I am the cheese.* Pantheon, 1977. Dell, 1978.
Dahl, R. *Charlie and the chocolate factory.* Knopf, 1964. Bantam, 1979.
Danziger, P. *Can you sue your parents for malpractice?* Delacorte, 1979. Dell, 1980.
———. *The cat ate my gymsuit.* Delacorte, 1974. Dell, 1979.

————. *The pistachio prescription*. Delacorte, 1978. Dell, 1978.

Donovan, J. *I'll get there. It better be worth the trip*. Harper & Row, 1969. Dell, 1973.

Duncan, L. *A gift of magic*. Little, Brown, 1971. Pocket Books, 1972.

————. *Down a dark hall*. Little, Brown, 1974. New American Library, 1975.

————. *Killing Mr. Griffin*. Little, Brown, 1978. Dell, 1979.

Eareckson, J., and J. Musser. *Joni*. Zondervan, 1976. Bantam, 1978.

Eckert, A. *Incident at Hawk's Hill*. Little, Brown, 1971. Dell, 1978.

Fitzgerald, F. S. *The great Gatsby* (1925). Scribner's, 1970.

Fox, P. *The slave dancer*. Bradbury, 1973. Dell, 1975.

Gaines, E. J. *The autobiography of Miss Jane Pittman*. Dial, 1971. Bantam, 1972.

George, J. C. *Julie of the wolves*. Harper & Row, 1972.

Greene, B. *Summer of my German soldier*. Dial, 1973. Bantam, 1974.

Guest, J. *Ordinary people*. Viking, 1976. Ballantine, 1980.

Gunther, J. *Death be not proud* (1949). Modern Library, 1953. Pyramid, 1979.

Haley, A. *Roots*. Doubleday, 1976. Dell, 1977.

Hall, L. *Gently touch the milkweed*. Follett, 1970. Avon, 1970.

Hamilton, V. *The planet of Junior Brown*. Macmillan, 1971. Dell, 1978.

Hartley, A. B. *Unexploded bomb* (1958). Norton, 1959.

Herriott, J. *All creatures great and small*. St. Martin's, 1972. Bantam, 1975.

————. *All things bright and beautiful*. St. Martin's, 1974. Bantam, 1975.

Hinton, S. E. *The outsiders*. Viking, 1967. Dell, 1982.

————. *Rumble fish*. Delacorte, 1975. Dell, 1975.

————. *Tex*. Delacorte, 1979. Dell, 1982.

————. *That was then, this is now*. Viking, 1971. Dell, 1980.

Holland, I. *Alan and the animal kingdom*. Lippincott, 1977. Dell, 1979.

————. *Of love and death and other journeys*. Lippincott, 1975. Dell, 1977.

Hopkins, L. B., and S. Rosch, eds. *I really want to feel good about myself*. Nelson, 1974.

————. *Mama*. Knopf, 1977. Dell, 1978.

Hunter, K. *The Soul Brothers and Sister Lou*. Scribner's, 1968. Avon, 1970.

Irwin, H. *Moon & me*. Atheneum, 1981.

————. *We are Mesquakie; we are one*. Feminist Press, 1980.

Kerr, M. E. *Gentlehands*. Harper & Row, 1978.

————. *Is that you, Miss Blue?* Harper & Row, 1975. Dell, 1976.

Klein, N. *Sunshine*. Avon, 1974.

Lash, J. P. *Eleanor and Franklin*. Norton, 1971. New American Library, 1973.

L'Engle, M. *A swiftly tilting planet*. Farrar, Straus & Giroux, 1978. Dell, 1979.

————. *A wind in the door*. Farrar, Straus & Giroux, 1973. Dell, 1981.

————. *A wrinkle in time*. Farrar, Straus & Giroux, 1962. Dell, 1976.

Lewis, C. S. *The lion, the witch, and the wardrobe*. Macmillan, 1950. Collier, 1976.

Lipsyte, R. *The contender*. Harper & Row, 1967. Bantam, 1979.

————. *One fat summer*. Harper & Row, 1977. Bantam, 1978.

McCracken, M. *A circle of children*. Lippincott, 1973. New American Library, 1975.

Mathis, S. B. *Teacup full of roses*. Viking, 1972. Avon, 1972.

Ney, J. *Ox: The story of a kid at the top*. Little, Brown, 1970. Bantam, 1971.

O'Dell, S. *The black pearl*. Dell, 1977.

————. *Island of the blue dolphins*. Houghton Mifflin, 1960. Dell, 1975.

Paterson, K. *Bridge to Terabithia*. Crowell, 1977. Avon, 1979.

————. *The great Gilly Hopkins*. Crowell, 1978. Avon, 1979.

Peck, R. *Ghosts I have been.* Viking, 1977. Dell, 1979.
————. *The ghost belonged to me.* Viking, 1975. Avon, 1976.
Peck, R. N. *Soup.* Knopf, 1974. Dell, 1979.
————. *Soup and me.* Knopf, 1975. Dell, 1979.
————. *A day no pigs would die.* Knopf, 1972. Dell, 1978.
Petry, A. *Harriett Tubman, conductor on the underground railroad.* Crowell, 1955. Archway, 1971.
Place, M. T. *The resident witch.* Washburn, 1970. Avon, 1973.
Raskin, E. *The Westing game.* Dutton, 1978. Avon, 1980.
Rhue, M. *The wave.* Dell, 1981.
Rockwell, T. *How to eat fried worms.* Franklin Watts, 1973. Dell, 1980.
Rockwood, J. *Long Man's song.* Holt, Rinehart & Winston, 1975. Dell, 1978.
————. *To spoil the sun.* Holt, Rinehart & Winston, 1976. Dell, 1979.
Scoppetone, S. *The late great me.* Putnam, 1976. Bantam, 1977.
Sebestyen, O. *Words by heart.* Little Brown, 1979. Bantam, 1981.
Sendak, M. *Where the wild things are.* Harper & Row, 1963.
Speare, E. G. *The witch of Blackbird Pond.* Houghton Mifflin, 1958. Dell, 1975.
Taylor, T. *The cay.* Doubleday, 1969. Avon, 1970.
Wier, E. *The loner.* McKay, 1963. Scholastic, 1973.
Zindel, P. *The pigman.* Harper & Row, 1968. Bantam, 1978.
————. *The undertaker's gone bananas,* Harper & Row, 1978. Bantam, 1979.

Suggested Readings

Bauer, C. F. *Handbook for storytellers.* American Library Association, 1977, 1979.
Busch, J. S. Television's effect on reading: A case study. *Phi Delta Kappan,* June 1978, pp. 668–71.
Blostein, F. *Invitations, celebrations. A handbook of ideas for promoting reading in junior and senior high schools.* Ontario Library Association, 1980.
Commire, A. ed. *Something about the author.* 33 vols. Gale Research Co. 1971–1983.
Cullinan, B., and M. J. Weiss, eds. *Books I read when I was young.* Avon, 1980.
Dale, E. *Audiovisual methods in teaching.* 3rd ed. Holt, Rinehart & Winston, 1969.
Danziger, P. I followed the sweet potato. *Voice of Youth Advocates,* June 1979, pp. 7–8.
de Montreville, D., and D. Hill, eds. *Third book of junior authors.* H. W. Wilson, 1972.
Eyerly, J. Writing for today's youth. *ALAN Review,* Winter 1981, pp. 1–3.
Flynn, E. W., and J. L. LaFaso. *Designs in affective education.* Paulist Press, 1974.
Fraim, E. C. Book reports—tools for thinking. *Journal of Reading,* November 1973, pp. 122–24.
Fuller, M. *More junior authors.* H. W. Wilson, 1969.
Fusco, E. Authors' week in a middle school. *Journal of Reading,* May 1981, pp. 676–79.
————. *Everybody reads: A step-by-step guide to establishing a book discussion group program in your school.* Dell, 1983.
Giermak, E. A. Reading to high school students: A painless method of improving language skills. *English Journal,* September 1980, pp. 62–63.
Hamilton, H. T.V. tie-ins as a bridge to books. *Language arts,* February 1976, pp. 129–30.

Hopkins, L. B. *Books are by people.* Scholastic/Citation, 1969.

————. *More books by more people.* Scholastic/Citation, 1974.

Kunitz, S. J., and H. Haycraft. *The junior book of authors.* H. W. Wilson, 1951.

Locher, F. C. *Contemporary authors: A bio-bibliographical guide to current authors and their works.* Gale Research Co., 1962. Semiannual since 1964.

Miles, B., et al. When writers visit schools: A symposium. *Children's literature in education,* Autumn 1980, pp. 133–46.

Parker, M. A visit from a poet. *Language Arts,* April 1981.

Parker, M., and J. Hickman. Teacher feature: An author is coming to school! *The WEB: Wonderfully exciting books,* Spring 1981, pp. 24–26.

Paterson, K. *Gates of excellence: On reading and writing books for children.* Nelson, 1981.

Rockwood, J. Can novelists portray other cultures faithfully? *The Advocate,* Fall 1982, pp. 1–5.

Sawyer, R. *The way of the storyteller.* Penguin, 1962, 1976.

Scales, P. *Communicate through literature: Introducing parents to books their teens are reading and enjoying.* Putnam, 1984.

Shachter, J. Learning from authors in person and in mixed media. *Gifted Child Quarterly,* Spring 1980, pp. 68–71.

Singer, D. G. Television "tie-ins" in the school library. *School Library Journal,* September 1979, pp. 51–52.

Stewig, J. W. *Storyteller: Endangered species.* Language Arts, March 1978, pp. 338–45.

Trelease, J. *The read-aloud handbook.* Penguin, 1979, 1982.

Weiss, M. J., ed. *From writers to students: The pleasures and pains of writing.* International Reading Association, 1979.

Nonprint Sources

I couldn't put it down: Hooked on reading. Sound-slide program. The Center for the Humanities, 2 Holland Ave., White Plains, NY 10603.

Meet the authors. Audiocassettes. Imperial International Learning Corp., Kankakee, Ill. 609012.

Meet the Newbery author. Filmstrip and audiocassette. Miller-Brody, Inc. 342 Madison Ave., New York, NY 10017.

The poetry of rock: A reflection of human values. Sound-slide program. The Center for the Humanities.

Profiles in literature. Video cassettes. Temple University, Ritter 443, Philadelphia, PA 19122.

The wave. Film that became the basis for Rhue's book. Available from T.A.T. Communications, Hollywood, Calif. 90028.

Young adult novels on film, filmstrips, records, and cassettes. Weston Woods, CT 06883.

Young adult novels on filmstrips, records, and cassettes. Guidance Associates, Communications Park, Box 3000, Mount Kisco, NY 10549.

Young adult novels on records. Caedmon, 1995 Broadway, New York, NY 10023.

Young adult novels on video cassettes and film. Learning Corporation of America, 1350 Ave. of the Americas, New York, NY 10019.

Part Four
Reviewing and Selecting Young Adult Books for Classroom Use

BEVERLY PARDEE

# 12 Selecting and Obtaining Appropriate Young Adult Books for the Classroom

"Best Book" Lists

Every year several organizations list what they consider to be the best books for young adults. The categories vary from books of great literary merit, to books that are likely to be popular with the young adult reader, to books of political or social value (as defined by the organization compiling the list). Teachers can use these lists as one tool to aid in the selection of young adult books for the classroom. It is important that teachers be aware of the criteria used to compile the "best book" lists so that they can suggest the books to the appropriate readers. Just because a book appears on a "best book" list does not mean that it will be enjoyed by all young adults, or that it has great value as a piece of young adult literature.

Many "best book" lists use selection criteria established by adults. Each year the Young Adult Services Division of the American Library Association publishes "Best books for young adults." It presents books that are published during the previous year "which are recommended for reading by young adults." The selections are made by a committee of adults, mostly librarians, called the Best Books for Young Adults Committee. The committee selects books that meet the following standards: "*Fiction* must have believable characters and dialogue and plausible plot development; *nonfiction* must have a readable text and an appealing format." To receive the list of approximately fifty books, teachers should write to Young Adult Services Division, American Library Association, 50 East Huron St., Chicago, IL 60611.

The New York Public Library compiles "Books for the teenage." The list, which is revised annually, is on subjects of special "interest and appeal to teenagers." The Committee on Books for Young Adults of the New York Public Library chooses books that are "clear, vivid, appealing, and imaginative." This list, which is grouped thematically, is available late in February from the New York Public Library, Office of Branch Libraries, 455 5th Ave., New York, NY 10016.

Several publications regularly compile "best book" lists. The *New York Times Book Review,* published each Sunday, has a section on books for children and young adults. The most interesting issues for teachers of young adults appear in the spring (usually April) and fall (usually late November or early December), when the review is devoted almost exclusively to children's books. The fall issue usually includes a roundup of the "best books" of the year.

The *School Library Journal* is a comprehensive review journal for both recommended and nonrecommended books. The highly recommended books are starred in each issue, and the reviewers provide teachers with information about books that they consider to be exceptionally good. Titles of interest to young adults appear in the children's listings by grade levels (fifth grade up, sixth grade to eighth grade, ninth grade to twelfth grade), if they come from the juvenile division of publishing houses. If, however, they come from the adult division, they are listed in a special young adult category.

Some "best book" lists are based on judgments made by young adults and children. Each year the Books for Young Adults poll is conducted under the direction of Dr. G. Robert Carlsen at the University of Iowa. The poll contains reading choices of young adults between the ages of sixteen and nineteen. Approximately 300 new books are presented to individualized reading classes near the university. The research team meets individually with participating readers to explore and record their reactions to the books. The most popular books appear on the annual list. At the end of the listing Carlsen suggests several titles that are particularly appropriate for classroom study. The list, containing approximately thirty fiction and nonfiction titles, usually appears in the January issue of the *English Journal*. The list can be obtained by sending a stamped, self-addressed envelope and 10¢ per copy to Books for Young Adults, N231 Lindquist Center, University of Iowa, Iowa City, IA 52242.

☐ *I believe that children are better judges of what constitutes a "good" book than adults. Children care nothing about best seller lists, what book has won an award and which one has not. Children know what they like and they read it—not once, but a half dozen times or more.*
JEANNETTE H. EYERLY

author of Good-bye to Budapest / in The ALAN Review / Winter 1981

A similar list for younger readers, "Children's choices," is available free of charge from the Children's Book Council. Many of the books on this list are appropriate for middle school and junior high school readers. This annotated list is prepared under the auspices of the International Reading Association–Children's Book Council Joint Committee. Books for the current year are read by ten thousand children annually and their favorites make the list. The list usually appears in the October issue of *The Reading Teacher,* published by the International Reading Association. To receive a copy of the current list, send a 6½ × 9 stamped, self-addressed envelope with first-class postage for two ounces to Children's Choices, Children's Book Council, 67 Irving Place, New York, NY 10003.

Award Books

THE NEWBERY MEDAL. The most prestigious and best-known award for a non-picture book in literature for young readers is the John Newbery Medal. First awarded in 1922, the medal is given annually to the author of the book that makes "the most distinguished contribution to American literature for children." It is presented by the Association for Library Service to Children, a division of the American Library Association. The award, named for an editor and author of children's books in mid-eighteenth-century England, is given to encourage original and creative work in literature for children. The criteria for the selection of the medal book are the author's "interpretations of the theme or concept; presentation of information including accuracy, clarity and organization; development of plot; delineation of characters; delineation of setting; appropriateness of style." In addition to the medal book, honor books are designated each year.

The selection of the book, by a committee of librarians, is not without controversy. Teachers who use Newbery Medal and Honor books in their classroom should be aware of the criticism before suggesting Newbery books to individual readers. The major criticism stems from the readability of the books and the books' interest to young people. Many critics of the award feel that the books selected should be ones that are likely to be popular with children. Often the Newbery Medal and Honor books are not best sellers. Critics point out that at times the books have underlying messages that are difficult for young readers to understand.

A teacher's comment about Newbery Medal winner *Jacob have I loved:*

> ☐ *A lot of the relationships in this book will go right over a kid's head. Things like the feeling between Louise's parents after they've been away together alone, for the first time in years, or even the title. One of the sixth graders who was reading the book asked me what it meant—*Jacob Have

I Loved—*so I explained the Bible story about Jacob and Esau. But she wasn't impressed with the symbolism at all.*
From THE WEB: Wonderfully exciting books / *Ohio State University College of Education* / *Spring 1981*[1]

Similarly, critics say, some of the books' subjects have no appeal to the average young reader. The award does not aim to promote acceptance of the books by the general public, but rather proclaims the literary quality of the work. The Association for Library Service to Children believes that the award is for originality and superiority, in contrast to popular appeal, which might mean imitativeness and mediocrity.

☐ *The 1940's, a Chesapeake Bay island, and its people come alive in Paterson's powerful first-person narrative* Jacob Have I Loved. *With wry humor, Sara Louise recalls her turbulent adolescence on Rass Island and her intense jealousy of her twin sister. Strength of characterization and memorable external and internal action mark this superbly-crafted novel about a quest for self-knowledge.*
From the American Library Association Public Information Office news release of February 3, 1981, announcing the 1981 Newbery and Caldecott awards[2]

However, the ease with which a particular student will read the book and the student's interest in the subject of the book must be considered by the teacher when recommending Newbery Award books. A current list of Newbery Medal books is available from the Association for Library Service to Children, American Library Association, 50 East Huron St., Chicago, IL 60611.

JANE ADDAMS CHILDREN'S BOOK AWARD. The Jane Addams Award is given annually by the Jane Addams Peace Association and the Women's International League for Peace and Freedom to honor the book that most effectively promotes peace, social justice, and world community. Authors of adolescent literature are frequent recipients of this award. In 1977, for example, Milton Meltzer won the award for his nonfiction work for young adults *Never to forget: The Jews of the Holocaust.*

THE ALAN AWARD. The ALAN Award is given annually by the Assembly on Adolescent Literature of the National Council of Teachers of English. The award honors authors, publishers, and/or teacher-scholars who have made significant contributions to the world of adolescent literature. Award recipients include author Robert Cormier and teacher-scholars Dwight Burton, Ken Donelson, and M. Jerry Weiss.

[1]Reprinted by permission.
[2]Reprinted by permission.

HANS CHRISTIAN ANDERSEN MEDAL. The Hans Christian Andersen International Medal is awarded every two years by the International Board on Books for Young People to a living author and a living artist for an outstanding body of work that has made a contribution to literature for young people. Several authors of young adult books, including Scott O'Dell, have won the award.

MILDRED L. BATCHELDER AWARD. The Batchelder Award is given annually to a publisher of children's books for a single book considered to be most outstanding of those originally published in a foreign language. It is given by the Association for Library Service for Children of the American Library Association. Often, this award goes to a publisher of a young adult book. In 1972, for instance, it was presented to Holt, Rinehart and Winston for the publication of Hans Richter's *Friedrich*.

BOSTON GLOBE–HORN BOOK AWARD. Awards for the best fiction and nonfiction books for children are given annually by the *Boston Globe* and *Horn Book* magazine. Announcement of the award and the acceptance speeches of the recipients appear annually in the *Horn Book*. A recent fiction award recipient is Andrew Davies's *Conrad's war,* about a boy's fascination with war. *M. C. Higgins the great* by Virginia Hamilton is another past winner.

LEWIS CARROLL SHELF AWARD. The award named for the author of *Alice in Wonderland* has been given by the University of Wisconsin School of Education since 1958. Winners include Joan Aiken for *The wolves of Willoughby Chase* and Norma Fox Mazer for *Saturday, the twelfth of October.* The purpose of the award is to recognize annually "those books worthy enough to sit on the shelf with *Alice in Wonderland*." A committee of five, representing librarians, teachers, parents, and writers, reviews the books submitted by publishers. They must agree unanimously on the winner.

CHILDREN'S BOOK AWARD. The International Reading Association annually presents an award to an author of a first or second book of fiction or nonfiction. The book, which "shows unusual promise," often falls within the young adult classification. In 1975, for example, T. Degens won the award for *Transport T-41-R.*

HUGO AND NEBULA AWARDS. The Hugo Award was established in 1953, and the winners are selected by participants to the annual World Science Fiction Convention. Because the awards, given for the best novel, short story, magazine, motion picture, fan letter, and dramatic presentation, are selected at a convention, they tend to emphasize popularity and the tastes of the audience. Though young adult writing is not specifically honored, the popular nature of the winning book often makes it appealing to teenagers. Young adult authors such as Ursula LeGuin have been honored by the convention.

Ursula LeGuin has also won the Nebula Award of the Science Fiction Writers of America. The awards, given for best novella, short story, and novel, consider style, characterization, plot structure, and imaginative style. The novella award is often presented to an author of young adult fiction.

THE AMERICAN BOOK AWARD FOR CHILDREN'S BOOKS. In 1979 the National Book Award became the American Book Award. Presented annually by the Association of American Publishers, the award recognizes the "best" children's books written, translated, or designed by U.S. citizens and published during the previous year. The award is designed not only to recognize literary merit, but to increase the public's awareness of books. In recent years it has been given to Betsy Byars for *The night swimmers,* Beverly Cleary for *Ramona and her mother,* Walter Wangerin for *The book of the dun cow,* and Madeleine L'Engle for *A swiftly tilting planet.*

EDGAR ALLAN POE AWARD. The Edgar Award, established in 1961, is given each spring by the Mystery Writers of America in several categories, including the best juvenile mystery published in the previous year, if one is considered worthy. Young adult authors such as Jay Bennett *(The long black coat)* and Virginia Hamilton *(The house of Des Drear)* have won the award.

LAURA INGALLS WILDER AWARD. The Wilder Award is given by the Association for Library Service to Children of the American Library Association. It is given "in recognition of an author or illustrator whose books, published in the U.S., have made, over a period of years, a substantial and lasting contribution to literature for children." Though most award recipients have been authors of books for young children, some, like Beverly Cleary, write books of interest to preteens and young teens.

CARNEGIE MEDAL. The Carnegie Medal has been awarded annually since 1936 to an outstanding book for children written in English and published initially in the United Kingdom during the preceding year. The award may be given in a variety of categories, including fiction and information books. The selection criteria for a work of fiction are plot, style, and characterization. Criteria for information books are accuracy, method of presentation, style, and format. The medal has been awarded to authors such as Edward Blishen and Leon Garfield for *The god beneath the sea* and Alan Garner for *The owl service.*

OBTAINING INFORMATION ABOUT AWARD BOOKS. In addition to the awards discussed above, many others are given for books appropriate to young adult audiences and the authors who write them. Teachers can gain current information about these award books by reading the "Hunt breakfast" column in each issue of the *Horn Book.* This column lists many of the awards given in the previous two months, discusses the criteria used, and briefly examines the books and authors. Another excellent source for comprehensive but less up-to-date information about award books is *Children's books: Awards and prizes,* published annually by the Children's Book Council. Many libraries will have a copy of Dolores Blythe Jones' *Children's literature awards and winners.*

Book Reviews

Book reviews, like "best book" lists, use a variety of criteria for evaluation. Teachers should be aware of the criteria used by the reviewing source before recommending particular books to individual students based on the reviews. Some reviewing sources pride themselves on strict codes of literary merit. Others favorably review books that they believe will be popular with the intended audience. Still other sources review books based on the presentation of a particular social issue or concern.

PRIMARY REVIEW SOURCES. There are numerous publications whose primary function is to review books. One of the most up-to-date review sources is the *Booklist,* published twice monthly from September through May and once in August by the American Library Association. The reviews range in size from brief annotations to long essays. A regular feature of the *Booklist* is "Books for young adults." Other young adult books appear in the children's and adult sections and are labeled YA. The books are reviewed for both high literary quality, in which case they are starred, and popularity. Books of high interest potential to poor readers are reviewed in a special section. The ALA's "Best books for young adults" listing appears in an early spring issue.

Kirkus Reviews devotes a complete section of each issue to young adult books. The reviews are thorough, usually averaging around 200 words, and up to date.

The *Bulletin of the Center for Children's Books* appears monthly except in August. Each issue reviews about sixty books for children and young adults. Edited by Zena Sutherland, a well-known authority on children's literature, the reviews are consistent, and recommended titles are likely to be appropriate for classroom use. Also included on the back cover of the bulletin are books, articles, and bibliographies of interest to teachers, librarians, and parents.

McNaughton Young Adult Reviews examine about thirty titles each issue. This monthly review sheet is free once you are on the mailing list. The reviews include descriptive paragraphs, intended audience, criticism, and feedback from young readers.

The *Horn Book* magazine, a bimonthly publication, is devoted to the literary criticism of books for children and young adults. The reviews, which emphasize literary quality, are approximately 200 words in length. Two columns that appear regularly discuss books appropriate for young adults. "Stories for older readers" examines about eight young adult books per issue. "Outlook tower" considers adult books that are appropriate for young readers. Other regular features, including acceptance speeches for the Newbery and Boston Globe–Horn Book awards, lists of new professional publications, announcements of awards, and information about professional conferences for teachers and librarians, make this magazine a valuable resource.

The *School Library Journal* is published nine times a year. It considers recommended and nonrecommended books. The "best books" are starred. Books are reviewed by a panel of 400 librarians who are sent books appropriate to their interests and backgrounds. Because the books are examined by people who work with young adults and who are interested in young adult literature, the value of the book to the reader and the accuracy of the presentation of the material in the book seem to be of primary importance in the reviews.

The *New York Times Book Review* is published weekly in the Sunday edition of the *Times.* The reviews are very up to date. Each issue features a section on books for young readers, some of which are appropriate to teenagers. One issue in the fall and another in the spring are primarily devoted to children's books.

The *ALAN Review,* published by the Assembly on Literature for Adolescents of the National Council of Teachers of English, is one of the few publications devoted entirely to adolescent literature. The journal is distributed three times per year (fall, winter, spring) to the members of ALAN. It contains articles about and by authors, information about media useful in the classroom, and clip-out reviews of hardbound and paperback releases in the young adult category. Most of the reviews are short enough to fit on a three-by-five file card, but many issues contain at least one long essay about a young adult book or several young adult books that relate to a single theme. Most of the reviews briefly summarize the book and even more briefly state the opinion of the reviewer. Each review lists the publishers of the hardbound and, when available, the paperback edition. The summaries and the brevity of the reviews make them valuable for the busy teacher who must learn as much as possible about young adult books in a short time. Membership in ALAN is important for teachers and librarians who are interested in adolescent literature. Members receive the *Review,* information about conferences, reprints of the Books for Young Adults poll, and other useful materials.

SECONDARY REVIEW SOURCES. Many professional journals have sections that review books on a regular basis. The *English Journal,* a publication of the National Council of Teachers of English, regularly presents adolescent books. The reviews are usually short, fewer than 200 words, and emphasize information about the book that is of interest to English teachers. Often the books reviewed are grouped thematically. The *English Journal,* published monthly from September through April, also has many articles about teaching English in the junior and senior high school classroom. Many of the articles, often written by junior and senior high school teachers, discuss the use of young adult literature. Also included are announcements of conferences, book awards, reviews of professional publications, the yearly printing of the Books for Young Adults poll, and other information of interest to English teachers.

Language Arts, also published by the National Council of Teachers of English, regularly reviews young adult books. The journal, published monthly from September through November and January through May, has a regular feature entitled "Books and Children: The Readers' Connection!" by Ronald Jobe. The column tends to feature books for the preteen and young teenage audience since the majority of the readers of *Language Arts* are elementary and middle school teachers. Books that are considered inferior by the reviewer are marked with a minus sign; those considered superior are marked with a plus sign. The reviews are short and to the point.

The *Journal of Reading,* published by the International Reading Association, is of particular interest to junior and senior high school teachers. In the past the only teacher who would be interested in this journal was the reading teacher. However, an increasing emphasis has been placed on the teaching of reading in all subject areas, from social studies to physical education. The *Journal of Reading,* published monthly October through May, has short reviews of adolescent books in every issue. M. Jean Greenlaw edits the column "Books for Adolescents." Many articles relate to a particular theme within adolescent literature or the use of the literature in the classroom. Announcements of conferences, awards, articles about teaching reading in a variety of subjects, reviews of recent research in reading, and other information of use to teachers make this an invaluable resource for all teachers.

Voice of Youth Advocates (VOYA) is a newcomer to the journal market. The journal, of primary interest to librarians, has the goal of changing the traditional placement of young adult literature in the children's section of the library. To reach this goal the journal publishes articles about young adults, library services for young adults, authors, thematic listing of young adult books, announcements of conferences and publications, reviews of books written for or of interest to young adults, reviews of pamphlets of interest to young adults and their parents, information about periodicals for teens, information about teachers' guides and "other goodies," and news about new paperback publications. The reviews are interesting for two reasons. They give good, brief summaries of the books, and they rate books on both quality and popularity. The highest-quality mark, 5Q, is given if the reviewer finds it "hard to imagine it being better written." The highest mark for popularity, 5P, is given if "every YA was dying to read it yesterday."

Top of the News is a quarterly of the Association for Library Service to Children and the Young Adult Services Division of the American Library Association. The publication, which is free to members of the two divisions, contains articles on services and materials for children and young adults in all types of libraries. Young adult books are reviewed in some but not all issues. The publication is of interest because of the feature articles about using young adult literature in the library and a column reviewing professional publications.

The *Wilson Library Bulletin,* published ten times per year by the H. W. Wilson Company, focuses on more than young adult literature. However, two columns are of particular interest to young adult librarians. "The young adult people," edited by Patty Campbell, regularly reviews current books. A column edited by Jana Varlejs, "Cine-Opis," reviews media of interest to young adult audiences.

Special-interest journals also review young adult books. *Interracial Books for Children Bulletin* is published eight times a year by the Council on Interracial Books for Children. The bulletin examines books for their treatment of social issues.

Appraisal: Science Books for Young People is published three times per year by the Children's Science Book Review Committee, sponsored by the Department of Science and Mathematics Education of Boston University School of Education and the New England Roundtable of Children's Librarians. This comprehensive review source rates books from unsatisfactory to excellent, assigns approximate grade levels, and includes at least two brief reviews for each book: one from a specialist and one from a librarian. The journal, which is divided thematically, primarily reviews nonfiction works. This is an invaluable review source for science teachers and librarians.

Several sources for locating specific book reviews are available. Often the busy teacher, librarian, or parent wants to find information about a specific young adult book without reading it. Possibly a young adult has asked about a particular title, an advertisement about the book looks intriguing, or an interview with the author was seen by the teacher. To gain information without reading the entire book, the teacher, librarian, or parent can read a review. The difficulty

Building a paperback classroom library can be an enjoyable chore for busy teachers.

is in locating a review that will be helpful in learning the necessary information about the book. Two excellent indexes of book reviews are available.

Children's book review index, published by Gale Research Company and edited by Gary C. Tarbert, lists current and past reviews of children's books. To find a review of the book, all the adult needs to know is the title or author. If the book has been reviewed during the time period covered by the index, and the review appeared in a journal listed in the front of the index, the source of the review will be listed. If the source of the review is likely to be appropriate for the information needed, the review can be examined. This index is particularly valuable to adults working with younger adolescents.

Reviews of books of interest to older adolescents are likely to be listed in the more complete index by the same editor and publisher, *Book review index.* This index lists books for adults and young adults. It can be used in the same way as *Children's book review index.*

Bibliographies

Bibliographic listings can save hours of searching time. Compiling course bibliographies is time-consuming for the teacher. The comprehensiveness of these teacher-made bibliographies is limited by the individual's knowledge of the books on the subject. Because teachers of young adults are often unfamiliar with recent books written for teenagers, these resources are often omitted from the bibliography. It is impossible, of course, for the classroom teacher to keep up with all the current offerings in the young adult literature field. Therefore, bibliographic listings, particularly those that are annotated, carefully indexed with good cross-referencing, and thematically or generically grouped, are exceedingly useful to the busy teacher.

The librarian is often faced with the dilemma of ordering books that will be attractive to young readers as well as to teachers. At times the teachers are so busy that it is difficult to develop library order request lists for their classes. Therefore, the librarian must order books that are likely to be appropriate for the subjects being taught, the reading tastes of all the young readers, and the wide range of reading levels in the school. Some bibliographic sources are particularly helpful in the search.

Many bibliographies are also designed to help young adults find books that interest them. For the young adult who enjoyed a particular book, locating a similar book can be difficult. The card catalogue may be of little or no help, searching the stacks may take too much time, and the student may be reluctant to ask for help. This young adult can often find books of interest listed in annotated bibliographies designed for young readers.

HELPFUL GENERAL BIBLIOGRAPHIES. *The book finder* (1977; 2nd ed., 1981) by Sharon Spredemann Dreyer, is a wonderfully useful guide for teachers and guidance counselors. The major purpose of the guide is contained in its subtitle:

A guide to children's literature about the needs and problems of youth aged 2–15. It is actually two books in one: an index, cross-referenced by subject, author, and book title, and a book of excellent summaries, publication information (including hard- and soft-cover publishers, Braille editions, cassette recordings of books, and other forms in which books are available), thematic headings, and age levels for which the book is appropriate. This is an invaluable source for recommending "a good book just like the other one," for suggesting books that relate to problems that students are facing, and for the development of thematic bibliographies. No school library should be without a copy.

Books and the teenage reader (1980) by G. Robert Carlsen is in its second edition and contains narrative about the types of literature of interest to young adults as well as excellent annotated bibliographies for fiction and nonfiction books. The basic premise of the book is that teenagers enjoy a wide range of literature, and so they should be introduced to literature written specifically for the young adult, literature written for the popular adult audience, biography, fantasy and science fiction, and nonfiction. The annotated bibliographies on "The teenager's world" (hobbies, personal advice, career and college information), "The adolescent novel" (about young women, about young men, animal stories, mystery, suspense, adventure, books about foreign cultures, U.S. history, world stories, sports stories), "the popular adult books," "significant modern literature," poetry, drama, nonfiction (personal experience, archaeology and anthropology, social sciences, science, mathematics, communications, fine arts, the environment), literature about women, and science fiction and fantasy are particularly helpful. *The best of best books, 1970-1983* (1984) is an annotated booklist of books selected as the best of each year by the Young Adult Services Division of the American Library Association.

Adventuring with books (1977 and 1981) is a booklist for preschool through eighth grade. It contains over 2,500 listings, all published since 1970. The annotations include information about the plot or factual content, style, and illustrations, suggest age level, and provide the publishers' names. The list is divided into thirteen categories, including novels and short stories, biography, biological sciences, social studies, crafts and hobbies, and "just for fun." The list, edited by Patricia Cianciolo in 1977 and M. L. White in 1981, is of use to teachers of young adolescents in the middle and junior high schools. *Children's fiction, 1896-1984* (1984) surveys children's books, from picture to junior high school, in one extensive volume. There are over 100,000 entries in this most complete reference source on children's books. Though expensive, it is a must for every library.

There are many bibliographies of books that are of interest to older students who read poorly. These are very important lists because they help the teacher select books on the subject that will be readable by all, or most, of the students in the class.

High interest–easy reading (1984), edited by Hugh Agee, is in its fourth edition. The book contains over 350 annotations of best-selling books for "hard-to-interest adolescent readers." Subject categories in the book include love and friendship, families, cars and cycles, problems and young people, sports, growing up, adventure, ethnic themes, science fiction, and others. This is an invaluable guide for all teachers of reluctant readers. The books are labeled J (junior high interest), S (senior high interest), or both.

Easy-to-read books for the teenage (1981) is available from the Office of Young Adult Services, New York Public Library. The list contains brief annotations to books under the headings of fiction and nonfiction. Many of the selections are published as "high interest, low vocabulary" titles. However, others have been selected because they "just happen to be easy to read." The list, prepared by the staff of the Office of Young Adult Services, is based on books that are popular with the young readers of New York City.

The Young Adult Services Division of the American Library Association also publishes a frequently updated *High-interest, low-reading-level booklist*. The list annotates approximately fifty books for teenagers with reading levels from first to fifth grade.

Good reading for the disadvantaged reader: Multi-ethnic resources (1975) by George Spache emphasizes the need for the development of a positive self-concept. In addition to annotated lists of books and other resources, ranging from primary to secondary levels, the book contains guidelines for teachers in helping minority children to gain a positive self-concept.

Many public library and school library bibliographies are helpful. Teachers should not ignore local sources of bibliographic information about books appropriate for young readers. Many libraries prepare lists of books that are available in the local library on a particular theme or in a specific literary genre. These thematic or generic listings are particularly useful since all of the books on the bibliography are locally available.

Two poetry indexes help the teacher to select poetry for the classroom. *Subject index of poetry for children and young people* (1977) by Dorothy B. F. Smith and Eva L. Andrews lists poems from 263 anthologies, published between 1957 and 1975, by author and topic. Each listing indicates the grade levels for which the poem is appropriate. *Index of poetry for children and young people* by John E. Brewton, G. M. Blackburn, and Lorraine A. Blackburn includes poems from 110 collections. Though the number of collections is fewer, the listings are more complete than in the Smith and Andrews book. This resource, which includes anthologies published from 1976 through 1981, indexes poems by title, subject, author, and first line. Appropriate grade levels are also indicated.

SPECIAL-INTEREST BIBLIOGRAPHIES. There are several useful bibliographic sources that list multicultural literature. *Black literature for high school students* (1978) by Barbara Dodds Stanford and Karim Amin is a guide for teachers who want to introduce black literature into the curriculum. In addition to the 370 books listed in the bibliography, which includes adult fiction, adolescent literature, biography and autobiography, poetry collections, anthologies, and literary criticism, there are discussions of issues and problems involved in teaching black literature. Commentary on more than fifty important black authors is included in the survey of black American literature from the colonial period to the present.

We build together: A reader's guide to Negro life and literature for elementary and high school use (1967), edited by Charlemae Rollins, is an intercultural annotated and indexed reading list. It includes books appropriate for preschoolers to ninth-graders under subject headings such as fiction, history, biography, poetry and folklore, science, and sports.

Reading ladders for human relations (1981), edited by Eileen Tway, is an annotated bibliography of over 1,300 titles selected to assist young readers in developing a sensitivity toward all peoples, their values, and their way of life. The resource is divided into sections such as growing into self, relating to wide individual differences, interacting in groups, coping in a changing world, and appreciating different cultures. Within each section books are listed by maturity level, from primary through adult. Instructional strategies are included.

Literature by and about the American Indian: An annotated bibliography (1979), edited by Anna Lee Stensland, identifies more than 700 titles published since 1973. The books are annotated, including comments from Indian critics and recommendations from Indian-sponsored bibliographies. The bibliography is divided into categories such as myth, legend, poetry, fiction, biography, history, and the arts. Each title is classified by reading level: elementary, junior high, and senior high and adult. The resource also contains essays about American Indian literature, recommended teaching materials, and biographies of American Indian authors.

Booklists for college-bound readers, distributed by the Young Adult Services Division of the American Library Association, are useful to both teachers and students. Five such lists are currently available: *Outstanding biographies for the college bound, Outstanding books on the current scene for the college bound, Outstanding fiction for the college bound, Outstanding nonfiction for the college bound,* and *Outstanding theater for the college bound.* Each list is in pamphlet format and contains approximately fifty annotated titles.

A role-free booklist is prepared by the Young Adult Services Division of the ALA Committee on Sexism in Adolescent Materials. The annotated list contains thirty-one titles that are sex-role-free and present positive sex-role images, according to the committee.

A guide to books about the handicapped is *Notes from a different drummer: A guide to juvenile fiction portraying the handicapped* (1977) by Barbara H. Baskin and Karen H. Harris. The bulk of it is an annotated bibliography of fiction portraying the handicapped from 1940 to 1975. Other sections of the book include chapters on the society and the handicapped person, the treatment of the handicapped in literature, and how to assess and use fiction about the handicapped.

Several subject-oriented bibliographic guides are available to teachers. *Sports: A multimedia guide for children and young adults* is useful to teachers and students. The extensive annotated guide is by Calvin Blickle and Frances Corcoran. Two free subject-oriented annotated booklists, available from the

Children's Book Council, are *Notable children's trade books in the field of social studies,* compiled under the direction of the National Council of Social Studies–Children's Book Council Joint Committee, and *Outstanding science trade books for children,* prepared by the National Science Teachers Association–Children's Book Council Joint Committee. Both of the lists appear in spring issues of journals of the associations, *Social Education* and *Science and Children.*

ESPECIALLY FOR TEACHERS. Two "too good to be missed" book resource listings available to teachers are *The WEB* and *The Calendar.* Though both are applicable primarily to teachers of younger adolescents, much of the information they contain will be of interest to teachers of older teenagers as well. *The WEB* (Wonderfully Exciting Books) is published quarterly by the Center for Language, Literature and Reading, College of Education, Ohio State University, under the editorship of Charlotte Huck and Janet Hickman. It is devoted to reviewing books and suggesting ways in which they can be used in the classroom. This unusual publication includes information about books that are appropriate for a wide age range. Often the articles about the books contain the comments of young people who have read them. The age level for which the book is appropriate is included. The centerfold of *The WEB* contains "a web of possibilities" for using books of a particular theme or by a particular author in the classroom. Recent editions have included webs for Folk and Fairy Tales, Nature: A Source of Wonder, *Bridge to Terabithia,* Life Stories, Poetry on Parade, The Middle Ages, Madeleine L'Engle, Sharing the Art of Picture Books, Eats, and Generations.

The Calendar, published by the Children's Book Council three times every two years, is an interesting resource which lists recent book titles under specific themes. Also included in the publication are interviews with people in the publishing business, articles about topics of interest to teachers, listing of free and inexpensive materials available to teachers from publishers and other sources, information about Children's Book Council materials, and useful professional publications. The booklists include books under three headings: lower elementary, upper elementary, and junior and senior high school. This is an invaluable publication for all teachers available for the low one-time fee of $10.

BIBLIOGRAPHIES FOR SCHOOL LIBRARIES. Some bibliographic sources are particularly useful for school or young adult librarians. *Junior high school library catalog,* edited by Ilene R. Schechter and Gary L. Bogart, is a particularly useful resource for librarians who work with young adolescents. Designed as a suggested basic book collection for junior high school libraries, it is divided into two major sections, fiction and nonfiction. Nonfiction is annotated and listed by Dewey decimal number. Fiction is catalogued by author or editor as well as alphabetically by title and subject. The resource is cumulated every five years, and yearly supplements are available.

A similar guide, *Senior high school library catalog,* edited by Gary L. Bogart and Karen R. Carlson, is available for high school libraries or librarians who work with older adolescents. Some books appropriate for both junior and senior high school libraries are listed in this catalogue. In addition, books for tenth-through twelfth-grade readers are included. Like the junior high catalogue, it is cumulated every five years with a yearly supplement.

BIBLIOGRAPHIES FOR YOUNG ADULTS. Several bibliographic sources are useful to young adult readers. Many of those mentioned above are useful for young adults as well as teachers. However, two guides are published specifically for young readers. *Books for you: A booklist for senior high school students* (1982) is a comprehensive, annotated guide to young-adult and adult books appropriate for teen readers. The book, edited by Robert C. Small, Jr., is grouped by topics such as mystery and crime, adventure and adventurers, westerns, science fiction, history: fact, love and romance, problems: social and personal, sports and sports figures, careers and people on the job, improving yourself, poetry and poets, ethnic experiences, music and musicians, essays, biography, languages, myths and legends, philosophies and philosophers, religion and religious leaders, drama, ecology, art and architecture, animals, and others. The index includes cross-referencing by title and author. *Your reading: A booklist for junior high students* (1984), edited by Jane Christensen, annotates more than 3,100 books of interest to junior high readers. The guide is divided into sections designed to help students locate books they are interested in reading. The book is divided into two main sections: fiction and nonfiction. Other sections include humor and satire, poetry, plays, and short stories. The fiction annotations sketch the plot and introduce the characters. The annotations on nonfiction books discuss the scope and aims of the book.

PAPERBACK BOOK BIBLIOGRAPHIES. Since most young adults buy paperback books for their own libraries, bibliographic sources that help identify books in paperback editions are important. Similarly, many teachers have found that with paperback books they can stock the shelves of the classroom library without depleting the budget. Even libraries now circulate paperbacks. Many young adults are more comfortable with paperbacks in their pockets than hardbacks in their hands. The circulation of the paperback library books is often more frequent than hardback books of the same title.

Good guides for locating young adult books in paperback include *Paperback books for young people: An annotated guide to publishers and distributors* by John T. Gillespie. The *Kliatt paperback book guide,* published eight times a year with periodic newsletter updates, reviews paperbacks (originals, reprints, and reissues) recommended for young readers from ages twelve through nineteen. The guide is divided into subjects and has a title index. The books are identified as appropriate for readers at differing levels including students with low reading abilities, junior high students, general young adult readers, advanced students, and emotionally mature students (readers who can handle "explicit sex, excessive violence and/or obscenity"). A useful guide is the *Paperback index to "Books for the teenage."* The index lists all of the books in the New York Public

Library bibliography that are available in paperback and gives each book's publisher and price.

Publisher's catalogues are sometimes overlooked as a resource for the selection of paperback books for the classroom. Most of the catalogues contain annotated listings, often with comments from positive reviews. The awards received by the book and/or the author are usually listed in the annotation. Reading and/or interest levels are often included in the annotations. Most of the catalogues are organized by topic, theme, genre, and subject area. Each book is carefully cross-referenced and appears in all appropriate sections of the catalogue. Title and author indexes appear in the back. Several of the paperback companies have well-qualified educational consultants who write brief articles for the catalogues. Limited information about authors also appears in some catalogues. Most of the companies prepare some type of promotional material and/or study guides to use when studying the books, the authors, or a particular topic covered by the publisher's books. Many of these materials are well done and are available either free or for a minimal charge. Most publishers have a single-copy review policy that allows the teacher to obtain a review copy of a book at minimal cost.

A BIBLIOGRAPHY OF BIBLIOGRAPHIES. A very special resource for obtaining information about additional bibliographies of young adult books is *Selecting materials for children and young adults: A bibliography of bibliographies and review sources* (1980). The guide is prepared by the joint committee of the Young Adult Services and Association for Library Service to Children divisions of the American Library Association. Over 300 bibliographies and review sources useful in selecting books for children and young adults are listed in the seventy-four-page annotated guide.

Obtaining Books for the Classroom

Even the classroom teacher without a budget and with no financial resources can begin a classroom paperback lending library of young adult books with a few simple tricks. The only thing needed is a little bit of time and the willingness to beg, borrow, and . . .

BEG. One of the problems with beginning a classroom young adult library is that one book leads to two books leads to twenty books. In other words, you never have enough. Therefore, the books you purchase at full price, even in paperback, whet your appetite for more books.

One day one of my students brought in a shopping bag of paperback books from her home library. I thanked her, but in skimming the books I found only three or four that were appropriate for the shelves in the classroom. However, since books are very much a part of my life, I never throw one away. I stored the rest in a closet in my classroom. Sometime later it occurred to me that if fifty students were to bring in a bag full of books, and if each bag had four useful books, I would gain 200 new books for my classroom library. So I sent a notice home, and, as expected, many students brought in paperback and hardback books from their home libraries. Several hundred titles were added to the classroom shelves, and several dozen shopping bags full of books were added to my closet. Thus began my home scavenger campaign, which eventually produced recent copies of dozens of magazines, many in multiple copies, day-old newspapers, and books, books, books. Pretty soon my classroom looked like the storeroom of the recycling center, and the friendly janitors were becoming a bit perturbed. However, my search for additional materials continued.

BORROW. The problem I faced was that I had hundreds of books and wanted to incorporate them into my cirriculum. Since I was teaching English and much of my teaching was thematic and generic, I was able to develop classroom bibliographies that allowed students to select books on the topic or in the genre from the classroom library. At times, however, there were not enough books on a particular theme to allow each student to have one book. Similarly, the students who read more rapidly were not always able to find another book from the bibliography on the shelves after they returned a completed one. This dilemma brought me first to the school library and later to the public library.

The school librarian agreed to set aside several shelves in the library that related to the topic we were studying. On these shelves she placed books, journals, and pamphlets that addressed the theme. Unfortunately, I had several students who would not enter any library unless they were shackled and dragged there. Therefore, if I wanted them to read, I had to add more books to my classroom library.

I visited my friends in the public library and discovered that they had a long-term loan policy for teachers. Not only could I borrow fifty books on the same theme, but I could keep them in my classroom for up to eight weeks. And, to make my life even easier, the public library staff searched the stacks and put together a group of books for me on the topic at a variety of different reading levels. All I had to do was give them one week's notice and I could pick up the books to use in my classroom. Since that time I've discovered that many libraries have a similar lending policy for teachers. The length of the checkout time usually varies from four to eight weeks. The number of books allowed may also have a ceiling, but the long-term use of the library materials is invaluable. Of course, the teacher is responsible for returning all of the books on time. However, in the ten years I have been using long-term loan books from public libraries in my classroom, I have lost only one book. There have been a few other times when I thought a book was lost, but it turned up in the library book drop.

Today's libraries not only lend books; many give teachers access to a free film and media lending library. Through our local public library teachers can borrow films of ABC afterschool specials, for example, which include film presentations of many young adult books. Most public libraries also lend records and cassettes. Many lend reproductions of famous paintings. Some even lend audiovisual equipment. The local public library can provide many invaluable resources for teachers.

AND. . . . The overcrowded conditions in my classroom were becoming unbearable. I could not even fit my winter coat in my closet. I had to do something with all those books. In a class I was taking at the time one of the students suggested that I take the books to a used-book store and trade them for the books that I could use in my classroom. It would be a new way to get more books for my classroom library.

One day I borrowed a van from the athletic department. In the van I piled all of the books and four of my strongest students. We drove approximately forty-five minutes to a used-book store with a large stock of young adult books that I had investigated the previous weekend. We deposited the home library books with the clerk, who told us we could have one book for each two "acceptable" books we brought in. The clerk was willing to accept over 300 books. The students, aware of the guidelines I had set, were allowed to select books from the bookstore shelves. The four of them, two young men and two young women, had a wonderful time grabbing books off the shelves. I sat and looked over each book before leaving the store. The only problem we encountered was getting out of the store before it closed. The students were having so much fun reading the books that it was difficult to pry them out of the store. In that single afternoon, using books we had received free as barter, we obtained over 150 new titles for the classroom library.

Another way to get many books from a used-book store is to find one that sells books that have been on the shelves for a long period of time at a reduced rate, often as low as ten to twenty-five cents per cpoy. One teacher I know collected fifty cents from each of her students. Armed with over fifty dollars and one student representative from each of her classes, she went to a local used-book store. In two hours the teacher and five students collected more than 300 paperback books for the classroom library. The students understood when they made their fifty-cent contributions that at the end of the year they would each be allowed to select one paperback from the classroom library to keep. Even after each student received a favorite book, the classroom library had over 150 titles with which to begin the new year.

Used-book stores are good sources of paperbacks for the classroom. A Saturday tour of the used-book stores in your community can be well worth the few delightful hours you spend. One rainy Saturday this spring I went into a shop about five miles from my home. The proprietor had a bin of books she was selling for ten cents each. Many of them were young adult titles. She said that her customers did not purchase these books and she was getting them off the shelves to make room for others. She told me that for five dollars I could have as many of the books in the bin as I wanted. I gave her five dollars, and in less than an hour I left with over seventy-five books for my classroom library.

Several companies have set up student book clubs. Each month the classroom receives a catalogue, geared to the appropriate age levels, containing approximately thirty offerings the students can buy at reduced rates. As in adult book clubs, dividend books are given after a certain number have been purchased. Not only do the students get dividend books, but so also do the classrooms. In this way the teacher can encourage the students to read as well as provide additional dividend books for the classroom library each month. Many of the companies also provide posters and promotional material with each month's catalogue. The three biggest student book clubs are Scholastic Book Services, Xerox Education Publications, and Troll Book Clubs.[3] Investigation of these clubs will allow the teacher to select the one that best fits the needs and interests of the students and the class. One word of caution about book clubs. If there are students in the school who cannot afford to purchase books from a club, the teacher should carefully weigh the frustrations these students will experience against the motivational advantage of the club.

Even today there are many free or inexpensive materials available to the teacher who takes the time to look. Knowing where to look can greatly cut down the time the search takes. Publishers provide free and inexpensive materials about their books, authors, and the publishing industry. Study guides are often available to teachers who plan to use particular books in the classroom. The best source of information about these freebies (or near-freebies) are the publishers' catalogues. Usually the back of the catalogue lists materials available to teachers. (About fifty publishers of young adult books, both hardbound and paperback, are listed in the Appendix of this book.) Information about material available from publishers free or for a small charge appears in the *Calendar.* Careful reading of this publication can help the teacher get free materials that relate to the young adult books and authors they introduce in their classrooms. Major national conferences, such as the annual convention of the National Council of Teachers of English the week prior to Thanksgiving and the International Reading Association Conference in early May, provide access to many publishers and much free material. Most of the major publishers set up booths at these conferences. Many of them give out posters, biographical information about authors, study guides, bookmarks, and sometimes books. Even if books are not given away, they can often be purchased at convention rates. The teacher who stays until the end of the conference can buy many of the paperback display books at "give-away" rates. Most of the paperback companies would rather sell the display books than ship them back to their warehouses.

Several guides that help direct teachers to free and inexpensive materials have been published. Most school libraries subscribe to at least one guide. If not, request a subscription. Although expensive, subscriptions can help one to find valuable materials that are often unavailable from any other source. For example, one of the best films I have ever used in the classroom is *Art is.* The film, produced by the Sears Foundation, is available only by free loan. That

---

[3]Scholastic Book Services, 904 Sylvan Ave., Englewood Cliffs, NJ 07632; Xerox Education Publications, 1250 Fairwood Ave., Columbus, OH 43216; Troll Book Clubs, 320 Rte. 17, Mahwah, NJ 07430.

means one cannot get it through any lending services that purchase or lease their films, even if the films are distributed free. Spending some time with this guide can save the school money and provide the classroom with many teaching aids. Ask your school librarian if you can check the guide out for several weeks over the summer, and get your name on the many mailing lists by requesting free material. Some of it will be useless, but much of it will be valuable.

Local businesses can be a great source of useful materials for the classroom. If it wasn't for the ends of the rolls of newsprint I collect from the local newspaper office, I might have to quit teaching. Posters and travel brochures obtained from travel agencies have been useful in units on foreign culture, particularly when used in conjunction with the many young adult books on the topic. The teacher's imagination is the only limit to finding useful free materials locally. Use your local resources; don't be afraid to ask. I have gotten free fabric to make costumes for plays from a local fabric company, carpet for the reading nook from a carpet manufacturer, strangely colored paper on which to print programs and creative writing journals from a paper company throw-away bin, and even a sound-slide show on dealing with death from a group of local funeral home directors.

Conclusion

Finding good young adult literature to use in the classroom is not difficult. Obtaining the books does not have to be expensive. Every classroom can have a good paperback lending library of young adult books. The teacher need not read every young adult book that is published, but can become familiar with them by reading current reviews, keeping track of award books, and developing a professional library of bibliographies.

Once familiar with the market, the teacher can begin developing a classroom library of young adult titles and adult titles that are appropriate for young adult readers. Parents, used-book stores, libraries, book clubs, and students are all helpful in developing a good lending library in the classroom.

As the library grows, the teacher adds to it information about the books and authors, posters, magazines, and other supplemental materials that help make reading an enjoyable experience.

Suggested Readings

"Best Books" Lists

Association for Library Services to Children. *Notable children's books.* Yearly. American Library Association.
————. *Notable children's books 1940–1970.* American Library Association.
The best of children's books, 1964–1978. Superintendent of Documents, Government Printing Office, Washington, DC 20402.

Carlsen, G. R., et al. *Books for young adults.* Yearly. Books for Young Adults, N494 Linquist Center for Measurement, University of Iowa, Iowa City, IA 52242.

Children's choices. Yearly. Children's Book Council.

New York Public Library. *Books for the teen age.* Yearly.

New York Times Book Review. Weekly. 229 W. 43rd St. New York, NY 10036.

Young Adult Services Division. *Best books for young adults.* Yearly. American Library Association.

Award Books

Association for Library Services to Children. *Choosing the Newbery and Caldecott Medal Winners and Newbery and Caldecott Medals: Authorization and terms.* American Library Association.

———. *The Laura Ingalls Wilder Award.* American Library Association.

———. *Newbery Medal Books.* Yearly. American Library Association.

Children's books: Awards and prizes. Children's Book Council, 1981.

Jones, D. B. *Children's literature awards and winners.* Gale, 1983.

Book Review Sources

ALAN Review. Three issues per year. Assembly on Literature for adolescents. National Council of Teachers of English.

Appraisal: Science books for young people. Three issues per year. Children's Science Book Review Committee, a nonprofit organization sponsored by the Department of Science and Mathematics Education of Boston University and the New England Roundtable of Children's Librarians.

Booklist. Twenty-three issues per year. American Library Association.

Brewton, J. E.; G. M. Blackburn III; and L. A. Blackburn. *Index of poetry for children and young people, 1976–1981.* Wilson, 1983.

Bulletin of the Center for Children's Books. Eleven issues per year. University of Chicago Graduate Library School, University of Chicago Press, 5801 Ellis Ave., Chicago, IL 60637.

English Journal. Nine issues per year. National Council of Teachers of English.

Horn Book. Six issues per year. The Horn Book, Inc., Park Square Building, 31 James Ave., Boston, MA 02116.

Interracial Books for Children Bulletin. Eight issues per year. Council on Interracial Books for Children, 1841 Broadway, New York, NY 10023.

Journal of Reading. Nine issues per year. International Reading Association, 6 Tyre Ave., Newark, DE 19711.

Kirkus Reviews. Twenty-six issues per year. Kirkus Service, Inc., 200 Park Ave. South, New York, NY 10003.

Language Arts. Eight issues per year. National Council of Teachers of English.

McNaughton Young Adult Reviews. Monthly. McNaughton Book Service, P.O. Drawer 926, Williamsport, PA 17705.

School Library Journal. Nine issues per year. R. R. Bowker Co., 1180 Ave. of the Americas, New York, NY 10036.

Tarbert, G. C., ed. *Book review index.* 1969–present. Gale Research Co.

———. *Children's book review index.* Gale Research Co.

Top of the News. Quarterly. American Library Association.

Voice of Youth Advocates (VOYA). Six issues per year. P.O. Box 6569, University, AL 35486.

Wilson Library Bulletin. Ten issues per year. H. W. Wilson Co., 1950 University Ave., Bronx, NY 19452.

Bibliographic Sources

Agee, H., ed. *High interest–easy reading.* 4th ed. National Council of Teachers of English, 1984.

American Library Association. *The best of best books,* 1970–1984.

———*Selecting materials for children and young adults: A bibliography of bibliographies and review sources.* 1980.

Baskin, B. H., and K. H. Harris. *Notes from a different drummer: A guide to juvenile fiction portraying the handicapped.* Bowker, 1977.

Blickle, C., and F. Corcoran. *Sports: A multimedia guide for children and young adults,* Neal-Schuman, 1980.

Bogart, G. L., and K. R. Carlson. *Senior high school library catalog.* Wilson.

Carlsen, G. R. *Books and the teenage reader.* 2nd rev. ed. Harper & Row, 1980. Bantam, 1980.

Children's Book Council. *The Calendar.* Three times every two years.

Children's fiction, 1876–1984. Bowker, 1984.

Christensen, J., ed. *Your reading: A booklist for junior high and middle school students.* National Council of Teachers of English, 1984.

Cianciolo, P., ed. *Adventure with books.* National Council of Teachers of English, 1977.

Dreyer, S. S. *The book finder: A guide to children's literature about the needs and problems of youth aged 2–15.* American Guidance Service, 1977, 1981.

Gillespie, J. T. *Paperback books for young people: An annotated guide to publishers and distributors.* American Library Association, 1977.

Huck, C., and J. Hickman, eds. *The WEB: Wonderfully exciting books.* Quarterly. Ohio State University, Room 200, Ramseyer Hall, 29 West Woodruff, Columbus, OH 43210.

Kliatt paperback book guide. Eight times per year. 425 Watertown St., Newton, MA 02158.

National Council of Social Studies–Children's Book Council Joint Committee. *Notable children's trade books in the field of social studies.* Children's Book Council.

National Science Teachers Association–Children's Book Council Joint Committee. *Outstanding science trade books for children.* Children's Book Council.

New York Public Library. *Easy-to-read books for the teenage* (1981).

Paperback index to "Books for the teenage." School and Library Division, Golden-Lee Book Distributors, Inc., 664 Bergen St., Brooklyn, NY 11238.

Rollins, C. W. *We build together: A reader's guide to Negro life and literature for elementary and high school use.* National Council of Teachers of English, 1967.

Schechter, I. R., and G. L. Bogart. *Junior high school library catalog.* Wilson

Small, R., ed. *Books for you: A booklist for senior high students.* National Council of Teachers of English, 1982.

Smith, D. B. F., and E. L. Andrews. *Subject index of poetry for children and young people, 1957–1975.* American Library Association, 1977.

Spache, G. *Good reading for the disadvantaged reader: Multi-ethnic resources.* Gerrard, 1975.

Stanford, B. D., and K. Amin. *Black literature for high school students.* National Council of Teachers of English, 1978.

Stensland, A. L. *Literature by and about the American Indian: An annotated bibliography.* National Council of Teachers of English, 1979.

Tway, E., ed. *Reading ladders for human relations.* 6th ed. National Council of Teachers of English, 1981.

White, M. L., ed. *Adventuring with books.* National Council of Teachers of English, 1981.

Young Adults Services Division. *High-interest, low-level booklist.* American Library Association.

————. *Outstanding biographies for the college bound. Outstanding books on the current scene for the college bound. Outstanding fiction for the college bound. Outstanding nonfiction for the college bound. Outstanding theater for the college bound.* American Library Association.

————. *Role-free booklist.* American Library Association.

Other Information Sources

The Yellow Pages of the telephone directory.

Aubrey, R. H. *Selected free materials for classroom teachers.* 6th ed. Pitman, 1978.

Diffor, J. C., and M. F. Horkheimer, eds. *Educators' guide to free filmstrips.* 32nd ed. Educators' Progress, 1982.

Duval, C. R. *Educators' index of free materials.* 89th ed. Educators' *Progress, 1980.*

Fader, D. N. *The new hooked on books.* Berkley Books, 1981.

Saalheimer, H. *Free for the asking: A super treasury of valuable things you can get for free or for next to nothing.* Parker, 1979.

Suttles, P. H., et al., eds. *Educators' guide to free teaching aids.* 26th ed. Educators' Progress, 1980.

————. *Educators' guide to free social studies materials.* Educators' Progress, 1980.

Trevarrow, W. M. *The book of free books.* Domus, 1979.

Important Addresses

Before ordering materials from any of these sources, send for catalogues, price lists, and other information.

Association for Library Service to Children and Young Adult Services Division
American Library Association
50 East Huron St.
Chicago, IL 60611

Children's Book Council, Inc.
67 Irving Place
New York, NY 10003

International Reading Association
800 Barksdale Road
P.O. Box 8139
Newark, DE 19711

National Council of Teachers of English
1111 Kenyon Road
Urbana, IL 61801

The New York Public Library
The Office of Branch Libraries
455 Fifth Ave.
New York, NY 10016

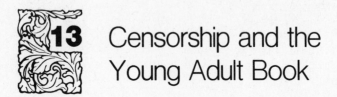

13 Censorship and the Young Adult Book

Censorship sends terror up and down the teacher's and the librarian's and the administrator's spine. No educator has failed to reexamine the materials used in the classroom or library when well-publicized cases of censorship, book-banning, and book-burning have occurred. No creative teacher feels safe from the censor's wrath when he or she reads about teachers who were fired for using particular books in their classrooms. Often these censored books fall into the category of young adult literature.

> Censorship is an act born of fear. Something is perceived to be dangerous, to pose a threat, and the censor moves to suppress it. The protesting parent may see the danger of moral corruption lurking in an "obscene" book. The teacher may see no danger in the book but sense a very real threat from the parent. Both are acting out of fear, and the deeper the fear, the stronger the action each is likely to take. (LaConte 1975)[1]

The less secure teachers are in what they are teaching, the less comfortable librarians are with their selections, and the less knowledge the principal has of the material used in the classrooms, the more likely each is to react strongly to the pressure put on him or her by the person criticizing the material. Teachers

[1]Reprinted by permission of the *Arizona English Bulletin*.

must have extensive knowledge of the material used in their classrooms and must be able to carefully defend their selections. Librarians must know a great deal about the books they order and recommend. The principal must understand the selection policies of the classrooms and the library. Without knowledge of the material being used and the reasons for selecting it, the person whose choice is being criticized is likely to take the criticism personally and be unable to defend the material.

The person criticizing the material is not a censor, but is exercising the right to question. Teachers or librarians or principals who act out of lack of knowledge of material and alternatives may become censors when, out of fear, they remove or force the removal of criticized material. Insecurity in one's own knowledge and fear of criticism may cause the professional to overreact and become the censor. Lack of knowledge and security creates fear, and censorship is an act of fear.

Differing Views of Censorship

THE CHANGING VIEWS OF THE COURTS. What is censorship? Who has the right to select books for the classroom? Who has the right to remove books from the classroom? What books are appropriate for classroom use? These questions have been argued in classrooms, in school board meetings, in legislatures, and in the courts. The courts have provided us with their interpretation of the First Amendment, which guarantees freedom of speech and of the press, and of how it applies to the selection and removal of classroom material.

In 1957 the Warren Supreme Court heard the case *Roth* v. *U.S.* The ruling in that case became a precedent for many other censorship cases until the early 1970s, when a shift in the Court's views began to be voiced. The majority decision in *Roth* stated, in part, "All ideas having even the slightest redeeming social importance—unorthodox ideas, controversial ideas, even ideas hateful to the prevailing climate of opinion—have full protection of the First Amendment guarantees unless excludable because they encroach upon the limited area of more important areas." Until the early 1970s all materials had to be shown to have no redeeming social value to be censored as obscene. This case proved to be very important as a precedent for the censorship cases that followed during the next decade and a half.

In 1973, however, the Supreme Court handed down a decision in *Miller* v. *California* that provided a new set of guidelines to determine obscenity:

1. Whether the "average person, applying contemporary community standards" would find that the work, taken as a whole, appeals to purient interest.
2. Whether the work depicts or describes, in a patently offensive way, sexual conduct specifically defined by the applicable state law.
3. Whether the work, taken as a whole, lacks serious literary artistic, political, or scientific value.

Richard Peck's *Are you in the house alone?* has been criticized for being too realistic. On the basis of "community standards," it has been removed from the shelves of classrooms and libraries in many towns.

> ☐ [*I owe my readers*] *entertainment and truth. Young people, in fact most people won't read anything unless they are entertained on some level, and I can't write through a book without believing in its truth. This can be a very light truth or it can be a very heavy one. I have written a book called* Are You in the House Alone? *and I have written it because the typical victim of the crime of rape is a teenage girl in our country. That's a very hard truth. Yet, I wanted my readers to know some things about this crime, that our laws are stacked against the victim and in favor of the criminal. I wanted them to know what it's like to be a victim. I had to do a lot of research and interview a lot of people and go to a lot of places. I had to talk to doctors and lawyers and police personnel and victims. I had to deal only in the truth. I couldn't put a happy ending on this story because we don't have any happy endings to this problem in our society.*
>
> RICHARD PECK
>
> *in Weiss (1979)*

The guidelines make it very difficult to determine whether a work is obscene. Who is the "average person"? How do we determine "community standards"? What does "contemporary" mean? Who decides?

The decision does, however, give increased control to the community in determining obscenity in censorship cases. Justice William O. Douglas, in a dissenting opinion, expressed concern about this increased control.

> *What we do today is rather ominous as respects librarians. The anti-obscenity net now signed by the court is so finely meshed that taken literally it could result in raids on libraries. . . . Libraries, I had always assumed, were sacrosanct, representing every part of the spectrum. If what is offensive to the most influential person or group in the community can be purged from a library, the library system would be destroyed.*

The courts, possibly realizing the difficulty in determining a work's obscenity, have moved from an earlier attempt to examine the quality of a work to an examination of an individual's or group's right to select a book. In earlier cases the courts examined the work to determine its appropriateness. In *Keefe* v. *Geanokos* (1969), a teacher assigned to his students an article from the *Atlantic Monthly* that dealt with student revolts of the 1960s in which the word *motherfucker* was used several times. The case was ruled in favor of the teacher. The Massachusetts Supreme Court said that the article was acceptable since it was written in a scholarly manner and the word was an integral part of the thesis of

424

the article. In a similar case a short autobiographical story, containing the phrase "White-mother-fuckin' pig," was read to a class of tenth-graders by Stanley Lindros. The California Supreme Court reversed a decision of a lower court saying that by reading the article Mr. Lindros was pursuing a "bona fide educational purpose" and no disruption was created by the reading of the story.

Kurt Vonnegut's "Welcome to the monkey house" was ruled appropriate for high school students by the U.S. District Court in Alabama in 1970. As in the California case, the court ruled that there was no disruption to the educational process and the school had no policy for the selection of works. In this case the court upheld the teacher's right to "academic freedom."

In more recent cases, however, particularly since the 1973 *Miller* decision, the courts have ruled against teachers. The decisions have been based not on the applicability of the work, but rather on the board of education's right to select the material and to remove it from use. Though there have been a few state court exceptions to this shift in censorship opinions, the vast majority have not attempted to judge the material.

The U.S. District Court in a Strongsville, Ohio, case found that the board of education had not violated First Amendment rights when it rejected faculty recommendations of books to be ordered for the library. The U.S. Court of Appeals upheld the decision, saying that the board's decision was neither "arbitrary" nor "capricious." As in most of the recent cases, the books were not on trial; obscenity was not the issue. In a similar case, *Cary* v. *Board of Education of Adams-Arapahoe (Colo.) School District,* the court ruled that the local school board had the right to rule on course content. The case involved a board-approved elective English course in contemporary literature for juniors and seniors. The books for the course were selected by the teacher and the students. The board objected to several of the selections. In its decision the court agreed that English teachers and students should be permitted to conduct an open discussion of free inquiry. "The student must be given an opportunity to participate openly if he is to become the kind of self-controlled individually motivated and independent thinking person who can function effectively as a contributing citizen." However, according to the court, free inquiry was not the issue at hand. The court decided in favor of the board, based on the question of who had the authority to select appropriate materials for the curriculum. It was claimed that when teachers submit to a collectively bargained contract, they agree to allow the board to decide everything, including the materials they use in the classroom.

The actual removal of books already in school libraries has been the issue in several recent court cases. A case that was first heard in 1972, appealed to the U.S. Court of Appeals, and argued in 1979 is *President's Council* v. *Community School Board.* In this case Piri Thomas's *Down these mean streets* was removed from all junior high school libraries in a particular New York school district. The court upheld the lower court's ruling that the power to remove books is in the hands of the board. A similar question argued in 1979 in Vermont is *Bicknell* v. *Vergennes.* In this instance the board of education ordered two books removed from the school library, calling them "obscene, vulgar, immoral, and perverted." The court ruled in favor of the board, not agreeing with the board's opinion of the books (again the books were not on trial), but affirming the authority of the elected board to control all curricular matters, including the removal of library books. Librarians, according to the court, do not have the right to control the library collection under the "rubric of academic freedom." The decision also stated that the board need not give any reason for refusing to purchase any book for the school library.

A third case dealing with the removal of library books was first heard in 1979. In *Pico* v. *Board of Education of Island Trees Free School District,* the court determined that "one of the principle functions of public education is indoctrinative, to transmit basic values of the community." For this reason the board has the right to remove any book from the school library that it believes is inconsistent with community values. The court again asserted the power of the school board to make decisions about the daily operation of the school. According to the decision, the court should not intervene, even if, as in this case, the court believes the decision to remove the books "reflects a misguided educational philosophy." However, in 1980 a federal district court of appeals reversed the decision in the *Pico* case.[2]

To summarize, recent court decisions, particularly since the 1973 *Miller* obscenity guidelines, have examined the right of elected officials to make decisions about the curriculum and materials used in the classrooms and school libraries. This is a shift in emphasis from the cases that followed the 1957 *Roth* decision. In obscenity cases from 1957 until the early 1970s, the courts ruled on the inherent value of the material being questioned. This shift in emphasis probably relates to two things: the new conservative leaning toward the autonomous decision-making of local elected officials, and the difficulty associated with the courts' making decisions about the obscenity of a written work based on the three guidelines set forth in the *Miller* case.

MAJOR PROFESSIONAL ORGANIZATIONS. The American Library Association (ALA) has clearly voiced its opposition to any form of censorship since 1939, when it responded to attacks on John Steinbeck's *The grapes of wrath.* Its response to the criticism leveled against the book was the precursor to today's "Library Bill of Rights."

The stand of the ALA regarding censorship is that all materials, no matter "the race or nationality or the social, political, or religious views of the authors," must be made available to all people. According to the Library Bill of Rights, all people, no matter their "origin, age, background, or views," should have free and open access to the library and all materials contained therein. The Library Bill of Rights further asserts that the library should cooperate with all groups or individuals who resist "abridgement of free expression and free access to

---

[2]*Pico* was heard by the U.S. Supreme Court in March 1982. The Court upheld the opinion of the court of appeals, saying, "petitioner's [Board of Education's] reliance upon duty is misplaced where they attempt to extend their claim of absolute discretion beyond the compulsory environment of the classroom into the school library."

ideas." In other words, the ALA believes that free access to ideas is essential in a democracy and that this freedom must be defended.

The detailed history of the ALA's fight against censorship is included in the second edition of the *Intellectual freedom manual,* published by the organization. The manual also includes a helpful list of suggestions for librarians in resisting censorship of library materials.

In conjunction with the Association of American Publishers (AAP), the ALA further defines its stand in the "Freedom to Read" statement. The statement says, in part, that it is the responsibility of publishers and libraries to make available to the public a wide diversity of views and expressions, including those which appear unorthodox or unpopular. The statement further asserts that it is in conflict with the public's interest for publishers, booksellers, and librarians to use their own personal political, moral, or aesthetic views as the standard for selecting materials to distribute, publish, or sell. Similarly, no author should be discriminated against, no matter what his or her political affiliation or personal history. Further, the reading tastes of the reader and the artistic freedom of the author should never be challenged. According to the statement, the librarian and publisher must contest any encroachments on an individual's freedom to read. The library and the publisher must make available materials that express the diversity of life and thought. "The suppression of ideas is fatal to a democratic society. Freedom itself is a dangerous way of life, but it is ours." The joint statement by the American Library Association and Association of American Publishers was subsequently endorsed by more than twenty other groups.

The National Council of Teachers of English (NCTE), like the ALA, has fought a battle against censorship for many years. The major publication of the NCTE which reflects its views on censorship is *The students' right to read.*[3] This publication, revised by Ken Donelson, is divided into two sections: "The right to read" and "A program of action." The "right to read" statement upholds students' right to choose their own reading material: " . . . education is an effort to improve the quality of choices open to man. But to deny the freedom of choice in fear that it may be unwisely used is to destroy the freedom itself," according to the NCTE statement. The statement further claims that the right of individuals to read whatever they want is "basic to a democratic society." The statement contends that the "reading man possesses judgment and understanding and can be trusted with the determination of his own actions."

In recent years the threat to free choice and open access to materials has come not only from groups or individuals who seem to want to destroy the rights of citizens, but also from groups and individuals who hope to protect the right of citizens. Minority and women's groups who object to the language or stereotypical image of minorities or women portrayed in classroom and library materials have been requesting that they be removed from the shelves. According to young adult author John Donovan:

[3] *The student's right to read* and *The student's right to know* (ed. Lee Burress and Edward B. Jenkinson) are available free of charge from National Council of Teachers of English, 1111 Kenyon Road, Urbana, IL 61801.

> *... pressure groups are not only persuading school boards and librarians to remove certain children's books from circulation, but are attempting to control the content of children's books at the source. ... [Donovan] cited, in particular, the vigorous campaign against* The Cay *by Theodore Taylor and described a recent action by the Task Force on Gay Liberation of the American Library Association which has advised children's book editors that there must be more children's books with gay themes in which gay persons are presented positively and that, moreover, a person who is proudly identified as gay should review such books in manuscript form. (NCTE Convention News Release, November 28, 1975)*

The situation is complicated not only by the fact that the sterotypes presented are often unattractive and unfair to the group, and so most librarians and teachers are uncomfortable with the view presented in the material; but also by the fact that the very groups (ALA and NCTE) who so vocally maintain the right of free access of materials and free choice of materials have member organizations that work for the fair portrayal of minorities and women in textbooks and other materials used in the classrooms. When are the guidelines set by the various member organizations of the NCTE and the ALA and by other organizations (such as the National Organization for Women and the Council on Interracial Books for Children) censorship and when are they guidelines for selection? In other words, what is censorship?

WHAT IS THE DIFFERENCE BETWEEN SELECTION AND CENSORSHIP?

> *Selection ... begins with a presumption in favor of liberty of thought, censorship, with a presumption in favor of thought control. Selection's approach to the book is positive, seeking its value in the book as a book and in the book as a whole. Censorship's approach is negative, seeking for vulnerable characteristics wherever they can be found—anywhere within the book, or even outside it. Selection seeks to protect the right of the reader to read; censorship seeks to protect—not the right—but the reader himself from the fancied effects of his reading. The selector has faith in the intelligence of the reader, the censor has faith only in his own.*
>
> *In other words, selection is democratic while censorship is authoritarian, and in our democracy we have traditionally tended to put our trust in the selector rather than in the censor. (Asheim 1953)*

The line between guidelines that assist teachers and librarians in selecting materials and guidelines that attempt to censor materials to remove from students the free access to ideas and the right to self-selection is a very fine one. Lester Asheim suggests that the difference lies in the intent of the selector. If the selector's intent is to look for value in the book, if it is to give the reader a choice and protect the right to read, if the selector believes that the reader is intelligent enough to detect biased, poorly written materials, then the selector is merely a selector of materials. If, on the other hand, the selector crosses the fine line and tries to protect the reader from unpopular or unorthodox ideas, if the selector does not assume the reader has the intelligence to be a "crap detector," if the selector looks for the negative aspects of the book, then the selector has become the censor.

Both the ALA and the NCTE defend librarians' and teachers' rights to select materials for a particular purpose or for a particular age group. Both organizations understand the difficulty in knowing the difference between selection and censorship. The NCTE organized a group in December 1980 to examine the issue and determine what censorship is. The group issued a position statement on the distinction between censorship and guidelines in December, 1982. The statement reaffirms the teacher's role as selector of classroom materials. It defines professional guidelines in terms of their goal to provide criteria for selection of materials and methods. Inclusion of material and methods rather than exclusion distinguishes professional guidelines from censorship, according to the statement.

At the November 1980 convention of NCTE, a workshop explored the guidelines-versus-censorship question. At the workshop a variety of viewpoints were expressed. Edward B. Jenkinson, past chair of the NCTE Committee Against Censorship, said that guidelines should be "voluntary, not mandatory . . . they [should] allow freedom of choice, not mandated selection. . . . [They should be] sound attempts at consciousness raising . . . [they should not] give the protectors of the young the license to go hunting through libraries and classrooms looking for the targets they can shoot down."

Robert Moore, director of the Racism and Sexism Resource Center for Educators, Council on Interracial Books for Children, expressed the concern that "indiscriminate charges of censorship are having a chilling effect on the discussion of racism and sexism in children's books and textbooks, causing many to avoid active consideration of these issues." He cautioned that if the cry of censorship is heard every time a person expresses a "concern for educational materials," we will lose the "forum for alternative views that are not usually heard in the standard review media."

Lallie Coy, chair of the Women's Committee of NCTE, examined the common elements of all kinds of guidelines and determined that "those dealing with minority groups [seem] . . . to have a common theme: pluralism. It is the theme that saves such guidelines from being censorial." She went on to describe censorship as the act of "exclusion," of removing books. Guidelines, on the other hand, "specifically those for minority groups, demand inclusion of different images" and "acknowledge the right of dissent. They are inclusive not exclusive in scope and philosophy." Therefore, Coy contends, "it is impossible for guidelines to act as censors."

The debate will continue for many years. What is censorship? When do guidelines become censorial? When is the selector of materials the censor? Ronald T. LaConte, in a 1975 article on the teacher as self-censor, tries to answer those questions.

> *Maybe the most important thing we [the teachers] can do is to keep reminding ourselves that only we can censor, that parents have a right to complain if they don't like what's happening in the schools, and that protest, no matter how strident, is not censorship. If we keep asking what they are afraid of, we might all find out that the monster is nothing more than a little kitten with a big shadow.[4]*

It is the professional who finally removes the books from the classroom or the library. It is the professional who understands the reasons for selecting particular materials for the classroom. If materials are not selected because the teacher or librarian fears the complaints of parents, if materials are not selected because the teacher or librarian fears that students will be unable to handle them, than perhaps the professional is acting as censor rather than selector. Similarly, if the guidelines are written to be inclusive rather than exclusive and the professional follows these guidelines, then the professional is acting as a selector rather than a censor.

Dealing with Censorship

No matter how careful the librarian and teacher are about the selection of reading material for the classroom and library, complaints are likely to occur. The ideal way to mitigate these complaints is for the school to work together with the community to answer the questions: What constitutes censorship? What is the difference between censorship and guidelines? What guidelines do we want for the selection of materials in our school? The open forum that encourages questions such as these is a positive step in the development of an environment that makes censorship unnecessary.

Margherite LaPota, in an article in the April 1976 *Arizona English Bulletin*, reports on one community / school solution to the issue.

> *After a traumatic experience testifying before a Grand Jury to answer charges of misusing public funds in the purchase of "obscene" books (which resulted in no indictments), the English staff in a local junior high in an affluent neighborhood was understandably nervous the following year when it came time to compile new reading lists for literature classes. How were they to please everyone—themselves, students and patrons— while avoiding a repetition of public criticism? The students did not want to read "dumb" stuff.... Parents wanted their children to read the "classics" and good stuff with "happy" endings. Teachers wanted their students to read and enjoy well-written literature; the principal wanted students to learn and everybody to be happy.[5]*

To help reach an accord on the problem, the English staff decided to involve students and parents in the making of the ninth-grade reading list. A committee

---

[4]Reprinted by permission of the *Arizona English Bulletin.*
[5]Reprinted by permission of the *Arizona English Bulletin.*

Patsy Scales, Greenville (SC) Middle School, holds literary discussion groups with parents in which the children recommend a book for their parents to read. The concern of parents has switched from keeping the book out of the hands of the students to a desire to understand why the children have selected a particular book.

of students and parents began reading books and book reviews that had been recommended by a variety of sources. The students selected fifty titles. These books were then read by the parents. The rest of the students voted on the books they would most like to read based on short summaries of each title. Twenty titles were selected. Finally, the students wrote a defense for each title selected and invited the parents to attend discussion sessions about the books. The books were discussed. When a parent objected to a work, a student verbally defended the selection of the students. "Often students were able to change parental opinion. One mother said, 'I read that book but I guess I was too busy looking for dirty words to understand what the story was saying. I just didn't see what a good message the book had for young people.'" As a result of the meetings an approved reading list was developed. The efforts of these teachers, students, and parents resulted in far more than an approved reading list. LaPota reports that the PTA decided to purchase paperbacks for the school, the students' attitude toward reading improved, and the parents expressed a respect for the quality of the educational program in the school.

Unfortunately, forming a joint committee of parents, teachers, students, librarians, and administrators is not always immediately possible, though it should be worked toward as an ultimate goal for all schools. When the development of such a committee is not feasible, there are several intermediate steps a school, department, or classroom teacher can take.[6] The school and/or the individual department should develop a policy for the selection of books, if one does not already exist. The school board should be involved in the policy-writing as early as possible and should approve the policy as soon as it is completed. The school and/or the individual department should work toward a consensus on what the curriculum should include. A consensus does not mean the opinion of the "most powerful" member of the department, but rather an agreement hammered out by the entire department. A consensus is never a majority opinion; it must be agreed upon by all the members of the department. Teachers, librarians, and administrators should do everything in their power to encourage the board of education to adopt a "students' right to read" policy.

Classroom teachers can involve parents in their child's reading by making them aware of the books the student has selected for reading and encouraging the parents to examine the books and discuss them with the child. In my own English classes every student was required to read a minimum of five books every quarter. The books were always available in the classroom or school library, were listed in an annotated bibliography dealing with the theme or genre to be studied, were selected by the students, and were available for parental reading. At the beginning of each quarter the students completed a contract in which they indicated the books they planned to read during the next nine weeks (see p. 433). On the contract the students also listed other materials they would be using as well as requirements for the awarding of the course grade. The contract was taken home with a copy of the annotated bibliography and returned with each parent's signature. A completed copy of each contract was filed in the English office and could be renegotiated with the initialing of the parents and the student on the changed item. The percentage of grade value of the contract for each course varied, depending on other course requirements. The contracts were valued at as little as 50 percent or as much as 100 percent of the course grade.

During the three years that I used the contract system in a rural Ohio school district, I had several parental requests to examine the books, not more than a handful of parents who asked their children to select a different book, and only one complaint about a book a student was reading. When the complaining parent entered my classroom for a scheduled conference, I expressed surprise at the complaint since she had signed the contract. "What contract?" she asked. I pulled the signed contract from the file. She had neither seen nor signed the contract. After explaining to her that all books were available for her to review, and a signed contract was an indication of her understanding of what her son was reading, the complaint was dropped. The issue was no longer the book her son was reading, but the fact he had chosen to forge the contract rather than

---

[6]A helpful reprint of a February 1978 article in *Language Arts* is available free of charge from the National Council of Teachers of English, Committee on Bias and Censorship. *Censorship: Don't let it become an issue in your school.* NCTE, 1111 Kenyon Road, Urbana, IL 61801.

GRADE CONTRACT

I, _____, agree to meet the requirements for the grade of _____,[1] in the course of _____, for the quarter of _____, set forth in this grade contract. I further agree to fulfill the assignments set forth in this contract to the best of my ability.

I understand that if I am unable to meet or would like to change the manner in which I meet the requirements, I may renegotiate them with my teacher, _____, any time prior to the seventh week of the said quarter.

I further understand that if I do not meet the agreed-upon requirements and do not renegotiate my contract, I will receive an incomplete or an F for the contracted portion of my course grade.

The following requirements are those I agree to meet for the aforementioned course, grade, and quarter:[2]

The following books, articles, short stories, poems, etc., have been selected by me to fulfill the requirements:[2]

I understand that this contract is not valid unless it is completed (including listing of requirements and reading material(s)), signed by all appropriate parties, and returned by ____ (date).

I further understand that this contract will be produced in triplicate. One copy will be kept in my file in the English office, and one copy will be returned to me and my parent or guardian.

Signed:
Student _____ Teacher _____

Parent or Guardian _____ Date _____

[1]This contract will equal ____ percent of the course grade.
[2]Use the reverse side if additional space is needed.

bring it home. After this incident the parent became a great supporter of the system, often asked for copies of the books her son was to be reading, and reported to me that she and her son had gained a new appreciation for each other through their discussions of the books; in addition, the young man learned a very valuable lesson.[7]

When a teacher plans to use a single book for reading by the entire class, or one of four or five books from which all of the students in the class may select, the teacher must read the book(s). A teacher should never select a book based only on a review or a recommendation from a colleague. After selecting the book(s), the teacher should prepare a carefully written, educationally sound reason for selecting the book(s). A copy of the dated statement should be given to the department chair and principal, and filed in a safe place for future teacher reference. If the school district, school, and/or department has guidelines for the selection of classroom materials, the teacher must be sure to examine these guidelines before making final selections. The teacher should always allow a student to read a book other than the one selected by the teacher, and should never penalize the student for not reading the selected book. One of the best ways to avoid criticism about the books being used in the classroom is never to require that any one title be read by every student. Allowing the student to select from an annotated list of books and encouraging parental review and discussion of the selections are likely to minimize criticism.

If someone complains about a book being used in the classroom, the teacher must be prepared to handle the complaint in a friendly, nondefensive manner. The teacher should not feel as if he or she is being criticized; rather, a book being used in the classroom is the object of the criticism. Every parent has the right to complain about what is being taught in the classroom. Removal of this right is as damaging as removal of the diversity of books from the cirriculum. If the teacher has alerted the principal and department chair to the books being used, has given them a written reason for the selection of the books, and has discussed the reasons for using the books with them, the administrators are likely to feel as if they have a role in the selection and are therefore likely to support the teacher. The complaint usually can be handled during a conference with the parent. Most often the objection is withdrawn when the parent discovers the child is not required to read a particular book, is free to select another, and will not be penalized for the change. Usually, the parent is objecting to the child's reading the book, and when informed that the child need not read the book, in a friendly, nonthreatening way, the objection will go no further.

However, the simple conference may not end the complaint, and the parent may insist that the book be removed from the classroom or library. If this is the case, two excellent forms—"Statement of Concern about Library/Media Center Resources" (ALA) and "Citizen's Request for Reconsideration of a Work" (NCTE)—can be given to the person requesting the removal. (See pp. 435 and

[7]A pamphlet, *Communicate through literature: Introducing parents to the books their teens are reading and enjoying*, by Pat Scales, describes a parents' outreach program that can keep censorship from becoming an issue.

■ ■ STATEMENT OF CONCERN ABOUT LIBRARY/MEDIA CENTER RESOURCES

[This is where you identify who in your own structure has authorized use of this form—Director, Board of Trustees, Board of Education, etc.—and to whom to return the form.]

Name _____ Date _____

Address _____

City _____ State _____ Zip _____ Phone # _____

1. Resource on which you are commenting:
   ____Book   ____Audiovisual Resource
   ____Magazine   ____Content of Library Program
   ____Newspaper   ____Other
   Title _____

   Author/Producer _____

2. What brought this title to your attention?

3. Please comment on the resource as a whole as well as being specific on those matters which concern you. (Use other side if needed.) Comment:

Optional:
4. What resource(s) do you suggest to provide additional information on this topic?

Reprinted by permission of the American Library Association from *Intellectual Freedom Manual,* 2nd ed., p. 167; copyright © 1983 by the American Library Association. Revised by the ALA Intellectual Freedom Committee, January 12, 1983.

■ ■ CITIZEN'S REQUEST FOR RECONSIDERATION OF A WORK

Hardcover _____

Author _____ Paperback _____

Title _____

Publisher (if known) _____

Request initiated by _____

Telephone _____ Address _____

City _____ State _____ Zip code

Complainant represents

_____ Himself
_____ (Name organization) _____
_____ (Identify other group) _____

1. To what in the work do you object? Please be specific; cite pages. _____

2. What of value is there in this work? _____

   _____

3. What do you feel might be the result of reading this work?
   _____

   _____

4. For what age group would you recommend this work? _____

   _____

5. Did you read the entire work? _____ What pages or sections?
   _____

   _____

6. Are you aware of the judgment of this work by critics?

   _____

7. Are you aware of the teacher's purpose in using this work? __

   _____

8. What do you believe is the theme or purpose of this work? _____

_____

9. What would you prefer the school do about this work?
   _____ Do not assign or recommend it to my child.
   _____ Withdraw it from all students.
   _____ Send it back to the English department for re-evaluation.

10. In its place, what work of equal value would you recommend that would convey as valuable a picture and perspective of a society or a set of values? _____

_____

_____   _____
(Date)   (Signature of Complainant)

436.) Often the simple acknowledgment that the citizen has the right to complain is enough to quell the complaint. At other times the questions asked on the form convince the person that the complaint is not valid. On these forms the complainant must indicate whether he or she has read the book, what part of the book or resource is objectionable, whether he or she would recommend the book for another group, awareness of critical comments about the book or resource, understanding of the theme, suggestions of alternative courses of action, and recommendation of another to be used in its place. These forms should be available in each classroom, office, and library. If the school is not currently using these forms, the teacher or librarian should suggest their adoption to the appropriate administrative officer.

Suggested Readings

American Library Association. *Intellectual freedom and the rights of youth—information packet.* American Library Association, 1979.

Asheim, L. Not censorship but selection. *Wilson Library Quarterly.* September 1953, pp. 63–67.

Burress, L., and E. B. Jenkinson, eds. *The student's right to know.* National Council of Teachers of English, 1982.

Committee on Bias and Censorship. *Censorship: Don't let it become an issue in your school.* National Council of Teachers of English, 1973.

Committee on the Right to Read. *The student's right to read.* National Council of Teachers of English, 1982.

Cox, C. B. *The censorship game and how to play it.* National Council for Social Studies, 1977.

Cullinan, B., and M. J. Weiss, eds. *Books I read when I was young: The favorite books of famous people.* Avon, 1980.

Davis, J. E., ed. *Dealing with censorship.* National Council of Teachers of English, 1979.

Donelson, K. Obscenity and the chill factor: Court decisions about obscenity and their relationships to school censorship. In J. E. Davis, *Dealing with censorship.* National Council of Teachers of English, 1979, pp. 63–75.

———. Some tentative answers to some questions about censorship. *English Journal,* April 1974, pp. 20–21.

Edwards, J. A new twist to an old problem: Recent court decisions on school book censorship. *English Journal,* March 1981, pp. 50–53.

Grossberg, K. Literature of adolescence: The inevitable battleground. *Journal of Reading,* October, 1977, pp. 76–80.

Hentoff, N. *The first freedom: The tumultuous history of free speech in America.* Delacorte, 1980. Dell, 1981.

Jenkinson, E. B. *Censors in the classroom: The mind benders.* Southern Illinois University Press, 1979.

———, ed. Organized censors never rest. *Indiana English,* Fall 1977.

LaConte, R. T. In K. Donelson, ed., Censorship and the teaching of English, *Arizona English Bulletin,* February 1975.

LaPota, M. Censorship and adolescent literature: One solution. In K. Donelson, ed., Adolescent literature revisited after four years, *Arizona English Bulletin,* April 1976, pp. 173–75.

Norwick, K. P. *Lobbying for freedom: A citizen's guide to fighting censorship at the state level.* St. Martin's, 1975.

Office for Intellectual Freedom. *Intellectual freedom manual.* American Library Association, 1974.

Right to Read Committee. *The right to read and the nation's libraries.* American Library Association, 1974.

Scales, P. *Communicate through literature: Introducing parents to books their teens are reading and enjoying,* Putnam, 1984.

Shugert, D. P., ed. Rationales for commonly challenged taught books. *Connecticut English Journal,* Fall, 1983.

Stanek, L. W. *Censorship: A guide for teachers, librarians, and others concerned with intellectual freedom.* Dell, 1976.

APPENDIX A

Publishers of Young Adult Books

Addison-Wesley Publishing Co., Jacob Way, Reading, MA 01867 (hard and paper)

Archway Paperbacks, c/o Pocket Books, 1230 Avenue of the Americas, New York, NY 10020 (paper)

Atheneum Publishers, 597 Fifth Avenue, New York, NY 10017

Avon Books, 959 Eighth Avenue, New York, NY 10019 (paper)

Ballantine Books (Division of Random House), 201 East 50th Street, New York, NY 10022 (paper)

Bantam Books, 666 Fifth Avenue, New York, NY 10103 (paper)

Bradbury Press, 2 Overhill Road, Scarsdale, NY 10583

Coward, McCann & Geoghegan (Putnam Publishing Group), 200 Madison Avenue, New York, NY 10016

Crowell Junior Books, 10 East 53rd Street, New York, NY 10022

Crown Publishers, 1 Park Avenue, New York, NY 10016

Delacorte Press, 1 Dag Hammarskjold Plaza, 245 East 47th Street, New York, NY 10017

Dell Publishing Co., 1 Dag Hammarskjold Plaza, 245 East 47th Street, New York, NY 10017 (paper)

Dial Press, 1 Dag Hammarskjold Plaza, 245 East 47th Street, New York, NY 10017

Dodd, Mead & Co., 79 Madison Avenue, New York, NY 10016

Doubleday & Co., 501 Franklin Avenue, Garden City, NY 11530

E. P. Dutton & Co., 2 Park Avenue, New York, NY 10016 (hard and paper)

Farrar, Straus and Giroux, 19 Union Square West, New York, NY 10003

Fawcett Books Group, 1515 Broadway, New York, NY 10036 (paper)

Follett Publishing Co., 1010 West Washington Boulevard, Chicago, IL 60607 (hard and paper)

Four Winds Press, c/o Scholastic Inc., 50 West 44th St., New York, NY 10036

Greenwillow Books, (Division of William Morrow & Co.), 105 Madison Avenue, New York, NY 10016

Harcourt Brace Jovanovich, 757 Third Avenue, New York, NY 10017 (hard and paper)

Harper and Row, Publishers, 10 East 53rd Street, New York, NY 10022

Hastings House, Publishers, 10 East 40th Street, New York, NY 10016

Hawthorn Books, c/o E. P. Dutton, 2 Park Avenue, New York, NY 10016

Holiday House, 18 East 53rd Street, New York, NY 10022

Holt, Rinehart and Winston, 383 Madison Avenue, New York, NY 10017 (hard and paper)

Houghton Mifflin Co., 2 Park Street, Boston, MA 02107 (hard and paper)

John Day Junior Books, c/o Harper and Row, Publishers, 10 East 53rd Street, New York, NY 10022

Alfred A. Knopf (Division of Random House), 201 East 50th Street, New York, NY 10022

Lippincott Junior Books, c/o Harper and Row, Publishers, 10 East 53rd Street, New York, NY 10022 (hard and paper)

Little, Brown & Co., 34 Beacon Street, Boston, MA 02106 (hard and paper)

Lothrop, Lee & Shepard (Division of William Morrow & Co.), 105 Madison Avenue, New York, NY 10016

Macmillan Publishing Co., 866 Third Avenue, New York, NY 10022

McGraw-Hill Book Co., 1221 Avenue of the Americas, New York, NY 10036

Julian Messner (Division of Simon & Schuster), 1230 Avenue of the Americas, New York, NY 10020

William Morrow & Co., 105 Madison Avenue, New York, NY 10016

New American Library, 1633 Broadway, New York, NY 10019 (paper)

Pantheon Books (Division of Random House), 201 East 50th Street, New York, NY 10022

Penguin Books, 625 Madison Avenue, New York, NY 10022 (paper)

Pocket Books (Division of Simon & Schuster), 1230 Avenue of the Americas, New York, NY 10020 (paper)

Scholastic, Inc., 730 Broadway, New York, NY 10003 (paper)

G. P. Putnam's Sons, 200 Madison Avenue, New York, NY 10016

Charles Scribner's Sons (Division of Macmillan), 597 Fifth Avenue, New York, NY 10017

Simon & Schuster, Inc., 1230 Avenue of the Americas, New York, NY 10020

Viking Press, 625 Madison Avenue, New York, NY 10022

Walker & Co., 720 Fifth Avenue, New York, NY 10019

APPENDIX B

The History of Young Adult Literature at a Glance

Books and Authors	Events

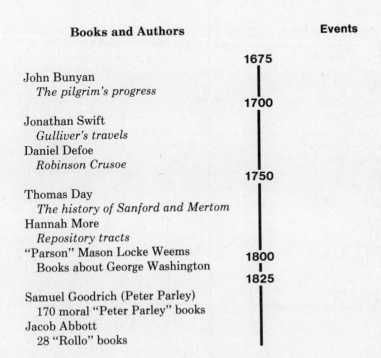

Books and Authors

1675

John Bunyan
The pilgrim's progress

1700

Jonathan Swift
Gulliver's travels
Daniel Defoe
Robinson Crusoe

1750

Thomas Day
The history of Sanford and Mertom
Hannah More
Repository tracts
"Parson" Mason Locke Weems
Books about George Washington

1800

1825

Samuel Goodrich (Peter Parley)
170 moral "Peter Parley" books
Jacob Abbott
28 "Rollo" books

Events

Books and Authors	Events

Susan Warner (Elizabeth Wetherell) **1850**
  More than 20 "domestic" novels   The first "dime" novel appears
Augusta Jane Wilson   (June 7, 1860).
  St. Elmo
The most popular of the "dime" novel
  characters: Seth Jones, Davy Crockett,
  "Old Sleuth" Nick Carter, Deadwood
  Dick
Louisa May Alcott
  Little women

Horatio Alger **1870** University entrance exams require
  "Ragged Dick" books   specific "classic" books for
  "Richard Hunter" books   college-bound.
  1875

Series books   "Dime" novels attacked for
  Harry Castlemon, "Frank" books   sentimentality and ability to
  Oliver Optic, "Boat Club" books   corrupt.
  Martha Farquharson, "Elsie
    Dinsmore" books
George Wilbur Peck
  Peck's bad boy
Mark Twain
  Tom Sawyer
  Huckleberry Finn
Adventure writers
  Howard Plyle, "Robin Hood"
  Jules Verne   *Huckleberry Finn* banned by
  Robert Louis Stevenson   Concord Public Library.
  Arthur Conan Doyle, "Sherlock **1890**
    Holmes"
  1900

Stratemeyer Syndicate
  (formula fiction)
  "Admiral Dewey" books
  "Lakeport" books
  "Rover boys"
  "Hardy boys"
  "Dana girls"
  "Ruth Fielding"
  "Tom Swift"
  "Nancy Drew"
Booth Tarkington
  Seventeen
William Gilbert Patton
  "Frank Merriwell" sports books
Books about the West
  Owen Wister
  The Virginian

Books and Authors	Events

Zane Grey
Kate Douglas Wiggin
   Rebecca of Sunnybrook Farm
Lucy Maud Montgomery
   Anne of Green Gables
John Fox, Jr.
   The little shepherd of Kingdom Come

> National Council of Teachers of English formed to protest college entrance exams.

1911

The Reverend Harold Bell Wright
   The winning of Barbara Worth
Eleanor Porter
   Pollyanna

1917 *Reorganization of English in the Secondary Schools*, U.S. Bureau of Education, add modern works to English curriculum.

Edgar Rice Burroughs
   Tarzan
John Buchan
   The thirty-nine steps
Ralph Henry Barbour
   "St. Marys"
   "Fairview High"
   "Lansing"
   School-Sports Series

1920

> First Newbery Medal awarded to *The story of mankind*, Hendrick Van Loon.
> *Comic Monthly* founded.
> *Funnies on Parade*

Joseph Gollomb
   Lincoln High Series
Charles Nordhoff and James Norman
   Hall
   "Mutiny Trilogy"

1930

Big-Little Books
   "Dick Tracy"
   "Flash Gordon"
   "Moon Mullins"
   "Our Gang"
   "Donald Duck"

> *Detective Comics*
> *Marvel Comics*
> Career books gain popularity and continue through the 1950s.

1938

John Tunis
   Iron duke
"Nancy Drew," "Hardy Boys," and
   "Tom Swift" live on

> First "paperback" published by Pocket Books, Pearl Buck, *The good earth*.

1940

Janet Lambert
   Star spangled summer

> Rise of paperback industry increases availability of popular books.

Maureen Daly
   Seventeenth summer

1942 A touch of realism appears in young adult fiction.

Henry Gregor Felsen
   Navy diver (1942) and other World War II books until 1947

> War books popular throughout the 1940s.

John Tunis
   All American (1942) and other sports books until 1964

Books and Authors	Events

Esther Forbes
 Johnny Tremain (1943)
Florence Crannell Means
 The moved outers   **1945**
The wonderful high school years books: Books of the 1940s and 1950s
 Rosamond DuJardin   usually avoided sex, smoking,
  Wait for Marcy   profanity, social or racial
  Boy trouble   injustice, and anything that might
 Betty Cavanna   be considered controversial.
  Going on sixteen
 Anne Emory   Robert Havighurst outlines the
  Going steady   "developmental tasks" of the
 James Summers   adolescent.
  Girl trouble   **1950**
Paul Annixter
 Swiftwater (1950)
Henry Gregor Felsen   Car and sports books popular
 Hot rod (1958) and other car books   throughout the 1950s and early
  through 1958   1960s. Formula romances also
William Gault   popular during the 1950s and
 Thunder Road (1952)   1960s.
Philip Harkin
 Road race (1953)
C. H. Frick
 Five against the odds (1955) and other
  sports books through 1961
John F. Carson
 Floorburns (1957) and other sports
  books through 1961
J. D. Salinger
 The catcher in the rye (1951)   Nonfiction emerges as popular
Elizabeth Yates   reading fare for young adults.
 Amos Fortune, free man (1950)
Anne Frank's *The diary of a young girl*
  (1952)
Shirley Graham
 Booker T. Washington   **1955**
Lorenz Graham   Realistic black characters emerge in
 South town   fiction for young adults.
Christine Arnothy   Criticism of and articles about
 I am fifteen and I do not want to die   young adult literature begins to
Ian Fleming's "James Bond" series from   appear in professional journals by
  1954 through the 1960s   scholars such as G. Robert
Clifton Fadiman   Carlsen, Dwight Burton, Emma
 Fantasia mathematica   Patterson, and Margaret Edwards.
Harper Lee   **1960** Dwight Burton, *Literature study in
 To kill a mockingbird   the high schools* (1959)
John Knowles   Margaret Early's study on
 A separate peace   developmental reading stages

Books and Authors	Events

Scott O'Dell
  Island of the blue dolphins
Robert Heinlein
  Stranger in a strange land
Howard Fast
  April morning
John Howard Griffin
  Black like me
Joan Aiken
  The wolves of Willoughby Chase
Madeleine L'Engle
  A wrinkle in time
Hal Borland
  When legends die
Irene Hunt
  Across five Aprils
Lloyd Alexander
  The book of three
Hannah Green
  I never promised you a rose garden
Frank Bonham
  Durango Street
Nat Hentoff
  Jazz country
Ann Head
  Mr. and Mrs. Bo Jo Jones
Zoa Sherburne
  Too bad about the Haines girl
Virginia Hamilton
  Zeely
S. E. Hinton
  The Outsiders
Robert Lipsyte
  The Contender
Richard Bradford
  Red sky at morning
James Forman
  My enemy, my brother
Nancy Larrick
  On city streets
Kin Platt
  The boy who could make himself
    disappear
Paul Zindel
  The pigman
Kristin Hunter
  The Soul Brothers and Sister Lou
John Donovan
  I'll get there. It better be worth the trip
	A new realism in young adult
	literature begins.
	
	1965
	
	Dan Fader, *Hooked on books:*
	Program and proof (1966)

Books and Authors	Events

John Neufeld
  Lisa bright and dark
Vera Cleaver and Bill Cleaver
  Where the lilies bloom
Judy Blume
  Are you there, God? It's me, Margaret
Maya Angelou
  I know why the caged bird sings
Anonymous
  Go ask Alice
Robbie Branscum
  Me and Jim Luke
Gunnel Beckman
  Admission to the feast
Robert Newton Peck
  A day no pigs would die
Jean Craighead George
  Julie of the wolves
Elliot Wigginton, editor
  Foxfire
Isabelle Holland
  Man without a face
R. R. Knudson
  Zanballer
William Armstrong
  Sounder
Norma Klein
  Mom, the Wolfman and me
Alice Childress
  A hero ain't nothin' but a sandwich
Rosa Guy
  The friends
Jeanne W. Houston and James D.
  Houston
  Farewell the Manzanar
Tim O'Brien
  *If I die in a combat zone, box me up
    and ship me home*
Sandra Scoppettone
  Trying hard to hear you
Robert Cormier
  The chocolate war
Paula Danziger
  The cat ate my gymsuit
 	
Richard Peck
  Are you in the house alone?
Judith Guest
  Ordinary people
	1970
	
	G. Robert Carlsen, *Books and the
	  teenage reader* (1971).
	
	ALAN Review first published (1973).
	  Supreme Court ruling (1973) on
	  censorship placed decision-
	  making power on boards of
	  education.
	
	1975

Books and Authors		Events
Judy Blume *Forever*		
Norma Fox Mazer *Dear Bill, remember me?*		
Linda Bird Franke *The ambivalence of abortion*		Formula romances reintroduced and very popular.
Robin Brancato *Blinded by the light*		
Ellen Raskin *The Westing game*	**1980**	
Jean Auel *Clan of the cave bear*		
Zibby Oneal *The language of goldfish*		
Katherine Paterson *Jacob have I loved*		

Nancy Willard
  A visit to William Blake's inn:
    Poems for innocent and
    experienced travelers		

Jean Fritz *Homesick: My own story*		

Index of Titles

Index of Titles

Index of Titles

Index of Titles

Index of Titles

Index of Titles

Index of Titles

Index of Titles

Index of Titles

Index of Titles

Index of Titles

Index of Titles

Index of Titles

Index of Authors

Index of Authors

Index of Authors

Index of Authors

Subject Index

Subject Index

objective biography, 159, 162
obtaining books, 413–417
occult books, 85–86
onomatopoeic language, 237

paperback book bibliographies, 412–413
paperback book program, 42–43, 255, 257–260, 323
parenthood, teenage, 64, 66
parent-teenager relationships, 116–122
past, projection into, 92–93
peer approval, 117
peer group, 11, 15
persuasion, 240–246
physical education classroom, 324
  thematic unit for, 325–336
physical handicaps, 68–70, 115, 295
physical maturation, 64–65, 143–144
plot, 230, 250–251, 305
poetry, 158, 172–180
poetry indexes, 409
point of view, 251–252
politics, 269, 275
population mobility, 275, 277
poverty, 114–115
pregnancy, 64, 66, 166
prejudice, 79–81, 276, 278, 280, 294–295, 427, 429
  heroes battling, 70–71
problem novels, 64–67, 255
propaganda, 240–246
prostitution, 67
publishers' publicity departments, 350–351, 353
puzzle books, 171–172, 338

quest fantasies, 88–90

radio, 173
rape, 64, 66–67, 166, 295, 424
"read a book in an hour" technique, 238–240
reading
  motivation for, 195–196
  practice in, 37, 42–43
  stages in development of, 3–5
  and television, 362–363
  writing skills and, 247
  see also reluctant readers

reading aloud, 367, 370–377
reading classroom, 320–323
read it and like it, 255, 257–260
realism, 64–81
  fantasy combined with, 86–90
  science fiction and, 96
recordings, 364–367
reform, 275
relationships
  developing, 116–117
  ending, 114
  with grandparents, 123
  with handicapped young adults, 115
  with nonfamily adults, 128–130
  parent-teenager, 116–122
  sibling, 116–119
  see also family relationships
religion, 96–98
religious cults, 167, 241–246, 295
reluctant readers, 15–16, 323n
  motivating, 35–36
  short-read books attractive to, 158
remarriage, 125
reviews, 403–407
Revolutionary War, 76, 290–291
rhyme, 237–238
rhythm, 237–238
rite of passage, 142–143
robots, 94
romantic mode, 227–228

saturation-diffusion program, 42–44
science books, 170–171
science classroom, 23, 319–320
science fantasy, 303–304, 306
science fiction, 86, 92–96, 401–402
  humor in, 133–134
  in the social studies classroom, 296, 302–307
scientists and careers in science, 310, 318–319
sea, 95
search plot, 85–86, 88–90
selection of books, 397–413
semantics, 232
sentimentality, 113–116
separation and divorce, 124–125
separation from childhood, 142–144
settings, 228–229, 231, 249–250, 304
sexuality, 64–66, 166